MICROCOMPUTER BASIC
Structures, Concepts, and Techniques

Edward J. Coburn

**UNIVERSITY OF TEXAS
AT EL PASO**

 DELMAR PUBLISHERS INC.

For my wife, Linda, and my two daughters, Shannon and Heather.

I wish to express special thanks to Greg Spatz, who had the confidence to accept the teaching package for publication; to Christina Gallagher for her unfailing efforts to push me to finish the manuscripts on time; to Sharon Rounds, who has been our important go-between; and to Gerry East for his invaluable editing skills, without which this series would be the same bundle of inconsistencies it was when it was turned in.

Cover Photos Courtesy of:
International Business Machines Corporation
Apple Computer, Inc.
Radio Shack, A Division of Tandy Corporation

Delmar Staff
Administrative Editor: Christina M. Gallagher
Production Editor: Gerry East

For information, address Delmar Publishers Inc.
2 Computer Drive West, Box 15-015
Albany, New York 12212-9985

Printed in the United States of America
Published simultaneously in Canada
by Nelson Canada
A Division of International Thomson Limited

10 9 8 7 6 5 4 3 2 1

Library of Congress Cataloging in Publication Data

Coburn, Edward J.
  Microcomputer BASIC.

  Bibliography: p.
  Includes index.
  1. BASIC (Computer program language)   2. Micro-
computers—Programming.   I. Title.
QA76.73.B3C63 1986   005.13'3   85-16108
ISBN 0-8273-2480-4

CONTENTS

CHAPTER 6
ARRAYS AND READ-DATA
139

CHAPTER 7
STRING HANDLING AND FUNCTIONS
182

CHAPTER 8
SEQUENTIAL FILE HANDLING
213

CHAPTER 9
MENUS AND REPORTS
242

CHAPTER 10
PROMPTS AND ERRORS
271

CHAPTER 11
RANDOM ACCESS FILE PROCESSING
291

CHAPTER 13
TREE STRUCTURES
354

CHAPTER 14
SORTING
383

PREFACE

It is hard to imagine that the world of the computer began only about forty years ago. What began as a roomful of equipment that needed specialized air-conditioning and seemed to break down about once every minute has now given birth to the microcomputer that can be set upon a desk or even carried in a pocket. Once only a handful of people could understand the computer; now almost anyone can at least experiment with programming on a microcomputer.

It was long believed by the public that only superintelligent technicians could handle the world of computers. And the computer workers did little to dispel this myth. Then, in 1965, Dr. John Kemeny and Dr. Thomas Kurtz of Dartmouth College designed a computer language that would be much easier to use, on the theory that if the language were easy to use, more people would be able to use it. How right they were! BASIC was the language they developed and it is now, without a doubt, the most widely used programming language.

For many years, programs written in any language were considered to be good programs as long as they worked and produced the correct results. We have now come to realize that just the fact that the program works for the moment does not necessarily indicate that it will continue to work without error. Also, very few programs are developed that will not need modification at some point because of changes in tax laws, accounting procedures, or company policies. Throwing together a program in any fashion just as long as it will work is a poor programming approach. It is difficult to modify or even understand such a program.

To help eliminate such haphazard programming practices, certain techniques have been expounded and widely accepted. *Structured programming* has become the best method of writing programs that are easy to maintain. These techniques allow the programmer to produce code that is easily read and understood.

Unfortunately, too many advocates of BASIC are under the impression that it is unsuited for structured programming. This is not the case. Structured programming does not deal with strict concepts but merely basic ideas. These basic ideas can be implemented in any language as long as one understands the concept of the structure itself.

Structured programming, then, *can* be implemented in the BASIC programming language. This text was developed around the three basic programming structures: the Simple Sequence, the IF-THEN-ELSE, and the Loop. We discuss these major structures in Chapter 2 and use them throughout our programming in the rest of the text.

ORGANIZATION

Microcomputer BASIC: Structures, Concepts, and Techniques offers complete coverage of both introductory and advanced BASIC programming topics and can be used in a variety of courses with the utmost flexibility. The text is de-

signed to discuss BASIC programming on microcomputers because the great majority of BASIC programming today is done on microcomputers. We discuss three different computers in the text: the IBM Personal Computer, the Radio Shack Model III, and the Apple II. In addition, the minor differences between the Radio Shack Model III and Model 4 are introduced, as well as those between the Apple II and II+ and the Apple IIe and IIc.

We begin with a general introduction to these machines and discuss many of the concepts that will be important throughout the remainder of the book. Chapter 2 covers flowcharting and structured programming techniques. The following six chapters cover what are traditionally considered to be introductory BASIC topics, including decisions and loops, arrays, string handling, and sequential file handling. Chapters 9 and 10 deal with important microcomputer programming techniques for developing menus and reports and understanding prompts and error trapping.

Beginning in Chapter 11, we progress to more advanced topics with a discussion of random access file processing. Chapter 12 then discusses indexed file processing, a concept that is vital to today's programming tasks. Chapter 13 covers the tree structure, a different and sometimes better technique to handle indexing. Following Chapter 14 on sorting techniques, the text concludes with an optional chapter on graphics and color, which really can be covered at any point in the course.

In addition, there are seven appendices. Appendix A contains additional programming aids and commands. Appendix B is a summary of all the commands used in the text, along with some interesting ones that were not covered earlier. An important feature of the command summary is the inclusion of commands used on seven microcomputers that were not included in the text (Timex, Atari, NorthStar, CBASIC, MBASIC, Commodore, and Texas Instruments). This will help you convert programs created for one microcomputer to another version of BASIC you may be using or want to learn in the future. The remaining appendices cover disk assistance, error messages and codes, project ideas, answers to selected questions, and ASCII sequence codes. The book concludes with a bibliography and index.

FEATURES   Throughout the text several features help the reader understand and make better use of the material presented.

■ **Differences** among the three versions of BASIC are treated within the body of the text rather than in appendices. All example programs are coded first in Microsoft BASIC, the version used on the IBM Personal Computer. Differences between the Microsoft version and the Radio Shack and Applesoft versions of BASIC are then highlighted immediately following the full program. A special symbol appears next to these highlighted variations (☒ for Radio Shack, and ◖ for Apple). So whether you are working consistently on the same computer or are in a lab with a variety of models, these symbols make finding the appropriate version of BASIC fast and simple.

■ At the beginning of each chapter an **Overview** lists each of the topics to be covered in the chapter. There are also several **Objectives** to give you an idea of what you will learn in the chapter.

■ Each **new term** introduced in a chapter appears in boldface type. These boldface words are defined in the Glossary at the end of each chapter. Each term in the Glossary is clearly defined in words other than those used in the text. This second definition will help clarify the meaning.

■ At the end of each chapter, four learning techniques are used. The **Summary** highlights all the important points covered in the chapter. The **Glossary** defines each new term introduced in the chapter. The **Questions to Aid Understanding** are specially designed to help you decide whether the Objectives at the beginning of the chapter have been met. Appendix F contains answers to selected questions; each question in the chapter that is answered in the appendix is marked with an asterisk. Finally, there is a **Quick Quiz** at the end of each chapter that contains fifteen true–false and five multiple-choice questions. The answers are given immediately after the quiz. In many cases, the answer includes an explanation of why that particular answer is the correct one. This lets you know immediately if you have mastered the chapter material.

■ Finally, the book features a special type of **Index.** Not only are page numbers listed, the subjects are also classified as to whether they are found in the Glossary or Summary, a figure, an appendix, or within the text material. This classification should prove useful in finding the exact information needed.

THE TEACHING PACKAGE

■ An Introduction to Basic: Structured Programming for Microcomputers

This book assumes no prior programming experience and covers BASIC techniques up to and including arrays, string handling, and sequential file handling. It can be used in a full quarter or semester course, a minicourse, or in conjunction with another text for those who teach BASIC as part of introductory data processing or other introductory computer courses.

■ Advanced BASIC: Structured Programming for Microcomputers

The coverage in this book overlaps slightly with that of the introductory book. While it assumes some prior programming experience, it makes no assumptions as to the extent of that experience. One or all of the first four chapters (covering BASIC review, string handling, sequential files, and menus and reports) may be skipped, assigned as review material, or covered as the first new topic of the advanced course.

■ Microcomputer BASIC: Structures, Concepts, and Techniques

This book is the most flexible. It combines the material in the introductory and advanced texts, allowing the instructor to individually tailor the course. It may be used in an introductory and advanced course sequence, providing consistency in coverage and eliminating the necessity of purchasing two separate texts. It is perfect for those instructors who wish to cover in their introductory course some advanced topics not found in conventional texts, or who want to give students the opportunity to continue learning

BASIC on their own. And finally, it is the ideal text for instructors whose students enter the introductory BASIC course with some prior programming experience gained in high school or an introduction to computers course. Based on the extent of that experience, the first chapters of *MICROCOMPUTER BASIC* can be used as review, and instructors are free to choose the depth of coverage desired for the rest of the course.

■ Instructor's Guide

Each of these three texts is accompanied by the same comprehensive *Instructor's Guide*. This extensive manual includes chapter outlines for all of the chapters in the three books discussed above; transparency masters for all illustrations; test questions; and suggested course outlines for using the texts in an introductory course, an advanced course, a two-course sequence, and an extended introductory course.

ACKNOWLEDGMENTS

I would like to thank the following reviewers for their comments and suggestions:

Anthony Basilco
Community College of Rhode Island
Warwick, RI 02886

Richard Fleming
Northlake College
Irving, TX 75038

Charlie Gohmiri
Delaware Technical and Community College
Dover, DE 19901

J. W. Lepenski, Sr.
Tarrant County Junior College
Fort Worth, TX 76179

Dennis Lundgren
McHenry County College
Crystal Lake, IL 60014

Kay Nelson
North Idaho College
Couer d'Alene, ID 83814

Jim Phillips
Lexington Community College
Lexington, KY 40506-0235

Jeffrey Sipkoff
Taylor Institute
Paramus, NJ 07652

Dennis Smirl
Central Piedmont Community College
Charlotte, NC 28235

Joseph Waters
Santa Rosa Junior College
Santa Rosa, CA 95405

ABOUT THE AUTHOR

Ed Coburn has been involved in the world of microcomputers and programming for over a decade. After receiving degrees from Colorado State University and Kearney State College, he was a senior programmer for several years before becoming a microcomputer programming analyst in 1979. At that time, he began teaching BASIC to people who had recently purchased microcomputers. He writes a popular column on microcomputers for a local newspaper and is the author of *Learning About Microcomputers: Hardware and Application Software* (Delmar, 1986) and *Microcomputers: Hardware, Software, and Programming* (Bobbs-Merrill, 1984). Professor Coburn has taught programming, computer science, and data processing courses at McLennan Community College, Waco, Texas, and at the University of Texas at El Paso.

1 MICROCOMPUTERS AND BASIC

OVERVIEW

OBJECTIVES

After completing Chapter 1, you will be able to:
- Explain what hardware and software are.
- Describe what memory is and the significance of the terms *bit* and *byte*.
- Explain what input, process, and output signify.
- Explain what a cursor is used for.
- Explain the significance of the RETURN and BREAK keys.
- Explain the setup of a diskette.
- Demonstrate how to get a directory.
- Demonstrate how to store a program and then get it back again.

1–1
INTRODUCTION

This is a textbook about how to write programs using the BASIC language. To help us along the way, we need to understand some terminology. We will begin this chapter with a short discussion of some of the more important terms that will be used throughout the book.

This is not a book about computer **hardware,** hardware being the computer equipment itself, such as keyboard, screen, disk drives, and printer. It is useful, however, to introduce some of the hardware of the computers referenced in this text to familiarize you with what you will be expected to use. Also, from time to time we will discuss certain aspects of the various computers because there are many differences. We will, however, only look at what we need in order to use the hardware, not at how it functions.

Our first topic of discussion, then, will be some important points about the machines this book was written for: the IBM Personal Computer, the Radio Shack Model III and Model 4, and the Apple II, II+, IIe, and IIc.

(*Note:* It is assumed that you are using a machine with at least one disk drive throughout all discussions. If you are using no disk drives, minor modifications to a few commands may be necessary and Chapter 8 on disk file processing will not be applicable to your machine.)

We will then discuss a little about what it means to write programs in BASIC or any other language. Disks and the amount of storage available are covered for each of the computers mentioned. Finally, a few of the more important and often-used commands for disk usage are covered for each machine.

The IBM Personal Computer with keyboard, monochrome display, and matrix printer. Courtesy of International Business Machines Corporation.

Radio Shack TRS-80™
Model III microcomputer.
Courtesy of Radio Shack,
a division of Tandy
Corporation. (TRS-80™ is
a trademark of the Radio
Shack Division of Tandy
Corporation)

Radio Shack TRS-80™
Model 4 microcomputer.
Courtesy of Radio Shack,
a division of Tandy
Corporation. (TRS-80™ is
a trademark of the Radio
Shack Division of Tandy
Corporation)

The Apple II Plus personal computer with monitor and two floppy disk drives. Courtesy of Apple Computer, Inc.

The Apple IIe personal computer with monitor and disk drive. Courtesy of Apple Computer, Inc.

The Apple IIc personal
computer with monitor.
Courtesy of Apple
Computer, Inc.

1–2
IN THE BEGINNING

Hardware is the equipment of the computer (keyboard, screen, disk drives, and printers), but it is only half of the story. To get our computers to do anything useful, they must be given instructions. These instructions are called **software,** or **programs,** and they are just as important as the actual equipment. These programs are written using special instructions which, when grouped together, are called a language.

There were many languages in use when microcomputers were first introduced, but only one seemed to be suited to the needs of the revolutionary new microcomputers. Back in 1964, John Kemeny and Thomas Kurtz of Dartmouth College developed **BASIC,** which stands for Beginners All-purpose Symbolic Instruction Code. BASIC proved to be the ideal beginner's language and easily fit the new microcomputers. BASIC is easy to learn, yet powerful enough to do even some of the most sophisticated tasks. Its few, simple commands have made the computer accessible to thousands upon thousands of people who otherwise might not have been able to understand the complexities of computer programming. In the past few years, other languages have tried to replace BASIC as the major microcomputer language. None have yet had as much impact as BASIC, which is still the most widely used language for **interactive programming** (entering information directly into the machine and getting immediate feedback).

1–3
STORAGE CONCEPTS

To use BASIC (or any other language) on a computer, information must be stored. This is accomplished in the computer in what is called **memory.** But the computer doesn't store numbers and words as numbers and words. The computer's memory is composed of a series of switches called transistors. These switches work on the same principle as a light switch. Just as the light is on when the switch is on, information is indicated in a computer as being stored by various on and off positions of these switches. One on–off switch is called a BInary digiT or **bit** for short. The word *binary*, meaning "two," refers to the two states of our bit. This on–off status means that each bit has the relative value of either 1 or 0, on or off.

To store information using only bits, some type of coding scheme must be used. The scheme that has been adopted in the microcomputers is called the **ASCII** code (pronounced ask' ee). ASCII stands for American Standard Code for Information Interchange. In the ASCII code, eight bits are grouped together to represent a **character,** which is also called a **byte.** (To be technically correct, a character is the information stored, while a byte refers to the storage for the character. The terms, however, have come to mean the same thing in common usage.) A character is merely a letter, number, or some special symbol such as a quotation mark ("), question mark (?), or asterisk (*). An example of a stored character would be the letter A, which has the ASCII configuration 01000001.

1–4
INPUT AND OUTPUT FUNCTIONS

All computers, whether microcomputer or larger, have three basic functions. They **input** information, perform some type of **process** or processes on that information, and then **output** the results of the processes. Pictorially it would look like this:

$$INPUT \rightarrow PROCESSING \rightarrow OUTPUT$$

For example, suppose you have to process the payroll for the place where you work. You gather all the information about who worked, how many hours they worked, and what they are supposed to be paid, and you give that information to the computer. That would constitute the input. Then the programs (payroll programs in this case) would calculate the employees' gross pay, the Social Security to be deducted, and the federal and state taxes to be withheld. That would constitute the processing of the information. Finally, the computer would print the payroll checks and probably some reports for management. That would be the output. Throughout this book, we will be doing many examples of just this type of processing.

When we are interacting with the computer, we use the keyboard to input the information, and we get our output on either a printer or (most of the time) the display screen.

1–5
THE DISPLAY SCREENS

On the display screen there is an indicator that tells you where you are working on the screen. This display indicator is called the **cursor.** It takes different forms in our computers as follows:

- The IBM cursor is a blinking underline.
- The Radio Shack cursor is a blinking half box.
- The Apple cursor is a blinking square.

When we are entering information on the screen (when using BASIC), the computer will prompt us that it is our turn in various ways. The IBM will print **Ok** on the screen, while the Radio Shack will display the word READY. In addition, the Radio Shack will display the > symbol as an indicator. The Apple uses the] symbol. In the programming examples in the book, we will use the IBM "Ok" response in the illustrations.

The upper left-hand corner of the screen is known as the **home position** (Figure 1–1). When you clear the screen, either by keyboard key or program command, the cursor returns to the home position. With some of the machines discussed in this book, the cursor can be homed without clearing the screen. That will come in handy later. The screens on our machines display a different number of characters, also defined as rows (horizontal character positions) and columns (vertical character positions), as follows:

- The IBM screen is either 40 columns or 80 columns by 24 rows. (There is a 25th row, but it is not generally used as part of the normal screen. It is reserved for special displays.) To change from a 40-column screen to an 80-column screen you type in the command **WIDTH** 80; to change to 40 columns you type in the command WIDTH 40. If you are using a monitor, 80 columns are probably okay, but if you are using a TV for a monitor, 80

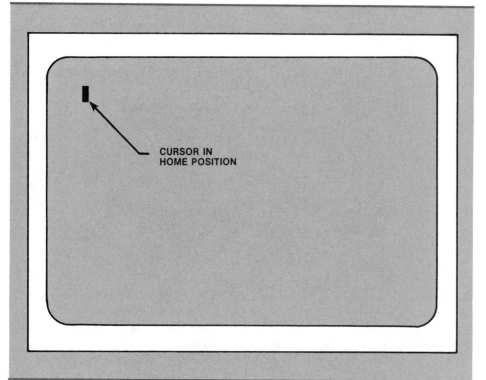

CURSOR IN
HOME POSITION

Figure 1–1
Diagram of a display screen with the cursor located in the home position.

columns may be hard to read. You will have to make the decision yourself.

- The Radio Shack Model III screen is 64 columns by 16 rows.
- The Radio Shack Model 4 screen is 80 columns by 24 rows.
- The Apple screen is 40 columns by 24 rows. (Boards are available to increase the Apple display to 80 columns.)

1–6
THE KEYBOARDS

On the keyboards there are a few keys that you need to become familiar with immediately. The first one is the key that signals to the computer that you have tried to communicate something. We will always refer to this as the **RETURN** key though it has a different label on each machine:

- The IBM key is labeled with an arrow ⟵⏎.
- The Radio Shack key is labeled ENTER.
- The Apple key is labeled RETURN.

Remember, any time reference is made to the RETURN key, we mean the above-listed keys.

Another important key will stop the execution of a program that is running. We shall call this the **BREAK** key; it is labeled on the machines as follows:

- The IBM uses the Ctrl (Control) and Scroll Lock keys in combination. To do this, you press the Ctrl key and hold it down like a shift key and then press the Scroll Lock key. Notice that the front of the Scroll Lock key is labeled "Break".
- The Radio Shack key is labeled BREAK.
- The Apple key is labeled RESET.

Any time we make reference to pressing the BREAK key, these are the keys we are referring to.

Though the Apple II and II+ don't use lowercase letters, the others do (including the Apple IIe and IIc). They have a shift key that functions when held down while pressing another key. The machines also have a key that will lock the entry into all capital letters. Only the Radio Shack Model III has any problem with the change from one case to the other. The instruction to change cases is indicated by holding the shift key and pressing the zero key. After this, all the alphabetic characters pressed will be lowercase (you begin in capitals); to switch back you use the same procedure. (This procedure works on the Model 4 also, but it is not needed since the Model 4 has a shift lock key.)

If you wish to key in a whole series of the same character, it can be done more easily than pressing the key several times. This is called a **repeat function,** and on the IBM, Radio Shack, and Apple IIe and IIc, all you have to do is hold the key down and it will begin to repeat. There is a short delay built in so that it doesn't happen by accident. On the older Apples there is a **REPEAT key** that you hold down while pressing the other key.

One final key of interest will clear the screen. This function (clearing the screen) can be accomplished in a program, but sometimes it is handy to be able to do it from the keyboard. We will refer to this key as the **CLEAR** key. It is important to realize that the CLEAR key affects only the screen. It has no effect on anything stored in memory. The clear function works as follows on the machines:

- On the IBM the Ctrl and Home keys together do the job.
- On the Radio Shack the key is labeled CLEAR.
- On the Apple there is no key for clearing the screen.

The IBM also uses function keys (the keys on the left side of the keyboard labeled F1 through F10) to produce commands. These commands are listed on the bottom of the screen (the 25th line).

1–7
GETTING STARTED
ON THE MACHINES

Before we continue to the next section on external storage, we should pause for a moment and discuss how to get started in BASIC on our machines. The machines differ slightly and will be covered separately.

IBM

First, insert a system disk (the DOS disk furnished with the computer or one that has been copied for use) in the correct drive (drive A if you have more than one) and then turn on the machine. After the disk is in drive A, it will take a few seconds and then you will be prompted for the current date. The date you enter can be in several different formats, such as 8-31-86 or 12/1/86. The date is edited to be sure it is valid, although the machine has no way of knowing if it is the correct date. If you enter an invalid date, you will merely be asked again. You can bypass this entry by pressing RETURN.

Then you will be asked for the current time. You may enter the entire time or only the hour, such as 16:00:05 or simply 16. You can also bypass this entry by pressing RETURN.

Finally, you will see some information and then A>. You can use either of two available versions of BASIC on the IBM, either BASIC or advanced BASIC. We will use BASICA (advanced) in our discussions, so you will need to enter BASICA next to the A> and press RETURN. You will now be in BASIC, ready to enter your programs.

Radio Shack

First, turn on the machine (the machine must be on *before* you insert your disk in order to avoid damage to the disk), and then insert a system disk (the DOS disk furnished with the computer or one that has been copied for use) in the bottom drive (drive 0 if you have more than one). Next, you press the orange switch, and after a few seconds you will be prompted for the current date. The date you enter must be just as the machine specifies. This date is edited to be sure it is valid, although the machine has no way of knowing if it is the correct date. If you enter an invalid date (or forget the slashes), you will merely be asked again.

Then you will be asked for the current time. You may enter this if you wish, but it is not generally used and can be bypassed by pressing RETURN. (The date prompt cannot be bypassed.)

Finally, you will see a TRSDOS and dotted line display. Here you key in the word BASIC and press RETURN. You will be asked two more questions, which you should merely press RETURN in response to. They are of no concern at this time. Some information will display at the top of the screen and you will see a > sign. You will now be in BASIC, ready to enter your programs.

The Apples First, insert a system disk (the DOS disk furnished with the computer or one that has been copied for use) in the drive numbered 1. Then turn on the machine, and after a few seconds you will be in BASIC (Applesoft), ready to enter your commands.

1–8
EXTERNAL STORAGE

There are two predominant forms of external storage used with microcomputers. They are the cassette and the diskette. Though cassettes are inexpensive and useful for storing games and additional copies of important information, they are not much use for the day-to-day processing necessary in a business environment because they are too slow. This being the case, we will only deal with the diskette in this book. We will use the diskette throughout the remainder of the book to store our programs as we create them. (At least we will save the important ones.) Those of you using a cassette-only machine can still use this book until you reach Chapter 8, which deals with sequential disk storage. Then Chapter 9, as an aid to the discussion, deals with programs that store and

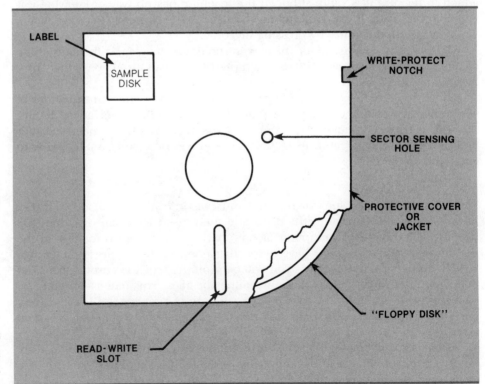

Figure 1–2
Diagram of a typical diskette.

retrieve information from the diskettes. Chapter 9 may be completed with the use of cassette-stored information, if necessary.

The **diskette** (or simply *disk*) is also known as a **floppy disk** because it is flexible and can "flop" back and forth. This flexible diskette is placed inside a protective plastic cover called a **jacket,** which also helps keep it a little more rigid and a little less floppy. The jacket is lined with special material to clean the surface of the disk as it rotates in the disk drive. The typical diskette looks like the one shown in Figure 1–2.

The disk itself is a round plastic sheet covered with a magnetic coating. This magnetic coating is the recording surface, which is set up in a series of concentric circles known as **tracks** (Figure 1–3).

Because the amount of potential storage on a single track is too large to manage effectively, each track is subdivided into several pie-shaped areas called **sectors** (Figure 1–4).

The amount of storage that is available on each of our machines is shown in Table 1–1. The amount of storage listed is the amount of storage on the disk. (Note that the IBM generally uses both sides of the diskette, which doubles the storage figure given.) The actual amount available to the programmer, however, is less because the machine uses some of it to mark where the tracks and sectors are. Additionally, since information is stored on the disk, the machine must have some method of keeping a record of what is stored where. It does this by recording in a **directory** all the programs and **files** (a file is a collection of data, discussed in depth in Chapter 8) and where they are stored. This directory also requires some of the disk's storage area.

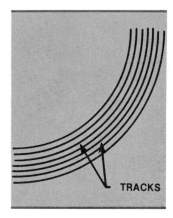

Figure 1–3
Tracks on a diskette.

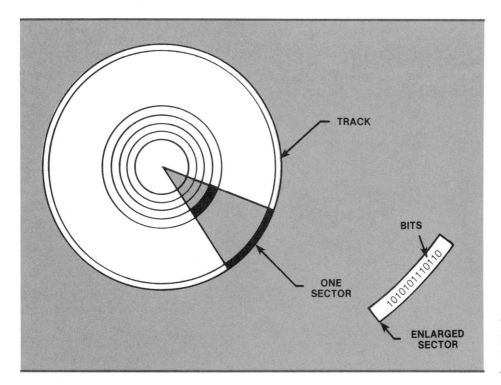

Figure 1–4
Diagram of a sector.

TABLE 1–1 Available Diskette Storage

MACHINE	BYTES/SECTOR	SECTORS	TRACKS	TOTAL BYTES
IBM	512	9	40	184,320
Radio Shack	256	18	40	184,320
Apple	256	16	35	143,360

We can look at what files and programs are stored on our disks by telling the machine to give us a directory listing. This command is different on each of our machines.

IBM On the IBM the disks are labeled as A, B, C, etc. To view the directory on drive A you would use the command **FILES A:** and the directory on drive B can be displayed with **FILES B:**. (The command FILES by itself will display the directory of the drive currently in use, which is generally A.) A directory might look like the following:

```
A:ASSIGN  .BAS 24K : A:TEST    .COM 5K : A:ERRORS  .BAS 14K
A:USER    .BAS 10K
```

This directory shows the file names (ASSIGN, TEST, etc.), the length of the files (24K, 5K), and an extension that tells the type of file it is. The .BAS means it is a BASIC program, and the .COM means it is a command file.

Radio Shack To access the directory on the Radio Shack you use the command **CMD"D:O"** or **CMD"D:1"** depending on whether you wish the directory from drive 0 (bottom drive) or drive 1 (top drive). A typical directory from the Radio Shack will look like the following:

```
DRIVE:O     LPC/CMD      MEMTEST/CMD       SAMPLE
PAYROLL     GLENT
READY
```

Notice that this directory lists only the file names. There is another type of directory listing, but it cannot be used with BASIC.

The Apples On the Apples the disks are labeled 1 and 2 and the command to display the directory is **CATALOG,D1** or **CATALOG,D2**. A typical display will look like the following:

```
DISK VOLUME 254
A 003 HELLO
A 004 ERRORS
T 006 USER
A 008 SUBS
T 003 PROMPTS
```

This directory shows the file names (HELLO, ERRORS, etc.), the length of the file (003, 004, etc.), and a code that tells the type of file it is. The A means it is an Applesoft program, and the T means it is a text (data) file.

1–9
AN IMPORTANT NOTE

It should be noted that before you can use a diskette to store your programs, you will need to make a copy of a system disk. This is an easy procedure and is discussed in Appendix C.

1–10
STORING PROGRAMS ON DISK

In Chapter 3 we will begin to write programs and you will probably want to store some of them on disk for further reference (or for finishing later if you run out of time). The command to do this is **SAVE.** The IBM and Radio Shack command is:

```
SAVE "PROGTEST"
```

The Apple does not require the quotes:

```
SAVE PROGTEST
```

1–11
RETRIEVING PROGRAMS FROM DISK

After a program is stored on the disk, you may wish to get it back from the disk. It is important to realize, however, that the act of storing the program on disk does nothing to the program that is in memory. The program on disk is simply a copy of that program. The program does not need to be brought from the disk unless the machine has been turned off, there was a power shortage, or you modified the program in memory and want the original back again.

To get the program back into memory, you use a **LOAD** command. The IBM and Radio Shack use:

```
LOAD "PROGTEST"
```

The Apple again drops the quotes:

```
LOAD PROGTEST
```

SUMMARY

1. This book is not about hardware but about the creation of software. We will create this software by writing programs in BASIC.
2. When we write these programs, the information is stored temporarily in memory in little on–off switches called bits. Eight of these bits put together form a byte, which is sufficient room to store one character such as a letter, numeric digit, or special symbol. The eight-bit code used in microcomputers is called ASCII.

3. Every computer has three basic functions: to input information, to process that information, and to output the results.
4. The position indicator on the display screen is called the cursor. When entering information, the machines will commonly respond with Ok when it is your turn to enter some information.
5. There are a few important keys that you need to know how to use. The RETURN key signals to the computer that you are finished entering your information. The BREAK key will allow you to stop the execution of the program.
6. Though some people use cassette storage, this book deals only with storage on diskettes. A disk stores information on tracks that are logically broken up into sectors to manage the information more effectively. Some of this storage area is required for the disk directory, which contains information about what programs and files are stored on the disk.
7. When you are finished typing in a program, it is useful to store the program on the disk where it can be saved or brought back into the machine as the need arises.

GLOSSARY

ASCII (American Standard Code for Information Interchange) The coding scheme used on microcomputers to represent the characters that are stored in memory.

BASIC (Beginners All-purpose Symbolic Instruction Code) An easy-to-learn language with relatively few instructions.

Bit An acronym for BInary digiT, which is a single on–off storage switch in a computer.

BREAK The key that allows you to stop the execution of a program while it is running. It has various names on our computers.

Byte A group of eight storage bits that is used to store a character of information.

CATALOG,D1 (or CATALOG,D2) The command on the Apple to get a disk directory listing.

Character A letter, numeric digit, or special symbol such as a dollar sign ($) or asterisk (∗).

CLEAR The key that will clear the screen of information. The labeling of this key varies on our machines.

CMD"D:0" (or CMD"D:1") The Radio Shack command to display the disk directory.

Cursor The position indicator on the display screen.

Directory The list of the programs and files stored on the disk.

Diskette A small, plastic, magnetically coated disk that is used to store information. Also called simply *disk.*

File A group of information stored on some device (in this book that device will be a disk).

FILES A: (or FILES B:) The directory command used on the IBM.

Floppy disk *See* **Diskette.**

Hardware The equipment of the computer itself, such as the keyboard, screen, disk drive, and printer.

Home position The upper left-hand corner of the display screen.

Input The operation of getting information into the computer.

Interactive programming A type of programming whereby you receive immediate feedback from the computer as you enter commands.

Jacket The protective covering on a diskette.

LOAD The command to get a program into memory from the disk.

Memory The series of transistors in a computer where information is stored.

Ok   The message the computer displays to tell you it is your turn to enter information. This message is READY on the Radio Shack and] on the Apple.

Output   The operation of getting processed information out of the computer.

Process   The manipulation of data that has been input into the computer.

Program   Instructions for the computer that have been put together into a logical format that can be translated so the computer can understand them.

Repeat function   This function allows you to repeat a character continuously by holding the key down.

REPEAT key   A key on the older Apples (II, II+) which, when held down while pressing another key, will repeat that character until you let up on one of the keys.

RETURN   The key that signals to the machine that you have finished entering.

SAVE   The command to copy a program from memory to the disk.

Sectors   The divisions of a track of storage on a diskette.

Software   *See* **Program.**

Tracks   Concentric circles of storage on a diskette.

WIDTH   The command on the IBM to change the width of the display screen from 40 to 80 columns or from 80 to 40.

QUESTIONS TO AID UNDERSTANDING

1. Explain the difference between hardware and software.
2. Explain what memory is and the significance of the terms *bit*, *byte*, and *character*.
3. What are input, process, and output?
4. What is a cursor and why is it important?
5. What are the RETURN and BREAK keys used for?
*6. Describe how a diskette is structured for storage and how much storage the disk used with your machine has.
*7. What is a directory and why is it important?
8. What is the command to store a program on disk? To get it back into memory?
9. Key in the appropriate program just as it is listed here. Do not concern yourself with trying to understand what the program is doing for the moment. That understanding will come later. This is merely an exercise to familiarize you with the keyboard and screen. After you key in the program, enter the command RUN and press RETURN.

9–A. IBM

```
NEW
10 REM ***** PROGRAM NAME: SCREXER
20 REM
30 CLS
40 WIDTH 40
50 FOR I=1 TO 4
60     PRINT "1234567890";
70 NEXT I
80 FOR I=2 TO 24
90     IF I<>2 THEN PRINT
100    PRINT MID$(STR$(I),2,1);
110 NEXT I
120 LOCATE 10,5
130 PRINT "THERE ARE 40 COLUMNS AND 24 LINES."
140 END
```

Note: To have this program display 80 columns change it to the following:

```
NEW
10 REM ***** PROGRAM NAME: SCREXER
20 REM
30 CLS
40 WIDTH 80
50 FOR I=1 TO 8
60     PRINT "1234567890";
70 NEXT I
80 FOR I=2 TO 24
90     IF I<>2 THEN PRINT
100    PRINT MID$(STR$(I),2,1);
110 NEXT I
120 LOCATE 10,5
130 PRINT "THERE ARE 80 COLUMNS AND 24 LINES."
140 END
```

9–B. Radio Shack Model III (64 columns)

```
NEW
10 REM ***** PROGRAM NAME: SCREXER
20 REM
30 CLS
40 FOR I=1 TO 8
50     PRINT "12345678";
60 NEXT I
70 FOR I=2 TO 16
80     IF I<>2 THEN PRINT
90     PRINT MID$(STR$(I),2,1);
100 NEXT I
110 PRINT @(524),"THERE ARE 64 COLUMNS AND 16 LINES."
120 END
```

9–C. Radio Shack Model 4 (80 columns)

```
NEW
10 REM ***** PROGRAM NAME: SCREXER
20 REM
30 CLS
40 FOR I=1 TO 8
50     PRINT "1234567890";
60 NEXT I
70 FOR I=2 TO 24
80     IF I<>2 THEN PRINT
90     PRINT MID$(STR$(I),2,1);
100 NEXT I
110 PRINT @(10,15),"THERE ARE 80 COLUMNS AND 24 LINES."
120 END
```

9–D. Apple (40 columns)

```
NEW
10 REM ***** PROGRAM NAME: SCREXER
20 REM
30 HOME
40 FOR I=1 TO 4
50     PRINT "1234567890";
60 NEXT I
70 PRINT
80 FOR I=2 TO 24
90     VTAB I
100    HTAB 1
```

Program continues

```
110     PRINT I;
120  NEXT I
130  HTAB 5
140  VTAB 10
150  PRINT "THERE ARE 40 COLUMNS AND 24 LINES."
160  END
```

10. After you have RUN the program, SAVE it on the disk, then do a directory listing and see that it is on the disk. Use the name listed in the first statement of the program for the program name. If the directory indicates the program is there, enter NEW (which will erase the program from memory) into the machine. Clear the screen (press the CLEAR key) and then enter LIST (which will display the program stored in memory). You should get no display on the screen, which indicates that the program is no longer in the memory. Now LOAD the program back into memory and enter LIST again. This time you should see the program displayed on the screen. You may wish to RUN the program again just to verify that it still works.

•

QUICK QUIZ

The answers to the questions follow immediately after the quiz. Questions 1–15 are true–false, while 16–20 are multiple choice.

1. A program is considered to be hardware.   T F
2. BASIC is the most powerful programming language available.   T F
3. A diskette is called memory.   T F
4. A bit is the smallest unit of storage measurement.   T F
5. A bit is storage for a character.   T F
6. All computers have the three basic functions of input, process, and output. T F
7. Calculating taxes on a payroll would be considered output.   T F
8. The READY key is the key that signals the computer you are "ready" for   T F
   something else.
9. The upper right-hand corner of the screen is known as the home position.   T F
10. The BREAK key signals the machine to stop program execution.   T F
11. The CLEAR key will clear out memory.   T F
12. A floppy disk is more commonly known as a cassette.   T F
13. Concentric circles known as tracks are where the information is stored.   T F
14. The bytes used for the directory on a disk are not available for use by the T F
   programmer.
15. The directory is simply a list of what is stored on the disk.   T F
16. Which of the following terms does not relate to storage on a computer?   _____

   a. bit   **c.** byte
   b. memory   **d.** they all do

_____ **17.** Which of the following is *not* a function of computers?

        a. input   **c.** generate

        b. output   **d.** process

_____ **18.** Calculations would be considered which of the following functions?

        a. input   **c.** output

        b. process   **d.** generate

_____ **19.** Printing a report would be considered which of the following functions?

        a. input   **c.** output

        b. process   **d.** generate

_____ **20.** Which key generally signals the computer you are trying to communicate?

        a. RETURN   **c.** BREAK

        b. CLEAR   **d.** READY

ANSWERS TO QUICK QUIZ

1. F (A program is software.)
2. F (Many languages are more powerful than BASIC. BASIC is useful because it is easy to learn.)
3. F (Memory is internal storage; a diskette is an external storage device.)
4. T
5. F (A bit is one eighth of a byte; a byte is storage for a character.)
6. T
7. F (That would be a process.)
8. F (There is no READY key.)
9. F (The upper left-hand corner is called the home position.)
10. T
11. F (The CLEAR key will only clear the screen. It will not affect memory at all.)
12. F (A floppy disk is called a diskette.)
13. T
14. T
15. T
16. d
17. c
18. b
19. c
20. a (Though b and c are also keys and any key sends a signal to the computer, the RETURN key is generally considered to be the most significant.)

2 FLOWCHARTS, PSEUDOCODE, AND STRUCTURES

OBJECTIVES

After completing Chapter 2, you will be able to:

- Explain why flowcharts are important to programmers.
- List all the symbols used in this chapter and explain how each is used.
- List and explain the three programming structures.
- Explain the purpose of pseudocode.
- Demonstrate knowledge of flowchart symbol usage by drawing several charts.
- Demonstrate the ability to describe a problem using pseudocode.
- Describe the function of a counter, and demonstrate the use of one in a flowchart and pseudocode.
- Describe the function of an end-of-data marker, and demonstrate the use of one in a flow-chart and pseudocode.

2–1

INTRODUCTION

It is widely accepted today that the biggest problem in business is communication or, rather, the lack of communication. People have great difficulty expressing their ideas. But this problem, like most problems in business and society as a whole, is not new. People have had difficulty communicating information as long as there have been methods of communication. Many methods have been devised to help solve this problem. One of the best methods is to describe the information pictorially. If we can get others to visualize the problem, it is normally easier for them to understand what we are trying to convey.

A picture or diagram is a simple, easy-to-understand method of expressing ideas. All fields of endeavor use graphs and pictorial representations to communicate more effectively. Think for a moment of all the things we see every day that use graphs or drawings: television weather reports, business forecasts and reports, magazines, government bulletins, etc.

In data processing we use pictorial diagrams to describe solutions to problems. This diagrammatic form is called the **flowchart.** We use the flowchart to show the flow of information through a system or program. A **system** is merely a group of programs that together perform a function. An example would be a payroll system, which consists of many programs.

To be able to write a program you must understand how one event relates to another and how they relate to the whole task. This ability is the most difficult thing a programmer has to learn. As an aid to becoming proficient at these relationships, flowcharts are invaluable.

Flowcharts used to be the panacea for everything in data processing. There were system flowcharts, subsystem flowcharts, program flowcharts, and subprogram flowcharts. It has become apparent over the years that **program flowcharting** is generally an unnecessary task for those programmers who know their way around the language and the job to be programmed. That's not to say that programmers don't ever flowchart. On the contrary, all good programmers flowchart unfamiliar routines that may be complex or especially difficult. Flowcharts are also used occasionally with familiar routines if the programmer is looking for a better or faster way to do something.

Even programmers who never actually draw a chart on paper go through the same thought processes as when designing a flowchart. Many times they use an informal language known as **pseudocode** to chart their way through the task. All good programmers decide the best way to approach a problem before they begin, even if they do not use a formal flowchart. In this text, we will use both flowcharts and pseudocode to design our programs before we code them. (There will be times when the programs will be trivial or consist merely of a few lines of code for demonstration purposes that we will do neither. You will discover that many times it is quicker just to key in small programs since they need no planning.)

Since most programmers do not do a great deal of flowcharting, the flowchart has mainly become the tool of **systems analysts.** They are the ones responsible for designing the overall system. The analyst's plan depicts the operations performed on information as it flows through the entire system. This chart is called the **systems flowchart.** The program flowchart is generally a subset of the systems chart.

Because the purposes of the charts are different, a systems flowchart uses more symbols than are used in program flowcharts. Nevertheless, the flowcharting process is the same. The representation of the flow of information is the same whether the entire system or only a small part is depicted. Even if a programmer never has a need to draw a program flowchart, the charts prepared by the systems analyst must be used. All the programs of a system will be represented in the systems flowchart. Therefore, a thorough understanding of the flowcharting process is a necessity. Also, as mentioned previously, the process of analyzing a problem is the same whether a chart is drawn or the steps are written in pseudocode. Understanding the necessary process is of prime importance.

The symbols in this book have been internationally adopted through the efforts of the American National Standards Institute, or **ANSI.** This chapter introduces the flowcharting process with a group of those symbols that programmers use to depict program processes. We will also use pseudocode as we progress so you will become familiar with both methods of illustration. We discuss each of the symbols in depth and use each in several sample charts along with the appropriate pseudocode. The logic associated with each problem will be clearly illustrated with the few symbols used.

Before we begin to study the problem-solving process, you first need to realize that there is never only one way to solve a problem or prepare a flowchart. Like many things in life, flowcharting allows for many correct solutions. Although some ways might be better than others, such as by using fewer steps, that doesn't mean the others are necessarily incorrect. Of course, we want to strive for the best solution, but being correct must be of primary importance. Since there are many correct solutions, each one proposed in this book is only one of several possible solutions. The solutions you arrive at, though they may differ from the ones furnished, should not be considered incorrect solely on that basis.

2–2 A WORD ABOUT STRUCTURED CONCEPTS

BASIC, like most other languages, is relatively easy to learn, and in the beginning little care needs to be exercised in getting programs to work. We can simply throw together a few commands and there it is, the solution. This is the concept that many programmers were taught and unfortunately continue to use as professional programmers. The problem is that, regardless of the language used, if programs are written in this haphazard fashion, they will invariably be difficult and time consuming to write and maintain. The programmer usually thinks that the project is going well because much of the coding is done quickly. The flaw in this logic is that much more time will be necessary to debug the program (get the errors out) than if the programmer had taken time to develop the program in a logical, instead of thrown-together, fashion.

One method of overcoming these haphazard programming practices is becoming popular, that of **structured programming.** The basic idea behind structured coding was presented by Edsger Dijkstra in the late 1960s. His concept was that any programming problem can be solved using only three different programming structures:

1. The simple sequence of instructions; that is, one instruction (or group of instructions) following another in a linear fashion.
2. A selection based on the testing of a condition.
3. A repetitive block where instructions can be repeatedly executed.

Both 2 and 3 are based on a block structure and can actually be thought of as a single step in the linear sequence discussed in item 1. In fact, every program can be designed as a single set of instructions regardless of how complicated the program is. We will see this concept developed time and again throughout the remainder of this book.

Structured programming, then, is merely a disciplined way of putting programs together. It may take a bit longer to write structured programs initially, but the rewards are many: less time to finish the program (after debugging is taken into account) and much less maintenance time because the programs are easier to read through to locate the area that needs to be repaired.

Structured programming as used in this text will follow a limited set of guidelines:

1. All programming will be done using the recommended structures.
2. All programs will be well documented as an aid to understanding.
3. All programs will be modular. This means that each program will be written so that each function in the program will be in a separate module.

These concepts may seem a bit fuzzy to you now, but as we develop them in this chapter and later in the text, they will become clear.

2–3
BEGINNING SYMBOLS AND PSEUDOCODE

We begin our introduction to program design with the explanation of a few common symbols. These symbols are drawn using an ANSI standard flowcharting template. Each symbol is large enough to allow labeling inside the symbol. The standard procedure for labeling symbols is followed throughout.

The first symbol to discuss is the **terminal symbol.** Each chart must begin and end with this symbol. Since every problem must have a beginning, this symbol indicates where the processing of the program starts. It is labeled **START.** There are no symbols before the START symbol. Similarly, the conclusion of the flowchart uses the **END** terminal symbol. There are no symbols that follow the END. There is, of course, only one START symbol since a process can only begin once. There could be many different points in a program that function as ending points, but structured programming dictates that there should only be one END point. The symbols for the START and END are labeled as in Figure 2–1. When using pseudocode, the beginning and the end of the program are labeled with Start and End as they are on the flowchart.

The **process symbol** denotes some type of data manipulation within the program. With this symbol we can indicate mathematical calculations, move-

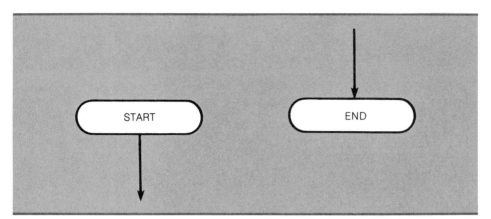

Figure 2–1
The two terminal
symbols.

ment of data, sorting, or other types of data handling. The labeling within the
symbol may be in the form of a calculation or a statement; pseudocode would
state explicitly what is occurring. There are two examples of such labeling in
Figure 2–2.

Input and output of data from the program are indicated by a parallelogram. The same symbol is used for input and output; it is called the **I/O symbol.** You indicate the process by appropriate labeling, such as that shown in
Figure 2–3.

Since there are several forms of input and output and they use the same
symbol, it is important to label the inputs and outputs as such. The most common form of input in BASIC is the **INPUT** (or READ), which was used in the
symbol shown in the left-hand side of Figure 2–3. The INPUT command de-
scribes the process of getting information into the program whether from the
keyboard or from some external storage source. **PRINT** is the most prevalent
type of output (see the right-hand side of Figure 2–3). It relates the process of
outputting to some printed or displayed form. Again, the labeling used in the
pseudocode representation will be similar to the labeling of the flowchart.

There are two ways the I/O symbol can appear, one of which is incorrect.
Beginning programmers sometimes have difficulty deciding on the proper form.
Figure 2–4 shows the correct and incorrect methods. Note that the correct par-
allelogram slants to the right, not to the left.

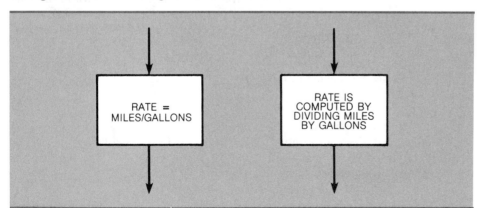

Figure 2–2
Two ways to label the
process symbol.

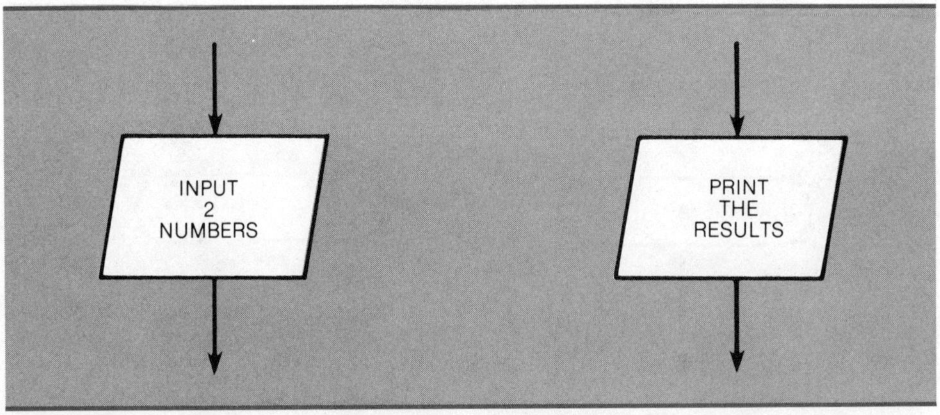

Figure 2–3
Labeling of the I/O
symbol.

Figure 2–4
Correct and incorrect
methods of labeling the
I/O symbol.

2–4
OUR FIRST STRUCTURE

As we mentioned in an earlier section, the first structure is called the **SIMPLE SEQUENCE,** one symbol following another in a linear fashion. We now know enough flowchart symbols that we can construct an instruction sequence.

In Chapter 1 we mentioned a payroll process of inputting all the information about the employees into the computer, where the gross pay was calculated and the checks and reports were written. This procedure really entails more of a system procedure, since checks and reports are not generally generated in the same program. We can, however, take a piece of that procedure and create a SIMPLE SEQUENCE chart.

We will develop a chart that details the inputting of the amount of time an employee worked for the week and then the writing of the check. This assumes that all the other necessary information about the employee is already in the computer. This is not an invalid assumption since that is generally how payroll is processed. The pseudocode for such a procedure would look like the following (the flowchart can be seen in Figure 2–5):

Start
Input the hours worked.
Calculate gross pay and deduct FICA, taxes, and miscellaneous deductions
    (calculate net pay).
Print the payroll check.
End

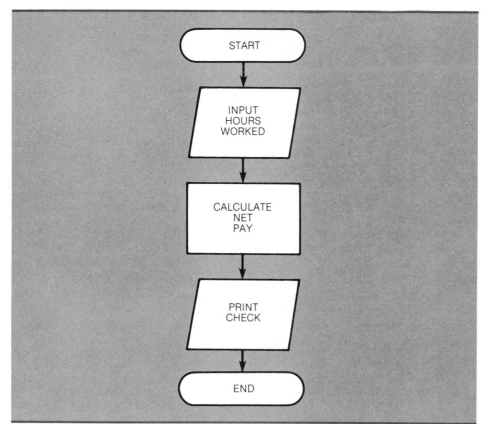

Figure 2–5
Flowchart of payroll
procedure.

Notice on the chart how the symbols are connected with lines. These lines are called **flow lines** and indicate the direction of flow of the logical processes (Figure 2–6). In flowcharts the assumed directions are top-to-bottom and left-to-right, but arrows should always be used on the flow lines to avoid any possible confusion.

You will probably notice that the previous process will only generate the payroll check for one employee. This would not be very useful since we would no doubt have many employees that want to be paid. This introduces us to another concept called the **loop** or **iteration.** A loop is simply a method of using the same instruction or group of instructions many times. We shall soon see that loops can be created with the use of the next type of structure.

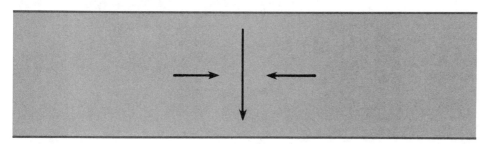

Figure 2–6
Flow lines.

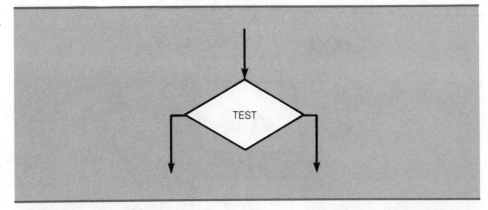

Figure 2–7
Decision symbol.

2–5
THE IF-THEN-ELSE STRUCTURE

One of the most important operations of a computer is its capability to make logical decisions based on certain conditions. It can make a choice between two items: Is item A larger than item B? Are two items equal? We have a symbol to indicate such decisions (Figure 2–7). The diamond is called the **decision symbol,** and it brings us to another structure, the **IF-THEN-ELSE** structure. The basic structure design can be seen in Figure 2–8. The pseudocode can be stated as:

IF a THEN b ELSE c

It means that a test is performed, and if condition *a* is true, then statement *b* is performed and statement *c* is skipped; otherwise (else), statement *c* is performed and statement *b* is skipped.

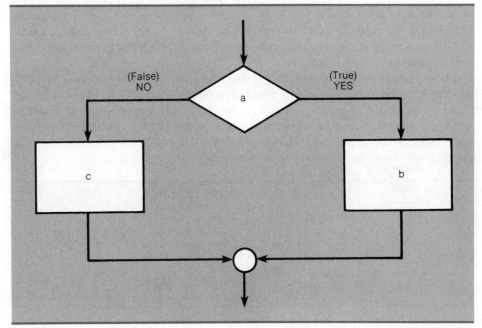

Figure 2–8
Basic IF-THEN-ELSE
structure.

Perhaps an example might make this clearer. Let's say you are planning to go to a concert but have only $10 to purchase the ticket. Your decision would be stated as:

IF the ticket is less than or equal to $10 THEN
    I shall go to the concert.
ELSE
    I shall stay home.
END-IF

Although the BASIC language has no END-IF statement (we will cover the IF-THEN-ELSE in Chapter 5), we will use it in our structures for the sake of clarity. Figure 2–9 presents the above structure in flowchart form.

Even though our charts and pseudocode show only one item on each selection (true and false) this is not always the case. Suppose you still have $10 for your ticket. We could change the structure to the following:

IF the ticket is less than $9 THEN
    I shall go to the concert.
    I shall buy popcorn.
ELSE
    I shall stay home.
END-IF

Notice that now we are going to do two things if the condition is true. The flowchart for this can be seen in Figure 2–10.

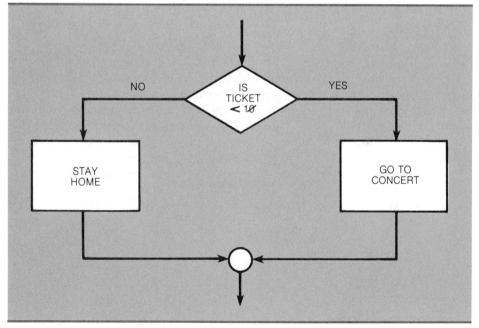

Figure 2–9
IF-THEN-ELSE example.

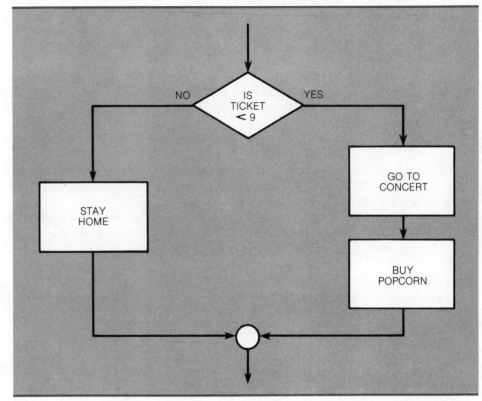

Figure 2–10
IF-THEN-ELSE with two
actions on true test.

One more thing about the two previous figures. The small, circular symbol is called a **connector symbol** and is used here as a collector, emphasizing that the IF-THEN-ELSE structure has only one entry point and one exit point. This is important as this makes the entire structure a single element, which can then be used as a part of a SIMPLE SEQUENCE chart. Recall that it was mentioned that the entire procedure should always be presented as a SIMPLE SEQUENCE no matter how many structures are within the sequence. When we use a connector as shown, it will always have two flow lines entering and only one exiting. This shows that it is not permissible for both paths to extend beyond the IF-THEN-ELSE structure itself. This allows us to prepare well-structured, SIMPLE SEQUENCE programs.

Let's look for a moment at a somewhat different problem. Suppose that before we print our payroll checks, we have to run a program that prints out all those employees that have worked more than 40 hours. The flowchart can be seen in Figure 2–11; the pseudocode follows:

```
Start
IF hours greater than 40 THEN
    Print information on report.
(ELSE)
END-IF
End
```

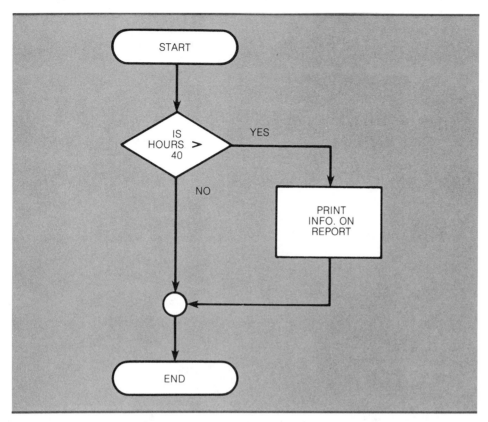

Figure 2–11
Null ELSE example.

We need an IF-THEN-ELSE structure, but since there is only one thing to do and it is only done under a certain condition, our structure really has no ELSE. This is what is called a **null ELSE.** It is simply a case whereby something is to be done in the program only if the condition is true. There will be many cases later when we will use the null ELSE. Notice the symbolism in the pseudocode: (ELSE) will be used to signify the null ELSE.

2–6
THE DO-WHILE STRUCTURE

With the use of a decision test we can modify the payroll procedure we used before to process any number of employees. We will use the DO-WHILE structure for this exercise.

The general form of the DO-WHILE structure can be seen in Figure 2–12. First, condition *a* is tested. If condition *a* is true, statement *b* is executed and control returns to the test. If condition *a* is false, control passes through the structure to the next process. This is the basic design of the structure; the steps in the loop are executed when the test is true, and control passes through when the test is false.

Notice that the first thing the DO-WHILE does is the test. The first time through the loop, if the decision test is false, control passes through. It is possible that none of the statements in the loop will be executed.

In our payroll example, let's assume we have 25 employees. We can create

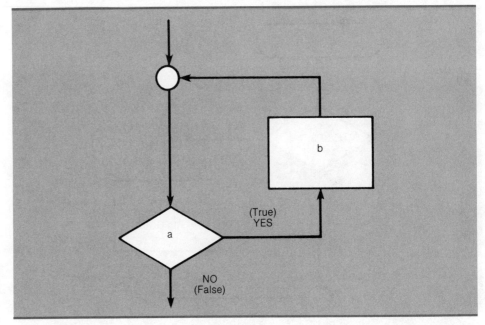

Figure 2–12
Basic DO-WHILE
structure.

a new procedure as shown in the following pseudocode (see Figure 2–13 for
the flowchart):

    Start
    Set counter to 0.
    DO-WHILE counter is less than 26.
        Input the hours worked.
        Calculate gross pay and deduct FICA, taxes, and miscellaneous deduc-
            tions.
        Print the payroll check.
        Increase the counter by 1.
    END-DO
    End

Now our process has the loop that we mentioned before. On the flowchart
you can see that if the test is true (counter < 26), the flow indicates the processing to be done and then connects back with the main line. This forms the
loop. The connector symbol serves as a collector at the beginning of the loop
just as it was used before on the IF-THEN-ELSE. It has two flow lines entering
and only one exiting. It indicates that there is only one entrance to this structure (at the connector symbol) and one exit (at the decision symbol).

This loop pattern is another of our three basic structures. As you have
probably gathered from looking at the pseudocode, this is called the **DO-
WHILE** structure. Note the keywords DO-WHILE and END-DO in the pseudocode. The END-DO, of course, signifies the end of the DO-WHILE. It does not
replace the End of the code itself, it simply marks the end of the DO-WHILE.
We still have an End in the pseudocode.

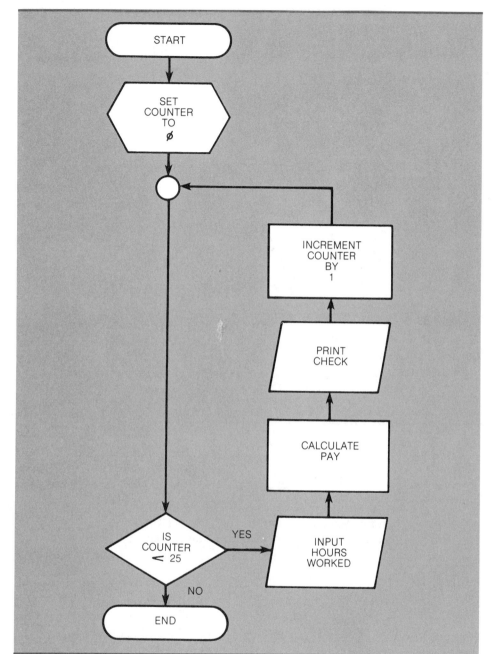

Figure 2–13
DO-WHILE payroll
example.

We have introduced a new symbol in our flowchart. The **preparation symbol** (Figure 2–14) is used to prepare data for a sequence of instructions. Many times this preparation takes the form of the **initialization** or initial setting up of a value. In this example, what we initially set up was a **counter** or a place to keep track of the number of times the input information has been processed.

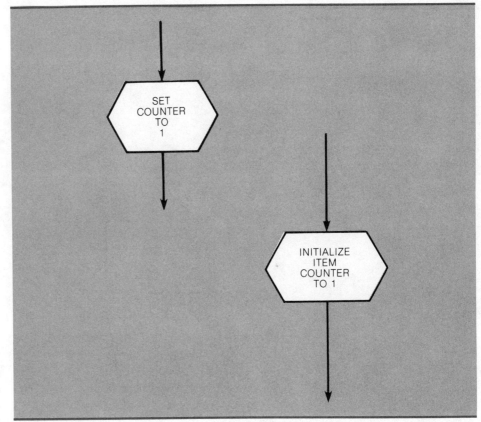

Figure 2–14
Examples of preparation
symbols.

It is again important to note that our new structure has only one entrance and one exit. This allows us to visualize it as a single part of the entire SIMPLE SEQUENCE. Each process we do should be able to be viewed as a SIMPLE SEQUENCE. When we have IF-THEN-ELSE or DO-WHILE structures within our SIMPLE SEQUENCE, they are said to be **nested.** This simply means the secondary structure is totally contained within the major. DO-WHILE structures can also be nested within IF-THEN-ELSE structures and vice versa.

2–7
ANOTHER
DO-WHILE

In the previous DO-WHILE structure we used a counter to determine when we were finished. There is another method that is used frequently. It is an **end-of-data marker,** which is simply a method of finding the end of the data by checking for some type of marker. The type of indicator varies, but it is always something suitable for the situation. One method used with numeric data is to put a dummy number in the data that would not ordinarily be found there to stop execution of the program. Usually a negative number is suitable. In our payroll example, we are inputting the hours worked. Hours could conceivably be zero, but not negative, so we would be safe using a negative for our end-of-data marker.

The flowchart for our reconstructed process can be seen in Figure 2–15; the pseudocode would look like the following:

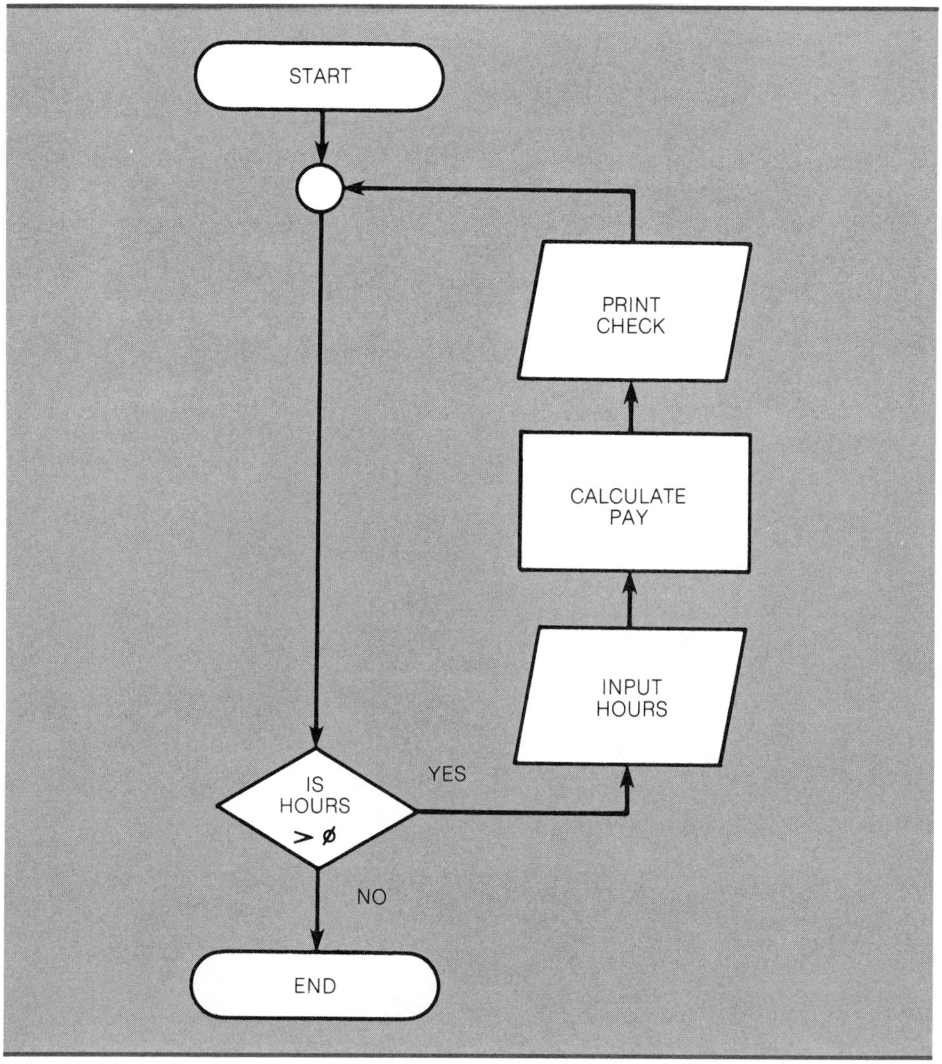

Figure 2–15
End-of-data marker
example with one input.

Start
DO-WHILE hours not negative.
   Input the hours worked.
   Calculate gross pay and deduct FICA, taxes, and miscellaneous deduc-
      tions.
   Print the payroll check.
END-DO
End

It should be readily apparent that we have a problem. We are testing for
negative hours before we have ever input any hours. That is not even the worst
problem. If the hours are negative, the processes will take place anyway since
the test is not done until after the processes. Obviously we need another step
somewhere. What we need to do is input the hours *before* we get into the loop.
But if we do that, then there will not be an input inside the loop where there

needs to be one. The solution is to use two input statements as shown in Figure 2–16 and below:

Start
Input the hours worked.
DO-WHILE hours not negative.
   Calculate gross pay and deduct FICA, taxes, and miscellaneous deductions.
   Print the payroll check. *(continues on page 35)*

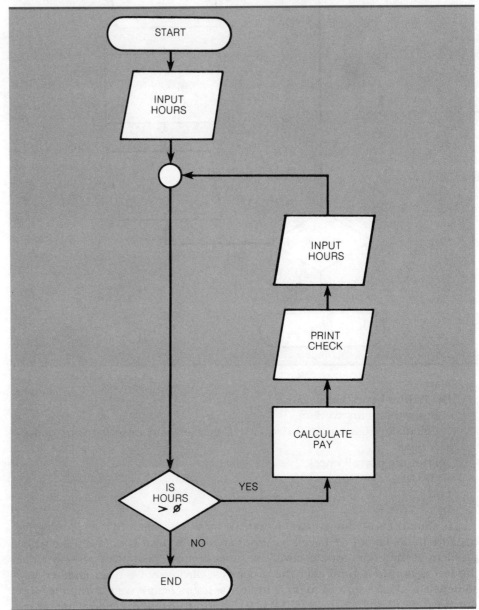

Figure 2–16
End-of-data marker example with two inputs.

Input the hours worked.
END-DO
End

Notice also that the second input, the one inside the loop, was moved to the end of the processing loop. It has to be the last thing done in the loop. It may seem strange to you that two input statements are used. But it is necessary to have the input hours to test before entering the loop; remember, the test is the first thing done within the loop. That means that we have to have a second input statement.

2—8
OTHER SYMBOLS

We mentioned that the connector is used in the IF-THEN-ELSE structure as a collector. But the connector has another use also. It is called a connector because it can be used to connect one area of a flowchart with another area. Say, for example, that our program is so large that it takes several columns on our paper to draw the entire chart. Instead of drawing a long flow line from the bottom of the first column of symbols to the top of the second column, we use connectors. Each connector is labeled with either a number or a letter so that if other connectors need to be used, there is no confusion about which goes with which. A sample of how this might be labeled is shown in Figure 2–17.

The standard procedure with connectors is to label them sequentially from the beginning of the chart. This allows us to tell approximately what relationship the connectors have in a large flowchart.

The symbols we use in flowcharting are not large, and sometimes there is

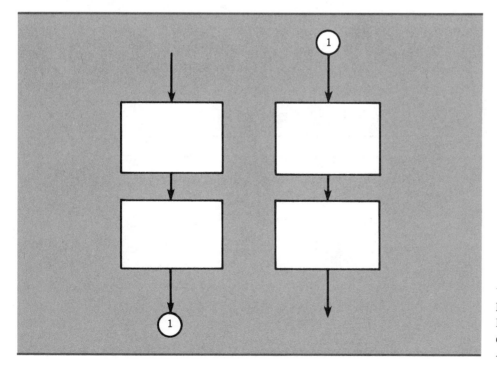

Figure 2–17
Example of second use of connectors.

need for more information than will comfortably fit within one symbol. There is
another symbol for just such situations. It is called the **annotation symbol** and
is used to add descriptive comments to a flowchart. The comments found in
the symbol do nothing to affect processing but serve merely to clarify a processing point. An example of a comment in an annotation symbol is shown in
Figure 2–18.

One final symbol that we will find handy later is the **predefined process
symbol** (Figure 2–19). This symbol is a means of referring to another routine (or
routines) that is specified elsewhere. This type of predefined process allows us
to build more modular programs, one of our basic guidelines.

Suppose, for example, when we print our payroll check that we need the
date printed on the check. The date we want to print is stored in the machine
and requires a few simple instructions to retrieve it. But since we have access
to the date, we use it for other things also (such as part of a screen display).
This being the case, we would probably want to set up some type of routine to
get the date so that we don't have to use the entire routine in our loop. We can
add the process to our flowchart (Figure 2–20) and our pseudocode easily (we

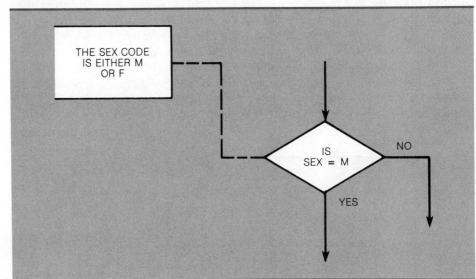

Figure 2–18
Use of the annotation
symbol.

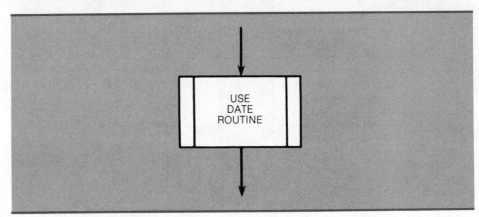

Figure 2–19
Example of predefined
process symbol.

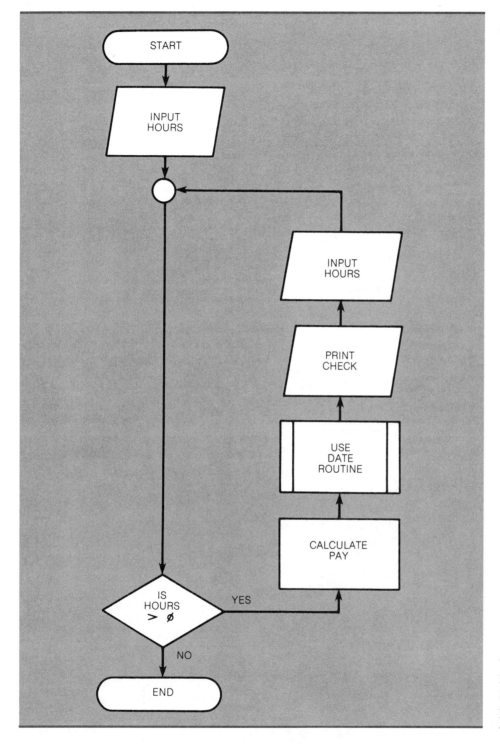

Figure 2–20
Flowchart using
predefined process.

won't concern ourselves with the routine itself, just how we would use the notation):

> Start
> Input the hours worked.
> DO-WHILE hours not negative.
>> Calculate gross pay and deduct FICA, taxes, and miscellaneous deductions.
>> Get the date.
>> Print the payroll check using the date.
>> Input the hours worked.
> END-DO
> End

SUMMARY

1. Flowcharts have become the tool of the systems analyst, and most charts produced are system flowcharts. Programmers, however, still must understand the processes necessary to produce a flowchart. The steps used when drawing flowcharts are the same steps necessary for solving any problem. Also, most programmers still use the program flowchart to help analyze difficult or unfamiliar routines.

2. Another tool that is becoming more popular with programmers is pseudocode.

3. Structured programming is a concept that can go a long way in helping you develop programs that are easy to write and easy to care for. The concepts of structured programming suggest that all programs can be written using only three basic structures:
   1. The SIMPLE SEQUENCE
   2. The IF-THEN-ELSE
   3. The DO-WHILE

4. All our programs in this text will follow an additional set of guidelines:
   1. They will be written using the recommended structures.
   2. They will be well documented.
   3. They will be modular.

5. The programming symbols we will use are ANSI standard symbols. The terminal symbol indicates the start or end of the procedure. A process symbol is used when charting a calculation or other manipulation of the data. The I/O symbol represents inputting or printing of information. Decisions are indicated by putting the conditional statement inside the decision symbol. When we have a statement that indicates a one-time process, preparing for a procedure, we use the preparation symbol. The annotation symbol is used when there is not enough room in the other symbol to indicate thoroughly the procedure; the annotation is used strictly for comments. Flow lines with arrows connect all the symbols to show the direction of the flow of data. A predefined process symbol refers to a process that is defined somewhere else and can be used many different times in the same chart.

6. Whenever we use the DO-WHILE structure, we must test for something to exit the loop. We can do this in two different ways. We can use a counter and exit when the counter exceeds a certain value; we continue the loop while the counter is less than that value. We can also test for an end-of-data marker.

GLOSSARY

Annotation symbol The symbol used for adding comments inside a flowchart. These comments have no effect on the logic of the chart but are merely additional information.

ANSI (American National Standards Institute) The committee responsible for the standardization of flowchart symbols (and many other things).

Connector symbol This symbol is used for two different things. First, it is used as a point of collection on our structures; second, it is used to connect one area of a flowchart with another.

Counter A marker that is increased each time through the loop until a maximum value is reached.

Decision symbol This diamond-shaped symbol is used for decisions in the flowchart.

DO-WHILE A structure that will do the processes contained within the structure while a condition is true.

END This is the marker used in the terminal symbol to signify the end of processing.

End-of-data marker An indicator placed at the end of the information being input to indicate to the program that all the data has been input.

Flowchart A series of symbols indicating the flow of information within a program or system.

Flow line The indicator of the path from one flowchart symbol to the next.

IF-THEN-ELSE The structure that allows one of two types of processing to be done based on a condition.

Initialization The process of setting a beginning value into a counter or other data item.

INPUT The most common method of getting data into a program.

I/O symbol The symbol used for input and output.

Iteration *See* **Loop.**

Loop The process of reusing a series of steps in a flowchart.

Nested Refers to one structure being wholly contained within another.

Null ELSE The condition in the IF-THEN-ELSE structure when there is no ELSE needed; something is done in the program only if the condition is true.

Predefined process symbol The symbol used to denote that a series of instructions are defined elsewhere.

Preparation symbol The symbol used to denote an operation performed on data to get it ready for processing.

PRINT A method of visually displaying the results of a computer process.

Process symbol The flowchart symbol used to indicate the manipulation of data in a program.

Program flowchart A flowchart of the operations on data as it passes through a program.

Pseudocode An informal language used by programmers to design programs to be coded in any programming language.

SIMPLE SEQUENCE The structure that dictates that each process within the structure is self-contained; the entire structure flows straight through from one process to the next.

START A flowchart label signifying the beginning of the chart.

Structured programming A method of programming that follows a certain set of rules devised to enable the creation of easy-to-write and maintain programs.

System A series of programs that are put together to perform a specific task.

Systems analyst The person responsible for designing the flow of data through an entire system or organization.

Systems flowchart The chart that depicts the flow of data through an entire system or organization.

Terminal symbol The symbol used at the beginning and end of the program.

1. Explain what flowcharts are for and why they are important.
*2. Name the two types of flowcharts and explain the differences and who uses each.
3. Explain what pseudocode is for and why it is important.
4. List all of the flowchart symbols used in this chapter, and explain what each is used for.
5. List and explain the purpose of the three programming structures used in this chapter. Use an example flowchart for an illustration.
*6. Explain why a counter is used and in which structure(s) it is used.
7. Explain why an end-of-data marker is used and in which structure(s) it is used.
8. Analyze Figure 2–21 and write the pseudocode for the process developed in the flowchart. The problem depicts the processing necessary to study for a test.
9. Design a flowchart to depict the following pseudocode for figuring gas mileage:

Start
Input miles traveled.
Compute the mileage rate.
Print out the results.
End

10. Design a flowchart and pseudocode for question 9, changing it so that it will figure the mileage for five different cars. (Use a counter.)
*11. Design a flowchart and pseudocode for question 9, changing it so that it will figure the mileage for any number of cars. End the process with a negative input (end-of-data marker).
12. XYZ Corporation has to prepare a payroll at the end of each week. There are 50 employees, and the payroll must be prepared so that deductions are made from the gross pay for social security, federal taxes, state taxes, and insurance. Design a flowchart and pseudocode for XYZ's payroll showing input of each employee's name, hours, and pay rate, calculation of the payroll including the deductions, and output of the payroll checks.

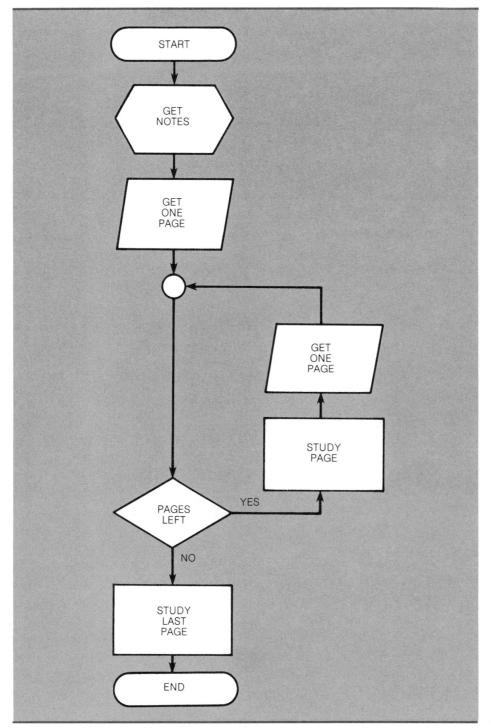

Figure 2–21
Flowchart of studying for
test.

The answers to the questions follow immediately after the quiz. Questions 1–15 are true–false, while 16–20 are multiple choice.

T F 1. Programmers must develop skill with using flowcharts, but systems analysts rarely use them.

T F 2. The two most prevalent forms of flowcharts in data processing are the systems chart and the program chart.

T F 3. Flowcharts are only used in data processing applications.

T F 4. Most programmers do a great deal of flowcharting, and this is the main reason they must learn to use flowcharts.

T F 5. Systems charts use different symbols from program charts, but the flowcharting principles are the same.

T F 6. The ANSI has been a strong force in the adoption of a set of standard symbols for use in flowcharting.

T F 7. All symbols except the START must have two exits.

T F 8. There are separate symbols for input and output.

T F 9. According to Dijkstra, all programs can be constructed from only three structures.

T F 10. A loop is called a noniterative process.

T F 11. Communication problems are most often associated with data processing.

T F 12. The IF-THEN-ELSE structure must always have two exits.

T F 13. The first step in the DO-WHILE structure is the decision.

T F 14. An end-of-data marker is generally a negative number when used with numeric data.

T F 15. A connector is used for two different purposes on our flowcharts.

_____ 16. The symbol for extra comments is the
  a. decision   c. annotation
  b. I/O   d. terminal

_____ 17. The shape of the decision symbol is
  a. parallelogram   c. rectangle
  b. diamond   d. square

_____ 18. Which of the following structures is the one that uses the decision test?
  a. SIMPLE SEQUENCE   c. IF-THEN-ELSE
  b. DO-WHILE   d. both b and c

_____ 19. An initialization process is depicted by which of the following symbols?
  a. decision   c. annotation
  b. preparation   d. predefined process

_____ 20. Which of the following structures is defined as conditional?
  a. IF-THEN-ELSE   c. SIMPLE SEQUENCE
  b. DO-WHILE   d. none of them

1. F (Programmers create flowcharts occasionally, but they are mainly the analyst's tool.)
2. T
3. F (They can be useful for many other things.)
4. F (Programmers do little flowcharting, but they need to be able to flowchart particularly complex programs and understand those the analysts create.)
5. T
6. T
7. F (Only the decision test has two exits.)
8. F (They both use the parallelogram.)
9. T
10. F (It is an iterative process.)
11. F (Communication problems are universal.)
12. F (There are two exits from the decision symbol, not from the structure itself.)
13. T
14. T (Though it can be any piece of data that is out of context with the data being input.)
15. T
16. c
17. b
18. d (However, so can the SIMPLE SEQUENCE since both of the others can be nested within it.)
19. b
20. a

3 BEGINNING BASIC

OBJECTIVES

After completing Chapter 3, you will be able to:

- Describe the difference between the immediate mode and the program mode.
- Use the PRINT command in both modes with both numeric and literal data.
- Explain the three types of delimiters for the PRINT command and why the blank is not an acceptable method.
- Explain why line numbering is done by 10s.
- Describe the different methods of using the LIST command on your particular machine.
- Describe the method of deleting one line from your program.
- Describe the only structure used in this chapter.
- Use the DELETE (or similar) command to delete a series of lines from your program.
- Describe the two types of variables and explain how they are used.
- Use assignments in several simple programs to show how they are used.
- Decide what assignments are valid and invalid in a list and explain what is wrong with the invalid ones.
- Demonstrate the use of pseudocode and flowcharts in the programs written.

44

BASIC has been touted as an easy-to-learn language, but as with any language, there are many rules. The computer expects these rules to be followed and will tell you when they are not. In this chapter a few of the more important rules and commands of BASIC are introduced.

Many of the new terms and methods may be foreign to you. But don't worry! After some experimentation, they will become a part of your everyday vocabulary. Also, don't be concerned about doing something wrong. The computer is very forgiving. It will tell you when you have made an error and tell you it is ready for something else by displaying **Ok** or READY. (Remember we will use the IBM response of Ok in our examples.)

One important point to remember is that the computer does not know you have tried to communicate with it until you press RETURN. The **RETURN** key is the signal to the machine that you have finished whatever you were entering and it can now execute the instruction. Until you press RETURN, the machine will wait. And you will find the computer to be very patient when waiting. So, when you are finished making an entry, press RETURN.

One reason microcomputers are so popular is that they generally use an **interactive** version of BASIC. That is, you are in direct and continual dialogue with the machine. It asks you a question and you answer it, then it asks another. BASIC uses this interactive approach to good advantage in the **immediate mode.**

Before we discuss the immediate mode, however, we need to examine a message with which you will become increasingly familiar. Any time you try to communicate with the machine and it doesn't understand what you entered, you will receive **Syntax error** on the screen. As an example, let's enter:

```
HI THERE
```

and press RETURN. You will see on the screen:

```
Syntax error
Ok
```

This just means that the computer didn't understand what you meant by HI THERE.

You will, however, sometimes see Syntax error when you don't think you have done anything wrong. If you do get Syntax error, examine the offending statement closely. If you cannot see anything wrong (there is always something wrong), try rekeying the line. Occasionally, a special character that does not register on the screen gets put into the statement, perhaps as a result of accidentally pressing two keys simultaneously. If you rekey the statement, you will replace the erroneous line with a new one. Usually, you have entered something incorrectly. Rekeying the statement will help you see what is incorrect. This may clear up the problem. If it does not, consult this book or your user's manual to discover what is wrong.

There are, of course, many errors that may occur other than syntax errors, but syntax errors are the most common. Most error messages are self-explanatory, and with a little thought you will understand what is incorrect. For a list of the various errors each machine will generate, consult Appendix B.

One important command in BASIC concerns output from the computer. When we give the computer information, we generally expect it to give us back some kind of response. This response is usually displayed on the screen. The BASIC command to display something on the screen is **PRINT.** PRINT is the microcomputer's output command. It outputs from the processor to the screen. Some BASICs have an abbreviation for the PRINT command. All our versions use the question mark (?) as a substitute. That is, instead of entering PRINT you can simply enter ? and the machine will assume you mean PRINT.

There are basically two types of information that can be printed: numbers or calculations of numbers and literals or characters within quotes. For example, if you entered these numbers:

    PRINT 4+5

(or you could enter ? 4 + 5) and pressed the RETURN key, the following would appear on the screen:

    9
    Ok

The 9 is the total of 4 + 5, and the Ok is, of course, the machine telling you that it is now ready for something else to do. The computer uses the plus (+) symbol for addition and the minus (−) symbol for subtraction. (Section 3–3 covers the rest of the operators.)

Notice that there is a blank in front of the 9 in the previous example. (The Apple doesn't leave the blank.) Most versions of BASIC print the sign of the number with the number. No sign is printed in this example because it is standard in mathematics to interpret no sign as a positive sign. Instead, a blank space is printed. If the number had been negative, the sign would have been printed. For example, if you enter:

    PRINT 5-6

and press the RETURN key, the following will appear on the screen:

    −1
    Ok

Notice that the minus sign (−) is right over the O in Ok. There is now no leading blank because the sign takes up the empty spot.

Let's try another calculation just to be clear. If you enter:

    PRINT 44-5

and press the RETURN key, you should get 39. What appears on the screen is:

    39
    Ok

Just as we expected, and notice the leading blank (not on the Apple). Now let's try it again a little differently. Try using spaces around the operator (the minus sign):

and press RETURN. Should this be a different result than the other one? Of course not. The point is that spaces do not generally matter to most versions of BASIC. (There are a few places, however, where blanks do have a meaning. These will be discussed when relevant.) Spaces are normally simply ignored. The computer will verify this when it does the calculation:

```
 39
Ok
```

This point is important to remember. Blank spaces *generally* do not make any difference in most versions of BASIC. One exception is in the words of the language, the commands. For example, PRINT is not the same as PR INT, and the machine would not understand the latter method. Let's try it. (We will stop mentioning to press RETURN. It is important, however, to always remember to do it after keying a line of code.)

```
PR INT 44-5
Syntax error
Ok
```

Take care when using commands to ensure that the actual command words are used precisely as designated. Unpredictable results may occur if this rule is not followed.

The commands we have been discussing are sometimes called **keywords.** A keyword is simply some word that has a special meaning in the language. All languages have keywords; most have many more than BASIC.

The other data type the computer can print is called a **literal.** A literal is any piece of data that is enclosed in quotes. For example, if you entered:

```
PRINT "HI THERE"
```

you would see appear on the screen:

```
HI THERE
Ok
```

Notice the lack of quotes in the output. The quotes are simply indicators to the computer that what you are telling it to print should be printed literally, as is. When the command is executed, the quotes are dropped and the display is only the literal itself. The computer prints exactly what it reads within the quotation marks. We know that if you key:

```
PRINT 4+5
```

you would see:

```
 9
Ok
```

on the screen. If you keyed:

```
PRINT "4+5"
```

you would get:

```
4+5
Ok
```

The command prints precisely what you put between the quotes.

In a literal, a blank or space also has a meaning. Everything is valid in a literal, including blanks. Therefore, within a literal, any number of blanks will be placed in the output exactly as you specify, such as:

```
PRINT "HI   THERE    WHAT ARE YOU DOING?"
HI    THERE     WHAT ARE YOU DOING?
Ok
```

Notice that the blanks that were specified in the PRINT statement appear in the output the same way. All blanks in quotes will be printed as they are stated.

Even though the quotes do not appear in the output, they are important. Let's try this one without quotes:

```
PRINT HI THERE
```

Your output will be something like:

```
 0
Ok
```

What this indicates is that what you had intended as a literal, the computer interpreted incorrectly as a variable (discussed in Section 3–9, but basically a location in storage where a value is placed). There was no value in the variable so the computer printed 0 (zero). Don't worry right now where the zero came from, just recognize that if you see a zero when you were attempting to print a literal, you probably forgot the quotes.

The PRINT command can print more than one item on each statement. It can also print mixed types of information, such as:

```
PRINT "4 + 5 = ";4+5
```

The resulting display would be:

```
4 + 5 =  9
Ok
```

The semicolon between items is called a **delimiter** and is used to indicate where one item ends and another begins. There are three different types of delimiters that may be usable on your machine. The semicolon is the first. It tells the machine to print the second item immediately after the first. With numerics, a blank is left after each number. For literals, the two items are printed with no space between them. (In the Apple, no space is left between numeric items.)

The second type of delimiter is the comma. If you use a comma, the second item will print in the next print zone. All our computers use various locations across the screen known as **print zones.** On the IBM, Radio Shack Model 4, and Apple the print zones are 14 columns wide. This gives an 80-column display—five zones of 14 and one (the last one) of 10. The 40-column display will have two zones of 14 and one of 12. On the Radio Shack Model III the zones are 16 columns wide. Consider the following example:

```
PRINT "4 + 5 = ",4+5
```

which displays as:

```
4 + 5 =                 9
Ok
```

Note the many blanks between the equal sign and the 9. (Depending on your machine, there may be more or fewer blanks than shown above.) Here the next item printed, the 9, is put in the next print zone.

To make sure you understand what we have done, let's try it again using a semicolon:

```
PRINT "HI THERE ";"I AM A COMPUTER"
HI THERE I AM A COMPUTER
Ok
```

Then try it with a comma:

```
PRINT "HI THERE ","I AM A COMPUTER"
HI THERE             I AM A COMPUTER
Ok
```

The third type of delimiter is a blank or space. It normally functions as does the semicolon. This is not recommended because it is much better to indicate precisely what you mean by using the appropriate symbol. Using blanks may create confusion for someone else who tries to read your program (or for yourself when you return to the program after a period of time).

Another, more flexible way to direct the item to be printed to the appropriate column is to use the **TAB** statement. It has the form TAB(xx) where the xx is the column number to print in. As an example, let's try the following:

```
PRINT "HI THERE";TAB(10);"GEORGE";TAB(20);"HOW ARE YOU?"
HI THERE  GEORGE    HOW ARE YOU?
Ok
```

This is how your output would look. The TAB statement moves the cursor to the specified cursor location. That is, if TAB(10) is used, the cursor is moved to the tenth column. (Actually, the next character prints in the eleventh column on the IBM and Radio Shack, but on the Apple it would appear in the tenth column. Thus, for the IBM and Radio Shack the output will differ by one column from the number in the TAB statement.)

There is another important thing to remember about the TAB statement on the IBM and Radio Shack. If you leave a space between the B in TAB and the open parenthesis, you will get an error known as a **subscript out of range error.** You don't need to be concerned about what the error means except to recognize that it is telling you that you left a space where you shouldn't have.

On the IBM and Apple (IIe and IIc) there is also a **SPC** statement. This statement prints the specified number of spaces between the PRINT items. For example, here is how the statement above would look if we changed the TABs to SPC:

```
PRINT "HI THERE";SPC(10);"GEORGE";SPC(20);"HOW ARE YOU?"
HI THERE          GEORGE                    HOW ARE YOU?
Ok
```

Note: When using a printer with the Apple, the TAB statement will function the same as the SPC statement.

Remember one important point about the immediate mode. The computer does not store anything entered in the immediate mode. The command is executed directly and then the computer waits for you to give it more instructions. Once the screen is cleared, all record of what you have done is lost.

3–3
MATHEMATICAL OPERATORS

We have already discussed how the plus (+) symbol is used as the mathematical operator for the addition process. Most of the other **mathematical operators** are also ones you're used to seeing. Table 3–1 covers each of the symbols:

TABLE 3–1   Mathematical Operators

SYMBOL	USE
+	addition
−	subtraction
*	multiplication
/	division
∧	exponentiation (up arrow on Radio Shack)
( )	parentheses

The symbol for multiplication is not the traditional ×. The reason for this is simple: The computer must follow a precise set of rules, and it has only one definition for each character. Since none of the keyboards have a special × for multiplication and the X is used in programs as a character, the machine would have no way of knowing when you were using the X for multiplication and when for a character. The problem is avoided by using a slightly different symbol for multiplication: the asterisk (*).

Let's see how mathematical symbols are used in the PRINT statement.

Addition:

```
PRINT 4+5
 9
Ok
```

Subtraction:

```
PRINT 9-5
 4
Ok
```

Multiplication:

```
PRINT 4*5
 20
Ok
```

```
PRINT 18/3
 6
Ok
```

Exponentiation (to the power of):

```
PRINT 5∧2
 25
Ok
```

Math operations have a particular order in which they must be done. This is known as the "order of operation." The standard procedure is that multiplication and division are completed before addition and subtraction. Thus, if you used the following statement:

```
PRINT 4+5*6
 34
Ok
```

the result, as shown, would be 34, not 54. The multiplication is done first and then the addition. If there are two operations to be performed that have the same priority, then the process is left to right. For example, a statement with both addition and subtraction would execute the calculation on the left first.

As in mathematics, parentheses are used to indicate the order of operations. Operations in parentheses have higher priority than multiplication and division. They are always calculated first. Within a set of parentheses, the regular order prevails again. That is, within the parentheses, whatever has priority will be done first. Thus, if we had a PRINT statement such as:

```
PRINT 5*(4+6)
 50
Ok
```

the result is 50 because the 4 + 6 would be done first, and 10*5 yields 50. Without the parentheses:

```
PRINT 5*4+6
 26
Ok
```

the result is 26. In the following PRINT statement:

```
PRINT 4+5*6-2+(8/2)
 36
Ok
```

the result is 36, but if we moved the parentheses:

```
PRINT (4+5)*((6-2)+8)/2
 54
Ok
```

we get 54. You could arrange the problem several other ways for several other solutions.

The other BASIC mode allows the computer to store your commands and execute them a multiple of times. It is called the **program mode.** In the program mode each command you enter is a line that has two elements.

First, each line is numbered. You may begin your **line numbering** with 0 (or anything higher) and number as high as 65529 on the IBM and Radio Shack and 63999 on the Apple.

The second element for each line is the command that you wish to execute. For example, a line to print 4+5 would be:

```
10 PRINT 4+5
```

The big difference here is that after you enter this into the computer, nothing happens. The program mode does not respond immediately as did the command mode. What happens is that the computer stores the program line in memory and will retain it until you either replace the line by entering another line numbered 10, or empty memory (described later). To execute the program line, you need to enter another command. This command is entered in the immediate mode and thus is executed immediately. The **RUN command** causes the program stored in memory to execute. Thus, when you enter RUN, you will see the result as:

```
 9
Ok
```

This is the same result as in the immediate mode, but in the program mode you can run the program as many times as you wish without having to rekey. All you have to do is enter RUN, and the program will execute again.

Now, let's try a literal. Enter:

```
20 PRINT "HI THERE"
```

We should now have two lines in our program because first we had line 10 and we just entered line 20. Remember, line 10 will stay in memory until we clear it out somehow.

We can now execute the stored program with the RUN command. The display will be:

```
 9
HI THERE
Ok
```

Recall that you may print several items on the same statement by using a delimiter between the items. You can also leave a delimiter on the end of the PRINT statement to turn off the carriage return and line feed. Normally, the carriage return and line feed put the cursor at the beginning of the next line (similar to what a typewriter does). The delimiter will cause the cursor to remain where it is. That is, the next item (even when it is on the next program line) will print right after the last item printed. This will become clear if you rekey line 10. It will automatically replace the line 10 in memory. Let's change it to:

```
10 PRINT 4+5;
```

When run, the program will display:

```
 9 HI THERE
Ok
```

This may also be done on one line with the same results, as follows:

```
10 PRINT 4+5;"HI THERE"
```

After the RUN command:

```
 9 HI THERE
HI THERE
Ok
```

Of course, the program printed HI THERE twice because line 20 is still in the program. Note also that there is a blank between 9 and HI THERE. The semicolon did not cause this. As we mentioned before, BASIC will put a blank after a number (except on the Apple).

3–5
LINE NUMBERING

In the previous program we used lines 10 and 20. When it was run, 10 executed before 20. As might be expected, the lines of a program are executed in sequence, low number to high number.

Why did we number the lines 10 and 20? Since we can start the program with any number 0 or higher and use any number higher than the first for the second, why didn't we just use 0 and 1 or 1 and 2? The reason is simple: If we used 0 and 1, there would be no empty lines between them. If we ever needed to insert a line between them, it would not be possible without renumbering. But if we number by 10s, then there are nine different lines that can be inserted between them if necessary. For example, line 15 might be put in as:

```
15 PRINT "INSERTED LINE"
```

The program would then be:

```
10 PRINT 4+5;"HI THERE"
15 PRINT "INSERTED LINE"
20 PRINT "HI THERE"
```

After the RUN command, execution would be:

```
 9 HI THERE
INSERTED LINE
HI THERE
Ok
```

Note that the printed output is in the order of the line numbers. 15 is used as the number of the inserted line for the same reason that we used 10 and 20. Using 15 allows the most room for adding additional lines both before and after the inserted line.

Suppose we wish to have a blank line printed between our other print lines. We could insert a program line with a literal of several blanks, and this inserted line would appear as a blank line in proper numerical order in the program lines. Such an insert would look like:

```
17 PRINT "     "
```

And when executed we would see:

```
 9 HI THERE
INSERTED LINE

HI THERE
Ok
```

Note the blank line between INSERTED LINE and HI THERE. This is the result of line 17. It is unnecessary, however, to print the literal of blanks on the PRINT statement. Just using the PRINT statement by itself will cause the carriage to return and go to the next line. Since that is all that is really needed, we don't need the blanks. Instead let's use line 17 as follows:

```
17 PRINT
```

The execution would be the same as before:

```
 9 HI THERE
INSERTED LINE

HI THERE
Ok
```

BASIC does have a renumber command (the Apple has one as a special system program) that allows the programmer to resequence the program so there is room to insert needed statements. But even when we have the command, it can sometimes cause some problems, so care should be taken to always number your programs to allow for expansion. (See Appendix A for renumbering commands.)

3–6
ADDITIONAL COMMANDS

Recall that in the program mode, whatever is entered is stored in memory. To verify what is in memory, we need another command. The **LIST** command will allow you to examine the program that you have entered. If you key LIST and press RETURN, you should see the entire program as you have entered it:

```
10 PRINT 4+5;"HI THERE"
15 PRINT "INSERTED LINE"
17 PRINT
20 PRINT "HI THERE"
Ok
```

The LIST command works several different ways depending on your version of BASIC. We will discuss each as we progress. To better demonstrate the LIST command, we will add two more lines to the program. Let's put lines 30 and 40 in our program as follows:

```
30 PRINT "I AM A COMPUTER"
40 PRINT "AND I GUESS YOU'RE A PROGRAMMER."
```

Now enter LIST and press RETURN, and your whole program will be:

```
10 PRINT 4+5;"HI THERE"
15 PRINT "INSERTED LINE"
17 PRINT
20 PRINT "HI THERE"
30 PRINT "I AM A COMPUTER"
40 PRINT "AND I GUESS YOU'RE A PROGRAMMER."
Ok
```

When you have more program than the screen will hold, the program will push up from the bottom and disappear at the top. This is called **scrolling.** The program will continue to scroll until either you stop it or the computer comes to the end of the program. To stop the listing at any particular point you would press the BREAK key.

Since programs are usually longer than can be seen on just one screen, you will often want to view only a portion of the program. You can view a particular portion by scrolling to the appropriate area then stopping, or you can list just a small section of code using one of the available list options.

Listing one line is done by entering LIST XX. XX is the number of the line you want listed; only that line would be listed on the screen. Key LIST 20, for example, and you will get:

```
20 PRINT "HI THERE"
Ok
```

To list from the beginning of the program to a certain line number, you would enter, say, LIST -15. All lines from the beginning of the program to line 15, including line 15, would list on the screen. Key LIST -15, and you will get:

```
10 PRINT 4+5;"HI THERE"
15 PRINT "INSERTED LINE"
Ok
```

You can examine a section of the program by entering, for example, LIST 15-30. Lines 15 through 30 *inclusive* would display on the screen. Key LIST 15-30, and you will get:

```
15 PRINT "INSERTED LINE"
17 PRINT
20 PRINT "HI THERE"
30 PRINT "I AM A COMPUTER"
Ok
```

To begin at a certain line and continue until the end, enter, for example, LIST 20-, and you will get:

```
20 PRINT "HI THERE"
30 PRINT "I AM A COMPUTER"
40 PRINT "AND I GUESS YOU'RE A PROGRAMMER."
Ok
```

Another thing you might want to do is delete a line that you do not want from the program. To remove a line from a program, enter the line number and then press RETURN. The line will then be gone. As an example enter:

15

Then when you press RETURN and key LIST, you will get:

```
10 PRINT 4+5;"HI THERE"
17 PRINT
20 PRINT "HI THERE"
30 PRINT "I AM A COMPUTER"
40 PRINT "AND I GUESS YOU'RE A PROGRAMMER."
Ok
```

Notice that line 15 is now gone from the listing.

If you wish to replace a line, you need only reenter the line in question, and the newly keyed line will be in its place:

```
30 PRINT "I AM A FRIENDLY COMPUTER"
```

Then on keying LIST, you will get:

```
10 PRINT 4+5;"HI THERE"
17 PRINT
20 PRINT "HI THERE"
30 PRINT "I AM A FRIENDLY COMPUTER"
40 PRINT "AND I GUESS YOU'RE A PROGRAMMER."
Ok
```

If you need to remove a section of a program, most of our versions of BASIC have a **DELETE command.** Its use is usually similar to the method of using the LIST command as described above. An example might be:

```
DELETE 20-30
```

Then key LIST:

```
10 PRINT 4+5;"HI THERE"
17 PRINT
40 PRINT "AND I GUESS YOU'RE A PROGRAMMER."
Ok
```

This works on the IBM and Radio Shack. On the Apple a comma is used instead of the dash and the command is DEL. For example, to use the DELETE command above, the Apple would require the command:

```
DEL 20,30
```

If you need to remove an entire program from the memory, such as when you're ready to begin keying a new program, you can enter **NEW,** press RETURN, and the program will be gone.

If you want to try this procedure, enter NEW and press RETURN. Now key LIST, and you will get no listing of your program since it has been erased from memory.

3–7
PRINTING ON THE PRINTER

The PRINT statements we have been using will display the output on the screen. If you should wish to output to the line printer (assuming you have one), the form of the statement must be altered slightly.

On the IBM and Radio Shack, you merely change the PRINT statement to **LPRINT.** On the Apple, it is a bit more complicated. You first need to tell the computer you want to print on the printer. You do this by issuing the command:

```
10 PR#1
```

This tells the computer to channel the print through slot 1. (The Apple has slots where boards for accessory devices, such as a printer, are put. If your printer board is in a slot other than 1, you would use a variation of the **PR#** command, such as PR#4.) Then you use the PRINT statement just as you have been using it. After you are finished printing on the printer, you have to send the output back to the screen by issuing:

```
10 PR#0
```

If you wish to list a program on the printer, the IBM and Radio Shack use a simple **LLIST** command. On the Apple you use the same commands as above to turn the printer on, and then LIST the program as normal.

3—8 CLEARING THE SCREEN

We saw in Chapter 1 how we can clear the screen by pressing a key, but we can also do it with a program command. On the IBM and Radio Shack, the command is **CLS.** On the Apple, the command is **HOME.**

3—9 VARIABLES

There are two methods of using data in a program: constant and variable (data that is allowed to change). We have already looked at constant data, that is, data that doesn't change, such as when we printed 4 + 5:

```
PRINT 4 + 5
```

Since every time we enter this statement we will get 9 as a result, the 4 and 5 are called **constants.** We will now examine those types of data that can change or vary. Since they can vary, they are called **variables.** When data that varies among several possible values is used in a program, it is assigned to a variable, which means it is stored in memory. The computer keeps track of the current value of each of the variables.

Just as there are two types of constants, numeric and literal, there are two types of variables. The two variables are **numeric variables** and **string variables.** Numeric variables can contain only numbers, a decimal, and a sign (positive or negative). String variables may contain anything, similar to the literals we discussed earlier. The values of variables are represented by letters of the alphabet, which are called variable names since the values represented by the letters can change. The value represented by each letter is stored in a separate location in memory; thus, each different letter or variable represents a different value.

There is a slight difference between the IBM version and our other versions of BASIC when it comes to variable names. However, they all follow a couple of simple rules: The initial character of a variable name must be a letter. Following the letter is either another letter or a number. (You can, however, have a one-character variable.) The IBM version will also allow any of the characters following the first to be a period. Variable name length is where the main difference in our versions lies. On the Radio Shack and Apple the variable names can be any length up to 255 characters long. However, only the first two characters are recognized as the variable name. For example, the two variables CAT and CAR would be the same variable, CA, to the computer. On the IBM, variable names are unique out to the fortieth character. Thus CAT and CAR would be totally different variable names and represent different stored values.

The second type of variable, string variables, may be represented in the same way as the numeric variables, with the exception that the last character in the variable name must be the dollar sign ($). The dollar sign signifies to the machine that this variable is a string variable.

As an example of variable name usage, let's say we have 15.5 stored in A. That means that out in memory somewhere, the computer has the number 15.5 stored and knows that the variable name A represents that location in storage. Now, every time we reference A in our program, 15.5 will be used.

Instead of using A for the variable name, I could have used B, C, D9, T8, CAT, DOG, HAROLD, or any of a virtually unlimited supply of variable names. (Actually, there are 962 different possibilities for the Radio Shack and Apple. The IBM is virtually unlimited since it allows variable names up to 40 characters long.) The variable name is strictly the programmer's choice. It is, however, a good practice to use a variable name that represents the type of information you are storing. If you are working with gas mileage, for example, it would be a good idea to use G, M, or possibly GAS or MILEAGE for your variable name. If you were using some character information, such as a person's name, in your variable, a good choice would be N$ or NAME$. (Remember, characters that are not numeric can be stored only in string variables.) Table 3–2 is a sample list of valid and invalid variable names.

TABLE 3–2 Valid and Invalid Variable Names

VALID		INVALID	
A1	numeric	9B	letter must be first
A$	string	T@	wrong character
B9	numeric	$T	letter must be first
T$	string		
DOG$	string		
S	numeric		
T85GR9	numeric		

We have another difference in our versions of BASIC. On the IBM and Apple, whenever string variables are used, unlimited storage is automatically set aside. In the Radio Shack, however, only a limited amount of string space is automatically set aside. Unless specifically told, the machine will set aside only 50 characters of string storage space. Once you run out of that space (which is easy to do, 50 is not much), you will get an **Out of string space error.** To rectify this error, you need to use a statement that tells the machine to reserve extra string space. That statement is **CLEAR,** and it has the form:

```
10 CLEAR number
```

where the number is simply any number within the size of available memory. How much should you clear? Well, the Radio Shack manual suggests you figure out how much string space you will need by calculating the size of all the strings used in your program and reserve that much string space. This would be exceptionally difficult to do. We suggest that instead you set aside 5000 characters (10 CLEAR 5000). This amount of string space should be sufficient for most programs. Then, if you run out of memory (unlikely), you can reduce the number on the CLEAR statement.

3–10
ASSIGNMENT

Since we now have access to the storage areas of the computer by virtue of the variables, we need some method of assigning values to those variables. The statement to store values is called an **assignment statement** and in our versions is the **LET statement.** The form of a LET statement follows:

```
10 LET variable = expression
```

where the variable is the variable name you have chosen. It can be a name for a numeric variable or a string variable, but it can be for only one variable. It is not valid to have anything other than just one variable name on the left side of the equal sign (other than the word LET, of course).

The equal sign is called the assignment operator. When discussing an assignment, it is proper to say the variable is *assigned* the expression. It is inaccurate and incorrect to say the variable *is equal to* the expression.

The expression can be a numeric calculation, a literal, a numeric variable, a string variable, or a combination of compatible elements. It is, of course, also necessary that the variable and the expression be compatible. That is, if the variable is numeric, then the expression must be numeric, either a constant, a variable, or a combination. If the variable is a string variable, then the expression must be a literal, another string variable, or a combination. An example of an assignment statement would be:

```
10 LET B=5
```

This assigns the value of 5 to the numeric variable B. From that point forward in the program, every time a reference is made to B, its value would be 5. That is, it would be 5 until another assignment is given to B.

The word LET is not necessary in an assignment statement. That is,

```
10 LET B=5
```

and

```
10 B=5
```

are the same statement as far as the computer is concerned. Since this is the case, from this point on we will cease to use the word LET. (Few programmers use LET, although it is usually recommended for beginners.)

Let's look at an example using the assignment statement. The first thing we need to do is clear out the memory so we can begin our new program. We don't want programming conflicts with the program that is already in memory. Remember that the previously used program will remain in memory until we do something to remove it. Recall that the command to do this is NEW.

Your new program will start as follows:

```
10 B=5
20 PRINT B
```

(recall that ? also means PRINT) and when you run the program you will get:

```
 5
Ok
```

Of course, that is just what we would have expected. We stored 5 in B so that every time B is referenced in the program, such as in a PRINT statement, the value 5 is used. Now let's add a couple more lines to the program:

```
30 B=6
40 PRINT B
```

Now when you LIST, you get:

```
10 B=5
20 PRINT B
30 B=6
40 PRINT B
Ok
```

And when you run the program, you get:

```
 5
 6
Ok
```

Again, just what we might have expected. On line 20 when you printed B, its value was 5, but we changed that value on line 30. Line 40, then, printed B with the new value of 6. Keep in mind that each storage location can contain only one value. When 6 was assigned to B, it replaced the former value of 5.

Again, the only concern we have when using the assignment is that the two sides be compatible. The right side must be either string or literal if the left side is a string, and the right side has to be either a numeric variable or constant if the left side is a numeric variable. For example, B would be incompatible with A$ since B is numeric and can contain only numbers while A$ can contain any valid character. B=A$ would not be correct no matter what had been stored in A$. Since the computer does not check the data on an assignment, but merely moves the information, even if A$ contained a number, 5 for example, it would not know that A$ was 5, because it would not check memory for the value of A$. Also, if A$ contains 5, the 5 is no longer a number. Any number assigned to a string can no longer be used as a number. It has become a character and can only be used as such.

Think for a moment of the following multiplication problem, and you will understand the concept:

```
A = "TIME OF DAY" * "HI"
```

It is, of course, silly to talk of multiplying two such items.

By the same token, A$ = B would not be a valid assignment. Numeric variables are stored differently in BASIC and, therefore, cannot be assigned to a string.

Examples of valid and invalid assignment statements are shown in Table 3–3.

TABLE 3–3   Valid and Invalid Assignment Statements

VALID	INVALID	
10 A = 6	70 A = TH@S	TH@S is not an expression of any kind
20 B = 5 + 4		
30 B$ = "HI THERE"	80 A$ = TH@S	TH@S is not an expression of any kind
40 A$ = " "		
50 C = A + 5	90 A = "THIS"	A numeric (A) and literal are incompatible
60 Z7$ = "5 + 4 = 9"		
70 A$ = "TH@S"	100 A$ = 5	A string cannot be assigned a numeric

Note that line 50 assigns the sum of variable A and 5 to the variable C. A + 5 is a numeric expression, specifically a calculation, and as such is valid to be assigned. But let's look more closely at exactly what is taking place.

Somewhere in the program a value is assigned to A (assume A is 6). This value, then, is copied from storage by the computer, added to the next element, 5, and then assigned back to the variable C. If the above assignments constitute a program, then the stored value of C would be 11. One important point about this is that the value of A does not change. Only the variable on the left side of the assignment operator (equal sign) is affected by an assignment statement. None of the variables on the right side of the equal sign are changed. They are only used in whatever calculation is done.

Let's try this point again. First, clear out whatever you still have stored by keying NEW. Then set up a different program:

```
10  B=6
20  A=10
30  PRINT A,B
40  B=A+5
50  PRINT A,B
```

Execute the program by keying RUN:

```
10          6
10          15
Ok
```

Line 30 printed A as 10 and B as 6, as they were assigned. The important point here is that line 50 printed A as still being 10 while B is 15 at that point. The calculation on line 40 changed B; however, since A was only used, not changed, it was still 10. The point is worth emphasizing one more time. Only the assigned variable is changed. The variables on the right-hand side of any assignment remain unchanged.

There is only one special situation in BASIC when the above does not seem to hold true. That is when the same variable is on both sides of the equal sign. Clear out the old program (using NEW) and try this one:

```
10 A=5
20 PRINT A
30 A=A+1
40 PRINT A
```

Before we run the program, let's examine what we are doing and decide what the PRINT statements should give us. Line 20 will, of course, print 5, but what amount will line 40 print? Since on an assignment statement only the left-hand side variable is altered (even when the left-hand side variable can also be found on the right-hand side), line 30 should take A with a value of 5, add one to it, and the result, which would be stored back into A, would be 6. Thus, A would from now on have the new value 6. When we run the program, we find out that is just what does happen:

```
5
6
Ok
```

A few points should be mentioned here. In the previous discussion we stated that we could add to a variable that already had a value assigned to it somewhere in the program. A variable always has a value. All numeric variables used in a program are automatically assigned a value of zero if not otherwise assigned by the programmer. String variables not otherwise assigned are assigned a value of **null,** which simply means they have nothing in them. Null does not mean blank, null means empty. Because of these assignments, when a variable is referenced in a program, it always has a value, even if that value is zero or null.

As an example, take the last program and delete line 10. (Remember, enter 10 and press RETURN to delete this one line.) Then key LIST, and the program will look like this:

```
20 PRINT A
30 A=A+1
40 PRINT A
Ok
```

What should the PRINT statements produce? Line 20 will yield 0, and line 40 will print 1. Run the program to verify this:

```
0
1
Ok
```

In line 20, A is 0 because it has been assigned no other value yet. Then in line 30, 1 is added to 0, which, of course, yields 1. Therefore, line 40 prints 1.

Let's try some work with strings now. To assign values to string variables, we have to mark the data so the computer knows we are using literal information. We discovered how to do this earlier when we were using the PRINT statement. To specify literal information, we enclosed the information within quotes. (It might be noted here that our versions of BASIC do not require the quote at the end of the literal. You may use something like "TEST leaving off the second quote. You should, however, always use the second quote as it will sometimes cause problems with other versions of BASIC. Even though our versions of BASIC will allow you to leave it off, there are versions of BASIC that will give you an error should you leave an open quote.)

Let's try a sample of string assignments. First get rid of the last program (NEW), then enter:

```
10 N$="ED COBURN"
20 C$="MY NAME IS "
30 PRINT C$;N$
```

(You may use your own name.) When run, the program would yield:

```
MY NAME IS ED COBURN
Ok
```

Let's try one that is a little more difficult. Clear out the last one and try:

```
10 A$="HI THERE"
20 PRINT A$
30 PRINT "LET'S TRY SOME CALCULATIONS"
40 A$="THE SUM OF"
50 B$="AND"
60 C$="IS"
70 A=5
80 B=10
90 PRINT A$;A;B$;B;C$;A+B
```

When run, the program will yield:

```
HI THERE
LET'S TRY SOME CALCULATIONS
THE SUM OF 5 AND 10 IS 15
Ok
```

If we wanted to add two different numbers, we would need to rekey lines 70 and 80, perhaps as follows:

```
70 A=15
80 B=4
```

Then run:

```
HI THERE
LET'S TRY SOME CALCULATIONS
THE SUM OF 15 AND 4 IS 19
Ok
```

3—11 ONE FINAL PROGRAM STATEMENT

Recall that when we were doing our flowcharts in Chapter 2 we used a terminal symbol. There were two points in the program that were terminal points. There was one START point and one END point. Although our programs could have more than one end point, structuring dictates that they do not. With BASIC programs, there is no START statement. The first statement of the program is always the beginning point. But the same thing is not necessarily true for the end of the program. The statement that allows us to end our programs is the **END statement.** Although our versions of BASIC do not require an END statement, it is nevertheless important to use the END statement to signify the physical (and logical) end of the program to prevent future problems, especially when we begin creating larger programs.

3–12
PUTTING IT ALL TOGETHER

Let's use all the things we have learned thus far and solve a few simple problems. Suppose, for example, we want to write a program to figure the gas mileage our car gets. First, we need to decide what we need to know:

1. How many miles did we travel in a given period?
2. How many gallons of gas did we use to travel those miles?
3. Miles per gallons is miles divided by gallons.

Since we want the program to be at least a little flexible, we will assign the miles and gallons to variables. Let's now write the pseudocode necessary for the program, given that we will assign the miles and the gallons to variables:

Start
Assign number of miles traveled (M).
Assign number of gallons used (G).
Divide miles by gallons.
Print out result.
End

We can now flowchart our program. The assignments will use the preparation symbol as shown in Figure 3–1. The division statement will use the process symbol as shown in Figure 3–2. And the print statements, of course, use the I/O symbol, which is shown in Figure 3–3.

The chart could be put together in either of the formats shown in Figure 3–4. Notice how we eliminated a step on the second chart by printing the cal-

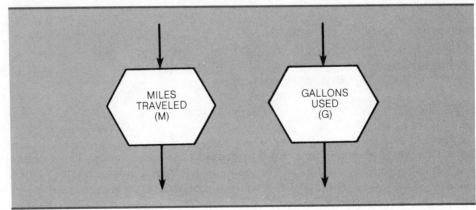

Figure 3–1
Assignment statements.

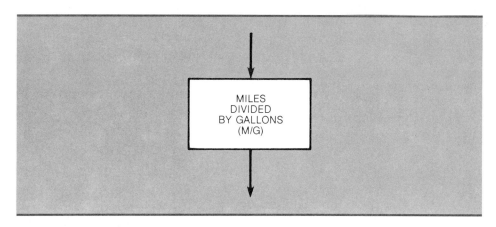

Figure 3–2
The division symbol.

culation of M/G instead of using an assignment and then printing the rate R. Either method is perfectly correct.

Now let's code the program. The first statement will be the first assignment. You could do it as:

```
10 M=200
```

The next line assigns the gallons:

```
20 G=5
```

Now you need either the calculation or PRINT statement, whichever method you decide to use. Although the PRINT statement is shorter, let's use the other method this time. Therefore, the next statement should be:

```
30 R=M/G
```

followed by the PRINT statement:

```
40 PRINT R
```

And add the END statement to terminate the program:

```
50 END
```

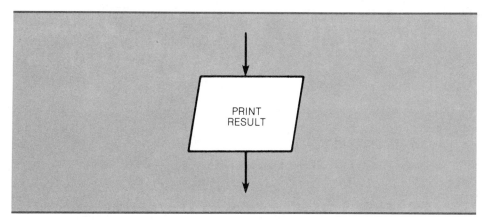

Figure 3–3
The output (PRINT) symbol.

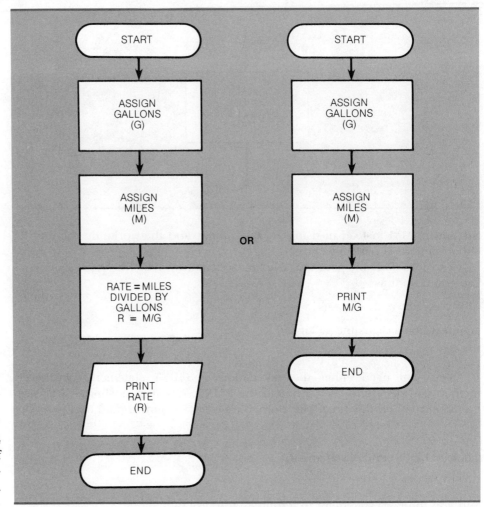

Figure 3–4
Two different methods of
flowcharting the miles-
per-gallon problem.

But just printing R really doesn't convey much. Let's put a message in the
PRINT statement to tell exactly what's been done. Try something like:

```
40 PRINT "YOUR USE RATE WAS";R;"MILES/GALLON"
```

Now if you list the program, you should have:

```
10 M=200
20 G=5
30 R=M/G
40 PRINT "YOUR USE RATE WAS";R;"MILES/GALLON"
50 END
Ok
```

When you run the program using 200 miles with 5 gallons, you should get
40 miles per gallon for your result since 200 divided by 5 is 40. See if you do.
Key RUN:

Not bad! But the big bonus is that you can run the program hundreds of times with different data each time by merely changing lines 10 and 20. Try:

```
10 M=100
20 G=10
```

Key RUN:

```
YOUR USE RATE WAS 10 MILES/GALLON
Ok
```

Or try:

```
10 M=216
20 G=16
```

Key RUN:

```
YOUR USE RATE WAS 13.5 MILES/GALLON
Ok
```

SUMMARY

1. There are two modes of operation in BASIC. The immediate or command mode, which handles the commands you give it immediately, and the program mode, which stores your commands until you use the command that executes the program. That command is RUN.
2. When you use the program mode, always number your lines by 10s so that you will be able to insert lines between the others.
3. There are two items that may be printed using BASIC's output command PRINT. These are numerics and literals. A numeric is any numeric digit, a sign, and a decimal. A literal is any type of data that is enclosed in quotes. When printed, the quotes don't print; only the characters within the quotes are printed.
4. More than one item may be printed on one statement. These multiple items are separated by either a comma or a semicolon. These separators are called delimiters. A third type of delimiter, the blank, is allowed but is not recommended for general use. Also, items may be printed in specific columns by using the TAB statement.
5. The LIST command allows you to display your program on the screen. The command has several different options to allow you to display sections of your program if you don't need or want to see the entire program.
6. You can delete one line of your program by entering the line number followed by the RETURN. Whole sections of the program can be removed by the DELETE (DEL on the Apple) command. The NEW command clears the entire program from memory.
7. Constant data is used in a program when you do not need to change the information, but usually you need data to be variable. BASIC handles this by

having two types of variables. Numeric variables can contain numbers, a sign, and a decimal and are represented by a letter followed by any number of other letters or numeric digits (though all but the IBM only use the first two characters as the variable name). String variables use the same type of variable name followed by a dollar sign. String variables can contain character data regardless of the type of data.

8. The form of the assignment statement is 10 LET variable = expression, but LET is optional. Both sides of the assignment must be compatible: both numeric or both string. Only the variable on the left side of the assignment operator (equal sign) is modified. Those on the right side do not change.

GLOSSARY

Assignment statement The statement that assigns numbers or literals to storage locations called variables.

CLEAR The statement necessary in Radio Shack BASIC to set aside additional string space.

CLS The command in IBM and Radio Shack BASIC to clear the screen.

Constant Information used in a program that is constant, that does not change.

DELETE command The command to remove blocks of program from the memory. This command is DEL on the Apple.

Delimiter An indicator on a PRINT statement that tells the computer where one item being printed ends and the next item begins. There are two recommended types of delimiters: the semicolon and the comma.

END statement The command that signals the logical (and usually physical) end of the program.

HOME The command on the Apple to clear the screen.

Immediate mode The BASIC mode in which instructions are executed immediately upon pressing RETURN.

Interactive A type of computer usage in which you are in direct and continual dialogue with the machine.

Keywords Words that have a special meaning to the BASIC language.

LET statement The assignment statement. The word LET is optional on the assignment statement.

Line number The numerical indicator of a line in BASIC to indicate to the computer the order of processing of the steps in the program.

LIST The command to display the program in memory on the screen.

Literal Any piece of data enclosed in quotation marks, which is either printed or stored as a variable by using an assignment statement.

LLIST The command in the IBM and Radio Shack to print the LIST on the printer.

LPRINT The command in the IBM and Radio Shack to print output on the printer.

Mathematical operators The symbols used to indicate mathematical operations in BASIC.

NEW The BASIC command to clear the entire stored program out of memory.

Null The automatic assignment value of a string variable, null represents a value of being empty.

Numeric variable A symbol indicating a storage location for numbers, a sign, and a decimal.

Ok The computer's display indicating it is ready for the user to do something.

Out of string space error The Radio Shack error indicating insufficient string space reserved for your variables.

PR#0 The command on the Apple that turns off the printer mode.

PR#1 The command on the Apple that turns on the printer mode.

PRINT The command for the display of information on the screen.

Print zone The distance between the automatic tab positions on the screen.

Program mode The BASIC mode in which instructions are placed on lines and stored in memory to be executed with the RUN command.

RETURN The key that signals to the machine that we have tried to communicate with it. On the Apple it is the RETURN key, on the IBM it is the ⟵⏎ key, and on the Radio Shack it is the ENTER key.

RUN command The command to execute a program mode program.

Scrolling The method by which the computer lists a program that is too long to fit on the screen. If there are more lines than will fit on the screen, the lines will push up from the bottom toward the top of the screen, with the excess lines disappearing off the top.

SPC The IBM and Apple PRINT statement command to print the specified number of spaces.

String variable A symbol indicating a storage location for literal information.

Subscript out of range error An error that occurs when you put a blank between the TAB statement and the parenthesis.

Syntax error An error the machine will display to you when it does not understand what you have tried to tell it.

TAB A part of a PRINT statement that instructs the computer to position the cursor to a particular location.

Variable A symbol indicating a storage location where either numerics or literals may be stored. The symbols are letters, numeric digits, and, for character storage, the dollar sign ($). There are two types of variables: numerics (which contain numbers, a sign, and a decimal) and strings (which contain anything that may be represented as a literal).

QUESTIONS TO AID UNDERSTANDING

All programming exercises should be developed using pseudocode and/or flowcharts according to the teacher's instructions.

1. Explain the immediate mode.
2. Explain the program mode.
*3. Describe the differences between the immediate mode and the program mode.
4. Explain why line numbering is done by 10's versus 1's.

Sample Program

```
10 PRINT "HI THERE"
20 N$="ED COBURN"
30 D$="WEDNESDAY"
40 PRINT "HOW ARE YOU DOING TODAY,";
50 PRINT N$
60 PRINT "SEE YOU NEXT ";D$
70 PRINT "I'LL BE WAITING FOR YOUR RETURN"
80 END
```

5. Given the above Sample Program, write down the command to display on the screen:
   a. the entire program
   b. lines 10 through 50
   c. lines 30 through the end of the program
   d. beginning of the program through line 60
6. Given the above Sample Program, write down the command to remove line 10 from the program.

*7. Using the following list of variable names, tell which are numeric, which are string, and which are invalid. For the invalid ones, tell why they are wrong.

a. A$ d. 9B   g. N
b. H@GH   e. 1   h. B29
c. D9$ f. SKR$ i. *

*8. Using the following list of assignments, indicate which are valid and which are invalid. For the invalid ones, tell why they are wrong.

a. A = B + 5   f. Q51$ = "HI THERE"
b. C + 5 = A   g. K = "TEST"
c. A$ = 5   h. T = A + "5"
d. B + 6(Y + 7)   i. G = 6* − Y
e. G$ = "4 + 5"   j. B$ = TEST

9. Using:

```
10 A=10
20 B=25
```

complete the program to print the variables multiplied together.

10. Using the assignment statement, write a program to add 41 and 68 together and print out the result.

*11. You have five course grades of 80, 90, 95, 63, and 75. Write a program to find your average grade. (Average = total divided by number of grades.)

12. Write a program to print a mailing label using your name, address, etc. The label should look like the following:

```
EDWARD J. COBURN
1400 SOUTH STREET
EL PASO, TEXAS   76708
```

13. Write a program to print a multiplication table as:

```
MULTIPLICATION TABLE
        !   1   2   3   4
     ---------------------
1    !   1   2   3   4
2    !   2   4   6   8
3    !   3   6   9   12
4    !   4   8   12  16
```

14. Write a program to produce the following picture of a tree:

```
   X
  XXX
 XXXXX
XXXXXXX
  XXX
  XXX
```

15. The XYZ Corporation has five employees. Design (flowchart and pseudocode) a program to write out the payroll checks for these employees. Calculate gross pay using hourly wage and number of hours worked and then deduct 9% for social security taxes, 20% for federal income taxes, and 5% for state income taxes. Your assignments should be made using the following data:

NAME	HOURLY WAGE	NUMBER OF HOURS
John Smith	4.56	40
Henry Thompson	7.65	35
Sara Hendricks	3.75	40
Jason Roberts	5.44	38
Tina Richards	10.50	40

The payroll checks that you print should look like the following (you can print them on a printer if one is available; otherwise, just print them on the screen):

```
XYZ Corporation
854 South Street
El Paso, Texas  78678

PAY TO THE ORDER OF      name

                    $ Amount
```

QUICK QUIZ

The answers to the questions follow immediately after the quiz. Questions 1–15 are true–false, while 16–20 are multiple choice.

1. Commands used in the immediate mode are stored in memory and can be executed many times without reentry. **T F**

2. The PRINT command can correctly be called an input command. **T F**

3. If you enter "HI" and press RETURN on your computer, you will get Syntax error. **T F**

4. A syntax error is the computer's way of telling you it doesn't understand what you tried to tell it. **T F**

5. Blanks are always ignored in BASIC. **T F**

6. There are two recommended delimiters used on PRINT statements. **T F**

7. The line number 0 is valid. **T F**

8. If you ran a one line program with: **T F**

```
10 PRINT "HI THERE","ED"
```

you would see:

```
HI THERE ED
Ok
```

printed on the screen.

9. The LIST command has the facility to remove entire blocks of the program from memory. **T F**

T　F　10. We use NEW to clear the entire program from memory.

T　F　11. The BASIC command to execute a program is RUN.

T　F　12. The word LET is optional on the assignment statement.

T　F　13. The END statement should be used to signify the end of the program.

T　F　14. B = "HI THERE" is a valid assignment.

T　F　15. T9$ is a valid variable name.

_____　16. Which of the following is an invalid variable name?

       a. A$ **c.** 7C

       b. T9   **d.** B9$

_____　17. Which one of the following is a valid assignment?

       a. B$ = HI THERE   **c.** A$ = B

       b. B = "4 + 5"   **d.** G9 = 47 + X*(3 + Y)

_____　18. In the following display

```
10 A=5*(6+5)+4-6
```

A would be:

       a. 93   **c.** 33

       b. 53   **d.** 44

_____　19. The result of:

```
PRINT "4+9"
```

would be:

       a. 13   **c.** "4 + 9"

       b. 4 + 9   **d.** Syntax error

_____　20. The command to display the program from memory is:

       a. LIST   **c.** RUN

       b. DELETE   **d.** PRINT

ANSWERS TO QUICK QUIZ

1. F (Commands stored in the immediate mode are not stored in memory.)
2. F (It is an output command.)
3. T (There is no command here. The immediate mode requires a command.)
4. T
5. F (Blanks are not ignored if they appear in a literal.)
6. T (The comma and semicolon)
7. T
8. F (The comma would cause ED to print in the next print zone.)
9. F (LIST displays the program; DELETE removes lines.)

10. T
11. T
12. T
13. T (Though our BASICs do not require the END statement, you should always use one.)
14. F (The B is numeric and "HI THERE" is a literal; therefore, they are incompatible.)
15. T
16. c (C7 would be valid, but a number cannot be the first character of a variable name.)
17. d (a, b, and c are all invalid because the two sides of the statements are not compatible.)

18. **b** (6 + 5 would be done first to give 11; then 11*5 would be done to give 55; finally, 55 + 4 − 6 would yield 53.)

19. **b** (This term is a literal; therefore, the computer prints what is between the quotation marks. Remember, the quotation marks will not print as in choice c.)

20. **a**

4 DOCUMENTATION AND INPUT

OVERVIEW

OBJECTIVES

After completing Chapter 4, you will be able to:

- Name the program documentation statement, and tell why it is important.
- Demonstrate how to document a program.
- Use documentation in all your future programs.
- Explain the use of the INPUT statement, and describe the two methods of using it.
- Demonstrate the use of the INPUT statement in several sample programs.
- Explain what a GOTO is and how it is used.
- Explain the difference between the STOP and END statements and why the STOP is used for program testing.

In Chapter 3 we introduced BASIC and discovered some important commands. But of course, that is not all there is to BASIC. There are many more commands that are useful. In this chapter we will explore additional commands. We will also pseudocode, flowchart, and code some more practice programs.

One of the largest problems facing the data processing industry is that most software produced today lacks adequate **documentation.** There are three kinds of documentation: program, programmer, and user.

Program documentation consists of comments that are put into the program itself to enable programmers to follow the logic of the code more easily. Comments are used to describe special routines, to separate areas of the program (modules), to embed blank lines, to label variables that might be used for special functions, and for many other purposes.

Programmer documentation consists of the documents that help the programmer understand the workings of the program. Pseudocode, flowcharts, layouts of the disk storage, and special written comments on the program are considered programmer documentation.

User documentation is a manual that is prepared to enable the user of a program to understand what the program is supposed to be used for and how to use it.

Why do we need documentation? The reason for documentation of a program is easy to understand. As you write a program, you have certain ideas as to the method of accomplishing the necessary task. These ideas are incorporated into the program as you write it. After a short period of time, however, you will not remember what those ideas were or how you accomplished the task. You will probably remember the overall purpose of the program, but the details will become fuzzy. To get the idea, try to remember the details of the last movie you saw at a theater. Even if it was very recently, you will find that you can recall only the overall plot of the movie and possibly a few details. Most of the movie is beyond your power of recall. Now look at it from a programmer's point of view. Many times programmers write a program and then don't see it again for many months. By that time, they remember little, if any, of the code. You can easily see why comments in the code become important if there is anything out of the ordinary in the program.

The comment or documentation statement used in a BASIC program is the **REM** statement. REM stands for REMark, and all words following a REM statement are treated as comments having no effect on the program. The form of the REM statement follows:

```
10 REM with anything in the rest of the line
```

Remarks may be used to separate areas of the program that serve a specific purpose, such as a date conversion routine and a report print routine. These are the modules we mentioned in Chapter 2. An example follows:

```
1000 REM
1010 REM ***** PRINT HEADING ROUTINE
1020 REM
:::
:::
:::
4030 REM
4040 REM ***** PRINT ITEM LINE ROUTINE
4050 REM
```

Remarks may also be used to identify the program. It is important to label each program with the name of the program so you will be able to easily identify what is stored on disk (or tape). Other remarks that are useful are the purpose of the program, a list of the variables used, the date of initial writing, the date(s) of update(s), the name of the person who originally wrote the program, and possibly the name of the person who made the last modification. A sample of such labeling follows:

```
10 REM ***** PROGRAM NAME: GLREP
20 REM
30 REM ***** GENERAL LEDGER REPORT PROGRAM
40 REM
50 REM ***** BY EDWARD J. COBURN
60 REM
70 REM THIS IS A MONTHLY PRINT PROGRAM.  IT
80 REM SHOULD BE RUN AFTER GLGEN, THE REPORT
90 REM GENERATOR.
100 REM
110 REM DATE FINISHED:        02/16/85
120 REM LAST MODIFICATION DATE: 05/15/85
130 REM
140 REM ***** VARIABLE LIST
150 REM P = THE PAGE COUNTER
160 REM L = THE LINE COUNTER
170 REM I = THE LOOP COUNTER
180 REM J = THE SECONDARY LOOP COUNTER
190 REM S = THE SUBTOTAL
200 REM T = THE GRAND TOTAL
```

Program 4–1

Notice in the above examples that some REM statements are left blank. This is merely to space out the remarks, making them easier to read. Most programmers use some type of spacing for this purpose.

Remarks may also be used to label important variables as they are used (instead of or in addition to the variable list), such as when you have a special variable that is used to indicate a particular condition:

```
10 F=1
20 REM ***** F INDICATES THE TYPE OF REPORT
30 P=1
40 REM ***** P IS THE PAGE NUMBER
```

Remarks about variables many times are necessary, but placing them as shown above can make the program more difficult to read since the remarks are interspersed between the commands. Because of this, most versions of BASIC allow a substitute character for the REM statement. The IBM and Radio Shack both allow the use of the apostrophe (') as a substitute for REM. The Apple does not have a substitute character for REM, but there is a way to put comments on the end of statements in Applesoft also. At the end of the first statement, you put a colon and then the REM command. The colon signifies to the machine that you are ending the first statement and creating another. Any type of statement can be used beyond the colon, but only the REM is recommended, since multistatement lines can easily cause confusion. Incidentally, the multistatement line also works in IBM and Radio Shack BASIC.

Using the apostrophe on the IBM and Radio Shack we would change the previous remarks to something similar to:

```
10 F=1 ' F INDICATES THE TYPE OF REPORT
30 P=1 ' P IS THE PAGE NUMBER
```

Using the colon and REM they would look like:

```
10 F=1 : REM  F INDICATES THE TYPE OF REPORT
30 P=1 : REM  P IS THE PAGE NUMBER
```

Remarks are a vital part of any program, and their use cannot be overemphasized. From now on, in this text we will use comments in every program we do. We strongly suggest that as you do the programming exercises you use the REM statement in your programs. In some of our programs, remarks may seem a little silly because the purpose of the program or statement is perfectly clear. Two points need to be emphasized about this. First, just because the purpose of a particular statement is clear when you write the program does not mean that in six months the purpose will still be clear. Second, there is an old saying that you do as you have practiced. If we practice putting comments into our small programs, we will automatically put them into our larger programs later on.

There is only one problem associated with using many comments. If you are writing an exceptionally long program, the overabundant use of comments may cause you to run out of memory. If this happens, however, it is easy to remove some comments of lesser importance, whereas it is difficult to add comments to the program after it is already written. Put the comments in your programs as you write them, and don't be concerned with running out of memory. It probably won't happen.

Note: In our programming examples in this book, we will, as mentioned in the Preface, always use the IBM for our example. Because of this, many program lines will have the ' on the end before the needed comments. If you are using an Apple, you should realize that the Apple cannot use the comments this way and must use the : REM format instead.

4–3
INPUT

We discovered in Chapter 3 how to assign values in our programs so we could change the data just by changing the variables. The only problem with that is that every time we need new data in the program, the program has to be changed; each of the variables must be reassigned. When you were doing this in the exercises, you probably thought there must be an easier way to change the data in the program. And there is. That easier way is called an **INPUT statement.** An INPUT statement allows the user of the program to assign values to variables as the program executes, instead of changing the program each time beforehand. In other words, the INPUT statement is another, more flexible form of assignment statement; more flexible, that is, in being able to assign variables as the program executes. (The regular assignment, of course, is useful for calculations and similar things that you cannot do with the INPUT statement.) One form of the INPUT statement follows:

```
10 INPUT A
```

The word INPUT is the command. The A is simply a variable and could be any valid variable, such as A9 or CATBIRD, or a string variable, such as A$, Y4$, or THOMAS$. Either type of variable, string or numeric, may be used on an INPUT statement.

The statement functions by printing a question mark (?) on the screen, signaling to the user that the computer is waiting for a reply. This question mark is called a **prompt** because it prompts the user for information. When the user enters the appropriate information and presses RETURN, the program stores that information in the area of memory reserved for that variable, just as if the program had specifically assigned that value to the variable. From that point on in the program, that variable will contain the input value.

Recall that the computer never knows that you are communicating with it until you have pressed RETURN. That is also true when using the INPUT statement. Therefore, when you are finished with your data entry, always remember to press RETURN.

You probably noticed in the above paragraph the words "appropriate information." What is "appropriate information"? In Chapter 3 when we were discussing variables, we said that the assignment is valid only when both sides of the assignment are of the same variable type. That is, if the right-hand side of the assignment is a string or literal, then the left-hand side must be a string variable. If one side is numeric, then the other side must be numeric also. The same thing holds true when using the INPUT statement. If the variable you use in the INPUT statement is a numeric, then the data entered by the user must be numeric type data. (Recall that numeric data is a number, sign, and decimal.) If the variable for receipt of the information on the INPUT statement is a string, any data may be entered in response to the prompt because any data is valid in a string.

Let's try a short program to get acquainted with the INPUT statement:

```
10 REM ***** PROGRAM NAME: SAMPINP
20 REM
30 REM ***** SAMPLE INPUT PROGRAM
40 REM
50 INPUT N$
60 PRINT N$
70 END
```
                                                        Program 4–2

When you execute (RUN) this program, you will see:

```
?
```

which prompts you to input a value for N$. Because the input variable is a string (N$), we can use any data we want in response. Let's use our name:

```
? ED COBURN
ED COBURN
Ok
```

What did the program do? First, it prompted you for some data (?). (Note that the Apple does not leave the blank after the question mark.) It didn't specify what type of data, so you could have entered any kind of data you wished. Then, since the INPUT statement assigned your data to the variable N$, you could print it out. Finally, the computer told you that it was ready for something else to do. Note how, on entering the string variable N$, we did not use quotation marks around what we entered. Since the INPUT statement knows what type of variable you are using, you don't need to use quotation marks around your entry. You could use them if you wished, but it is usually not necessary. However, later we will see an example where using quotation marks *is* necessary.

Let's run the program again with different data:

```
? WHATEVER WE WANT TO ENTER
WHATEVER WE WANT TO ENTER
Ok
```

That is much easier than changing the program each time we need to use different information. But let's try something that is a little more demonstrative. Assume for a moment that we need to be able to add two numbers and print out the sum. This is easy with the INPUT statement. Your program should look like this:

```
NEW
10 REM ***** PROGRAM NAME: SAMPADD
20 REM
30 REM ***** SAMPLE ADDITION PROGRAM
40 REM
50 INPUT A ' THIS IS THE FIRST NUMBER
60 INPUT B ' THIS IS THE SECOND NUMBER
70 PRINT "THE SUM IS =";A+B
80 END
```
                                                        Program 4–3

When you execute it, you will have to respond to two question marks. Let's use 7 and 45:

```
? 7
? 45
THE SUM IS = 52
Ok
```

Let's run it again with different data:

```
? 19
? 36
THE SUM IS = 55
Ok
```

Of course, you could run the program as many times as you wished, each time with different data. Each time you would get a different result. Again, it is much easier than having to change the program to use the new data.

We mentioned briefly before that we need to make sure that the data we enter in response to the question mark is compatible with the variable that was used in the program. What will happen if we don't? Only one variable type will give us any problem in that respect, the numeric. Recall that anything entered is okay for the string variable. Let's run the program again, using invalid data this time in response to the question mark.

```
? TEST
? Redo from start
? 1
? 2
THE SUM IS =  3
Ok
```

The **Redo from start** message simply means that the computer did not accept whatever you entered. (The Apple displays REENTER rather than Redo from start, and the Radio Shack merely displays REDO.) It prints this error message, then displays the question mark again and waits for another entry. It evaluates the new entry. If it too is inappropriate, it will give you the same Redo from start message. It will keep asking you (with additional question marks) for an entry until you have given it the proper, or at least valid, information as we did in the example by entering 1 and 2.

Since the INPUT command is used to bring information into the program from the user, it is useful to indicate to the user what is expected. This is called prompting the user. The computer automatically prompts the user on executing an INPUT statement by printing the question mark on the screen. But a question mark does not indicate to the user the type of data the program is expecting. It is much better to indicate explicitly what type of data the user should input. This prompting may be done in two ways. The first way is by using a PRINT statement followed by the INPUT statement.

```
NEW
10 REM ***** PROGRAM NAME: SAMPPRMT
20 REM
30 REM ***** SAMPLE PROMPT PROGRAM
40 REM
50 PRINT "WHAT IS YOUR NAME"
60 INPUT N$
70 PRINT "I SEE YOUR NAME IS ";N$
80 END
```
Program 4–4

When run, the program shows the following on the screen:

```
WHAT IS YOUR NAME
?
```

Then you enter your name to cause:

```
? ED COBURN
I SEE YOUR NAME IS ED COBURN
Ok
```

That's good, except for the prompt or question mark, which showed up on the next line down from the prompt. When the machine printed the prompt, the carriage return and line feed were active so that whatever printed on the screen next would print on the next line. Since the question mark is printed on the screen, it constitutes the next PRINT statement and, therefore, is printed on the next line. We can, however, turn off the carriage return and line feed by using a comma or semicolon on the end of the PRINT line. The semi-colon will cause the next item to print right next to the one previously printed, while the comma will take the cursor to the next print zone. The best choice, then, would probably be the semicolon. Let's try it. Change line 50 to:

```
50 PRINT "WHAT IS YOUR NAME";
```

Now, if you list the program, it is:

```
10 REM ***** PROGRAM NAME: SAMPPRMT
20 REM
30 REM ***** SAMPLE PROMPT PROGRAM
40 REM
50 PRINT "WHAT IS YOUR NAME";
60 INPUT N$
70 PRINT "I SEE YOUR NAME IS ";N$
80 END
```

When you run the program, you get:

```
WHAT IS YOUR NAME? ED COBURN
I SEE YOUR NAME IS ED COBURN
Ok
```

There is an easier (and more-often-used) method of prompting. The INPUT statement allows the use of a prompt as part of the statement itself. The form for the above prompt would be (you would need to delete line 60 since it is no longer needed):

```
50 INPUT "WHAT IS YOUR NAME";N$
```

Now when you run the program you get the same result as before:

```
WHAT IS YOUR NAME? ED COBURN
I SEE YOUR NAME IS ED COBURN
Ok
```

The prompt is a normal literal, and as such, anything may be used within the quotes (except another quote). The following are examples of other prompts you could use:

```
10 INPUT "WHAT IS YOUR AGE";A
20 INPUT "ADD, CHANGE, OR DELETE";A$
30 INPUT "ENTER A, B, AND C";A,B,C
```

Notice that the delimiter between the prompt and the first variable is a semi-colon. Anything else (such as a comma) will cause a different result or a syntax error.

On the Apple, neither the question mark nor space will appear when you use a prompt on the INPUT statement. To have it appear as in the example, you would have to use a statement such as 50 INPUT "WHAT IS YOUR NAME? ";N$.

On line 30 above, the prompt asks for three different values corresponding to the INPUT statement's three variables, A, B, and C. More than one variable can be used in an INPUT statement, and they can be mixed any way the pro-grammer chooses. Commas must be used between the different variables on the INPUT statement.

When run, an INPUT statement with multiple variables allows entry either of two ways on the Radio Shack and Apple. (Only the first method works on the

IBM.) You may enter them on separate lines or put all entries on the same line separated by commas. Remember to key in NEW to delete the old program.

```
10 REM ***** PROGRAM NAME: TWOINP
20 REM
30 REM ***** SAMPLE OF 2 INPUTS ON SAME STATEMENT
40 REM
50 INPUT "ENTER A NUMBER, THEN A STRING";A,A$
60 PRINT "THE NUMBER =";A;"  THE STRING = ";A$
70 END
RUN
ENTER A NUMBER, THEN A STRING? 5,TEST
THE NUMBER = 5    THE STRING = TEST
Ok
```
Program 4–5

)))DIFFERENCES

As mentioned earlier, the Apple will not print the ? or the blank following it. To get them, the INPUT prompt has to include the ? and blank, such as:

```
50 INPUT "ENTER A NUMBER, THEN A STRING? ";A,A$
```

This will be true of all the INPUT statements for the Apple throughout the remainder of the book. We will mention this difference in subsequent programs only occasionally as a reminder. It will be up to the student to remember this difference.

Another way to answer these program prompts follows (but not for the IBM):

```
ENTER A NUMBER, THEN A STRING? 5
?? TEST
THE NUMBER = 5    THE STRING = TEST
Ok
```

Notice the double question marks on the second line. Here the program is indicating that you haven't finished your input. Notice also that on the INPUT statement in line 50 the delimiter (after the initial one) between variables is a comma, not a semicolon. (Note: the previous example will not work on the IBM, as it will not give you the second prompt. If you do not enter both inputs, a Redo from start message will appear.)

Even though you can use more than one variable on an INPUT statement, as we have shown, it is generally not a good idea. The user of the program has enough to be concerned about without trying to figure out which variable is being responded to at any particular moment. It is a better practice to put each variable on a separate INPUT statement.

We mentioned previously that we don't usually need to put quotation marks around input data. There is one time when it is necessary, however. Since the comma is the delimiter between items when we are inputting data, if we have a comma appear in our data, it will be treated as a delimiter, not as data. We can take care of that problem by using quotes around the data. An example of this concept follows:

```
10 REM ***** PROGRAM NAME: QUOTEST
20 REM
30 REM ***** TEST FOR QUOTED INPUT
40 REM
50 INPUT "TWO STRINGS";N$,A$
60 PRINT "THE FIRST STRING IS ";N$
70 PRINT "THE SECOND STRING IS ";A$
80 END
RUN
TWO STRINGS?
```

Program 4–6

Now we want input data with a comma. A logical thing to try would be an address such as WACO, TEXAS 76708.

```
RUN
TWO STRINGS? WACO,TEXAS
THE FIRST STRING IS WACO
THE SECOND STRING IS TEXAS
Ok
```

We expected a second prompt line with two question marks. But we did not get to enter our second item (the zip code) because the computer interpreted the comma as a delimiter between WACO and TEXAS. If we answer the prompt with quotes around WACO, TEXAS, we'll get a different result:

```
RUN
TWO STRINGS? "WACO, TEXAS"
?? 76708
THE FIRST STRING IS WACO, TEXAS
THE SECOND STRING IS 76708
Ok
```

This time the computer printed the first item, which was WACO, TEXAS, as one item. The zip code was treated as the second separate item because the comma within the quotes was treated as part of the literal and not as a delimiter.

Now that you know all about INPUT statements, let's try an experiment with a simple multiplication program. (First, key in NEW.)

```
10 REM ***** PROGRAM NAME: MULTSAMP
20 REM
30 REM ***** SAMPLE MULTIPLICATION PROGRAM
40 REM
50 INPUT "TWO NUMBERS TO MULTIPLY";A,B
60 P=A*B
70 PRINT A;"*";B;"=";P
80 END
RUN
TWO NUMBERS TO MULTIPLY? 5,10
 5 * 10 = 50
Ok
```

Program 4–7

 **)))DIFFERENCES**

A final reminder about the Apple INPUT statement. Line 50 should be:

```
50 INPUT "TWO NUMBERS TO MULTIPLY? ";A,B
```

Also, since the Apple doesn't leave spaces in front of or behind the numbers, the output here would be:

5*10=50

To get it to print with the spaces, you need to change line 70 to:

```
70 PRINT A;" * ";B;" = ";P
```

Next, let's try the gas mileage program that we used in Chapter 3. The pseudocode was:

Start
Assign number of miles traveled (M).
Assign number of gallons used (G).
Divide miles by gallons (M/G).
Print out the results.
End

The pseudocode using INPUT statements in place of the assignments is only slightly different:

Start
Input number of miles traveled (M).
Input number of gallons used (G).
Divide miles by gallons (M/G).
Print out the results.
End

The flowchart is also only slightly different. Instead of the hexagons, which we used for the assignments, we will use parallelograms, which signify I/O. Why? Because input is, of course, an I/O procedure. The chart looks like the one in Figure 4–1. Now we can code the program:

```
NEW
10 REM ***** PROGRAM NAME: MPGCALC
20 REM
30 REM ***** MILES PER GALLON CALCULATION
40 REM
50 REM ***** BY EDWARD J. COBURN
60 REM
70 INPUT "HOW MANY MILES";M
80 INPUT "HOW MANY GALLONS";G
90 PRINT "YOUR USE RATE WAS";M/G;"MILES/GALLON"
100 END
```
                                                              Program 4–8

)))DIFFERENCES

To receive the same output on the Apple, line 90 needs a blank after WAS and before MILES/GALLON. Again, this is a common difference so we will cease to mention it; the student should become familiar with this difference very quickly.

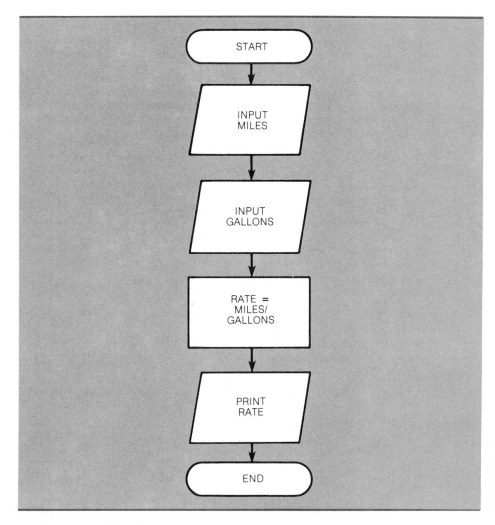

Figure 4–1
Flowchart of mileage
problem.

Let's execute the program with several different values:

```
RUN
HOW MANY MILES? 50
HOW MANY GALLONS? 10
YOUR USE RATE WAS 5 MILES/GALLON
Ok
```

And:

```
RUN
HOW MANY MILES? 150
HOW MANY GALLONS? 20
YOUR USE RATE WAS 7.5 MILES/GALLON
Ok
```

And finally:

```
RUN
HOW MANY MILES? 5000
```

Program continues

```
HOW MANY GALLONS? 150
YOUR USE RATE WAS 33.3333 MILES/GALLON
Ok
```

4—4
UNCONDITIONAL BRANCH

We now have the capability to input data from the keyboard and thus change our program every time it runs. But to get several different results from our program, we have to run it several different times. Wouldn't it be nice to have some type of a loop in the program so we could do the same routine over and over again without having to rerun the program? BASIC comes to the rescue again. Whenever we need to return to a particular point in a program from any other point, all we do is use a **GOTO statement.** The form of the GOTO is:

```
100 GOTO line number
```

When a BASIC program encounters GOTO 10, it branches to line 10 and begins executing at that point. Of course, any line number may follow GOTO, the 10 is merely an example. The GOTO statement used in this fashion is called an **unconditional branch.** It directs the program to the line number specified in the statement, and the program begins executing at that point.

It should be noted before we go any further into the use of the GOTO that structured programming concepts dictate careful use of the GOTO statement. Unrestricted use of the statement can have damaging effects on even the most carefully structured programs; branches jumping here and there can make the logic of the program extremely difficult to follow.

The GOTO statement does not have to return to a previous statement. The branch can be used to go to any line number if that number exists in the program. Let's see what happens when you try to go to a line number that isn't in the program. First, key in NEW.

```
10 GOTO 100
RUN
Undefined line number in 10
Ok
```

As might be expected, we get an error. (The error message shown is the IBM version, the other computers use a slight variation.) We will always get this type of error when we try to GOTO a line number not in the program.

Now let's try the GOTO in a valid situation.

```
NEW
10 REM ***** PROGRAM NAME: GOTOTEST
20 REM
30 REM ***** TEST PROGRAM FOR THE GOTO
40 REM
50 INPUT "GIVE ME A NUMBER";A
60 T=T+A
70 PRINT "THE TOTAL THUS FAR IS";T
80 GOTO 50                ' RETURN FOR ANOTHER INPUT
90 END
```
                                                      Program 4—9

What will this program do when you run it? First, it will prompt for a number. After you enter one, it will add that number to the variable T. But what is in T? Recall that each new variable in a BASIC program is initially given an appropriate value of either null or, as here, zero. So it will initially contain zero. After the input, the value in A is added to T and the new T is printed. Finally, the program will go to line 30, which will prompt for another input. As used in this program, the variable T is called an **accumulator** since it accumulates the values that are input. (It is also called a running total.) Let's run the program and observe how T accumulates and how the GOTO functions:

```
GIVE ME A NUMBER? 5
THE TOTAL THUS FAR IS 5
GIVE ME A NUMBER? 7
THE TOTAL THUS FAR IS 12
GIVE ME A NUMBER? 3
THE TOTAL THUS FAR IS 15
GIVE ME A NUMBER?
```

The program will continue to ask the same question if you continue to answer it. There is no exit from this program. Every time you respond, it will total your response to the accumulative total in T, print it, and then ask for another. Notice how T increases each time you input another number.

This is what is called a **nonending** or **infinite loop.** There is only one way to stop this program: Press the BREAK key. The BREAK key comes in handy for many things; in this case, to stop the nonending loop.

Of course, the use of the GOTO as we have described it is not structured. It does not fit any of our structures. We do not yet have the decision test to create the structure. We are merely practicing with the GOTO. In structured programming, such a loop would need some type of test because it needs an exit.

The GOTO will be an integral part of most of the programs that we will create but, as mentioned previously, the indiscriminate use of it can be hazardous to your code. Remember, you are writing programs, above all, for yourself. Even if the program is for someone else's use, you are the one who will have to fix it if there is a problem. The better job you do of coding the program, the easier it is to fix. Structuring of your code cannot be overemphasized.

Let's expand upon our gas mileage program and add a loop. As we mentioned, there is no structure used with this type of branch, so we cannot construct the pseudocode. The flowchart, however, should look like the one in Figure 4–2. Note that there is no END symbol in the flowchart since the program does not end unless you press the BREAK key. The BREAK key is a function of the machine, not the program, so the flowchart cannot reflect the end of the program.

The program could be coded as:

```
NEW
10 REM ***** PROGRAM NAME: GASMILE
20 REM
30 REM ***** MILES PER GALLON CALCULATION
40 REM
50 REM ***** BY EDWARD J. COBURN
60 REM
70 INPUT "HOW MANY MILES";M
80 INPUT "HOW MANY GALLONS";G
90 PRINT "YOUR USE RATE WAS";M/G;"MILES/GALLON"
100 GOTO 70    ' RETURN FOR MORE INPUT
110 END
```
Program 4–10

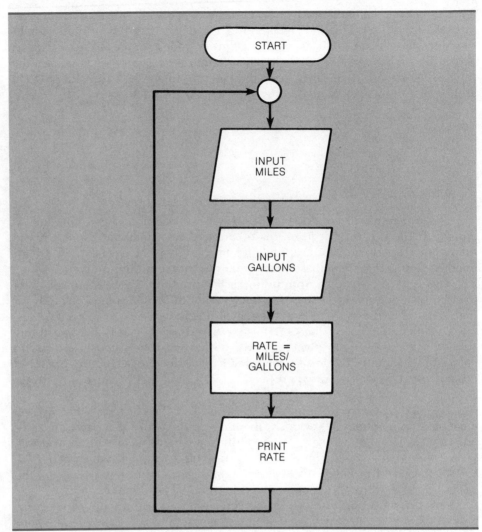

Figure 4–2
Flowchart with
nonending loop.

Even though we just said that the program cannot designate an end, our program has an END statement. We use it because it is important to always signify the physical end of the program even though the code will not actually ever encounter the END statement.

Now when you run the program, you will see:

```
HOW MANY MILES? 50
HOW MANY GALLONS? 10
YOUR USE RATE WAS 5 MILES/GALLON
HOW MANY MILES? 150
HOW MANY GALLONS? 20
YOUR USE RATE WAS 7.5 MILES/GALLON
HOW MANY MILES? 5000
HOW MANY GALLONS? 150
YOUR USE RATE WAS 33.3333 MILES/GALLON
HOW MANY GALLONS?
Break in 70
Ok
```

Again, we had to use the BREAK key to stop this program.

We have mentioned several times that the END statement causes the execution of your program to halt and that there should be only one end in your program. But sometimes, when you are using a large program, you will want to halt the program (as a debugging aid), check some intermediate data, and then restart the program where it left off. All our versions allow you to end the program, check the data by printing any variables you wish to see, and then restart the program by entering a **CONT command** to CONTinue the program. If you wish, you may substitute the **STOP statement** for the END statement and then continue from there.

Why would we use STOP instead of END? Because there is one fundamental and important difference between the two statements. The STOP statement will print on the screen the line number where you stopped in the program. This is valuable in long programs where you may be using many STOP statements to help you debug the program. It is useful to know exactly where the program stopped.

When you stop or end the program, all variables will retain their values until you either modify (add a line, delete a line, etc.) or rerun the program. Therefore, you can examine the value of any variables in the program where you have stopped it. This is useful when trying to find an error in a program. When you continue the program after a stop or end, the program will take up where it left off. That is, the value of all the variables will be as they were before the stop or end. Execution will continue as if the program had not been stopped or ended. (It is important to note that Applesoft sometimes has problems when continuing a program. It can give you errors that are really not there. This is a problem without solution. *The CONT statement should be used with caution on the Apple.*)

The CONT command may also be used to restart your program after you press the BREAK key. Everything we have said about the STOP command is also true of the BREAK key.

As an example of where this might come in handy, let's look at the gas mileage program we were using in Program 4–10 and insert a couple of steps, the STOP and a variable to keep track of the number of loops we have executed:

```
92 C=C+1
95 STOP
```

and see what the program looks like (we'll skip the flowchart this time since the change is subtle):

```
10 REM ***** PROGRAM NAME: GASMILE
20 REM
30 REM ***** MILES PER GALLON CALCULATION
40 REM
50 REM ***** BY EDWARD J. COBURN
60 REM
70 INPUT "HOW MANY MILES";M
80 INPUT "HOW MANY GALLONS";G
```

Program 4–11

Program continues

```
90 PRINT "YOUR USE RATE WAS";M/G;"MILES/GALLON"
92 C=C+1
95 STOP
100 GOTO 70     ' RETURN FOR MORE INPUT
110 END
RUN
HOW MANY MILES? 50
HOW MANY GALLONS? 10
YOUR USE RATE WAS 5 MILES/GALLON
Break in 95
Ok
```

Program 4–11 (cont.)

Now we can check the counter by using a simple PRINT statement in the command mode:

```
PRINT C
 1
Ok
```

If this were a large program we could check the value of any of the variables in use. This will later prove to be a valuable tool. Now enter CONT, and the program will resume:

```
HOW MANY MILES? 150
HOW MANY GALLONS? 20
YOUR USE RATE WAS 7.5 MILES/GALLON
Break in 95
Ok
```

PRINT again:

```
PRINT C
 2
Ok
```

And then key in CONT again:

```
HOW MANY MILES? 5000
HOW MANY GALLONS? 150
YOUR USE RATE WAS 33.3333 MILES/GALLON
Break in 95
Ok
```

We can let the program stop when we have entered enough data. We can also print in the command mode any variable used in the program to check its value at the time of the stop. For example:

```
PRINT M,G,M/G
 5000      150      33.3333
Ok
```

The values are as they last were before we stopped the program. Remember, all the variables in the program remain unchanged as we stop and continue the program. When we are doing complex programs and have to know what values our variables have taken on as our program has progressed, we can insert STOP statements and print the variables we are interested in. If we are satisfied that the program is functioning properly, we can then allow the program to continue. Always remember to remove the STOP statements when you are finished debugging.

1. One problem in the data processing industry is the lack of documentation of programs and programming systems. There are three forms of documentation that are used to help overcome this shortcoming. Program documentation consists of REM statements (remarks) in the program. Programmer documentation consists of flowcharts, tables of the variable usage in the program, notes on the program, etc. User documentation is a manual that accompanies the software to explain to the user how the program works.

2. The INPUT statement allows the user to assign different values to variables each time a program is run. This allows changing the variables of the program without having to change the program.

3. The INPUT statement can be used two different ways. In the first method the prompt is printed first and then the variable is input. The second method is more common. In this method the prompt is part of the INPUT statement along with the variable or variables.

4. It is not much fun to have to rerun a program every time you want to input new data. Therefore, we use a looping facility. The GOTO statement allows the program to return to a previous point in the program or even go forward to another point. It transfers control to the statement indicated by the line number in the GOTO statement.

5. GOTOs should be used only in the defined structures. We do not have the proper statements to do that yet, however.

6. A STOP statement is a useful tool when debugging a program, since the line number where the program stops will be printed on the screen. You may continue the program from the point where it stops, and all the variables will contain the same values they contained before the program halted.

' (apostrophe) The apostrophe may be used as a substitute for the REM statement in the IBM and Radio Shack versions of BASIC. It allows the addition of a remark on the end of a regular statement. On the Apple the same thing is accomplished by using a colon followed by REM.

Accumulator A variable used in BASIC to add a newly input value to a total that keeps increasing with each new entry. Also called a running total.

CONT command The command to restart a program after a STOP or END statement has halted execution. It may also be used to restart the program after pressing the BREAK key. CONT stands for continue.

Documentation There are three types of documentation. Program documentation consists of comments that may be placed anywhere within a program to clarify its logic. Programmer documentation consists of the program flowchart, tables of variable usage, etc., that help a programmer understand how a program functions. User documentation is a manual that accompanies a program and explains to the user the prompts used, the data the prompts expect from the user, etc.; in other words, the way the program functions from the user's point of view.

GOTO statement The unconditional branch of BASIC. The program will transfer control to the line number that is specified in the GOTO statement.

Infinite loop *See* **Nonending loop.**

INPUT statement A statement that allows values to be assigned to variables as the program executes.

Loop   The process of repeating a routine in a program.

Nonending loop   A program loop with no exit, either accidental or intentional. Also called an infinite loop.

Program documentation   Comments put into a program to give information about the coding in the program.

Programmer documentation   Documents, such as pseudocode, flowcharts, and layouts of file storage to help a programmer understand how a program is put together.

Prompt   A statement that is printed on the screen to indicate to the user what kind of input is expected.

Redo from start   An IBM error that will occur if you key in string data in answer to a prompt for numeric data. On the Radio Shack this is REDO; on the Apple it is REENTER. On the IBM this can also indicate that too much data has been entered in response to the input prompt.

REM   A statement that allows comments to be added to a BASIC program.

STOP statement   A statement to halt program execution. It prints on the screen the line number where program stopped.

Unconditional branch   A GOTO statement in the program that will always branch to the line number indicated in the GOTO statement.

User documentation   A manual that explains step-by-step how to use a program.

QUESTIONS TO AID UNDERSTANDING

In the programming exercises that follow, always use the appropriate documentation (including pseudocode and/or flowchart) and attempt to use prompts that are meaningful to the situation.

*1. What are the three types of documentation and how do they differ?

2. What is the statement that allows you to put comments in a BASIC program?

*3. Explain the two different methods of using the INPUT statement.

4. What is the difference between the STOP and END statements?

5. Why is it important to know how to use the STOP statement?

*6. There are several errors (syntax and logic) in the following program. Find them and explain how you would correct them.

```
10 RME ***** SAMPLE PROGRAM WITH ERRORS
20 REM
30 INPUT "WHAT IS YOUR NAME?";N5$
40 PRIN "I SEE, YOU NAME IS";N5$
50 PRINT "HOW OLD ARE YOU ";N5$
60 INUPT A ' A STANDS FOR THE AGE
70 PRINT MY BUT YOU ARE GETTING ON IN YEARS"
80 GOTO 25
90 END
```

*7. Some of the following statements have errors in them. Indicate which have errors and what the errors are.
a. 10 PRINT
b. 10 INPUT A;B
c. 10 INPUT 'WHAT IS YOUR NAME";N
d. 10 PRINT 5 "+" 6 "=" 5+6
e. 10 GOTO LINE 10
f. "INPUT A$"

8. We have been given the task of writing a maintenance program for a payroll system. The program will need to be able to add records to the file, change records in the file, delete records (remove them), and print the file. Create the remarks that should appear at the beginning of such a program. Only the remarks are to be prepared; the program to do such processing is beyond your present knowledge.

9. Write a program to input the information necessary to produce a mailing label in the form:

```
ED COBURN
1400 SOUTH STREET
EL PASO, TEXAS   76708
```

*10. Write a program to input three course grades and find and print the average. (Average = total of grades/number of grades)

11. Write a program that will figure your bank balance by successively reducing the starting balance by the amount of each check. Print each new balance. The starting balance should be input before beginning to input the check amounts.

12. Write a program to input five numbers and print them and the total of them as:

total = number 1 + number 2 + number 3 + number 4 + number 5

For example, if we input 1, 2, 4, 7, and 10, the print line would be:

```
24 = 1 + 2 + 4 + 7 + 10
```

13. XYZ Corporation has to write a payroll list detailing gross pay, deductions, and net pay. Use pay rate and number of hours worked to determine gross pay. Then deduct social security (9%), federal income tax (20%), and state income tax (5%) to determine net pay. Totals for all three figures should be shown at the end of all the input. Design (flowchart and pseudocode) and code the program, using the following information to input:

NAME	RATE OF PAY	HOURS WORKED
John Smith	3.56	40
Leslie Thompson	4.56	35
Sara Harrison	7.89	40
Jill George	3.90	38
Henry Stevens	10.75	40

The output generated should have the following format (the totals should appear after all five employees have been input):

```
GROSS PAY = XXX.XX    DEDUCTIONS = XXX.XX
NET PAY  = XXX.XX

TOTAL GROSS PAY  = XXXXX.XX
TOTAL DEDUCTIONS = XXXXX.XX
TOTAL NET PAY    = XXXXX.XX
```

The answers to the questions follow immediately after the quiz. Questions 1–15 are true–false, while 16–20 are multiple choice.

T F **1.** No software should ever be produced without adequate documentation.

T F **2.** Program documentation is a manual that is prepared to enable the user to understand the program.

T F **3.** Comments in a program are a vital part of the program and should never be omitted under any circumstances.

T F **4.** Fixing or repairing (maintenancing) a program is one of the easiest jobs a programmer has to do.

T F **5.** Remarks can be used in a variety of ways in a program to allow for easier understanding of the code.

T F **6.** The single quote (') at the end of a statement allows the use of remarks following the quote (in IBM and Radio Shack BASIC).

T F **7.** There are two types of variables allowed on an INPUT statement: literal and string.

T F **8.** The INPUT statement allows the user to assign values to variables as the program executes.

T F **9.** Anything may be used as data when the variable is a numeric; however, the string variable is particular.

T F **10.** Only one item may be input on each INPUT statement.

T F **11.** The separator used between the prompt and the variable on the INPUT statement is the semicolon.

T F **12.** If you enter string data in response to a numeric input, a Redo from start message will appear.

T F **13.** When you see two question marks on an input prompt, it indicates that you have done something wrong.

T F **14.** A GOTO as used in this chapter is called a conditional branch.

T F **15.** The STOP statement differs from the END statement in one fundamental way. A STOP statement prints on the screen the line number where the program stopped.

_____ **16.** Which of the following statements is invalid?

    a. 10 REM   **c.** 10 GOTO A
    b. 10 INPUT A   **d.** 10 STOP

_____ **17.** Which of the following assignments is invalid (review from Chapter 2)?

    a. 10 K$ = "THIS IS A TEST"   **c.** 10 Y = (16 + 7)*5Y
    b. 10 K5 = Y + 7   **d.** 10 A9 = B6 + Z4*(G3 + 3)

_____ **18.** A STOP statement will do all the following *except:*

    a. halt execution of the program
    b. indicate the line number where it stopped

c. zero or null out all variables

d. allow continuation of the program

```
10 REM ***** QUESTION 4-19
20 REM
30 INPUT A$,A
40 PRINT A$,A
```

19. In response to the program displayed above, each of the following shows _____
the data input and the printed results. Which is correct?

    a. ? WACO, TEXAS, 5   c. ? "WACO, 5"

      WACO, TEXAS   5   WACO   5

    b. ? WACO, 5   d. ? 5, WACO

      WACO   5   5   WACO

20. Which of the following INPUT statements is incorrect? _____

    a. 10 INPUT A$,A,B$

    b. 10 INPUT "WHAT IS YOUR NAME";N$

    c. 10 INPUT A$;N$,C$

    d. 10 INPUT "HOW OLD ARE YOU";A$

ANSWERS TO
QUICK QUIZ

1. T (Few systems have "adequate" documentation.)
2. F (That's the definition of *user* documentation.)
3. T (With the understanding that they can be removed should the need arise.)
4. F (Fixing programs is the most difficult job for any programmer; it is also the most disliked.)
5. T
6. T
7. F (The two types are numeric and string.)
8. T
9. F (It is the numeric variable that is particular; anything may be used for the string.)
10. F (Many items may be input on one statement, though this is not recommended.)
11. T
12. T
13. F (It only indicates that you didn't enter all the values the computer expected.)
14. F (It is an *un*conditional branch.)
15. T
16. c (You can't use a variable as a line number.)
17. c (5Y is not a valid variable name.)
18. c (It does not affect the variables.)
19. b (a is incorrect because there is extra data; the first comma ends the first data input, and 5 is extra. c is incorrect because "WACO, 5" would fill only the first variable; there is no data for the A variable. d is incorrect because WACO is not numeric and would not be accepted into the variable A.)
20. c (The semicolon should be a comma.)

5 DECISIONS AND LOOPS

OBJECTIVES

After completing Chapter 5, you will be able to:

- Name the command BASIC uses for testing.
- List the six relational operators and explain how they are used.
- List the three boolean operators and explain how they are used.
- List at least three actions of an IF-THEN or IF-THEN-ELSE statement.
- Explain the three structures used in the chapter.
- Demonstrate how to use the FOR-NEXT (DO-WHILE) loop in several simple programs.
- Explain and demonstrate how the STEP value works.
- Demonstrate the concepts of BASIC thus far learned by writing and executing several simple and several complex programs using the defined structures.

In the preceding chapters, we studied methods of inputting data, storing that data, calculating with it, and then printing it. In this chapter, we learn about one of the most useful commands in BASIC: the decision test. With this test and the related structures, we can create much more intricate and complicated programs with only a little more effort. We also learn a new and easier way of creating a **DO-WHILE** loop in our programs.

Computers can make decisions within the logic of a program. This important capability allows certain tasks to be performed if and only if certain conditions are met. The BASIC decision statement is the **IF-THEN** statement. The form of the statement follows:

```
10 IF condition THEN action
```

The conditional part of the statement tests some type of relationship between two quantities. That is, two quantities are compared and, based on that result, the THEN part of the statement is either executed or not. If the condition is met, meaning that the relationship is true, then the specified action is done. If the condition is not met, the condition is said to be false, and the execution of the program falls through to the statement following the IF-THEN. (In the case of a condition on line number 10, the next statement would probably be line 20.) This would constitute the ELSE (in certain cases) on our IF-THEN-ELSE structure. More on that later.

An example of the IF-THEN might help clarify this discussion:

```
IF it is raining THEN
    I will use my umbrella.
(ELSE)
END-IF
```

This means that if it is raining out, then I will use my umbrella, otherwise I will not use the umbrella. Notice that we used the null ELSE structure. This was done because there is no ELSE.

The condition is specified with **relational operators,** which define a relationship between two elements. Table 5–1 lists relational operators and their meanings, along with a sample of the way the comparison might look.

Each of these operators may be used in an IF-THEN statement as a test. Let's examine for a moment how they work. Suppose we have the following part of a program:

```
10 A = 5
20 B = 8
```

Now, if we ask the following question (let's omit the THEN for the moment; just keep in mind that the IF condition is only part of the whole statement):

```
30 IF A = B
```

TABLE 5–1   Relational Operators

OPERATOR	MEANING	SAMPLE
=	equal to	A = B
<	less than	A < B
>	greater than	A > B
<>	not equal to	A <> B
<=	less than or equal to	A <= B
>=	greater than or equal to	A >= B

Here, the condition would be false because A is 5, B is 8, and 5 and 8 are not equal. But if we asked:

```
30 IF A < B
```

then the answer would be true because 5 is less than 8. If we asked:

```
30 IF A <= B
```

the answer would again be true and for the same reason. The equal sign would not make the statement true, the less than sign does that, but the equal sign would also not make the statement false. It tests less than *or* equal to, and A is less than B.

Now consider:

```
30 IF A <> B
```

This, of course, would also be true. We already decided that they were not equal. Since <> means not equal to, then the condition must be true. It is interesting to note that the symbol for not equal to is a combination of the less than and greater than symbols. That means that if it is either less than or greater than, the statement is true; which means the statement is true in any case except equal, meaning not equal to.

We can use relational operators to compare strings and literals also. For example, let's use this part of a program:

```
10 A$ = "HI"
20 B$ = "BYE"
```

Now if we ask:

```
30 IF A$ = B$
```

the answer is again obvious; of course, HI and BYE are not equal. How about:

```
30 IF A$ < "HIGH"
```

Is this true? Let's look at what is taking place. When the computer does a numeric comparison, it compares the value of the numerics. But when it compares strings, it begins on the left-hand side and makes a character-by-character comparison with the right-hand side. Since H is equal to H, it moves to the next letters which are both I's. Again equal. On to the next characters. But A$ has no more characters while the literal does. Because of this, A$ is automatically less than the other string. The statement is true. When the computer is able to determine whether there is a difference, the comparison stops. In this case, the difference is that one string is longer than the other. In such a case, the shorter string is always less.

Now let's look at the action part of the IF-THEN statement. Recall that if the result of the condition check is false, execution falls through to the next statement. When it is true, however, the THEN part of the statement is carried out. That action can be any valid BASIC statement. Anything that would be valid as a BASIC statement can be used as the action part of an IF-THEN statement, including another IF-THEN statement. However, multiple IF-THEN statements, though syntactically (and structurally) correct, should be used with caution since they can be confusing. Some examples of the way an action may be used in an IF-THEN statement follow. We will pseudocode and flowchart each.

An assignment statement may be coded as:

```
Start
Input A.
Input B.
IF A is not equal to B THEN
   Add 1 to A.
(ELSE)
END-IF
Print A.
END
```

Notice we have a null ELSE. We will continue to have one until we specify a certain action for ELSE. The flowchart is shown in Figure 5–1, and the program can be coded as follows:

```
NEW
10 REM ***** PROGRAM NAME: IFASSG
20 REM
30 REM ***** SAMPLE OF IF-THEN ASSIGNMENT
40 REM
50 INPUT "ENTER FIRST NUMBER";A
60 INPUT "ENTER SECOND NUMBER";B
70 IF A<>B THEN A=A+1
80 PRINT "A =";A
90 END
```
Program 5–1

When you run the program you will get the following results:

```
RUN
ENTER FIRST NUMBER? 10
ENTER SECOND NUMBER? 20
A = 11
Ok
RUN
ENTER FIRST NUMBER? 10
ENTER SECOND NUMBER? 10
A = 10
Ok
```

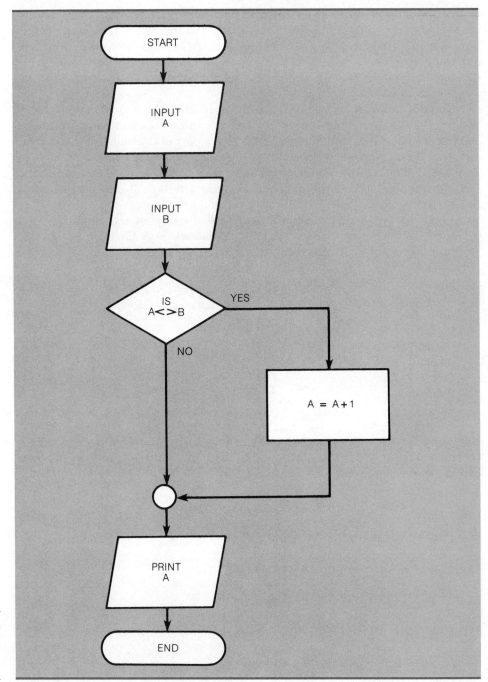

Figure 5–1
IF-THEN assignment
example.

Notice that in the first run the numbers were not equal so 1 was added to A, while the second time A was printed out as its initial value since A and B were equal.

A program can be stopped or ended based on a condition as shown in Figure 5–2; the program can be coded as:

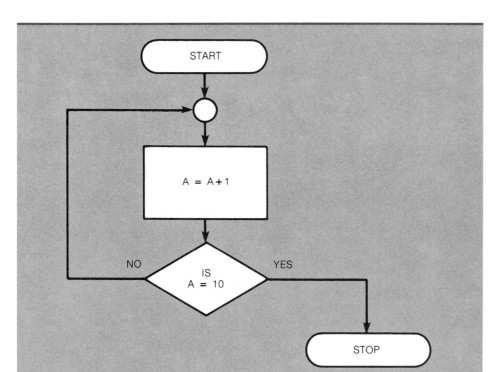

START

A = A+1

NO   IS
A = 10   YES

STOP

Figure 5–2
IF-THEN STOP example.

```
NEW
10 REM ***** PROGRAM NAME: IFSTOP
20 REM
30 REM ***** SAMPLE OF IF-THEN STOP
40 REM
50 A=0
60 A=A+1
70 PRINT A
80 IF A=10 THEN STOP
90 GOTO 60
100 END
RUN
 1
 2
 3
 4
 5
 6
 7
 8
 9
 10
Break in 80
Ok
```

Program 5–2

This program will loop until A has accumulated to 10. Line 60 will increase A until it has reached 10 as printed by line 70. The program will then stop in line 80.

Recall that all numeric variables begin automatically as 0. We have initialized A as 0, however, since it is not wise to have BASIC doing things for us automatically. (Not all languages will automatically initialize the variables as zero.)

Another type of action can be pseudocoded as:

Start
Input A.
Input B.
IF A is not equal to B THEN
   Print message.
(ELSE)
END-IF
End

The flowchart can be seen in Figure 5–3; the program could look like the following:

```
NEW
10 REM ***** PROGRAM NAME: IFPRT
20 REM
30 REM ***** SAMPLE OF IF-THEN PRINT
40 REM
50 INPUT "ENTER FIRST NUMBER";A
60 INPUT "ENTER SECOND NUMBER";B
70 IF A<>B THEN PRINT "A AND B ARE NOT EQUAL"
80 END
```

Program 5–3

When you run the program you will get the following results:

```
RUN
ENTER FIRST NUMBER? 10
ENTER SECOND NUMBER? 20
A AND B ARE NOT EQUAL
Ok
RUN
ENTER FIRST NUMBER? 10
ENTER SECOND NUMBER? 10
Ok
```

On the first run, A and B are not equal so the message is printed. On the second run, no message is printed since the numbers are the same.

A final use of the IF-THEN statement that we will examine is the conditional branch (with an understood GOTO), such as:

```
NEW
10 REM ***** PROGRAM NAME: IFBRCH
20 REM
30 REM ***** SAMPLE OF IF-THEN BRANCH
40 REM
50 A=5
60 PRINT "A IS NOW =";A
70 A=A+1
80 IF A<>10 THEN 60
90 PRINT "A CONCLUDES AS";A
100 END
RUN
A IS NOW = 5
```

Program 5–4

Program continues

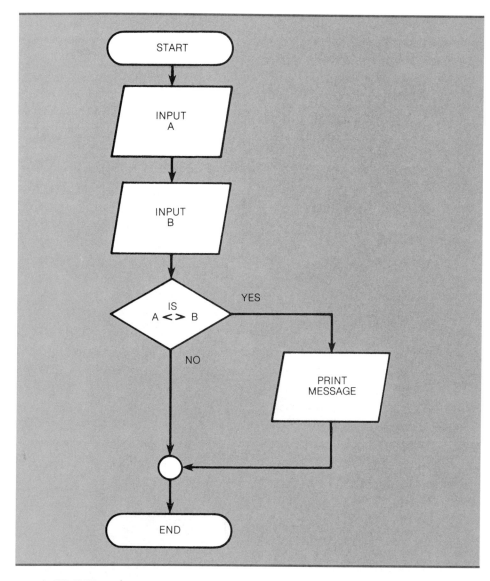

Figure 5–3
IF-THEN PRINT example.

```
A IS NOW = 6
A IS NOW = 7
A IS NOW = 8
A IS NOW = 9
A CÓNCLUDES AS 10
Ok
```
                                            Program 5–4 (cont.)

Here, the THEN 60 is actually a THEN GOTO 60 but the GOTO here is understood. This type of test is called a **conditional branch.** Control in the program
will branch based on the condition of the test.

How does the program work? Originally, A=5, then 1 is added each time
statement 70 is executed. Line 80 compares A to 10 to see if it is unequal to 10.
Since the first time A is tested it will be 6 (5+1=6), control will return to line
60. It will continue to return to line 60 until line 70 has been executed five times,

whereupon A will be 10 and control will fall through to whatever is after 70, in this case another PRINT statement. If there are no more lines after an IF-THEN (except the END), execution simply ends at that point.

We skipped doing the pseudocode and the flowchart for Program 5–4 for a reason. This use of the IF-THEN requires a new structure. You may recall that the DO-WHILE structure leads off with an IF-THEN statement. That is, the first statement in the DO-WHILE structure is the IF-THEN statement. The loop in

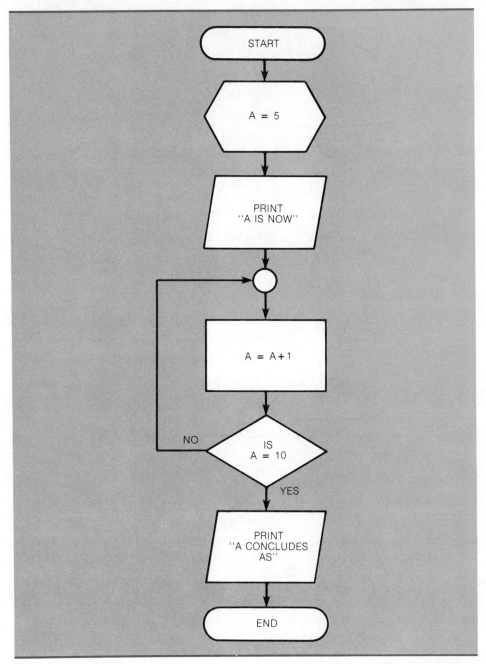

Figure 5–4
REPEAT-UNTIL structure.

Program 5–4, however, has the calculation first and then the IF-THEN. Such a loop is called a **REPEAT-UNTIL.** That is, the action is continued until the specified condition is true, and the control passes out of the loop. In this structure, the test is the last thing in the block rather than the first thing. The flowchart for this structure is shown in Figure 5–4, and the pseudocode should look like the following:

```
Start
Assign 5 to A.
Print message.
REPEAT-UNTIL A = 10.
   Increment A by 1.
END-REPEAT
Print message.
End
```

Notice that we now use an END-REPEAT to mark the end of the loop. Now that we can create a REPEAT-UNTIL, how do we construct the DO-WHILE we introduced back in Chapter 2? A simple example is shown in Figure 5–5; the pseudocode follows:

```
Start
Assign 5 to A.
DO-WHILE A<>10.
   Print A.
   Increment A by 1.
END-DO
End
```

The program can be coded as:

```
NEW
10 REM ***** PROGRAM NAME: DOWHILE
20 REM
30 REM ***** SAMPLE OF DO-WHILE
40 REM
50 A=5
60 IF A=10 THEN 100
70 PRINT A
80 A=A+1
90 GOTO 60
100 END
RUN
 5
 6
 7
 8
 9
Ok
```

Program 5–5

This program is actually more complicated than the REPEAT-UNTIL. Sometimes one structure is superior to the other in developing the necessary logic for the program. It merely takes practice and experience to decide which structure is the one best suited to the task.

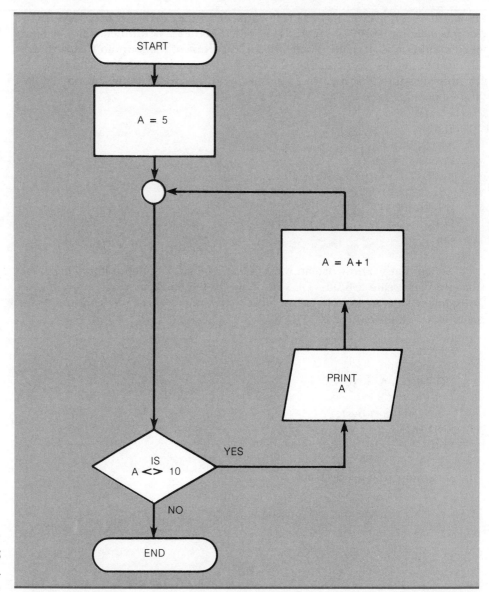

Figure 5–5
DO-WHILE structure.

It is important to remember that the difference between the DO-WHILE and REPEAT-UNTIL is the placement of the test. In the DO-WHILE, the test is the first thing in the structure. In the REPEAT-UNTIL, the test is the last thing in the structure. Other than this, the loops are the same.

5–3
THE ACTUAL
IF-THEN-ELSE

There is actually an **IF-THEN-ELSE** statement in IBM and Radio Shack BASIC. The form of the statement is much like you would expect:

```
10 IF condition THEN action ELSE action
```

As we discussed in Chapter 2, if the condition is true, the THEN action is carried out; otherwise (else), the ELSE action is done. Let's suppose, for example, that we have a variable and if it is a certain value, we want to print one message, and if it is another value, we want to print a different message. The flowchart for this is shown in Figure 5–6, and the pseudocode follows:

```
Start
Input A.
IF A is 5 THEN
    Print A IS 5.
ELSE
    Print A IS NOT 5.
END-IF
End
```

The program to perform this code is shown on page 108.

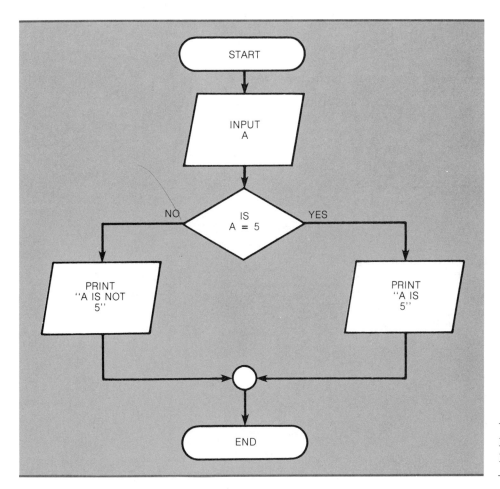

Figure 5–6
IF-THEN-ELSE example.

```
NEW
10 REM ***** PROGRAM NAME: IFELSE
20 REM
30 INPUT "ENTER A NUMBER";A
40 IF A=5 THEN PRINT "A IS 5" ELSE PRINT "A IS NOT 5"
50 END
```
Program 5–6

If we execute the program we will see:

```
RUN
ENTER A NUMBER? 5
A IS 5
Ok
RUN
ENTER A NUMBER? 6
A IS NOT 5
Ok
```

Although the Apple doesn't have an actual IF-THEN-ELSE statement, we can construct one fairly easily using *two* IF-THEN statements. We will use the same logic as in Program 5–6, except we will use two IF-THEN statements:

```
NEW
10 REM ***** PROGRAM NAME: IFELSE
20 REM
30 INPUT "ENTER A NUMBER";A
40 IF A=5 THEN PRINT "A IS 5"
50 IF A<>5 THEN PRINT "A IS NOT 5"
60 END
```
Program 5–7 (Apple)

If we execute the program we will see:

```
RUN
ENTER A NUMBER? 5
A IS 5
Ok
RUN
ENTER A NUMBER? 6
A IS NOT 5
Ok
```

The same result we had from Program 5–6. If A is 5, then the PRINT statement on the first IF-THEN is executed. Control then falls to the second IF-THEN, but since A is 5, that test is false so no printing is done. On the second input, the first IF-THEN is false, so control falls through to the second IF-THEN, which is true so the message is printed. Notice that the two IF-THEN statements are opposites. Such will always be the case when constructing an IF-THEN-ELSE without the appropriate statement.

5–4
USING THE COLON TO CONTINUE THE ACTION

We mentioned in Chapter 4 that a second statement can be put at the end of another by a colon. We use it in this manner only for putting comments on statements:

```
10 P=1 : REM P IS THE PAGE NUMBER
```

But it can actually be used to put two different statements on the same line:

```
10 P=1 : R=5
```

This use is not recommended except in one instance: an IF-THEN statement. The action of the THEN part of the statement can be followed by a colon and more statements. For example, suppose we needed to print a message and increase the value of a variable if a certain condition is true. We could construct a statement such as:

```
10 IF A=5 THEN PRINT "MESSAGE" : A=A+1
```

Both statements are performed if the condition is true. If the statement is false, control merely passes to the next line statement as always. The structure would look like that shown in Figure 5–7, and the pseudocode would look like:

Start
IF A is equal to 5 THEN
    PRINT ''MESSAGE''.
    Increment A by 1.   *(continues on page 110)*

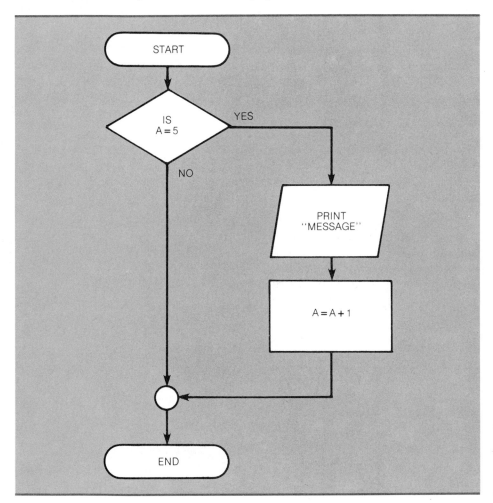

Figure 5–7
Example of IF-THEN with two actions on THEN.

```
      (ELSE)
      END-IF
      End
```

In the case of the IBM and Radio Shack, the colon also works after the ELSE part of the IF-THEN-ELSE. Such a statement might look like:

```
10 IF A=5 THEN PRINT "MESSAGE" : A=6 ELSE PRINT "NO" : A=7
```

This example is not something you would ordinarily use. It merely serves to demonstrate how the statement works. In this instance, if A is 5, then MESSAGE is printed and A is set to 6. Control would then fall through to the next statement. If A is not 5, NO is printed and A is set to 7.

5–5
BOOLEAN OPERATORS

Many times we need a program in which an action is performed only when *two* relationships are true. For example, suppose we want to print a message if both A and B are 5. We could do this with convoluted logic, such as:

```
NEW
10 REM ***** PROGRAM NAME: MESS
20 REM
30 INPUT "A NUMBER";A
40 INPUT "ANOTHER NUMBER";B
50 IF A<>5 THEN 70
60 IF B=5 THEN PRINT "MESSAGE"
70 END
```

In this example, if A is 5, then the condition in line 50 would be false and control would fall to statement 60. If the condition in line 60 is true, then the message would be printed. We would achieve the desired result, but the logic is not too clear. It would be much better if we could test both A and B on one statement. We can do just that by using **boolean operators,** which are also known as **logical operators.** A boolean operator is simply an operator that allows two (or more) conditionals to be combined into one test. There are three boolean operators: AND, OR, and NOT.

The best way to explain boolean operators is to show some examples. Let's use the above example. We want to print the message if A and B are both 5. The statement, then, should be:

```
50 IF  A=5 AND B=5 THEN PRINT "MESSAGE"
```

This means that the message will only be printed when both A and B are 5. If either one of them is not 5, the condition will be false and the message will not be printed.

The second operator is OR. Suppose we want to print the message if either A is 5 or B is 5. We can do that with:

```
50 IF A=5 OR B=5 THEN PRINT "MESSAGE"
```

Now the message will print if A is 5, or B is 5, or both are 5. The only time it would not print is when neither A nor B is 5.

NOT is an operator used infrequently. (There are a few times, however, when it is useful.) It specifies the opposite of the condition. If the condition is true, the NOT will make it false; and if the condition is false, the NOT will make it true. Suppose we want to print the message only when A is not equal to 5. We could do it like:

```
50 IF NOT(A=5) THEN PRINT "MESSAGE"
```

If A is 5, the message will not print. It will only print should A not be 5. This same statement could be constructed in a more straightforward manner like:

```
50 IF A<>5 THEN PRINT "MESSAGE"
```

For this reason, the NOT is used infrequently, but there are times when it is useful. In Chapter 8 we will see just such a time.

5–6
A COUPLE OF PROGRAM SEGMENTS

Now that we understand a bit about IF-THEN, let's look at some simple problems using this most useful tool.

Suppose for a moment that we have a program that will do certain actions when the user is a female and other actions when the user is male. If we were to input the male/female code, the flowchart would look like the one in Figure 5–8, and the pseudocode would be:

Start
Input male or female code.
DO-WHILE not male or female.
    Print error message.
    Input male or female code.
END-DO
IF male THEN
    Accomplish male routines.
ELSE
    Accomplish female routines.
END-IF
End

The program would look like this:

```
NEW
10 REM ***** PROGRAM NAME: MFCODE
20 REM
30 REM TEST FOR MALE-FEMALE CODE
40 REM
50 INPUT "ARE YOU FEMALE (F) OR MALE (M)";C$
60 IF C$="F" THEN 820 ' GOTO FEMALE ROUTINE
70 IF C$="M" THEN 1020 ' GOTO MALE ROUTINE
80 REM
90 REM ***** ERROR ROUTINE
100 REM
110 REM THIS FOR C$ <> F OR M
```

Program 5–8

Program continues on page 113

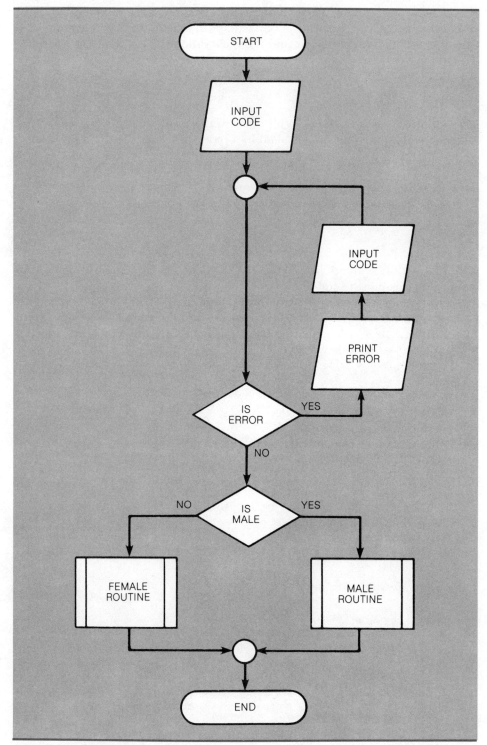

Figure 5–8
Flowchart using error
trap.

```
120 REM
130 PRINT "VALID ENTRY IS ONLY F OR M.   TRY AGAIN."
140 GOTO 50
::::
::::
::::
770 REM
780 REM ***** FEMALE ROUTINE
790 REM
800 REM DISPLAY AREA FOR FEMALE INFORMATION
810 REM
::::
::::
::::
970 REM
980 REM ***** MALE ROUTINE
990 REM
1000 REM DISPLAY AREA FOR MALE INFORMATION
1010 REM
::::
::::
::::
```

Program 5–8 (cont.)

Notice that the program statements are not in the same order as the pseudocode or the flowchart, but they follow the logic associated with the stated problem. The pseudocode indicates that there should be a test for the male/female code (the DO-WHILE), but as we see, that test is not necessary. It is accomplished by **default,** that is, if not male and not female, control falls through to the error routine.

The program begins by inputting for the type of user, male (M) or female (F). If the user enters an F, the program jumps down to line 820 and does whatever is intended (not displayed in example). If the user enters an M, the program goes to line 1020 and does whatever is appropriate for a male respondent (not displayed in example). If the user enters neither one, the program will fall through to an error routine that will tell the user that the wrong key for the code was entered and to try again; then it will have another INPUT statement or a branch to the original INPUT statement as shown in the example. This is called **error trapping,** and it is an important part of every program. Whenever a user enters erroneous information into a program, an error should indicate as much.

Some programmers use other defaults in their programs. A default is created by writing a test so that if it is false, control will fall through to the next option automatically. Consider when M is entered, for example. The program goes to the male routine, otherwise it might fall into the female routine. Sometimes this is an appropriate thing (such as defaulting into the error routine), but most of the time, defaults will lead to trouble. Users may not know how they got into the routines they are in. Take for example, a user of a program with a male/female test who intended to enter an M but accidentally pressed N. If the program simply defaulted into the female routine, that user might have a little trouble understanding why he was being asked the female-type questions when he pressed (or at least he thought he did) the key for the male questions.

Users appreciate error routines. You are a user of your own programs as much as anyone else who might use them. You will like your programs better with proper error handling.

You might note that the program branches to actual functioning lines in the program rather than to the comments at the beginning of the routine. Though it is not incorrect to branch to a REM, it is bad practice. Remember that if your program needs to be reduced in size, the first things to remove are the remarks. If you have GOTO statements set for lines that are REM statements and those remarks have to be removed from the program, you will have a line number error in the program. You'll have to figure out just what line number the GOTO should jump to. Sometimes that can be a difficult task. The safest thing to do is to always make sure each GOTO statement branches to an actual functioning line number. Although a functioning line may be removed occasionally, it is still a safer choice.

Let's try another simple problem to test your knowledge of the IF-THEN. Suppose you have a program that you wish only a few people to use. Each of these people has been given a code to use to get into the program. You will ask them for this code and, based on their answer, they will either gain access or be given some error message. This is a type of password protection routine. The flowchart can be seen in Figure 5-9, and the pseudocode follows:

Start
Input password.
DO-WHILE password not correct.
   Print error.
   Input password.
END-DO
Accomplish remainder of program.
End

Your program should look something like this:

```
NEW
10 REM ***** PROGRAM NAME: PASSWORD
20 REM
30 REM TEST FOR PASSWORD TO GAIN PROGRAM ACCESS
40 REM
50 INPUT "WHAT IS YOUR PASSWORD";P$
60 IF P$="SAM" THEN 1000  ' VALID PASSWORD
70 IF P$="JOE" THEN 1000  ' VALID PASSWORD
80 IF P$="ED " THEN 1000  ' VALID PASSWORD
90 REM
100 REM ***** PASSWORD ERROR
110 REM
120 PRINT "PASSWORD IS INCORRECT.  PLEASE REENTER."
130 GOTO 50
:::
:::
:::
970 REM
980 REM ***** BEGIN PROGRAM
990 REM
:::
:::
:::
```

Program 5-9

This program has several acceptable responses to the prompt for the pass-

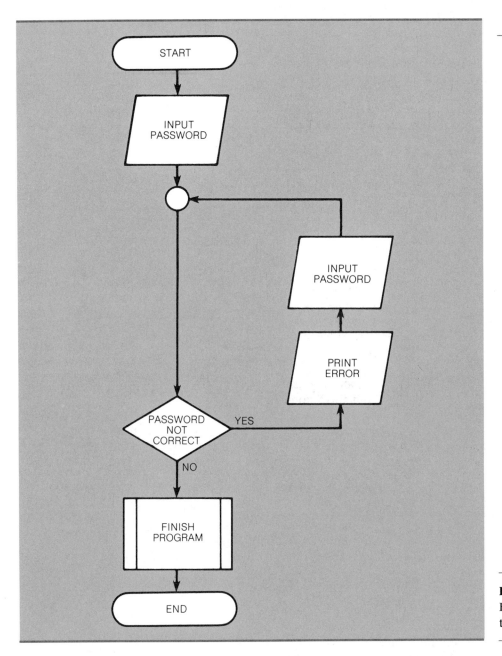

Figure 5–9
Flowchart of password
testing program.

word. If any of them are entered, the program will branch to line 1000 and begin the processing of the program. If none of the correct responses is entered, the program will fall through to an error routine such as the one shown. For password protection, the routine would probably flash an error message and then stop the processing of the program so that unauthorized use could be halted. The routine in our example program simply branches back to the INPUT statement.

Let's go back for a moment to Chapters 3 and 4. In the Questions to Aid Understanding in each of those chapters, there was a problem dealing with grade averaging. Let's expand on that program, add a test, and end up with a much more versatile program. The problem in Chapter 4 directed you to input three grades and then print out the average. The average was found by dividing the total of the three grades by 3. The pseudocode to accomplish this task follows:

> Start
> Input grade 1.
> Input grade 2.
> Input grade 3.
> Print total of grades divided by 3.
> End

Now, we must expand the program to be able to input any number of grades and find the average. We need to add three things. First, since we want to be able to input any number of grades, the program needs to be in a loop. Second, because we have to be able to divide the total by the number of grades we have input, we need an accumulator for the total and a counter to know how many grades there were. Finally, we have to have some kind of indicator of the end of the program. The user needs to be able to indicate when the entry is finished. Recall that in Chapter 2 such an indicator was called an **end-of-data marker.**

We need to decide what would be a good choice for our end-of-data marker. Since the input is grades, we should use something that would be inappropriate for grades. Since we are going to be calculating with grades, or numerics, that rules out any special keys for a marker, such as an asterisk or something similar, since the data must be a number of some type. We could use zero to indicate that we are finished, but it is possible for a student to receive a zero (perhaps for work not turned in). Therefore, the best choice would be a negative number. It is unlikely that a grade will ever be negative.

The flowchart for such a program can be seen in Figure 5–10, and the pseudocode follows:

> Start
> Initialize counter and accumulator.
> Input a grade.
> DO-WHILE grade is not negative.
>   Add grade to accumulator.
>   Increment counter by 1.
>   Input a grade.
> END-DO
> Calculate the average by accumulator divided by counter.
> Print the average.
> End

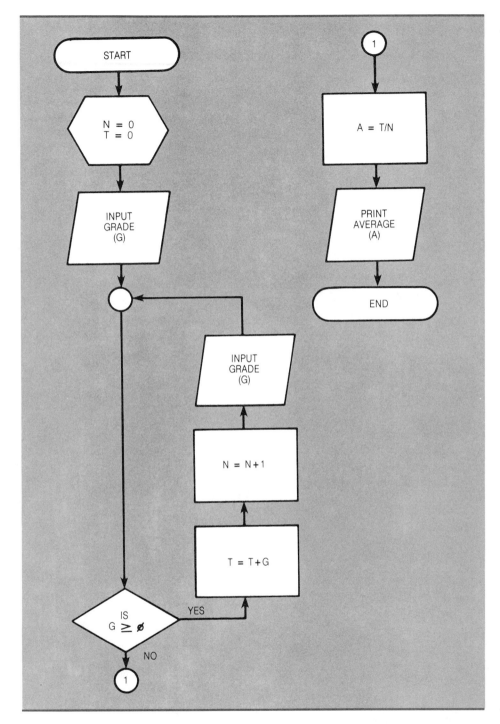

Figure 5–10
Flowchart for grade-averaging program.

One way to code such a program would be:

```
10 REM ***** PROGRAM NAME: GRADING
20 REM
30 REM CALCULATE GRADE AVERAGES
40 REM END-OF-DATA MARKER IS NEGATIVE NUMBER
50 REM
60 REM ***** WRITTEN BY EDWARD J. COBURN
70 REM
80 T=0                  ' INITIALIZE ACCUMULATOR
90 N=0                  ' INITIALIZE COUNTER
100 INPUT "WHAT IS THE GRADE";G
110 IF G<0 THEN 200' END INPUT - GO CALCULATE
120 T=T+G               ' TOTAL THE GRADES
130 N=N+1               ' GET THE NUMBER OF GRADES
140 GOTO 80             ' RETURN FOR ANOTHER GRADE
170 REM
180 REM ***** GRADE CALCULATION AND PRINT
190 REM
200 A=T/N               ' CALCULATE AVERAGE
210 PRINT "YOUR AVERAGE FOR";N;"GRADES IS";A
220 END
```

Program 5–10

When you run the program you should get:

```
WHAT IS THE GRADE? 100
WHAT IS THE GRADE? 95
WHAT IS THE GRADE? 97
WHAT IS THE GRADE? 90
WHAT IS THE GRADE? -1
YOUR AVERAGE FOR 4 GRADES IS 95.5
Ok
```

You are prompted for the grades as long as you keep entering valid data. When you enter the negative number (-1), the program branches down, calculates the average, then prints it out. If you were calculating grades for an entire class of students, only minimal changes would be needed. These changes are left as an exercise at the end of the chapter.

You may note that we initialized the counter and accumulator, which BASIC will do for us automatically. Although BASIC will do it for us, it is always a good idea to do things explicitly. It keeps us from getting into bad habits that we will regret later.

5–8
ANOTHER METHOD OF LOOPING

Using the previously learned information, we can construct loops that will operate a certain number of times and then exit. The loop is created by using a GOTO to return to the beginning of the routine we are using.

BASIC gives us another method of performing loops in our programs that handles most of the testing, counting, etc., for us. The **FOR-NEXT** loop allows us to specify a loop that will have an automatic counter, an end-point test, and an automatic branch. The form of the FOR-NEXT is:

```
10 FOR counter variable = start point TO end point

      body of loop (what the loop accomplishes)

100 NEXT counter variable
```

The **counter variable** can be any numeric variable and is the counter of the loop. It begins with the starting-point value and is increased by one every time the loop executes. When the counter value exceeds the ending-point value, the loop terminates and execution passes to the line following the NEXT statement. The NEXT statement does not require the counter variable to be specified on it in our versions of BASIC. It is, however, a good idea to put the variable both places even though our versions of BASIC do not require it. It is sometimes difficult in larger programs to tell where a particular loop ends unless the NEXT statement is labeled with the counter variable.

The execution of a FOR-NEXT loop begins with the FOR statement setting the counter to the starting-point value. Then each statement in the body of the loop is executed until the NEXT is reached and the counter is incremented. Then control returns to the FOR again, and the counter is compared to the ending-point value. If it is less than or equal to that ending-point value, the loop will execute again. Otherwise, the control passes out of the loop to the statement following the NEXT. If there are no other statements, the program ends at that point.

An actual FOR-NEXT loop looks something like:

```
NEW
10 REM ***** PROGRAM NAME: FNSAMP
20 REM
30 REM ***** SAMPLE FOR-NEXT
40 REM
50 FOR I = 1 TO 10
60     PRINT I
70 NEXT I
80 PRINT "WE ARE DONE AND THE VALUE OF I IS";I
90 END
```
Program 5—11

The counter variable is I, the starting value is 1, and the ending value is 10. That means the loop will execute 10 times. It will begin with I being 1. Then the loop functions. The loop does only one thing: it prints the value of I. (We will explain later why this line is indented.) This causes the value of the counter to be displayed on the screen. In this first loop it will be 1. Line 70 then sends control back to the FOR statement where I is incremented by 1. This is compared to the ending value of 10. Since I is now 2, which is less than 10, the loop functions again. This process continues until I has been incremented beyond the ending value of 10. At that point, control passes to the statement following the NEXT, which will print "WE ARE DONE" and the last value of I on the screen. What will be the value that will print after the loop finishes? Let's run the program and find out:

```
RUN
 1
 2
 3
 4
 5
 6
 7
 8
 9
 10
WE ARE DONE AND THE VALUE OF I IS 11
Ok
```

Of course, the value of I is 11. Since that is the first value greater than 10, that is the value at which the loop would have to stop.

It is important to note that some versions of BASIC, specifically the IBM, require that spaces be used on the FOR statement surrounding the TO. *Except on the IBM*, we could construct our statement as:

```
10 FOR I=1TO10
```

This is, of course, harder to read than a FOR statement with spacing such as:

```
10 FOR I = 1 TO 10
```

This example is the form required on the IBM. You should use spacing whether it is necessary or not since it is much clearer, *but it is required on the IBM*.

This loop is a slight variation on our standard DO-WHILE structure. The DO-WHILE specifies that the test be performed and if the test is true, then the loop is executed. If the test is false, then control bypasses the loop. This is precisely what takes place in the FOR-NEXT with one slight exception. In our versions of BASIC (this is not true in all versions of BASIC), the test of the counter variable is not done the first time through the loop. That is, if the starting point is greater than the end point, the loop will function anyway. In our versions of BASIC, the loop will *always* function at least once. If we are facing a situation where this would be a problem, we can put an IF-THEN test right after the FOR-NEXT to test before the loop is executed. But in such a case it would be better to use a GOTO loop such as we were using before. It would be much easier to understand.

We can begin our FOR-NEXT loop at any starting value we choose. The usual choice is 1, but it does not have to be. Let's change Program 5–11 to begin at a different point. Change line 50 to:

```
50 FOR I = 8 TO 10
```

So the program now looks like:

```
10 REM ***** PROGRAM NAME: FNSAMP
20 REM
30 REM ***** SAMPLE FOR-NEXT
40 REM
50 FOR I = 8 TO 10
60     PRINT I
70 NEXT I
80 PRINT "WE ARE DONE AND THE VALUE OF I IS";I
90 END
```

Let's see how many times it loops when we run it:

```
RUN
 8
 9
 10
WE ARE DONE AND THE VALUE OF I IS 11
Ok
```

The program began at 8 and concluded after 10. It ran through the loop three times because it took only three loops for the counter to exceed the ending point value. We can also change the ending point in the same fashion.

The starting and ending points for a FOR-NEXT loop do not have to be constants. We can use variables to allow more flexibility in our programs. Let's expand this program to use variables for the starting and ending points. Insert lines 42 and 44 as:

```
42 INPUT "STARTING POINT";S
44 INPUT "ENDING POINT";E
```

Then we need to change line 50 to allow for flexible start and end points:

```
50 FOR I = S TO E
```

And the program follows:

```
10 REM ***** PROGRAM NAME: FNSAMP
20 REM
30 REM ***** SAMPLE FOR-NEXT
40 REM
42 INPUT "STARTING POINT";S
44 INPUT "ENDING POINT";E
50 FOR I = S TO E
60      PRINT I
70 NEXT I
80 PRINT "WE ARE DONE AND THE VALUE OF I IS";I
90 END
```

When we run our program, we will be asked for two inputs: the starting point and the ending point. Let's try it:

```
RUN
STARTING POINT? 5
ENDING POINT? 8
 5
 6
 7
 8
WE ARE DONE AND THE VALUE OF I IS 9
Ok
```

Of course, we can use whatever values we wish. Let's try running the program again, using different values for the starting and ending points. The loop will execute only the appropriate number of times.

```
RUN
STARTING POINT? 5
ENDING POINT? 6
 5
 6
WE ARE DONE AND THE VALUE OF I IS 7
Ok
```

As the loop executes, only the value of the counter changes. The starting and ending points remain the same. In fact, even if you change the values of the start and end variables in the body of the loop, the start and end points will not change. When the computer begins a FOR-NEXT loop, the starting-point value is set into the counter variable and from that point forward, the starting value does not change. Also, when the computer reads the FOR statement, the value of the ending point is stored in memory in a special location that is separate from the ending variable itself. The comparison for ending point is then made with this special location and not with the ending-point variable. There-fore, changing the ending-point variable in the body of the loop will have no effect.

Let's test this with Program 5–11. Insert line 65 as follows:

```
65 E=100
```

When we run the program, let's use 10 for the ending value and see what hap-pens.

```
RUN
STARTING POINT? 6
ENDING POINT? 10
  6
  7
  8
  9
  10
WE ARE DONE AND THE VALUE OF I IS 11
Ok
```

If changing the value of E in the loop made any difference, the loop should have run through 100 before it ended. It didn't, however, so changing the value must not matter.

The same does not hold true for changing the counter variable. When the loop functions, it depends on the counter variable to know when it is finished. This value is derived strictly from the storage setup for that variable, so chang-ing that variable will modify the loop. Let's experiment with that for a moment. Change line 65 to:

```
65 I=10
```

Now the program looks like:

```
LIST
10 REM ***** PROGRAM NAME: FNSAMP
20 REM
30 REM ***** SAMPLE FOR-NEXT
40 REM
42 INPUT "STARTING POINT";S
44 INPUT "ENDING POINT";E
50 FOR I = S TO E
60 PRINT I
65 I=10
70 NEXT I
80 PRINT "WE ARE DONE AND THE VALUE OF I IS";I
90 END
```

When we run it, we will see:

```
RUN
STARTING POINT? 1
ENDING POINT? 10
  1
WE ARE DONE AND THE VALUE OF I IS 11
Ok
```

What happened? Shouldn't it have looped through 10 times? Look at the ending value. It's 11 just as it was before. Why? In line 65 we set I to 10, so when the computer hit the NEXT statement (line 70) it increased I by 1 to 11. Then when control returned to line 50, I was compared to the ending-point value (which was 10) and found to be too large, so control passed through the loop to line 80 to print.

Because the counter variable can be changed, which could damage the processing of your loop, be extremely careful with FOR-NEXT loops so that you don't change the counter variable within the'loop unless you intend to. There are times when you need to modify the counter for a specific purpose, but again, be careful when doing this.

The body of the loop of a FOR-NEXT loop can be whatever routine you need to be done a number of times. You can print the counter variable, but that is usually just a convenience (it is handy sometimes). Let's take an example of a loop where the counter value is not printed. Let's use a simple addition program. Here we want to input two numbers, add them, print the total, and then keep track of the cumulative total for a series of three sets of numbers. The flowchart would look like the one in Figure 5–11, and the pseudocode would look like the following:

```
Start
Initialize counter to 1.
DO-WHILE counter is less than 4.
   Input two numbers.
   Total the numbers.
   Accumulate the total.
   Print the total and the accumulative total.
END-DO
End
```

The program would be:

```
NEW
10 REM ***** PROGRAM NAME: ADDPROG
20 REM
30 REM ***** ADDITION PROGRAM
40 REM
50 FOR I = 1 TO 3
60    INPUT "WHAT IS THE FIRST NUMBER";N1
70    INPUT "WHAT IS THE SECOND NUMBER";N2
80    T1=N1+N2  ' TOTAL OF THE TWO NUMBERS
90    T2=T2+T1  ' ACCUMULATED TOTAL
100   PRINT "TOTAL =";T1;
110   PRINT " ACCUMULATIVE TOTAL =";T2
120 NEXT I
130 END
```
                                                    Program 5–12

When we run this program, we will see something like the following:

```
RUN
WHAT IS THE FIRST NUMBER? 4
WHAT IS THE SECOND NUMBER? 5
TOTAL = 9  ACCUMULATIVE TOTAL = 9
WHAT IS THE FIRST NUMBER? 7
```

Program continues on page 125

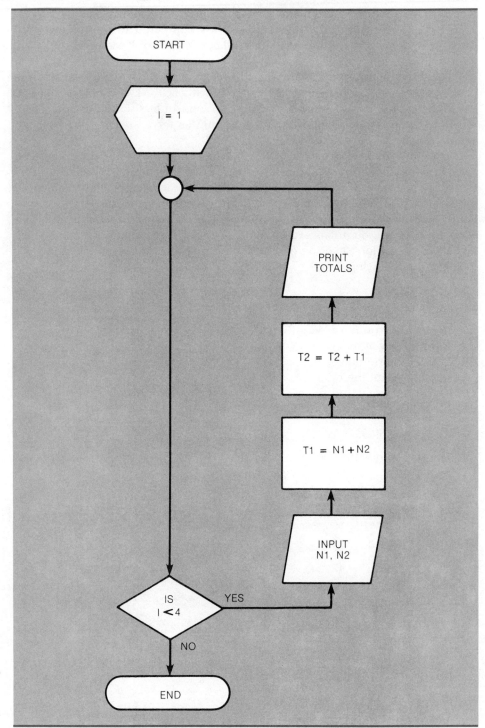

Figure 5–11
Example of FOR-NEXT
loop (accompanies
Program 5–12).

WHAT IS THE SECOND NUMBER? 12
TOTAL = 19   ACCUMULATIVE TOTAL = 28
WHAT IS THE FIRST NUMBER? 15
WHAT IS THE SECOND NUMBER? 6
TOTAL = 21   ACCUMULATIVE TOTAL = 49
Ok
```

chapter 5 **125**

decisions and loops

Notice in Program 5–12 that the body of the loop was indented several spaces. This is done by the careful programmer to indicate the levels of control of the program and is similar to what we have been doing with our pseudocode. It marks which program lines lie within the control of which statements. It is a good practice because you can tell at a glance where the guiding statements are by finding those without the indentation. Programs that do not use such indentation are much more difficult to follow and understand.

Those of you programming an Apple will notice that any spacing put into your program is messed up by the machine when you list your program back out. This happens because as Applesoft stores your program in memory, it removes all the spaces. Then when it lists the program back, spaces are put in predescribed places. Thus, whatever indentation or spacing you use will not be retained.

The FOR-NEXT loop has a special feature that is important in certain instances. How would you write a FOR-NEXT loop if you needed the loop to count backwards, say, starting at 10 and reducing to 1? Right now you can't. But with an addition to the FOR statement, you can. By adding a **STEP command,** you can increment your counter variable by whatever amount you choose, including a negative amount. The form of the FOR-NEXT loop is now:

```
10 FOR counter = start value TO end value STEP value

        Body of loop

100 NEXT counter
```

The STEP value can be either a constant or a variable. Like the ending point value, its value won't change even if the variable assigned to the step value is changed. An example of how the STEP might function within a FOR-NEXT loop follows:

```
NEW
10 REM ***** PROGRAM NAME: STEPSAMP
20 REM
30 REM ***** INITIAL STEP SAMPLE
40 REM
50 FOR I = 10 TO 6 STEP -1
60     PRINT I
70 NEXT I
80 END
RUN
 10
 9
 8
 7
 6
Ok
```

Program 5–13
```

The program began with I set to 10 and a step value of −1. Therefore, when I printed the first time it was 10. The step value was then added (−1), and I was 9. This process continued until the value was less than the end point. Ordinarily the computer checks the counter to see if it is larger than the end point, but for a negative step value, it compares the counter to see if it is *less than* the end point. In this example, the counter variable (I) is 5 at the end of the loop. You can verify this by entering PRINT I as a command. The result will be 5, the current value of I.

The step value can also be a decimal number (.5, for example) if desired. The counter is increased (or decreased) by the amount of the step value regardless of the size of that value.

5—9
ONE FINAL NOTE ABOUT THE FOR-NEXT

The FOR-NEXT loop should not be used for every loop in your program. It should only be used when a counter is needed to dictate the number of cycles the loop should run through. For example, if you want to perform a loop until an end-of-data marker is keyed in, you shouldn't use a FOR-NEXT loop. This would be contrary to our structures. Such an improper program might look like the following:

```
NEW
10 REM ***** PROGRAM NAME: BADPROG
20 REM
30 REM ***** A SAMPLE OF WHAT NOT TO DO
40 REM
50 FOR I = 1 TO 1000      ' DON'T KNOW END POINT
60     INPUT "GRADE";G
70     IF G<0 THEN 100    ' EXIT THE LOOP
80     T=T+G
90 NEXT I
100 PRINT "AVERAGE OF";I-1;"GRADES IS";T/(I-1)
110 END
```

There is no pseudocode for this program since there is no structure for the logic we used. The DO-WHILE (or REPEAT-UNTIL) is perfect for such a program, and the FOR-NEXT logic is just not suited to this type of problem since the upper limit of the counter is not known nor is it needed since we have an end-of-data marker (G<O).

The proper development of such a program would be the following:

```
NEW
10 REM ***** PROGRAM NAME: GOODPROG
20 REM
30 REM ***** A SAMPLE OF WHAT TO DO INSTEAD
40 REM
50 INPUT "GRADE";G
60   IF G<0 THEN 100    ' EXIT THE LOOP
70   T=T+G
80   I=I+1              ' COUNTER
90   GOTO 50            ' DO-WHILE LOOP
100 PRINT "AVERAGE OF";I;"GRADES IS";T/I
110 END
```

Program 5–14

This is a much cleaner program than the last one because it uses the DO-WHILE structure. Notice that this program also uses indentation for the body of the loop. Since everything after the INPUT statement is a part of the loop, it makes sense to indent the lines to show where the loop is. Remember, it is important to do this indentation because it makes the program much easier to read and follow.

We have seen how to have our programs make decisions and how to perform loops more easily and in a more straightforward manner than with GOTOs. It is now time to put all we know together in one program. Let's set up a program to figure out the amount of pay that commissioned salespersons earn. We will take into consideration their salaries and their earned commissions. We will follow these steps:

5–10 PUTTING IT ALL TOGETHER

1. INPUT the employee's number, salary, and the amount of sales made.
2. Check the amount of sales against the five amounts as follows:
   a. For amounts less than $501 use no commission
   b. For $501 to $2000 use 1% commission
   c. For $2001 to $4000 use 2% commission
   d. For $4001 to $10,000 use 3% commission
   e. For all amounts over $10,000 use 4% commission.
3. Combine salary and commissions to come up with total pay.
4. Print the information in a list.

We have left out only one thing. How many employees are there? Well, let's assume there are five and set up the program appropriately. The flowchart for this program can be seen in Figure 5–12, and the pseudocode would look like the following:

```
Start
Initialize counter to 1.
DO-WHILE counter is less than 6.
   Input number, salary, and sales.
   IF sales are less than 501 THEN
      Commission = 0.
   ELSE IF sales are less than 2001 THEN
      Commission = .01.
   ELSE IF sales are less than 4001 THEN
      Commission = .02.
   ELSE IF sales are less than 10001 THEN
      Commission = .03.
   ELSE Commission = .04.
   END-IF
   Total salary = salary + sales * commission.
   Print salesperson information.
   Accumulate totals.   (continues on page 130)
```

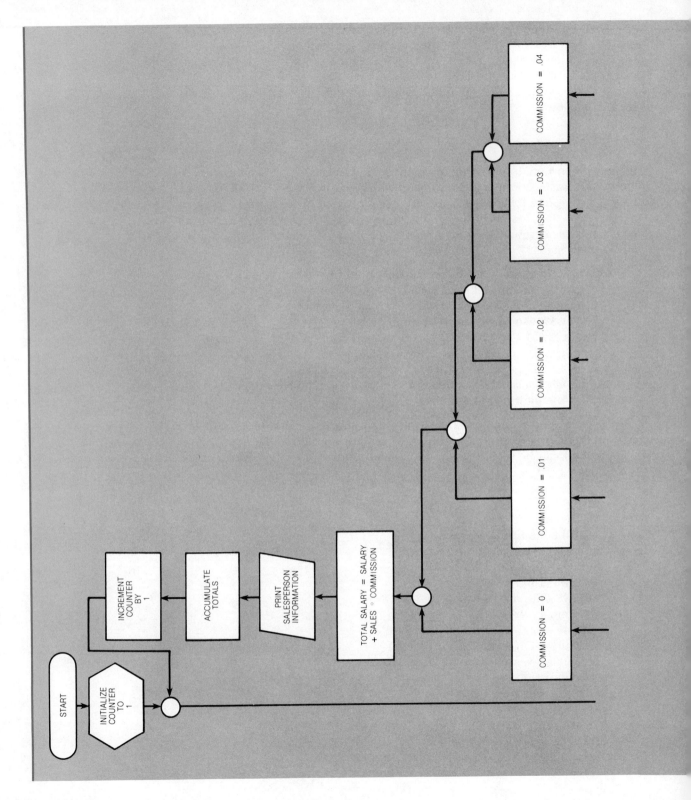

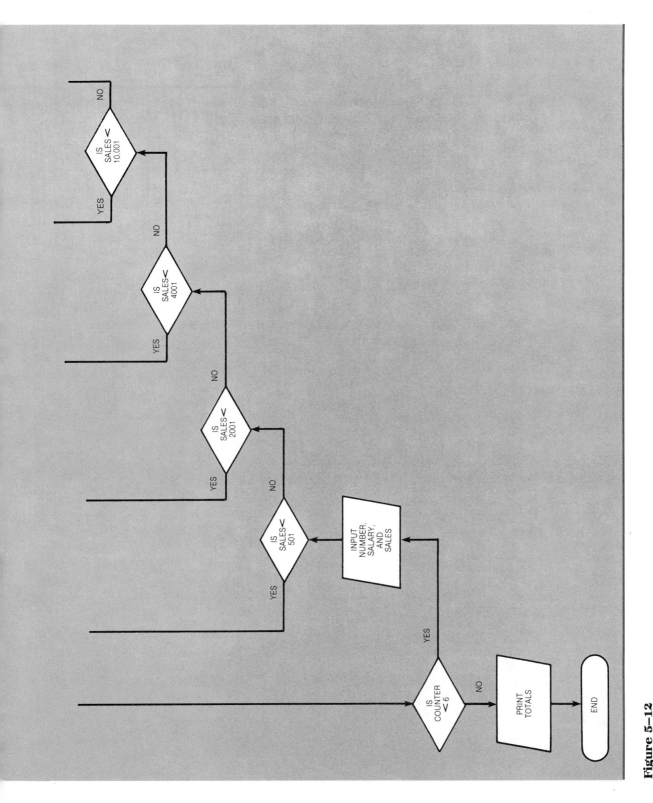

Figure 5–12
Flowchart for sample commission program (accompanies Program 5–15).

129

Increment counter by 1.
END-DO
Print totals.
End

You will notice that there are several IF-THEN-ELSE statements connected together. This is done anytime there is a need to check an INPUT item against several possibilities. You must take care when constructing such routines in your programs that two or more of the IF tests will not be TRUE. For example, this would be a problem if we defined one test for less than or equal to 500 and another for greater than or equal to 500.

One way of coding our sales commission program follows:

```
NEW
10 REM ***** PROGRAM NAME: COMISION
20 REM
30 REM ***** SAMPLE COMMISSION PROGRAM
40 REM
50 REM ***** WRITTEN BY EDWARD J. COBURN
60 REM
70 FOR I=1 TO 5
80     INPUT "WHAT IS THE EMPLOYEE NUMBER";N$
90     INPUT "WHAT IS THE SALARY DRAW";D
100    INPUT "WHAT IS THE SALES AMOUNT";SL
110    IF SL<501 THEN C=0
120    IF SL>500 AND SL<2001 THEN C=.01
130    IF SL>2000 AND SL<4001 THEN C=.02
140    IF SL>4000 AND SL<10001 THEN C=.03
150    IF SL>10000 THEN C=.04
160    G=D+SL*C       ' GROSS = DRAW + COMMISSION
170    PRINT "COMMISSION =";SL*C;"   GROSS PAY =";G
175    PRINT          ' LEAVE A BLANK LINE
180    TD=TD+D        ' TOTAL DRAW
190    TS=TS+SL       ' TOTAL SALES
200    TC=TC+SL*C     ' TOTAL COMMISSIONS
210 NEXT I
220 PRINT             ' LEAVE A BLANK LINE
230 PRINT "TOTAL DRAW        =";TD
240 PRINT "TOTAL SALES       =";TS
250 PRINT "TOTAL COMMISSIONS =";TC
260 PRINT "TOTAL GROSS PAY   =";TD+TC
270 END
```

Program 5–15

It is important to note a couple of things about the program. First, notice how the multiple IF tests are constructed. The first one asks for less than 501, while the second asks for greater than 500 and less than 2001. This allows the range of 501 to 2001, including 2000 but not 2001. This is the way we originally specified the test. (This will work as long as the data is in whole dollars. If we allow cents, we will have to change the tests a bit.) Second, note that we have to accumulate three of the totals separately while the fourth, the total gross pay, is calculated from the others.

Now let's run the program and see how we do:

```
RUN
WHAT IS THE EMPLOYEE NUMBER? 100
WHAT IS THE SALARY DRAW? 500
```

Program continues

```
WHAT IS THE SALES AMOUNT? 3500
COMMISSION = 70    GROSS PAY = 570

WHAT IS THE EMPLOYEE NUMBER? 256
WHAT IS THE SALARY DRAW? 500
WHAT IS THE SALES AMOUNT? 4567
COMMISSION = 137.01    GROSS PAY = 637.01

WHAT IS THE EMPLOYEE NUMBER? 300
WHAT IS THE SALARY DRAW? 750
WHAT IS THE SALES AMOUNT? 8975
COMMISSION = 269.25    GROSS PAY = 1019.25

WHAT IS THE EMPLOYEE NUMBER? 55
WHAT IS THE SALARY DRAW? 800
WHAT IS THE SALES AMOUNT? 12600
COMMISSION = 504    GROSS PAY = 1304

WHAT IS THE EMPLOYEE NUMBER? 60
WHAT IS THE SALARY DRAW? 800
WHAT IS THE SALES AMOUNT? 7500
COMMISSION = 225    GROSS PAY = 1025

TOTAL DRAW        = 3350
TOTAL SALES       = 37142
TOTAL COMMISSIONS = 1205.26
TOTAL GROSS PAY   = 4555.26
Ok
```

SUMMARY

1. Computers possess the useful ability to make decisions by test. In BASIC, this test is done with an IF-THEN test.
2. The IF-THEN statement consists of two parts. The conditional part yields a true or false statement based on the results of a comparison of two quantities using one of the six relational operators. The THEN part specifies actions based upon whether the condition is true or false.
3. If the IF-THEN test is false, control falls through to the next statement. If, however, the statement is true, the action part of the IF-THEN is done. This action can be any valid BASIC statement, but it is typically a PRINT, assignment, or GOTO.
4. The IF-THEN-ELSE structure can be created using just the IF-THEN command, though the IBM and Radio Shack do have a complete IF-THEN-ELSE structure.
5. Use of the IF-THEN is necessary for the IF-THEN-ELSE, DO-WHILE, and RE-PEAT-UNTIL structures.
6. We used loops in Chapter 2, but now we know an easier and more flexible way to do loops using the FOR-NEXT statement. It can be used like the DO-WHILE structure as a substitute for the decision test and the branches.
7. Of the four numbers on the FOR statement—counter variable, start point, end point, and step value—only the counter variable must be a variable. The other three can be either constants or variables. When using the counter variable within the loop, extra caution must be exercised so that the value of

the counter is not changed unless you have a distinct purpose in mind. Changing the value of the counter can have adverse effects on the loop and possibly the rest of the program.

8. Most versions of BASIC require the counter variable to appear in the NEXT statement also. Though our versions do not require it, you should do this anyway. Using the variable on the NEXT statement makes your programs much easier to read and the logic easier to follow.

9. The step value allows you to set up loops with an increment (or decrement) of any value you choose instead of the automatic 1 that is used if there is no step specified.

GLOSSARY

Boolean operator An operator used to allow a test of two (or more) conditions at the same time. The three boolean operators are AND, OR, and NOT.

Conditional branch A branch that is executed based on the result of an IF-THEN test.

Counter variable The variable that counts the number of loops when using a FOR-NEXT loop. The variable should be used on the NEXT statement as well as on the FOR.

Default The construction of a program such that if a specific option is not selected, a value is assumed that fits within the specifications of the program.

DO-WHILE A loop created with the decision test as the first part of the structure.

End-of-data marker When input, this type of data signals to the program that the data is at an end.

Error trapping This is used in all well-constructed programs to keep the user from entering erroneous data. Usually some type of error message is flashed to the user, and then another opportunity is given to enter whatever data was entered incorrectly.

FOR-NEXT This is an easier way to do a loop in a program than a GOTO. It automatically has a loop counter, a test for ending the loop, and an automatic branch.

IF-THEN This is the test statement for BASIC. It does a comparison of two elements. If the condition comparing the two elements is true, the program performs the action that follows the word THEN. If the statement is false, control falls through to the first statement immediately following the IF-THEN.

IF-THEN-ELSE This statement is like the IF-THEN, except that if the test is false, the ELSE action is done. This is also the name of the structure that uses the decision test.

Logical operator *See* **Boolean operator.**

Relational operators These are operators that compare two elements in the IF-THEN test. There are six relational operators.

REPEAT-UNTIL A loop created with the decision test as the last part of the structure.

STEP command This may be used to specify the value of the increment (or decrement) on the FOR-NEXT loop as something other than 1.

QUESTIONS TO AID UNDERSTANDING

In the programming exercises that follow, always use the appropriate documentation (including pseudocode and/or flowchart) and attempt to use prompts that are meaningful to the situation.

1. List three possible actions of an IF-THEN statement.

2. List the six relational operators and the three boolean operators, and explain how they are used.

*3. Given the following:

```
10  A=5
20  B=8
30  C=9
```

answer the following questions:

a. Which of the following branch to line 110?

```
40  IF  A<B   THEN 110
```

```
40  IF  C>=B  THEN 110
```

```
40  IF  A<C   THEN 50
```

```
40  IF  A<>B  THEN 110
```

b. Adding line 40:

```
40  B=B+1
```

which of the following branch to line 110?

```
50  IF  B=C    THEN 110
```

```
50  IF  B>=C   THEN 110
```

```
50  IF  B<=C$  THEN 110
```

```
50  IF  A<=C   THEN 110
```

```
50  IF  A=B    THEN 110
```

*4. What will be the value of A when each of the following programs ends?

a.
```
10  A=5
20  B=6
30  IF A<B THEN A=A+A
40  END
```

b.
```
10  A$="HI"
20  B$="HILITE"
30  IF A$=B$ THEN A=5
40  END
```

c.
```
10  A$="ED"
20  B$="ED"
30  IF A$<=B$ THEN A=1
40  END
```

d.
```
10  A=10
20  B=20
30  IF A=B THEN A=B
40  END
```

5. List three of the elements in every FOR-NEXT loop.

*6. Why is it important to use the counter variable on the NEXT statement?

7. Explain why it doesn't matter if we reuse the start and end point values within the loop.

8. Explain why we should use the counter variable within the loop only with extreme caution.

*9. Which of the following are incorrect and why?

   a. 10 IF A="5" THEN 20
   b. 10 FOR I = I TO 10
   c. 10 IF B$=A$ THEN B
   d. 10 FOR I = 1 to 10 STEP −1
   e. 10 FRO J = 2 TO 5 STEP A
   f. 10 FOR 2 TO 8
   g. 10 IF A>=< THEN 100
   h. 10 IF A<B THNE A<5+B
   i. 10 IF A=5 THEN B=6

10. List and explain the functioning of the three structures used in this chapter.

11. As the computer executes the following program, it will print out the values of I, J, and A on line 50. Make a table of the values that will be printed for each of the variables. Do not key in the program. Figure out the values by following the logic of the loop.

```
10 REM ***** EXERCISE 5-11
20 REM
30 FOR I = 1 TO 4 STEP 2
40      IF J>I THEN 90
50      PRINT I,J,A
60      J=J+1
70      A=I*J
80      GOTO 40
90 NEXT I
100 END
```

12. Write the pseudocode for and draw a flowchart of the program displayed in question 11.

13. Write a program to loop from 10 to 5 by − .25, printing out the counter variable each step of the way.

14. Look back to the problem in the text for averaging student grades. Change the program so that you can enter any number of separate groups of grades. Print the average of each set of grades, and print the overall average at the end.

*15. Write a program to build a table of squares of numbers. (A square is a number multiplied by itself.) Input a number to determine the size of the table. The table should look something like:

NUMBER	SQUARE
1	1
2	4
3	9

16. Write a program to build a multiplication table such as the following:

	1	2	3
1	1	2	3
2	2	4	6
3	3	6	9

Use at least one FOR-NEXT loop in the program.

17. Write a program with your name as a password. Input the password from the user. If it is not input correctly, print "INCORRECT PASSWORD. PROGRAM TERMINATED." and end the program. If it is input correctly, print "PASSWORD ACCEPTED" ten times on the screen. The user should get only one opportunity to enter the correct password.

18. Sending a telegram will cost $1.60 for the first five words and 12 cents for each additional word. Write a program to find the cost of a given number of words input. (Input the number of words, not the words themselves.)

19. One often-used concept in business programming is date comparison. Write a program to input three numerics, one for the month, one for the day, and one for the year. Validate each, and print an appropriate error message should one be invalid (for example, if a day is entered as 32). Don't concern yourself with the number of days in a particular month, such as only 28 days in February. If the date is valid, print it out as MM / DD / YY, for example 12 / 15 / 84.

20. Print a tax table for amounts from $100 to $1000 in increments of 100. It must have columns for 1 through 5 dependents. The amount of tax should be 15% for one dependent, decreased by 2% for each dependent thereafter. It should be printed similar to:

```
            1        2        3        4        5
            15%      13%      11%      9%       7%
$100        15       13       11       9        7
$200        30       26       22       18       14
ETC.
```

(Recall the TAB statement from Chapter 3.)

21. You need to do the payroll for XYZ Corporation. Design and write a program to input the information for five employees. Input the number of hours each employee worked and the hourly wage. Calculate and print the total wages giving time-and-a-half for all hours over 40. Use deductions of 9% for social security, 20% for federal income tax, and 5% for state income tax. Use the following input information:

NAME	RATE OF PAY	HOURS WORKED
Sam Smith	5.65	45
Tom Jefferies	4.25	50
Sam Spade	10.35	35
Lisa Harris	6.75	40
Tara Simpson	5.85	36

The output you generate should look like the following (totals appear after all five inputs):

```
REGULAR PAY = XXXXX.XX   OVERTIME = XXXXX.XX
DEDUCTIONS = XXXXX.XX   NET PAY = XXXXX.XX
```

Program continues

```
TOTAL REGULAR PAY = XXXXX.XX
TOTAL OVERTIME = XXXXX.XX
TOTAL DEDUCTIONS = XXXXX.XX
TOTAL NET PAY = XXXXX.XX
```

QUICK QUIZ

The answers to the questions follow immediately after the quiz. Questions 1–15 are true–false, while 16–20 are multiple choice.

T F **1.** The decision test can be used to assign values to variables.

T F **2.** If the condition of an IF-THEN statement is met (is true), control falls through to the next statement.

T F **3.** Relational operators test a relationship between two elements.

T F **4.** 10 IF A = B PRINT "HI"

If the above statement is executed, HI will print.

T F **5.** After 10 and 20 below are executed, A will be 15.

```
10 A=5
20 IF A>0 THEN A=A+A
```

T F **6.** The IF-THEN could rightfully be called an unconditional branch in certain cases.

T F **7.** If a STOP is used on an IF-THEN statement, it would usually be permissible to use the CONT command to restart the program from that point.

T F **8.** Care should always be exercised when using unconditional branches in your programs.

T F **9.** We could not use an INPUT statement as the result of an IF-THEN.

T F **10.** The FOR-NEXT loop will always branch down to the statement following the NEXT statement when the counter variable exceeds the ending value.

T F **11.** The counter is always a variable but the start, end, and step values can be constants or variables.

T F **12.** You should always use the same variable names on your FOR-NEXT loops so you will know what variables not to use in other places in your program.

T F **13.** If a FOR-NEXT loop has the FOR as follows:

```
10 FOR I = 4 TO 25 STEP 3
```

then the loop would execute seven times.

T F **14.** It is generally a good idea not to use your counter variable within a loop because this will cause your loop to execute in some way other than that originally planned.

T F **15.** If we were to print a variable that we had used in our program after the program ended, its value would be the last value it had before the program ended.

16. Which of the following is *not* a function of a FOR-NEXT loop? _____

    a. Establishes a counter for the number of times through the loop.

    b. Automatically branches to the statement following the NEXT when the loop concludes.

    c. Automatically increments the counter by one each time through the loop.

    d. Automatically tests the counter to see if it is outside the range of the end point value.

17. Given that A$ = "10/15/86", which of the following strings would be less than _____ A$?

    a. "10/15/86"   **c.** "10/16/78"

    b. "11/13/81"   **d.** "04/15/86"

18. How many times would the following loop? _____

```
10 FOR I = 10 TO 8 STEP -.2
```

    a. 10   **c.** 12

    b. 11   **d.** 22

19. Which of the following is invalid? _____

    a. 10 IF A=B THEN A

    b. 10 IF A=B THEN STOP

    c. 10 IF A=B THEN B=C

    d. 10 IF A<B THEN A=A+B

20. Which of the following variables will affect the execution of a FOR-NEXT _____ loop if the variable is changed within the loop?

    a. end point   **c.** start point

    b. counter   **d.** step value

ANSWERS TO QUICK QUIZ

1. T

2. F (When the IF test is *false*, control falls through to the next statement.)

3. T

4. T (Unassigned, A and B would both be zero.)

5. F (With A=5, A+A would be 10.)

6. F (It is always a conditional branch.)

7. T (If the program were designed that way.)

8. T

9. F (An input is a valid executable statement, and any such statement can be the result of an IF-THEN.)

10. F (It will not always exceed the end point. If the step is negative, the counter will need to be less than the end point to drop out of the loop.)

11. T

12. T (If you do this, you are less likely to reuse a counter variable accidentally, thus causing problems in your loop.)

13. F (It would execute eight times: 4, 7, 10, 13, 16, 19, 22, 25.)

14. T

15. T

16. c (It would decrement the counter if the step value were negative.)

17. d (The computer makes a character-by-character comparison from left to right. 04 in d is less than the 10 in A$. a is equal to A$. b is greater because 11 is greater than 10. c is greater because 16 is greater than 15. However, the only valid way to test dates is to turn them around so the year is the first thing tested.

137

That is the way we look at dates to determine which is larger (i.e., which is later). The computer cannot look at them backwards however, so we have to help it by turning the date around.)

18. b (The counter values would be 10, 9.8, 9.6, 9.4, 9.2, 9.0, 8.8, 8.6, 8.4, 8.2, 8.0)

19. a (The implied GOTO must go to a line number, not a variable.)

20. b (The others are stored in special locations, so changing them within the loop does not matter.)

6 ARRAYS AND READ-DATA

OBJECTIVES

After completing Chapter 6, you will be able to:

- Explain why the default value limits the size of an array.
- Name the command that allows you to expand your arrays beyond the default size.
- Explain why your DATA statements should all be in the same relative area of your programs and why that area should be either the top or the bottom.
- Explain what errors might occur when using the READ-DATA statements and how to correct them.
- Explain what errors might occur when using arrays and how to correct them.
- Explain what error might occur when using a subroutine and how to correct it.
- Describe the new structure introduced in this chapter.
- Explain what the two ON... statements are and what they are used for.
- Demonstrate the concepts of BASIC we have learned thus far by writing and executing several programs.

6–1
INTRODUCTION

In this chapter we will cover three more important commands. We will learn how to store information in a series and how to access that information. We will discover how to set up tables of constant information in our program so that we can access it. Finally, we will learn how to set up routines so that they will execute any number of times without losing our code continuity, and how to branch to several different areas based on a numeric test.

6–2
ARRAYS

Thus far in our study of BASIC, when we needed to store a number, we used a variable as an indicator. This let us know where the number was stored so we could use it later in the program. Each variable could store only one number at a time. So, if we needed to store two numbers, we had to use two variables. The more numbers we needed to store, the more variables we had to use. Imagine the difficulty of using a program that had 100 variables. Just setting the numbers into the variables would take 100 assignment statements or 100 INPUT statements.

BASIC gives us a much easier way to store large amounts of similar data. We simply tell the computer that we want a series of storage locations set aside; BASIC will then allow us to access the information stored in these locations by merely referencing the locations. These locations are stored adjacent to one another in a block of memory called an **array.** The entire array is labeled with a single variable that follows the same variable name rules that we have been using thus far. Each of the single stored items is referenced by number. Suppose, for example, that you had five grades that you wished stored for further use by the program. You could store all five in an array called G, and grade #1 would be stored in the first location of the array. That first location is referenced by calling for G(1) (pronounced G sub 1), the second location or number is called G(2), and so forth. If we were to look at the storage pictorially, it would look like:

$G(1)$ = first item
$G(2)$ = second item
$G(3)$ = third item
$G(4)$ = fourth item
$G(5)$ = fifth item

It might be helpful to think of an array as an apartment complex. The apartment complex has a name but to address a particular apartment, the number of the apartment must be known. A single variable, on the other hand, would be considered a single family home. For access, only the name of the house (address) is needed.

For an array, the number within the parentheses is called the **index** or **subscript,** and it can be either a number or a numeric variable. This allows a lot of freedom in accessing the arrays. You can use loops with the loop counter as the index for the array going from 1 to 100, for example. In this way, you can automatically access each element of a 100-element array in sequence.

You can store the items in the array by using either an assignment statement or an INPUT statement. Array items are just like any other variables. They are simply easier to use. Suppose you need to input all five of the grades. Without an array, you could do something like:

```
10 REM ***** PROGRAM NAME: SAMPINP1
20 REM
30 REM ****** SAMPLE INPUT PROGRAM
40 REM
50 INPUT "FIVE NUMBERS";G1,G2,G3,G4,G5
60 END
```

This type of entry is extremely difficult for the user. A better method for the user, but a pain for the programmer, would be something like:

```
10 REM ***** PROGRAM NAME: SAMPINP2
20 REM
30 REM ***** ANOTHER SAMPLE
40 REM
50 INPUT "GRADE NUMBER 1";G1
60 INPUT "GRADE NUMBER 2";G2
70 INPUT "GRADE NUMBER 3";G3
80 INPUT "GRADE NUMBER 4";G4
90 INPUT "GRADE NUMBER 5";G5
100 END
```

This uses one variable for each of the grades. If you were to use an array instead, you could create a much simpler version of the same program with a FOR-NEXT loop:

```
10 REM ***** PROGRAM NAME: SAMPINP3
20 REM
30 REM ***** SAME SAMPLE USING ARRAY
40 REM
50 FOR C = 1 TO 5
60     INPUT "ENTER GRADE";G(C)
70 NEXT C
80 END
```

Program 6–1

Now as the loop executes, C will begin as 1 and increase to 5, so the input values are stored in G(1), G(2), G(3), G(4), and G(5). If you need to do other things with this information, you now have easy access to it. If you wish to access the third item, simply use G(3). You do not need to remember a name for the third variable.

This looks simple even if you do it as in the first version (SAMPINP1). In fact, the first version of the program is actually shorter than the FOR-NEXT loop version. But we were using only five grades. Problems arise with SAMPINP1 when you need to input 1000, or even 100, grades. However, using the array in Program 6–1 you would only need to change the end point of the loop to reflect the new number of items needed. In the original program, all the new items would need their own INPUT statements. Also, if we only have a few items, the variable names are easy to remember, G1, G2, etc. But what happens when there are more than ten variables? You then need other variable names. You can get into a mess using different letters for different groups of numbers, say G0–G9 for the first ten, H0–H9 for the second ten, etc. It's much easier to have G(1)–G(10) for the first ten, G(11)–G(20) for the second ten, etc.

There is an additional statement that is necessary to expand an array beyond eleven items. Our versions of BASIC have a default of eleven items automatically set aside for every array accessed. Those items are elements 0 through 10. This means that we cannot access any element of an array past 10. To do that we need to use a **DIM** or **DIMension statement.** The DIM statement simply tells the computer how many storage locations to set aside for the array. Without it, we could not reference any element in our array beyond the defaulted value. That is, we could not use a statement like the following:

```
10 B(15)=156
```

If B had not been dimensioned to at least 15 and we tried to use the above statement in our program, we would get a **Subscript out of range error** on the IBM and Radio Shack and a **Bad subscript error** on the Apple. The form of the DIM statement is:

```
10 DIM variable(value),variable(value),...
```

The variable can be any valid variable name, and the value can be any size that does not exceed the memory size of the machine. (Remember that any variable we use requires memory to be stored.) Also, as with the index of an array, the size of the array may be specified by a variable. This is usually done in cases in which the expected number of elements for an array is going to be input. When input, that variable may be used to dimension the array.

Most versions of BASIC have virtually no limit on the number of elements we can have in our arrays. We can dimension as many variables as we want on each DIM statement, or we can use separate statements for each array. For an example of the DIM statement, suppose we need to expand our grade program to allow for 100 numbers. We then would add line 45 to our program as follows:

```
45 DIM G(100)
```

Then we would need to change line 50 to reflect the new number of inputs:

```
50 FOR I = 1 TO 100
```

The program would now look like:

```
10 REM ***** PROGRAM NAME: SAMPINP3
20 REM
30 REM ***** SAME SAMPLE USING ARRAY
40 REM
45 DIM G(100)
50 FOR I = 1 TO 100
60    INPUT "ENTER GRADE";G(I)
70 NEXT I
80 END
```

The variable we use for an array does not use the same storage area as an ordinary variable. That is, G(1) is not the same variable as G or G1. A totally different storage area is set up for each by the computer.

The real benefits of using arrays come when you need to examine each of the items. Suppose you need to know how many grades were above 75 out of a sample of 100 grades. If you had 100 different variables, you would need 100 different IF tests. Because you used an array, you can compare all 100 items within one small loop.

```
NEW
10 REM ***** PROGRAM NAME: TESTSAMP
20 REM
30 REM ***** SAMPLE WITH TEST
40 REM
45 DIM G(100)
50 FOR I = 1 TO 100
60     INPUT "ENTER GRADE";G(I)
70 NEXT I
80 FOR I = 1 TO 100
90     IF G(I)>75 THEN C=C+1
100 NEXT I
110 PRINT "THERE ARE";C;"ITEMS LARGER THAN 75"
120 END
```
Program 6–2

You will notice that in both loops the loop counter is used as the index for the array. This is a common technique and one of the values in having and using a FOR-NEXT loop.

In the program, the second loop compares each item of the array against 75 and counts those that are larger. When the loop finishes, C will contain the number of items that are larger than 75, and you can print it out. Let's make a few changes to the program and run a test sample to see just how well the program works. Change lines 50 and 80 to:

```
50 FOR I = 1 TO 5
80 FOR I = 1 TO 5
```

Then run the program:

```
ENTER GRADE? 10
ENTER GRADE? 80
ENTER GRADE? 90
ENTER GRADE? 45
ENTER GRADE? 30
THERE ARE 2 ITEMS LARGER THAN 75
Ok
```

The two larger items are, of course, 80 and 90. Why, when we changed the program, didn't we change the DIM statement? Isn't G now dimensioned much too large? Yes, it is. But we only have to make sure in our programs that the arrays are dimensioned large enough. Having them too big does not matter. Storage is reserved for the number of elements we specify in the DIM statement. While it is better to reserve only as much memory as we are going to need, there is no harm in reserving extra space as long as our programs do not exceed the memory size of the machine. Occasionally, when you begin to write longer programs, you will discover that you will even need to DIM those arrays with fewer than ten elements, such as DIM B(5). This will conserve the memory required for the other five elements and possibly save your program from running out of memory.

Arrays can be used in all types of statements in the same manner as ordinary variables. Another common usage is in calculating statements such as:

```
10 C(I) = B(I) + 5
```

If we were to use such a statement in a loop, all the values in the B array would be copied into the C array and increased by 5. Let's build a quick sample. First, we will assign the first three elements of each array, run through a loop assigning the C array as shown above, and then print each element. The program would look something like the following:

```
10 REM ***** PROGRAM NAME: ARRLOOP
20 REM
30 REM ***** ARRAY LOOP EXAMPLE
40 REM
50 B(1)=3
60 B(2)=6
70 B(3)=2
80 C(1)=6
90 C(2)=7
100 C(3)=8
110 FOR I = 1 TO 3    ' ASSIGNMENT LOOP
120    C(I)=B(I)+5
130 NEXT I
140 REM
150 FOR I = 1 TO 3  ' PRINT LOOP
160    PRINT B(I);"+ 5 =";C(I)
170 NEXT I
180 END
```

Program 6–3

If we ran it, the output would look like:

```
3 + 5 = 8
6 + 5 = 11
2 + 5 = 7
Ok
```

Note that C(1), C(2), and C(3) changed in value just as we would expect.

String arrays are also used in our versions of BASIC. A string array is the same as a numeric array except that the elements are strings instead of numerics. An example of this would be storing a list of names in your program using the string array N$(I) in much the same fashion as we used the numeric array before. Again, any arrays that will be larger than the default size, which is ten, will have to be dimensioned. A typical string DIM statement might be:

```
10 DIM N$(25),I$(11)
```

Let's take a simple example. Let's assume that we need to use two arrays, one with names and the other with addresses. We will input them into two string arrays. The program will look like the following:

```
10 REM ***** PROGRAM NAME: STRARRAY
20 REM
30 REM ***** PRACTICE WITH STRING ARRAYS
40 REM
50 REM ***** PROGRAM WRITTEN BY EDWARD J. COBURN
60 REM
70 DIM N$(5),A$(5)
80 FOR I=1 TO 5
90    INPUT "WHAT IS THE NAME";N$(I)
100    INPUT "WHAT IS THE ADDRESS";A$(I)
110 NEXT I
120 PRINT
130 PRINT "NAME 3 = ";N$(3)
140 PRINT "THE ADDRESS IS = ";A$(3)
150 END
```

Program 6–4

Program continues

```
RUN
WHAT IS THE NAME? TINA SMITH
WHAT IS THE ADDRESS? 1414 SOUTH STREET
WHAT IS THE NAME? JOHN JONES
WHAT IS THE ADDRESS? P.O. BOX 15
WHAT IS THE NAME? ED COBURN
WHAT IS THE ADDRESS? 1400 SOUTH STREET
WHAT IS THE NAME? TOM HARRIS
WHAT IS THE ADDRESS? TWIN TOWERS APT. 16
WHAT IS THE NAME? JOE FRANKS
WHAT IS THE ADDRESS? 2345 BROWN STREET

NAME 3 = ED COBURN
THE ADDRESS IS = 1400 SOUTH STREET
Ok
```

Program 6–4 (cont.)

6–3
PROGRAM EXAMPLE USING ARRAYS

We could do other useful things with our array in Program 6–4 simply by modifying it again. But instead of continuing with this example, let's take a real-world example of inventory. We have inventory items, and we wish to know which items need to be reordered because we seem to be running low on some of them. We begin our program in the same fashion as the previous grade program, by inputting the inventory item numbers, the quantity-on-hand or the amount of stock currently in inventory, and the order point or the quantity at which new orders should be processed. Let's set up the program so that we can enter any number of inventory items by checking for an end-of-data marker, which will be a zero. We want to be able to compare the quantity-on-hand with the order point and print the item numbers of those that need to be reordered. The generalized steps might be stated as follows:

1. Loop through inputting the item numbers, quantity-on-hand, and order point until the item number is 0.
2. Loop through the items, printing those that have a quantity-on-hand less than or equal to the order point.

These steps are generalized and must be expanded into pseudocode and a flowchart. Since we don't know how many items are going to be input, we really don't know how large to dimension our arrays. Let's assume that more than ten items are to be entered. Therefore, we need to dimension our arrays with some value. We need, then, to arbitrarily pick something we can be reasonably sure is large enough; 1000 should be enough. We will use 1000 in the DIM statement for our arrays. The pseudocode follows, and the flowchart for this program is shown in Figure 6–1. Notice in the flowchart that the dimension statement is indicated with a preparation symbol.

Start
Dimension the arrays.
Initialize the counter to 1.
Input item number.
DO-WHILE inventory number not 0.
   Input quantity-on-hand. *(continues on page 147)*

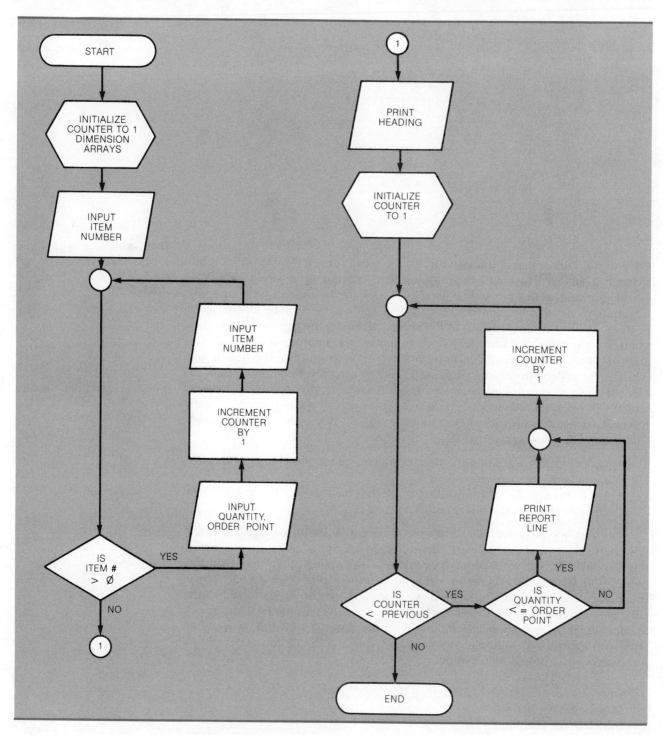

Figure 6–1
Flowchart of inventory program.

        Input order point.
        Increment counter by 1.
        Input item number.
    END-DO
    Print report heading.
    Initialize counter to 1.
    DO-WHILE counter is less than previous counter.
        IF quantity-on-hand < = order point THEN PRINT report line.
        (ELSE)
        END-IF
        Increment counter by 1.
    END-DO
    End

One way to code the program follows:

```
10 REM ***** PROGRAM NAME: INVPROG
20 REM
30 REM ***** INVENTORY PROGRAM
40 REM
50 REM CALCULATES WHICH INVENTORY ITEMS
60 REM NEED TO BE REORDERED.
70 REM
80 REM ***** INPUT ITEMS
90 REM
100 DIM N(1000),Q(1000),P(1000)
110 I=1
120     INPUT "INVENTORY ITEM NUMBER (0 TO END)";N(I)
130     IF N(I)=0 THEN 220   ' END-OF-DATA MARKER
140     INPUT "QUANTITY-ON-HAND";Q(I)
150     INPUT "ORDER POINT";P(I)
160     I=I+1
170     PRINT                ' PRINT A BLANK LINE
180 GOTO 120
190 REM
200 REM ***** CHECK AND SAVE THE ITEMS
210 REM
220 PRINT                    ' PRINT A BLANK LINE
230 PRINT "ITEM      QTY     ORD PT     AMOUNT BELOW"
240 FOR J = 1 TO I-1 ' I-1 IS NUMBER OF ITEMS
250     IF Q(J)<=P(J) THEN PRINT N(J);TAB(11);Q(J);
                           TAB(18);P(J);TAB(29);P(J)-Q(J)
260 NEXT J
270 END
```
                                            Program 6–5

When we run the program, we should get the following:

```
INVENTORY ITEM NUMBER (0 TO END)? 1
QUANTITY-ON-HAND? 5
ORDER POINT? 8

INVENTORY ITEM NUMBER (0 TO END)? 2
QUANTITY-ON-HAND? 100
ORDER POINT? 50

INVENTORY ITEM NUMBER (0 TO END)? 3
QUANTITY-ON-HAND? 45
ORDER POINT? 50
```
Program continues

```
INVENTORY ITEM NUMBER (O TO END)? 4
QUANTITY-ON-HAND? 15
ORDER POINT? 10

INVENTORY ITEM NUMBER (O TO END)? 5
QUANTITY-ON-HAND? 32
ORDER POINT? 35

INVENTORY ITEM NUMBER (O TO END)? 6
QUANTITY-ON-HAND? 85
ORDER POINT? 30

INVENTORY ITEM NUMBER (O TO END)? O

ITEM        QTY      ORD PT      AMOUNT BELOW
1            5         8          3
3           45        50          5
5           32        35          3
Ok
```

The program prompts for the three pieces of information (item number, quantity-on-hand, and order point) until we enter zero for the item number. Then the program jumps down to the loop to print those item numbers that need to be reordered. The counter of the second loop goes from 1 through $I-1$, since that was how many items were input before 0 was entered. The small report indicates which items need to be reordered, what the on-hand quantities are as compared to the order point, and how much the on-hand was below the order point.

6–4
THE READ AND DATA STATEMENTS

BASIC allows us to set up arrays of values in our programs quickly and easily by putting the values in our programs to begin with. This is much more efficient, though sometimes not practical, than using INPUT statements to get the data in. These values may be assigned to variables or array elements by using the **READ statement,** which appears as follows:

```
10 READ variable,variable,...
```

The variables may be either string or numeric. There is no limit to how many (or how few) variables can be used on each READ statement. The values to be read into the variables are placed in the program via a **DATA statement.** The form of the DATA statement follows:

```
10 DATA constant,constant,...
```

Again, there are no limits to how many (or how few) constants can be placed on each DATA statement. Consider the following READ-DATA combination:

```
NEW
10 REM ***** PROGRAM NAME: SAMPRD
20 REM
30 REM ***** SAMPLE READ-DATA
40 REM
50 READ A,B,C
60 DATA 5,10,15
70 END
```

Program 6–6

The DATA statements may be placed anywhere in the program; they will be found when the program executes. A DATA statement is not a statement that the computer executes, but rather a storage place for constant data. The above program will read the items A, B, and C and from the data list 5, 10, and 15. This means that when finished, A has the value of 5, B has the value of 10, and C has the value of 15.

Since we can put as many variables on each statement as we wish, the previous program might also appear as:

```
NEW
10 REM ***** PROGRAM NAME: SAMPRD
20 REM
30 REM ***** SAMPLE READ-DATA
40 REM
50 READ A
60 READ B
70 READ C
80 DATA 5
90 DATA 10
100 DATA 15
110 END
```

The same values are in each of the variables as before. That is, A is 5, B is 10, and C is 15.

As mentioned before, the DATA statements can be placed anywhere in the program, but many programmers prefer to put the data next to the statement that reads that data. Many times, however, it is a better choice to put all the DATA statements in the same location in the program so we know precisely where to find them if we ever need to change one item on the statement. It is recommended to put the DATA statements either at the beginning or the end of the program. They are out of the way at the bottom of the program, but the location is up to the individual programmer. Above all, remember always to be consistent in your programming. Don't put them at the beginning of the program one time and then at the bottom the next time.

Many times a READ statement is used in a loop to assign values to an array. Such an example might be:

```
NEW
10 REM ***** PROGRAM NAME: ARREAD
20 REM
30 REM ***** ARRAY ASSIGNMENT WITH A READ
40 REM
50 FOR I = 1 TO 10
60     READ A(I)
70 NEXT I
80 DATA 2,5,6,5,4,3,8,3,5,6
90 END
```

Program 6–7

As the loop executes, the values in the DATA statement get stored in the array variables A(1), A(2), A(3), etc. Figure 6–2 shows which array variables receive which values.

We can also use literal information on a DATA statement, as well as intermix literal and numeric if we need to. An example of this follows on page 151 (notice that we also take advantage of arrays in this example):

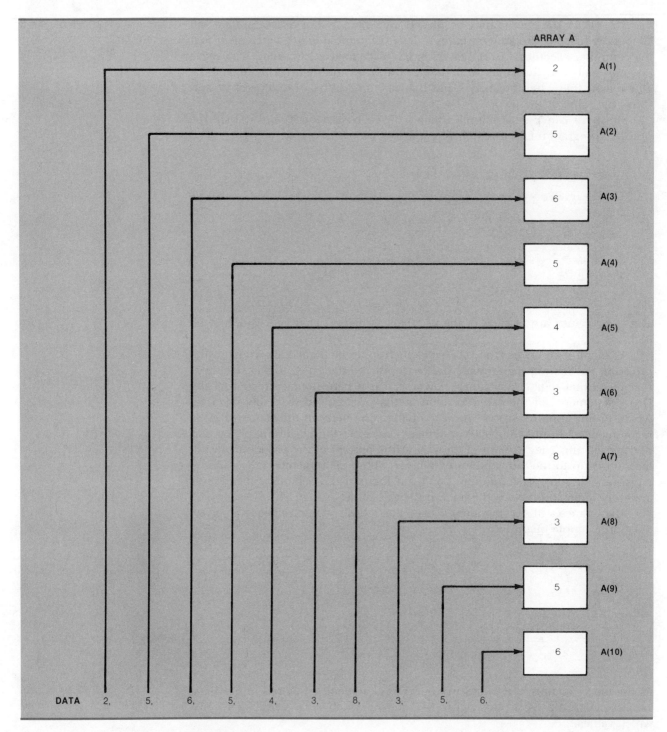

Figure 6–2
Assigning data into an array.

150

```
NEW
10 REM ***** PROGRAM NAME: READST
20 REM
30 REM ***** STRING AND NUMERIC READ MIX
40 REM
50 FOR I = 1 TO 3
60     READ N$(I),A(I)
70 NEXT I
80 FOR I = 1 TO 3
90     PRINT "THE NAME IS ";N$(I);" AND THE AGE IS";A(I)
100 NEXT I
110 DATA SAM,15,TIM,20,GEORGE,3
120 END
```

Program 6–8

If we run the program, we get:

```
THE NAME IS SAM AND THE AGE IS 15
THE NAME IS TIM AND THE AGE IS 20
THE NAME IS GEORGE AND THE AGE IS 3
Ok
```

There are a couple of important things to remember when using READ-DATA statements. First, if the READ variable is numeric, only numeric data can be read into that variable. This is the same rule as stated before—data type and variable must match. We can never put nonnumeric data in a numeric variable. Also, we must have at least as many items on our DATA statements as we have variables in the READ statements. If we try to read more items than are available, we will get an **Out of data error.** This simply means that we have read past the end of our data and that we should examine our program to see where it is wrong.

Finally, since the delimiter on the DATA statement is a comma, a comma cannot be part of an item on the DATA statement unless we enclose the item in quotes. If we do that, it indicates to the machine that what is in the quotes is the entire item. Consider:

```
100 DATA WACO, TEXAS, "WACO, TEXAS"
```

This statement requires three variables to hold all the data. The first variable is to hold WACO because the first comma tells the machine that we have reached the end of the data for that item. The second value is TEXAS, and the third is WACO, TEXAS because of the quotes around the whole thing. Also, leading and trailing blanks are ignored. If you wish leading or trailing blanks to be part of the data, you must use quotation marks.

Sometimes it is easier to leave the constants in the DATA statements rather than reading them into the program, which takes up additional storage. Storage area for the constants in DATA statements is already taken up because the statements are stored in the computer as the program is functioning. Therefore, when you load the data into an array, two areas in memory are taken up, the area for the DATA statements and the area for the array. But if we need to access the information many times, how can we do it if they are not in an array or at least in single variables? BASIC has a command that allows us to reuse the constants in DATA statements. A **RESTORE statement** allows the program to restart at the beginning of the data. The form of the RESTORE is simply:

```
10 RESTORE
```

To understand how the RESTORE statement works, let's look at the way the computer uses DATA statements. Now, assume that we have the following DATA statement in our program:

```
10 DATA 10,20,30,40,50,60,70
```

The computer sets up a **pointer** that indicates to it where in the data it will read the next item. It might be pictured something like:

```
10 DATA 10,20,30,40,50,60,70
         ↑
```

Now, after the program reads the first value, the pointer is moved to the second value:

```
10 DATA 10,20,30,40,50,60,70
            ↑
```

As each of the values is read, the pointer moves along the list until finally there are no more values to point at. When we try to read a value that the computer can no longer find, we get the Out of data error.

Executing a RESTORE tells the computer that we want the pointer to be put back to the beginning of the data. Assume that the pointer is still on the second item. When the RESTORE is done, the pointer would move back to the start:

```
10 DATA 10,20,30,40,50,60,70
         ↑
```

And all the data can then be read again.

Let's try a small program to see exactly how the RESTORE works:

```
NEW
10 REM ***** PROGRAM NAME: RESTSAMP
20 REM
30 REM ***** SAMPLE FOR THE RESTORE
40 REM
50 READ A,B,C
60 RESTORE
70 READ D
80 DATA 1,2,3,4
90 PRINT "A =";A;"  B =";B;"  C =";C;"  D =";D
100 END
RUN
A = 1   B = 2   C = 3   D = 1
Ok
```

Program 6–9

As the program functions, A is 1, B is 2, and C is 3. Then the RESTORE resets the pointer to the beginning of the data, so D is 1, not 4 as it would have been without the RESTORE.

On the IBM, the RESTORE allows even more flexibility. If you have a series of DATA statements, the pointer can be directed to the first item of any of the DATA statements by using the line number of the statement as part of the command. For example:

This statement would RESTORE the pointer to the beginning of the DATA statement in line 200. If line 200 is not a DATA statement, BASIC would find the first one after 200. Remember, you cannot RESTORE to a particular DATA item, only to the first item of a particular statement.

6-5
AN EXAMPLE USING ARRAYS AND THE READ-DATA

In our programming example in Program 6–5, we used an INPUT statement to bring the data into the program. The READ statement now provides an easier way to get some of the data into usage. We used three fields in Program 6–5: the item number, quantity-on-hand, and order point. The item numbers and the order point sometimes need to be changed, say when we need to add or remove an inventory item or change an order point; but, on the whole, they remain fairly constant. This makes them perfect for the READ-DATA statements. Let's take Program 6–5 and modify it to use the READ and DATA statements. The steps are now:

> Start
> Dimension the arrays.
> Initialize the counter to 1.
> DO-WHILE counter is less than 11.
>> Read item number and order point.
>> Print item number and order point.
>> Input quantity-on-hand.
>> Increment counter by 1.
> END-DO
> Print report heading.
> Initialize counter to 1.
> DO-WHILE counter is less than 11.
>> IF quantity-on-hand $<=$ order point
>> THEN PRINT report line.
>> (ELSE)
>> END-IF
>> Increment counter by 1.
> END-DO
> End

Now we know how many items we are going to read, so we can use a FOR-NEXT loop instead of an end-of-data marker. We will use ten items for our DATA statements as an example. The new flowchart is shown in Figure 6–3.

The program could be coded as follows:

```
NEW
10 REM ***** PROGRAM NAME: INVREAD
20 REM
30 REM ***** INVENTORY PROGRAM
40 REM
50 REM CALCULATES WHICH INVENTORY ITEMS NEED
60 REM TO BE REORDERED AND PRINTS THEM OUT
```

Program 6–10

Program continues on page 155

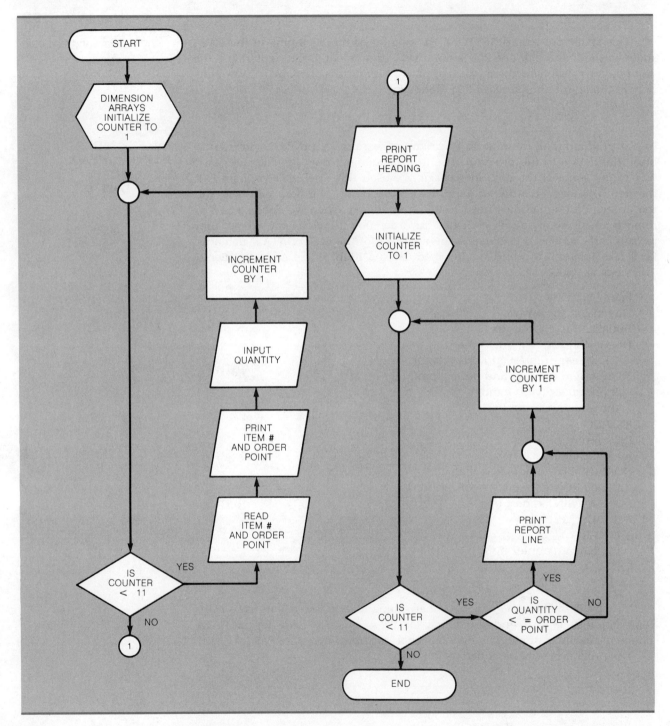

Figure 6–3
Flowchart of inventory program using READ-DATA and arrays.

```
70 REM
80 REM ***** READ THE ITEMS
90 REM
100 DIM N(10),Q(10),P(10)
110 FOR I = 1 TO 10
120     READ N(I),P(I) ' ITEM NUMBER AND ORDER POINT
130     PRINT "ITEM NUMBER =";N(I);" AND ORDER POINT =";P(I)
140     INPUT "QUANTITY-ON-HAND";Q(I)
150     PRINT           ' BLANK LINE
160 NEXT I
170 REM
180 REM ***** CHECK AND PRINT THE ITEMS
190 REM
200 PRINT "ITEM      QTY     ORD PT      AMOUNT BELOW"
210 FOR J = 1 TO 10    ' NUMBER OF ITEMS
220     IF Q(J)<P(J) THEN PRINT Q(J);TAB(11);Q(J);
                              TAB(18);P(J)TAB(29);P(J)-Q(J)
230 NEXT J
240 DATA 1,5,2,25,3,45,4,44,5,66,6
250 DATA 34,7,8,8,14,9,2,10,6
260 END
```

Program 6–10 (cont.)

When we run the program, we should get the following:

```
ITEM NUMBER = 1 AND ORDER POINT = 5
QUANTITY-ON-HAND? 5

ITEM NUMBER = 2 AND ORDER POINT = 25
QUANTITY-ON-HAND? 30

ITEM NUMBER = 3 AND ORDER POINT = 45
QUANTITY-ON-HAND? 5

ITEM NUMBER = 4 AND ORDER POINT = 44
QUANTITY-ON-HAND? 50

ITEM NUMBER = 5 AND ORDER POINT = 66
QUANTITY-ON-HAND? 70

ITEM NUMBER = 6 AND ORDER POINT = 34
QUANTITY-ON-HAND? 32

ITEM NUMBER = 7 AND ORDER POINT = 8
QUANTITY-ON-HAND? 15

ITEM NUMBER = 8 AND ORDER POINT = 14
QUANTITY-ON-HAND? 8

ITEM NUMBER = 9 AND ORDER POINT = 2
QUANTITY-ON-HAND? 5

ITEM NUMBER = 10 AND ORDER POINT = 6
QUANTITY-ON-HAND? 5

ITEM       QTY     ORD PT      AMOUNT BELOW
3          5       45          40
6          32      34          2
8          8       14          6
10         5       6           1
Ok
```

The program reads the item number and order point into the two arrays N and P. Each time it prompts for the quantity-on-hand and stores that in the array Q. After the loop finishes, the program jumps down to the next loop to print those item numbers that need to be reordered in the same report format as before.

6—6
USING MULTIDIMENSIONAL ARRAYS

Now that we have had the opportunity to use and become familiar with single-dimension arrays, it is time to turn our attention to arrays with more than one dimension. We have thus far used arrays that are called one-dimensional, i.e., arrays of a single column. Many times, however, we need to be able to work with data that requires two or more dimensions. A simple example is data in a table such as a tax table. Such data is really better examined by using an array with two dimensions so that the storage will match the way the table is constructed. Let's use an example to help us understand this concept better. The following small table of costs and sales prices of items will assist us:

ITEM NUMBER	COST	SELLING PRICE
100	1.05	1.50
105	2.25	2.69
200	3.25	5.50
207	1.25	2.05

Now, this table is set up to allow us to determine the cost to us and the price to our customers of items we are selling. For example, item 100 cost us 1.05 and we are selling it for 1.50, which yields us a gross profit of .45. We could, of course, use this table by using three arrays, one for the item number, one for the cost, and one for the selling price. But it is easier to keep track of one array than three. Plus, if we were to expand the table into about 10 or 20 columns, we would need 10 or 20 different one-dimensional arrays to handle the table when only one multidimensional array will do the same task.

In order to establish a two-dimensional array, we must dimension it just like a single-dimensional array except that we use two dimensions. Recall that the DIM statement looks like:

```
10 DIM variable(value),variable(value),...
```

Well, we are not going to change it much; we will simply add the second dimension as follows:

```
10 DIM variable(rows,columns),variable(rows,columns),...
```

Note that we listed the first dimension as the row and the second dimension as the column. That is going to be our convention, but actually the two numbers can work either way. It merely depends on how the information in the table is put into the array. We will put them in row first; thus the first number will represent the rows. In the case of the table we constructed before, the DIM statement would require 4 rows by 3 columns and would look like the following:

```
50 DIM A(4,3)
```

Now let's look at how we go about loading our data into the array. We will use a small loop to put the data, row first, into the A array. The routine would look like the following:

```
10 REM ***** PROGRAM NAME: ARRLOAD
20 REM
30 REM ***** TO LOAD A TWO-DIMENSIONAL ARRAY
40 REM
50 DIM A(4,3)
60 FOR I=1 TO 4      ' FOUR ROWS
70     FOR J=1 TO 3 ' THREE COLUMNS
80         READ A(I,J)
90     NEXT J
100 NEXT I
500 REM
510 REM ***** THE DATA
520 REM
530 DATA 100,1.05,1.50
540 DATA 105,2.25,2.69
550 DATA 200,3.25,5.50
560 DATA 207,1.25,2.05
570 END
```

Program 6–11

How does the routine work? Well, first notice that the DATA statements are lined up with the data in the same rows and columns as in the original table. If we can manage to store it in the array in the same fashion, it should be easy to determine which index point relates to which part of the table. The program stores the data as follows. The first time through the loops (there are two loops) I is 1 and so is J. That means that the first DATA item is put in A(1,1). Then J increases, which means that the second DATA item, which is the item in the first row, second column of the table, is placed into array location A(1,2), that is, row 1, A(1,), and column 2, A(,2). The third item read is placed in A(1,3). This drops us out of the inside loop and the outside loop is increased to 2. Notice that now the DATA is on the second statement. That is, we have moved to the second row of the table. This fourth item will then be placed in the array in A(2,1), which is row 2, column 1. Perfect placement! And the rest of the array gets the same treatment, every item going exactly where it is supposed to.

Now that we have the data in the array, how do we find the particular piece of data we need? For example, if we are visually examining the table and are asked "What is the cost of item 105?", we would merely scan down column 1 (the item numbers), find item number 105 (row 2), and then look in the cost column (the second column) for the cost of 2.25. We can do the same thing in our program by knowing which columns relate to the item number, cost, and selling price. We merely scan through column 1 (in the array), which is items A(1,1), A(2,1), A(3,1), and A(4,1), until we find the item number we are looking for. How do we determine that we have found it? With an IF test, of course. Such a routine is easy to write, as follows:

```
110 REM
120 REM ***** SCAN ROUTINE
130 REM
140 INPUT "WHAT ITEM NUMBER DO YOU WANT";A
```

Program 6–12

Program continues

```
150 IF A=0 THEN 300 ' END THE PROGRAM
160 FOR I=1 TO 4    ' 4 ROWS
170     IF A=A(I,1) THEN J=I : I=6
180 NEXT I
190 IF I=5 THEN PRINT "ITEM NUMBER NOT FOUND" : GOTO 140
```

Program 6–12 (cont.)

Notice that we INPUT the item number (and checked for the end-of-data marker) and then looped to find it. We stored the counter and changed it to 6 so that the loop will terminate. If the loop terminates naturally, I will be 5 (one more than 4) and we can test for it, which we do in line 190. If I is 5, we know it is an error because for the loop to conclude naturally, it would mean no match of the item number was found and, therefore, we have an error.

Let's finish our program by inputting the quantity purchased of each item and determine how much profit we made on the sale. We will need to determine the total cost by multiplying the quantity by the cost and the quantity by the selling price and then taking the difference. The pseudocode for the entire program follows; the flowchart is shown in Figure 6–4.

```
Start
Dimension the array.
Initialize counter I to 1.
DO-WHILE I is less than 5.
   Initialize counter J to 1.
   DO-WHILE J is less than 4.
      Read data into array A(I,J).
   END-DO
END-DO
Input item number.
DO-WHILE item number not 0.
   Initialize counter I to 1.
   DO-WHILE I is less than 5.
      IF item number = A(I,1) THEN
         Set holder J to I.
         Set counter I to 6.
      (ELSE)
      END-IF
   END-DO
IF counter I = 5 THEN
   Print error message.
ELSE (when I = 6)
   Input quantity sold.
   Calculate profit of item using A(J,2) for cost and A(J,3) for selling price.
      Print profit on the screen.
   END-IF
   Input item number.
END-DO
End
```

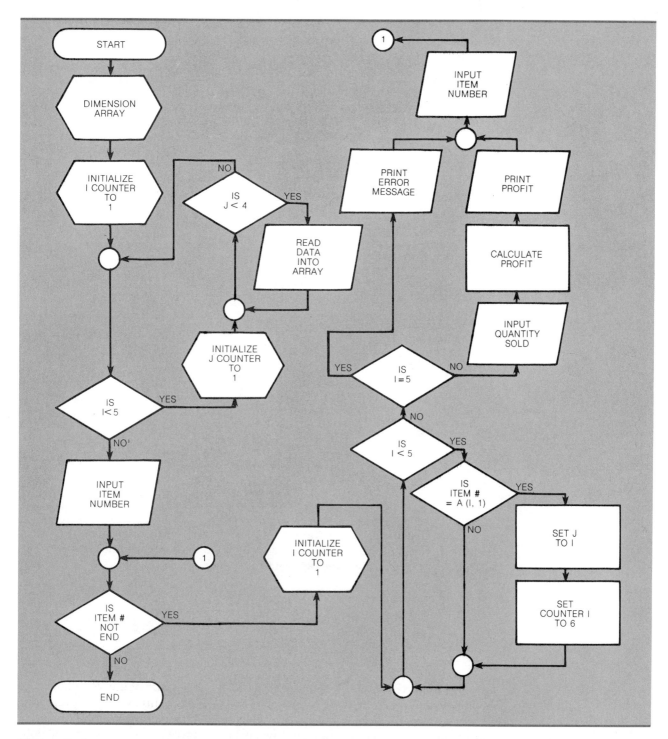

Figure 6–4
Flowchart of two-dimensional array example.

With the design as above, we will now code the rest of the program as follows:

```
10 REM ***** PROGRAM NAME: ARRLOAD
20 REM
30 REM ***** TO LOAD A TWO-DIMENSIONAL ARRAY
40 REM
50 DIM A(4,3)
60 FOR I=1 TO 4      ' FOUR ROWS
70     FOR J=1 TO 3 ' THREE COLUMNS
80         READ A(I,J)
90     NEXT J
100 NEXT I
110 REM
120 REM ***** SCAN ROUTINE
130 REM
140 INPUT "WHAT ITEM NUMBER DO YOU WANT";A
150 IF A=0 THEN 300 ' END THE PROGRAM
160 FOR I=1 TO 4     ' 4 ROWS
170     IF A=A(I,1) THEN J=I : I=6
180 NEXT I
190 IF I=5 THEN PRINT "ITEM NUMBER NOT FOUND" : GOTO 140
200 REM
210 REM ***** CALCULATION AREA
220 REM
230 INPUT "WHAT QUANTITY WAS SOLD";Q
240 C=A(J,2)           ' COST
250 P=A(J,3)           ' SELLING PRICE
260 PR=Q*P-Q*C         ' PROFIT
270 PRINT "THE PROFIT ON THIS SALE WAS";PR
280 GOTO 140
290 REM
300 END
500 REM
510 REM ***** THE DATA
520 REM
530 DATA 100,1.05,1.50
540 DATA 105,2.25,2.69
550 DATA 200,3.25,5.50
560 DATA 207,1.25,2.05
570 END
```

Program 6–13

Note that we assigned the cost and selling price to other variables. This was done for demonstration purposes only. In actual practice lines 240 and 250 would be dropped, and line 260 would become

```
260 PR=Q*A(J,3)-Q*A(J,2) ' PROFIT
```

Actually, we could go even further and eliminate line 260 and put the entire calculation on line 270:

```
270 PRINT "THE PROFIT ON THIS SALE WAS";Q*A(J,3)-Q*A(J,2)
```

An important point to remember is that though many of our programs can be shortened by combining statements, we are attempting to write programs that are easy to maintain. By combining many statements, we save program area in the memory of our machine, but we make our programs much more difficult to follow. Many times it is better to write slightly longer programs (and possibly a bit less efficient) to make the programs easier to maintain. You must keep uppermost in your mind the idea that these are your programs, and *you* will be responsible for their upkeep.

Now let's execute the program and see if it does what it is supposed to:

```
RUN
WHAT ITEM NUMBER DO YOU WANT? 120
ITEM NUMBER NOT FOUND
WHAT ITEM NUMBER DO YOU WANT? 105
WHAT QUANTITY WAS SOLD? 20
THE PROFIT ON THIS SALE WAS 8.8
WHAT ITEM NUMBER DO YOU WANT? 0
Ok
```

Only one sample is needed to determine if the program works. We know the error check works since there is no item number 120. Item 105 would have a cost of 2.25, which gives us a total cost of 45 for a quantity of 20. The selling price would be 2.69 for a total selling price of 53.8. The difference between 53.8 and 45 is indeed 8.8. Well, how about that! The program works.

Though we didn't practice with them, arrays can have more than two dimensions. A three-dimensional array can be visualized as a cube, but though up to 255 dimensions are allowed, they are difficult to visualize. Such multidimensional arrays are only used in very specialized applications.

6–7
GOSUB (SUBROUTINE)

Many times we have certain routines in our programs that we need to execute from various points in the program, always in the same manner. There are basically two ways to do this. One way is to retype the same routine each time it is needed in the program. Let's try a simple program to demonstrate. Suppose we need to input two numbers, print the total, the square of the numbers, and again print the total. We could do it like the following:

```
10 REM ***** PROGRAM NAME: SAMPDEMO
20 REM
30 REM ***** SAMPLE DEMONSTRATION
40 REM
50 INPUT "FIRST NUMBER";A
60 INPUT "THE NEXT NUMBER";B
70 T=A+B
80 PRINT "THE TOTAL IS";T
90 A=A*A          ' THE SQUARE OF A
100 B=B*B         ' THE SQUARE OF B
110 PRINT "THE SQUARE OF A IS";A
120 PRINT "THE SQUARE OF B IS";B
130 T=A+B
140 PRINT "THE TOTAL IS";T
150 END
```

Program 6–14

When we run the program, we should see the following:

```
FIRST NUMBER? 5
THE NEXT NUMBER? 7
THE TOTAL IS 12
THE SQUARE OF A IS 25
THE SQUARE OF B IS 49
THE TOTAL IS 74
Ok
```

Another easier and more useful way of accomplishing the same thing is to put the repeated program parts, the addition and the print, in a **subroutine.** A subroutine is simply a series of instructions set apart from the main program so that they may be referenced as a unit. Generally, there are two reasons for using subroutines. First, if there is a group of instructions that the program will need to use several times, a subroutine is used so that the coding need be done only once. Second, in large programs with many functions, it is many times easier to break the program apart into separate routines to facilitate testing and debugging. The subroutine is what we called in Chapter 2 a **predefined process,** and we will use that symbol for subroutines in our flowcharts.

The instructions in a subroutine are executed by using a **GOSUB statement,** such as:

```
10 GOSUB line number
```

This statement works like a GOTO statement in that it transfers program control to the statement at the specified line number. It differs from the GOTO in that, when the subroutine is completed, control will return to the next statement immediately following the GOSUB. This return is accomplished with a **RETURN statement** that is coded:

```
100 RETURN
```

The statements in the subroutine will execute until a RETURN statement is found, and then control will transfer back to the statement following the line that sent the program to the subroutine. Let's try an example to illustrate the point:

```
10 REM ***** PROGRAM NAME: SUBRSAMP
20 REM
30 REM ***** SAMPLE SUBROUTINE
40 REM
50 PRINT "START HERE"
60 GOSUB 110
70 PRINT "SECOND STEP"
80 GOSUB 110
90 END
100 REM
110 REM ***** SUBROUTINE
120 REM
130 PRINT "YOU ARE IN THE SUBROUTINE"
140 RETURN
```

Program 6–15

When we run the program, we should see the following:

```
START HERE
YOU ARE IN THE SUBROUTINE
SECOND STEP
YOU ARE IN THE SUBROUTINE
Ok
```

The program prints START HERE and then transfers to the subroutine beginning at 130. There it prints YOU ARE IN THE SUBROUTINE and returns to line 70 to print SECOND STEP. It then goes to the subroutine again and ends. Notice that after it was in the subroutine the first time, it went back to the line right after the GOSUB statement.

There is only one concern when using a subroutine: to make sure that program control does not fall into the subroutine without first executing a GOSUB. If it does, when the computer finds the RETURN statement, it will not know where to return, and we will receive a **Return without GOSUB error.** This is why in Program 6–15 we have the END statement prior to the subroutine.

We can now use this subroutine concept to simplify Program 6–14. Recall that we input two numbers, added them, printed the total, squared them, added the squares, and printed the total again. Let's rewrite the program so that the add and the print are in the subroutine. It might look like:

```
NEW
10 REM ***** PROGRAM NAME: SUBRSAM2
20 REM
30 REM ***** SAMPLE DEMONSTRATION
40 REM
50 INPUT "FIRST NUMBER";A
60 INPUT "THE NEXT NUMBER";B
70 GOSUB 170
80 A=A*A      ' THE SQUARE OF A
90 B=B*B      ' THE SQUARE OF B
100 PRINT "THE SQUARE OF A IS";A
110 PRINT "THE SQUARE OF B IS";B
120 GOSUB 170
130 END
140 REM
150 REM ***** ADDITION SUBROUTINE
160 REM
170 T=A+B
180 PRINT "THE TOTAL IS";T
190 RETURN
```

Program 6–16

This program doesn't look any simpler than before. Keep in mind, however, that our subroutine had only two things to do so we saved very little coding by using the subroutine. Most subroutines, however, are many lines long and much coding can be saved by not using the same instructions over and over. It is difficult with a small program to demonstrate how much better a program with a subroutine can be. When we get into writing larger programs, you will find that subroutines are extremely handy.

Another advantage that subroutines have is that since the coding for the repeated routine is in only one place in the program instead of several, if there is a change to be made in the routine (maybe we want to multiply instead of add the two numbers), only one change needs to be made. Without a subroutine, all the places in the program where the routine is used would have to be found and modified.

A third advantage of subroutines is their suitability for use in creating modular programs. That is, we can break our programs up into separate modules that each perform a separate task. With subroutines, we can travel from one complicated routine to another in a straightforward manner by putting each routine in a separate module and then calling them in order. Also, if we have a program with several different functions, we can set each into a separate module and be able to access them quite easily. We will see this concept in the next section.

6–8
THE CASE
STRUCTURE

We had a program example in the last chapter in which we input a male/female code, and the program performed some procedure based on whether the person was a male or female. The IF-THEN test was fine for this because there were only three choices; the input was either male, female, or an error. But what if we had to input any of four different numbers and the program had to do something different in response to each of the possible inputs? And if we can input four different numbers, there is actually a fifth possibility, that of an error.

As an example of this, let's take a program that has the options of adding information to a file, changing the information that is already in the file, deleting the information, and printing a report of the information. Figure 6–5 shows the flowchart for this; the pseudocode would look like the following:

```
Start
Input code.
IF add code THEN
    Execute add routine.
ELSE
    IF change code THEN
        Execute change routine.
    ELSE
        IF delete code THEN
            Execute delete routine.
        ELSE
            IF print code THEN
                Execute print routine.
            ELSE
                Execute error routine.
            END-IF
        END-IF
    END-IF
END-IF
End
```

This is what is called a nested IF-THEN-ELSE. We discussed nested routines in Chapter 2. This structure seems to work okay, but there is a problem when we have to add even more choices to the program: the number of levels on the pseudocode and flowchart quickly become unmanageable. The program for this pseudocode would have an IF-THEN test for each one designated in the pseudocode; if we had to add more, the program could get to be quite large. There is a fifth structure (recall that we have used the SIMPLE SEQUENCE, IF-THEN-ELSE, DO-WHILE, and REPEAT-UNTIL) that is much easier to manage than the nested IF-THEN. It is called the **case structure.** The pseudocode for using this structure for the previous example follows on page 167; the flowchart can be seen in Figure 6–6.

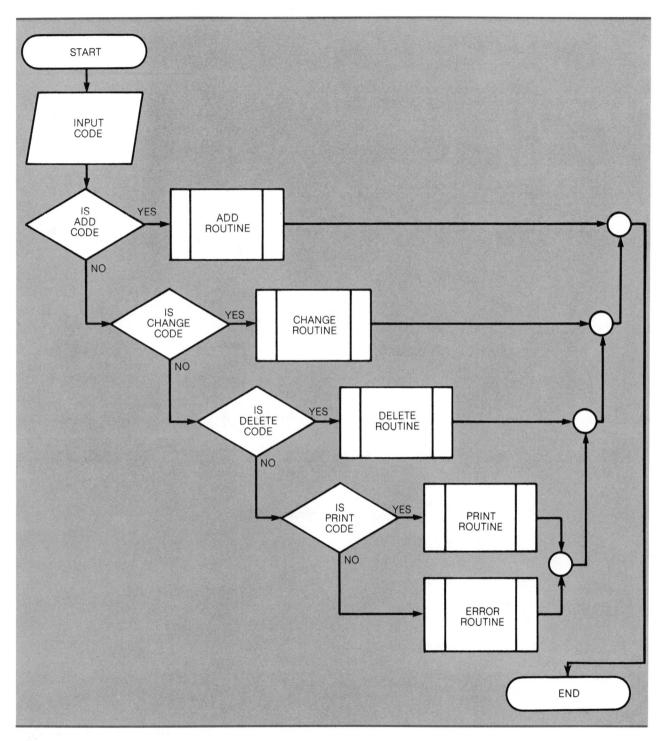

Figure 6–5
Flowchart with nested IF-THEN-ELSE.

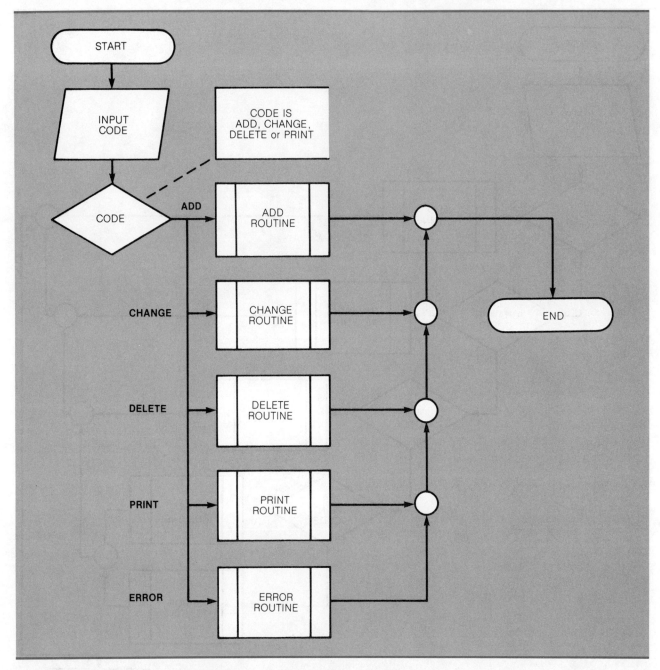

Figure 6–6
Flowchart of CASE structure.

```
Start
Input code.
CASE-TEST
Case 1
   Add routine.
Case 2
   Change routine.
Case 3
   Delete routine.
Case 4
   Print routine.
Case error
   Error routine.
END-CASE
End
```

BASIC gives us a statement (actually two statements) that follows the case structure. The **On...GOSUB** statement has the form:

```
10 ON numeric expression GOSUB line number,line number,...
```

There is a similar statement that has the form:

```
10 ON numeric expression GOTO line number,line number,...
```

Both statements function the same way except for the obvious difference that one uses subroutines and the other is purely a branch statement. In using modular programming, the ON...GOSUB is used more often, though occasionally the ON...GOTO can prove to be useful.

The statement functions much like a multiple IF-THEN. The numeric expression (it can simply be a numeric variable) is evaluated and based on the value, the appropriate branch is taken. That is, if the evaluation yields 1, the first line number listed is branched to; if the evaluation yields 2, the second line number is branched to; and so forth. If the evaluation yields zero or a number higher than the number of line numbers listed, control simply falls through to the next statement. For example, if A = 5, what line number would the following statement branch to?

```
10 ON A GOSUB 70,30,80,60,90,100
```

That's right, the program would branch to line 90 since that is the fifth line number listed in the statement. If A were zero or more than 6, control would fall through to the next statement. Notice on the statement that the line numbers are not in sequence. They do not need to be, but for the sake of ease of use, you should always put the line numbers in sequence. It makes for a much cleaner program.

As an example of how to use the statement, we will write a program segment based on the previous pseudocode dealing with the file functions. The program segment follows:

```
NEW
10 REM ***** PROGRAM NAME: ONGOSUB
20 REM
30 REM ***** SAMPLE ON...GOSUB PROGRAM
40 REM
50 PRINT "ENTER THE NUMBER OF YOUR CHOICE"
60 INPUT "ADD (1), CHANGE (2), DELETE (3), PRINT (4)";A
70 IF A<1 OR A>4 THEN PRINT "ERROR" : GOTO 50
80 ON A GOSUB 130,500,1000,1500
90 GOTO 50                          ' ASK FOR ANOTHER FUNCTION
100 REM
110 REM ***** ADD ROUTINE
120 REM
130                                          Program 6-17
```

Of course, there would be much more program. Notice that on line 70 we have a small error routine. This is helpful in letting the user know a mistake was made.

This is a perfect example of what we discussed earlier about modular programming. Notice that the program has five different functions (counting the error routine), each one set apart in its own area of the program. By utilizing this type of modular programming, you can write programs that are not only easier to understand, but easier to maintain.

6–9
SORTING FOR PRACTICE

There are many occasions when it is useful to have information in some type of sequence. Putting items in sequence is known as **sorting.** As an example, suppose we have a list of people who have contributed to our favorite charity. We need to know how long it has been since everyone on the list contributed. We could, then, sort the list into order by the date of last contribution. Then we would know who contributed recently and who has not done so for a long time.

How does one go about putting a list into sequence? Well, many sorting techniques exist; some are better than others. Probably the most often learned technique is the **bubble sort.** This is a sort whereby you start at the beginning of the list and move the biggest items to the end. When you finish, the list is in sequence. Though the bubble is the most widely taught, it is not, by any means, the best sort. It is extremely slow as sorts go. Therefore, instead of using the bubble sort, we will use one that is twice as fast and just as easy to learn called the **selection sort.** Keep in mind, however, that there are many sorts that are even faster than the selection sort. We are using it because it is easy to understand and will give us a good look at how a list can be put into sequence.

The idea of the selection sort is to scan through the array and find the smallest element. This element is then switched with the element at the beginning of the array. Take, for example, this line of data that we will use in our program:

```
1010 DATA 403,625,556,379,775,260,14,455,694,745
```

If we were to use the selection sort on these ten numbers, we would examine them and find the smallest number in the list. In this case, 14 is the smallest.

Then this element is switched with the first element in the array, 403. After this, the list would be:

    14,625,556,379,775,260,403,455,694,745

Then, because we know the first element is now the smallest in the array, we begin to search again starting at the second element, 625. This time, the low number is 260. This is switched with the starting element, 625. The list becomes:

    14,260,556,379,775,625,403,455,694,745

Now the search begins at the third element, and 379 is the smallest. The list becomes:

    14,260,379,556,775,625,403,455,694,745

Search from position 4 to find 403, and the list is:

    14,260,379,403,775,625,556,455,694,745

Search from position 5 to find 455, and the list is:

    14,260,379,403,455,625,556,775,694,745

Search from position 6 to find 556, and the list is:

    14,260,379,403,455,556,625,775,694,745

Search from position 7 to find 625, and the list doesn't change. Search from position 8 to find 694, and the list is:

    14,260,379,403,455,556,625,694,775,745

Search from position 9 to find 745, and the list is completely sorted:

    14,260,379,403,455,556,625,694,745,775

To find the smallest item in a list, we need to set up a save variable; that is, a variable we can use to store the least value. To begin with, we will place in this variable a number larger than any number in the list. This way, when we scan through the list, any number in the list will be less than the save variable. Then, when we find a number less than the save value, it will be stored in the save variable as the smallest. This way, by the time we have scanned through the list, the save variable will contain the smallest value that was in the list.

We will also keep another variable that will have the index number of the smallest array element. This is necessary for the switching. After the item is located, the switching is done through a temporary variable. This switch is an interesting point in itself.

For example, suppose we have two items: C, which contains 5, and N, which contains 10. We want to switch them so C is 10 and N is 5. The logical thing to do would be to use two assignments:

```
10 C=N
20 N=C
```

The only problem with this is that they both now have the same value. Line 10 will indeed give C the value of 10, but since line 20 assigns the value of C to

N and the value of C is now 10, both variables end up with the value of 10. Somehow, we lost a value. The only way to do an exchange is by using a temporary storage variable for one of the numbers, such as:

```
10 T=N          ' T IS TEMPORARY STORAGE
20 N=C          ' ASSIGN THE FIRST
30 C=T          ' NOW WE CAN ASSIGN THE SECOND
```

Now, the value of N (10) is stored in T; then line 20 puts the value of C (5) into N, and line 30 will take the temporary value of 10 and put it in C. This gives C the value of 10 and N the value of 5, just like we wanted.

Now that we have discussed how the sort should work, let's see how we could construct it. The pseudocode follows, and the flowchart can be seen in Figure 6–7.

Start
***** INPUT MODULE *****
Read number of items.
Dimension array to number of items.
Initialize counter to 1.
DO-WHILE counter is less than or equal to number of items.
　　Read item into array (counter).
END-DO
***** SORT MODULE *****
Set array position counter to 1.
DO-WHILE array position counter < number of elements −1.
　　Initialize comparison value to 1000.
　　Initialize loop counter to array position counter.
　　DO-WHILE loop counter < number of elements.
　　　IF array item < comparison value THEN
　　　　Comparison value = array item
　　　　Array marker = loop counter.
　　　(ELSE)
　　　END-IF
　　　Increase loop counter by 1.
　　END-DO
　　Switch array items.
　　Increase array position counter by 1.
END-DO
***** OUTPUT MODULE *****
Initialize item counter to 1.
DO-WHILE item counter < number of items.
　　Initialize loop counter to item counter.
　　DO-WHILE loop counter <= item counter +4.
　　　Print item.
　　END-DO
　　Increase item counter by 5.
END-DO
End

A couple of things are worth noting here. First, notice that the data we are going to sort will come from a DATA table in the program. The first item in the DATA table is the number of items in the table; that number is used to guide the loops. Also note that the output is done so that five numbers are displayed across the screen (there will be 100 numbers). This will allow the output to fit on a 40-column display. You can adjust the output loop if you want a wider display.

The program should look like the following:

```
10 REM ***** PROGRAM NAME: SORTSEL
20 REM
30 REM ***** WRITTEN BY EDWARD J. COBURN
40 REM
50 REM ***** PRACTICE SELECTION SORT
60 REM
70 READ NE                      ' NUMBER OF ELEMENTS
80 DIM A(NE)                    ' ARRAY TO SORT
90 FOR I=1 TO NE
100    READ A(I)                ' READ IN ARRAY
110 NEXT I
270 REM
280 REM ***** SELECTION SORT MODULE
290 REM
300 FOR I=1 TO NE-1             ' TO ELEMENTS -1
310    CV=1000                  ' COMPARISON VALUE
320    FOR K=I TO NE            ' COMPARISON LOOP
330       IF A(K)>=CV THEN 360
340       CV=A(K)               ' STORE SMALLER ITEM
350       AM=K                  ' SAVE THE ARRAY SPOT
360    NEXT K
370    T=A(AM)                  ' STORE ITEM TO SWITCH
380    A(AM)=A(I)               ' BEGINNING ITEM DURING LOOP
390    A(I)=T                   ' PUT IN SMALLEST
400 NEXT I                      ' END SORT LOOP
870 REM
880 REM ***** OUTPUT MODULE
890 REM
900 J=1
910    FOR I=J TO J+4
920       PRINT A(I);
930    NEXT I
940 J=J+5
950 PRINT                       ' CARRIAGE RETURN
960 IF J<NE THEN 910
970 END
980 REM
985 REM ***** DATA TABLE
990 REM
1000 DATA 100
1010 DATA 403,625,556,379,775,260,14,455,694,745
1020 DATA 55,553,738,392,513,401,273,816,101,435
1030 DATA 227,537,315,446,727,605,642,22,753,2
1040 DATA 608,429,244,377,520,985,545,160,171,584
1050 DATA 500,812,258,671,516,828,693,990,795,385
1060 DATA 897,859,430,253,459,522,843,750,902,782
1070 DATA 87,484,507,369,321,541,246,581,462,389
1080 DATA 523,161,587,78,939,343,969,436,79,543
1090 DATA 677,142,310,279,460,669,266,707,495,66
1100 DATA 154,702,528,387,943,150,916,706,4,517
```

Program 6–18

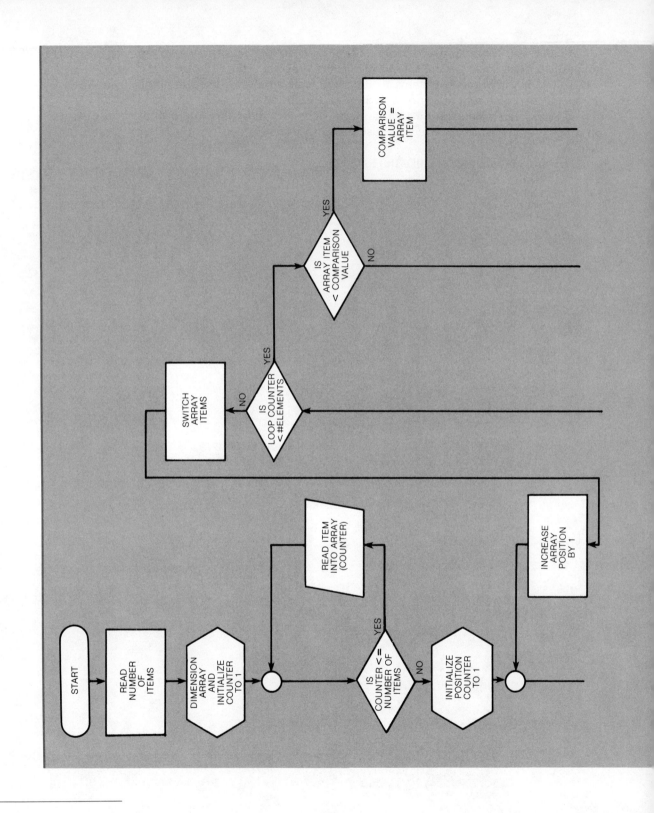

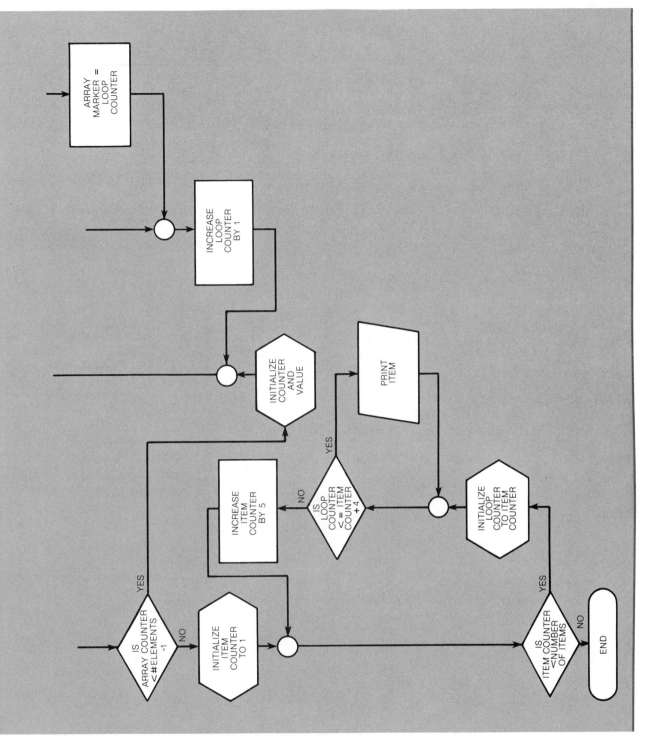

Figure 6–7
Flowchart of selection sort.

On the Apple, you will want to put a space or two before printing each item. Otherwise, the numbers will run together. Remember that the Apple doesn't leave a space around the numbers as the other machines do.

Now, when you execute the program, it will seem as if it isn't doing anything. That's because there is no visual indication that anything is taking place. You may want to cause something to be printed as the sort functions. Perhaps print the items as they are switched. The reason we are not using such an indicator is that anything extraneous only serves to slow down the processing. As it is, this sort takes about 50 seconds (on the IBM). Pretty slow as sorts go, but remember, this is not the fastest sort, merely one that was easy to understand.

SUMMARY

1. The array is a much easier way to store and use a series of related items than using a separate variable for each item. An array gives us the capability to store numbers in series and reference each simply by its subscript or index number. We can use either one-dimensional or multidimensional arrays.

2. We can use string arrays as well as numeric arrays. A string array functions in the same manner as the numeric array except it contains string data instead of numeric.

3. Arrays are useful when combined with both a READ and DATA statement. The READ statement allows values stored in the program to be assigned to variables as the program executes. These values are stored in a DATA statement. As many variables as you wish may be on a READ statement, and as many constants as you wish may be on each DATA statement.

4. When using READ and DATA statements, don't try to read string information into a numeric variable. Also, be sure that you have enough data items for all your READ variables.

5. When there are certain sections of code in a program that will be executed several times, it is easier to use a subroutine than to key in the same code every time it is needed. The subroutine is also useful in a large program; subroutines allow you to code in smaller segments that are easier to test and debug. Also, in a large program, a great deal of coding can be saved by using subroutines.

6. The case structure is easier to manage then a series of nested IF-THEN-ELSE statements. The BASIC statements for the case structure are the ON...GOTO and the ON...GOSUB.

7. A sort is useful for putting a list of items into sequence. One such sort is the selection sort. Though it is easy to understand and program, it is not one of the best sorts because it is too slow to be practical.

Array A series of storage locations referenced by one variable name and a number or a variable called an index or subscript. Any value in the array may be accessed by using the index.

Bad subscript error The error message that appears on the Apple when the program tries to access an array variable outside the allocated dimension.

Bubble sort A procedure for arranging items in a list in order by moving the largest items to the end of the list.

Case structure The structure that allows the program to transfer control to several different routines without having to use a confusing nested IF-THEN-ELSE.

DATA statement A statement for storage of constant values in a program by assigning them to variables in a READ statement.

DIM or dimension statement A statement that allows the programmer to specify the size of the arrays to be used.

GOSUB statement The statement that transfers control to a subroutine.

Index *See* **Subscript.**

ON...GOSUB One of the BASIC case structures. The other is the ON...GOTO.

Out of data error The error that will occur when your program has tried to read more data items than there are in the program.

Pointer An internal marker used by the computer to keep track of which item in a DATA statement is to be read next.

Predefined process The symbol used on a flowchart to depict a subroutine.

READ statement The statement that allows constant values stored in DATA statements to be assigned to variables as the program executes.

RESTORE statement The statement that returns the pointer to the first constant in the first (or specified) DATA statement. It allows DATA statements to be used more than once.

RETURN statement The statement that transfers control from the subroutine back to the line following the GOSUB statement that called the subroutine.

Return without GOSUB error This error will occur when the program finds a RETURN statement without previously executing a GOSUB statement.

Selection sort A procedure for arranging items in a list in order by switching the smallest item with the element at the beginning of the list.

Sorting The process of putting items into sequence.

Subroutine A series of statements that may be executed any number of times but are coded in the program only once.

Subscript The number or variable that allows an individual item in an array to be accessed.

Subscript out of range error The error message that appears on the IBM and Radio Shack when the program tries to use an array element that was not dimensioned.

QUESTIONS TO AID UNDERSTANDING

1. What is the default value for the number of array elements?
2. What command do you use to set aside more storage for an array than the default automatically assigns?
*3. Explain why your DATA statements should all be in the same area of the program and why that should be either the bottom or the top of the program.
4. How many variables can be used on a single READ statement?
5. What error will occur if you try to read more data items than are on the DATA statement?
*6. What instruction tells the machine that you need to read your data again?

7. Explain why the case structure is useful.
8. Examine the following program and then answer the questions that follow.

```
10 REM ***** PROBLEM 6-8
20 REM
30 FOR I = 1 TO 50 STEP 3
40     READ B(I)
50 NEXT I
60 DATA 5,7,9,1,2,4,6,7,5,4,7,8,4,5,3,2
70 DATA 6,7,2,8
80 END
```

   a. After the program executes, what will be the value of:
     $B(1)$, $B(3)$, $B(4)$, $B(8)$, $B(10)$, and $B(13)$?
   b. This program will cause an error. What type of error will occur?
   c. What statement could we add to the program so the error would not occur?
   d. How many loops will the program go through before the error causes the program termination?

*9. Which of the following statements are incorrect and what is wrong with the incorrect ones?
   a. 10 RETURN 100
   b. 10 DIM A
   c. 10 GOSUB 10000
   d. 10 READ A;B,C,D
   e. 10 FOR 1 TO 100
   f. 10 A(I) = B(J) + C$(R)
   g. 10 READ A,A$,B,B$,D,C$,R,G$,H,H,J
   h. 10 READ "WHAT IS YOUR NAME";N$
   i. 10 DATA "WACO",2,12/15/57
   j. 10 ON A$ GOSUB 50,100,500,60,80,90

*10. Which of the following pairs of READ and DATA statements are incorrect and why? Assume that the DATA statement is to be processed by the READ statement.
   a. 10 READ A,B,C
     90 DATA 5,7,8
   b. 10 READ A,A$,B,B$
     90 DATA HI,5,BYE,6
   c. 10 READ A$,B$,C$
     90 DATA 7,8,9,THIS
   d. 10 READ A,B,C
     90 9,8,7
   e. 10 READ A,B
     90 DATA 5,6,2,334,6,7,333
   f. 10 READ A,B,C
     90 DATA MARY,5,2

11. Write a program using a READ-DATA pair to produce the following small table:

1	3	7	15
6	5	9	89
5	8	14	22

12. Write a program that takes a data list of names and wages and prepares a report like the following:

```
LAST NAME        FIRST NAME        WAGES EARNED
COBURN           ED                1000
SMITH            JOHN              3000
SIMPSON          TAMMY             4000
```

Use the following DATA statements in your program:

```
500 DATA ED,COBURN,1000,JOHN,SMITH,3000
510 DATA TAMMY,SIMPSON,4000,STEVE,WOODS,1500
520 DATA AMY,THOMPSON,3500
```

13. You have used an array in a program, and you need to be able to reuse it; but in order to reuse it, it must be all zeros. Write the part of the program you would need to zero out the array. The first part of the program is as follows:

```
10 REM ***** ARRAY WITH VALUES TO ZERO OUT
20 REM
30 DIM B(20)
40 B(1)=15
50 B(4)=25
60 B(19)=55
```

Add the rest of the program to zero out the array, and then print the entire array to be sure that all values are zero.

14. The following income tax table (fictitious) is to be used as data in a program:

GROSS PAY	1 DED.	2 DED.	OVER 2 DED.
0 TO 100	0	0	0
100 TO 200	12	9	6
200 TO 400	42	30	24
400 TO 800	168	120	96
800 AND UP	580	394	300

Read the data into an array and use it to determine the amount of tax to withhold on each employee input. Input the employee name, hourly rate, number of hours worked, and the number of deductions. Print a report showing the employee name, amount of gross pay, amount of tax, and amount of net pay (what is left after taxes).

15. Given the following DATA statement:

```
10 DATA 10,11,6,12,54,76,43,65,9
```

write a program that will print the numbers in the reverse order (use an array):

```
9   65   43   76   54   12   6   11   10
```

16. Using the following DATA statement:

```
500 DATA 100,15,68,95,45
```

write a program to input a number and then check it against the data to see if it matches any of the numbers. Print a message for each input telling whether it matched or not.

17. XYZ Corporation uses a table of raw materials and parts to manufacture several different products. The table shows the weight needed for each raw material and the number of each part needed to produce the finished goods. The table is as follows:

PRODUCT	RAW A	RAW B	PART A	PART B	PART C
1597	100	200	3	4	5
1497	3	1500	2	0	17
12478	15	25	10	0	0
1342	2	0	0	0	9
1458	2	2	5	6	0

Write a program that will store all the table data in a two-dimensional array. Then input the product code and the quantity and determine how many pounds of each raw material and how many of each part it will take to complete the specified quantities. Keep a total of all the materials and parts to be printed at the end of the list. Use the following data for input (use an end-of-data marker):

PRODUCT	QUANTITY	
1400	100	(should print an error—no such product)
1597	10	
12478	25	
1597	100	
1342	35	
1458	20	

Your output should look like the following (the final totals coming after all six entries):

```
RAW A = XXXXX     RAW B = XXXXX
PART A = XXXXX     PART B = XXXXX     PART C = XXXXX
TOTAL RAW = XXXXX     TOTAL PARTS = XXXXX

TOTAL RAW A = XXXXXX     TOTAL RAW B = XXXXXX
TOTAL PART A = XXXXXX     TOTAL PART B = XXXXXX
TOTAL PART C = XXXXXX
TOTAL QUANTITY PRODUCED = XXXXXX
```

The answers to the questions follow immediately after the quiz. Questions 1–15 are true–false, while 16–20 are multiple choice.

1. The variables B1 and B(1) are stored in the same place in memory.   **T**   **F**
2. There is virtually no limit to the number of elements you can specify for your arrays.   **T**   **F**
3. You can access any array element up to 20 without specifically dimensioning it.   **T**   **F**
4. The DIM statement simply tells the computer to reserve storage for the specified number of elements for the variable(s) named in the statement.   **T**   **F**
5. You can specify up to ten different variables on each DIM statement.   **T**   **F**
6. Care should always be exercised when using arrays that you don't dimension your arrays larger than is necessary because this can cause problems in your program execution.   **T**   **F**
7. When using string arrays you need to be careful that you use only compatible data types when assigning values.   **T**   **F**
8. The following READ-DATA pair is compatible: **T**   **F**

```
10 READ A,B,C
100 DATA 5,TOM,6
```

9. There are no specific limits to the number of items that can be put on each READ and DATA statement.   **T**   **F**
10. A READ statement is another type of assignment statement.   **T**   **F**
11. The value of D would be 30 after execution of the following program.   **T**   **F**

```
10 REM ***** QUICK QUIZ #11
20 REM
30 READ A,B
40 RESTORE
50 READ D
60 DATA 10,20,30,40
70 END
```

12. DATA statements should always be in the same relative position in the program, but where they are is strictly up to the programmer.   **T**   **F**
13. If you have more items to read than you have constants on the DATA statements, you will get a RESTORE error.   **T**   **F**
14. In a DATA statement we have the old problem of commas separating our data. If we wish to read a data item with a comma in it, we must enclose the entire item within quotes.   **T**   **F**
15. Subroutines should not be used unless the instructions in the routine are to be used a number of times. If they are not, you should code the program straight through from top to bottom.   **T**   **F**

16. Which of the following statements is invalid?

    a. 10 GOSUB 1000   **c.** 10 DIM A(100),B(100)

    b. 10 RETURN   **d.** 10 READ A;B,C

17. Given the following program, which of the choices is incorrect?

```
10 REM ***** QUICK QUIZ #17
20 REM
30 FOR I = 1 TO 4
40    READ B(I)
50 NEXT I
60 RESTORE
70 READ B(3),B(1)
80 DATA 1,2,3,4,5
90 END
```

    a. B(1)=2   **c.** B(5)=5

    b. B(3)=1   **d.** B(2)=2

18. If you executed each of the following statements by itself, which would *not* give you an error?

    a. 10 GOSUB 1000   **c.** 10 B(14)=3

    b. 10 RETURN   **d.** 10 DIM B$(15)

19. Using the program below, which of the statements would be correct?

```
10 REM ***** QUICK QUIZ #19
20 REM
30 FOR I = 1 TO 20
40    IF I>10 THEN 70
50    B(I) = I*I
60 NEXT I
70 END
```

    a. A Subscript out of range error will occur.

    b. B(3)=6

    c. The loop and the IF-THEN should be changed and combined.

    d. The branch on the IF test should be 60.

20. In which of the following programs will B(2) *not* be 4?

    a.
```
10 REM ***** SAMPLE A
20 REM
30 B(1)=2
40 B(2)=B(1)*B(1)
50 END
```

    b.
```
10 REM ***** SAMPLE B
20 REM
30 FOR I = 1 TO 10 STEP 2
40    READ B(I)
50 NEXT I
60 DATA 3,4,8,10,11
70 END
```

    c.
```
10 REM ***** SAMPLE C
20 REM
30 B(1)=1
40 GOSUB 100
50 GOSUB 100
60 B(2)=B(1)
```

Program continues

```
70 GOTO 120
100 B(1)=B(1)+B(1)
110 RETURN
120 END
```

d.
```
10 REM ***** SAMPLE D
20 REM
30 READ B(1),B(2)
40 DATA 5,4,6,4
50 END
```

---

1. F (B1 and B(1) are different variables and are stored in different places in memory.)
2. T (Provided you don't run out of memory.)
3. F (The default value for arrays is 10 not 20.)
4. T
5. F (The only limit to the number of variables that can be specified on the DIM statement is the length of your line.)
6. F (You would only have a problem in specifying more array elements than you need if your program ran out of memory.)
7. T (This is true because all assignments to any variable must be compatible data types. Though string variables and string arrays are less specific about what they will accept, they still have to be assigned in the proper manner.)
8. F (The variable B cannot contain TOM.)
9. T (Line length is the only limit.)
10. T
11. F (The RESTORE would make the value of D = 10.)
12. T (The DATA statements may be anywhere in the program, but the programmer should be consistent in their placement.)
13. F (You will get an Out of data error.)
14. T (That's the only way you will be able to do it.)
15. F (Subroutines are useful for a variety of things besides multiple-use routines, such as for creating modular programs.)
16. d (The semicolon between A and B should be a comma.)
17. c (The loop only goes to 4. B(5) would not be assigned and would, therefore, be zero.)
18. d (This is the only statement that would not cause an error. Choice a would give you an Unidentified line number error, b would yield a Return without GOSUB error, and c would cause a Subscript out of range error.)
19. c (For a, there would be no subscript error because you would branch out before I was larger than 10. For b, B(3)=9. For d, there is nothing wrong with branching to the END statement. Branching to the NEXT statement would simply prolong the program.)
20. b (The program assigns B(1) and then B(3). B(2) would not be assigned and would, therefore, be zero.)

7 STRING HANDLING AND FUNCTIONS

OBJECTIVES

After completing Chapter 7, you will be able to:

- Concatenate strings and literals.
- Move any part of one string into another string.
- Describe the instruction and technique for searching one string for another string.
- Convert a string to a numeric and a numeric to a string.
- Load a string with any number of the same character.
- Use the character input function to input information without the computer stopping for prompting.
- Demonstrate how to generate random numbers and explain why the technique is useful.
- Demonstrate how to get an integer from a decimal number and explain why the technique is useful.

There are only a few things that place a computer a class above a calculator, and one of them is the capability of the computer to handle string information. Unfortunately, some programmers are not versed in many of the techniques of handling strings. In this chapter we shall look at many ways to handle strings and a few techniques to make use of the functions that are available to us.

There are many times when we are using two or more strings and need to combine them into one string. This combining is called **concatenation,** and though we use the addition sign (+) as the symbol for this function, we are not really adding the strings in the numeric sense. We are merely combining the two strings end to end. As an example, suppose A$ = "CAT" and B$ = "TOM". We can concatenate them as C$ = B$ + A$, and C$ will contain the word "TOM-CAT". The following program offers a further example:

```
10 REM ***** PROGRAM NAME: CONCAT
20 REM
30 REM ***** CONCATENATION EXAMPLE
40 REM
50 A$="COBURN"
60 B$="ED"
70 C$=A$+", "+B$
80 PRINT "THE NAME IS NOW ";C$
90 END
RUN
THE NAME IS NOW COBURN, ED
Ok
```

Program 7–1

C$ became the combination of COBURN, the comma and space, and ED. Notice that variables and constants may be combined in series with the concatenation function. There is no limit to the number of literals and variables that may be combined in this manner.

Just as sometimes we need to put several strings together to make one larger string, there are times when we need to be able to pull from a large string only one small segment of the string. This segment is called a **substring,** and there are three functions that enable us to manipulate substrings: LEFT$, RIGHT$ and MID$.

The **LEFT$** function allows you to pull off the first few characters from the left side of a string. The form of the statement is:

```
10 string variable = LEFT$(string,number of characters)
```

The string variable on the left side of the equal sign can be the same string as the one in parentheses or a different one. The string in the parentheses is the one you want to take the substring from; it can be either a variable or a literal string, though most often it is a variable. The number of characters refers to how many characters you want to put in the substring.

An example of this command would be:

```
10 A$=LEFT$(B$,4)
```

This statement would take the first four characters from the left side of B$ and store them into A$. Thus, if B$ were "123456", A$ would be "1234" after the statement was executed. For another example, examine the following program:

```
NEW
10 REM ***** PROGRAM NAME: LEFTEX
20 REM
30 REM ***** LEFT$ EXAMPLE
40 REM
50 B$="TOMCAT"
60 A$=LEFT$(B$,3)
70 PRINT A$
80 END
RUN
TOM
Ok
```

Program 7–2

The LEFT$ function took the first three characters of TOMCAT and stored them into A$. Those three characters were, of course, TOM and were printed out by line 70.

The LEFT$ function doesn't have to be used in an assignment. The previous program could have been written as:

```
10 REM ***** PROGRAM NAME: LEFTEX
20 REM
30 REM ***** LEFT$ EXAMPLE
40 REM
50 B$="TOMCAT"
60 PRINT LEFT$(B$,3)
70 END
```

And on execution the result would be the same:

```
RUN
TOM
Ok
```

The LEFT$ can also be used in some of the other statements we have been using, such as the IF-THEN statement:

```
NEW
10 REM ***** PROGRAM NAME: LEFTIF
20 REM
30 REM ***** IF-THEN AND LEFT$ EXAMPLE
40 REM
50 A$="TOM"
60 IF A$=LEFT$("TOMCAT",3) THEN PRINT "MATCH"
70 END
RUN
MATCH
Ok
```

This is not much of a program; it merely serves to demonstrate that the LEFT$ can be used in an IF test and that a literal can be used for the string in the LEFT$ command. Both options can be handy sometimes.

Just as the LEFT$ gives us the first few characters of a string, the **RIGHT$** **RIGHT$** will give us the last few characters of the string. The form of the RIGHT$ is:

```
10 string variable = RIGHT$(string, number of characters)
```

This statement functions basically the same way the LEFT$ does except that the count of the number of characters is done from the right end of the string. That is, if we ask for three characters, we get the last three characters on the right side of the string. An example of this function would be:

```
10 A$ = RIGHT$(B$,4)
```

This would store the four right-most characters of B$ into A$. If B$ contained TOMCAT, then after the statement executed, A$ would contain MCAT. An example of this statement used in a program can be seen in the following:

```
NEW
10 REM ***** PROGRAM NAME: RIGHTEX
20 REM
30 REM ***** RIGHT$ EXAMPLE
40 REM
50 B$="123456"
60 PRINT RIGHT$(·B$,3)
70 END
RUN
456
Ok
```

Program 7–3

Just as you would have expected. When the last three characters of B$ were printed, the result was 456.

Another substring command with a bit more flexibility is the **MID$** command. It can do the job of either the LEFT$ or the RIGHT$ and can also take substrings from the middle of the named string. The form of the MID$ is:

```
10 string variable = MID$(string,beginning position,# of characters)
```

Notice that the MID$ function requires the specification of not only how many characters, but also the starting position in the string. Thus, if we specified the starting location as the first position (from the left side of the string), we would have a function just like the LEFT$ function. As an example:

```
NEW
10 REM ***** PROGRAM NAME: MIDLEFT
20 REM
30 REM ***** MID$ AND LEFT$
40 REM
50 A$="123456"
60 PRINT "THE LEFT$ IS = ";LEFT$(A$,3)
70 PRINT "THE MID$  IS = ";MID$(A$,1,3)
```

Program continues

```
80 END
RUN
THE LEFT$ IS = 123
THE MID$  IS = 123
Ok
```

Notice that MID$ gave exactly the same result as LEFT$. MID$ can also function like RIGHT$ by using a starting position the exact number of positions from the end as the number of characters you ask for. For example, if B$ = "123456" and with RIGHT$ you ask for three characters, you will get 456. You can get the same result with MID$ by using MID$(B$,4,3). This begins the substring at position 4 (the 4) and gives you the next three characters including the one specified, thus 456.

The real power of the MID$ function, however, is that it can take substrings from the middle of the string. For example, if B$ = "123456", the specification MID$(B$,2,3) would yield "234". The following program provides another example:

```
NEW
10 REM ***** PROGRAM NAME: MIDSAMP
20 REM
30 REM ***** SAMPLE MID$
40 REM
50 B$="TOMCAT"
60 PRINT MID$(B$,2,4)
70 END
RUN
OMCA
Ok
```

Program 7–4

The program prints four characters from B$, starting at the second character (O), to yield the OMCA shown.

A feature of IBM BASIC is that the MID$ function can have a string assigned to it. For example, an instruction such as the following is possible with IBM BASIC:

```
10 MID$(B$,3,4)=A$
```

Let's assume for the moment that B$ contains 123456 and A$ contains ABCD. After executing the above statement, B$ would be 12ABCD since A$ would replace the characters in B$ starting at position 3 (the 3) for four characters. If there are not enough characters in the second string (A$) as are asked for by the MID$ function, only as many as are available are assigned. For example, suppose A$ was AB. Using line 10 again, B$ would be 12AB56; the assignment would start at position 3 and take only two characters since A$ only contains two characters.

To do this same type of assignment with our other versions of BASIC requires a bit more work. Let's assume that B$ still contains 123456 and A$ contains AB. To make B$ contain 12AB56 as we did above, with the Radio Shack and Apple we would have to use a statement similar to the following:

```
10 B$=MID$(B$,1,2)+A$+MID$(B$,5,2)
```

This statement will assign B$ using the first two characters from B$ (12) concatenated with A$ (AB) and concatenated with the last two characters of B$ (56).

```
10 B$=LEFT$(B$,2)+A$+RIGHT$(B$,2)
```

We have been using these functions in samples that no one would probably ever use. Let's use them to do something that is needed all the time in the business world. Many times to facilitate sorting, we store names by last name first, then first name. If we want to look up someone, it is much easier if the list of names is sorted by last name. But when we want to send a letter to someone through the mail, it doesn't look good to send the letter addressed to COBURN, ED. It is much more pleasing to address the letter to ED COBURN. The following program shows a method of turning a name around:

```
NEW
10 REM ***** PROGRAM NAME: REVERSE
20 REM
30 REM ***** NAME STRING REVERSAL
40 REM
50 B$="COBURN, ED"
60 L$=LEFT$(B$,6)  ' LAST NAME
70 F$=RIGHT$(B$,2) ' FIRST NAME
80 PRINT F$;" ";L$
90 END
RUN
ED COBURN
Ok
```
Program 7–5

7–4
INSTR (STRING SEARCH FUNCTION)

The previous example has a problem. If we need to input the name string, how would we know how many characters long the first and last names are? We specified the LEFT$ with a length of 6, but we knew how many to specify by looking at the string. If we are unable to look at the string, we would not be able to do that. In Radio Shack and IBM BASIC there is a function that will help us with this problem. It can help us find a particular character by searching the string for us. The function is called **INSTR** and has the form:

```
10 INSTR(beginning position, search string, searched for string)
```

As you can see, two strings are specified. The first string is the one we want searched and the second string is what we are searching for. For example, suppose we have a string that has, as our example before, the last name, comma, and then first name. To determine how long the last name is we could search for the comma by specifying the INSTR function as follows:

```
10 A=INSTR(1,B$,",")
```

The function will look for a comma (,) in B$ starting at position 1 and store its numerical position in A. As an example, if B$ contains COBURN, ED, line 10 will yield 7 for A since the comma is in the seventh position (starting from the left end as always). Notice that we specified position 1 in the INSTR function. If we want the function to begin in position 1, it is not necessary to specify it. We could use the simpler command:

```
10 A=INSTR(B$,",")
```

But don't forget that you can specify which column to begin with. That is useful when you want to search a string for a character that might appear in the first column, but you want to find an occurrence beyond the first character.

What will be the value of A in the INSTR function should a comma not be found? You probably guessed zero, and if you did you are correct. Anytime the searched-for string is not found, the number returned is zero.

Now that we have the position of the comma, it can be used for any purpose we choose. One example might be in a LEFT$ function to assign the last name, such as:

```
20 L$=LEFT$(B$,A-1)
```

Why did we use A−1? Since A contains the position of the comma, we want to assign one character less than the comma. If we used A, we would get the comma also.

The INSTR function is fine for those versions of BASIC that have it (the IBM and Radio Shack), but what of the Apple version? We can do this same type of thing, but we have to write the routine ourselves. We can use a loop to search for the character with an IF test. Such a routine might look like the following:

```
NEW
10 REM ***** PROGRAM NAME: CHSRCH
20 REM
30 REM ***** CHARACTER SEARCH
40 REM
50 B$="COBURN, ED"
60 A=1
70 IF MID$(B$,A,1)="," THEN 100
80 A=A+1
90 GOTO 70
100 L$=LEFT$(B$,A-1)
110 PRINT L$
120 END
RUN
COBURN
Ok
```

Program 7–6

This is obviously more work than letting a prepared function do the work for us (it is also slower), but in those versions where such a function doesn't exist, we do what we can. It is important to know how to do this process. In later chapters we will run across other times when this will become useful.

7–5
LEN (STRING LENGTH FUNCTION)

We now have the method (useful for many other purposes also) of finding the last name in a name string, but how do we get the first name? We could use a command that takes the rest of the string beyond the comma as the first name, but how much string is left? Since the functions will allow you to specify more characters than are actually available, you could specify the MID$ function as follows:

```
100 F$=MID$(B$,A+2,25)
```

This would assure you of getting all the string that is remaining. Notice that we specified beginning F$ with character A + 2. Recall that A points to the comma.

Since we don't want the comma to be part of the first name, we have to tell the machine to bypass it. The next character following the comma is a blank. We don't care to use the blank either, so we don't specify A + 1. We skip the blank by specifying one character beyond A + 1, that is, A + 2.

Notice also that we specified the length of the substring as 25 characters. This will, as we mentioned, get us all the remaining characters, but it is sloppy programming. But to specify the length exactly, we have to know how long the string is. Well, we can find this out with another BASIC function, the **LEN** function. This function tells us the length of a string. The form of the LEN function is simply:

```
10 LEN(string)
```

An example of how the function might be used is:

```
10 A=LEN(B$)
```

If B$ contains COBURN, ED, then A would be 10 since there are 10 characters in the string.

We can also use the LEN function within a BASIC statement. We will do just that to find the first name by specifying the string length precisely:

```
100 F$=MID$(B$,A+2,LEN(B$)-(A+2))
```

What are we doing now? Well, the statement is basically the same as before, except now we are specifying the number of characters by determining the length of the string with the LEN function and then subtracting from that length the number of characters that we have already used (A + 2). This is much more difficult to do and understand than just to stick 25 in the end of the function. No argument there. But many times we will not be able to use default values such as 25. We will have to be able to figure out just how long every string is.

Now that we know how to use the functions, let's do a little more experimentation. Let's take a name that is specified in the normal fashion and turn it around. As an example, we will turn ED COBURN around so that it is COBURN, ED and ready to be sorted. We will input the name, search for the blank between the first and last names, then print them out using the RIGHT$ and LEFT$ functions. Such a program might look like:

```
NEW
10 REM ***** PROGRAM NAME: NAMESTR
20 REM
30 REM ***** NAME STRING MANIPULATION
40 REM
50 INPUT "NAME";B$
60 A=INSTR(B$," ")              ' FIND THE BLANK BETWEEN
70 L$=RIGHT$(B$,LEN(B$)-A)      ' GET THE LAST NAME
80 PRINT L$;", ";LEFT$(B$,A)    ' LEFT$ WILL PRINT FIRST NAME
90 END
RUN
NAME? ED COBURN
COBURN, ED
Ok
```
                                                    Program 7–7

The program inputs ED COBURN as B$. Then the function searches for the blank, which gives A the value of 3 since the blank is the third character. Then the program assigns to L$ the part of the string to the right of the blank by subtracting the position (3) from the length of the whole string (LEN(B$)) to give us 6, the length of just the last name. Finally, the program prints the name out using L$ (the last name) first and then LEFT$ to get the first name and the blank. It is not necessary to print the blank, but it doesn't hurt anything.

The same program can be constructed on the Apple without the INSTR function by substituting a loop like the following for line 60:

```
60 FOR A = 1 TO LEN(B$)
64     IF MID$(B$,A,1)=" " THEN 70
67 NEXT A
68 A=0     ' THE BLANK WAS NOT FOUND
```

This will find the blank, and A will be 3 just as if we had used the INSTR function.

What would happen in the program if we input a name without a blank? Let's experiment (you should always do this kind of thing to test your programs to make sure they will handle whatever may be given them):

```
RUN
NAME? EDCOBURN
EDCOBURN,
Ok
```

What happened? Since we are searching for a blank and there is no blank, A would be zero. As such, statement 70 would give us the whole string since the RIGHT$ would use the LEN of 9 minus zero, or all 9 characters. Then, when the program printed the LEFT$, we get nothing since the number of positions to print would be zero (A). This result is for the program using the INSTR function. If you use the Apple, you will get an "Illegal quantity error" since you have a zero in the function.

Our previous program still has a small problem. What would happen if we input a name with a middle initial? Let's try it and see.

```
RUN
NAME? EDWARD J. COBURN
J. COBURN, EDWARD
Ok
```

Just as we might have suspected. The first blank stops the search and we get the last name as "J. COBURN". Not really what we were after. Is there another way we can handle the problem? Well, we could search for one blank and then search for another blank. If we don't find a second blank we can assume that there is no middle initial and print the string as we did before. If we find the second blank then we can use the same routine as we used before for the last name, except that the location of the second blank is used as the starting point of the last name.

We will examine how such a program might look, but we are beginning to get into a bit more complicated program. We should take the time to pseudo-code and flowchart the routine this time to make sure we know how the routine is going to work. The pseudocode of the program should be:

Start
Input the name. (*continues*)

Search for the first blank (predefined process).
Search for the second blank (predefined process).
IF the second blank is not found THEN
    Use the first blank position to locate the last name.
ELSE
    Use the second blank position to locate the last name.
END-IF
Put the two strings together and print the result.
End

Figure 7–1 shows how the flowchart would look for this program. But let's take a good look at what we're doing. Both RIGHT$ and LEFT$ routines are similar except for the position variable. So, by using the first position variable if the second is zero (or equal to LEN(B$) in Apple BASIC), we could use the same assignments for the two RIGHT$ and LEFT$ routines. A new flowchart depicting this is shown in Figure 7–2, and the new pseudocode is:

Start
Input the name.
Search for the first blank (predefined process).
Search for the second blank (predefined process).
IF the second blank is not found THEN
    Assign the second position.
(ELSE)
END-IF
Use the second position to locate the last name.
Put the two strings together and print the result.
End

Using the flowchart in Figure 7–2, we would write the program similar to the following:

```
NEW
10 REM ***** PROGRAM NAME: NEWSRCH
20 REM
30 REM ***** NEW NAME STRING SEARCH
40 REM
50 INPUT "NAME";B$
60 A=INSTR(B$," ")               ' FIRST BLANK
70 B=INSTR(A+1,B$," ")           ' SECOND BLANK
80 IF B<>0 THEN A=B              ' IF SECOND SEARCH OK
90 L$=RIGHT$(B$,LEN(B$)-A)       ' GET THE LAST NAME
100 F$=LEFT$(B$,A)               ' GET THE FIRST NAME
110 PRINT L$;", ";F$
120 END
RUN
EDWARD J. COBURN
COBURN, EDWARD J.
Ok
RUN
ED COBURN
COBURN, ED
Ok                                        Program 7–8
```

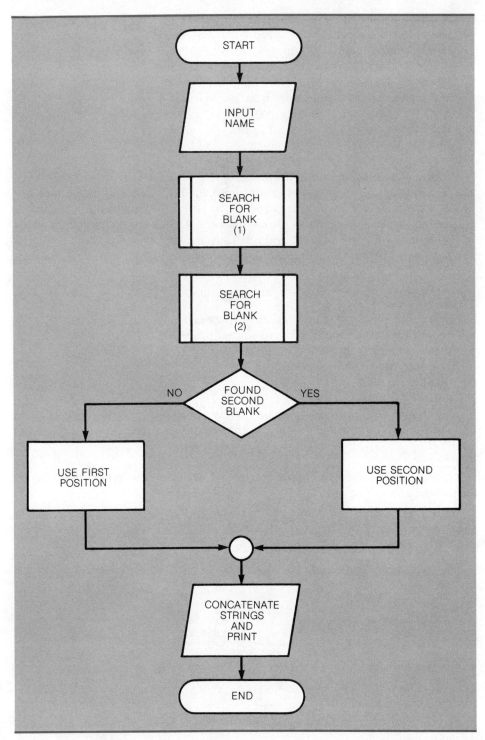

Figure 7–1
Flowchart of search for
blank.

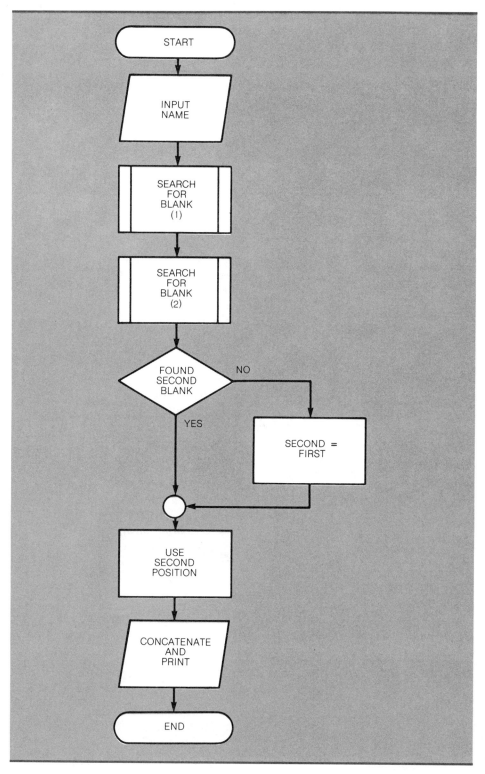

Figure 7–2
Better solution for search problem.

On the Apple, there is no INSTR function, so the routine discussed on p. 190 will have to be substituted for lines 60 and 70 as follows:

```
60 FOR A = 1 TO LEN(B$)
64     IF MID$(B$,A,1)=" " THEN 70
67 NEXT A
68 A=0      ' THE BLANK WAS NOT FOUND
70 FOR B = A+1 TO LEN(B$)
74     IF MID$(B$,B,1)=" " THEN 80
77 NEXT B
78 B=0      ' THE BLANK WAS NOT FOUND
```

Now the program works for both types of input (with and without a middle initial). There are a couple of things worth noting about the program. First, notice on line 70 that the second search begins beyond the first search (A + 1). This is necessary because we have to bypass the first blank to find the second blank. Also notice that line 80 stores B into A if the second blank is found. If it is not found, then the original blank must be the only one and no storage is necessary.

7–6
STRING CONVERSION

It is sometimes necessary to be able to convert a string to a numeric or a numeric to a string. For example, if you input string information and want to use the answer to the prompt as the value on an ON...GOTO or ON...GOSUB, it would have to be changed to a number since a string won't work with these commands. We have BASIC statements for both conversions, from string to numeric and numeric to string.

VAL (String to Numeric Conversion)

The value function, **VAL,** will allow us to change string data to numeric data. The form of the VAL statement is:

```
10 VAL(string)
```

A sample VAL statement is:

```
10 A=VAL(B$)
```

If B$ contains "15", then using line 10 would give A the value of positive 15. If the string has no *leading* numeric digits, the numeric will be given the value of zero. That is, should the value of the string B$ be something like HI-15, then A would be assigned the value of zero. If only the first part of the string is numeric, the value will be only that portion which is numeric. For example, if B$ = "155 SOUTH STREET" and we used line 10, A would be 155.

As mentioned before, we can use this function to allow the input of string data to be used on the ON... commands. Let's try a small example:

```
NEW
10 REM ***** PROGRAM NAME: VALSAMP
20 REM
30 REM ***** VAL SAMPLE
40 REM
50 INPUT "ADD (1), CHANGE (2), DELETE (3)";A$
60 A=VAL(A$)
70 IF A<1 OR A>3 THEN 50
80 ON A GOSUB 100, 200, 300
90 END
RUN
ADD (1), CHANGE (2), DELETE (3)? 1
Undefined line number in 80
Ok
```
Program 7–9

The error is, of course, caused by having no line 100 in the program. Notice that line 70 edits the input to make sure it is only 1, 2, or 3. Anything else will cause the input to be done again.

Now you may wonder why we didn't just use a numeric variable for the input instead of the string; then no conversion would be necessary. In this particular example such an argument is valid. We shall learn later an instruction whereby the use of the VAL function becomes important because the input cannot be done with a numeric.

STR$ (Numeric to String Conversion)

The **STR$** function is useful for changing numerics to strings. It has the form:

```
10 STR$(numeric)
```

A sample of the statement in use is:

```
10 B$=STR$(A)
```

When this statement is executed, B$ will contain the characters of whatever number is stored in A. For example, suppose A contains 15. B$ will then become 15 also. But how long (how many characters) will B$ be? It may be logical to assume that B$ will be two characters long since 15 has only two characters. But if you recall, when numbers are printed a blank is printed in front of them. This is for the understood positive sign. The same thing holds true when a numeric is converted to a string. The blank is carried with the number, and the string is here going to be three characters long. (The Apple version of BASIC does not follow this convention; the string would be only two characters long.)

So, the string is going to be three characters long. But we don't want three characters. We only want the 15. We can get just the characters beyond the blank by using the RIGHT$ function and specifying the number of characters as one less than the length of the string. (The same thing could be done using the MID$ function with the substring beginning in the second location.) The following short program will demonstrate this use of the RIGHT$ function:

```
NEW
10 REM ***** PROGRAM NAME: STRSAMP
20 REM
30 REM ***** SAMPLE STR$
```
Program 7–10

Program continues

```
40 REM
50 A=15
60 B$=STR$(A)
70 PRINT LEN(B$)            ' PRINT FOR VERIFICATION
80 B$=RIGHT$(B$,LEN(B$)-1) ' GET ALL BEYOND THE FIRST
90 PRINT B$,LEN(B$)
100 END
RUN
 3
15          2
Ok
```

Program 7–10 (cont.)

Notice that we printed the LEN of B$ to satisfy ourselves that it was indeed three characters long. Then, line 80 takes all the characters except the first one and moves them into the string, giving it the length now of 1 less than the length of the original string. The new string will have a length, as our print in line 90 shows, of 2.

ASC (Character to ASCII Code Conversion)

In order for the computer to keep track of which character is which, each character is stored with a unique storage configuration (see Chapter 1). Each storage code has a different decimal value, which is the numeric equivalent of the binary storage code the machine uses. Any value from 0 to 255 may represent a character.

However, since there are only 52 letters (counting lowercase), 10 numeric digits (0–9) and about 20 special symbols (*, &, $, etc.), there are more codes than there are printable characters. Other keys, such as the RETURN key, send out codes also. There is a command that will allow these codes to be converted from their character code to its decimal value. This command is the **ASC** command and has the form:

```
10 ASC(string)
```

A sample of the statement is:

```
10 C=ASC(B$)
```

If B$ = "A", then after executing line 10, C would have the value of 65 since the decimal value of the character A is 65. This function can be useful for converting input characters to numbers to be used in other types of commands. Say, for example, we used Program 7–9 and changed the prompt to something easier to use, such as A for add, C for change, and D for delete. The ON...GOSUB could still be used by using the ASC function. The following program will illustrate:

```
NEW
10 REM ***** PROGRAM NAME: ASCSAMP
20 REM
30 REM ***** ASC SAMPLE
40 REM
50 INPUT "ADD (A), CHANGE (C), OR DELETE (D)";B$
60 IF B$<>"A" AND B$<>"C" AND B$<>"D" THEN 50 ' EDIT
70 A=ASC(B$)-64                 ' GIVES THE DECIMAL VALUE
```

Program continues   **Program 7–11**

```
 80 ON A GOSUB 120,50,200,300  ' 50 IS A DUMMY ENTRY
 90 GOTO 50
 95 REM
100 REM ***** ADD SUBROUTINE
110 REM
120 PRINT "ADD SUBROUTINE"
130 RETURN
170 REM
180 REM ***** CHANGE SUBROUTINE
190 REM
200 PRINT "CHANGE SUBROUTINE"
210 RETURN
270 REM
280 REM ***** DELETE SUBROUTINE
290 REM
300 PRINT "DELETE SUBROUTINE"
310 RETURN
320 END
RUN
ADD (A), CHANGE (C), OR DELETE (D)? Q
ADD (A), CHANGE (C), OR DELETE (D)? A
ADD SUBROUTINE
ADD (A), CHANGE (C), OR DELETE (D)?
Break in 50
Ok
```

Program 7–11 (cont.)

Notice that line 60 checks B$ to verify that it is A, C, or D. If it is not, the program returns to the input statement. Next, line 70 changes the string to its decimal equivalent number and subtracts 64. This lowers the values of A from the 65, 67, and 68 it would have, to the 1, 3, and 4 we need to have for the ON...GOSUB. Finally, the A variable is used as the indicator on the ON...GOSUB. Notice also that on the ON...GOSUB, line 50 is used as the second entry. The value of A will never be 2 since we edited that letter out in line 60, but in order for the ON...GOSUB to function properly, there must be four line numbers. The number 50 could have been any number, but it is more logical to put the number of the line where a "B" entry will go, line 50.

When we executed the program, the first entry was a Q to test the edit. Since the letter entered was not an acceptable one, the prompt reappeared. Next we entered an A, and the message ADD SUBROUTINE was printed on the screen, signifying that the add subroutine was reached using the ON...GOSUB. Then the prompt reappeared as we had a branch back to the input statement after returning from the subroutine. Here we pressed the BREAK key to drop out of the program. How could the program have been written to avoid having to use the BREAK key? Another code, such as EXIT (E), could have been added so the ON...GOSUB could branch to the end of the program.

CHR$ (ASCII Code to Character Conversion)

The function that is the direct opposite of the ASC function is the **CHR$** function. This function yields the string equivalent of the ASCII code. The form of the instruction is:

```
10 CHR$(number < 255)
```

An example of this function would be:

```
10 A$=CHR$(B)
```

If B has the value of 65, then A$ would contain "A" after the execution of line 10 since "A" is the character equivalent of the decimal value 65. This function is useful in cases where you need either to interpret input data as a string when it is not a printable character (RETURN key or backspace key), or to use numeric codes as characters. Let's use an example of the latter to illustrate. Suppose we need to print alphabetic characters when processing a FOR-NEXT loop. A program to do this might look something like the following:

```
NEW
10 REM ***** PROGRAM NAME: CHRSAMP
20 REM
30 REM ***** SAMPLE FOR CHR$
40 REM
50 PRINT "YOUR OPTIONS ARE:"
60 PRINT
70 FOR I = 65 TO 69
80     READ A$
90     PRINT CHR$(I);". ";A$
100 NEXT I
110 DATA ADD,CHANGE,DELETE,PRINT,EXIT
120 PRINT
130 INPUT "WHAT OPTION DO YOU WANT";A$
140 END
RUN
YOUR OPTIONS ARE:

A. ADD
B. CHANGE
C. DELETE
D. PRINT
E. EXIT

WHAT OPTION DO YOU WANT? A
Ok
```

Program 7–12

In this example, there is no more to our program. If it were an actual program, we would probably have continued with a subroutine for each of the options.

Remember, all these illustrations of the string functions are merely that, illustrations. There are many uses of each of these functions, and we will see more of them as we progress through the book.

7–7
FILLING A STRING

Another useful function in the IBM and Radio Shack versions of BASIC is the **STRING$** function. It allows a string to be filled or partially filled with a particular character. The form of the statement is:

```
10 STRING$(number, "character" or number)
```

And an example of its use is the following:

```
10 A$=STRING$(5,"A") or STRING$(5,65)
```

Both statements create the same string in A$, five A's or AAAAA. In the first example, the "A" is specified and in the second, the ASCII decimal number is given. This function could also be done by using the following:

```
10 A$="AAAAA"
```

But the STRING$ function is useful for assigning as many characters as needed. As an example, you may want to assign a string of 50 dashes to print an underline for totals on a report.

In the Apple, you will have to construct your own routine to assign a string of characters. One way to do this would be the following:

```
NEW
10 REM ***** PROGRAM NAME: STRFILL
20 REM
30 REM ***** STRING FILLING
40 REM
50 FOR I = 1 TO 50
60     A$=A$+"-"
70 NEXT I
80 PRINT A$
90 END
RUN
--------------------------------------------------
Ok                                    Program 7-13
```

)))DIFFERENCES

If you are using a machine with only a 40-column display (either an Apple or the IBM in 40-column mode), the dashes display will wrap around the screen in this program (and in Program 7–14 since there are 64 dashes).

The above program will fill A$ with 50 dashes. The problem with a routine like this is that if you have to use such routines often in your program, they might slow down your program. A much faster way to do this type of manipulation is as follows:

```
NEW
10 REM ***** PROGRAM NAME: NEWFILL
20 REM
30 REM ***** NEW STRING FILLING ROUTINE
40 REM
50 A$="-"
60 FOR I = 1 TO 6
70     A$=A$+A$
80 NEXT I
100 PRINT A$
110 END
RUN
--------------------------------------------------
Ok                                    Program 7-14
```

Notice that this routine begins by assigning A$ as the first dash. Then the loop successively doubles the size of A$. That is, the first time through the loop A$ becomes "--". The second time it becomes "----". So, by the sixth loop, A$ will be 64 dashes long. The problem is that we only wanted 50 of them. One final statement will rectify that situation:

```
90 A$=MID$(A$,1,50)
```

This will put only 50 of the dashes back into A$.

7–8
INPUTTING A
CHARACTER

The final string function command we are going to discuss in this chapter allows the inputting of a character from the keyboard without the user having to press RETURN. On the IBM and Radio Shack, the command is **INKEY$,** and the form usually is:

```
10 A$=INKEY$
```

though the INKEY$ doesn't actually have to be assigned. It can be used in other commands such as the IF-THEN. On the Apple, the command is **GET,** and it takes the form:

```
10 GET A$
```

Other than the form, the two commands function the same.

When a user keys in a response to an INPUT statement, the characters that are pressed appear on the screen. Such is not the case when using the character input. If you want the characters to print on the screen as they are input, they must be programmed to print. This is called **echoing** the characters. Another difference between the character input and the INPUT statement is that the character input command does not wait for the user to press a key. The key must be pressed *before* the character input command executes. That is, a statement such as A$ = INKEY$ will not work by itself. For example, key in this small program and see what happens when you execute it:

```
NEW
10 REM ***** PROGRAM NAME: INKEYSAM
20 REM
30 REM ***** INKEY$ SAMPLE
40 REM
50 A$=INKEY$
60 PRINT A$
70 PRINT "WE ARE DONE"
80 END
RUN

WE ARE DONE
Ok
```
Program 7–15

)))DIFFERENCES

On the Apple, line 50 should be:

```
50 GET A$
```

On the Apple IIe and IIc, the program will automatically pause and wait for your entry with the use of the GET command. It will not continue as the others will do. We will now see how to get the others to wait for your entry.

Notice that the program did not wait for you to press any key, it immediately printed a blank line (line 60) because there was nothing in A$; it then printed "WE ARE DONE" on the screen. If we want the program to wait for us to enter something, we have to write a small routine for this:

```
NEW
10 REM ***** PROGRAM NAME: INKEYPAZ
20 REM
30 REM ***** INKEY$ PAUSE ROUTINE
40 REM
50 A$=INKEY$
60 IF A$="" THEN 50
70 PRINT A$
80 PRINT "WE ARE DONE"
90 END
RUN
A
WE ARE DONE
Ok
```

Program 7–16

)))DIFFERENCES

On the Apple, line 50 should be:

```
50 GET A$
```

On the IIe and IIc, this pause routine is not necessary since the machine will automatically pause until a key is pressed. The Apple will always require the written INKEY$ to be changed to a GET. We will not list this change in the rest of the chapter. The student will be expected to remember the difference.

Now, the program will wait until you press a key before it continues. (Here we pressed A.) How did it do this? Line 60 checks A$ to see if there is anything in it. If there isn't, it will be null or empty. This is tested with the double quotes (" "). If there is nothing in A$, then the program returns to the INKEY$ command. When a key is pressed, the program goes past line 60 and completes its operation. Notice that line 70 prints A$. This is the echo. If it were not there, the key pressed would not be displayed at all. To show this to yourself, delete line 70 and run the program again. It will function as before except that the key pressed will not be displayed.

To experiment with this command a bit more we will use the following program as a demonstration:

```
NEW
10 REM ***** PROGRAM NAME: INKEYDEM
20 REM
30 REM ***** INKEY$ DEMO PROGRAM
40 REM
50 A$=INKEY$
60   IF A$="" THEN 50
70   PRINT A$,ASC(A$)
80   IF A$<>"Q" THEN 50
90 END
RUN
A            65
```
Program continues

Program 7–17

```
B                       66
C                       67

                        13
Q                       81
Ok
```

This program will appear to be doing nothing until a key is pressed. Then the character pressed and its decimal equivalent will print on the screen. Notice that the fourth item printed was 13 with no corresponding character printed, and a blank line printed before it. Recall that the decimal code for the RETURN key is 13. That is the key that was pressed to give this display. The blank line was printed because A$ was the carriage return and line feed that the RETURN key causes. Then the 13 printed because that is the decimal code for the RE-TURN key. Our end-of-data marker was Q.

Another popular use for the character input function is in password protection. Generally, when passwords are used a character other than the one entered is printed on the screen. This is done so that if someone is looking over the shoulder of the person entering the password, the password cannot be read. Let's write the program routine to input a password of four characters.

```
NEW
10 REM ***** PROGRAM NAME: INKEYPAS
20 REM
30 REM ***** INKEY$ PASSWORD ROUTINE
40 REM
50 FOR I = 1 TO 4
60      A$=INKEY$
70      IF A$="" THEN 60
80      B$=B$+A$              ' STORE THE PASSWORD
90      PRINT "X";
100 NEXT I
110 PRINT
120 PRINT "THE PASSWORD IS ";B$
130 END
RUN
XXXX
THE PASSWORD IS TEST
Ok
```
Program 7–18

Notice that line 80 concatenates each new character to the end of B$. When the loop is finished, B$ will have all four of the characters entered. Also, line 90 prints X's instead of echoing the character. Of course, this program would continue or end depending on whether or not the password that was entered was correct.

7–9
INTEGER FUNCTION

It is sometimes useful to be able to remove and keep the integer value from a decimal number. This may be done with the **INT** or integer function. The function gives us the value of the largest integer that is less than or equal to the decimal value. The form of the function is:

```
10 numeric variable=INT(numeric variable)
```

A sample of the command follows:

```
10 A=INT(B)
```

If B is 5.65, then the above statement would give A the value of 5 since 5 is the largest integer that is less than 5.65. It is important to realize that this function does not round the number off. It drops the decimal part of the number.

This function is useful for many things. In fact, you will see one use in the next section. For now, however, we will use it to test the **mod** of a number. The mod is simply a fancy way of saying a number is evenly divisible by a certain other number. For example, if a number is mod 4, it is evenly divisible (no remainder) by 4. Of what use is this? If we are doing calculations based on a date, it may be important to know if the year is a leap year since February has more days during leap years. An easy test for leap year is to take the year from the date and do a mod 4 on it, that is, see if it is evenly divisible by four. That's how we know when a year is a leap year.

The formula needed to determine if it is leap year divides the year by 4 and compares that number to the integer of the year divided by 4 as in:

```
10 IF YY/4 = INT(YY/4)
```

Now, if YY/4 is equal to INT(YY/4) it will mean that YY is evenly divisible by 4 and thus, a leap year.

Let's see how such a routine would work by writing a short program:

```
NEW
10 REM ***** PROGRAM NAME: MODSAMP
20 REM
30 REM ***** LEAP YEAR CHECK USING MOD
40 REM
50 INPUT "DATE (MM/DD/YY)";D$        ' DATE TO BE USED
60 IF D$="END" THEN 130             ' END-OF-DATA MARKER
70 YY$=RIGHT$(D$,2)                 ' PULL OFF YEAR
80 YY=VAL(YY$)                      ' CONVERT TO NUMERIC
90 PRINT YY;"IS ";
100 IF YY/4=INT(YY/4) THEN PRINT "LEAP YEAR"
110 IF YY/4<>INT(YY/4) THEN PRINT "NOT LEAP YEAR"
120 GOTO 50
130 END
RUN
DATE (MM/DD/YY)? 10/15/84
 84 IS LEAP YEAR
DATE (MM/DD/YY)? 12/16/83
 83 IS NOT LEAP YEAR
DATE (MM/DD/YY)? END
Ok
```

Program 7–19

7–10
RANDOM NUMBERS

Many times it is useful to be able to generate random numbers. A **random number** is an unpredictable number produced by chance. Actually, a computer cannot generate random numbers. What we end up with are called **pseudo-random numbers.** These are numbers that, though not completely random (which can be proven mathematically), are sufficiently random for practical uses.

What good are random numbers? For one thing random numbers can be useful in games such as dice games or card games. Suppose you are writing a program that uses a die. How are you going to pick which of the six possible rolls the die is going to have? The only practical way is to use random numbers.

If you are not interested in games, random numbers have many uses in the business world. Suppose you are running a contest and want to randomly select 100 numbers for awards from the 10,000 numbers that have been distributed to customers. Random numbers could prove useful. Another common use for them is in **sampling.** Suppose we have a list of 10,000 subscribers to our newsletter and want to send a sample mailing to 500 of them. This is also done by using random numbers.

How do we generate random numbers (remember they are actually pseudorandom)? We do it by using a **RND** statement that has the form:

```
10 numeric variable = RND(1) (RND(0) on the Radio Shack)
```

A sample command would be:

```
10 A=RND(1)
```

This will put into A a random number greater than or equal to 0 but less than 1 (thus a decimal). This random number does us little good if we are trying to use the number for rolling dice. We need the number to be from 1 to 6. This can be accomplished with a simple calculation. The numbers that will be generated by the statement will be, as we said, between 0 and 1. That means the lowest number will be (using five significant digits) .00000, and the highest number will be .99999. If we multiply this generated number by 6 we will get from .00000 to 5.9994. Now if we use the integer function on this decimal we will get from 0 to 5. Since we want from 1 to 6, all we have to do is add 1 to this product and we come up with a range of 1 to 6. Just what we were after. Our formula, then, looks like the following:

```
10 A=INT(RND(1)*6)+1
```

If we want to use the generator for playing cards (52 cards in a deck), all we have to do is change the 6 to 52, and we will get numbers from 1 to 52.

On the Radio Shack, you can get these same results by using a zero in the parentheses, that is, RND(0). But you can also do away with the calculation altogether by putting the highest number you are looking for in the parentheses. For example, if we are looking for 1 through 6, put 6 in the parentheses, such as RND(6), and the function will generate a number 1 through 6 just as we had calculated with our previous formula.

Let's experiment with our new formula for a moment by trying a bit of sampling. We will create a list of ten names (in a DATA statement) and then randomly select five of them for our sample. Normally, the list and the sample both would be much larger, but a smaller number will serve well as an example.

A bit of explanation about what we are going to do is in order. We will set up two arrays. The first array will have ten elements, one for each name in our list. The second array will have five elements, one for each name we will select. We will generate a random number and then check the first array (we will call it L for list) to see if that element has been selected yet. We do that by checking the value. If the value is 0 (automatically initialized), then that element has not been selected. We will then assign that index to the first element in our second array (called S for sample) and change the list element to 1 so we will know it has been selected.

For example, suppose we generate a 5 for the first random number. We will check the value of element 5 of array L; since it is zero, we change that value to 1 to indicate that it has been selected and then assign the first element of array S the value 5 to signify the element selected. We then move on to the next selection. After generating five numbers, five elements of the L array would be 1 and all five elements of the S array would have values. This is assuming there are no duplicates. It is possible (likely) that sometime during the generation of the five numbers the same number will be generated twice. That's why we change the element in L to 1. Even if we generate the same number, we will not use that element again because its value is 1, not 0.

After we have generated the five numbers, we will print the five names associated with those positions. To do that, we will have to create a third array to load the names into. Keep in mind that the five generated numbers will not be in sequence. After we load the string array, we can use the selected numbers to print the names.

The pseudocode to create such a program follows; the flowchart can be seen in Figure 7–3.

```
Start
Dimension arrays.
Initialize arrays to zero (done automatically).
Initialize counter to 1.
DO-WHILE counter is less than 6.
   Generate random number R.
   IF list array (R) is zero THEN
      List array (R) = 1.
      Sample array (counter) = R.
      Increment counter by 1.
   (ELSE)
END-DO
Read names into array.
Print name array element corresponding to sample array.
End
```

Notice that we only increment the counter should the list array element be zero. If it is not, a new number will be generated because of the loop. The program to accomplish this pseudocode would look like the following:

```
NEW
10 REM ***** PROGRAM NAME: RNDNAMES
20 REM
30 REM ***** GENERATE LIST OF RANDOM NAMES
40 REM
50 DIM L(10),S(5),N$(10)        ' NOT ACTUALLY NECESSARY
```

Program 7–20

Program continues on page 207

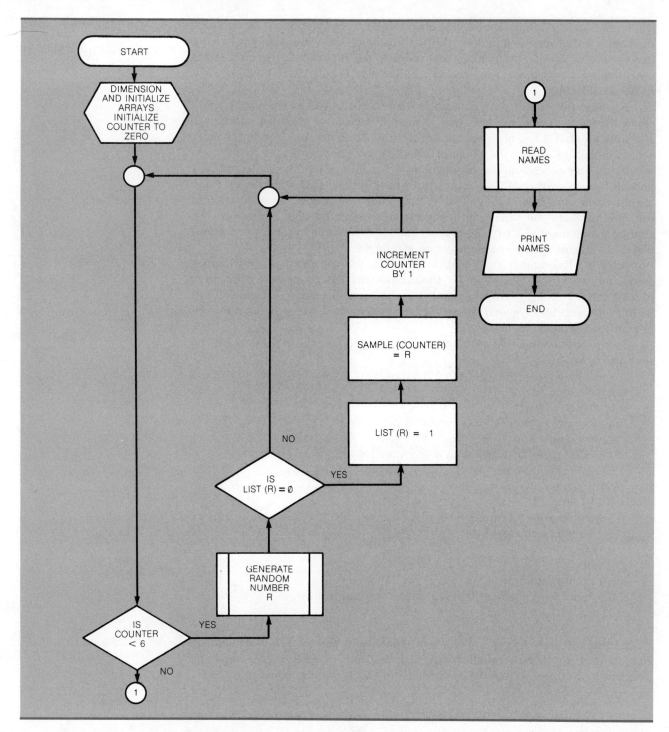

Figure 7–3
Flowchart of random names list.

```
60 FOR I = 1 TO 5
70     R=INT(RND(1)*10)+1     ' GENERATE THE RANDOM NUMBER
80     IF L(R)<>0 THEN 70     ' LOOP BACK
90     S(I)=R                 ' SAMPLE ITEM
100    L(R)=1                 ' CANNOT USE AGAIN
110 NEXT I
120 REM
130 REM ***** GET NAMES
140 REM
150 FOR I = 1 TO 10
160    READ N$(I)
170 NEXT I
180 FOR I = 1 TO 5
190    PRINT N$(S(I))         ' PRINT SAMPLE NUMBER
200 NEXT I
210 END
220 DATA TOM,SAM,GEORGE,LISA,FRED,TAMMY,SAMANTHA
230 DATA HARRY,HOWARD,LINDA              Program 7-20 (cont.)
```

))) DIFFERENCES

On the Radio Shack, line 70 should read:

```
70 R=RND(10)                   GENERATE RANDOM NUMBERS
```

If we run the program we should get results similar to the following (of course, a different list may appear):

```
TOM
LINDA
TAMMY
LISA
HARRY
```

Note: On the IBM, you will always get the same result every time you run the program unless you add another statement to the program. IBM has a **RANDOMIZE** statement to make each running of the program different. The form of the statement to use in Program 7–20 would be:

```
55 RANDOMIZE VAL(RIGHT$(TIME$,2))
```

This statement gives the RANDOMIZE statement the seconds from the internal time-of-day clock (TIME$). The TIME$ function gives the time of day as HH:MM:SS (hours, minutes and seconds). The RIGHT$ (TIME$,2) will yield the SS portion of TIME$. This means that each time the program runs, there is only a 1 in 60 possibility that it will be the same as the last time.

SUMMARY

1. Combining several strings into one is called concatenation, and though the command looks like the strings are being added, they are merely being stored back to front.

2. There are three commands that allow assignment of substrings from a main string. The LEFT$ will assign from the beginning of the string (the left side) for a designated number of characters. The RIGHT$ will assign a certain number of characters from the end of the string (the right side). The MID$ will allow the assignment of any size substring from inside the original string.

3. In IBM and Radio Shack BASIC, we may search for a substring within a string with the INSTR command. It will reveal at what position the string being searched for lies within the string being searched. In the Apple, a search routine must be written to accomplish this function.

4. The LEN function allows the determination of how many characters are contained in a string.

5. A string may be converted to a numeric in two different ways. Either the numeric value of the characters in the string or the ASCII decimal code for the characters may be assigned to a numeric variable. The reverse conversion may be done by assigning the character associated with the decimal code to a string or simply converting a number to a string.

6. The INKEY$ function in the IBM and Radio Shack versions of BASIC and the GET function in the Apple versions allow data to be input a character at a time without the computer having to prompt or pause for the entry of the data.

7. The INT function may be used to extract from a decimal number the largest integer less than or equal to the number. This can prove useful in many applications.

8. Random numbers can be generated with the RND function. They are useful in games and for many business applications, such as sampling.

GLOSSARY

ASC The command to convert a string character into its ASCII decimal code.

CHR$ The command to convert the ASCII decimal code to its related character.

Concatenation The process of combining several strings into one.

Echoing Printing of the character input with the INKEY$ or GET.

GET *See* **INKEY$.**

INKEY$ (IBM and Radio Shack) or **GET** (Apple) A character input command that allows the input of data without the printing of a prompt or waiting for the user's response.

INSTR The command that allows one string to be searched for within another string. There is no such command on the Apple.

INT The function to remove the integer portion of a decimal number.

LEFT$ The command that allows the assignment of a substring from the beginning of the string and continuing for a specified number of characters.

LEN The command that determines the length of a string.

MID$ The command that allows the assignment of a substring from within another string.

Mod A function to determine if a number is evenly divisible by another number.

Pseudorandom numbers Numbers that can be mathematically proven to be less than random but that are used as random numbers.

RANDOMIZE An IBM statement to cause the random number function to generate a different random number each time the program is run.

Random number An unpredictable number produced by chance.

RIGHT$ The command that allows the assignment of a substring beginning at a specified point in the middle of the string to the end of the string.

RND The command used to generate a random number.

Sampling A method of taking a random selection of elements from a list.

STR$ The command that converts a numeric to a string.

STRING$ The command that permits a string to be filled with a specified character. The Apple does not have this command.

Substring A partial string extracted from a larger string.

VAL The command that converts a string to a numeric value.

QUESTIONS TO AID UNDERSTANDING

1. Describe each of the string manipulation functions and explain how they differ.
2. Explain the purpose of the INSTR command.
3. What is the LEN function used for, and why is it important to know how to use it?
4. What is the name of the function to change a string of numbers to a numeric?
5. What is the name of the function to change a numeric to a string of numbers?
*6. What is the significance of the ASCII decimal code?
7. What is the name of the command to convert a character to its related ASCII decimal code?
8. What is the name of the command to convert the ASCII decimal code to its related character?
9. What does the STRING$ function do?
*10. What are three differences between the INPUT command and the INKEY$ (or GET) command?
11. Of what use is the RND function?
12. Write a routine to print the alphabet without assigning the letters to a string.
13. Write a routine to print the alphabet backwards by assigning the letters to a string.
*14. Write a routine to print the alphabet backwards without assigning the letters to a string.
15. Write a program that will randomly generate years from 1900 through 2000 and print each year with a message that states whether or not the year is a leap year.
*16. Write a program that will input a word, check it against a list of words already in the program (DATA stored in an array), and verify if it is spelled correctly. Any word that does not check against the list should be printed out as having been misspelled.
17. Use the INKEY$ (or GET) to input a character and print a message if the character is not a printable character. The message should be "NOT

PRINTABLE CHARACTER - CODE IS XX". Character codes less than 32 (32 is the ASCII code for a blank) are generally nonprintable characters. Keys such as backspace and RETURN are nonprintable characters.

18. Use the INKEY$ (or GET) to input any of the alphabetic characters A–Z (edit to make sure). Then change the character to its decimal value and accumulate the total of the characters until the number 300 is reached and then end the program. Print the character, the decimal value, and accumulated total.

19. Use the random number function to generate numbers that range from 65 to 90 and change the number to a letter. Use three letters in conjunction and print out a list (on paper) of three-letter "words". Print at least 100 words and then visually determine if any of them are actually the correct spelling of any words.

20. XYZ corporation uses a list of inventory part numbers. The designation following the first dash is for the color of the item, and the number following the slash is the quantity-on-hand. As an example, the part number 123-RE-BG45/15 has a color designation of RE and quantity-on-hand of 15. Using the color designation of RE for red, GR for green, YE for yellow, and BL for black, write a program to read the inventory items listed below from a data statement and print the inventory number, the color designation from within the number, the appropriate color designation, and the quantity-on-hand. The report should appear as:

```
NUMBER              COLOR DES.      COLOR     QUANTITY

123-RE-BG45/15      RE              RED       15

133-BL-GD67/95      BL              BLACK     95
```

The inventory numbers are 123-RE-BG45/15, 133-BL-GD67/95, 147-YE-HQ668/46, 1-BL-4/67, 33574-GR-TG/456, 4569-RE-HH/78.

QUICK QUIZ

The answers to the questions follow immediately after the quiz. Questions 1–15 are true–false, while 16–20 are multiple choice.

T   F   1. There is no limit on the number of strings that can be concatenated together.

T   F   2. Random numbers are basically just used for games.

The following assignment is to be used to answer questions 3 through 10.

```
10 B$="ABCDEFGHIJK"
```

T   F   3. The command LEFT$(B$,5) would yield the string "ABCDE".

T   F   4. The command MID$(B$,5,2) would yield the string "DE".

T   F   5. The command INSTR(B$,"1") would yield the string "A".

T   F   6. The command LEN(B$) would yield the number 11.

7. The command ASC(B$) would yield the number 0 since there are no numbers in the beginning of the string.   **T F**

8. The command ASC(MID$(B$,7,1)) would yield the number 71.   **T F**

9. The command CHR$(B$) would yield the string "A".   **T F**

10. The command LEN(MID$(B$,5,2)) would yield the number 7.   **T F**

11. The CHR$ and STR$ functions are similar functions in that they both convert numbers to strings.   **T F**

12. The INKEY$ (or GET) function doesn't allow prompts.   **T F**

13. If we need to print quotes, we can do it by using the CHR$ function.   **T F**

14. If we want a string of 100 asterisks, we could create it by using the STR$ function.   **T F**

15. The INSTR function allows a search of a number for a specific numeric digit.   **T F**

16. To convert the number 13 to one printable character we would use which of the following commands?   _____

    a. CHR$ **c.** VAL
    b. ASC   **d.** none of them

17. If we used ASC("I") we would get which of the following?   _____

    a. 71   **c.** 65
    b. 73   **d.** none of them

18. If B$ = "ABCDEFG", which of the following commands could be used to get a substring of "CDEF"?   _____

    a. RIGHT$(B$,4)   **c.** MID$(B$,2,4)
    b. MID$(B$,INSTR(B$,"CDEF"),4)   **d.** LEFT$(B$,3,4)

19. If B$ = "ABCDEFG", which of the following commands could *not* be used to get a substring of "DEFG"?   _____

    a. RIGHT$(B$,5)   **c.** MID$(B$,4,10)
    b. MID$(B$,INSTR(B$,"D"),LEN(B$))   **d.** MID$(B$,4,4)

20. We used a null string to test to see if any characters had been entered into the INKEY$ (or GET). We could use a different command for the same function. Which of the following would work?   _____

    a. 10 IF A$ = " " THEN   **c.** 10 IF LEN(A$) = 0 THEN
    b. 10 IF VAL(A$) = 0 THEN   **d.** 10 IF ASC(A$) = 0 THEN

---

1. T (Except that strings cannot exceed 255 characters in length.)
2. F (Random numbers are useful for many business applications.)
3. T
4. F (It would yield "EF".)
5. F (The INSTR function will give a number as a result. Here, the number would be 0 since there is no "1" in B$.)
6. T
7. F (The ASC function translates the

ANSWERS TO QUICK QUIZ

string to its decimal equivalent code. The A, as the first character, would yield the value 65.)

8. T (The seventh character is "G", and the decimal code for G is 71.)
9. F (This command would give you a Syntax error.)
10. F (The LEN would be the 2 specified in the MID$ function.)
11. T (In the loosest sense. The type of conversion, however, is completely different.
12. F (It doesn't use a prompt, but a programmer can create and use one.)
13. T (The command would be CHR$(34) since 34 is the decimal code for quotes (").)
14. F (We would have to use the STRING$(100,"*") function. IBM and Radio Shack only.)

15. F (The INSTR searches strings only.)
16. d (None of the commands will translate 13 to a printable character since 13 is the decimal code for the RETURN key, which is a nonprintable character.)
17. b (The decimal code for I is 73.)
18. b (Though b would only be necessary when the construction of B$ is unknown. a will give "DEFG", c will give "BCDE", and d is not proper syntax.)
19. a (We would get five characters: "CDEFG".)
20. c (a would only branch should a blank be keyed. b would only work if no number key were pressed. d will yield an error because the ASC function will not work on a null string.)

8 SEQUENTIAL FILE HANDLING

OBJECTIVES

After completing Chapter 8, you will be able to:

- Explain why disk files are important.
- Explain the significance of the terms *field, record,* and *file.*
- Explain what a file extension is.
- Describe how a sequential file works.
- Define and explain the OPEN, PRINT, INPUT, and CLOSE statements for your machine.
- Demonstrate how sequential disk access is accomplished by writing several programs that use disk access.

8–1
INTRODUCTION

As I'm sure you have seen from our programming examples thus far, data is what a computer is all about. Getting the data into a program for manipulating is one of the most important functions of a programming language. But having to continually input the same information over and over again or having to store the information in DATA statements severely limits the flexibility of the computer system. What we need is some way to enter the information into a program and then store that information permanently (or at least semipermanently). We can do this by storing the information on some external device, such as a cassette or diskette.

Although it is true that information can be stored on cassette, we will not cover that concept in this book. Cassette storage is simply too slow and cumbersome for use in serious programming. In this book, we will cover only disk storage.

Thus far, our versions of BASIC have been very similar. There have been a few commands that one or two machines used that the others didn't, but by and large the major differences have been in the form of the error messages. This is not true when it comes to disk processing. Virtually every version of BASIC (not just the ones we are using) handles disk processing differently. This is not to say that the concepts are different. Absolutely not! The concepts of data storage are universal. It is merely the implementation of these concepts that varies from computer to computer. We will cover these basic ideas and branch into the differences when it becomes necessary.

Throughout the chapter, we will discuss how information is formatted for storing into files, how those files are created on the disk, and how to get the information into and out of those files.

8–2
STORAGE METHODOLOGY

We discussed in Chapter 1 that information is stored in the computer in a series of on–off switches called BInary digiTs or **bits.** Eight of these bits are put together into a single storage location called a **byte,** which is enough storage for one character. Since then, we have used variables of two different types: string and numeric. Well, in data storage, these variables can also be called **fields.** A field is merely a group of related characters. Some examples of fields are a name field, social-security-number field, and hours-worked field. Just as there are two types of variables, there are two types of fields, numeric and character.

Now, when we refer to information about an item, such as an inventory item, that information is not only a number, though items are usually referenced by number. The information about that inventory item is made up of an entire collection of different fields, such as the item number, item description, cost, date of purchase, selling price, and many other things that would be related to an inventory item. If we group all these related fields together, we have what is called a **record.** A record is simply a collection of related fields.

We keep saying *related.* Why is that important? Well, it would do no good, when trying to keep track of inventory, to have the number of one inventory item, the description of a second item, and the cost of a third item all stored together. We should have a record made up of information about a particular item, information that is related to that item.

Generally, reference is made to a particular inventory item record that is stored on disk. But when such a record is stored, it is not usually stored by itself; it is stored with many other records to make up the inventory of the entire store or plant. Such a collection of records is called a **file.** A file is simply a collection of related records.

There are many different file types that may be found in a typical business installation. There are general ledger files that contain information about how money has been allocated in the business, accounts payable files that have information about whom the company owes money to, accounts receivable files that contain records about who owes the company money, and inventory files that contain records about what is currently in the warehouse.

Let's look for a moment at how such an inventory file might be set up. To set up a file, we first must decide what information we need to have in our file. Information important to processing inventory records would probably include the following:

1. Inventory item number
2. Item name
3. Item description
4. Quantity-on-hand
5. Cost at last purchase
6. Sales price per item
7. Date of last purchase of item

The next thing we have to decide is what type of information each of these fields is going to contain. Recall that they can contain either numeric or character information. Some of them are obvious choices: the quantity-on-hand, cost, and sales price should be numeric, while the item name and item description should be character. But what about the item number? Should it be numeric? Reflect back to the previous chapter. We had a programming exercise that used inventory item numbers. They were not just numeric since they also contained dashes and letters. One of them was 123-RE-BG45/15. Of course, these item numbers were designed merely for the exercise, but they reflect the variety of information that the typical inventory item number contains. Admittedly, some inventories are kept strictly by part number, i.e., 1 through the total number of items. In such cases, the item number could indeed be numeric. More often, however, the item numbers contain more than just numeric digits and would have to be stored as characters.

What about the other field that we have not yet decided about, the date? Normally, a date is given in the form 12/15/85, but we don't need to store the slashes since we can put them in the date when it prints out. That leaves us with six characters. Should they, then, be stored in a numeric or character field? Since dates are generally not used in calculations, there is no mathematical reason for the date to be numeric. Therefore, since strings are easier to manipulate (to put in the slashes), we would leave the date as a string.

8–3
FILE NAMES

Just as we have variable names to keep track of stored information, we have file names to keep track of where our information is stored on the disk. Our versions of BASIC vary a little in the way they use file names, but they all follow the same basic rules. Generally, a file name can be any mixture of letters and numeric digits as long as it begins with a letter. The file names can be up to eight characters long, except on the Apple where they can be up to thirty characters long. Some examples of file names are "SAMPLE", "GLAR5", and "PAYROLL".

File extensions can be used in the IBM and Radio Shack versions. A file extension is a method of marking the file with the type of information that is stored in it. Since no extensions are necessary for storing data files, we will not use them, but let's discuss them briefly.

In the IBM, the extension is placed after a period following the file name. For example, SAMPLE.BAS would be a BASIC program named SAMPLE; the extension BAS stands for BASIC. There is a long list of extensions used on the IBM, but the only ones that we will be concerned with are the .BAS and possibly the .DAT for data files. The extensions are a maximum of three characters long.

The Radio Shack also uses extensions that are a maximum of three characters long, but they follow a slash instead of a period. A file name of SAMPLE/CMD would be a system file as indicated by the CMD extension. The only ones you will probably ever see when using the Radio Shack are the CMD, BAS for BASIC programs, and DAT for data files. Again, we will not use extensions since they are not necessary.

There are no extensions in Applesoft BASIC.

8–4
HOW TO USE A FILE

Whenever you intend to use a file on disk, there are always three things that you must do. First, you must open the file. In all our versions, if you open a file for outputting and the file is not there, the machine will create a new file for you.

Second, you must put some records into the file. There are basically two ways to do this, with **sequential access** or **random access,** which is also called **direct access.** A sequential file (the type we are going to use in this chapter) is a file wherein information is stored one field after another and must be retrieved the same way. For example, suppose we have three records to store and each of these records has five fields. With sequential processing, we write the five fields of the first record on the disk and then the five fields of each of the other records following the first record. To retrieve the third record, we must read the first two records first. There is no way to get to the third record without reading the other two records first. When records are processed randomly, any records that are stored can be accessed individually. That is, if we store the three records as before, we can access record three without having to bother with the other two records.

Third, you must close the file after you are finished inputting or outputting the records. This is necessary so that the system will not continue to put information into the file.

Each of our machines uses a different open command, so we will discuss each of them separately. You should definitely read the section for your machine, but it would be instructive to read the others also.

The form of the file **OPEN** statement in IBM BASIC is:

```
10 OPEN "file name" FOR mode AS #file number
```

The words FOR and AS are part of the command and must always be specified exactly as shown.

The file name on the OPEN command simply refers to the name you have given (or are going to give) the file and must be enclosed in quotes.

The mode is the code that specifies the type of file processing that we are going to do. The possible modes are:

INPUT is for input files; that is, information coming into the program from the disk.

OUTPUT is for output files; that is, information being stored on the disk from the program.

APPEND is for appending to the end of files. After a file has been created with records in it, if you open that file as output, it will start writing the new records at the beginning of the file again. If you want instead to put the new records at the end of the records already in the file, then you must use this APPEND option. With it, all new entries into the file are put on the end of the file.

The file number specified on the command requires a number between 1 and 3 in normal usage. If you use any number beyond 3, you will get an error. It is possible to use higher numbers, but it requires special handling of the machine that is beyond the scope of this text. Normally, the file number is 1, but if you have two or three files open in your program at the same time, the number can be 1, 2, or 3.

A sample OPEN command might look like the following:

```
10 OPEN "SAMPLE" FOR OUTPUT AS #1
```

This tells the machine to open the file SAMPLE for output and give it the file number 1. Then every time we reference file number 1, it will refer to the file SAMPLE.

The form of the file **OPEN** statement in Radio Shack BASIC is:

```
10 OPEN "code",file number,"file name"
```

The code specifies the type of file processing that we are going to do. The possible codes, which must be enclosed in quotes, are:

I is for input files; that is, information coming into the program from the disk.

O is for output files; that is, information being stored on the disk from the program.

E is for **extending** the files. After a file has been created with records in it, if you open that file as output, it will start writing the new records at the beginning of the file again. If you want instead to put the new records at the end of the records already in the file, then you must use this extend option. With it, all new entries into the file are put on the end of the file.

The file number specified on the command requires a number between 1 and 3 in normal usage. If you use any number beyond 3, you will get an error. It is possible to use higher numbers, but it requires special handling of the machine that is beyond the scope of this text. Normally, the file number is 1, but if you have two or three files open in your program at the same time, the number can be 1, 2, or 3.

The file name on the OPEN command simply refers to the name you have given (or are going to give) the file; it must be enclosed in quotes.

A sample OPEN command might look like the following:

```
10 OPEN "O",1,"SAMPLE"
```

This tells the machine to open the file SAMPLE for output and give it the file number 1. Then every time we reference file number 1, it will refer to the file SAMPLE.

APPLE   Because of the construction of the Apple computer, all output to peripheral devices is done using the **PRINT** statement. Because of this, we have to have some way of signaling to the machine that we are communicating with a device other than the CRT screen. This is done by using a **control-D** on the keyboard (by holding down the Control key and then pressing the D key). But because we will be doing much device switching in our programs, we don't want to have to stop the program each time to press the control-D. Instead, we will use a code that, to the machine, is the same as the control-D. That code is the **CHR$(4).** We could use this code in all our print statements, but it is easier to assign it to a string variable and then use that variable in our print statements. We usually do it as:

```
10 D$=CHR$(4)
```

If you are using the CHR$(4) to switch between devices, never use a semicolon on the end of the previous print statement. The computer will only recognize the CHR$(4) as control-D when it immediately follows a carriage return.

In the following discussions involving the commands necessary for disk access using the Apple, we will assume that D$ contains CHR$(4).

The form of the file **OPEN** statement in Apple BASIC is:

```
10 PRINT D$;"OPEN file name"
```

The file name on the OPEN statement simply refers to the name you have given (or are going to give) the file; it must be enclosed within quotes.

A sample OPEN statement might look like the following:

```
10 PRINT D$;"OPEN SAMPLE"
```

This tells the machine to open the file SAMPLE. If we are opening for outputting a file that already exists, when we start writing into it, the storage will be done at the beginning of the file. This is a problem because the Apple puts no marker at the end of the file. New data will simply overlay old data, and there will be no way to tell when you have reached the end of the valid data when reading it back in. To solve this problem, we need to **DELETE** the old file before we use it. If we try to delete a file that does not exist, however, we will get an error. So the best thing to do is open the file, delete it, and then reopen it. Now, it may seem a bit silly to open a file we intend to delete, but if we don't open the file to create it, we will get an error if we try to delete the file and it is not found. The form of the DELETE command is:

```
10 PRINT D$;"DELETE file name"
```

The best way to delete and reuse a file is to use three statements, as in this sample:

```
10 PRINT D$;"OPEN SAMPLE"
20 PRINT D$;"DELETE SAMPLE"
30 PRINT D$;"OPEN SAMPLE"
```

Using the DELETE command will remove the old file, but suppose we want to write new data onto the end of a file that already has data in it. In that case, instead of opening the file, we **APPEND** to the file. The form of the command is the same as the OPEN except that the word APPEND replaces OPEN. For example, an APPEND statement similar to the OPEN statement we used before would look like the following:

```
10 PRINT D$;"APPEND SAMPLE"
```

The PRINT# Command

To put information into the disk file once it is opened for output, we need to use a **PRINT#** command. The form of the command is simply:

```
10 PRINT#file number,field
```

And a sample of the command would be:

```
10 PRINT#1,A,B,C
```

In this case we are using file number 1, and we are putting into the file three numeric fields, A, B, and C.

This form is used on the IBM and Radio Shack. The Apple requires the use of the PRINT D$ and two steps. First, we must issue a **WRITE** command and then PRINT into the file. The WRITE command has the form:

```
10 PRINT D$;"WRITE file name"
```

And using the file name we used in the OPEN statement (it must be the same), our sample statement would look like:

```
10 PRINT D$;"WRITE SAMPLE"
```

Once a write command has been issued, all subsequent PRINT statements will print into the file instead of onto the screen. For example,

```
20 PRINT A,B,C
```

will print the three numerics into the file.

Although the PRINT command will put three fields onto the disk in all our versions of BASIC, because of the way the output is structured, when we read the fields back in, we will get only one field. One way around this problem is to write the fields independently on separate PRINT statements. Thus, our PRINT statement (for the IBM and Radio Shack) should really be broken up into three:

```
10 PRINT#1,A
20 PRINT#1,B
30 PRINT#1,C
```

And the Apple output would look like:

```
20 PRINT A
30 PRINT B
40 PRINT C
```

This will ensure that when we read the fields back in, we will indeed get three fields.

There is another way to do this same thing. We can write the fields into the file on one statement with a comma between them; not the comma that we used before on the statement, that is a delimiter. We need to cause a comma to actually be written into the file by enclosing the comma in quotes. An example of this for the IBM and Radio Shack statements would be:

```
10 PRINT#1,A,",",B,",",C
```

And for the Apple the statement would be:

```
10 PRINT A,",",B,",",C
```

Notice that the comma is enclosed in quotes between each of the variables. This functions the same as putting the fields on separate PRINT statements. Generally, however, we will write our programs with separate statements to help clarify the processing.

On the Apple, when we have finished writing into the file and want the next PRINT statement to go to the screen, we have to issue a control-D to switch devices. The command would be a simple

```
50 PRINT D$
```

All the PRINT statements from then on would go to the screen. If we are then ready to write into the disk again, we would have to reissue the write command.

The INPUT#
Command

Once the fields are stored on the disk, we need to be able to get them back for use in our program. This is done with the **INPUT#** command. The form of this statement is:

```
10 INPUT#file number,field,field,field,...
```

And a sample of the command would be:

```
10 INPUT#1,A,B$,C
```

Again, this is for the IBM and Radio Shack. The Apple requires two statements. Just as we have to use a WRITE statement to put data into a disk file, we have to issue a **READ** command to tell the machine we want to read information in. The form of the statement is:

```
10 PRINT D$;"READ file name"
```

And a sample would look like:

```
10 PRINT D$;"READ SAMPLE"
```

This simply tells the machine that we want to get the information from the disk. To get that information we use an INPUT statement, such as:

```
20 INPUT A,B,C
```

These INPUT statements allow the retrieval from the file of A, B, and C. Although putting more than one field on a PRINT command without quoted commas can cause problems, no such problems are encountered by having more than one field on an INPUT command.

On the Apple, just as with the write command, when we are finished inputting information and want to set the INPUT command back to the normal user INPUT type, we have to issue a control-D:

```
30 PRINT D$
```

End-of-File Check

The input command has a bit of a problem. Most of the time we will not know exactly how many records are stored in our files. How, then, will the program know when to stop inputting? It is logical to assume that if we input more records than are in the file we will get an error, and indeed we will. We will now examine a way to avoid this on each of our machines by using an **end-of-file check.**

IBM and Radio Shack

On the IBM and Radio Shack, we can test for the end of the data on the disk by using the **EOF** command. The form of the command is:

```
EOF(file number)
```

where the file number is the number of the file you are reading the information from. The EOF command is usually used in an IF-THEN statement, such as:

```
100 IF NOT EOF(1) THEN 30
```

whereby it checks the next byte in the file to see if it is the special end-of-file marker that the machine puts there automatically when the file is closed after creation. If statement 100 does not find the code, then it will branch back to 30, presumably to continue the input loop. Notice that we found a use for the NOT boolean operator.

APPLE

On the Apple, we need to use a special routine to test for the end of the file. Actually, this routine will check for an error, but since reading past the end of the file is an error, it will work. The routine is the **ONERR GOTO,** and it has the form:

```
100 ONERR GOTO line number
```

This statement may be put anywhere in the program *before* you begin reading the file. Any kind of error in the program will be captured by this statement (including syntax errors). When an error is encountered, the program will branch to the line specified on the GOTO. Since this line will capture any error, we will need to be sure it has found the end of the file and not some other type of error. To do this we need to use another statement, the **PEEK** statement. This statement allows you to look at what is stored in a particular byte in memory. Whenever an error occurs, the type of error is given a number and that number is stored at a particular location in memory. That location is 222, and the command to examine it is:

```
1000 E=PEEK(222)
```

As we mentioned, this type of routine will pick up any error. The particular error number of the end of file is 5 (see Appendix D). Therefore, if E is 5, the end of file was reached. Any other code would indicate some other type of error.

The CLOSE Command

After we have finished accessing the file, we need to close it. This is done with the **CLOSE** command, which has (on the IBM and Radio Shack) the form:

```
10 CLOSE #file number
```

or:

```
10 CLOSE
```

The first statement will cause only the file specified by the number to be closed, while the second statement will cause all open files to be closed. It is suggested that, for most uses, the first statement be used since it specifies exactly which files you are using in your program and when they should be closed.

Open files are automatically closed on using certain other commands in IBM and Radio Shack BASIC. For example, if you BREAK out of the program and modify it by adding, deleting, or changing a line, the files are closed. Also, loading in a different program will close the files, as will rerunning the same program. Despite this, you should never depend on the computer to close your files for you. It is important for you to always close your files with the program command; sometimes, if the file is not closed with a program command, information can be lost. There is a temporary storage location in the computer called a *buffer,* and the information to be stored on the disk is dumped into the buffer before it is put into the file. If you don't close your file, the information left in the buffer will not be dumped into the file and will be lost.

As you might expect, the Apple files are closed with a PRINT statement, such as:

```
10 PRINT D$;"CLOSE file name"
```

or:

```
10 PRINT D$;"CLOSE"
```

As with the IBM and Radio Shack commands, the first statement above closes only the named file, while the second will close all files that are open. It is again suggested that you use the first type of statement since it lends itself to closer care of the processing in your program.

On the Apple, files are not automatically closed; if you do not close one, some information may be lost. You may also run into an error in another program that is using files if you leave some open. The Apple will only use a limited number of files (3 on default), and if you leave one or two open, it may limit file usage in subsequent programs.

We will now experiment with our new information for a moment. We will write a program to create a file, store a couple of fields, and then read them back. As always, our sample program is for the IBM; changes (if necessary) for the other machines will be listed at the end of the program.

We have to start the program with an OPEN statement, such as:

A Simple Example

```
NEW
10 REM ***** PROGRAM NAME: DISKSAMP
20 REM
30 REM ***** SAMPLE DISK PROGRAM
40 REM
50 OPEN "SAMPLE" FOR OUTPUT AS #1
```

)))DIFFERENCES

The Radio Shack OPEN statement should be:

```
50 OPEN "O",1,"SAMPLE"
```

The Apple OPEN statement will also require the assignment of D$:

```
50 D$=CHR$(4)
55 PRINT D$;"OPEN SAMPLE"
```

This will open the file for output, using file number 1 for the file named SAMPLE on the IBM and Radio Shack; only the file name SAMPLE is needed for the Apple. Recall that if the file is not on the disk, it will be created by the open statement automatically. Before you execute this program (or any program with disk access), you should check the disk using the directory command (IBM uses FILES, or FILES "A:" or "B:"; the Radio Shack uses CMD"D:O" or :1"; and the Apple uses CATALOG or CATALOG,D1 or ,D2) to be sure there isn't already a file out there with the name you have chosen.

Now we are ready to put some information into our file SAMPLE. Let's add a few lines to our program:

```
60 B$="HI."
70 B=35
80 PRINT#1,B$
90 PRINT#1,B
100 PRINT#1,"ED COBURN"
```

)))DIFFERENCES

On the Apple, we need to add line 75 and change lines 80 through 100:

```
75 PRINT D$;"WRITE SAMPLE"
```

```
80 PRINT B$
```

```
90 PRINT B
```

```
100 PRINT "ED COBURN"
```

This will write all the indicated information on the disk. Notice that we used three different PRINT# (or PRINT) statements to avoid running the information together and causing us to retrieve only one field. Recall that we could also use one statement by putting quoted commas between each field.

After we print the information into the file, we need to close the file so we can input the information back into the program.

For the IBM and Radio Shack this would be:

```
110 CLOSE #1
```

For the Apple we would use:

```
110 PRINT D$;"CLOSE SAMPLE"
```

We didn't have to use the file number (or file name); it is not necessary if we are only using one file. But as we mentioned earlier, it is good practice to be explicit in our programming. We therefore used the explicit CLOSE statement.

We are now ready to input the information back from the file. We must first open the file for input. We could use file number 1 again for the IBM and Radio Shack, but just for practice let's use 2. Remember, the file *name* tells the machine which file is being accessed. The file *number* is used in the commands. Since we are accessing SAMPLE, we may use any file number.

```
120 REM
130 REM ***** GET THE INFORMATION FROM THE FILE
140 REM
150 OPEN "SAMPLE" FOR INPUT AS #2
```

)))DIFFERENCES

On the Radio Shack, line 150 needs to be:

```
150 OPEN "I",2,"SAMPLE"
```

On the Apple, line 150 needs to be:

```
150 PRINT D$;"OPEN SAMPLE"
```

Now we can use our INPUT# (or INPUT) statements to input the information. We will use different variables when we input just to be sure we are not printing the information already assigned to our variables. Remember, as long as we don't reassign values to our variables, they will still have the same values originally assigned. By using new variables, we will be sure that we are actually retrieving the data from the disk.

The IBM and Radio Shack statement will be:

```
160 INPUT#2,C$,C,C1$
```

Notice that we used file number 2 on the INPUT# statement. This was necessary because that is the file number we opened.

The Apple requires the READ statement also:

```
160 PRINT D$;"READ SAMPLE"
165 INPUT C$,C,C1$
```

Finally, let's print our information on the screen to verify that we indeed did retrieve it from the file:

```
170 PRINT C$;" MY NAME IS ";C1$;" AND I AM";C
180 CLOSE #2
190 END
```

On the Apple, before we PRINT, we first need to print control-D to switch devices, which means we need to add line 168:

```
168 PRINT D$
```

Also, line 180 needs to be changed to:

```
180 PRINT D$;"CLOSE SAMPLE"
```

Now that we have constructed the program, let's take a look at the whole thing for the IBM and Radio Shack:

```
LIST
10 REM ***** PROGRAM NAME: DISKSAMP
20 REM
30 REM ***** SAMPLE DISK PROGRAM
40 REM
50 OPEN "SAMPLE" FOR OUTPUT AS #1
60 B$="HI."
70 B=35
```

Program 8–1

Program continues

```
80 PRINT#1,B$
90 PRINT#1,B
100 PRINT#1,"ED COBURN"
110 CLOSE #1
120 REM
130 REM ***** GET THE INFORMATION FROM THE FILE
140 REM
150 OPEN "I",2,"SAMPLE"
160 INPUT#2,C$,C,C1$
170 PRINT C$;" MY NAME IS ";C1$;" AND I AM";C
180 CLOSE #2
190 END
```
Program 8–1 (cont.)

)))DIFFERENCES

The only difference for the Radio Shack was the OPEN statement:

```
50 OPEN "O",1,"SAMPLE"
```

The entire Apple program should look like:

```
LIST
10 REM ***** PROGRAM NAME: DISKSAMP
20 REM
30 REM ***** SAMPLE DISK PROGRAM
40 REM
50 D$=CHR$(4)
55 PRINT D$;"OPEN SAMPLE"
60 B$="HI."
70 B=35
75 PRINT D$;"WRITE SAMPLE"
80 PRINT B$
90 PRINT B
100 PRINT "ED COBURN"
110 PRINT D$;"CLOSE SAMPLE"
120 REM
130 REM ***** GET THE INFORMATION FROM THE FILE
140 REM
150 PRINT D$;"OPEN SAMPLE"
160 PRINT D$;"READ SAMPLE"
165 INPUT C$,C,C1$
168 PRINT D$
170 PRINT C$;" MY NAME IS ";C1$;" AND I AM";C
180 PRINT D$;"CLOSE SAMPLE"
190 END
```
Program 8–2 (Apple)

Very nice. Let's run it and see what we get.

```
RUN
HI. MY NAME IS ED COBURN AND I AM 35
Ok
```

Did you notice the small red disk access light light up as the information was written to and read back from the disk? The whole process took only a few seconds.

Of course, we have only scratched the surface of what can be accomplished with disk access. We will now write two programs that will be a bit more extensive. We will write one program to create a file in which we will store mailing labels by inputting them from the keyboard. We will then write a second program that will read them from the disk and print them out. The pseudocode necessary for the first program is:

```
Start
Open the file for output.
Input the name.
DO-WHILE name is not "END".
   Print the name in the file.
   Input the address, city, state, and zip code.
   Print them to the file.
   Input the name.
END-DO
Close the file.
End
```

Figure 8–1 shows the flowchart for this program. Notice that the file open statement is drawn with a process symbol, while the PRINT is shown, of course, with an I/O symbol.

The second program needs to read the information back from the disk and print it out in mailing label form. Since we will not know how many records were put in the file, we will have to test for the end of the file (or use error trapping). The pseudocode for this second program should look like:

```
Start
Open the file for input.
DO-WHILE not EOF.
   Input name, address, city, state, and zip.
   Print the information as a label.
END-DO
Close the file.
End
```

The flowchart for this program can be seen in Figure 8–2.

We are now ready to write the programs. The first program should look something like the following:

```
NEW
10 REM ***** PROGRAM NAME: MAILLIST
20 REM
30 REM ***** MAILING LIST STORAGE PROGRAM
40 REM
50 REM ***** WRITTEN BY EDWARD J. COBURN
60 REM
```

Program 8–3

Program continues on page 229

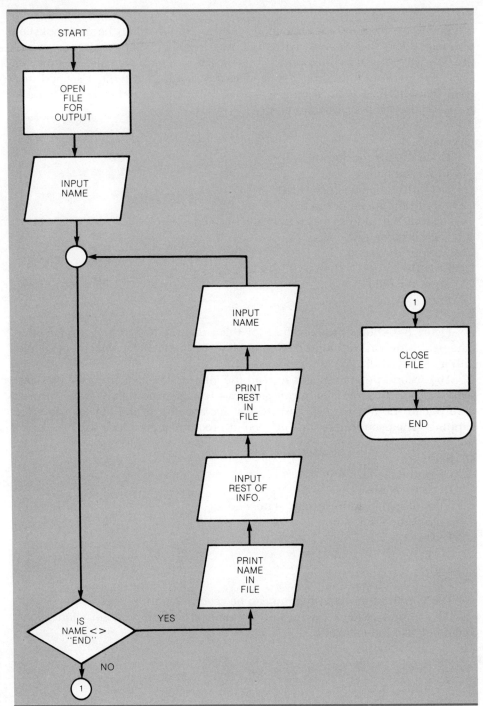

Figure 8–1
Flowchart of program to store mailing labels.

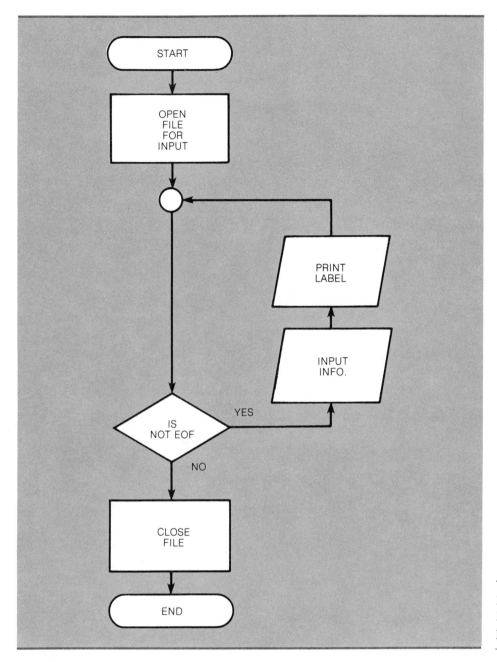

Figure 8–2
Flowchart of program to
print mailing labels.

```
70 REM THIS PROGRAM STORES MAILING LABELS
80 REM
90 OPEN "MAILFILE" FOR OUTPUT AS #1  ' OPEN THE FILE
100 INPUT "WHAT IS THE NAME";N$
110 IF N$="END" THEN 250      ' END-OF-DATA MARKER
120    INPUT "WHAT IS THE ADDRESS";A$
130    INPUT "WHAT IS THE CITY";C$          Program 8–3 (cont.)
```

Program continues on page 230

```
140     INPUT "WHAT IS THE STATE (USE CODE XX)";S$
150     INPUT "WHAT IS THE ZIP CODE";Z$
160     PRINT#1,N$                ' PUT THE NAME IN FILE
170     PRINT#1,A$
180     PRINT#1,C$
190     PRINT#1,S$
200     PRINT#1,Z$
210     GOTO 100                  ' RETURN FOR MORE INPUT
220 REM
230 REM ***** END OF THE PROGRAM
240 REM
250 CLOSE #1                      ' CLOSE THE FILE
260 END
```
Program 8-3 (cont.)

)))DIFFERENCES

On the Radio Shack we need to add the CLEAR statement to set aside more room for our string data:

```
85 CLEAR 5000
```

And line 90 needs to be changed to:

```
90 OPEN "O",1,"MAILFILE"        ' OPEN THE FILE
```

On the Apple, we need line 85:

```
85 D$=CHR$(4)
```

And then line 90, the OPEN statement, needs to be:

```
90 PRINT D$;"OPEN MAILFILE"    : REM OPEN THE FILE
```

All the INPUT statements are slightly different (as always); for example, line **100** should be:

```
100 INPUT "WHAT IS THE NAME? ";N$
```

The PRINT# statements should all be PRINT statements, and line 155 is needed:

```
155 PRINT D$;"WRITE MAILFILE"
160 PRINT N$                        : REM PUT THE NAME IN THE FILE
170 PRINT A$
180 PRINT C$
190 PRINT S$
200 PRINT Z$
```

Line 205 is also needed:

```
205 PRINT D$    : REM SET TO PRINT TO SCREEN
```

And finally, line 250 needs to be:

```
250 PRINT D$;"CLOSE MAILFILE"
```

A few things are worth noting about the program. First, the name of the file in which we are going to store our labels is "MAILFILE". This is important because we will have to use that same name to get the records back in the second program. Also, notice that we again store all the fields in the file on separate PRINT# (PRINT) statements.

Let's go ahead and run the program and store some labels:

```
RUN
WHAT IS THE NAME? ED COBURN
WHAT IS THE ADDRESS? 1400 SOUTH STREET
WHAT IS THE CITY? EL PASO
WHAT IS THE STATE (USE CODE XX)? TX
WHAT IS THE ZIP CODE? 76708
WHAT IS THE NAME? TOM SMITH
WHAT IS THE ADDRESS? 415 SOUTH STREET
WHAT IS THE CITY? CINCINNATI
WHAT IS THE STATE (USE CODE XX)? OH
WHAT IS THE ZIP CODE? 98709
WHAT IS THE NAME? AMY JOHNSON
WHAT IS THE ADDRESS? 458 WEST WESTWOOD
WHAT IS THE CITY? NASHVILLE
WHAT IS THE STATE (USE CODE XX)? TN
WHAT IS THE ZIP CODE? 64578
WHAT IS THE NAME? HARROLD ROBBINS
WHAT IS THE ADDRESS? 896 TERRANCE SQUARE
WHAT IS THE CITY? NEW YORK
WHAT IS THE STATE (USE CODE XX)? NY
WHAT IS THE.ZIP CODE? 10056
WHAT IS THE NAME? END
Ok
```

Now we are ready to store the program on the disk so we can enter the next program. Recall that to store the program on the IBM and Radio Shack requires a command such as:

```
SAVE "MAILLIST"
```

On the Apple the command is:

```
SAVE MAILLIST
```

Before we leave this program, we need to look at one more thing. Recall that when we were discussing the OPEN statement, we mentioned another way to open the file for output other than OUTPUT for the IBM, "O" for the Radio Shack, and OPEN for the Apple: APPEND. If we were to execute this program again, we would write right on top of the addresses we had already entered. If we need to put more addresses into the file, we need to use the other open option: APPEND for the IBM and Apple and "E" for extend on the Radio Shack. The only thing we would have to do to the program to allow it to add to the file is to change the open statement. No other changes would be needed.

The second program to read the records back from the file should look something like the following:

```
NEW
10 REM ***** PROGRAM NAME: MAILPRT
20 REM
30 REM ***** PROGRAM TO PRINT THE MAILING LABELS
40 REM
50 REM ***** WRITTEN BY EDWARD J. COBURN
60 REM
70 REM THIS PROGRAM PRINTS THE MAILING LABELS
80 REM THAT WERE STORED BY THE MAILLIST PROGRAM
```

Program 8–4

Program continues

```
90 REM
100 OPEN "MAILFILE" FOR INPUT AS #1
110 IF EOF(1) THEN 210          ' CHECK FOR END OF FILE
120    INPUT#1,N$,A$,C$,S$,Z$
130    PRINT N$
140    PRINT A$
150    PRINT C$;", ";S$;"   ";Z$
160    PRINT
170    GOTO 110
180 REM
190 REM ***** END OF THE PROGRAM
200 REM
210 CLOSE #1                    ' CLOSE THE FILE
220 END
```
Program 8–4 (cont.)

)))DIFFERENCES

The Radio Shack needs line 95:

```
95 CLEAR 5000
```

And the OPEN statement needs to be:

```
100 OPEN "I",1,"MAILFILE"
```

On the Apple, line 95 needs to be added:

```
95 D$=CHR$(4)
```

To check for the end of file we need to insert the ONERR statement before the OPEN statement and change the OPEN statement:

```
98 ONERR GOTO 210
100 PRINT D$;"OPEN MAILFILE"
```

Before the changed INPUT statement we need the READ statement:

```
110 PRINT D$;"READ MAILFILE"
120 INPUT N$,A$,C$,S$,Z$
```

Then we need to add line 125:

```
125 PRINT D$                   : REM SWITCH TO SCREEN
```

And finally, the end-of-file routine needs to be expanded:

```
210 E=PEEK(222)                : REM CHECK THE ERROR BYTE
214 IF E<>5 THEN PRINT "UNKNOWN ERROR CODE = ";E;"  TERMINATING."
216 PRINT D$;"CLOSE MAILFILE" : REM CLOSE THE FILE
220 END
```

Notice that we input the labels from the MAILFILE. Also note that we input all the fields on the same INPUT# (INPUT) statement.

Let's execute this program to see how well it works:

```
RUN
ED COBURN
```

Program continues

```
1400 SOUTH STREET
EL PASO, TX  76708

TOM SMITH
415 SOUTH STREET
CINCINNATI, OH  98705

AMY JOHNSON
458 WEST WESTWOOD
NASHVILLE, TN  64578

HARROLD ROBBINS
896 TERRANCE SQUARE
NEW YORK, NY  10056
Ok
```

8—6
PROGRAM REWRITE

Now that we have written the programs, it is time to experiment a little with all the things we have learned. Look back at the MAILLIST program for a minute. Notice that there are five input statements that have virtually the same format. That is, they all start with "WHAT IS THE". The difference comes in what is being asked for. If we used a variable for the rest of the prompt, we could use a subroutine for the input routine. Suppose we have P$ assigned as the prompt. Then we could use a routine such as the following:

```
1000 REM
1010 REM ***** INPUT SUBROUTINE
1020 REM
1030 PRINT "WHAT IS THE ";P$;
1040 INPUT A$
1050 RETURN
```

Notice that there is no prompt on the input statement. Since we want a variable prompt, we can't put it on the input statement itself. Now, if we put the name of each of the things we want to ask for in P$, we can use the routine.

Look again at the original program. Notice that the PRINT statements used are virtually identical. Why can't we put them in the subroutine also? All we have to do is add one statement to the subroutine, such as:

```
1050 PRINT#1,A$
1060 RETURN
```

for the IBM and Radio Shack. *Or:*

```
1050 PRINT A$
1060 RETURN
```

for the Apple.

Now the routine will input the information and dump it to the file. The only problem with the way we have developed this routine is that it will automatically dump the information into the file, but there is one time when we don't want that to happen. On the input of the name, we need to check for the end-of-data marker. We can also put that in the routine by renumbering a bit:

```
1050 IF A$="END" THEN 1070
1060 PRINT#1,A$
1070 RETURN
```

for the IBM and Radio Shack. For the Apple, line 1060 will be:

```
1060 PRINT A$
```

We still have a problem. If someone were to enter "END" in response to any prompt except the name, we would get only a partial record stored. What we have to do is have the program check for the "END" only when it is processing the name. But how can we tell the program to do it that way? What is true when we are processing the name? That's right, P$ should contain "NAME". We can check for that by changing line 1050 to:

```
1050 IF A$="END" AND P$="NAME" THEN 1070
```

Let's look at our routine now:

```
LIST
1000 REM
1010 REM ***** INPUT SUBROUTINE
1020 REM
1030 PRINT "WHAT IS THE ";P$;
1040 INPUT A$
1050 IF A$="END" AND P$="NAME" THEN 1070
1060 PRINT#1,A$
1070 RETURN
```

)))DIFFERENCES

Line 1060 is different for the Apple:

```
1060 PRINT A$
```

Now we need to change the program to be able to use this routine. In place of the inputs, we need an assignment of P$ and then a GOSUB. For example, the input for the name should be changed from:

```
100 INPUT "WHAT IS THE NAME";N$
```

to:

```
100 P$="NAME"
105 GOSUB 1030
```

Then the end-of-data check on the next line needs to have the variable name changed from N$ to A$:

```
110 IF A$="END" THEN 250
```

We could now change the rest of the program the same way as we changed the first input. But let's do one more thing. Recall a few chapters ago that we used the READ statements. Since the assignments and GOSUBs are virtually the same, we can change the program to use a READ and thus have a much smaller program. The final program should appear as:

```
10 REM ***** PROGRAM NAME: MAILLIST
20 REM
```

Program 8–5

Program continues

```
30 REM ***** MAILING LIST STORAGE PROGRAM
40 REM
50 REM ***** WRITTEN BY EDWARD J. COBURN
60 REM
70 REM THIS PROGRAM STORES MAILING LABELS
80 REM
90 OPEN "MAILFILE" FOR OUTPUT AS #1 ' OPEN THE FILE
100 READ P$
110 GOSUB 1030
120 IF A$="END" THEN 250
130 IF P$="ZIP CODE" THEN RESTORE
140 GOTO 100
220 REM
230 REM ***** END OF THE PROGRAM
240 REM
250 CLOSE #1                     ' CLOSE THE FILE
260 END
1000 REM
1010 REM ***** INPUT SUBROUTINE
1020 REM
1030 PRINT "WHAT IS THE ";P$; ' P$ IS THE TYPE
1040 INPUT A$
1050 IF A$="END" AND P$="NAME" THEN 1070
1060 PRINT#1,A$                  ' DUMP THEM IN THE FILE
1070 RETURN
2000 DATA NAME,ADDRESS,CITY,STATE (USE CODE XX),ZIP CODE
```
Program 8–5 (cont.)

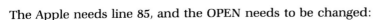

)))DIFFERENCES

The Radio Shack needs the CLEAR statement and a different OPEN statement:

```
85 CLEAR 5000
90 OPEN "O",1,"MAILFILE"        ' OPEN THE FILE
```

The Apple needs line 85, and the OPEN needs to be changed:

```
85 D$=CHR$(4)
90 PRINT D$;"OPEN MAILFILE"
```

The CLOSE statement also needs to be changed:

```
250 PRINT D$;"CLOSE MAILFILE"
```

Finally, lines 1055 and 1065 need to be added to write to the disk, and line 1060 needs to be changed:

```
1055 PRINT D$;"WRITE MAILFILE"
1060 PRINT A$                : REM DUMP THEM IN THE FILE
1065 PRINT D$                : REM SWITCH BACK TO SCREEN
```

Notice that we had to check for the "END" (line 120) when we came back from the subroutine as well as in the subroutine. Also notice that we had to check which input we were doing (line 130) since once we ran out of DATA we needed to RESTORE.

This example shows how a program can be made dramatically cleaner and neater looking simply by using some of the concepts that we have been covering.

SUMMARY

1. Many times when we are writing programs we have need for large amounts of data. Though we can use DATA statements or input all the information, it is slow and cumbersome to do so with large amounts of data. In such cases, storage on diskette becomes invaluable.

2. A single on–off storage switch is called a bit. Eight bits form a byte, which is storage enough for a character. A collection of characters is called a field. Variables are actually just fields. Whenever we refer to something, such as an inventory item, many fields are necessary to describe that item. These fields together form a record and when we store a group of these records on disk, they are stored in a file.

3. Though the Apple allows file names up to thirty characters, our other versions allow names only up to eight characters. The file name must begin with a letter; there are only a few file names that are not permitted (i.e., keywords). File extensions in IBM and Radio Shack BASIC are handy to mark file types.

4. To use a sequential file, three steps are necessary: (1) the file must be opened; (2) records must be written into or read from the file; and (3) the file must be closed.

5. All our versions operate basically the same way throughout these three operations, but their command structures are slightly different.

6. There are two ways that information may be written into a sequential file; the choice is guided by the way the file is opened. If it is opened for new writing to replace the old then the file writing begins at the beginning of the file. On the other hand, if the file is being appended to (extended in Radio Shack BASIC), the new information is added to the end of the old information already in the file.

GLOSSARY

APPEND The command to cause information stored in a file to be put at the end of existing data. (On the Radio Shack the command is E for Extend, not APPEND.)

Bit An acronym for BInary digiT, a bit is a single on–off switch used to store information in the computer.

Byte A group of eight bits, a byte is enough to store one character.

CHR$(4) *See* **Control-D.**

CLOSE The command necessary to end access to a data file when processing is concluded.

Control-D The code necessary on the Apple to switch the print output command from the screen to another device, or back to the screen from the device.

DELETE The Apple command to remove a file from disk. It is necessary on the Apple to delete sequential files before writing into them.

Direct access *See* **Random access.**

End-of-file check The command used to find the end of the data when inputting from a file. *See also* **EOF** and **ONERR GOTO.**

EOF The command for the IBM and Radio Shack that checks a file to see if the end of the data contained in the file has been reached.

Extend The command used on the Radio Shack to add more information to the end of an existing file.

Field A group of related characters.

File A group of related records stored on some type of storage device (in this text only diskette storage is discussed).

File extension A marking appended to the end of a file name that indicates the type of file.

INPUT The specification on the IBM OPEN statement to set up a file for inputting data. Also, the command in Apple BASIC to get information from a file.

INPUT # The command in IBM and Radio Shack BASIC to get information from a file.

ONERR GOTO The error trapping command necessary in the Apple to find the end of the data when reading information from a file.

OPEN The command used to indicate to the machine that you want to either read from or write to a disk file.

OUTPUT The specification on the IBM OPEN statement to set up a file to receive data.

PEEK The command that allows the examination of what is stored in a particular byte in memory. (Introduced for the Apple error trap, but all versions of BASIC can use the PEEK command.)

PRINT The disk output command used on the Apple.

PRINT# The disk output command used on the IBM and Radio Shack.

Random access A type of file processing that allows access to any record stored in the file without having to access any of the previous records. Also called **direct access.**

READ The command necessary on the Apple to set the file input mode.

Record A collection of related fields.

Sequential access A type of file processing whereby records must be accessed in the same order in which they were stored.

WRITE The command necessary on the Apple to set the file output mode.

QUESTIONS TO AID UNDERSTANDING

*1. Explain why disk files are necessary.

2. Explain bit, byte, field, record, and file and how they relate to each other.

3. Define file extensions and indicate why they are important.

*4. Describe the difference between a sequential file and a random file and how each processes data.

5. Discuss how disk files are accessed.

*6. Select the part of this question for the machine you are using and indicate which commands have errors in them and what those errors are.

6A. IBM
a. 10 OPEN "OUTPUT" AS #1, FOR INPUT
b. 10 INPUT#1,A,B,C,D$,B$,C$,B
c. 10 PRINT#1,A,B,C
d. 10 DCLOSE #1
e. 10 OPEN "SAMPLE" FOR EXTEND AS #1
f. 10 IF A$ = 5 THEN INPUT#1,A$
g. 10 IF EOF THEN CLOSE
h. 10 FOR I = 1 TO INPUT#1,A
i. 10 CLOSE
j. 10 INPUT "FROM FILE 1";#1,A

237

6B. Radio Shack

a. 10 OPEN "OUTPUT",1,"TIME"

b. 10 INPUT#1,A,B,C,D$,B$,C$,B

c. 10 PRINT#1,A,B,C

d. 10 DCLOSE #1

e. 10 OPEN#1, "O", "SAMPLE"

f. 10 IF A$=5 THEN INPUT#1,A$

g. 10 IF EOF THEN CLOSE

h. 10 FOR I = 1 TO INPUT#1,A

i. 10 CLOSE

j. 10 INPUT "FROM FILE 1";#1,A

6C. Apple (Assume D$=CHR$(4))

a. 10 PRINT D$;"OPEN 'OUTPUT' "

b. 10 INPUT A,B,C,D$,B$,C$,B

c. 10 PRINT A,B,C

d. 10 PRINT D$;"DCLOSE OUTPUT"

e. 10 PRINT D$;"OPEN#1"

f. 10 IF A$=5 THEN PRINT "WRITE SAMPLE"

g. 10 IF ONERR=5 THEN PRINT D$;"CLOSE"

h. 10 FOR I = 1 TO INPUT A

i. 10 CLOSE

j. 10 PRINT D$;"APPEND SAMPLE"

7. Write a program to create a file that will contain student information. Each record should contain the student ID (use social security number), student name, class number, and five grades. Use the following records (and others you make up) for the file (INPUT the records into the program):

STUDENT ID	NAME	CLASS	GRADES
555667777	COBURN, ED	DP100	100,56,75,88,95
664569899	HILL, SAM	EG205	88,86,85,92,76
759898878	THOMAS, TERRY	MA106	45,88,96,92,99
878200280	HARRISON, TOM	EG445	40,60,70,55,63

Write a second program to read the records back from the file and generate a report. Put the dashes in the social security numbers (555-66-7777), turn the names around (ED COBURN), print out the class name with DP=DATA PROCESSING, EG=ENGLISH, MA=MATH, and average the grades using the following ranges for the letter grade:

A: $>= 90$

B: <90 and $>= 80$

C: <80 and $>= 70$

D: <70 and $>= 60$

F: <60

Each record should be printed out as follows:

```
STUDENT ID = 555-66-7777      STUDENT NAME = ED COBURN
DEPARTMENT = DATA PROCESSING  CLASS = 100
GRADES = 100, 56, 75, 88, 95
AVERAGE = 82.8  FOR A GRADE OF B
```

8. Use the inventory record items on page 215 to store information in a file using at least five inventory records. Write a second program to read the inventory items back off the file and write a report, such as (note that only some of the fields are used for the report):

```
ITEM NUMBER        ITEM NAME        QUANTITY     COST    TOTAL COST
123-RE-BG45/15     HORSE COLLAR       100        15.56     1556.00
                                                 TOTAL     1556.00
```

9. One of the advantages of random access files is their ease of updating. Updating is difficult with sequential files. Use the program in the chapter to generate a file of mailing labels. Then write a program that will input the label, print the name on the screen, and input a new address writing all the old information with the new address on a second file. This means both files need to be opened at the same time. Then use the program shown in the chapter to print the original file and then modify it (or use a new program) to print the new file.

*10. Write a program to create a file of thirty random numbers from 1 to 10. Then modify the program so it will create another file of thirty random numbers. Write a second program to read the files and compare the two numbers. If two numbers match, print the number and an appropriate message. If two numbers don't match, print both numbers and the difference with an appropriate message.

11. You need to write the payroll programs for the XYZ Corporation. Write a program to INPUT the following payroll information: social security number (leave out the dashes), employee name, salary code (S for salaried, H for hourly), and hourly rate if hourly or weekly salary if salaried. Input the records given for five employees and store them in a file. Use the following data:

NAME	SOCIAL SEC. #	CODE	SALARY or HOURLY RATE		HOURS
ED COBURN	497-88-1906	S	450		40.5
SARA SMITH	687-95-8392	H		2.56	40.0
TOM HARRIS	487-85-9374	H		3.85	35.6
SALLY THOMAS	837-69-4872	S	325		40.0
FRED FILSTER	847-82-2929	H		6.75	38.5

Write a second program to input the information from the file. Print the employee name on the screen as a prompt for the number of hours worked if the employee is hourly. If the employee is salaried, skip the prompt since the weekly pay (the salary) is already known. Generate a report that shows the following:

```
SOCIAL SEC. #    NAME          CODE   RATE     HOURS   WEEKLY PAY
497-88-1906      ED COBURN      S     SALARY   40.5           450
687-95-8392      SARA SMITH     H     2.56     40.0         102.4
                                                           ------
                                              TOTAL         552.4
```

QUICK QUIZ

The answers to the questions follow immediately after the quiz. Questions 1–15 are true–false, while 16–20 are multiple choice.

T F   **1.** Cassette file processing is not covered in this text because cassettes are too expensive for most operations.

T F   **2.** A byte is the smallest unit of storage used with microcomputers.

T F   **3.** A field is composed of several individual records.

T F   **4.** Record is a term that relates mainly to use of a storage device.

T F   **5.** One of the first things to do when creating a file is to decide what fields you need for the file.

T F   **6.** Normally, a social security number would be stored without the dashes to save disk storage.

T F   **7.** Normally, a file name can be virtually any length.

T F   **8.** Sequential file processing is discussed because it is the best method for processing data.

T F   **9.** Random files allow the access of any individual record.

T F   **10.** Whenever we are creating a file for the first time, it is necessary to open that file.

T F   **11.** It is always best when writing information into a file to close that file before attempting to read from it.

T F   **12.** We can open as many as three files at the same time in our versions of BASIC.

T F   **13.** The file CLOSE command can work to close either one file or all the open files.

T F   **14.** It's a good idea to print several variables on the same print statement to make a more compact and easy to read program.

T F   **15.** We always want to append (or extend in Radio Shack) records to the end of a file we have used before.

_____   **16.** Which of the following statements is the same in all three versions of BASIC discussed in this text?

  a. 10 CLOSE #1   **c.** 10 PRINT#1,A
  b. 10 INPUT#1,A   **d.** none of them

17. Which of the following is not always necessary when accessing a disk file? _____

    a. open the file   **c.** close the file

    b. read the file   **d.** all are always necessary

18. When inputting information from a disk, which one of the following is true? _____

    a. We can use up to five files at the same time.

    b. We must close one file before opening another.

    c. We can input from one file while writing to another.

    d. We should delete the file before reusing it.

19. Think back to when we rewrote Program 8–4. Which of the following did _____ we *not* do?

    a. Use a subroutine.

    b. Use READ and DATA statements.

    c. Use a variable prompt.

    d. Check for end of file.

20. The advantages of random file processing would include all of the following _____ *except:*

    a. accessing any record

    b. storage sequentially

    c. retrieval can be sequential

    d. all of the above

---

1. F (Cassettes are too slow, not too expensive.)
2. F (A bit is the smallest.)
3. F (A record is made up of fields.)
4. T (This is also true of the term file.)
5. T
6. T
7. F (In the Apple, it can be up to thirty characters; in the others it can be no longer than eight.)
8. F (It is the easiest to use and understand, but not the best).
9. T
10. T
11. T
12. T
13. T
14. F (Printing more than one variable on one print statement can cause problems in your program when reading the records back.)
15. F (Many times we want to rewrite the entire file.)
16. d (Unfortunately, disk processing has few common commands even between two versions of BASIC, much less three.)
17. b (Perhaps you want to write to the file.)
18. c (a stipulated five files, but the maximum is defaulted to three. b is incorrect because we can use up to three files at the same time. d is incorrect because we would never delete a file we were going to input.)
19. d (It was a file output program so no end-of-file check was necessary.)
20. d (All are advantages.)

9 'MENUS AND REPORTS

OVERVIEW

OBJECTIVES

After completing Chapter 9, you will be able to:

- Explain what it means to write user-oriented programs.
- Explain what menu-driven means.
- Describe how to use direct cursor addressing on your machine and demonstrate its use in several programs.
- List and explain at least six of the nine screen display guidelines.
- Explain why error messages are used, and demonstrate the techniques by writing a program that uses error messages.
- List and explain three factors that need to be considered when designing a report program.
- Explain what a control break is and why it is used.
- Demonstrate a knowledge of report generation techniques by designing and writing several report programs.

A new phrase has evolved in the microcomputer industry over the past few years. **User-oriented programming** refers to writing programs that are easy for a user to understand and use. However, no one is exactly sure how to go about doing that.

In this chapter we will explore two methods that help us write programs that are, in fact, easier to use and help us structure the output so it will be easier to understand. The first will be accomplished by using menu-driven programs. The second will be achieved by using various methods that have been developed involving the printing of subtotals and other types of structured output.

One programming procedure has become almost standard practice on microcomputers in an effort to produce user-oriented programs. That practice is the use of **menu-driven** programs. Menu-driven simply means that the various functions of a program are arrived at through selection of options from a screen display called a **menu.**

Suppose, for example, that we have a program to add records to a file, change existing records, delete records, and print a report of the records. These four options could be displayed on a menu for the user to choose which function to use. Such a menu might look like the following:

```
              RECORD MAINTENANCE PROGRAM


YOUR OPTIONS ARE:

1.   ADD RECORD
2.   CHANGE EXISTING RECORD
3.   DELETE EXISTING RECORD
4.   PRINT RECORD LIST
5.   QUIT THE PROGRAM


WHAT OPTION DO YOU WANT (1-5)?
```

Putting such a menu on the screen is a fairly simple matter. You need to clear the screen (recall the command from Chapter 3), then use several PRINT statements. A sample of this type of display program might look like the following:

```
NEW
10 REM ***** PROGRAM NAME: SCRDSPLY
20 REM
30 REM ***** SAMPLE SCREEN DISPLAY PROGRAM
40 REM
50 REM ***** WRITTEN BY EDWARD J. COBURN
60 REM
70 CLS                      ' CLEAR THE SCREEN
80 PRINT TAB(10);"RECORD MAINTENANCE PROGRAM"
90 PRINT                    ' LEAVE BLANK LINE
100 PRINT                   ' LEAVE BLANK LINE
110 PRINT "YOUR OPTIONS ARE:"
```

Program continues

Program 9–1

```
120 PRINT                        ' LEAVE BLANK LINE
130 PRINT "1.   ADD RECORD"
140 PRINT "2.   CHANGE EXISTING RECORD"
150 PRINT "3.   DELETE EXISTING RECORD"
160 PRINT "4.   PRINT RECORD LIST"
170 PRINT "5.   QUIT THE PROGRAM"
180 PRINT
190 PRINT
200 INPUT "WHAT OPTION DO YOU WANT (1-5)";A
210 IF A<1 OR A>5 THEN 190
220 ON A GOSUB 500, 1000, 1500, 2000, 2500
```

Program 9–1 (cont.)

)))DIFFERENCES

For the Apple, line 70 needs to be:

```
70 HOME                    : REM CLEAR THE SCREEN
```

And (as always) the INPUT statement is different:

```
200 INPUT "WHAT OPTION DO YOU WANT (1-5)? ";A
```

Of course, the program would continue after line 220 with the various routines for each of the functions. Notice that line 210 is an error trap for the option code that the user enters. An error trap is used in case the user presses some number outside the range of the options. But this is a sloppy way to do the input. Why? Well, what happens if the user presses a nonnumeric key? That's right. The machine will display a Redo from start message. Though we, as programmers, understand this message, the user probably wouldn't. Therefore we should trap the error before it occurs. How do we do that? The easiest way is to change the INPUT statement from a numeric input to a string. Having a string input is no problem for us because we can use the VAL function to change it to a number; the advantage of using a string is that it will eliminate the Redo message. This way we can control the error messages. The changed INPUT statement should look something like:

```
200 INPUT "WHAT OPTION DO YOU WANT (1-5)";A$
```

Then we need to add a conversion; we will be able to use the same check (line 210) since any nonnumeric character entered will have a value of zero. So the new line should look like:

```
205 A=VAL(A$)
```

The problem with this is that if the user enters incorrect data, the input prompt will reappear below the first one. If this is done enough times, the screen display of options will scroll off the top of the screen. Not very good from the user's standpoint. It would be much better if, when the user makes an error, the input prompt would reappear right where it was before. But how can we do this? There is a technique in BASIC called **direct cursor addressing.** Direct cursor addressing refers to using a program command to put the cursor anywhere on the screen without destroying any of the information already on the display. In our example, we need to put the cursor back to the beginning of the line where the INPUT statement displayed its prompt. The commands for direct cursor addressing are explained in the next few sections.

The direct cursor addressing command for the IBM is the **LOCATE** command, and its form is simply:

```
10 LOCATE row,column
```

An example would be:

```
10 LOCATE 10,5
```

This would position the cursor to column 5 on row 10. Recall that the IBM has 80 columns by 24 lines. In most of the other computers, the cursor positioning is a bit more difficult and is easier to use as a subroutine. So, to be consistent in the programs in the text, we will put the IBM cursor positioning statement in a subroutine also, though it is not really necessary. The form of the subroutine would be:

```
4970 REM
4980 REM ***** CURSOR POSITIONING SUBROUTINE
4990 REM
5000 LOCATE R,C
5010 RETURN
```

R is for the row and C is for the column. Then we would merely assign the row and column values and do a GOSUB.

Radio Shack BASIC uses a **PRINT** @ command (the @ is the "at" symbol). The form of the command is:

```
10 PRINT @(cursor position),item;item;...
```

If you recall from Chapter 1, the screen size of the Model III is 64 columns by 16 rows. In Radio Shack BASIC, the positions on the screen are numbered beginning with 0 in the home position and continuing to the lower right-hand corner. This means the positions are numbered 0 through 1023. The PRINT @ command requires that you specify the screen position; a typical command would be:

```
10 PRINT @(596),"HI THERE"
```

which would print HI THERE on row 9, column 19. The problem with this command is that we have to do a conversion to figure out what position on the screen we want things printed. In other words, should we decide we want some message printed on row 10, column 15, we would have to do a calculation to figure out the cursor position.

Let's see how such a calculation would be done to figure out the actual position. We will use a screen size of 5 rows of 6 columns as a demonstration. Such a display would look like the following if each screen position were marked:

```
                    COLUMNS
      ROW      1    2    3    4    5    6
          +----------------------------------+
          !                                  !
       1  !   0    1    2    3    4    5     !
          !                                  !
       2  !   6    7    8    9    10   11    !
          !                                  !
       3  !   12   13   14   15   16   17    !
          !                                  !
       4  !   18   19   20   21   22   23    !
          !                                  !
       5  !   24   25   26   27   28   29    !
          !                                  !
          +----------------------------------+
```

Now let's say we want to position the cursor to row 3, column 4. That means the cursor should be located at position 15. Okay, to get this position, we have to take the row number and multiply it by 6 since there are 6 positions in each row. This will give us the number of positions to bypass to get the cursor to the correct row. If we do this, we get 3 * 6 or 18. But we wanted position 15, and we are already beyond that. What happened? We wanted the cursor on row 3, so we multiplied the number of columns by 3. But if we wanted the cursor to be on row 1, we wouldn't use any row count since on the first row all the column numbers are also the position numbers. Thus, if we want row 2, we have to displace the count by 1 row, not 2; for row 3, we displace the count by 2, not 3. To put that in mathematical form, we need to take the row number and subtract 1 from it to find the displacement for the row. This will give us $(3-1)$ * 6, or 12. Then we take the column number and add that, and we get $12 + 4 = 16$. But we're still off one column. That's because the first cursor position is 0, not 1. To make the calculation precisely correct, we need to subtract 1 from it. Now the whole formula will be: position $= (row-1)$ * 6 + column-1.

Now we need to translate this formula to 64 columns. It should look like the following:

$$position = (row-1) * 64 + column-1$$

The trouble is that we have to do this calculation every time we need to know a screen position. It's much easier to simply let the computer do the calculations for us. We can do this by using our new formula in the PRINT @ statement, such as:

```
10 PRINT @((R-1)*64+C-1),"";
```

In this statement, R is the row number and C is the column. Notice that we are printing " " on the statement (the semicolon is, of course, to turn off the carriage return). That is the symbolization for a null (we also used this on the INKEY$ check) and means we are printing nothing. The PRINT @ statement requires something to be printed on it, otherwise we will get an error. But why would we want to print a null? Why not just print what we want on the statement? It is much easier in our programs to make this statement into a subroutine. Then all we have to do is assign R, C, and then GOSUB. That's much easier than rekeying the entire PRINT @ statement many times.

Since we are processing this statement in a subroutine, it is easier to print a null and then print the message up in the program. Besides, there are times we will want to simply position the cursor without printing anything. That is what we will do for the INPUT statement. Remember, the prompt for the INPUT statement is already contained in the statement.

Our subroutine should look like the following:

```
4970 REM
4980 REM ***** CURSOR POSITIONING SUBROUTINE
4990 REM
5000 PRINT @((R-1)*64+C-1),"";
5010 RETURN
```

MODEL 4

Although the Model 4 will use the PRINT @ statement in the same manner as the Model III, there is an additional method that can be used. The form of the other type of statement is:

```
10 PRINT @(row,column),item;item;...
```

Using this command, you can specify the actual row and column where you want the cursor to be positioned. An example of this command in use would be:

```
10 PRINT @(10,5),"HI THERE"
```

This would cause HI THERE to print at column 5 on row 10. Recall that the Model 4 has 80 columns by 24 rows; the rows are numbered 0 through 23 and the columns 0 through 79. For the Model 4, the command is easy enough to use that each time it is needed it could be specified using the actual command. But for the sake of modular programming and consistency throughout the text, we will put the cursor positioning in a subroutine. The form of the subroutine would be:

```
4970 REM
4980 REM ***** CURSOR POSITIONING SUBROUTINE
4990 REM
5000 PRINT @(R,C),"";
5010 RETURN
```

In this routine, the R is the row number and the C is the column. Notice that we are again printing " " on the statement, as in the last section.

Apple Direct Cursor Addressing

To do direct cursor addressing on the Apple, you use two commands: one to position horizontally and one to position vertically. The horizontal statement is **HTAB** xx, and the vertical statement is **VTAB** xx, with the xx being the row or column number. Together they would look like:

```
100 VTAB 10
110 HTAB 15
```

These two commands together would position the cursor to row 10 and column 15. Recall that the screen on the Apple has 40 columns by 24 lines.

It is easier to use these two commands in a subroutine, such as the following:

```
4970 REM
4980 REM ***** CURSOR POSITIONING SUBROUTINE
4990 REM
5000 VTAB R
5010 HTAB C
5020 RETURN
```

The R is for the row number, and the C is for the column number. To use this routine, you would assign the row and the column and do a GOSUB.

9–3
BACK TO THE MENU PROGRAM

Now let's add our cursor addressing subroutine to the program we were working on (Program 9–1). Key in the subroutine as we discussed, using lines 4970 on, so the subroutine will begin in line 5000.

Now we will have to change lines 190 through 210 to put in the cursor positioning. Right now they are:

```
190 PRINT
200 INPUT "WHAT OPTION DO YOU WANT (1-5)";A$
205 A=VAL(A$)
210 IF A<1 OR A>5 THEN 190
```

But we can change them to something similar to the following:

```
190 R=23
194 C=1
196 GOSUB 5000            ' CURSOR POSITIONING ROUTINE
200 INPUT "WHAT OPTION DO YOU WANT (1-5)";A$
205 A=VAL(A$)
210 IF A<1 OR A>5 THEN 196
```

This is okay for all the machines except the Radio Shack Model III, which needs R = 15, since there are only 16 lines on the screen. We are using one line up from the bottom of the screen so the screen will not scroll up after RETURN is pressed on the entry.

You will note in the program that we changed line 190, which was a PRINT statement for printing a blank line, to our row designation; we also changed line 210 to GOTO (understood) 196 instead of 190. We don't need to reassign R and C if we have an error, so we simply branch to the GOSUB statement.

Now we have a new problem. Suppose that in response to the prompt, the user answered "THAT ONE". When we redisplay the input statement, "THAT ONE" will still be on the screen since the new prompt will simply lie on the top of the old one. What we need to do is erase the old line. We can do this by printing the screen's width of blanks to blank out anything on the screen. (Actually we print one less than the width, otherwise the screen would scroll.) That is, on the IBM we can print either 39 or 79 blanks before we redisplay the prompt. On the Radio Shack Model III, we will need 63 blanks before we redisplay the prompt. This can be done with the STRING$ command (only for IBM and Radio Shack, see Chapter 7), such as:

```
197 PRINT STRING$(39," ");
198 GOSUB 5000                   ' CURSOR POSITIONING ROUTINE
```

Notice that we also reposition the cursor, otherwise it would be sitting at the end of the blanks. Keep in mind that the 39 in the STRING$ command would be 79 for 80-column displays or 63 for the 64-column display of the Model III.

On the Apple, the easiest thing to do is load a string with 39 blanks and then print the variable, such as:

```
197 PRINT LEFT$(CL$,39);       : REM CLEAR THE LINE
198 GOSUB 5000                 : REM CURSOR POSITIONING ROUTINE
```

Of course, for this to work we must assign blanks to the CL$ variable. If you recall, we discussed how to do this in Chapter 7. A routine similar to the following would work fine in our current program:

```
62 CL$=""
64 FOR I=1 TO 6                : REM LOOP FOR BLANKS
65     CL$=CL$+CL$
66 NEXT I
```

Now when we execute this program, the cursor is positioned at the beginning of the bottom line on the screen, and it is blanked out. Then the INPUT is done and the prompt is printed. If the user enters something incorrect, the program branches back to statement 196, the line is blanked, and the prompt is printed again.

9–4 A FEW GUIDELINES ABOUT SCREEN DISPLAYS

Before we expand our program any more, we need to discuss a few simple guidelines about using displays.

1. Every screen display you use should have some type of heading at the top. In our example we used the heading "RECORD MAINTENANCE PROGRAM". This is done so that the user is sure that the correct program is being used before it's too late.
2. Try to make the display pleasing in appearance. Do this by balancing the screen from top to bottom and left to right. Don't scatter a couple of entries here and a couple there.
3. Don't clutter up the screen. If there are more items to display than will comfortably fit on the screen, use two screens and allow the program to switch back and forth between them. If you do have to set up two (or more) screens, do your best to make the transitions between screens as smooth as possible.
4. Use blank lines between items where appropriate. This makes the information on the screen much easier to read.
5. Prompts should always appear in the same place. We will always use the bottom line of the screen. This makes the prompts stand out; they are more noticeable than if they were intermingled with the rest of the screen display.

6. Keep your prompts as short as possible without using too many abbreviations. Above all, try to keep the length of your prompts to only one print line. Prompts that are longer than one line are often distracting. However, the prompt must have all the needed information. The user should have no trouble understanding what the program needs. It helps to be explicit. Tell the user exactly what the program is expecting. For example, if a date is to be input with slashes, the prompt should so specify. Such a prompt might look like:

```
INPUT TODAY'S DATE (MM/DD/YY)
```

7. When you are using error messages (we will do this next), they should not be cryptic. They should state explicitly what the user has done incorrectly. They should be as brief as possible while still conveying the appropriate message. Never use codes that will make the user consult a manual to find out what the error is.

8. Like prompts, error messages should always be displayed in the same location on the screen. We will use the bottom of the screen for our error messages also.

9. Finally, the error messages should be displayed to attract the attention of the user. Use color if you have it (we will not use color in our programs), or use some other method of attracting the user's attention, such as making the errors flash (this we will do).

9–5
DISPLAYING AN ERROR MESSAGE

The program we have been using does not display an error message when the user enters incorrect data. It simply returns and lets the user enter again. It is much better to tell the user that something was entered incorrectly. It can be stated simply as in the following example (using the same program we have been using):

```
210 IF A>0 AND A<6 THEN GOTO 250
220     M$="ONLY ENTER 1 THROUGH 5.  TRY AGAIN."
230     GOSUB 6000                 ' ERROR SUBROUTINE
240     GOTO 196
```

We changed the shape of our IF test. Now, it will branch around our error routine should the entered information fall within the proper range. Notice that we assign an error message to M$. We do this because the error routine is going to be located in a subroutine (6000). Since there are several things the error routine will need to do, it is best to put it in a subroutine. That routine will begin in line 6000. It might look like the following:

```
5970 REM
5980 REM ***** ERROR SUBROUTINE
5990 REM
6000 R=23
6010 C=1
6020 GOSUB 5000
6030 PRINT STRING$(39," ");
6040 GOSUB 5000
6050 PRINT M$;
6060 RETURN
```

Note: We will list the differences in our other BASIC versions after we have finished constructing the routine.

This routine has a problem. It will clear off the line, then reposition the cursor and print the message. The problem is, the message will only be displayed briefly and then the RETURN will return the program back to the input routine and the error message will be wiped off. The user would have no time to see the message. A much better way to create such a routine is to print the message and erase it several times so the error appears to be blinking. Such a routine might look like the following:

```
5970 REM
5980 REM ***** ERROR SUBROUTINE
5990 REM
6000 R=23
6010 C=1
6020 GOSUB 5000                    ' POSITION THE CURSOR
6030 PRINT STRING$(39," ");        ' WIPE OFF INPUT
6040 FOR I1 = 1 TO 3
6050     GOSUB 5000                ' POSITION THE CURSOR
6060     PRINT M$;                 ' PRINT THE MESSAGE
6070     FOR J = 1 TO 250          ' DELAY LOOP
6080     NEXT J
6090     GOSUB 5000                ' POSITION THE CURSOR
6100     PRINT STRING$(39," ");    ' BLANK THE LINE
6110     FOR J = 1 TO 100          ' DELAY LOOP
6120     NEXT J
6130 NEXT I1
6140 RETURN
```

 **)))DIFFERENCES**

On the Radio Shack Model III, R should be 15, and the number of blanks printed in the STRING$ statements should be 63. On the Model 4, the blanks should be 79.

On the Apple, lines 6030 and 6100 should print 39 blanks as:

```
6030 PRINT LEFT$(CL$,39);

6100     PRINT LEFT$(CL$,39);
```

Notice that this routine begins by wiping off the line. This will clear off any prompt that might be there. Then the routine has a loop of 1 to 3. This will cause the error message to print on the screen three times. Also notice the delay loops. They are necessary to slow down the program so the message can be read. The second delay loop is shorter in duration than the first. This is so the message will display longer than the blank line. This creates the best flashing appearance. The end points of these loops may have to be adjusted to make the message flash the way it looks best to you.

Now that we have the routines written to display the prompt and flash the errors, let's look at the whole program (the differences will not be listed here as they have already been noted; make sure you use the appropriate cursor positioning subroutine for your machine):

```
10 REM ***** PROGRAM NAME: SCRDSPLY
20 REM
30 REM ***** SAMPLE SCREEN DISPLAY PROGRAM
40 REM
50 REM ***** WRITTEN BY EDWARD J. COBURN
60 REM
70 CLS                          ' CLEAR THE SCREEN
80 PRINT TAB(10);"RECORD MAINTENANCE PROGRAM"
90 PRINT                        ' LEAVE BLANK LINE
100 PRINT                       ' LEAVE BLANK LINE
110 PRINT "YOUR OPTIONS ARE:"
120 PRINT                       ' LEAVE BLANK LINE
130 PRINT "1.   ADD RECORD"
140 PRINT "2.   CHANGE EXISTING RECORD"
150 PRINT "3.   DELETE EXISTING RECORD"
160 PRINT "4.   PRINT RECORD LIST"
170 PRINT "5.   QUIT THE PROGRAM"
180 PRINT
190 R=23
194 C=1
196 GOSUB 5000                  ' CURSOR POSITIONING ROUTINE
197 PRINT STRING$(39," ");
198 GOSUB 5000                  ' CURSOR POSITIONING ROUTINE
200 INPUT "WHAT OPTION DO YOU WANT (1-5)";A$
205 A=VAL(A$)
210 IF A>0 AND A<6 THEN GOTO 250
220    M$="ONLY ENTER 1 THROUGH 5.  TRY AGAIN."
230     GOSUB 6000              ' ERROR SUBROUTINE
240     GOTO 196
250 PRINT "CORRECT ENTRY OF";A
260 PRINT "THE PROGRAM WOULD CONTINUE"
270 END
4970 REM
4980 REM ***** CURSOR POSITIONING ROUTINE
4990 REM
5000 LOCATE R,C
5010 RETURN
5970 REM
5980 REM ***** ERROR SUBROUTINE
5990 REM
6000 R=23
6010 C=1
6020 GOSUB 5000                         ' POSITION THE CURSOR
6030 PRINT STRING$(39," ");             ' WIPE OFF INPUT
6040 FOR I1 = 1 TO 3
6050     GOSUB 5000                     ' POSITION THE CURSOR
6060     PRINT M$;                      ' PRINT THE MESSAGE
6070     FOR J = 1 TO 250               ' DELAY LOOP
6080     NEXT J
6090     GOSUB 5000                     ' POSITION THE CURSOR
6100     PRINT STRING$(39," ");         ' BLANK THE LINE
6110     FOR J = 1 TO 100               ' DELAY LOOP
6120     NEXT J
6130 NEXT I1
6140 RETURN
```

Program 9–2

You should try this program a bit. Notice that we added a couple of PRINT statements (lines 250 and 260) so you can check that the program is working. Of course, this program segment would need the rest of the routines added. It is only the first segment.

Earlier in the book, when we printed a report, we simply put things into columns, maybe used column headings, possibly used totals, and didn't concern ourselves with much more. But there is much more to printing reports than simply throwing together some output. There are actually three things we need to be concerned about:

1. *What the report should contain.* The purpose of printing a report is to give the user useful information. To do that we have to determine what information the user needs. If it is an inventory report, for example, the report should contain at least the item number and the quantity-on-hand. From that point on, it is a matter of need. The report could include item description, item name, date of last sale, cost, sale price, etc.
2. *Whether the report should be printed or simply displayed on the screen.* This will be largely a matter of what type of data is being presented on the output. If the data is such that a permanent record needs to be kept or if the data is needed for disbursement (such as checks), then it must be printed out. If, however, the information is going to be changed regularly, then perhaps a screen display would better suit the need.
3. *What format the report should have.* Formatting can fall into many different categories. First, most reports must have **detail lines.** These are the item lines of information, such as the information about each inventory item. The items on the detail line are sometimes edited using special procedures so that they appear more presentable; the decimal points on numbers all aligning under each other for example.

   Second, there are two different types of headings: the **page heading,** or the heading that appears at the top of the report to identify it, and **column headings,** which identify the contents of the columns printed on the report.

   Finally, there are two types of totals: **subtotals,** or totals that display the totals of certain subgroups within the main group, and **final totals,** which are the cumulative totals for the entire report. We will discuss subtotals in more depth shortly.

Other things are sometimes added to reports to make them more impressive looking, such as dashed lines between column headings and the detail lines and perhaps between the detail lines and the totals. Also, blank lines between detail lines are sometimes used for the sake of clarity.

Figure 9–1 shows a typical **line spacing chart.** This is a form that looks a lot like graph paper with the rows and columns numbered. There is a wide variety of different forms available, and many people simply use graph paper or program coding forms. A line spacing chart is simply a form on which you can design your reports to determine, before beginning to write your program, on which lines and in which columns everything should print.

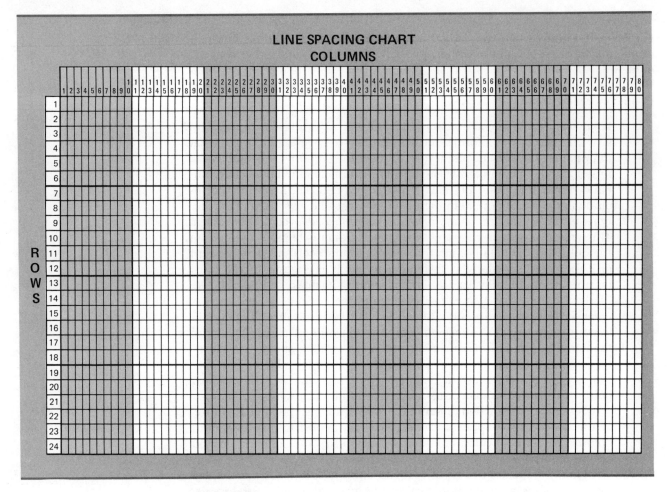

Figure 9-1
Typical line spacing chart.

Anytime you are designing a program for either a screen display or a report to be printed on paper, a spacing chart can be a valuable tool. Figure 9–2 shows a completed spacing chart for the layout of a report we will be using in section 9–9. Notice the use of both types of headings and both types of totals.

9–8
REPORT GENERATION— DATA EDITING

All stored numeric data does not have to take the same form. To this point, we have been letting all our numeric variables default to single precision. That is, without specifying the precision, BASIC will automatically default to **single precision,** which will allow numbers up to seven significant digits. That is, the smallest allowable number will be $-9,999,999$, and the largest will be $9,999,999$; or you can express them with decimal values, such as $99,999.99$, for the same seven digits.

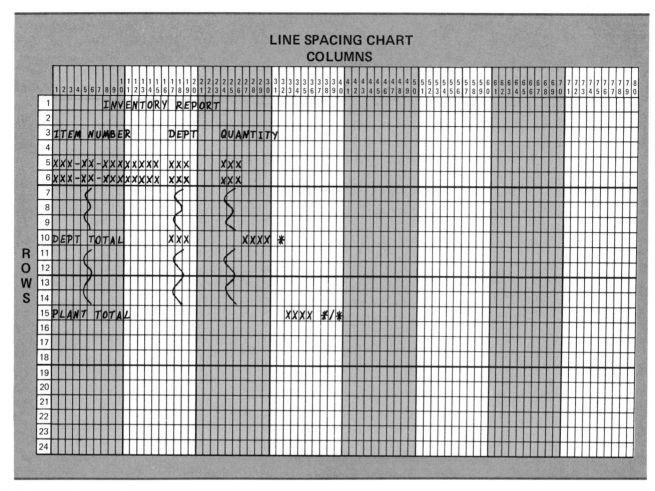

Figure 9–2
Design of report using line spacing chart.

Now, if your number exceeds the largest allowable number (or is smaller than the smallest allowed), the machine will still allow the number to be stored, but it will represent only seven significant digits and will display the number in scientific notation, such as 9.0097E15. **Scientific notation** is a method of specifying large numbers by keeping track of the number of decimal positions needed. 9.0E15 means there are 15 positions to the left of the decimal point (in addition to the 9). Thus, 9.0097E15 is actually the number 9,009,700,000,000,000. If the number were 9,009,700,056,897,345, all the trailing digits beyond the seven allowed would be rounded and the significance of the digits would be lost.

We can help alleviate this problem by specifying our storage to be **double precision.** (*Note:* The Apple does not use double precision variables.) This is done by specifying your variable name with a # symbol at the end, such as

AB#. This variable would be stored as double precision, i.e., with up to 17 significant digits printed. Thus, our last number would print exactly as stored since it has only 16 significant digits.

We can also specify numbers to be **integers.** This sometimes improves program speed since the computer can process integers faster than it can single precision numbers. You specify an integer by appending a % to the end of your variable name, such as AB%. The range of allowable integers is from -32768 to 32768; if you try to assign a number beyond those extremes, you will get an Overflow error.

The main difference in using one precision level over another is the amount of memory required to store the variables. An integer requires only two bytes of memory, a single precision variable requires four bytes, while a double precision requires eight bytes to store each number. Thus, if memory is tight, or your disk file is too large, or program speed is important, or your numbers are extra large, you may wish to use some precision level other than single.

It is important to note that variable names are made up of the characters of the name and the marking for the variable type. For example, A% and A are two different variables, just as A and A$ are different variables. Also (for the IBM and Radio Shack), A# and A% are different variables, and both can be used in the same program at the same time.

The PRINT USING for IBM and Radio Shack

Note: Despite the heading, this section should be read by those using Apple machines, since much of this information will be referred to in the following section on creating your own editing procedures.

Thus far, when we have printed numbers, the first digit of the numbers has always been aligned. A simple example of this (note that we use double precision variables since the numbers are large) is:

```
NEW (remember to store the previous program on disk)
10 REM ***** PROGRAM NAME: DATASAMP
20 REM
30 REM ***** DATA SAMPLE
40 REM
50 FOR I = 1 TO 5
60    READ A#            ' DOUBLE PRECISION
70    PRINT A#
80 NEXT I
90 DATA 123,134.5,132456.678,34.5675,23459.23
100 END
RUN
 123
 134.5
 132456.678
 34.5675
 23459.23
Ok
```

Program 9–3

Now, this type of alignment may be fine for character output, but it is extremely difficult for reading numeric output. What we would really like is for the data to appear as follows:

```
    123.0000       or possibly          123.00
    134.5000                            134.50
132,456.6780                        132,456.68
     34.5675                             34.57
 23,459.2300                         23,459.23
```

The difference between the two lists above is simply that the second list has the numbers rounded to two decimal places. IBM and Radio Shack BASIC have a statement that will allow us to output our numbers as depicted above. We can add other things also, such as dollar signs. The statement for data editing is **PRINT USING** and has the form:

```
10 PRINT USING "edit string";item;item;...
```

The edit string can be a variable if you so choose. It is simply a group of characters that specify to the machine the method of printing the items, which incidentally can also be strings. The following is a list of the edit characters that can be used and what they are used for:

This represents the placement of a numeric digit. The number of symbols used in the edit string dictate the number of digits printed. If there are not enough digits specified to the left of the decimal, then all the digits are printed and at the front a percent symbol (%) is printed to indicate an error. If there is more edit string than there are digits to the left of the decimal point, the extra spots are filled with blanks. If there are not enough digits to the right of the decimal point, then the extra spaces are filled with zeros. If the data contains too many decimal positions, the number is rounded.

The period represents the positioning of the decimal point. It can be used anywhere in the edit field if there are also some # signs. Rounding of the number will occur automatically if there are more digits to the right of the decimal point than are specified in the edit string.

The comma specifies that a comma should be placed every three digits to the left of the decimal point.

$ One dollar sign tells the machine to put a dollar sign in the position you specify. Two dollar signs ($$) indicate a **floating dollar sign,** which means the dollar sign will be placed immediately to the left of the left-most digit in each number.

/blanks/ This tells the machine that a string is to be printed and the characters should be placed between the / symbols. On the actual output, blanks are printed in the place of the / symbols, so the field is actually two characters longer than the number of blanks specified. On the Radio Shack, the percent symbol (%) is used instead of the slash.

There are other codes, but the above are the ones used most often. For a complete discussion, refer to your user's manual. These are the only ones we will use for our programs.

Let's put some edit strings together so we can see how they are actually used. Table 9–1 shows some edit strings and how the edited data would look.

TABLE 9–1 Data Editing Examples

DATA	EDIT FIELD	OUTPUT
12.5	"###"	13 (the decimal was rounded)
1245.6	"##,###.##"	1,245.60
Harold	"/ /"	Haro (only two blanks between)
12.345	"$$,###.##"	$12.35 (rounded)
12.345	"$#,###.##"	$ 12.35 (no float on $)

Now we will use the format in Program 9–3. We will write an edit field that will round off the decimal to two digits. We will need to use an edit string of "###,###.##" and can modify our program to print the appropriate number list by changing only line 70 to:

```
70 PRINT USING "###,###.##";A#
```

Our program will now look like:

```
10 REM ***** PROGRAM NAME: DATASAMP
20 REM
30 REM ***** DATA SAMPLE
40 REM
50 FOR I = 1 TO 5
60    READ A#            ' DOUBLE PRECISION
70    PRINT USING "###,###.##";A#
80 NEXT I
90 DATA 123,134.5,132456.678,34.5675,23459.23
100 END
```

Program 9–4

And the output will be:

```
RUN
     123.00
     134.50
 132,456.68
      34.57
  23,459.23
Ok
```

If we wanted all four digits after the decimal point to appear, the edit string would change only slightly to "###,###.####". Notice there are now four # to the right of the decimal. Suppose our numbers represented dollars and we wanted to print the dollar sign. As noted, this can be done in two different ways: either by a stationary dollar sign or a floating one. The edit pattern for the stationary dollar sign would be "$###,###.##", and for the floating sign it would be "$$##,###.##". Notice that we added the dollar sign to the left of the first edit pattern and overlayed one # with the floating sign. The output from these two patterns would be as follows:

```
STATIONARY        FLOATING
$     123.00        $123.00
$     134.50        $134.50
$132,456.68     $132,456.68
$      34.57         $34.57
$ 23,459.23      $23,459.23
```

Note: Apple users should read the previous section (page 256) before reading this section; much of the information contained there pertains to this Apple section.

On the Apple, there is no PRINT USING, so if you wish to do data editing, you have to create the routines yourself. It really isn't as hard as it might seem at first, given that we already know how to use the string manipulation functions.

When using the PRINT USING on the IBM and Radio Shack we assume when setting up the edit string that the number will not exceed a certain size. If we do that same thing in creating our own editing routine it will simplify matters. Let's create our editing for the same list of numbers we used in the previous section.

The first thing we need to do is to break up our numbers into decimal parts and integer parts. We can do this by using the INT function as follows:

```
8000 B=INT(A)          : REM INTEGER PART
8010 C=A-B             : REM YIELDS THE DECIMAL PART
```

Line 8010 yields the decimal portion of the number since the variable B has only the integer portion. For example, suppose A contains 5.6. Then line 8000 will assign 5 to B, and 5.6 − 5 will give C the value of .6, the decimal portion.

Now we have to determine how many characters are in the integer portion so we can insert commas if needed. We can do that by first changing the integer to a string:

```
8020 B$=STR$(B)
```

Then we find the length of the string. If it is larger than three, we need to insert a comma. The routine to find the length and insert the necessary comma is as follows:

```
8030 IF LEN(B$)>3 THEN B$=LEFT$(B$,LEN(B$)-3)+","+RIGHT$(B$,3)
```

The next thing is to round off the decimal to two places. This is an easy task. We merely multiply our number by 100, add .5 to round it, take the integer of it to drop any further decimal places beyond two, and then divide it by 100. For example, suppose our decimal is .556. We multiply by 100 to get 55.6, then add .5 to get 56.1. Next, we take the integer of 56.1 and divide by 100 to end up with .56. Just what we wanted. The statement to do this manipulation would look like the following:

```
8040 C = INT((C * 100) + .5) / 100
```

This will give us the rounded decimal, but if we print it as is, we will not get two digits for those numbers that have only one decimal place. To get the zero printed for these numbers, we will have to put one in as part of a string:

```
8050 IF C<>0 THEN C$=STR$(C)
8060 IF C=0 THEN C$=".00"
8070 IF LEN(C$)<3 THEN C$=C$+"0"
```

We have to check for 3 in the length (line 8070), since the decimal point will already be a part of this string. Notice that we added a special test (lines 8050 and 8060) because if C is zero, there will be no decimal places. Line 8060 takes care of that situation.

Now the rest is merely a matter of assigning the elements in the proper order. We can use either a static or floating dollar sign, but let's use a floating. The concatenation should look like the following:

```
8080 P$="$"+B$+C$      : REM P$ IS THE FORMATTED NUMBER
```

To print it in the proper column we need to test the length and TAB over the appropriate number of spaces. The longest the string can be is the number $132,456.68, which is 11 characters. So our PRINT statement should look like the following:

```
8090 PRINT TAB(12-LEN(P$));P$
```

Our entire program (using Program 9–4) will look like the following, using a GOSUB (you should save the subroutine on disk so you can use it in later programs):

```
10 REM ***** PROGRAM NAME: DATASAMP
20 REM
30 REM ***** DATA SAMPLE
40 REM
50 FOR I = 1 TO 5
60     READ A
70     GOSUB 8000
80 NEXT I
90 DATA 123,134.5,132456.678,34.5675,23459.23
100 END
7970 REM
7980 REM ***** DATA EDITING ROUTINE
7990 REM
8000 B=INT(A)          ' INTEGER PART
8010 C=A-B             ' YIELDS THE DECIMAL PART
8020 B$=STR$(B)
8030 IF LEN(B$)>3 THEN B$=LEFT$(B$,LEN(B$)-3)+","+RIGHT$(B$,3)
8040 C=INT((C * 100) + .5) / 100
8050 IF C<>0 THEN C$=STR$(C)
8060 IF C=0 THEN C$=".00"
8070 IF LEN(C$)<3 THEN C$=C$+"0"
8080 P$="$"+B$+C$
8090 PRINT TAB(12-LEN(P$));P$
8100 RETURN
RUN
    $123.00
    $134.50
$132,456.68
     $34.57
 $23,459.23
]
```

Program 9–5

To use this routine in later programs, you will need to delete the PRINT statement, line 8090. Then the program can RETURN from the subroutine with the formatted data in P$ for further use in the program.

Up to this point, any time a total was printed, the entire total was printed by using an accumulator. Many times, however, we need to be able to print a **subtotal.** A subtotal is simply a part of the overall total that is keyed to some type of **control field.** A subtotal is sometimes called a **control break** or **control total** for that reason. An example of a control break or subtotal is a sales report in which we want to print subtotals by salesperson and by department in addition to the overall total.

There is an important consideration when using control breaks. The data you are printing must be in some type of order. That is, it must either be sorted or entered into the file in sorted order. Given the assumption that the file is sorted, we can use control breaks.

If we use a file of inventory numbers such as we have used in past chapters, a report with subtotals might look like the following:

```
        INVENTORY REPORT

ITEM NUMBER     DEPT.   QUANTITY
123-BL-BG45/97  123     15
123-BL-HT32/132 123     25
123-RE-F4.6/2   123     32
DEPT TOTAL      123            72 *
135-BL-RD46/2   135     765
135-RE-RE3/45   135     952
DEPT TOTAL      135          1717 *
400-GR-4/2      400     45
400-GR-15/3     400     46
DEPT TOTAL      400            91 *
452-BL-RF15/2   452     386
DEPT TOTAL      452           386 *
542-BL-TF45/24  542     34
542-RE-TF14/35  542     45
DEPT TOTAL      542            79 *
PLANT TOTAL                  2345 */*
```

Notice that the department totals are printed each time that the control field, the inventory number here, changes. Beside each department total, which is indented to make it stand out, an asterisk is displayed. The plant total is indented even further and marked with two asterisks. This is a common technique when printing control totals.

When using control totals, there are a few things that must be done. Before the first record is read in, a control variable, called a **test field,** must be set up. This is the field that the control field will be compared against to determine when a control break has occurred. For example, a variable is initially set up as blanks; then when the first record is read, that variable is assigned the control field value. But since the two fields are not equal when the first record is read, and since we don't want subtotals printed at that point, some type of first-record switch must be set up. This keeps the control totals from being printed on the first record.

Two different accumulators must be kept since two different totals need to be printed. Each time the subtotals are printed, that subtotal accumulator has to be zeroed out so a new subtotal can be accumulated; but the grand total needs to be accumulated throughout. Finally, on the last record, the control total and then the final total must be printed.

If you recall from Chapter 7, the letter code on the inventory item number between the dashes is the color code. The department code is the first three digits of the item number. To test for the control break we can compare entire item numbers since they are strings of characters. To construct such a program we will need to do the following steps:

```
Start
Open the file for input.
Read a record.
DO-WHILE not end-of-file.
   If not first record and control break THEN
      Perform control subroutine.
   (ELSE)
   END-IF
   Print the detail line.
   Accumulate the subtotal.
   Read a record.
END-DO
Perform the control subroutine.
Print the grand total.
Close the file.
End
```

The control total subroutine would have the following steps:

```
Start (subroutine)
Print the subtotal.
Add the subtotal to the grand total.
Zero out the subtotal accumulator.
Assign the control field to the test field.
End (subroutine)
```

The flowchart for this program would look like the one shown in Figure 9–3.

We will now code this program. We will, however, modify the steps slightly. Instead of using a data file for the inventory numbers, we will READ them from DATA statements. It is left as an end-of-chapter exercise for you to put the file processing into the program. The program should look like the following:

```
NEW
10 REM ***** PROGRAM NAME: INVREPT
20 REM
```

Program 9–6

Program continues on page 264

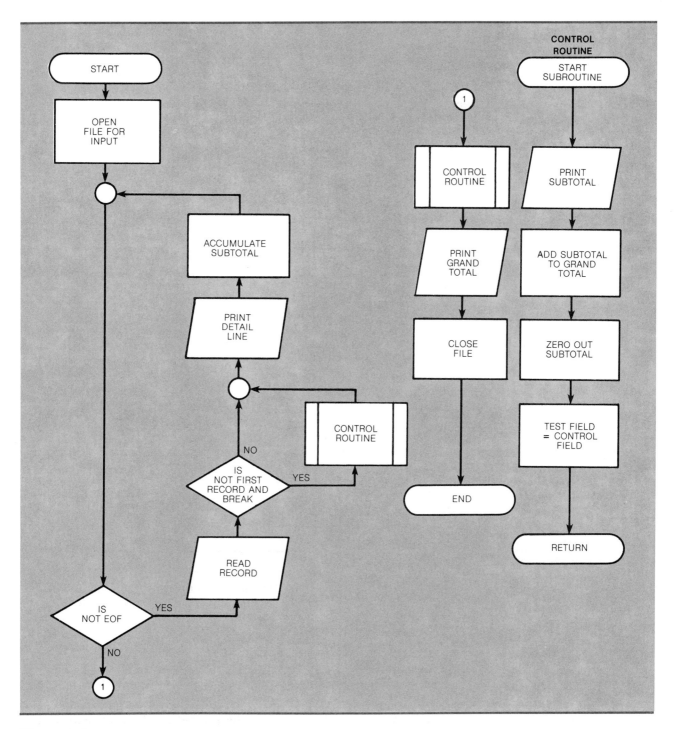

Figure 9–3
Flowchart of control break program.

```
30 REM ***** INVENTORY REPORT WITH CONTROL TOTALS
40 REM
50 REM ***** WRITTEN BY EDWARD J. COBURN
60 REM
70 CLS                                    ' CLEAR THE SCREEN
80 PRINT TAB(7);"INVENTORY REPORT"
90 PRINT
100 PRINT "ITEM NUMBER     DEPT.  QUANTITY"
110 READ I$
120 IF I$="END" THEN 230                  ' END OF DATA MARKER
130 READ Q                                ' READ QUANTITY
140 IF T$<>"" AND T$<>LEFT$(I$,3) THEN GOSUB 1000' CONTROL BREAK
150     S=S+Q                             ' ACCUMULATE SUBTOTAL
160     PRINT I$;TAB(16);LEFT$(I$,3);TAB(20);
170     PRINT USING "#####";Q
180     T$=LEFT$(I$,3)
190     GOTO 110                          ' GET MORE DATA
200 REM
210 REM ***** END OF DATA ROUTINE
220 REM
230 GOSUB 1000                            ' PRINT SUBTOTAL
240 PRINT "PLANT TOTAL";TAB(30);
250 PRINT USING "###### */*";T            ' PRINT TOTAL
260 END
970 REM
980 REM ***** CONTROL SUBROUTINE
990 REM
1000 PRINT "DEPT TOTAL";TAB(16);LEFT$(T$,3);TAB(24);
1010 PRINT USING"###### *";S
1020 T=T+S                                ' ACCUMULATE TOTAL
1030 S=0                                  ' ZERO OUT SUBTOTAL
1040 T$=LEFT$(I$,3)                       ' SET UP TEST FIELD
1050 RETURN
2000 DATA 123-BL-BG45/97,15,123-BL-HT32/132,25,123-RE-F4.6/2,32
2010 DATA 135-BL-RD46/2,765,135-RE-RE3/45,952
2020 DATA 400-GR-4/2,45,400-GR-15/3,46
2030 DATA 452-BL-RF15/2,386
2040 DATA 542-BL-TF45/24,34,542-RE-TF14/35,45
2050 DATA END
```
Program 9–6 (cont.)

)))DIFFERENCES

On the Apple, you will need to include the subroutine we wrote for the data editing and then change lines 170, 250, and 1010 to GOSUB statements, adding a PRINT statement afterwards to print the edited variable (P$) that is returned from the subroutine.

When we run this program, we will get a display like that shown on page 261. A report like this would most likely be printed on the printer instead of simply displayed on the screen. Inventory files would rarely contain few enough items to make screen display practical.

A report like the one we just programmed would consume a lot of paper should there be more than just a few items. Many times the detail lines are not needed, but the department totals are. In such a case we would run virtually the same program except the detail lines would not be printed, only the subtotals and final totals. Such a report is therefore called a **totals report** or a **summary report** since it summarizes the data. The previous report generated as a totals report would look like the following:

```
        INVENTORY REPORT

  ITEM NUMBER    DEPT.   QUANTITY
  DEPT TOTAL     123          72 *
  DEPT TOTAL     135        1717 *
  DEPT TOTAL     400          91 *
  DEPT TOTAL     452         386 *
  DEPT TOTAL     542          79 *
  PLANT TOTAL               2345 */*
```

About the only difference in the program is that we would not print the detail lines, only the total lines.

SUMMARY

1. Over the past few years user-oriented programming has become common. It simply refers to programs that are easy to use.
2. One way to approach user-orientation is with menu-driven programs. These are programs that spell out user options clearly on a full screen menu instead of simply listing them in a prompt.
3. BASIC has a method for positioning the cursor at a specific location on the screen. It is called direct cursor addressing and is usually done by specifying the row and column number of the screen to pinpoint the cursor location.
4. There are certain guidelines to follow in using screen displays. Every screen display should have a heading. The display should be pleasing in appearance and uncluttered. To aid this, blank lines should be used when feasible. Prompts and error messages should appear in the same location on the screen and be as short as possible while maintaining clarity. Prompts should state explicitly what the user is expected to enter, and errors should be displayed to attract the user's attention. A flashing error message is a good technique.
5. There are three things to be concerned about when printing reports: what the report should contain, whether the report should be displayed on the screen or printed on the printer, and what format the report should have.
6. A line spacing chart can be helpful when designing either screen or paper output.

7. The IBM and Radio Shack computers have a PRINT USING command that is exceptionally helpful in data editing. On the Apple, you have to create your own routine for data editing.

8. Many times, subtotals on a report can help the user get more information out of the report. Subtotals are generated using control breaks. Occasionally it is useful to have just the totals printed on a report, which is appropriately called a totals report.

GLOSSARY

Column heading   Information printed at the top of a column of output explaining what is contained in the column.

Control break   The break in processing that occurs when the value of the control field changes. *See also* **Subtotal.**

Control field   The field that is used when printing a report to determine when one grouping that is generating subtotals is completed.

Control total   *See* **Subtotal.**

Detail line   A line of item information on a report.

Direct cursor addressing   Locating the cursor anywhere on the screen without destroying any of the information that is already on the screen.

Double precision   The storage of a number allowing twice as many significant digits as single precision.

Final totals   The totals that appear at the end of a report showing the accumulation from the entire report.

Floating dollar sign   On data editing, the dollar sign that prints just to the left of the left-most digit. Indicated in the program by two $ signs.

HTAB   The direct cursor addressing command for horizontal movement of the cursor on the Apple.

Integer   A number that is stored without decimal digits.

Line spacing chart   A chart of small squares with the columns and rows numbered that can be used to design screen and report layouts.

LOCATE   The direct cursor addressing command on the IBM.

Menu   A selection of program options displayed on the screen.

Menu-driven   A program with options on the screen for the user to choose from, as opposed to a program with the options on a prompt.

Page heading   The information printed at the top of a report telling the user what type of report it is.

PRINT @   The direct cursor addressing command on the Radio Shack.

PRINT USING   A data editing command used on the IBM and Radio Shack computers.

Scientific notation   A method of writing large numbers by specifying, on the right side of the decimal point, the number of digits needed.

Single precision   The storage of a number that allows up to seven digits.

Subtotal   A partial total on a report that gives total information about a group or portion of the output.

Summary report   *See* **Totals report.**

Test field   The temporary field that is used for comparison with the control field to determine when a control break has occurred.

Totals report   A report containing only the subtotals and final totals. The detail lines are left off.

User-oriented programming   Writing programs that are easy for the user to use and understand.

VTAB   The direct cursor addressing command for vertical movement of the cursor on the Apple.

1. Define user-oriented programming and explain why it's important.
2. Describe a menu-driven program.
3. List and explain at least six of the nine screen display guidelines.
*4. Why are error messages important?
5. What are the three factors to be considered when designing a report?
6. What are control breaks and why do we use them?
7. Write a program to output a file of inventory information using the inventory numbers and quantities-on-hand that were used in the example in the text. Then modify the program shown to fit your machine and to input the information from the file. Add to the report the color codes, which are the letters between the dashes, and print out the color instead of the code. The color codes are RE for red, GR for green, BL for black, and YE for yellow. Also add to the report the class code, which is the number following the slash. Use appropriate page and column headings and print subtotals and a final total similar to the report shown in the text. Design the report using a line spacing chart before coding the program.
8. Change the program in question 7 to a totals only report.
9. Return to Chapter 8 and use the MAILFILE created there to print a report of the file instead of labels. Use appropriate page and column headings and use a line spacing chart to design the output.
10. Look back at question 11, page 239, in Chapter 8 and output the information into the file with all salaried employees first. Then print the report with a control break between the salaried and hourly employees and print the appropriate totals and headings on the report.
11. Add an FICA rate of 9.65% and federal tax rate of 22% to question 10 and figure gross and net pay totals and subtotals for each.
*12. Write a menu program that will allow the user to choose among changes in the fields of an inventory record. Display the record on the screen beside a message for the field and an option number. Then prompt the user for the new information and redisplay the new information beside the message on the screen. Design the display using a line spacing chart. A sample screen display might look something like the following:

```
        INVENTORY MAINTENANCE

YOUR OPTIONS ARE:

1.  INVENTORY ITEM      123-RE-BG45/15   ←——prompt should print
                                            here on the row of the
2.  ITEM DESCRIPTION      HORSE COLLAR      entry

3.  QUANTITY-ON-HAND             154

4.  LAST PURCHASE DATE      10/15/84

5.  COST AT LAST PURCHASE     $15.65


WHAT OPTION DO YOU WANT?
```

13. Write a menu display program with 13 options. Use your own option messages, but design the display using a line spacing chart and proper menu techniques.

14. The XYZ Corporation has a fleet of vehicles that it keeps maintenance records on. It is your job to create a file to keep the records in and generate a report giving vital information on the vehicles. You need to store information about the vehicle ID, purchase date, current mileage, date of last five maintenance checks, the mileage reading at each check, and maintenance codes for what repairs were done at the last five maintenance checks. The information you should use (for 3 vehicles) follows:

ID	PUR. DATE	MNT. DATES	MILEAGE @ CHK.	MAINT. CODES
1343	01/10/80	06/12/85	85,345	6,7,8
		05/15/85	84,287	2,5
		03/25/85	81,466	1,2,7
		01/15/85	75,255	5,9,10
		10/09/84	69,455	2
1556	03/15/83	07/01/85	28,345	5
		06/05/85	25,245	2,8,10
		04/03/85	22,345	1,2,3
		01/12/85	19,255	
		11/29/84	18,899	5,6
1666	04/25/85	06/18/85	9,255	2,4,5
		07/22/85	12,346	

Design and create a program to INPUT this information and store it on disk. Then create another program to read the information off the disk and print a report. You will need to print on the report the explanation for the maintenance codes that were stored. If a line in the list contains no maintenance codes, that means no maintenance was necessary. The codes are explained below:

CODE	EXPLANATION
1	Oil change
2	Replace fan belt
3	Carburetor kit
4	Tune up
5	Replace tires
6	Repair air conditioning
7	Coolant system
8	Complete engine overhaul
9	Safety sticker
10	Body work

The report program should appear as follows (only a small part of the report is shown):

```
             VEHICLE MAINTENANCE REPORT

                    MILAGE
   ID    MNT. DATE  BETWEEN   MNT. CODE    EXPLANATION
   1343  06/12/85   1058          6        REPAIR AIR CONDITIONING
                                  7        COOLANT SYSTEM
                                  8        COMPLETE ENGINE OVERHAUL

         05/15/85   2821          2        REPLACE FAN BELT
                                  5        REPLACE TIRES
```

Note that the "mileage between" refers to the mileage at the time of maintenance minus the mileage at the time of the previous maintenance. For the last maintenance date, leave the "mileage between" column blank.

QUICK QUIZ

The answers to the questions follow immediately after the quiz. Questions 1–15 are true–false, while 16–20 are multiple choice.

1. User-oriented programming is a new concept. **T F**
2. Menu-driven programs use menus of options for users to choose among. **T F**
3. The first thing to do when displaying a menu is to print the heading. **T F**
4. You have to be careful how you use the direct cursor addressing commands, as they can sometimes disturb what is already displayed on the screen. **T F**
5. Direct cursor addressing is done by positioning the cursor to the particular row and column where you want the cursor to be. **T F**
6. Flashing an error message can be accomplished by printing the message and then printing blanks in the same place to make the message disappear. **T F**
7. You should always use some type of heading at the top of your screen displays. **T F**
8. It is best to have as many different screen displays as possible in a program to avoid confusing the user. **T F**
9. Prompts and error messages should always appear on the screen under the item to be changed when doing on-screen changes. **T F**
10. Explain yourself as clearly as possible in all prompts using two lines or even three if necessary. **T F**
11. It is best to use a numeric code on your error messages to facilitate the user looking them up in the manual. **T F**
12. The first thing to do when writing a report program is to decide what information the user needs to see on the report. **T F**
13. Detail lines are always the first thing printed on a report. **T F**

T F **14.** A line spacing chart can help you decide where to put the information when printing a report or designing a screen layout.

T F **15.** Data editing is useful for printing character information in nice, straight columns.

_____ **16.** Which of the following commands is not available for the Apple?

    a. direct cursor addressing   **c.** LEN
    b. PRINT USING   **d.** all are available

_____ **17.** Which of the following is _not_ a part of the same structure as the others?

    a. subtotal   **c.** final total
    b. control total   **d.** control break

_____ **18.** The field that is compared to the control field is called the

    a. index field   **c.** pointer field
    b. test field   **d.** none of these

_____ **19.** Which of the following conveys information to the user directly from the data file?

    a. subtotal   **c.** detail line
    b. column heading   **d.** control field

_____ **20.** Which of the following commands is not used for direct cursor addressing?

    a. PRINT @   **c.** HTAB
    b. PRINT USING   **d.** all are used

ANSWERS TO QUICK QUIZ

1. T (It actually began with the introduction of microcomputers.)
2. T
3. F (The first thing to do is clear the screen.)
4. F (In general they do not disturb what is already on the screen, though the Radio Shack cursor addressing command is a PRINT statement.)
5. T
6. T
7. T
8. F (Having too many screen displays is very confusing.)
9. F (They should always appear in the same location, generally the bottom line of the screen.)
10. F (Try to avoid using more than one line, while maintaining clarity.)

11. F (You should never force the user to look up error messages.)
12. T
13. F (The page heading is the first thing.)
14. T
15. F (Characters are not generally a problem; it is with numeric output that data editing comes in handy.)
16. b (The PRINT USING is for the IBM and Radio Shack.)
17. c (The other three all deal with control breaks.)
18. b
19. c (The detail line is direct file information.)
20. b (PRINT USING is for data editing.)

10 PROMPTS AND ERRORS

OBJECTIVES

After completing Chapter 10, you will be able to:

- Explain the three differences between the INPUT statement and the character input command (the INKEY$ or GET).
- Explain how to program the character input statement.
- Explain the purpose of the asterisks printed after the prompt on the character input.
- Explain why a different character might be used for the character input statement.
- Explain how to compare for the RETURN and backspace keys.
- Use all the techniques described thus far to write several programs.

In the last chapter we learned to utilize the bottom line of the screen to display prompts and error messages. When we did the entry for the prompts we used the INPUT statement. In this chapter we will review how to use the INKEY$ (or GET on the Apple) to give us a much more flexible input format. Then we will examine how to recover from many of the errors that typically occur in business programming.

In Chapter 7 we learned how to use the **INKEY$** on the IBM and Radio Shack and the **GET** on the Apple. We will take a brief moment here to examine it again.

There are basically three differences between the character input function (we will use the INKEY$ for discussion purposes; remember that GET is used for the Apple) and the regular INPUT statement. First, the INKEY$ does not require the RETURN to be pressed to terminate the entry. The INKEY$ inputs only one character. Second, the INKEY$ does not **echo** the character back to the screen. If you want the character displayed, you must print it on the screen. Third, the INKEY$ retrieves only string characters. If you want a numeric entry, you have to convert the string.

Recall the form of the INKEY$ is:

```
10 string variable = INKEY$
```

While the GET looks like:

```
10 GET string variable
```

This function will examine the keyboard to see if any key has been pressed. If any key has been pressed, that key code is returned into the string variable. The keyboard is scanned so quickly that we have to check the variable to verify that something was entered. This is handled with the following routine (remember, the Apple IIe and IIc don't need the test):

```
10 A$=INKEY$
20 IF A$="" THEN 10        ' IF EMPTY THEN CHECK AGAIN
```

This small loop will return any key pressed, then check to see if one was. If A$ is null (empty), then no key was pressed and the program loops back to 10 to check again. It will continue to do this until a key is pressed.

Keep in mind that the INKEY$ will not cause the key pressed to display on the screen. If you want to see it displayed, it must be echoed to the screen with a print line such as the following:

```
10 A$=INKEY$
20 IF A$="" THEN 10        ' IF EMPTY THEN CHECK AGAIN
30 PRINT A$                ' THE ECHO
```

This type of routine can be used to trap keys that cause something to happen rather than display a character on the screen. Keys such as the RETURN key, ASCII code of 13, and backspace key, ASCII code of 8, can be trapped with the INKEY$. The following program shows a small example of this:

```
10 A$=INKEY$
20 IF A$="" THEN 10          ' IF EMPTY THEN CHECK AGAIN
30 IF A$=CHR$(13) OR A$=CHR$(8) THEN 10
40 PRINT A$
```

Now when you run the program, it will seem to do nothing if you press the RETURN key or backspace key. In reality, it is trapping the key on line 30 and returning to the INKEY$ command. Notice that we used the CHR$ function in the IF-THEN test. This test could also be done with the ASC function:

```
30 IF ASC(A$)=13 OR ASC(A$)=8 THEN 10
```

The result of running the program will be exactly the same as with the CHR$ program above. There is no particular advantage to either method. Use the method you prefer.

10–3
USING THE INKEY$ WITH PROMPTS

When we discussed prompting in the last chapter, we positioned the cursor on the bottom line of the screen and then used the INPUT statement. We can do virtually the same thing with the INKEY$, but it will be much more flexible. For example, we can construct the INKEY$ in a routine that allows only a certain number of characters to be entered (as the next routine shows). Notice in this routine that we are constructing it as a subroutine using relatively high line numbers. We are doing this so that when we finish with the routine we can use it as a subroutine in future programs. We also skipped several line numbers (for example, lines 60 and 70). This is so we can add needed lines as we continue to construct the routine.

```
10 REM ***** PROGRAM NAME: VARINKEY
20 REM
30 REM ***** WRITTEN BY EDWARD J. COBURN
40 REM
50 CLS
80 GOSUB 7130                    ' PROMPT INPUT ROUTINE
90 END
6970 REM
6980 REM ***** PROMPT AND INPUT ROUTINE
6990 REM
7130 FOR I9=1 TO 4
7140     A$=INKEY$
7150     IF A$="" THEN 7140      ' CHECK FOR CHARACTER
7260     B$=B$+A$                ' ACCUMULATE ENTIRE STRING
7270     PRINT A$                ' ECHO
7280 NEXT I9
7290 PRINT
7300 PRINT "THE WHOLE STRING IS ";B$
7310 RETURN
```
                                        Program 10–1

)))DIFFERENCES

Line 50 on the Apple should be:

```
50 HOME
```

Line 7140 on the Apple should be the GET statement, and on the IIe and IIc, line 7150 is not needed.

When we run the program, we will need to enter four characters, and then the whole string will be printed back. Notice that the characters will be echoed as the loop functions.

```
RUN
A
B
C
D
THE WHOLE STRING IS ABCD
Ok
```

This is not the way we would like the entry to be displayed. We can fix that by putting a semicolon on the end of line 7270. Let's do that and try the program again.

```
RUN
ABCD
THE WHOLE STRING IS ABCD
Ok
```

Now let's make the routine more flexible by using a variable length for the input. We can do this by changing the FOR statement to:

```
7130 FOR I9=1 TO L          ' INPUT LOOP L=PROMPT LENGTH
```

Of course we will have to set L before using the routine. Let's add line 70:

```
70 L=3                      ' LENGTH OF THE INPUT STRING
```

Now the length of the input will be 3. Let's see that by executing the program again:

```
RUN
ABC
THE WHOLE STRING IS ABC
Ok
```

Notice that the program released as soon as three characters had been input. This allows the length of our input to be whatever is necessary. For example, suppose you are asking the user for a number that can only be 1 through 9. It makes the user's job a bit easier if your program only accepts one digit. That keeps the user from entering a number 10 or above by mistake.

Earlier we mentioned prompting the user. The routine we have rigged thus far has no capacity for prompting, but we can do it simply by positioning the cursor where it needs to be and then printing the appropriate message. To position the cursor, we will use the cursor positioning subroutine we used in the last chapter. But we need to add two more things to our little routine. We need to set the row and column, GOSUB the cursor positioning routine, and then print the message. Let's begin properly and print the message as a variable. Add the following lines to your routine.

For the IBM, Radio Shack Model 4, Apple:

```
7000 R=24
7010 C=1
```

For the Radio Shack Model III:

```
7000 R=16
7010 C=0
```

Then for all of them:

```
7020 GOSUB 5000                      ' POSITION THE CURSOR
```

To have a prompt printed, we will put it in a string variable:

```
60 P$="THIS IS THE PROMPT"
```

And finally we will clear the line (the Radio Shacks will use more blanks in the STRING$ command) and print the prompt in the subroutine:

```
7030 PRINT STRING$(39," ");
7040 GOSUB 5000              ' POSITION THE CURSOR
7050 PRINT P$;              ' PRINT THE PROMPT
```

For the Apple we will print as follows:

```
7030 PRINT MID$(CL$,1,39);
7040 GOSUB 5000              : REM POSITION THE CURSOR
7050 PRINT P$;              : REM PRINT THE PROMPT
```

Line 7030 requires the addition of a fill routine for CL$ (Apple only):

```
52 CL$=""
54 FOR I=1 TO 6
56      CL$=CL$+CL$
58 NEXT I
```

Notice the semicolon at the end of the statement to print the prompt. This way the entry will follow the prompt just as with an INPUT statement. Note that we have changed the beginning line number of the subroutine, so line 80 will have to be changed to reflect the new routine line number.

Now the whole program should look like Program 10–2. Notice that we have added the prompt routine. This is the IBM version of the program; we will not list the differences for Radio Shack and Apple here since we looked at the differences as we constructed the routine.

```
10 REM ***** PROGRAM NAME: VARINKEY
20 REM
30 REM ***** WRITTEN BY EDWARD J. COBURN
40 REM
50 CLS                       ' CLEAR THE SCREEN
60 P$="THIS IS THE PROMPT"
70 L=3                       ' LENGTH OF THE INPUT STRING
80 GOSUB 7000                ' PROMPT INPUT ROUTINE
90 END
4970 REM
4980 REM ***** CURSOR POSITIONING ROUTINE
4990 REM
```

Program 10–2

Program continues

```
5000 LOCATE R,C
5010 RETURN
6970 REM
6980 REM ***** PROMPT AND INPUT ROUTINE
6990 REM
7000 R=24
7010 C=1
7020 GOSUB 5000                        ' POSITION THE CURSOR
7030 PRINT STRING$(39," ");
7040 GOSUB 5000                        ' POSITION THE CURSOR
7050 PRINT P$;                         ' PRINT THE PROMPT
7130 FOR I=1 TO L                      ' INPUT LOOP L=PROMPT LENGTH
7140    A$=INKEY$
7150    IF A$="" THEN 7140             ' CHECK FOR CHARACTER
7260    B$=B$+A$                       ' ACCUMULATE ENTIRE STRING
7270    PRINT A$;                      ' ECHO
7280 NEXT I
7290 PRINT
7300 PRINT "THE WHOLE STRING IS ";B$
7310 RETURN                            Program 10-2 (cont.)
```

Now when we run the program the display will look like the following (except that the prompt will be at the bottom line of the screen):

```
RUN
THIS IS THE PROMPTABC
THE WHOLE STRING IS ABC
Ok
```

Notice two things about this entry. First, there is no space between the prompt and the entry. This can be taken care of in the prompt printing statement. Also, there is no question mark as with a prompt from an input statement. This is deliberate. Many times a prompt is not a question, so a question mark is inappropriate. The way the prompt is structured using the INKEY$, we can use a question mark when it is appropriate and leave it off when it isn't.

We have constructed the input loop such that length of the input can be determined. That's fine for us as programmers. We know how many characters the input is supposed to be. But what about the user? There is no indication to the user as to how many characters to type. Well, there can be. Right after we print the prompt, we can print some type of marker so the user will know how many characters are expected. How many characters should be displayed? This has already been determined by the assignment of L, the length of the input. With only a couple of changes, we can display the size of the entry.

```
7080 FOR I9=1 TO L
7090   PRINT "*";                      ' PRINT PROMPT MARKERS
7100 NEXT I9
```

This will display L (in our example, 3) asterisks as an indication to the user. The asterisk is simply a matter of programmer choice. You can display any character you choose to. Some programmers like a period, some like an X, and some like different characters for different types of input; for example, an asterisk for characters, a number symbol (#) for numeric entries. Fancy programs will even display something like MM/DD/YY when a date is expected. For our examples we will go the simple route and use asterisks.

Note: If you are using the IBM or Radio Shack, you can substitute a PRINT

STRING$(L,"*") statement for the previously mentioned loop. The loop is used throughout the book for the sake of consistency.

You may have noticed that we have forgotten something. If we display the asterisks as we have specified, they will follow immediately after the prompt, such as:

```
THIS IS THE PROMPT***
```

This is not a good way to do it. We could change line 60 to print a blank after the prompt, but there is a better way to do it. If we use the INKEY$ after we print the asterisks, the echo will be at the end of the asterisks, such as:

```
THIS IS THE PROMPT***A
```

We haven't repositioned the cursor so it will still be at the end of the asterisks. Since we are going to have to determine where we are on the display line so we can position the cursor to the beginning of the asterisks for the INKEY$ echo, we might as well figure the position now and put the asterisks there in the actual position. We can determine the position for the asterisks by figuring the length of the prompt string and then moving over two spaces. We can do this with the LEN command, such as:

```
7050 PRINT P$;            ' PRINT THE PROMPT
7060 C=LEN(P$)+2          ' FIND THE COLUMN TO BEGIN
7070 GOSUB 5000           ' POSITION THE CURSOR
```

We move the cursor over *two* positions because the LEN of P$ puts the cursor on the last character of P$ and LEN P$ plus one puts the cursor in the first space after P$. Thus, if we want the cursor to be positioned with a blank between P$ and the first asterisk, we must move over two positions.

Now when we position the cursor, it will be right where we need the asterisks. Then we can print the asterisks and reposition the cursor back to the first asterisk. This requires an additional statement:

```
7110 GOSUB 5000                     ' POSITION THE CURSOR
```

It was not necessary to refigure either the row or column number here since the row is still the bottom of the screen and the column was specified in line 7060.

We need one final statement before we can begin to test the program. Since this routine will be used many times in the program, we need to empty the collection string so that our entry will not keep accumulating into it. We need to add:

```
7120 B$=""                          ' NULL THE STRING
```

Now let's run the program and see how it works. The first display you should see is:

```
RUN
THIS IS THE PROMPT ***
```

After you enter one character, you should see:

```
THIS IS THE PROMPT A**
```

And after you enter all three, you should see:

```
THIS IS THE PROMPT ABC
THE WHOLE STRING IS ABC
Ok
```

Now we have a much more user-oriented input routine. There are, however, a few more things that we can add to make the routine even better. We mentioned that we can trap nonprinting keys such as the RETURN and backspace keys. What will happen in our prompt if the user presses an incorrect key and wants to redo it? Our routine will not be able to handle it. Actually, the screen would seem to be backspacing (except on the IBM), but actually it would merely be printing the backspace character code. Our count will continue, and we will lose two characters. For example, suppose we pressed an A when we meant to press a B; we then press the backspace (which seems to work) and then press B. This, however, would give us a total of three characters: A, backspace, and B. We can fix the problem by trapping the backspace key.

To trap the backspace, we need a short procedure, which is different for the IBM than for the Radio Shack and Apple. We will describe the IBM procedure first.

Once we have decided that the backspace key was pressed, we need to determine where the cursor is currently located. We can do this with the **POS(O)** command. Then, since we are trying to backspace, we can assign the column number to be one less than the current location by using $C = POS(O) - 1$. Then we GOSUB to move the cursor back to the character we just echoed. Next, we need to redisplay an asterisk for answering the prompt. This, of course, moves the cursor over again so we have to do another backspace using the GOSUB again. We don't have to reassign C since it hasn't changed. The needed lines will look like the following:

```
7160      IF A$<>CHR$(8) THEN 7260 ' CHECK FOR BACKSPACE
7170          IF I9=1 THEN 7140 ' NO BACKSPACE WHEN 1ST CHAR.
7180          C=POS(O)-1          ' REDUCE THE COLUMN
7182          GOSUB 5000          ' POSITION THE CURSOR
7184          PRINT "*";          ' PRINT THE MARKER
7186          GOSUB 5000          ' POSITION THE CURSOR
7190          I9=I9-1             ' REDUCE COUNTER
7210          GOTO 7140           ' GET CHARACTER AGAIN
```

For the Radio Shack and Apple, we can use the same routine, except that lines 7180–7186 can be made one line. All we have to do is print a backspace, which is CHR$(8), the replacement asterisk, and another backspace. This can be done with one line as:

```
7180          PRINT CHR$(8);"*";CHR$(8); ' BACK, MARKER, BACK
```

Now let's try the program to see how it works.

```
RUN
THIS IS THE PROMPT ***
```

Enter an A:

```
THIS IS THE PROMPT A**
```

Now press the backspace:

```
THIS IS THE PROMPT ***
```

Very nice. Now press the backspace again, and nothing will happen. Since we are at the beginning of the prompt, line 7170 eliminates the backspace. Now fill in the three characters:

```
THIS IS THE PROMPT BCD
THE WHOLE STRING IS ABCD
Ok
```

Where did the A come from? There's a problem. When we input A, we concatenated it to the whole string (line 7260). But now that we backspaced, we need to remove it from the string. We can do that by adding line 7200:

```
7200         B$=MID$(B$,1,LEN(B$)-1) ' DROP END CHARACTER
```

Try it again, and don't forget to use the backspace a couple of times.

There is only one more addition we need to make to the input routine. We are printing a certain number of asterisks to indicate to the user how many characters are appropriate for the entry. Suppose, however, that the user doesn't need all the characters. Perhaps we are inputting a name. The length of a name field input would be in the range of 24 to 30 characters, but most names are shorter. After the user has entered all the characters necessary it would be good if, by pressing the RETURN key, the entry could be concluded. We can change our program slightly to include just such a routine. We merely need to add a check (and the routine conclusion) for the RETURN key. If you recall, the ASCII decimal code for RETURN is 13; that's what we will look for using the following lines:

```
7220    IF A$<>CHR$(13) THEN 7260 ' RETURN PRESSED?
7230        I9=L              ' INCREASE COUNTER TO MAX
7240        PRINT STRING$(L-LEN(B$)," ");
7250        GOTO 7280         ' THIS WILL END LOOP
```

──

)))DIFFERENCES

Here the Apple will use the MID$ command instead of the STRING$ command:

```
7240         PRINT MID$(CL$,1,L-LEN(B$));
```

──

When we add these lines, we need to go back to line 7160 and change the branch so that it will now branch to the appropriate line. Otherwise, the routine would merely branch around our new lines.

With this inclusion, when the user presses RETURN before filling the prompt field, the program will release as if all the characters had been entered. Notice that line 7240 prints blanks for the number of characters that are left on the prompt line. Since the length of the input field is L, if we subtract the number of characters that have been entered into B$, we are left with the number of asterisks that are remaining on the line. By printing those as blanks, we spruce up the appearance of our input line.

WIth this final addition, the program is now as follows (the differences have already been listed):

```
10 REM ***** PROGRAM NAME: VARINKEY
20 REM
30 REM ***** WRITTEN BY EDWARD J. COBURN
40 REM
50 CLS                              ' CLEAR THE SCREEN
60 P$="THIS IS THE PROMPT"
70 L=3                              ' LENGTH OF THE INPUT STRING
80 GOSUB 7000                       ' PROMPT INPUT ROUTINE
90 END
4970 REM
4980 REM ***** CURSOR POSITIONING ROUTINE
4990 REM
5000 LOCATE R,C
5010 RETURN
6970 REM
6980 REM ***** PROMPT AND INPUT ROUTINE
6990 REM
7000 R=24
7010 C=1
7020 GOSUB 5000                     ' POSITION THE CURSOR
7030 PRINT STRING$(39," ");
7040 GOSUB 5000                     ' POSITION THE CURSOR
7050 PRINT P$;                      ' PRINT THE PROMPT
7060 C=LEN(P$)+2                    ' FIND THE COLUMN TO BEGIN
7070 GOSUB 5000                     ' POSITION THE CURSOR
7080 FOR I=1 TO L
7090     PRINT "*";                 ' PRINT PROMPT MARKERS
7100 NEXT I
7110 GOSUB 5000                     ' POSITION THE CURSOR
7120 B$=""                          ' NULL THE STRING
7130 FOR I9=1 TO L                  ' INPUT LOOP L=PROMPT LENGTH
7140     A$=INKEY$
7150     IF A$="" THEN 7140         ' CHECK FOR CHARACTER
7160     IF A$<>CHR$(8) THEN 7220          ' CHECK FOR BACKSPACE
7170         IF I9=1 THEN 7140 ' NO BACKSPACE WHEN 1ST CHAR.
7180         C=POS(0)-1             ' REDUCE THE COLUMN
7182         GOSUB 5000             ' POSITION THE CURSOR
7184         PRINT "*";            ' PRINT THE MARKER
7186         GOSUB 5000             ' POSITION THE CURSOR
7190         I9=I9-1                ' REDUCE COUNTER
7200         B$=MID$(B$,1,LEN(B$)-1)     ' DROP END CHARACTER
7210         GOTO 7140              ' GET CHARACTER AGAIN
7220     IF A$<>CHR$(13) THEN 7260       ' RETURN PRESSED?
7230         I9=L                   ' INCREASE COUNTER TO MAX
7240         PRINT STRING$(L-LEN(B$)," ");
7250         GOTO 7280              ' THIS WILL END LOOP
7260     B$=B$+A$                   ' ACCUMULATE ENTIRE STRING
7270     PRINT A$;                  ' ECHO
7280 NEXT I9
7290 PRINT
7300 PRINT "THE WHOLE STRING IS ";B$
7310 RETURN
```

Program 10–3

Now you should understand this routine well enough to make any changes necessary, such as using the number symbol (#) to prompt numeric entry and MM/DD/YY to prompt date entry.

Now that we have this new routine, let's combine it with the information from the previous chapter about menus and write an add routine for adding records to a file. We will begin with the screen display of the fields to input: name, address, city, state, zip code, and phone number. We will create our program with a flexible format by using our field names and field lengths in a DATA table. We will then read the DATA into an array and print the field names on the screen. Designated cursor positions will then be used to input the data at the end of the field names. We can do this by positioning the cursor to the appropriate location. The program will look like the following:

```
10 REM ***** PROGRAM NAME: DATAIN
20 REM
30 REM ***** WRITTEN BY EDWARD J. COBURN
40 REM
50 REM THIS PROGRAM WILL INPUT VARIOUS FIELDS OF DATA
60 REM
70 DATA NAME, 24, ADDRESS, 24, CITY, 15, STATE, 2
80 DATA ZIP CODE, 9, PHONE NUMBER, 12
90 FOR I=1 TO 6
100    READ A$(I),A(I)         ' DISPLAY INFO, FIELD LENGTH
110 NEXT I
120 CLS                        ' CLEAR THE SCREEN
130 PRINT TAB(15);"RECORD ENTRY"
140 PRINT
150 FOR I=1 TO 6               ' DISPLAY LOOP
160    PRINT STR$(I);". ";A$(I)
170 NEXT I
180 FOR J=1 TO 6               ' ENTRY LOOP
190    L=A(J)
200    R=3+J-1                 ' ROW OF ENTRY
210    C=17                    ' COLUMN OF ENTRY
220    GOSUB 7070              ' PROMPT SUBROUTINE
230 NEXT J
240 END
```
Program 10—4

)))DIFFERENCES

On the Apple, line 120 should use HOME instead of CLS, and on line 160 the STR$ command is not needed. It is used in the program to eliminate the space that usually follows a number. The Apple does not print the space, so the STR$ is not necessary.

Notice that we GOSUB not to the beginning of the subroutine (which would be line 7000) but to a few lines past the beginning (line 7070). This way we skip past the prompting and go straight to the input part of the subroutine. Incidentally, on the machines with 24 lines, you may want to double space between the entry lines. To do that you insert line 165:

```
165 PRINT
```

and change line 200 to:

```
200      R=3+(J-1)*2              ' ROW OF ENTRY
```

Don't forget to put the subroutines for cursor positioning and prompting on the end of this program. Now let's run the program and see how it works. You should see the following display (the printed asterisks are programmed in the prompting subroutine):

```
RECORD ENTRY

1. NAME              **************************
2. ADDRESS
3. CITY
4. STATE
5. ZIP CODE
6. PHONE NUMBER
```

After you enter the name, you will be prompted for the address, then the city, and so on. Now, it would be nice if the user were able to change one of the entries if necessary. We can add a few lines to the end of the program to allow such changes. First, we need to prompt the user:

```
240 P$="WHAT FIELD TO CHANGE (0 TO END)?"
250 L=1                          ' LENGTH OF PROMPT
260 GOSUB 7000                   ' PROMPT SUBROUTINE
```

Now we edit (in B$) the answer returned from the prompt subroutine:

```
270 IF B$="0" THEN 400           ' ZERO TO END
280 A=VAL(B$)                    ' SHOULD BE NUMBER
290 IF A>0 AND A<7 THEN 330      ' VALID ENTRY BRANCH
300     M$="INVALID ENTRY.  TRY AGAIN"
310     GOSUB 6000               ' ERROR SUBROUTINE
320     GOTO 240                 ' RETURN FOR NEW INPUT
```

Line 270 checks for a zero, which is the indication that the user is finished. If a zero was entered, the record would be dumped into the file. (That part of the program will not be shown here. It is left as an exercise at the end of the chapter.) Then we convert the input to a number; if it is less than zero or greater than six, invalid data was entered so we set the error message and GOSUB the error routine that we set up in the previous chapter. You will, of course, need to put that routine into this program also.

Now we are ready for the actual reentry of the data. We begin by reassigning the appropriate column. Then we determine the proper row by using the input number (lines 270 and 280) and the length of the field by using the DATA in the array. Then we GOSUB the part of the prompt subroutine that we need. Finally, we branch back to the prompt for the field number to change. The code will look like the following:

```
330 C=17                         ' COLUMN OF ENTRY
340 R=3+A-1                      ' ROW OF ENTRY
350 L=A(A)                       ' LENGTH OF FIELD
360 GOSUB 7070                   ' PROMPT ENTRY
370 GOTO 240                     ' RETURN TO FIELD PROMPT
380 REM
390 REM
400 END                          ' HERE WE WOULD ADD THE RECORD
```

Notice that the end of the program at line 400 states that we would add the records here. This is the point where the program would continue.

Now when you execute the program, it will prompt for all the fields just as before. After all six of the fields are keyed in, the program will ask if you need to change any of them. If you enter a number between 1 and 6, that field will be reprompted. If you enter 0, the program will branch to the end where you can add the routine to put the records into a file.

This same prompting routine is appropriate for a record change routine. That is, if the user indicates that a particular record needs to be changed, the fields may be displayed on the screen and then the cursor positioned to the appropriate field to be changed. After the field has been reentered and the user indicates completion, the record may be put back into the file. However, to do this type of processing you need better file access than sequential processing. Further disk processing ideas will be covered in the next few chapters.

10–5
ERROR TRAPS

We have in the past few chapters used various error traps. The ones we have used, however, have been for trapping invalid data input by the user. In this section we will discuss the trapping of errors in our programs or in the machines. Such error trapping is necessary for disk processing so that programs will help the user instead of simply crashing. Suppose, for example, the user (via a program prompt) asks for a file to be opened in a disk drive that doesn't have a disk in it. The computer would print an error message such as "Device I/O error" and stop. Instead, we can trap that error, flash a message to the user describing the error, and then prompt again. This is the type of error trapping, then, that we will be looking at. (Appendix D has a complete list of the possible errors that occur in our versions of BASIC and the error codes that are associated with them.)

The IBM and Radio Shack

Many errors that would disrupt program execution can be trapped on the IBM and Radio Shack. The statement that makes this trapping possible is the **ON ERROR GOTO** statement, which has the form:

```
10 ON ERROR GOTO line number
```

Upon detection of an error, the program will branch to the line number specified and proceed from there.

Though error trapping techniques vary, many programmers will place an ON ERROR GOTO statement somewhere near the beginning of the program. The error routine is then used to determine the type of error that has occurred. Other programmers prefer to use separate error traps in various areas of the program.

The type of error is determined with the **ERR** command. The form of this command differs between the IBM and Radio Shack. The form of the statement in the Radio Shack is more complicated than the simple ERR used on the IBM. The Radio Shack uses **ERR/2 + 1** to determine the error number.

These statements are used to determine the error number, which can be used in the error routine to decide which course of action to follow. For example, on the IBM if the disk drive was left open as we mentioned before, the error message that would be printed without the error trap would be:

```
Device I/O error
```

and the trapped error number would be 57. Therefore, in your error routine you could put a test to determine the error number, and if it were 57 your program could print a message indicating some unidentified disk error. Then, after the user corrected the fault, the program processing could continue. Without the error trap, when the error occurred the program would simply crash.

In order for processing to continue, control of the program must be returned from the error routine to some point in the program. This is accomplished with the **RESUME** statement, which directs the computer to transfer control to one of three possible places:

1. If you use RESUME without a line number, the program will return to the statement where the error occurred. For example, if a disk access caused the error because the disk drive door was open, after the error message was flashed and the user prompted, the program would again check the drive to see if it could access the disk this time. Of course, if the problem was not corrected, the error would occur again.
2. If you use RESUME followed by a line number, the program will branch to that particular line number to begin processing again.
3. If you use a RESUME NEXT statement, the program will branch to the statement following the one where the error occurred.

It is vital when using an ON ERROR GOTO routine that control be returned with a RESUME statement. If your program simply branches back into the program, the next time an ON ERROR GOTO is needed, it will not function. Also, if the RESUME is not used and a STOP, END, or RETURN statement is encountered, an error will occur, but this error will not be trapped.

If you have set an error trap that you need disabled later in the program, you can do this with a special ON ERROR GOTO statement. When you add a zero to the statement, such as **ON ERROR GOTO O,** then the error trap your program is currently using is discontinued. That means that the next error that occurs will cause the program to print the error message and halt.

IBM and Radio Shack BASIC can handle only one error at a time. For example, if you have trapped an error and while processing is in your error routine another error occurs, the second error will not be trapped, and the program will halt with a system error.

One additional statement is sometimes useful. The **ERL** statement can be used to determine the line where an error occurred. If you have a routine that traps errors from several locations in the program, it might be necessary to determine in which area of the program an error occurred to determine the course of action to take. It can also be useful when debugging programs because sometimes you may have a syntax error or something similar that is trapped by your error trapping routine. Your error routine will not be set up for such a situation, but you can use the ERL to determine the line number of the error. After examining the line number, you can decide what to do. You may, in such cases, also want to print the error number to indicate the type of error that occurred.

The Apple

We discussed briefly the error trapping statements used on the Apple in Chapter 8. We will discuss them a bit more now.

Many errors that would disrupt program execution can be trapped on the Apple. The statement that makes this trapping possible is the **ONERR GOTO** statement, which has the form:

```
10 ONERR GOTO line number
```

Upon detection of an error, the program will branch to the line number specified and proceed from there.

Though error trapping techniques vary, many programmers will place an ONERR GOTO statement somewhere near the beginning of the program. The error routine is then used to determine the type of error that has occurred. Other programmers prefer to use separate error traps in various areas of the program.

The type of error is determined with the **PEEK (222)** command. This command will return the number of the error that occurred. The example we used in Chapter 8 was the error number 5 for end-of-file, but many other errors can be trapped. Appendix C has a complete list of Apple errors and their corresponding numbers.

The PEEK (222) statement is used to determine the error number, which can be used in the error routine to decide which course of action to follow. For example, on the Apple if the end-of-file was reached by trying to access too many records, the error message that would be printed without the error trap would be:

```
END OF DATA
```

and the trapped error number would be 5. Therefore, in your error routine you could put a test to determine the error number; if it were 5, your program could print a message indicating that the end-of-file was reached and the program could continue. Without the error trap, when the error occurred the program would simply crash.

If you have set an error trap that you need disabled later in the program, you can do this with a **POKE 216,0.** This will cause the error trap to be discontinued, which means that the next error that occurs will cause the program to print an error message and halt.

SUMMARY

1. Earlier we saw how to use the INPUT command to input data on a menu. In this chapter we learned a more flexible method using the INKEY$.
2. The INKEY$ is used on the IBM and Radio Shack; the Apple uses the GET command. There are three differences between the functioning of the char-

acter input and the regular input. First, the INKEY$ does not require the RETURN to be pressed to terminate entry; second, the INKEY$ does not echo the character; and third, it is used to input only string characters.

3. In this chapter we used the INKEY$ command to create a flexible prompting routine to print a prompt and then input however many characters are specified. We created the routine such that it would be able to backspace and terminate the entry with the RETURN key should the entire entry area not be necessary.

4. Utilizing this new routine, we created a data entry program for inputting several fields. This routine would be useful for adding records to a file or changing some of the records in the file.

5. Previously we used error traps to capture data input errors. In this chapter we looked at how our various versions of BASIC utilize error trapping commands to trap errors in the program or the machine.

The IBM and Radio Shack use an ON ERROR GOTO command to trap the error and the RESUME command to end the trap routine. In addition, the ERR command will return the error number, and the ERL command will indicate the line where the error occurred.

The Apple uses the ONERR GOTO command to begin the routine; you can determine the number of the error by using the PEEK (222) command.

GLOSSARY

Echo The display of an input character using the character input command. The character must be printed to be seen since the character input command does not display the character.

ERL The command in IBM and Radio Shack BASIC to get the line number of an error.

ERR The command in IBM BASIC to get the number of an error.

ERR/2+1 The statement in Radio Shack BASIC to get the number of an error.

GET The character input command for the Apple.

INKEY$ The character input command for the IBM and Radio Shack.

ONERR GOTO The Apple command to begin the error trapping procedure.

ON ERROR GOTO The command on the IBM and Radio Shack to begin the error trapping procedure.

ON ERROR GOTO O The command in the IBM and Radio Shack to turn off an error trapping routine.

PEEK (222) The command in Apple BASIC to get the number of an error. (PEEK may also be used on the IBM and Radio Shack.)

POKE 216,0 The Apple command to turn off an error trapping routine.

POS(O) The IBM command to find the cursor column position.

RESUME The command in IBM and Radio Shack BASIC to continue execution of a program after an error trap.

QUESTIONS TO AID UNDERSTANDING

1. What are the three differences between the INPUT statement and the character input command (either INKEY$ or GET)?

2. What is the second statement necessary when you use the character input command, and why is it necessary?

*3. What is the purpose of printing the asterisks on the screen after the prompt is printed?

*4. Why might you choose to use a character other than an asterisk for the purpose mentioned in 3 above?

5. Why do we need to determine the cursor column number for the IBM prompting routine and not for the other machines?

6. What ASCII code is used for the RETURN key?

*7. Construct a short entry routine that uses MM/DD/YY as the prompt. Construct it so that as the user enters the response, the program will automatically skip the slashes. The user should only have to press six characters to enter the entire date.

8. Use the routine designed in the program for the data entry menu screen (Program 10–4) to add records to a file. The add routine will need to follow the entry of the 0 code.

9. Add to the program in question 8 above a routine to retrieve the records from the disk and display them with the same type of display used for inputting the records. You will need to use an array to get the records out of the file. After all the records have been changed, close the file, reopen it, and write the records back into the file. This is one of the few ways to update a sequential file.

10. Create a program to read the sequential records you will have stored in question 8 above and write a report listing all the records. Use appropriate headings for the report.

11. Write a program, using the menu and prompting methods we have learned, to create a file with each record containing a name and eight grades that you randomly generate from 50 to 100. Input the name for the record, generate the eight grades, and then dump the record into the file. You should create at least ten records.

12. Write a program to read the records created by the program in question 11 and display them on a menu screen. Then use a prompt to allow the user to change the name or any of the grades. You will need to use an array to read the records into the program. After all the records have been changed, close the file, reopen it, and write the records back into the file.

13. Write a program to read the file created in question 11 and print a report detailing the average grade of each student. Also provide a total average at the end of the list. The total average should be calculated by adding all the averages and dividing that total by the number of students. Use appropriate headings on the report.

14. Write an entry program (using the techniques described in the chapter) to input payroll information of employee number, name, rate of pay, hours worked, and number of dependents. Store the records in a file.

15. Write a program to input the records from the file created in question 14 above and print a report detailing all the listed information—along with FICA at 9.25%; taxes at 22%; insurance deductions of $50 for one dependent, $75 for two dependents, and $100 for more than two dependents; gross pay; and net pay. Total the gross pay, FICA, taxes, deductions, and net pay and print the totals at the bottom of the report. Use appropriate headings on the report.

16. You are the payroll programmer for the XYZ Corporation, and you need a

program to input all the employee information for the permanent records. Design and write a program that will use a screen display for the entry of the records. The screen should look like the following:

```
        XYZ CORPORATION
        EMPLOYEE ENTRY

1. NAME

2. ADDRESS

3. CITY

4. STATE          5. ZIP

6. BIRTH DATE     7. PAY CODE

8. EMP. DATE      9. # EXEMPT.
```

Use the prompting techniques learned in the chapter to input the information on the line next to the entry. After accepting all nine entries, ask the user if any need to be changed. If they do, the prompt should reappear on the item line. When there are no more changes, store the record in a file. The fields should be the following lengths: name = 20; address = 20; city = 15; state = 2; zip = 5; birth date = 6 stored, 8 displayed (including slashes); pay code = 1 (S for salaried or H for hourly—edit for the proper entry); emp. date (employment date) = 6 stored, 8 displayed (including slashes); and # exempt. (number of exemptions) = 1. All the fields should be string, with the possible exception of the number of exemptions.

The data to be used follows:

NAMES	ADDRESSES	CITY	STATE	ZIP
ED COBURN	1400 SOUTH STREET	EL PASO	TX	76879
SARA SMITH	34567 WEST BLVD.	DENVER	CO	83789
TOM JONES	493 WESTERN	LOS ANGELES	CA	12837
HAROLD HARRIS	P.O. BOX 10	BROOKINGS	SD	68594
EVERITT JOHNSON	3246 BOSQUE	DES MOINES	IA	39849

The rest of the data is:

BIRTH DATE	PAY CODE	EMP. DATE	# EXEMPT.
05/16/43	H	12/15/84	3
03/22/50	S	05/18/80	1
02/02/65	H	06/16/84	5
03/15/44	S	05/15/76	3
04/18/22	H	04/16/53	2
06/16/37	H	03/22/57	2

The answers to the questions follow immediately after the quiz. Questions 1–15 are true–false, while 16–20 are multiple choice.

1. The Apple uses the GET statement for character input.   **T F**

2. It is necessary to check for a blank after a character input to be sure a key   **T F** was pressed.

3. Printing the character that was input with the character input statement is   **T F** called echoing the character.

4. The ASCII code for the backspace is 13 in all of our versions of BASIC.   **T F**

5. We can use either the CHR$ or ASC function when checking the character   **T F** returned by the character input statement.

6. In the prompting routine we created, we used the length of the prompt   **T F** itself to determine the position of the cursor in displaying the asterisks.

7. We used asterisks in our prompt, but we could have used any character we   **T F** wished to.

8. In order to trap the RETURN key we need to use a statement similar to   **T F** A$ = ASC(13).

9. If we want to use a data prompt such as MM/DD/YY, the program could   **T F** keep track of the column number and automatically skip over the slashes.

10. The field size of a phone number entry could be 12, or it could be 10 and   **T F** still retain all the necessary characters.

11. It is important to always blank out an accumulating string to be sure that   **T F** the variable will contain only what is entered during the particular entry.

12. The error trap command for the IBM and Radio Shack is ON ERROR GOTO.   **T F**

13. The Apple has no error trapping command.   **T F**

14. The RESUME statement is used on the IBM and Radio Shack when you   **T F** need the program to return to the original error line.

15. All our versions of BASIC use the PEEK command.   **T F**

16. Which of the following is the *least* valid reason to use the character input   _____ command?
    a. To input without a question mark appearing.
    b. To input numbers without a REDO message appearing should a character be input by accident.
    c. To input at a particular location on the screen.
    d. To have the input automatically terminate after a certain number of input characters.

17. Which is the best way to check for a null character?   _____
    a. ASC(O)   c. " "
    b. CHR$(8)   d. none are correct

18. When would you *not* want to echo the character to the screen when using   _____ the character input?

a. When you are entering something that might be considered private.
b. When the character entered is not a valid entry.
c. When the character entered is not a printable character.
d. All are valid answers.

_____ **19.** Which of the following commands is *not* used on the IBM and Radio Shack?

    a. ON ERROR GOTO   **c.** RESUME
    b. PEEK   **d.** they all are

_____ **20.** Which of the following commands is used to turn off the error trap on the IBM and Radio Shack?

    a. ON ERROR GOTO O   **c.** RESUME line number
    b. ERL   **d.** ERR

ANSWERS TO QUICK QUIZ

1. T
2. F (You check for a null, not a blank.)
3. T
4. F (That is the RETURN code. The backspace code is 8.)
5. T (However, the test differs depending on which function you use.)
6. T (The length plus 2)
7. T (Any printable character)
8. F (The statement should be either A$ = CHR$(13) or ASC(A$) = 13.)
9. T
10. T(It is not necessary to store the dashes in the phone number.
11. F (The variable should be nulled, not blanked.)
12. T
13. F (It uses the ONERR.)
14. F (It is used to terminate all error traps.)
15. T (It is used to examine the contents of a byte of memory.)
16. c (We can also use the INPUT command at any location on the screen.)
17. c (Is the only correct answer.)
18. d
19. d (Remember the PEEK is used for looking at what is stored in a byte of memory.)
20. a

11 RANDOM ACCESS FILE PROCESSING

OBJECTIVES

After completing Chapter 11, you will be able to:
- Describe the problems associated with sequential file processing and ways of handling those problems.
- Define random access file processing.
- Specify the record length necessary to store a series of fields of given lengths.
- Explain why it is necessary to know the record length of the file.
- Describe the differences of the commands that are used in both sequential and random processing.
- Explain how to use the FIELD, LSET, RSET, and numeric assignment statements.
- List all commands needed to create, write to, and retrieve records from a random file.
- Use all the commands discussed thus far to write several programs.

11–1

In Chapter 8 we discovered how to do sequential file processing. The one problem with sequential file processing is that the records are stored in order (record 1, record 2, record 3, and so on) and must be retrieved in the same order.

This is fine if all we need is sequential processing. Take payroll, for example. In order to process payroll, all the records in the file, one for each employee, must be processed. But what happens when we need to change one of the employee payroll records? Suppose someone moves and their address needs to be changed. How can we do this?

Well, there are basically two ways to change records in a sequential file. First, we can read all the records (the entire file) into memory, change the affected record, and store the file back out. The only problem with this technique is that we are limited in the amount of memory we have. Keep in mind that the records not only have to be in memory, but they must share this valuable space with the program. Unless the file is very small, there would not be room for all the records. This solution is, at best, impractical.

The other approach is to use two files: the original employee file and a new one to copy the modified record into. Suppose we have a file of ten records and need to change the fifth record. We would have to read the first four records into the program and store them on the second file. Then, we would read the fifth record, make the necessary changes, and write it back into the second file. Finally, we would need to read the other five records remaining in the file and store them in the second file. (See Figure 11–1 for an illustration of this sequential update process.)

Not too difficult to do, but we have just processed every record in the file when all we needed to change was one record. Still, it's not too slow as long as the number of records in the file is small. But suppose we had 10,000 records instead of just 10. You can imagine how much processing this would require. It is much more practical to simply read in the record to be modified, change it, and store it back in the file. Well, we can do just that with **random file processing.**

Random file processing, also known as **direct access,** is a method of creating the file so that any particular record can be accessed directly by knowing the position of that record in the file. For example, if we need to change record number five, we can read that record directly into the program. Then, after the record is modified, we merely put it back in the file.

Random file processing is not much more difficult than sequential processing, but there are a few more steps involved. These steps are the subject of this chapter. We will begin by looking at how to design the file. Then we will examine the OPEN statements in our different versions of BASIC. The IBM and Radio Shack then require a FIELD statement to set up the storage areas for the different fields we are going to store in our file. Finally, we will examine how to actually store the records on the file and how to close the file when we are done.

11–2
FILE DESIGN

In Chapter 8 we looked at how to decide which fields to store in our file. We neglected, however, to decide how long each field should be. That was done

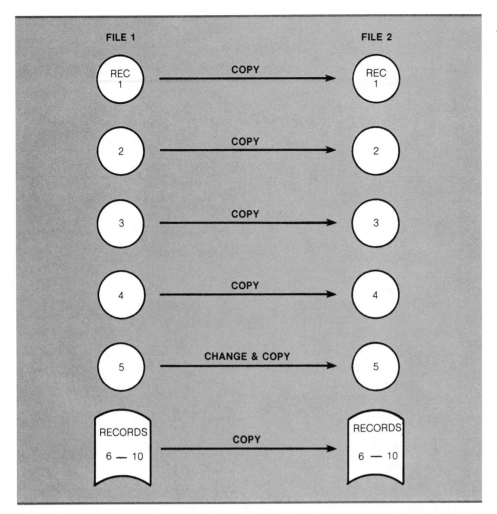

Figure 11–1
Sequential update.

deliberately because when using sequential files, it is not necessary to determine the lengths of the fields since they are simply stored one after another.

Suppose, for example, that we create records that each have a name, address, and date. The first three records might look like the following:

	RECORD 1	**RECORD 2**	**RECORD 3**
NAME	15 characters	12 characters	20 characters
ADDRESS	12 characters	17 characters	22 characters
DATE	6 characters	6 characters	6 characters

Notice that the only field that is the same in all records is the date. The other two fields are of varying lengths. This really doesn't matter with sequential storage since they would be stored one after the other, as depicted in Figure 11–2.

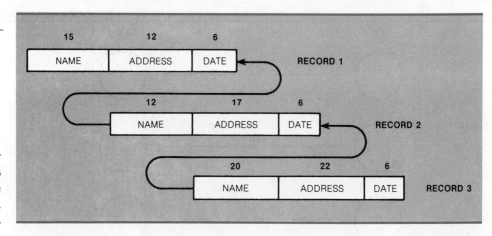

Figure 11–2
Example of sequential file storage.

With random records, however, the records must all be the same length. This is necessary so that the program can determine the beginning position in the file of the record we want to access. Take our sequential records above, for example. Notice that the first record is a total of 33 characters long, the second is 35 characters long, and the third is 48 characters long. It would be impossible to determine where each record begins and ends in such a file. The only way to determine the beginning of records is to have all the records the same size. To do this, the fields of each record must be the same size.

But how big should the fields be? This must be determined before a random file can be set up. We need to examine each of the fields, determine the largest possible entry, and then create the field large enough to accommodate that size of entry.

For example, in our above situation, field 1 would need to be at least 20 characters long, since the field in the third record is that long. Having a few extra characters is a good idea just in case, so a length of 24 characters for the name would be a good choice. This size is, in fact, quite often used in computer applications.

The address must be at least 22 characters long, so a length of 24 would be appropriate in this case also. It is common to create the name and address fields of the same size.

The third field, of course, presents no decision problems. It will need to be 6 digits long.

The total size needed then will be 24 for the name, 24 for the address, and 6 for the date, for a total of 54 characters. This means that we should set up our file such that our records will be 54 characters long. Then, when they are stored, the file will be as shown in Figure 11–3.

Notice that the file will take more room to store randomly than it took to store sequentially. This is because we have to leave room in our fields for more data than may actually be there. This extra room is a small price to pay, however, for the ease of use allowed by random processing.

For our beginning random file processing examples in this chapter, we will develop a small file that will contain information about contributions to a charity drive. The file will contain the name of the contributor and the amount of contribution. We will set up the name with a length of 24, but we will not yet

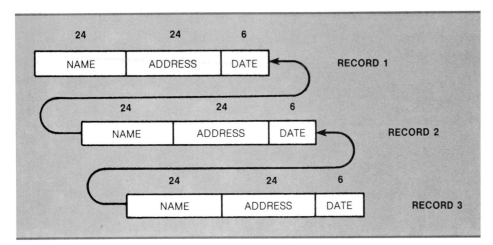

Figure 11–3
Example of random file storage.

attempt to determine the length of the numeric field since numeric data is handled differently in each of our versions of BASIC.

We shall process our file in three ways, such that the program we create will allow the addition of records to the random file, changes to the records, and sequential printing of the records. There are many differences in the way random files are processed on our four different versions of BASIC; the differences will be pointed out where they occur.

11–3 THE OPEN STATEMENT

The first step in any type of disk processing is always opening the file. Once a random file is opened, records may be read from or written into the file by record number without having to close the file first as with sequential files. The form of the open statement is nearly the same as it was in Chapter 8. There are a couple of differences, however, that are covered in the following sections.

IBM OPEN Statement

The IBM can use the same **OPEN** statement as the Radio Shack, but it can also use a modification of the IBM form discussed in Chapter 8:

```
10 OPEN "file name" AS #file number LEN=record length
```

You may note that part of this statement has been dropped and the LEN option added. If the file is to be random, the FOR option we used previously is left off. The particular statement we will be using would look like:

```
10 OPEN "RANDOM" AS #1 LEN=28
```

Notice that the record length is 28. We will see shortly where that length comes from.

Radio Shack OPEN Statement

The form of the OPEN statement for the Radio Shack is:

```
10 OPEN "code",file number,"file name",record length
```

We briefly mentioned in Chapter 8 the code R for random file processing. This OPEN statement is where that code is needed. Note that we also have added something to the OPEN command. The program needs to indicate the length of each of the records to be processed, and this is indicated by the record length on the end of the OPEN statement. The OPEN statement we will use in our program will be:

```
10 OPEN "R",1,"RANDOM",28
```

Notice that the record length is 28. We will see shortly where that length comes from.

Note: In order to use a file length other than 256, you need to indicate variable-length records to the machine. You do this by entering "3V" when you respond to the FILES? prompt when loading into BASIC. Otherwise, if you enter a file length, you will get an error.

IBM and Radio Shack Buffer and FIELD Statement

As soon as a file is opened for random processing in IBM and Radio Shack BASIC, an area of memory is set aside called a file **buffer.** This area is a temporary storage area for the records of the file as they are read from or written into the file. Since processing is done an *entire record* at a time instead of *one field* at a time, it makes more sense to write the whole record at one time. This is what the buffer is for. If our record has three fields, each of these fields is set up in the buffer area, and then we may process the data from the buffer. When we have done whatever processing is necessary, we write (PUT) the record into the file, and the system takes the record from the buffer and puts it in the file.

This buffer requires an additional statement to set up the fields necessary to use the buffer. Since the buffer is a special area of memory, special variables must be set up to be used by the buffer. This is done with the **FIELD** statement. The form of the FIELD statement is:

```
10 FIELD #file or buffer number, length AS string variable,...
```

Notice that the # is specified as file or buffer number. This is the same number used when opening the file. There we called it the file number, but on the FIELD statement it is called the buffer. It is the same number. That is, if you OPEN the file as #1, you FIELD the buffer as #1. Then you specify all the fields you wish to use in the buffer by the length of the field and the string variable name. Note that the statement does not call for a variable name; it calls for a *string* variable name. This is not an accident. All the fields on the FIELD statement must be strings. To store numerics, you must use a special statement to set the field into the buffer. (We will cover that statement shortly.)

An example of a FIELD statement would be:

```
100 FIELD #1, 30 AS N$, 20 AS B$, 4 AS A$(1), 4 AS A$(2)
```

This means that the first 30 characters of each record will be N$, the next 20 will be B$, then 4 will be A$(1), and the final 4 will be A$(2). What is the actual record length of file #1 as we have specified? You probably answered 58 since that is the total of all the field lengths. But that is not an indication of the record length. Many times a file will need to be fielded several different times with different types of records in it. These different types of records may or may not have the same lengths. If the FIELD statement does not fill the entire buffer area, the remaining area is automatically filled with blanks. Thus, the actual record length may or may not be the total of the lengths on the field statement.

It is important to realize that the fields on the FIELD statement are not the same fields as are stored in regular memory. For example, an assignment such as A\$ = "HI" stores "HI" in A\$ in regular memory, not in the buffer. Because the buffer is a special area, in order to store fields in it, you need to use a special type of assignment statement: either an **LSET** or an **RSET** statement. The form of the statement is:

Assigning the IBM and Radio Shack FIELD Statement Variables

```
10 LSET string variable = string, literal or numeric conversion
```

This will cause the information placed into the buffer string to be left-justified (the RSET would cause right-justification). *Left-justification* is a way of saying that the characters in the field are aligned on the left and any blank characters are on the right end. Thus, a left-justified field with a length of 6 might have three characters starting at the left with three blanks following. LSET is usually used for literals and RSET for numerics.

If you intend to store information into the buffer area, the assignment must be done with either the LSET or RSET. Otherwise, the stored information will be put into regular storage, and the FIELD variable will not be assigned. To put this another way, if you use A\$ = "HI", even when A\$ is in the FIELD statement, "HI" will not be put into the buffer. To get "HI" into the buffer, you must use LSET A\$ = "HI". If you misuse one of the variables, this will not affect any of the other variables that are in the buffer. Thus, if you use A\$ = "HI" and you have previously LSET B\$ and C\$, B\$ and C\$ will still be stored in the buffer area. For an illustration of the buffer concept, see Figure 11–4.

You may have noticed that the LSET command above mentions numeric conversion. But didn't we say previously that numeric storage requires a special statement? Well, actually, you have a choice of three special statements: one for integers, one for normal precision, and one for double precision. The three statements are **MKI\$** for integers, **MKS\$** for single precision, and **MKD\$** for double precision. The MKI\$ requires a two-character field for storage, MKS\$ requires four characters, and MKD\$ requires eight characters. This means that when you field the buffer, you need to set up the field for the appropriate size conversion. Sample conversion statements would be:

```
10 RSET A$=MKI$(A)      ' INTEGER FOR 2 CHARACTERS
20 RSET B$=MKS$(B)      ' NORMAL FOR 4 CHARACTERS
30 RSET C$=MKD$(C)      ' DOUBLE PRECISION FOR 8 CHAR.
```

Notice that we used RSET statements. Once again, to assign to fields in the buffer, the assignment must be done with either an LSET or RSET statement.

As you might expect, if you store the numbers in a special way, to get them back will also require special handling. The statements to convert from the buffered strings to numeric variables are **CVI** for integers, **CVS** for single precision, and **CVD** for double precision. Sample statements for these would be:

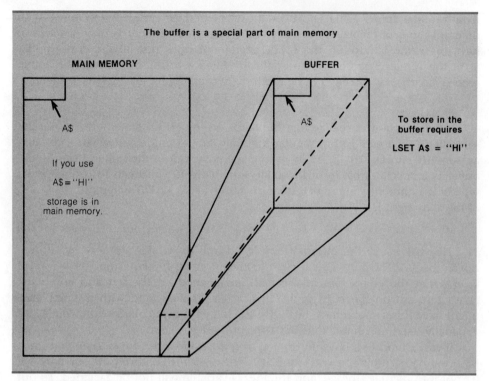

The buffer is a special part of main memory

MAIN MEMORY

BUFFER

A$

A$

To store in the buffer requires

LSET A$ = "HI"

If you use

A$ = "HI"

storage is in main memory.

Figure 11–4
Illustration of buffer memory.

```
10 A=CVI(A$)          ' INTEGER
20 B=CVS(B$)          ' NORMAL PRECISION
30 C=CVD(C$)          ' DOUBLE PRECISION
```

Now that we know how to use the FIELD statement, let's set up the one we will need for our program. To review, we stated that our file would contain the name of each of our contributors and the amount of contribution. The name would be 24 characters long, but we had not determined the length of the numeric field. We can now decide to use a length of 4, for single precision. This means that to assign the variable we will need to use the MKS$ function; to convert it back into a numeric we will need the CVS function.

Knowing this information, our FIELD statement should look like the following:

```
10 FIELD #1, 24 AS NF$, 4 AS CF$
```

Notice that the second character of each variable name is F. This is done so that the variables are easy to recognize as fielded variables. It is helpful to mark the fielded statements in some recognizable manner. Now we need to put the information into the buffer with the statements:

```
20 LSET NF$=A$
30 RSET CF$=MKS$(C)
```

Recall that disk processing on the Apple needs to be prefaced with the printing of the CHR$(4). The same is true of all the processing in this chapter. We will, therefore, again assign D$ to contain CHR$(4). The form of the OPEN statement is virtually the same as before. The only difference is that at the end of the statement there is a record length:

```
10 PRINT D$;"OPEN file name,Lrecord length"
```

The L is the marker indicating that you are using a record length. This is the only indication to the machine that we are using a random file. If it is left off, the file is opened for sequential processing. The OPEN statement we will use in our program will be:

```
10 OPEN D$;"OPEN CONTDATA,L33"
```

Data is written into a random file in the same manner as it is written into a sequential file; that is, on the Apple, once the random record is located, fields are written into and read from the file one after the other as with sequential processing. Therefore, to determine the record length, we take the maximum length of the fields *plus* the carriage return needed to terminate the fields. Thus, we have the field length of 24 for the name, plus one for the carriage return, which gives 25; the numeric field is determined to be sufficient with a length of 7 (no contribution will be larger than 7 figures!), plus one for the carriage return, which gives 8. Thus the total record length is 33 characters (25 + 8).

11–4
RANDOM I/O

Because we are using a random file, we can open the file at the beginning of the program and read from and write into it as many times and in whatever combination is necessary without having to close it first. Recall that with sequential processing, after we have stored the records in the file, we have to close it before we read them back. This is not necessary with a random file. We can write a record into the file and then immediately read it back again.

After all the information has been put into the buffer with the LSET and RSET statements, you are ready to store the record on the disk file. This is done with a **PUT #** command in the form:

```
10 PUT #file or buffer number,record number
```

Once again, the number after the # symbol can be thought of as either the file number or the buffer number. You then list the number of the record you want to store. If you leave off the record number, the next record in sequence is accessed. For example, if you have just accessed record 5 and PUT another record without specifying the record number, you would PUT record number 6.

A sample PUT command would be:

```
10 PUT #1,5                    ' STORE RECORD NUMBER 5
```

The record number on the PUT statement can, of course, be a variable. This way you can input the record number from the user and then access that particular record. Though not often used, the file number can also be a variable.

Storing Records on the Apple

Recall that on the Apple after a file is opened, another step is necessary before information can actually be written into or read from the file: A second statement is needed to indicate to the machine what function you intend. In the case of storing the records, that statement is a **WRITE** statement and has the following format:

```
10 PRINT D$;"WRITE file name,Rrecord number"
```

Notice that we have added an R and the number of the record we want to write into. This statement indicates to the computer that we want to store the records in the file and which particular record we want to use. A sample statement would be:

```
10 PRINT D$;"WRITE CONTDATA,R5"
```

The record number (along with the file name) can be a variable instead of a constant. Such a statement might look like the following with the record number stored in R$:

```
10 PRINT D$;"WRITE CONTDATA,R"+R$
```

After access is established with the WRITE statement, the actual fields are stored as before with the **PRINT** statement. Our particular record might create a statement pair like the following (keep in mind that the fields should still be written as separate statements, or with quoted commas between, to keep them from running together):

```
20 PRINT N$              : REM STORE THE NAME
30 PRINT C               : REM STORE THE CONTRIBUTION
```

Retrieving Records on the IBM and Radio Shack

After records are stored, they can be retrieved with a **GET #** statement in the form:

```
10 GET #file number, record number
```

A sample command would look like the following:

```
10 GET #1,5       ' GET RECORD NUMBER 5
```

Here, also, the file number and record number can be variables.

This will put the information from the file into the FIELD buffer. Then, the individual fields may be used from the buffer.

Retrieving Records on the Apple

After the records are stored, they can be retrieved by indicating the read function with the **READ** statement as before. The statement has the form:

```
10 PRINT D$;"READ file name,Rrecord number"
```

Notice that, as with the WRITE statement, we use an R and the record number here. An actual statement would look like the following:

```
10 PRINT D$;"READ CONTDATA,R5"
```

As before, the file name and record number can be variables to allow more flexibility in the program. This statement merely sets the computer into the proper mode; to access the records on the disk you need an **INPUT** statement, such as:

```
20 INPUT N$,C          : REM READ THE NAME AND CONTRIBUTION
```

11–5
THE CLOSE STATEMENT

As we mentioned, since we are using a random file, we can open the file at the beginning of the program and read from and write into it as many times and in whatever combination is necessary without having to close it first. However, we do need to close it before the end of the program. This is done with the same **CLOSE** statement we used before. As you may recall, the form on the IBM and Radio Shack is:

```
10 CLOSE #file number        ' WILL CLOSE A PARTICULAR FILE
```

Or:

```
10 CLOSE                     ' WILL CLOSE ALL OPEN FILES
```

The form on the Apple is:

```
10 PRINT D$;"CLOSE file name" : REM WILL CLOSE A PARTICULAR FILE
```

Or:

```
10 PRINT D$;"CLOSE"          : REM WILL CLOSE ALL OPEN FILES
```

11–6
CREATING THE PROGRAM

We are now ready to create the entire program to put the records into the file, retrieve them for updating, and print a list of them. The program will be broken up into five separate modules: one for each of the three functions, one for a menu of the available options so the user may choose the appropriate option, and an exit module.

We will pseudocode and flowchart the logic and then give the IBM program listing with the modifications necessary for the Radio Shack and Apple.

The Initial Module

We will pseudocode and flowchart the beginning module first. As we mentioned, since this is a random file, we can open the file (and set up the FIELD statement for the IBM and Radio Shack) at the beginning of the program and only close it when we need to exit the program.

There is, however, another consideration. Since this is a random file, there is no command to append newly added records onto the end of the file. Since we are going to allow the user to add records any time it is necessary, somehow we will have to keep track of how many records we have in the file. This will also stop the user from accessing records beyond the end of the file since we can test the number of file records against the record number indicated by the user.

We can keep track of the number of records by creating a "dummy" record at the beginning of the file, containing only the number of records in the file. That is, the first record in the file will be used as a storage place for keeping track of the number of records that we have added to the file. Thus, the first thing we will need to do when we open the file is to get the number of records in the file from the first record in the file. This means, for example, that when we access the third contributor's record in the file, the actual record number will be four since we have to bypass the first (dummy) record. See Figure 11–5 for an illustration of the construction of the file.

We will reflect the use of this dummy record access in our pseudocode and programs (see Figure 11–6 for the flowchart):

Start
Open the file (and field the variables).
Read the first record (dummy).
IF first record not found THEN   (*continues on page 304*)

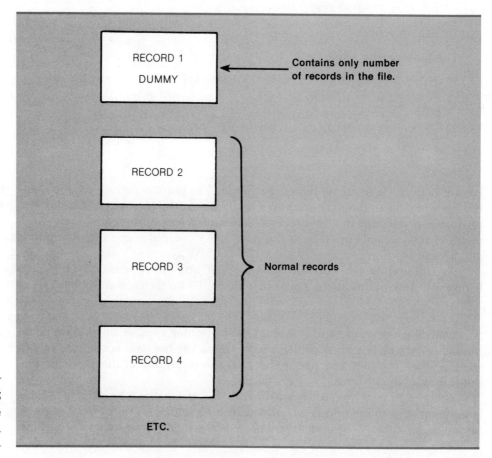

Figure 11–5
Illustration of file
construction.

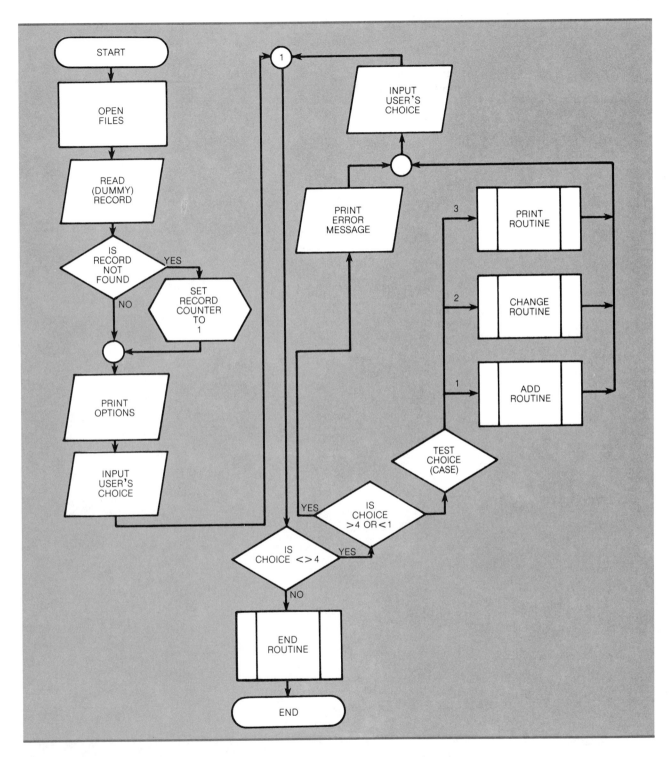

Figure 11–6
Flowchart of initial module.

            Set record counter to 1.
(ELSE)
END-IF
Print the options.
Input the user's choice.
DO-WHILE user's choice is <> 4.
  IF choice >4 or <1 THEN
    Print error message.
  ELSE
    CASE-ENTRY user's choice.
      CASE 1
        GOSUB addition routine.
      CASE 2
        GOSUB change routine.
      CASE 3
        GOSUB print routine.
    END-CASE
  END-IF
  Input the user's choice.
END-DO
GOSUB program end routine (CASE 4).
End

The program code follows:

```
10 REM ***** PROGRAM NAME: CONTRIB
20 REM
30 REM ***** WRITTEN BY EDWARD J. COBURN
40 REM
50 REM THE FIRST RANDOM FILE PROCESSING PROGRAM
60 REM
70 OPEN "CONTDATA" AS #1 LEN=28
80 FIELD #1, 2 AS RF$
90 GET 1,1                        ' GET THE FIRST RECORD
100 IF CVI(RF$)=0 THEN RECS=1 ELSE RECS=CVI(RF$)
110 FIELD #1, 24 AS NF$, 4 AS CF$
120 CLS                           ' CLEAR THE SCREEN
130 PRINT TAB(10);"CONTRIBUTIONS MAINTENANCE"
140 PRINT                         ' BLANK LINE
150 PRINT "1.  ADD NEW RECORDS"
155 PRINT
160 PRINT "2.  CHANGE EXISTING RECORD"
165 PRINT
170 PRINT "3.  PRINT THE FILE"
175 PRINT
180 PRINT "4.  EXIT THE PROGRAM"
190 PRINT
200 P$= "WHAT OPTION (1-4)"
210 L=1                           ' LENGTH OF PROMPT
220 GOSUB 7000                    ' PROMPT SUBROUTINE
230 IF B$>"0" AND B$<"5" THEN 270
240    M$="INPUT ERROR.  RETRY ENTRY"
250    GOSUB 6000                 ' ERROR SUBROUTINE
260    GOTO 200                   ' REPROMPT
270 ON VAL(B$) GOSUB 500, 2000, 3000, 4000
280 GOTO 120                      ' RETURN FOR ANOTHER INPUT
```

Program 11-1

First, on the Radio Shack, we need a CLEAR statement and a different OPEN statement:

```
65 CLEAR 5000                    ' SETUP THE STRING AREA
70 OPEN "R",1,"CONTDATA",28
```

Next, when reading a blank record, the Radio Shack will give you an error. Thus, the record number check in line 100 needs to be expanded. Also, we need to add line 85. The routine from 85–108 should be:

```
85 ON ERROR GOTO 100
90 GET 1,1                       ' GET THE FIRST RECORD
95 RECS=CVI(RF$)
98 GOTO 108
100 RECS=1                       ' ASSIGN THE NUMBER OF RECORDS
105 RESUME 108
108 ON ERROR GOTO 0              ' TURN OFF THE ERROR PROCESSING
```

On the Apple, the first thing is to add a routine to assign a string of blanks and D$:

```
62 CL$=""
64 FOR I=1 TO 6
66    CL$=CL$+CL$
68 NEXT I
69 D$=CHR$(4)
```

Then the OPEN statement and error routine need to be different:

```
70 PRINT D$;"OPEN CONTDATA,L33"
75 ONERR GOTO 120
80 PRINT D$;"READ CONTDATA,R1"
85 INPUT RECS                    : REM READ THE NUMBER
90 GOTO 130
95 RECS=1                        : REM ASSIGN THE NUMBER
100 PRINT D$;"CLOSE CONTDATA"    : REM CLOSE THE FILE
115 PRINT D$;"OPEN CONTDATA,L33"
120 PRINT D$                     : REM TURN OFF DISK ACCESS
124 POKE 216,0                   : REM TURN OFF ERROR PROCESSING
128 HOME                         : REM CLEAR THE SCREEN
```

The Addition Module

In the addition module, we will input the data from the user, store it in the fielded variables, and PUT the record. We will automatically put the new record on the end of the last one. To do this, we use the number input from the dummy record. Since that number represents the number of records currently in the file, the record to add will be one more than that number, or RECS + 1.

After we add the record, we have to update the number in the dummy record. Then the program will ask the user if there are more records to be added or if the function is completed. The pseudocode follows; the flowchart is shown in Figure 11–7.

Start ADD module
REPEAT-UNTIL input code is N (for no more records added).
(*continues on page 307*)

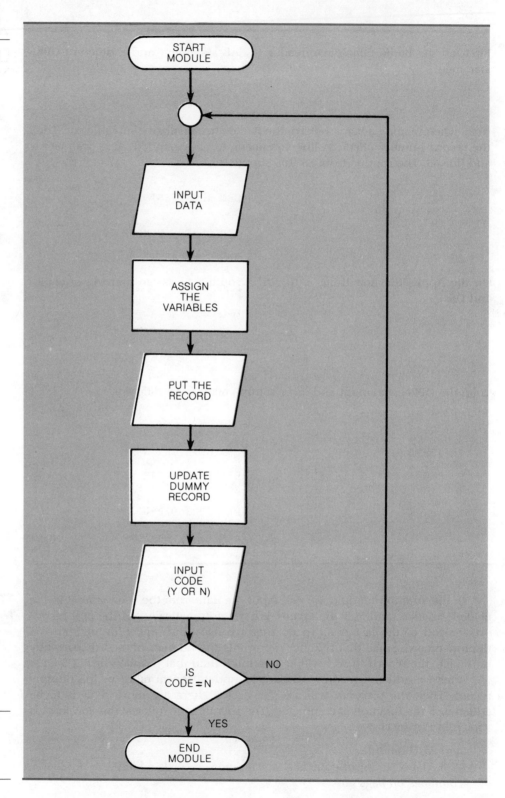

Figure 11–7
Flowchart of addition
module.

Input data.
Assign the variables.
Put the record.
Update the number of records in record 1.
Input for more records (Y or N).
END-REPEAT
End module

Notice that we used a REPEAT-UNTIL in this routine instead of a DO-WHILE. When we enter the routine, we know we need to add a record, so no test is necessary. The test only becomes necessary after the record is added. Therefore, the test is the last thing in the loop, and thus a REPEAT-UNTIL is needed. The programmed module follows:

```
470 REM
480 REM ***** ADD MODULE
490 REM
500 CLS                          ' CLEAR THE SCREEN
510 PRINT TAB(10);"CONTRIBUTIONS ENTRY"
520 PRINT                        ' BLANK LINE
530 PRINT "1. CONT. NAME"
535 PRINT
540 PRINT "2. CONT. AMOUNT"
550 R=3                          ' ROW NUMBER
560 C=17                         ' COLUMN NUMBER
570 L=24                         ' NAME LENGTH
580 GOSUB 7070                   ' PROMPT SUBROUTINE
590 LSET NF$=B$                  ' ASSIGN NAME
600 R=5                          ' ROW NUMBER
610 L=7                          ' CONTRIBUTION LENGTH
620 GOSUB 7070                   ' PROMPT SUBROUTINE
630 LSET CF$=MKS$(VAL(B$))       ' ASSIGN AMOUNT
635 RECS=RECS+1                  ' INCREMENT RECORD NUMBER
640 PUT 1,RECS                   ' PUT THE RECORD
650 FIELD #1, 2 AS RF$           ' FIELD RECORD 1
660 LSET RF$=MKI$(RECS)          ' SET THE FIELD
670 PUT 1,1                      ' PUT RECORD 1
680 P$= "DO YOU WANT TO ADD ANY MORE (Y OR N)"
690 L=1                          ' LENGTH OF PROMPT
700 GOSUB 7000                   ' PROMPT SUBROUTINE
710 IF B$<>"Y" THEN RETURN       ' RETURN TO INITIAL MODULE
720 GOTO 500                     ' GET ANOTHER RECORD
```

Program 11–2

)))DIFFERENCES

For the Apple, line 500 should be HOME. Next, we need ordinary assignments:

```
590 N$=B$                        : REM ASSIGN NAME

630 C=VAL(B$)                     : REM ASSIGN AMOUNT
```

And the file routine (635–670) should be:

```
635 PRINT D$ : PRINT D$;"WRITE CONTDATA,R";R
650 PRINT N$                      : REM STORE THE NAME
655 PRINT C                       : REM STORE THE CONTRIBUTIONS
```

Program continues

```
660 PRINT D$;"WRITE CONTDATA,R1"
665 PRINT RECS               : REM WRITE THE NEW RECORD NUMBER
670 PRINT D$                 : REM TURN OFF OUTPUT
```

Notice in lines 650 and 655 that we continue to write out the variables with separate PRINT statements. On each random record the fields are still sequential and have to be written out that way (or with a quoted comma between).

The Change Module

In the change module, the first thing to do is to ask the user what record is to be changed. We have to refer to the record by number since that is the way we access the records. (In the next two chapters we will learn other ways to access random files, but for now we shall have to be content with numeric access.) We will verify that the number is within the range of the records in the file by checking the input number against the number stored in the dummy record. This is one of the reasons we used the dummy record. If the record number input by the user is outside the range of the file, we will issue an error message and then reprompt for the record number. We will have problems if we try to access a record other than those that have been added to the file, so we must take care that the record number we give the program to read is always the correct one.

After we know which record to retrieve, we will input the record and display the fields on the screen. We will number the fields so we can ask the user to choose which field is to be modified. We will then let the user make the changes beside the field title on the screen.

After the changes have been made, we put record back into the file and reprompt for another record. When the user has finished and indicated so on the prompt (by entering 0), the program will exit the routine and return to the main program.

The pseudocode for this module follows (the flowchart is shown in Figure 11–8):

```
Start CHANGE module
Input record number to change.
DO-WHILE record number is not 0 (no more changes).
    Input the record.
    Print items on the screen by number.
    Input item number to change.
    DO-WHILE item to change is not 0 (end).
        Input the new field.
        Print the items on the screen by number.
        Input item number to change.
    END-DO
    Output the record.
    Input record number to change.
END-DO
End module
```

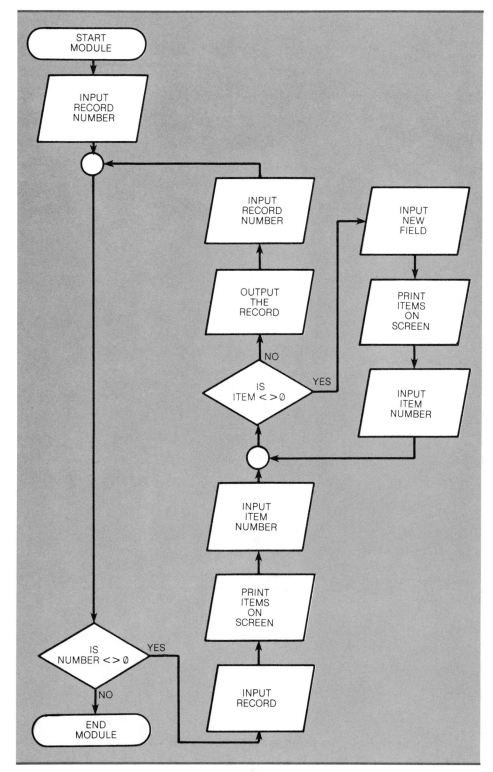

Figure 11–8
Flowchart of change
module.

Notice that to access the requested record we will have to access the record number plus one (VAL(B$)+1). This is necessary in order to bypass the dummy record. For example, if the user requests to change record 5, that record is actually record 6 in the file. The programmed module would look like the following:

```
1970 REM
1980 REM ***** CHANGE MODULE
1990 REM
2000 P$="RECORD NUMBER TO CHANGE (0 TO END)"
2020 L=3                          ' PROMPT LENGTH
2030 GOSUB 7000                   ' PROMPT SUBROUTINE
2040 IF VAL(B$)=0 THEN RETURN ' EXIT THE SUBROUTINE
2050 IF VAL(B$)<=RECS THEN 2080' RECORD OKAY?
2060      M$="RECORD NOT FOUND.  REENTER."
2070      GOSUB 6000             ' ERROR SUBROUTINE
2075      GOTO 2000              ' GET INDEX AGAIN
2080 RN=VAL(B$)+1                ' RECORD TO ACCESS
2082 FIELD #1,24 AS NF$, 4 AS CF$
2085 GET #1,RN                   ' GET THE RECORD
2090 CLS                         ' CLEAR THE SCREEN
2100 PRINT TAB(10);"CONTRIBUTIONS CHANGES"
2110 PRINT                       ' BLANK LINE
2120 PRINT "1. CONT. NAME    ";NF$
2130 PRINT                       ' BLANK LINE
2140 PRINT "2. CONT. AMOUNT ";CVS(CF$)
2150 P$="FIELD TO CHANGE (0 TO END)"
2160 L=1                         ' PROMPT LENGTH
2170 GOSUB 7000                  ' PROMPT SUBROUTINE
2180 IF B$>="0" AND B$<="2" THEN 2220
2190      M$="INVALID ENTRY.  TRY AGAIN"
2200      GOSUB 6000             ' ERROR SUBROUTINE
2210      GOTO 2150              ' REINPUT
2220 IF B$="0" THEN 2290         ' FIELD ENTRY
2230      IF B$="1" THEN L=24 : R=3
2240      IF B$="2" THEN L=7  : R=5
2250      C=17                   ' COLUMN
2260      GOSUB 7070             ' PROMPT SUBROUTINE
2270      IF R=3 THEN LSET NF$=B$ ELSE LSET CF$=MKS$(VAL(B$))
2280      GOTO 2090              ' REPROMPT
2290 PUT #1,RN                   ' STORE THE RECORD BACK INTO FILE
2300 GOTO 2000                   ' RETURN FOR NEW NUMBER
```

Program 11–3

)))DIFFERENCES

The first changes on the Apple are lines 2082–2090:

```
2082 PRINT D$;"READ CONTDATA,R";RN
2085 INPUT NF$,C              : REM INPUT THE FIELDS
2087 PRINT D$                 : REM TURN OFF THE I/O
2090 HOME                     : REM CLEAR THE SCREEN
```

Then the Apple doesn't need the conversion on line 2140:

```
2140 PRINT "2. CONT. AMOUNT ";CO
```

Line 2270 requires two statements since Applesoft has no ELSE:

```
2270      IF R=3 THEN NF$=B$   : REM STORE THE FIELD
2275      IF R=5 THEN CO=VAL(B$)
```

Finally, line 2290 requires several lines:

```
2290 PRINT D$;"WRITE CONTDATA,R";RN
2292 PRINT NF$                    : REM WRITE NAME
2294 PRINT CO                     : REM WRITE CONTRIBUTION
2296 PRINT D$                     : REM TURN OFF DISK ACCESS
```

The PRINT Module

In this module we will print out a sequential list of the records stored in the file. If you recall, we can automatically access the next record in a file by leaving off the record number. If we begin our access to the file without a record number, the first record accessed will automatically be record 1.

There is only one problem with this approach. If we try to access a record beyond the last record written into the file, the program will stop with an error. We can alleviate this problem by using the number we have stored in the dummy record to determine how many records are in the file, and then we can use a FOR-NEXT loop to access them. This is the approach we will use. The pseudocode for this module follows (the flowchart is shown in Figure 11–9):

```
Start PRINT module
Print headings.
Initialize counter to 1.
DO-WHILE counter <= number of records.
   Input record.
   Print fields.
   Add 1 to counter.
   Accumulate contribution.
END DO
Print total.
End module
```

Notice that we also have included a total of the contributions. The programmed module would be:

```
2970 REM
2980 REM ***** PRINT MODULE
2990 REM
3000 T=0                          ' ZERO OUT TOTAL FIELD
3005 LPRINT TAB(10);"CONTRIBUTIONS LIST"
3010 LPRINT " "                   ' BLANK LINE
3020 LPRINT "NAME";TAB(27);"AMOUNT"
3030 LPRINT " "                   ' BLANK LINE
3040 FOR I=2 TO RECS              ' TO NUMBER IN FILE
3050     GET #1,I                 ' GET RECORD BY NUMBER
3060     LPRINT NF$;TAB(25);USING "#,###.##";CVS(CF$)
3070     T=T+CVS(CF$)             ' ACCUMULATE TOTAL
3080 NEXT I                                    Program 11–4
```

Program continues on page 313

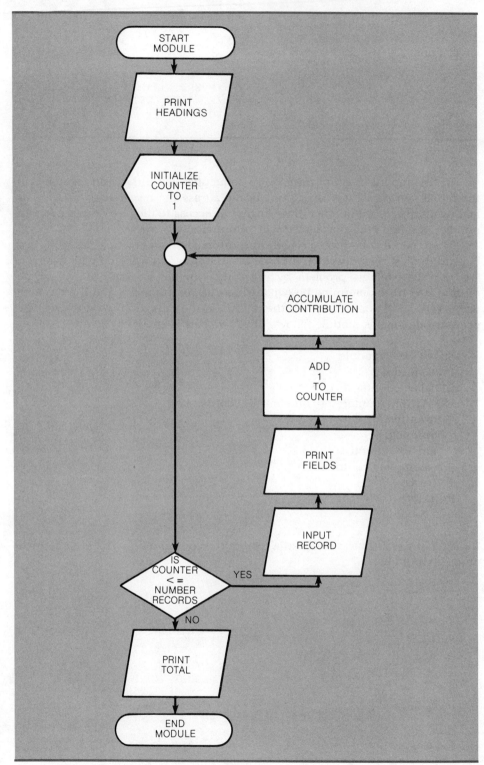

Figure 11–9
Flowchart of print
module.

```
3090 LPRINT TAB(24);"----------"'UNDERLINE
3100 LPRINT "TOTAL";TAB(24);USING "##,###.##";T
3110 RETURN
```

Program 11–4 (cont.)

On the Apple, we first need to turn the printer on. Earlier we were using PR#1 to turn on the printer. This works fine in the immediate mode, but in a program we need to use:

```
3002 PRINT D$;"PR#1"
```

The LPRINT statements should be PRINT statements. Then the input from the disk and the print routine need to be changed:

```
3050      PRINT D$;"READ CONTDATA,R";I
3052      INPUT NF$,CO          : REM INPUT FIELDS
3054      A=CO                  : REM PREPARE FOR SUBROUTINE
3056      GOSUB 8000            : REM FORMAT SUBROUTINE
3060      PRINT NF$;TAB(37-LEN(P$));P$
3070      T=T+CO                : REM ACCUMULATE TOTAL
3080 NEXT I
3090 PRINT TAB(22);"--------" : REM UNDERLINE
3092 A=T                       : REM PREPARE FOR SUBROUTINE
3094 GOSUB 8000                : REM FORMAT SUBROUTINE
3100 PRINT "TOTAL";TAB(32-LEN(P$));P$
3104 PRINT D$;"PR#0"           : REM TURN OFF PRINTER
3108 PRINT D$                  : REM TURN OFF I/O
3110 RETURN
```

The EXIT Module

The final module, the module for exiting the program, is very short. We need only to close the file and end the program. The pseudocode follows (the flowchart is shown in Figure 11–10):

Start EXIT module
Close the file.
End module and End program

The programmed module is:

```
3970 REM
3980 REM ***** EXIT MODULE
3990 REM
4000 CLOSE #1
4010 END
```

The Apple uses a different CLOSE statement:

```
4000 PRINT D$;"CLOSE CONTDATA"
```

Putting the Program Together

Don't forget that this program needs all the subroutines we have used up to this point (e.g., prompt subroutines) before it will be complete. If you put the various modules and subroutines together, you should be able to run to program and get results similar to what follows.

The menu should appear as:

```
          CONTRIBUTIONS MAINTENANCE

1.  ADD NEW RECORDS

2.  CHANGE EXISTING RECORDS

3.  PRINT THE FILE

4.  EXIT THE PROGRAM




WHAT OPTION (1-4) *
```

The add screen should appear as:

```
          CONTRIBUTIONS ENTRY

1. CONT. NAME    *************************

2. CONT. AMOUNT
```

And the change screen should look like:

```
          CONTRIBUTIONS CHANGES

1. CONT. NAME    TOM JONES


2. CONT. AMOUNT 1000




FIELD TO CHANGE (0 TO END) *
```

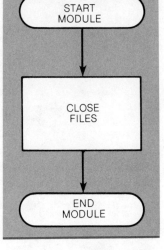

Figure 11–10
Flowchart of exit module.

A Final Note About IBM and Radio Shack

Although we wrote our program using a dummy record, the IBM and Radio Shack actually have a statement that eliminates the need for this technique. The **LOF** statement will tell us how much space (in bytes) the file is taking up. We can then use this number to calculate the number of records in the file. The form of the statement is:

```
10 numeric variable = LOF(file number)
```

An example would be:

```
10 R=LOF(1)
```

This will return the number of bytes taken up by the file. If the length of the file is given as 160 and our record length is 20, there must be 8 records in the file (160/20). Now we can eliminate some of the program, such as the first record rewrite every time a new record is added. Since we would no longer have the dummy record, this rewrite would not be necessary.

Other changes can also be made to simplify the program. These changes are left as an exercise at the end of the chapter.

SUMMARY

1. Prior to this chapter we used sequential file processing. The problem with this type of processing is that the records can be retrieved only sequentially. There are many applications, such as record maintenance, in which it is desirable, if not absolutely necessary, to access the records randomly, that is, to be able to access any record in the file for changing by simply referring to the record number.

2. When we design a random file, we have to decide the length of each of the records so that the machine will know how many bytes to bypass to access the desired record. The records must also be the same length so that accessing can always be done in the same manner. To determine the length of a record, the length of each field is determined, and then all the field lengths plus the appropriate count for delimiters (if necessary) are totaled. This length is used in several of the random access commands.

3. The first command that is necessary for random file processing is the OPEN statement. This statement is used in a fashion similar to that for sequential processing, but the file length is added to the command.

4. On the IBM and Radio Shack, a special area of memory, called a buffer, is set up for file accessing. Access to the buffer is established with a FIELD statement. Fields are stored in the buffer with a special assignment statement, LSET or RSET. If the special statement is not used, the variable used in the assignment is stored in regular memory, the buffer does not get fielded, and the information does not get stored in the file. Numerics must be converted to strings using special functions, since all fields in the FIELD statement must be string variables.

5. Records are stored on the IBM and Radio Shack with a PUT statement, which stipulates the number of the buffer assigned to the file in the OPEN statement. To get the records off the disk, a GET # statement is used. The data is returned into the buffer via the FIELD statement and is then accessed from the variables in the buffer.

6. On the Apple, the record is accessed by issuing a READ statement and then inputting individual fields with a simple INPUT statement. To store them, a WRITE statement is issued and the fields printed into the file. It is important when writing in the fields that you put a carriage return between fields, otherwise the fields will be run together and will be retrieved as only one field.

7. Because of its construction, a random file can be opened at the beginning of the program, and then records can be added, read from the file, and stored back into the file without closing the file in between. The file needs to be closed only at the end of the program. The CLOSE statements used for random file processing are identical to the CLOSE statements for sequential

processing. One file can be independently closed, or all open files can be closed with a single CLOSE statement.

8. In order to do random file processing, it is necessary to determine how many records are in the file. On the IBM and Radio Shack, this is done with the LOF statement. On the Apple, you must keep track with a separate routine. Probably the easiest method is to use a dummy record at the beginning of the file to store the number of records currently in the file. This number can then be used to determine the next record to be added, how many records there are to print when sequentially printing the file, and whether a particular record is within the range of the file when doing record maintenance. Though not actually necessary, this technique works well on the IBM and Radio Shack also, and for the sake of consistency it is the method we used.

GLOSSARY

Buffer A storage place reserved in memory for the accessing of records from a random access file. Access to the buffer is via a FIELD statement (on the IBM and Radio Shack).

CLOSE The IBM and Radio Shack command to close access to the file.

CVS, CVI, CVD The IBM and Radio Shack statements to convert numerics stored in the FIELD buffer as strings back into their appropriate numeric equivalent. CVS is for single precision, CVI is for integers, and CVD is for double precision.

Direct access *See* **Random file processing.**

FIELD The IBM and Radio Shack command to set up a record for storage in the buffer area.

GET # The IBM and Radio Shack command to retrieve a random record from the file.

INPUT The Apple command for retrieving the fields from the disk.

LOF The IBM and Radio Shack function to find the number of bytes in the file. This can be used to calculate the number of records.

LSET The IBM and Radio Shack command necessary to store information in the fielded variables. This command will left-justify the data in the field.

**MKS$, MKI$, MKD$** The statements in IBM and Radio Shack BASIC that translate numeric variables to strings for storage in the FIELD buffer. MKS$ is for single precision, MKI$ is for integers, and MKD$ is for double precision.

OPEN The command used to open a file for access. For random access, part of the command is the record length of the file.

PRINT The Apple output command used to write the fields into the file.

PUT # The IBM and Radio Shack output command used to write the record to the file from the buffer.

Random file processing The type of processing that allows direct access to any record in a file without the need to access other records in the file.

READ The Apple command used to set up access for inputting the random record.

RSET The IBM and Radio Shack command necessary to store information in the fielded variables. This command will right-justify the data in the field.

WRITE The Apple command used to set up access for outputting the random record.

QUESTIONS TO AID UNDERSTANDING

1. Describe the major problem with sequential files and two methods of handling this problem without random access.
*2. Define random file processing and give the other name for it.

3. Give the record length for a file with a name of 24 characters, date, social security number, and three numbers each with a maximum of seven digits. Specify the length that would be used in your machine.

*4. Explain why it is necessary to know the record length for random processing.

5. Give the form of the OPEN statement for your version of BASIC and explain how it differs from the OPEN statement used for sequential processing.

6. Explain what the FIELD statement is (IBM and Radio Shack) and what it is used for.

7. Explain what will happen if you don't use either LSET or RSET to field your FIELD variables (IBM and Radio Shack).

8. List the commands (and their proper form) in your version of BASIC to open the file, write records, retrieve the records, and close the file.

9. Go through the chapter's sample programs and make the changes necessary in the IBM and Radio Shack versions to use the LOF function instead of the dummy record.

*10. Write a program to input the following payroll information: social security number, employee name, salary code (S for salaried, H for hourly), and hourly rate if hourly or weekly salary if salaried. Store the records randomly. You will have to determine the proper record length. Write a module that will allow the user to change any of the fields on any of the records. Write another module to print a sequential report of the information.

11. Using the file created in question 10, write a program to read the file sequentially, print the employee name on the screen as a prompt, and input the number of hours worked for the hourly employees. No input is necessary for salaried employees. Generate a report giving total weekly pay, similar to the following:

```
SOCIAL SEC. #   NAME        CODE   RATE     HOURS    WEEKLY PAY
555-66-7777     ED COBURN     S    SALARY   40.0        1500.00
666-66-6666     TOM JONES     H    3.56     45.5         161.98
                                                        -------
                                            TOTAL       1661.98
```

12. Add FICA of 9.65% and federal tax of 22% to question 11 and create a new report with gross and net pay and totals for each.

13. Write a program to create a random file in which each record has ten different string fields and three numeric fields. Write the program so you can add records, change them, and print a sequential list of them. Use any type of data you choose, such as payroll, mailing list, etc. Use duplicate information in the first string field in some of the records as you create them. For example, if your first field contains the item number, use the same item numbers in several of the records. This will enable you to generate a control break report.

14. Use the first field of the records created in question 13 as a control field and generate a control totals report with subtotals and grand totals of the three numeric fields.

15. You are the payroll programmer for the XYZ Corporation, and you need a program to input all the employee information for the permanent records. Design and write a program that will use a screen display for the entry of the records, store them in a random file, and use a change and print rou-

tine as discussed in the chapter. The screen display should look like the following:

```
                    XYZ CORPORATION
                    EMPLOYEE ENTRY

1. NAME

2. ADDRESS

3. CITY

4. STATE              5. ZIP

6. BIRTH DATE         7. PAY CODE

8. EMP. DATE          9. # EXEMPT.
```

Use the prompting techniques shown earlier to input the information on the line next to the entry. After accepting all nine entries, ask the user if any need to be changed. If they do, the prompt should reappear on the item line. When there are no more changes, store the record in the file. The fields should be the following lengths: name = 20; address = 20; city = 15; state = 2; zip = 5; birth date = 6 stored and 8 displayed (with slashes); pay code = 1 (S for salaried or H for hourly—edit for the proper entry); emp. date (employment date) = 6 stored and 8 displayed; and # exempt. (number of exemptions) = 1. All the fields should be string, with the possible exception of the number of exemptions.

The data to be used follows:

NAMES	ADDRESSES	CITY	STATE	ZIP
ED COBURN	1400 SOUTH STREET	EL PASO	TX	76879
SARA SMITH	34567 WEST BLVD.	DENVER	CO	83789
TOM JONES	493 WESTERN	LOS ANGELES	CA	12837
HAROLD HARRIS	P.O. BOX 10	BROOKINGS	SD	68594
EVERITT JOHNSON	3246 BOSQUE	DES MOINES	IA	39849

The rest of the data is:

BIRTH DATE	PAY CODE	EMP. DATE	# EXEMPT.
05/16/43	H	12/15/84	3
03/22/50	S	05/18/80	1
02/02/65	H	06/16/84	5
03/15/44	S	05/15/76	3
04/18/22	H	04/16/53	2
06/16/37	H	03/22/57	2

The report you generate should look like the following (we show only two records):

```
                    XYZ CORPORATION                          chapter 11  319
                    EMPLOYEE LIST
                                                    random access file processing
     NAME            BIRTH DATE   CODE   EMP. DATE    # EXEMPT.

     ED COBURN       05/16/43      H     12/15/84        3
     SARA SMITH      03/22/50      S     05/18/80        1
```

Note: This program is an expansion of number 16 from Chapter 10.

QUICK QUIZ ___

The answers to the questions follow immediately after the quiz. Questions 1–15 are true–false, while 16–20 are multiple choice.

1. A random access file cannot be accessed sequentially.   **T**   **F**
2. Random file processing is also called direct access.   **T**   **F**
3. All random file records should be the same length.   **T**   **F**
4. A date field should always be stored as a number since that will take up less space.   **T**   **F**
5. The OPEN statement always requires the record length as a part of the statement.   **T**   **F**
6. The FIELD statement in IBM and Radio Shack BASIC is used to set up a buffer for data input and output.   **T**   **F**
7. The LSET and RSET statements are functionally identical.   **T**   **F**
8. All our versions use a form of the INPUT statement to retrieve random records from the file.   **T**   **F**
9. The Apple uses a READ statement to set up the record to be accessed.   **T**   **F**
10. It is relatively easy to keep track of the record number each particular record is stored with.   **T**   **F**
11. All our versions of BASIC can use their CLOSE statement to close one file or all open files.   **T**   **F**
12. The IBM and Radio Shack versions of the OPEN statement are the same.   **T**   **F**
13. The Apple stores records the same way with random processing as with sequential processing once the record is set up.   **T**   **F**
14. When using the dummy record, we need to add 1 to the record number input by the user to allow access to the correct record.   **T**   **F**
15. The CVS, CVI, and CVD statements are necessary to store numbers when using the FIELD statement, while the MKS$, MKI$, and MKD$ are used to access the numbers.   **T**   **F**
16. Which of the following commands is used to field integers?
    - **a.** CVS
    - **b.** MKD$
    - **c.** MKI$
    - **d.** CVI

_____ 17. Which of the following statements does *not* deal with random processing on the IBM and Radio Shack?

        a. FIELD   **c.** CVI

        b. INPUT #   **d.** PUT #

_____ 18. Which versions of BASIC uses the FIELD statement?

        a. IBM   **c.** Radio Shack

        b. Apple   **d.** None of them

_____ 19. Which of the following is *not* a random record access command?

        a. GET   **c.** INPUT #

        b. READ   **d.** All are

_____ 20. When changing random records, which of the following is *not* a vital part of the process?

        a. Getting the record from the file

        b. Displaying the record on the screen for changes

        c. Putting the record back in the file

        d. Updating the dummy record

ANSWERS TO QUICK QUIZ

1. F (We have already done this in printing sequential reports.)
2. T
3. T (Otherwise access would be difficult at best.)
4. F (As a numeric it would take up virtually the same amount of storage and would have to be converted when printing to insert the slashes.)
5. F (Only required with random processing.)
6. T
7. F (If they were, there would be no need for two statements. The LSET is left-justification, and the RSET is right-justification.)
8. F (The IBM and Radio Shack use a GET # statement.)
9. T
10. F (Not the way we have worked thus far. In the next chapter we will learn how to do indexed processing, which will keep track of the record numbers for us.)
11. T
12. T (Though the IBM can also use one of a different format.)
13. T
14. T (This is necessary because the dummy record is the first record. For example, record 6 is actually record 7 in the file.)
15. F (MKS$, MKI$, and MKD$ are used for storing; CVS, CVI, and CVD are used for accessing.)
16. c (d is used to retrieve the field.)
17. b (GET # is used for random access.)
18. a and c
19. c (The IBM and Radio Shack use the GET, and the Apple uses the READ.)
20. d (Updating of the dummy record is only necessary for adding records.)

12 INDEXED FILE PROCESSING

OBJECTIVES

After completing Chapter 12, you will be able to:
- Give at least one reason why indexed file processing is beneficial.
- Explain why indexed file processing is easier for the user.
- Explain why two files are necessary for indexed processing.
- Explain why the index file must be in sequence.
- Explain how the binary search works.
- Explain how the bubble insert works.
- Explain why we search the index file before adding a record.
- Use the techniques described in the chapter to create an indexed file that may have records added, changed, and printed.

12–1
INTRODUCTION

We discovered in the last chapter how to access records randomly. This type of access, however, has one inherent drawback. The user has to know which record to access by number. A list of the records (or something similar) must be available so the user can look up which record number to access. In other words, if a change is needed on the record of Tom Jones, the user will need to know the number of the Tom Jones record before it can be accessed.

There is a much better way to do random access files that eliminates this difficulty: the use of indexed files. In this chapter we shall examine how to create and use indexed files and how to do a binary search. We will create a small program to test the use of such a search, and we will look at a technique for inserting the indexes in the index file. We will then modify our random access file program so it can be used to access an indexed file.

12–2
INDEXED FILES

In order to use an indexed file, the file must contain some unique field. That is, there must be one field in each record that is not the same in any other record. This unique field is called the **index** and is used to determine which record to access. For example, our previous file of name and contribution amount contains a name field. If we are careful to make each name in the file unique, we could use the name as our index. We would need to make sure there are not two Tom Jones records, for example.

When we use an indexed file, we actually use two files. We set up one file for our data and another file to contain the list of indexes and the record numbers that those indexes are related to. For example, if the number of the Tom Jones record is 15, then the index file would have a record that contained only Tom Jones and 15. When we want to access the record for Tom Jones, we look up the name in the key file, find the actual record number (15 in this case), and use that number to find the record in the main file. (See Figure 12–1 for an illustration of this idea.)

Now you may wonder why we want to set up a separate file with the name and the record number in it when the main file only contains the name and the contributions amount. Though the file we are using contains only two fields, most of the time, a file will contain many fields. Take a payroll file, for example. It will typically contain the employee number, name, address, city, state, zip code, social security number, birth date, number of deductions, and probably other fields also. The index file for this type of record would contain only the index field (in this case, possibly an employee number) and the record number. So you see, the index file will contain only the index field and the random record number regardless of how much information is in the main file. This makes access of the index file easy to handle.

12–3
BINARY SEARCH

In order to use an index file to look up indexes, it must be in sorted sequence. That is, it must be in alphabetic or numeric sequence, sorted by the index field. We must be able to find the index we need in the least possible time. It would

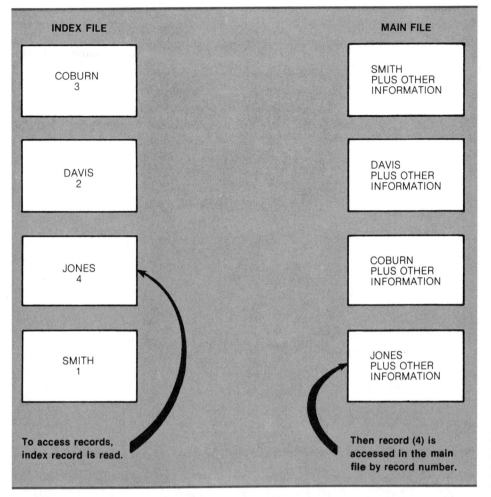

INDEX FILE

COBURN
3

DAVIS
2

JONES
4

SMITH
1

MAIN FILE

SMITH
PLUS OTHER
INFORMATION

DAVIS
PLUS OTHER
INFORMATION

COBURN
PLUS OTHER
INFORMATION

JONES
PLUS OTHER
INFORMATION

To access records,
index record is read.

Then record (4) is
accessed in the main
file by record number.

Figure 12–1
Illustration of index file processing.

be no help to have an index file that was just a jumble, since we would have to examine every entry until we found the correct index. It would be just as fast to access the main file.

But it would also do us little good to access the index file sequentially. Suppose, for example, we have an index file with 10,000 entries. If we had to look up an index near the end of the index file, it would take a long time to find the entry. What we need is some method of searching through the index other than sequential. Because the index will be in sorted sequence, we can use a method called a **binary search.**

A binary search works by finding the item that is in the middle of the list and then comparing that item to the item being searched for. If the searched-for item is less than the middle item, the search routine then drops down to the middle item in the lower half and compares again. If the searched-for item is larger than the middle item, the routine jumps to the middle of the upper half of the list and compares again. This process continues until either the list is exhausted or the item is found.

An example will help clarify the search technique (see Figure 12–2). Suppose we have a list of the numbers 1, 4, 6, 8, 9, and 15, and we are searching for 4. The binary search will take the number of items, 6 in this case, add 1 (we'll see why this is necessary in a moment), and divide by 2, throwing away the remainder, to yield 3. The third item, 6, is then compared to the one being searched for. Since 4 is less than 6, the search will continue on the lower half of the list. The current item number, 3, is divided in half (again throwing away the remainder), and that item is compared. Thus, list item 1, which is 1, is compared to the 4 we are searching for. Since 4 is larger, we now have to move in the other direction. To do this, we use the position number of the previous high, which was 3, subtract the current position number, 1, and get 2. We divide that by 2 and add the result to the current position, which is 1. This gives us 2, and the number in position 2 is the 4 we are looking for. We have a match.

Let's try another example with the same list of 1, 4, 6, 8, 9, and 15. This time let's look for 15 (see Figure 12–3). The search will take the total number of items plus one, 7, divide it in half, 3, and use that item for comparison. This time, 15 is larger than the third item, 6. Therefore, the item number (3) is subtracted from the total number of items plus one (7) and then halved. This number is then added to the item number to get the number halfway above the item number. In this case, $7 - 3 = 4$, $\frac{4}{2} = 2$, and $3 + 2 = 5$. The item to compare is the fifth item, or 9. 15 is larger than 9, so the process is done again: $7 - 5 = 2$, $\frac{2}{2} = 1$, and $5 + 1 = 6$. Item 6 is 15, and the match is found.

If we had used just the correct number of items, 6 (instead of 6 + 1), for the test, the top item, 15, could not have been found. Let's rework our calculations to discover this. The first calculation was the original midpoint, or $\frac{7}{2} = 3$. This is the same $(\frac{6}{2} = 3)$, but the second calculation is going to be different: $6 - 3 = 3$, $\frac{3}{2} = 1$, $3 + 1 = 4$. Then the next calculation would have been:

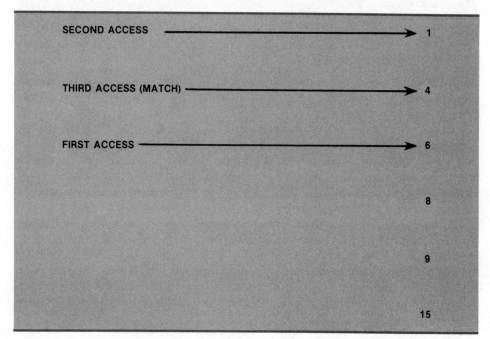

SECOND ACCESS ————————————————————————▶ 1

THIRD ACCESS (MATCH) ————————————————————————▶ 4

FIRST ACCESS ————————————————————————▶ 6

8

9

15

Figure 12–2
Illustration of binary
search.

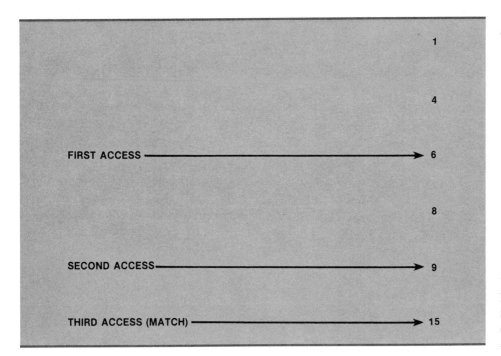

FIRST ACCESS ——————————————————————▶ 6

SECOND ACCESS——————————————————————▶ 9

THIRD ACCESS (MATCH) ——————————————————▶ 15

1

4

8

Figure 12–3
Second binary search
example.

$6 - 4 = 2$, $\frac{2}{2} = 1$, and $4 + 1 = 5$. Finally, we would have calculated $6 - 5 = 1$, $\frac{1}{2} = 0$, and we would be stuck on 5. We could not find the top item. So it is important to use one more than the total number of items in order to locate the very top-most item.

What do you suppose would happen if we searched for a nonexistent item? Well, let's see. Let's look for 7 in our list (see Figure 12–4). The first calculation, $\frac{7}{2} = 3$, gives us the third item, 6. Since the 7 we are searching for is larger, we calculate $7 - 3 = 4$, $\frac{4}{2} = 2$, $3 + 2 = 5$, and find 9, which is greater than 7. Then we calculate using the midpoint we found before (3) as our low end, since we have already discovered our number is larger than that: $3 + 5 = 8$, $\frac{8}{2} = 4$. Item 4, the 8, is too large, and we calculate again for lower: $3 + 4 = 7$, $\frac{7}{2} = 3$; but 3 is the low end again. Since we already checked it, we know it cannot be correct. Thus, we know there is no item in our list with the value of 7.

Now that we understand the logic of the binary search, let's construct one to see how well it works. In order to create the routine, we have to look at exactly what it will need to do. First, it will need a list of numbers, which we will supply with a DATA table. We will use the following statements:

```
290 DATA 1, 5, 8, 9, 15, 20, 42, 50, 65, 95
300 DATA 105, 125, 130, 140, 142, 144, 145, 148, 150, 190
```

Notice that there are twenty items and that they are in sequence. Recall that we will need to use one more than this number in the routine to give us the high end, but we also need the low end. If we begin the low end at 1, we will never get the bottom item for the same reason we cannot get the top item without adding one to the total number of items. We will, therefore, use 0 as the low end.

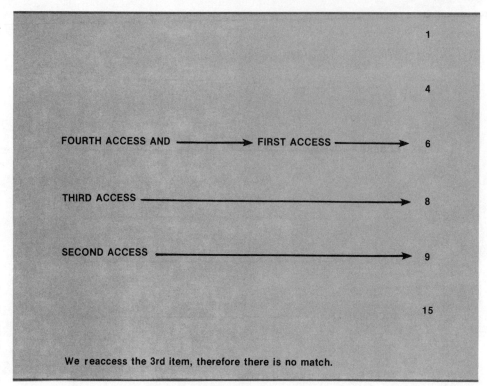

Figure 12–4
Example of search for nonexistent item.

Now, the first step in the program will be to input the item to be searched for. Then we need to determine the halfway point. Next, we check to see if this is the item we need. If it is more than the item we need, we use the lower half of the list, otherwise we use the upper half of the list. If we are going to use the lower half of the list, the total number of items will have to be reduced to half since we are throwing away all the upper-half items. If we are using the upper half, the halfway point of the list will be changed to the lowest number since we are throwing away the bottom items.

After we do the appropriate calculation for the new item, we compare the calculated item number against the low and high points. If it is the same as either one, that means that the item just calculated is one we already looked at, so we are finished because there is no match. If the calculated number doesn't agree with either one, then the search continues. The pseudocode follows (the flowchart is shown in Figure 12–5):

Start
Dimension DATA variable and read DATA into it.
Initialize low and high points.
Input the number to search for.
Find the halfway point.
DO-WHLE search item<> current item
  AND search item <> high or low.
    IF search item < current item THEN *(continues on page 328)*

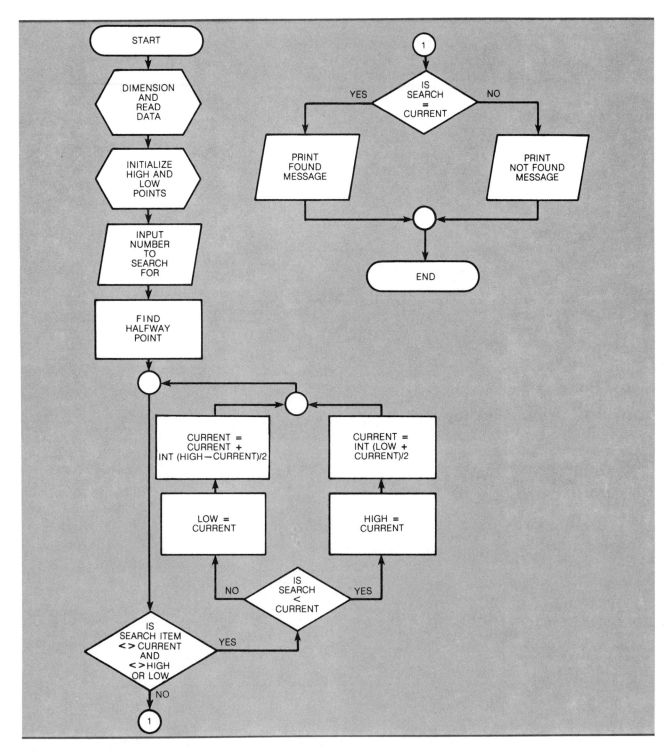

Figure 12–5
Flowchart of binary search.

```
    High = current
    Current = the integer of (low + current) / 2.
ELSE
    Low = current
    Current = current + integer of (high - current) / 2.
    END IF
END-DO
IF search item = current item THEN
    Print found message.
ELSE
    Print not found message.
END IF
End
```

The program should look like the following:

```
10 REM ***** PROGRAM NAME: BINARY
20 REM
30 REM ***** WRITTEN BY EDWARD J. COBURN
40 REM
50 REM THIS PROGRAM WILL TEST THE BINARY SEARCH ROUTINE
60 REM
70 CLS                     ' CLEAR THE SCREEN
80 DIM B(20)               ' ARRAY FOR THE LIST
90 FOR I=1 TO 20
100      READ B(I)         ' READ IN THE LIST
110 NEXT I
120 H=21                   ' HIGH POINT = NUMBER ITEMS + 1
130 L=0                    ' LOW POINT ALWAYS STARTS AT ZERO
140 INPUT "SEARCH FOR WHAT NUMBER";N
150 C=INT(H/2)             ' C=CURRENT ITEM NUMBER
160 PRINT "* ";            ' JUST A MARKER TO INDICATE LOOPS
170 IF N<>B(C) THEN 230    ' IS CURRENT = SEARCHED ITEM
180     PRINT "THERE IS A MATCH"
190     PRINT "SEARCHED FOR ";N
200     PRINT "FOUND        ";B(C)
210     GOTO 280
220 REM
230 IF N<B(C) THEN H=C : C=INT((L+C)/2)
             ELSE L=C : C=C+INT((H-C)/2)
240 IF H<>C AND L<>C THEN 160      ' NOT LOW OR HIGH
250     PRINT "THERE IS NO MATCH"
260     PRINT "SEARCHED FOR    ";N
270     PRINT "ENDED SEARCH AT ";B(C)
280 END
290 DATA 1, 5, 8, 9, 15, 20, 42, 50, 65, 95
300 DATA 105, 125, 130, 140, 142, 144, 145, 148, 150, 190
```

Program 12–1

)))DIFFERENCES

On the Apple, line 70 should be HOME instead of CLS, and line 230 will have to be two statements (no ELSE):

```
230 IF N<B(C)  THEN H=C : C=INT((L+C)/2) : GOTO 240
235 IF N>=B(C) THEN L=C : C=C+INT((H-C)/2)
```

Now let's execute the program and see how it works. Let's first use a number that is in the list, 142:

```
RUN
SEARCH FOR WHAT NUMBER? 142
* * THERE IS A MATCH
SEARCHED FOR 142
FOUND        142
Ok
```

Notice the printed asterisks. They indicate how many loops the routine went through in the search. Let's try another number. This time let's use 190 to be sure the routine will find the item at the top of the list.

```
RUN
SEARCH FOR WHAT NUMBER? 190
* * * * * THERE IS A MATCH
SEARCHED FOR 190
FOUND        190
Ok
```

Good, it will find the top item. How about the bottom item? Let's use 1 and find out.

```
RUN
SEARCH FOR WHAT NUMBER? 1
* * * * THERE IS A MATCH
SEARCHED FOR 1
FOUND          1
Ok
```

Terrific! Now let's see what happens when we enter a number not in the list. Let's use 10.

```
RUN
SEARCH FOR WHAT NUMBER? 10
* * * * * THERE IS NO MATCH
SEARCHED FOR    10
ENDED SEARCH AT 9
Ok
```

Well, now we know that works also. However, when we get ready to use this to search our index file, we will have to set up the routine to access the index file rather than merely compare items in an array, but we should have no difficulty with the changes necessary.

12–4
SEQUENCING THE INDEX FILE

We mentioned that the index file must be in sequence for any searching technique to work. It is up to us in our programs to make sure the index file is in sequence. We will discuss sorts again later, but there is a fairly simple sorting technique we can use that works well as long as there are not too many items in the file to be adjusted.

The technique is a **bubble insert.** This insert method allows an added entry to "bubble" to the appropriate location. Here's the way it works. We take the original list of sorted items and put the new item at the top (the highest point in the sequence). Then we compare the current item with the next item in the list. If the current item is less than the next item, the two items are switched.

Then the comparison is done again. This continues until the current item is greater than the next item, at which point it is in the correct spot and the bubbling can cease. (See Figure 12–6 for an illustration of this technique.)

An example will help clarify this technique (Figure 12–6). Suppose we have the list of numbers 1, 4, 7, 9, 14, 16, 18, and we need to insert 10 in the appro-

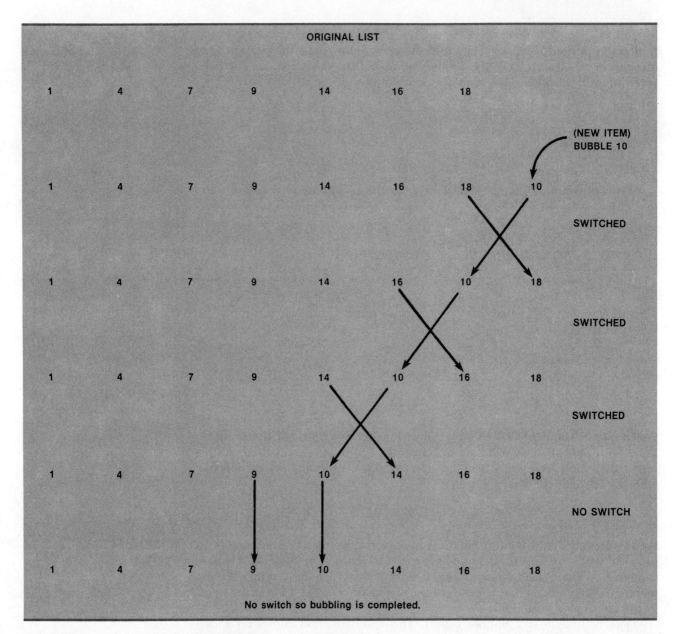

Figure 12–6
Bubble technique illustration.

priate location. First, 10 would be put on the end, and the list would become 1, 4, 7, 9, 14, 16, 18, 10. Then 10 would be compared to 18. Since 10 is less, 18 and 10 would switch places. The list would then become 1, 4, 7, 9, 14, 16, 10, 18. Then 10 and 16 would be compared, and again a switch would take place. Likewise when 10 is compared to 14. Finally, 10 would be compared to 9, but since 10 is greater than 9, no switch is necessary and the list is again in the correct sequence.

Before we experiment with this technique, we need to review how to switch the items. Let's suppose that C is the current item and N is the next item. We want to switch them, so the logical thing to do would be to use two assignments:

```
10 C=N
20 N=C
```

The only problem with this is that now both have the same value. If N contains 3 and C contains 4, line 10 will change C to 3. Then line 20 will assign 3 (we just changed C) to N. But N was supposed to get assigned 4. We lost a value. The proper way to do this exchange is by using temporary storage for one of the variables, such as:

```
10 T=N          ' T IS TEMPORARY STORAGE
20 N=C          ' ASSIGN THE FIRST
30 C=T          ' NOW WE CAN ASSIGN THE SECOND
```

Now, if N is 3 and C is 4, line 10 stores 3 in T, line 20 puts 4 into N, and line 30 puts 3 into C. They are now reversed, as we wanted.

Now let's write a small sample program to test this technique. The pseudocode follows; the flowchart is shown in Figure 12–7.

Start
Dimension array variable and assign with READ.
Initialize high value to number of items + 1.
Input item to insert.
Put item to insert (current item) into last array position.
DO-WHILE high value item > current item.
　　Exchange items.
　　Reduce high value by 1.
END-DO
Print new list
End

The program will look like the following:

```
10 REM ***** PROGRAM NAME: BUBBLE
20 REM
30 REM ***** WRITTEN BY EDWARD J. COBURN
40 REM
50 REM THIS PROGRAM WILL TEST THE INDEX FILE BUBBLE TECHNIQUE
60 REM
```
                                                              Program 12–2

Program continues on page 333

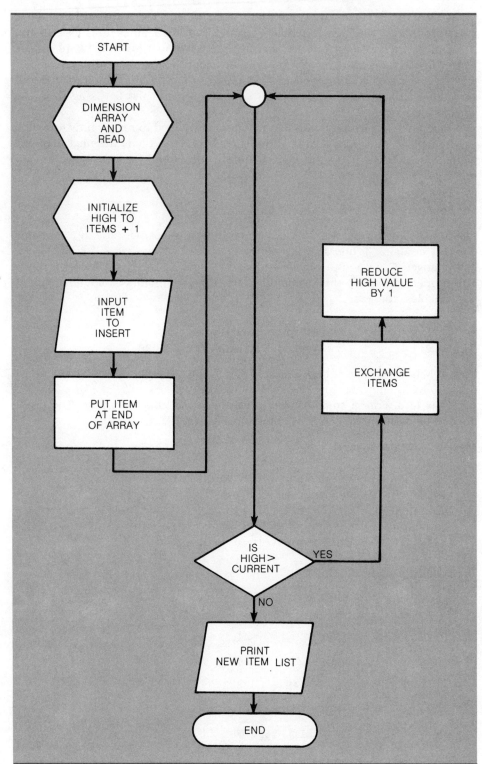

Figure 12–7
Flowchart of bubble
insert.

```
80 DIM B(21)                    ' ARRAY FOR THE LIST
90 FOR I=1 TO 20
100      READ B(I)              ' READ IN THE LIST
110 NEXT I
120 CLS                         ' CLEAR THE SCREEN
130 INPUT "WHAT ITEM TO INSERT";I
140 B(21)=I
150 H=21
160 IF B(H)>=B(H-1) THEN 220    ' EXIT THE LOOP
170      T=B(H-1)               ' TEMPORARY STORAGE
180      B(H-1)=B(H)
190      B(H)=T
200      H=H-1                  ' REDUCE THE HIGH
210      IF H>1 THEN 160        ' QUIT IF BOTTOM OF LIST
220 FOR I=1 TO 21
230      PRINT B(I);            ' PRINT LIST
240 NEXT I
250 END
290 DATA 1, 5, 8, 9, 15, 20, 42, 50, 65, 95
300 DATA 105, 125, 130, 140, 142, 144, 145, 148, 150, 190
```

Program 12–2 (cont.)

)))DIFFERENCES

The only Apple change is that line 120 should be HOME.

Let's try out the program to be sure it works. Let's insert 2:

```
RUN
WHAT ITEM TO INSERT? 2
 1   2   5   8   9   15   20   42   50   65   95   105   125   130   140
 142   144   145   148   150   190
Ok
```

Notice that 2 is now in the list. This routine will also insert a duplicate index. Let's try 20:

```
RUN
WHAT ITEM TO INSERT? 20
 1   5   8   9   15   20   20   42   50   65   95   105   125   130   140
 142   144   145   148   150   190
Ok
```

Now there are two 20s in the list. This would present a problem in the search routine. We will discuss this in the next section.

12–5 ADDITIONAL CONSIDERATIONS

Before we put these concepts together and write our indexed file accessing program, we need to discuss a few other considerations.

When we were discussing the binary search, we mentioned that in order for the search to work, the list must be in sequence. This also means that there can be no duplicate entries. Though the bubble insert routine will add duplicates to the index list, we have to make sure that it doesn't happen. If there are duplicates, there is no way to know which of the duplicates we are accessing at a particular time. Besides, if you were trying to find the Tom Jones record, you would want only one Tom Jones to be in your file.

So what do we do about duplicate entries? In the case of using a name for the index, duplicates are a definite possibility. Well, there are several solutions to this problem. Probably the easiest is to use some code for duplicate entries. For example, suppose we have two Tom Jones entries. We could use Tom Jones for one and Tom A. Jones for the other; or possibly Tom Jones for one and Tom Jones. for the other. Putting the period on the end of one Jones would make each of them unique but would not affect the use of the name. There would then be a problem for the user to keep track of which Tom Jones is which.

How can we ensure that duplicates do not invade our index file? The easiest way to do that is to check the index file before we store the records (remember there are two records now, the main file record and the index record) and make sure there is no duplicate entry in the index. Recall that our search program will indicate when no entry is found. We search the index file for our entry and if no entry is found, the records are added. If a duplicate is located, the user is informed and asked to change the index to eliminate the duplication.

Another consideration is file size. If disk space is a concern, the main file can be constructed without the index in it. For example, if the name field is the index, it can be put in the index file and left out of the main file. This will save some space in the main file since the index is really not needed in both places. However, this is sometimes a dangerous thing to do. Should some problem occur and you lose the index file, you would not be able to use the main file to reconstruct the index since the index field would not be in the main file. Also, doing this would limit file access to use of the index file along with the main file, since that would be the only way to get all the data. Therefore, unless space is a primary consideration, the index field should be used in both files.

Finally, the bubble insert technique works well as long as the number of entries in the file is not too large. Naturally, the more entries there are, the slower the insertion. Also, insertions at the end of the file will be faster than insertions at the beginning of the file. That is, if your list is of names, inserting a name beginning with Z would be much faster than inserting one beginning with A since the A will have to bubble to the beginning of the file. This technique is workable until the file grows beyond about 500 entries. After that, the delay in inserting becomes intolerable, and some other technique should be used. We will discuss another processing method for this in the next chapter.

One method to help alleviate the speed problem in adding records to the index is to load the entire index into memory. This can be done at the beginning of the program. Then, every time you access the records or add a new index, you will be getting them from memory instead of from the disk. This is much faster. The problem here is one you might expect: in order to load the index into memory, you have to have either a small index or only a few records. As microcomputers are designed with more memory, this method will become more viable.

To make our index file concept a bit more sensible, we will add two more fields to the random file we used in the last chapter. As you recall, our file had the name and contribution amount of each donor. We will now put in the date of the last contribution and the phone number of the contributor. The date will be six characters long, and the phone number will be 10 (we will include the area code).

We will build all our modules from scratch, though some of the code will be duplicated from the previous chapter. The only module that will remain totally unchanged is the exit module. We will begin with the initial module; the pseudocode and the flowchart (Figure 12–8) are the same as in the previous chapter.

Note: You can reuse the modules from the previous chapter and insert the needed lines, by loading the program from disk and deleting the unnecessary lines to leave you the skeleton. Be careful that you delete only what you are not going to need.

The Initial Module

As discussed in the previous chapter, this module merely opens the files to be used, then displays the program options on the screen for the user to choose from. As before, there are four choices on the menu, and the subroutines used for the choices are numbered as they were before. Notice that we now have two files to open at the beginning of the program.

Note also that we changed the ON ... GOSUB in line 270 so that the add module begins on line 1000 instead of 500. This was deliberate. Since the add module is much larger this time, we won't attempt to patch the one from the last chapter. We will write the routine from scratch. The change and print routines will also be rewritten from scratch, though we did use the same line numbers to start the routines. The only routine that is completely the same is the exit module.

The program for the initial module follows:

```
10 REM ***** PROGRAM NAME: CONTINDX
20 REM
30 REM ***** WRITTEN BY EDWARD J. COBURN
40 REM
50 REM THE INDEXED FILE PROCESSING PROGRAM
60 REM
70 OPEN "R",1,"INDXDATA",44     ' OPEN DATA FILE
75 OPEN "R",2,"CINDEX",28       ' OPEN INDEX FILE
80 FIELD #1, 2 AS RF$
90 GET 1,1                      ' GET THE FIRST RECORD
100 IF CVI(RF$)=0 THEN RECS=1 ELSE RECS=CVI(RF$)
110 FIELD #1, 24 AS F$(1), 4 AS F$(2), 6 AS F$(3), 10 AS F$(4)
115 FIELD #2, 24 AS ID$, 4 AS IN$
120 CLS                         ' CLEAR THE SCREEN
130 PRINT TAB(10);"CONTRIBUTIONS MAINTENANCE"
140 PRINT                       ' BLANK LINE
150 PRINT "1. ADD NEW RECORDS"
155 PRINT
160 PRINT "2. CHANGE EXISTING RECORDS"
```

Program 12–3

Program continues on page 337

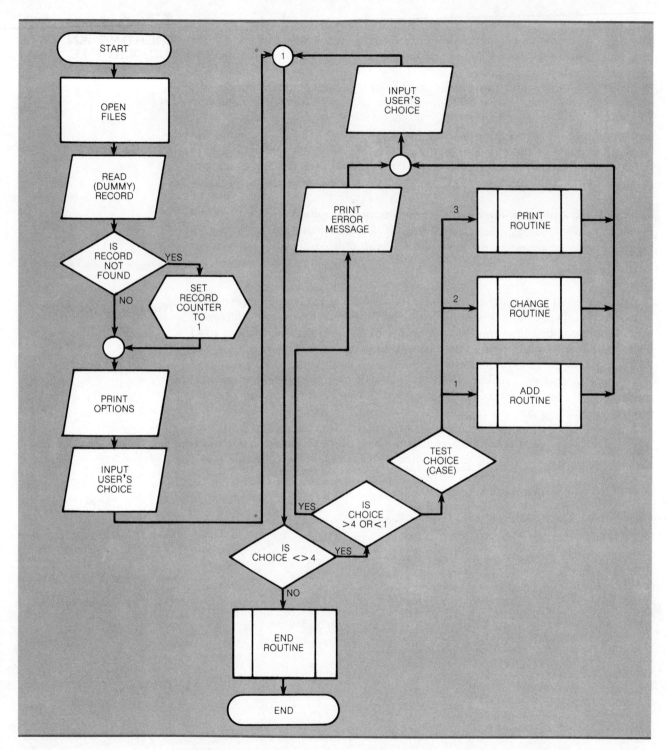

Figure 12–8
Flowchart of initial module.

```
165 PRINT
170 PRINT "3. PRINT THE FILE"
175 PRINT
180 PRINT "4. EXIT THE PROGRAM"
200 P$="WHAT OPTION (1-4)"        ' PROMPT
210 L=1                          ' PROMPT LENGTH
220 GOSUB 7000                   ' PROMPT SUBROUTINE
230 IF B$>"0" AND B$<"5" THEN 270
240    M$="INPUT ERROR.  RETRY ENTRY"
250    GOSUB 6000                    ' ERROR SUBROUTINE
260    GOTO 200                      ' REPROMPT
270 ON VAL(B$) GOSUB 1000, 2000, 3000, 4000
280 GOTO 120
```

Program 12–3 (cont.)

)))DIFFERENCES

On the Radio Shack, you need to change lines 70–100 and add lines 65, 105, and 108:

```
65 CLEAR                        ' SETUP THE STRING AREA
70 OPEN "R",1,"INDXDATA",44
75 OPEN "R",2,"CINDEX",28
80 FIELD #1, 2 AS RF$
85 ON ERROR GOTO 100
90 GET 1,1                      ' GET THE FIRST RECORD
95 RECS=CVI(RF$)
98 GOTO 108
100 RECS=1                      ' ASSIGN THE NUMBER OF RECORDS
105 RESUME 108
108 ON ERROR GOTO 0             ' TURN OFF THE ERROR PROCESSING
```

On the Apple, you need the assignment of the blanks and D$:

```
62 CL$=""
64 FOR I=1 TO 6
66     CL$=CL$+CL$
68 NEXT I
69 D$=CHR$(4)
```

Then the OPEN statement and the error routine need to be different:

```
70 PRINT D$;"OPEN CONTDATA,L50": REM OPEN DATA FILE
72 PRINT D$;"OPEN CINDEX,L32" : REM OPEN INDEX FILE
75 ONERR GOTO 120            : REM IF NO FIRST RECORD
80 PRINT D$;"READ CONTDATA,R1"
85 INPUT RECS                : REM READ THE NUMBER
90 GOTO 150
95 RECS=1                    : REM ASSIGN THE NUMBER
100 PRINT D$;"CLOSE CONTDATA" : REM CLOSE THE FILE
115 PRINT D$;"OPEN CONTDATA,L33"
120 PRINT D$                 : REM TURN OFF DISK ACCESS
124 POKE 216,0               : REM TURN OFF ERROR PROCESSING
128 HOME                     : REM CLEAR THE SCREEN
```

Before we look at the addition module, we will have to devise the binary search subroutine to access the records. This is necessary since this subroutine will be used in the add module and the change module. The routine will be virtually the same as Program 12–1, except now we will need to have the routine

The Binary Search Subroutine

access the index file rather than simply pull the index from the array. The routine will use the contributor's name for the index to search for. We will call this S$, and a search code will be set up to indicate whether or not the search was successful. Upon return to the original routine, this code will be used to determine the appropriate course of action.

The search routine follows:

```
8970 REM
8980 REM ***** BINARY SEARCH ROUTINE
8990 REM
9000 IF RECS=1 THEN RETURN        ' NO RECORD TO SEARCH
9010 H=RECS                       ' HIGH POINT = NUMBER ITEMS + 1
9020 L=0                          ' LOW POINT ALWAYS STARTS AT ZERO
9030 CO=INT(H/2)                  ' C=CURRENT ITEM NUMBER
9040 GET #2,CO                    ' GET THE RECORD
9050 I$=MID$(ID$,1,LEN(S$))       ' ONLY USE LENGTH OF SEARCH $
9060 IF I$<>S$ THEN 9090          ' IS CURRENT = SEARCHED ITEM
9070    SC=1                      ' SEARCH CODE=1 IF FOUND
9080    RETURN                    ' SUBROUTINE ENDED
9090 IF I$>S$ THEN H=CO : CO=INT((L+CO)/2)
             ELSE L=CO : CO=CO+INT((H-CO)/2)
9100 IF H<>CO AND L<>CO THEN 9040 ' NOT LOW OR HIGH
9110    SC=0                      ' SEARCH CODE, 0 IF NOT FOUND
9120    RETURN                    ' SUBROUTINE ENDED    Program 12—4
```

))) DIFFERENCES

On the Apple, we need line 9035 so that the bottom line won't scroll when using the PRINT statements:

```
9035 R=23 : C=1 : GOSUB 5000    : REM REPOSITION THE CURSOR
```

Then the disk access needs to be changed:

```
9040 PRINT D$;"READ CINDEX,R";CO
9050 INPUT I$,IN              : REM GET THE NAME INDEX
```

And we need a bit extra on the two RETURN statements:

```
9080       PRINT D$ : RETURN    : REM SUBROUTINE ENDED

9120       PRINT D$ : RETURN
```

The Addition Module

This module will require quite a few changes. First, we have to add two more fields to the display and to the input. The routine to add the records to the file will have to be upgraded to include the key file. We will actually add the records in several stages. We will first input the name as the index field and verify that it is not a duplicate. If it is, we will reprompt the user for a new one. Then we will input the rest of the fields and put the record in the main file and in the index file. You will notice that we will again use the dummy record concept to keep track of how many records are in the file. The same number can be used to add the record to the index file.

The new pseudocode follows; the flowchart can be seen in Figure 12–9.

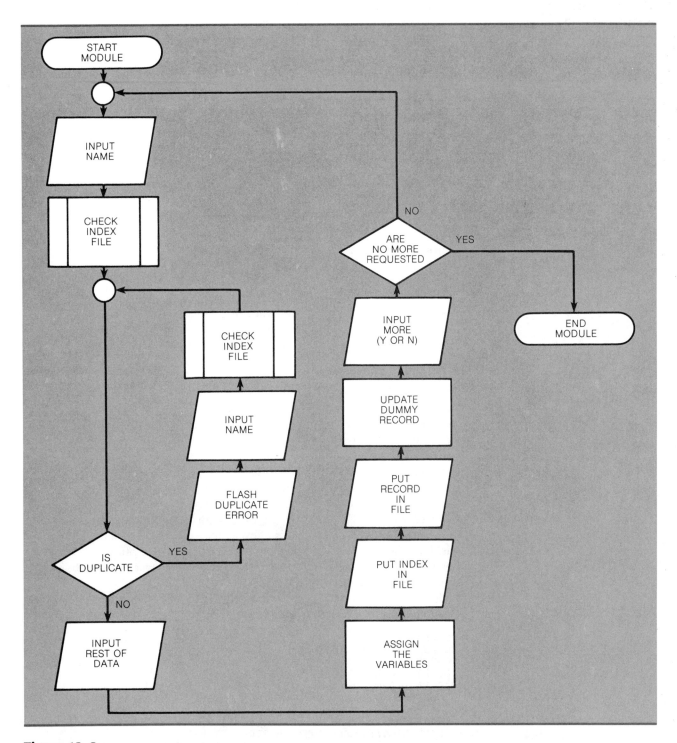

Figure 12–9
Flowchart of addition module.

Start ADD module
REPEAT-UNTIL input code is N (for no more records added).
    Input name.
    Check index file for duplicate (binary search module).
    DO-WHILE name is duplicate.
        Flash duplicate error.
        Input name.
        Check index file for duplicate (binary search module).
    END-DO
    Input the rest of the data.
    Assign the variables.
    Put the index in the index file.
    Put the record in the file.
    Update the number of records in record 1.
    Input for more records (Y or N).
END-REPEAT
End module

The main logic of this module will not change, but we do need to add a new loop. The binary search subroutine will be used for accessing the index, but the file addition routine will be part of the addition module.

We will also substantially change the routine to display and input the data for the fields. The program in the previous chapter simply displayed the name of the field and then input the data with two separate routines. This is a good approach when there are only a few fields, but when there are more, it becomes quite tedious. We will, instead, put the prompts and field lengths into a DATA statement and then display and input the fields using this information. We won't need to store the cursor positions for the input since the column will always be 18 and the row will be two beyond the previous display. The initial display will be on line 3. We will, however, include the row on the DATA statements because they will also be used in the change module and we will need the row number there. Notice that the date is input with eight characters and the phone number with twelve. This allows the user to enter them in the standard fashion, using slashes for the date and dashes for the phone number. We will, however, remove the slashes from the date and the dashes from the phone number before storing them in the file.

Again, note that the add routine was moved to line 1000 to avoid the problems that would have occurred if we had tried to patch the routine.

```
970 REM
980 REM ***** ADD MODULE
990 REM
1000 DATA CONT. NAME, 24, 3, CONT. AMOUNT, 7, 5
1010 DATA DATE OF CONT., 8, 7, PHONE NUMBER, 12, 9
1020 CLS                        ' CLEAR THE SCREEN
1030 RESTORE                    ' RESET DATA POINTER
1040 FIELD #1, 24 AS F$(1), 4 AS F$(2), 10 AS F$(3), 10 AS F$(4)
1050 PRINT TAB(10);"CONTRIBUTIONS ENTRY"
1060 PRINT                      ' BLANK LINE
```

Program continues

Program 12—5

```
1070 FOR I=1 TO 4
1080     READ D$(I),L(I),R(I)  ' THE PROMPT, LENGTH, ROW
1090     PRINT MID$(STR$(I),12,1);". ";D$(I) ' DISPLAY PROMPT
1100     PRINT                 ' BLANK LINE
1110 NEXT I
1120 FOR I8=1 TO 4
1130     L=L(I8)                   ' PROMPT LENGTH
1140     R=R(I8)                   ' ROW
1150     C=16                      ' COLUMN
1160     GOSUB 7070                ' PROMPT SUBROUTINE
1170     IF I8<>1 THEN 1260        ' SKIP THE SEARCH
1180         S$=B$                 ' ASSIGN THE SEARCH FIELD
1190         GOSUB 9000            ' SEARCH SUBROUTINE
1200         IF SC=0 THEN 1260     ' SKIP IF SEARCH OKAY
1210             M$="DUPLICATE INDEX.  REENTER"
1220             GOSUB 6000        ' ERROR SUBROUTINE
1230             R=3               ' ROW NUMBER
1240             C=16              ' COLUMN NUMBER
1250             GOTO 1130         ' REDO THE PROMPT
1260         G$(I8)=B$             ' STORE THE FIELD
1270 NEXT I8
1280 LSET F$(1)=G$(1)             ' ASSIGN THE FIELDS
1290 LSET F$(3)=MID$(G$(3),1,2)+MID$(G$(3),4,2)+MID$(G$(3),7,2)
1300 LSET F$(4)=MID$(G$(4),1,3)+MID$(G$(4),5,3)+MID$(G$(4),9,4)
1310 RSET F$(2)=MKS$(VAL(G$(2))
1320 PUT 1,RECS+1               ' PUT THE RECORD
1330 FIELD #1, 2 AS RF$         ' FIELD RECORD 1
1340 RECS=RECS+1               ' INCREASE RECORD COUNT
1350 LSET RF$=MKI$(RECS)        ' SET THE FIELD
1360 PUT 1,1                    ' PUT RECORD 1
1365 FIELD #2, 24 AS ID$, 4 AS IN$
1370 H=RECS-2                   ' NUMBER OF RECORDS
1380 IF H=0 THEN 1440           ' BYPASS IF NO RECORDS
1390 GET 2,H                    ' GET THE INDEX
1400 IF G$(1)>=ID$ THEN 1440    ' EXIT THE LOOP
1410     PUT 2,H+1             ' PUT THE OLD RECORD
1420     H=H-1                 ' REDUCE THE HIGH
1430     IF H>0 THEN 1390      ' GET THE NEXT INDEX
1440 LSET ID$=G$(1)            ' ASSIGN THE INDEX
1450 RSET IN$=MKS$(RECS)       ' USE THE ACTUAL NUMBER
1460 PUT 2,H+1                 ' STORE THE INDEX
1470 P$= "DO YOU WANT TO ADD ANY MORE (Y OR N)"
1480 L=1                       ' LENGTH OF PROMPT
1490 GOSUB 7000                ' PROMPT SUBROUTINE
1500 IF B$<>"Y" THEN RETURN
1510 GOTO 1020                 ' GET ANOTHER RECORD
```

Program 12–5 (cont.)

)))DIFFERENCES

For the Apple, line 1020 needs to be HOME, and we don't need line 1040. Next, we need a different output routine:

```
1280 PRINT D$;"WRITE CONTDATA,R";RN+1
1290 PRINT F$(1)                    : REM ASSIGN THE FIELDS
1300 PRINT MID$(F$(3),1,2);MID$(F$(3),4,2);MID$(F$(3),7,2)
1310 PRINT MID$(F$(4),1,3);MID$(F$(4),5,3);MID$(F$(4),9,4)
1320 PRINT VAL(F$(2))
1330 RECS=RECS+1                    : REM INCREASE RECORD COUNT
1340 PRINT "WRITE CONTDATA,R1" : REM WRITE RECORD 1
```

Program continues

```
1350 PRINT RECS                : REM WRITE THE RECORD NUMBER
1360 H=RECS-2                   : REM NUMBER OF RECORDS
1365 IF H=0 THEN 1450
1370 PRINT "READ CINDEX,R";H    : REM SET UP THE RECORD
1380 INPUT ID$,IN               : REM GET THE INDEX
1390 IF F$(1)>=ID$ THEN 1450    : REM EXIT THE LOOP
1400     PRINT D$;"WRITE CINDEX,R";H+1 : REM PUT THE OLD RECORD
1410     PRINT ID$
1420     PRINT IN
1430     H=H-1                  : REM REDUCE THE HIGH
1440     IF H>0 THEN 1370       : REM GET THE NEXT INDEX
1450 PRINT D$;"WRITE CINDEX,R";H+1 : REM PUT THE NEW INDEX
1455 PRINT F$(1)                : REM WRITE THE INDEX
1460 PRINT RECS                 : REM USE THE ACTUAL NUMBER
1465 PRINT D$                   : REM SET BACK TO SCREEN
```

The Change Module

The change module will be substantially the same as in the previous chapter. The differences will occur in the screen display and record access. When we get the index (this time the name rather than just the record number) from the user, that index must be looked up using the search routine. If it is not found, an error will be flashed. If it is found, the record number will be used from the index record, and the regular file record will be input and displayed. Then four fields may be changed instead of just two, but the prompting will be the same. We will use the DATA statement technique from the previous module (we can READ the same DATA statements) to display and prompt for the information. The pseudocode would be as follows (the flowchart is shown in Figure 12–10):

```
Start change module
Prompt for index of record to change.
DO-WHILE index<> 0.
   Assign search field.
   Search for the record (search subroutine).
   DO-WHILE search code <> 1.
      Print error message.
      Search for the record (search subroutine).
   END-DO
   Get the record.
   Display the data on the screen.
   Prompt for field to change.
   DO-WHILE field <> 0.
      IF field is invalid THEN
         Print error message.
      ELSE
         Input new field.
         Assign new field.
      END-IF
      Prompt for field to change.
   END-DO (continues on page 344)
```

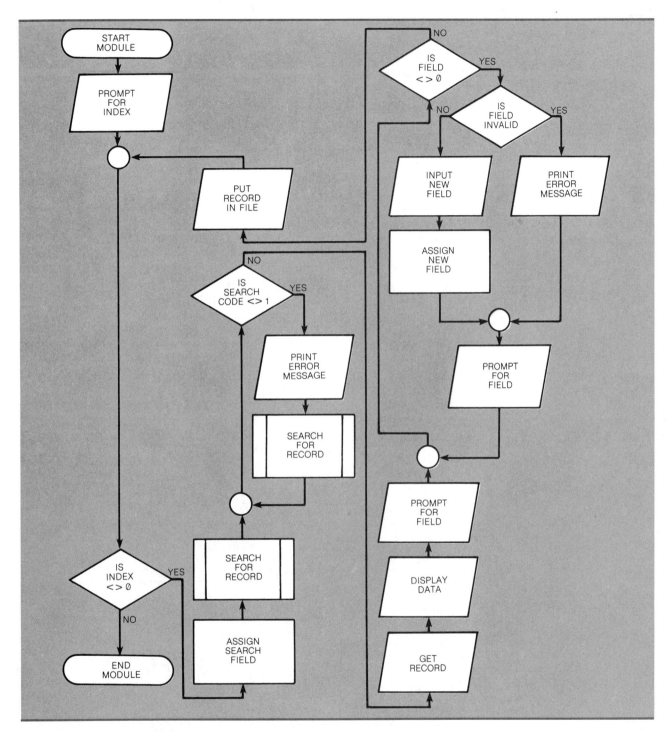

Figure 12–10
Flowchart of change module.

Put the changed record back in the file.
END-DO
End module

The programmed module follows. Recall that the module has too many additions to the one in the last chapter to try to reuse that one. You should erase the entire routine and rewrite it.

```
1970 REM
1980 REM ***** CHANGE MODULE
1990 REM
2000 P$="NAME (0 TO END)"
2010 L=24                           ' PROMPT LENGTH
2020 GOSUB 7000                     ' PROMPT SUBROUTINE
2030 IF B$="0" THEN RETURN          ' EXIT THE SUBROUTINE
2040 S$=B$                          ' ASSIGN SEARCH INDEX
2050 GOSUB 9000                     ' SEARCH SUBROUTINE
2060 IF SC=1 THEN 2100              ' SKIP IF SEARCH FOUND
2070     M$="RECORD NOT FOUND.  RETRY"
2080       GOSUB 6000               ' ERROR SUBROUTINE
2090       GOTO 2000                ' GET INDEX AGAIN
2100 RN=CVS(IN$)                    ' ASSIGN RECORD NUMBER
2105 FIELD #1, 24 AS F$(1), 4 AS F$(2), 6 AS F$(3), 10 AS F$(4)
2110 GET #1,RN                      ' GET THE RECORD
2120 CLS                            ' CLEAR THE SCREEN
2130 PRINT TAB(10);"CONTRIBUTIONS CHANGES"
2140 PRINT                          ' BLANK LINE
2150 RESTORE                        ' RESET DATA POINTER
2160 FOR I8=1 TO 4
2170     READ D$(I8),L(I8),R(I8) ' PROMPT, LENGTH, ROW
2180     PRINT MID$(STR$(I8),2,1);". ",D$(I8); ' DISPLAY PROMPT
2190     R=R(I8)                     ' ROW
2200     C=16                        ' COLUMN
2210     GOSUB 5000                  ' CURSOR POSITIONING
2220     IF I8=1 THEN PRINT F$(1)
2230     IF I8=2 THEN PRINT USING "####.##";CVS(F$(2))
2240     IF I8=3 THEN PRINT MID$(F$(3),1,2);"/";
                             MID$(F$(3),3,2);"/";
                             MID$(F$(3),5,2)
2250     IF I8=4 THEN PRINT MID$(F$(4),1,3);"-";
                             MID$(F$(4),4,3);"-";
                             MID$(F$(4),7,4)
2260     PRINT                       ' BLANK LINE
2270 NEXT I8
2280 P$="WHAT FIELD TO CHANGE (1-4, 0 TO END)"
2290 L=1                            ' PROMPT LENGTH
2300 GOSUB 7000                     ' PROMPT SUBROUTINE
2310 IF B$>"0" AND B$<"5" THEN 2350 ' IS ENTRY OKAY?
2320     M$="INVALID ENTRY. RETRY"  ' ERROR MESSAGE
2330     GOSUB 6000                 ' ERROR SUBROUTINE
2340     GOTO 2280                  ' REPROMPT
2350 IF B$="0" THEN 2460            ' END CHANGES
2360 B=VAL(B$)                      ' CONVERT INPUT
2370 R=R(B)                         ' ROW
2380 C=16                           ' COLUMN
2390 L=L(B)                         ' PROMPT LENGTH
2400 GOSUB 7070                     ' PROMPT SUBROUTINE
2410 IF B=1 THEN LSET F$(1)=B$' ASSIGN FIELDS
2420 IF B=2 THEN RSET F$(2)=MKS$(VAL(B$))
2430 IF B=3 THEN LSET F$(3)=MID$(B$,1,2)+MID$(B$,4,2)+MID$(B$,7,2)
```

```
2440  IF B=4 THEN LSET F$(4)=MID$(B$,1,3)+MID$(B$,5,3)+MID$(B$,9,4)
2450  GOTO 2120
2460  PUT 1,RN                    ' DUMP OUT RECORD
2470  GOTO 2000                   ' PROMPT FOR NEW RECORD
```

Program 12–6 (cont.)

)))DIFFERENCES

On the Apple, changes begin with the first file access:

```
2100  PRINT D$;"READ CONTDATA,R";RN
2110  INPUT F$(1),F$(2),F$(3),F: REM GET THE RECORD
2115  PRINT D$                   : REM SET BACK TO SCREEN
2120  HOME                       : REM CLEAR THE SCREEN
```

Then we need to change line 2230 so it doesn't use CVS:

```
2230      IF I8=2 THEN PRINT F$(2)
```

Then we need the format routine for the contribution amount:

```
2242      A=F                    : REM SETUP FOR SUBROUTINE
2244      GOSUB 8000             : REM FORMAT SUBROUTINE
2250      IF I=2 THEN PRINT P$
```

Finally, we need different assignments and output:

```
2420  IF B=2 THEN F=VAL(B$)
2430  IF B=3 THEN F$(2)=MID$(B$,1,2)+MID$(B$,4,2)+MID$(B$,7,2)
2440  IF B=4 THEN F$(3)=MID$(B$,1,3)+MID$(B$,5,3)+MID$(B$,9,4)
2450  GOTO 2120
2460  PRINT D$;"WRITE CONTDATA,R";RN
2470  PRINT F$(1)
2480  PRINT F$(2)
2490  PRINT F$(3)
2500  PRINT F
2510  GOTO 2000                  : REM RETURN FOR NEW RECORD
```

A Note About the Change Routine

You may have noticed in examining this routine that there is an oversight. If the name is changed in the record, a change in the index file would be necessary since the name is the index. This index file change is not done in our program.

To do this change requires several steps. First, when a new name is entered, it has to be checked against the current index to see if it is a duplicate (as we did for adding records). If it is a duplicate, an error message is flashed, and the name is reprompted for. If the name is verified as permissible, then the old index has to be removed from the index file and the new one inserted. The old one can be removed by moving all the records in the index up one position to fill in the position of the removed index. (See Figure 12–11 for an illustration of this process.) Finally, a routine similar to the one we used for the add routine could be used to put the new index in the file.

We will not add this routine to our program. It is left as an exercise at the end of the chapter. Just remember, when testing this routine, that although you can change the name in the record, this does not change the name in the index file.

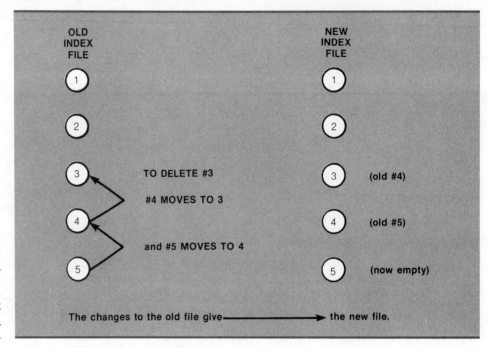

OLD
INDEX
FILE

NEW
INDEX
FILE

TO DELETE #3

#4 MOVES TO 3

and #5 MOVES TO 4

3 (old #4)

4 (old #5)

5 (now empty)

The changes to the old file give ————————▶ the new file.

Figure 12–11
Illustration of index
deletion.

The PRINT Module

In this module we will print a sequential list of the records stored in the file, as we did in the last chapter. This time, however, we will use our index file to determine the order of the list. This way the list will be in sorted sequence. The pseudocode follows; the flowchart is shown in Figure 12–12.

```
Start PRINT module
Print headings.
Initialize counter to 1.
DO-WHILE counter <= number of records.
    Input index record.
    Input file record using index number.
    Print fields.
    Add 1 to counter.
    Accumulate contributions.
END-DO
Print total.
End module
```

Notice that we have included a total of the contributions.

Again, the module is significantly different from before and should be re-keyed:

```
2970 REM
2980 REM ***** PRINT MODULE
2990 REM
3000 T=0                          ' ZERO OUT TOTAL FIELD
```

Program continues on page 348

Program 12–7

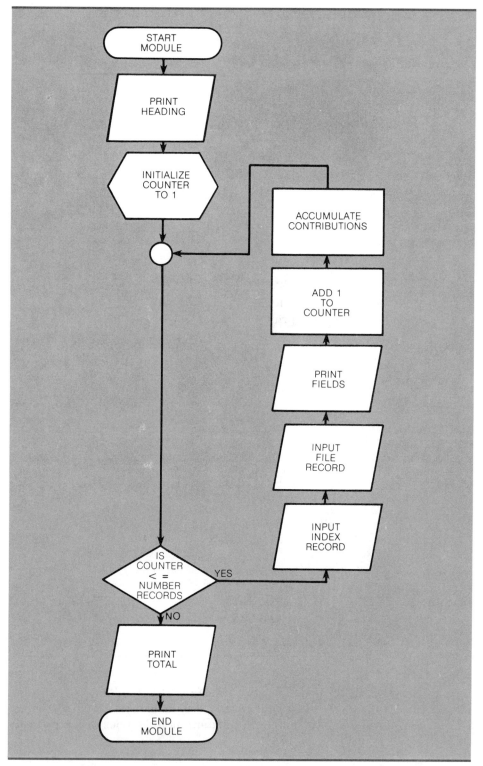

Figure 12–12
Flowchart of print
module.

```
3005 LPRINT TAB(25);"CONTRIBUTIONS LIST"
3010 LPRINT " "                    ' BLANK LINE
3020 LPRINT "NAME";TAB(28);"AMOUNT       DATE          PHONE NUMBER"
3030 LPRINT " "                    ' BLANK LINE
3040 FOR I=1 TO RECS-1             ' TO NUMBER IN FILE
3050     GET #2,I                  ' GET THE INDEX
3060     GET #1,CVS(IN$)           ' GET THE RECORD
3070     LPRINT F$(1);TAB(27);
3080     LPRINT USING "####.##";CVS(F$(2));
3090     LPRINT "     ";MID$(F$(3),1,2);"/";
                      MID$(F$(3),3,2);"/";
                      MID$(F$(3),5,2);
3100     LPRINT "     ";MID$(F$(4),1,3);"-";
                      MID$(F$(4),4,3);"-";
                      MID$(F$(4),7,4)
3110     T=T+CVS(F$(2))            ' ACCUMULATE TOTAL
3120 NEXT I
3130 LPRINT TAB(25);"----------"
3140 LPRINT "TOTAL";TAB(25);USING "######.##";T
3150 RETURN
```

Program 12–7 (cont.)

)))DIFFERENCES

On the Apple, all the LPRINT statements should be PRINT statements. Also, we need to add a line to turn the printer on:

```
3003 PRINT D$;"PR#1"                    : REM TURN ON THE PRINTER
```

Then the input routine needs to be different:

```
3050     PRINT D$;"READ CINDEX,R";I
3060     INPUT ID$,IN            : REM GET THE INDEX
3070     PRINT D$;"READ CONTDATA,R";IN
3080     INPUT NF$,DF$,PF$,F
3090     PRINT NF$;TAB(27);
3100     A=F                    : REM SET FOR FORMAT
3110     GOSUB 8000             : REM FORMAT SUBROUTINE
3120     PRINT TAB(37-LEN(NF$)-LEN(P$));P$;
3130     PRINT "     ";MID$(DF$,1,2);"/";MID$(DF$,3,2);"/";
                  MID$(DF$,5,2);
3140     PRINT "     ";MID$(PF$,1,3);"-";MID$(PF$,4,3);"-";
                  MID$(PF$,7,4)
3150     T=T+F                  : REM ACCUMULATE TOTAL
3160 NEXT I
3170 PRINT TAB(29);"----------"
3180 A=T                        : REM SETUP FOR FORMAT
3190 GOSUB 8000                 : REM FORMAT SUBROUTINE
3200 PRINT "TOTAL";TAB(32-LEN(P$));P$
3210 PRINT D$;"PR#0"            : REM TURN OFF PRINTER
3220 PRINT D$                   : REM TURN OFF I/O
3230 RETURN
```

The EXIT Module

The final module is for exiting the program. This module is exactly the same as in the last chapter. We need only to close the file and end the program. To see the pseudocode, flowchart, and program module, refer to the previous chapter.

Don't forget that this program needs all the subroutines we have used up to this point to make it complete. If you put the various modules and subroutines together, you should be able to run the program to add and change records and generate a report similar to the following:

```
              CONTRIBUTIONS LIST

NAME                 AMOUNT      DATE      PHONE NUMBER
ED JONES              200.00   10/15/83   777-185-8768
FRED SMITH           1200.00   03/17/84   777-786-9987
HARIOT THOMPSON        15.45   05/01/84   777-786-7648
SAMANTHA STEEL        235.16   11/16/83   777-856-8754
                    ---------
TOTAL                1650.61
```

SUMMARY

1. Random access files have one inherent difficulty: In order to access a record by number, you have to know the number of the record. The best solution to this problem is to create an index file using one of the fields of the record so that the record number can be looked up by that field. Access can then be gained to that record through the record number associated with the index.

2. Using an index file means actually setting up two files, one for the indexes and one for the records themselves. Looking up the index in the file can be done several ways. For one, we could simply start at the beginning of the file and look sequentially through the indexes. But this would gain us little time, so we devised a better way called a binary search. Using the binary search, we break the list into halves and decide in which half our desired index lies. Then we break that half into half and continue this process until we locate our record.

3. A binary search requires that the index file be in sequence, otherwise the search will not work. To put the index file in sequence, we used a bubble technique to move a new index into the appropriate place in the index file. We start at the top and switch indexes until the new index reaches the desired location.

4. In order to find an index in an index file, the file must have no duplicate entries. To ensure this, before we add a new record, we must check the index file to be sure the new index is not already in the file.

5. If file size is a consideration, the index can be left out of the main file since it is already in the index file. This is not generally a good idea because various problems may arise.

6. As long as there are only a few entries in the file, the bubble insertion technique works well. But as the file gets larger, it takes a great deal of time to insert the indexes. The bubble technique reaches an upper bound of usefulness at about 500 entries. After that, the insertion process takes too long.

7. One solution to this speed problem is to bring the entire index file into memory and use it there. The insertion and access are much quicker since

disk access is limited to the actual records; no access is necessary for only the indexes. The potential problem here is one of memory size. Unless your index is small, you will not have enough memory for the indexes.

GLOSSARY

Binary search   A technique for searching a sequential list for a particular entry. This technique continually divides the list in half until the desired entry is located.

Bubble insert   A method of inserting a new index; beginning at the top of the list, the new index is

"bubbled" to the appropriate location through a series of comparisons and exchanges.

Index   A field stored in a separate file to allow random access through something other than the record number.

QUESTIONS TO AID UNDERSTANDING

*1. Why is an indexed file easier for the user than a simple random access file?

2. Why are two files necessary when using an indexed file?

*3. Why must the index file be in sequence?

4. Explain how the binary search works.

5. Explain how the bubble insert works.

*6. Why do we search the index before adding another record to the file?

*7. Use the search technique described in the chapter to write a program to search for an entry in a list of names instead of numbers.

8. Use the techniques described in the chapter to add a check for a duplicate index to the change routine in Program 12–6.

9. Change Program 12–7 to input all the indexes into memory for processing rather than accessing the index file.

10. Return to page 317 and modify the program you wrote for question 10 to use indexed processing. Use the social security number as the index.

11. Use the information from question 11 on page 317 to generate a sequential report by social security number.

12. Add FICA tax of 9.65% and federal tax of 22% to question 11 and create a new report with gross and net pay and totals for each.

13. Write a program to create an indexed file in which each record has ten different string fields and three numeric fields. Write the program such that you can add records, change them, and print an index-sorted list of them. Use any type of data you choose (payroll, mailing list, etc.). Use the first string field as the index field.

14. You are the payroll programmer for the XYZ Corporation, and you need a program to input all the employee information for the permanent records. Design and write a program that will use a screen display for the entry of the records and store them in an indexed file using the name for the index. The display should look like the following:

```
    XYZ CORPORATION
    EMPLOYEE ENTRY
```

1. NAME

2. ADDRESS

3. CITY

4. STATE   5. ZIP

6. BIRTH DATE   7. PAY CODE

8. EMP. DATE   9. # EXEMPT.

Use the prompting techniques shown in Chapter 10 to input the information on the line next to the entry. After getting the name (index), check the file to make sure the index is not already in the file. If it is, print an appropriate error message and reprompt. After accepting all nine entries, ask the user if any changes are needed. If there are, the prompt should reappear on the item line. When there are no more changes, store the record in a file. The fields should be the following lengths: name = 20; address = 20; city = 15; state = 2; zip = 5; birth date = 6 stored, 8 displayed (with slashes); pay code = 1 (S for salaried or H for hourly—edit for the proper entry), emp. date (employment date) = 6 stored, 8 displayed; and # exempt. (number of exemptions) = 1. All the fields should be string, with the possible exception of the number of exemptions.

The data to be used follows:

NAMES	ADDRESSES	CITY	STATE	ZIP
ED COBURN	1400 SOUTH STREET	EL PASO	TX	76879
SARA SMITH	34567 WEST BLVD.	DENVER	CO	83789
TOM JONES	493 WESTERN	LOS ANGELES	CA	12837
HAROLD HARRIS	P.O. BOX 10	BROOKINGS	SD	68594
EVERITT JOHNSON	3246 BOSQUE	DES MOINES	IA	39849

The rest of the data is:

BIRTH DATE	PAY CODE	EMP. DATE	# EXEMPT.
05/16/43	H	12/15/84	3
03/22/50	S	05/18/80	1
02/02/65	H	06/16/84	5
03/15/44	S	05/15/76	3
04/18/22	H	04/16/53	2
06/16/37	H	03/22/57	2

The report you generate should look like the following (we only show two records):

```
                          XYZ CORPORATION
                          EMPLOYEE LIST

NAME                 BIRTH DATE    CODE    EMP. DATE      # EXEMPT.

ED COBURN            05/16/43       H      12/15/84          3
SARA SMITH           03/22/50       S      05/18/80          1
```

Note: **This program is similar to the one in question 15 on page 317 and question 16 on page 287.**

QUICK QUIZ

The answers to the questions follow immediately after the quiz. Questions 1–15 are true–false, while 16–20 are multiple choice.

T F 1. In order to do random access processing, the record number must be known.

T F 2. The only things we need to store in the index file are the index and the record number in the main file.

T F 3. Our programs should allow for duplicate entries in the index field.

T F 4. Our index file must be in sorted sequence to do a binary search.

T F 5. It is much faster to load the index file into memory and then access and add indexes with an array, than it is to use an index file.

T F 6. It is a good idea to construct our main file without our index field (putting it only in the index file), because this will save a lot of disk space.

T F 7. We always use a form of the INPUT statement to retrieve records from the index file.

T F 8. We should CLOSE the index file after each access so the file pointer will be repositioned to the beginning of the file.

T F 9. We have to include the length of the file on the OPEN statement when doing random access.

T F 10. The numbers 1, 3, 5, 10, 15, 25 are in sorted sequence.

T F 11. The strings "1", "3", "5", "10", "15", "25" are in sorted sequence.

T F 12. Detail lines are the first things printed on a report.

T F 13. When displaying a menu on the screen, you should always have a heading for the menu.

T F 14. The command MID$("ABCDEF",4,2) would yield "CD".

T F 15. The CHR$ and STR$ commands perform virtually the same function.

_____ 16. Which of the following fields would be sorted before "35"?

    a. "yes"   **c.** "YES"

    b. "4"   **d.** none of the above

17. What will ASC(MID$("ABCDE",1,1)) yield? _____

    a. "A"   **c.** "E"

    b. 65   **d.** none of the above

18. Which of the following is not an element of all OPEN statements for random _____
processing?

    a. the word OPEN   **c.** the file name

    b. the file length   **d.** all are

19. Which of the following is not always necessary when accessing an indexed _____
file?

    a. open the file   **c.** close the file

    b. read the index   **d.** all are necessary

20. When doing a control report, which of the following conveys data file infor- _____
mation?

    a. control field   **c.** subtotal

    b. detail line   **d.** column heading

ANSWERS TO QUICK QUIZ

1. T (Also, it must be stored in the index file for indexed processing.)
2. T
3. F (The index search will not work if there are duplicate entries. We have to make certain our programs do not allow duplicates.)
4. T
5. T (The only problem is with memory size.)
6. F (Though this will save disk space, it will limit us to doing access only through the index file.
7. F (GET is used also.)
8. F (This is unnecessary since we are accessing by record number.)
9. T
10. T
11. F ("10", "15", and "25" are all less than "3" because strings are compared from the left, one character at a time.)
12. F (Headings should be printed first.)
13. T
14. F (It would yield "DE".)
15. F (The CHR$ converts a number to its ASCII equivalent, while STR$ converts a number to characters.)
16. d
17. b
18. d
19. d
20. b (The detail line is the file information.)

13 TREE STRUCTURES

OVERVIEW

OBJECTIVES

After completing Chapter 13, you will be able to:

- Name two differences between a tree structure and an index file.
- Define the terms *tree, node, traverse, root node,* and *branch.*
- Explain when a tree is preferable to an index and when an index is preferable to a tree.
- Explain why you can't change an index in the tree structure without deleting it and then adding it back.
- Explain how to delete a record from a tree file.
- Diagram a tree structure given the items to be added.
- Explain how to store a number as one or more characters.
- Use all the techniques described thus far to write several programs.

There is a method of accessing random records by index without creating an index file. This method is called a **tree structure.** A tree has the advantage of access of the records in the file itself, eliminating the need for a separate index file. Also, though access is not necessarily any faster, adding records with a tree structure is much faster than with the bubble insertion technique used for the index file.

In this chapter we will introduce the tree structure, write a small program to test its use, and then continue our development of the contributions program.

A tree is fundamentally an indexing structure without cycles. That is, we access the indexes by examining each in sequence without jumping forward and backward as we did with the binary search. The first entry of the structure is called the **root;** all entries are called **nodes.** In Figure 13–1, node R is the root and the connections to the nodes at A and B are called **branches.** As we examine the nodes in search of a particular element, we are said to be **traversing** the tree.

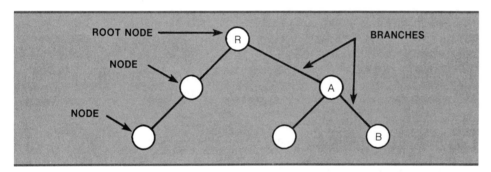

Figure 13–1
Diagram of a tree structure.

An example may help explain how a tree works. Suppose we need to add records to our file with indexes of 15, 10, 5, 16, 19, 7, 4, 17, and 20. Notice that they are not in order; our tree will create the order for us, not sequential order, but a branching sequence.

We will begin with 15 as the root node (Figure 13–2). The next index, 10, is then compared against the root node; since it is less than 15, the index 10 is added to the tree as the left branch (Figure 13–3). Any time the compared index is less than the node, the logic will branch to the left and follow the branch of the tree to the next node. If the compared index is greater, the branch will be to the right.

The third index is 5, which is compared to the root node, 15; since it is less, the branch to the left is followed. 10 is found on that branch, so a comparison is again performed. Since 5 is less than 10 and there are no more nodes to the left of 10, a node is added for index 5 as shown in Figure 13–4.

The next index, 16, is compared to 15; the branch is to the right since 16 is larger. There are no nodes to the right, so a node for 16 is set up as shown in Figure 13–5.

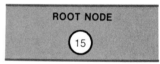

Figure 13–2
Diagram of root node.

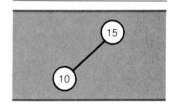

Figure 13–3
Diagram of addition of lower node.

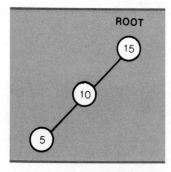

Figure 13–4
Addition of another lower node.

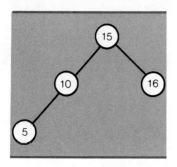

Figure 13–5
Addition of a higher node.

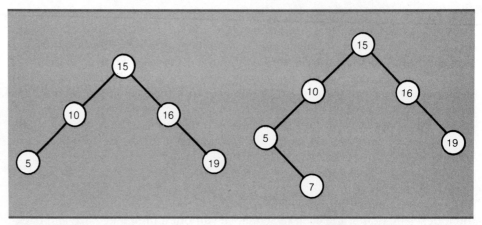

Figure 13–6
Addition of right node.

Figure 13–7
Addition of node for 7.

The next index is 19; it will branch to the right of 15 and again to the right of 16 to add another node (Figure 13–6). The next index is 7; it will branch left of 15, left of 10, and add a new node to the right of 5 as shown in Figure 13–7. The completed tree is shown in Figure 13–8 with the final three nodes added for 4, 17, and 20.

Indexes are located with the same method. Suppose we want to find index 7. We would begin the search at the root node and branch to the left (using the tree shown in Figure 13–8). At 10 we would again branch left and at 5 we would branch right and find our match. This search technique will work for changing and deleting records from the tree.

What would happen if we searched for an index not in the tree? In this case, we are not trying to add the index but merely find out if it is in the tree. Let's try one using Figure 13–8 and see what would happen. Let's search for 18. We begin by branching right at 15 and 16. We then go left at 19 and attempt to go right at 17, but we find no right node. That indicates that 18 does not exist in the tree.

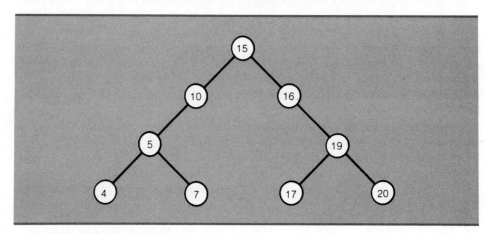

Figure 13–8
Final version of tree.

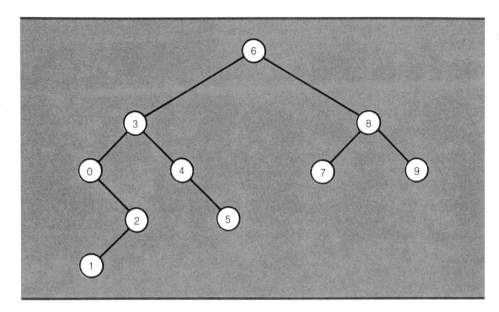

Figure 13–9
Second tree structure
example.

Let's try another short example to be sure we have the idea. This time, draw the nodes as we go through the problem and check your result against the final figure. We will use the numbers 6, 8, 3, 4, 9, 7, 0, 2, 1, and 5.

The root node will be 6. The 8 will be on the right, and the 3 will be the first node on the left. Then 4 is left of 6 and right of 3; 9 is right of 6 and right of 8. The 7 is right of 6 and left of 8; 0 is left of 6 and left of 3. The 2 is left of 6 and 3 and right of 0. Finally, 1 is left of 6 and 3, right of 0, and left of 2. Your finished tree should look like the one in Figure 13–9.

13–3
UTILIZING THE
TREE STRUCTURE

The branches on the tree structure are only for visual perspective. They do not actually represent anything, since a file is just a sequence of records. Therefore, we need some method of keeping track of each index's relationship to the others. We can do this by placing in each record two new fields: one for the record number of the next lower node and one for the record number of the next higher node.

To illustrate this, let's go back to our previous example of 15, 10, 5, 16, 19, 7, 4, 17, and 20. To keep track of the next lower node and the next higher node we will construct a small table. You may wish to follow along using Figure 13–8 as reference. The root node is again 15 and the first table entry then would be:

RECORD	VALUE	NEXT LOWER	NEXT HIGHER
1	15	0	0

Notice that the next lower and next higher nodes for the root are both zero. They will remain zero until something has been added to the list that is lower or higher on the tree. Also notice that the record number is 1. Now let's add the second index, 10. The record number will be 2, and the table will be:

RECORD	VALUE	NEXT LOWER	NEXT HIGHER
1	15	2	0
2	10	0	0

Now the next lower (to the left on the diagram) for the root is 2. That points to index 10 as being the first record with an index lower than the root. Of course, the next higher and lower nodes for 10 are both temporarily zero.

The next index is 5, and the table will become:

RECORD	VALUE	NEXT LOWER	NEXT HIGHER
1	15	2	0
2	10	3	0
3	5	0	0

The next lower node for 10 is now the record number of index 5, 3. The next addition is index 16, which is higher than 15, so the table will become:

RECORD	VALUE	NEXT LOWER	NEXT HIGHER
1	15	2	4
2	10	3	0
3	5	0	0
4	16	0	0

Notice that the next higher node (to the right on the diagram) for the root is now 4. This points to the first node higher than the root node. If you continue to add the remaining indexes, the table, completely filled out, will look like the following:

RECORD	VALUE	NEXT LOWER	NEXT HIGHER
1	15	2	4
2	10	3	0
3	5	7	6
4	16	0	5
5	19	8	9
6	7	0	0
7	4	0	0
8	17	0	0
9	20	0	0

Notice that records 6, 7, 8, and 9 have the next nodes all as zero. This is because they are all at the end of branches. All records at the end of branches will have the next nodes as zero since nothing branches from them.

13–4
A SAMPLE PROGRAM

In order to create the tree, we need our routine to do several things. First, we need to input an index and set it up as the root node. Then, for every subsequent input we need to traverse the tree until either there is a match or there are no more branches in the indicated direction. Also, we will have to keep track of the number of nodes currently in the tree and increase that number each time a new node is added.

We will set up the tree with a two-dimensional array, which is 100 items (the number of possible nodes) by 3 positions. The first position in the second dimension is for the value of the node, the second position is for the next lower node, and the third is for the next higher node.

Before we code the program we will pseudocode and flowchart it. This particular example is for the creation of the insert procedure only. After we verify that it works, we will add the rest of the search procedure. Therefore, when you key the program, make sure you pay particular attention to the line numbers because we will be inserting a few before we are finished. The flowchart can be seen in Figure 13–10; the pseudocode follows:

```
Start
Dimension the array
Input the root node.
Assign the root node to the first array element.
Set the node counter to 1.
Input the index to insert.
DO-WHILE insert <> 0
  IF input = current node THEN
     Print found message.
     Input the index to insert.
     Set node counter to 1.
  ELSE
     IF input < current node THEN
       Use left branch code.
     ELSE
       Use right branch code.
     END-IF
     IF node = 0 THEN
       Assign next node (low or high).
       Assign node value.
       Increase number of nodes.
       Input the index to insert.
       Set node counter to 1.
     ELSE
       Set node counter to low or high.
     END-IF (continues on page 361)
```

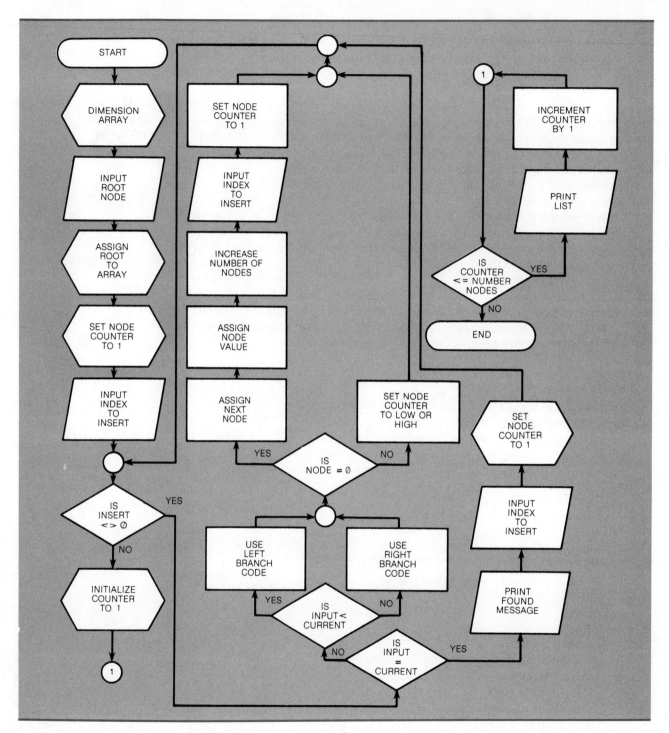

Figure 13-10
Flowchart of tree program.

```
END-IF
END-DO
Initialize counter to 1.
DO-WHILE counter <= number of nodes.
    Print the list.
    Increment counter by 1.
END-DO
End
```

The program follows:

```
10 REM ***** PROGRAM NAME: TREESAMP
20 REM
30 REM ***** WRITTEN BY EDWARD J. COBURN
40 REM
50 REM THIS PROGRAM WILL TEST THE TREE INSERTION TECHNIQUE
60 REM
65 CLS                                ' CLEAR THE SCREEN
70 DIM B(100,3)                       ' ARRAY FOR THE LIST
120 INPUT "WHAT NUMBER";X
130 IF X=0 THEN 360                   ' EXIT TO PRINT ROUTINE
140 IF B<>0 THEN 190
150     B(1,1)=X                      ' ASSIGN ROOT NODE
160     B=B+1                         ' COUNT THAT NODE
170     GOTO 120                      ' GET NEW INDEX
180                                   '
190 I=1                               ' BEGIN SEARCH LOOP
200     IF X=B(I,1) THEN PRINT "FOUND" : GOTO 120
210     IF X>B(I,1) THEN C=3 ELSE C=2 ' SET LOW OR HIGH CODE
220                                   ' CHECK NODE
230         IF B(I,C)<>0 THEN 320
240                                   ' AREA FOR NO NEXT NODE
270             B(I,C)=B+1            ' ASSIGN NEXT NODE
280             B(B+1,1)=X            ' ASSIGN VALUE
290             B=B+1                 ' INCREASE # OF NODES
300             GOTO 120              ' GET NEW INDEX
310             ' NEXT NODE FOUND - NEED TO CHECK AGAIN
320             I=B(I,C)              ' SET NEW NODE CHECK
330             GOTO 200              ' CHECK NEW NODE
340                                   '
350                                   '
360 FOR I=1 TO B
370     PRINT "ITEM=";I;"  VALUE=";B(I,1);
380     PRINT "  LOW=";B(I,2);"  HIGH=";B(I,3)
390 NEXT I
400 END
```

Program 13–1

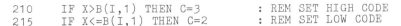

)))**DIFFERENCES**

The only changes for Applesoft are: line 65 should be HOME, and line 210 needs to be two lines because of the ELSE:

```
210     IF X>B(I,1) THEN C=3        : REM SET HIGH CODE
215     IF X<=B(I,1) THEN C=2       : REM SET LOW CODE
```

Before we test the program, a bit of explanation might help clarify the code. Lines 140–170 set the first input into the root node. Line 190 begins the search loop with the root node being searched as node 1. If that node is equal to what is being searched for (line 200), then the FOUND message is printed, and another input is asked for. If the input is not equal to the current node (line 210), then the array subscript code is set so the low or high node will be checked. Then line 230 checks to see if the node (either low or high) is 0. If it is, there is no node, and the input index is placed there for the node (lines 270–300). If the next node is there, then that node number is used to set a new current node (line 320) and the checking begins again. Lines 360–390 are there simply to print the table of array values after a few indexes have been inserted, so that the program function may be checked.

Now let's try the program to see how well it works. We will use the same series of numbers we used before: 15, 10, 5, 16, 19, 7, 4, 17, and 20.

```
RUN
WHAT NUMBER? 15
WHAT NUMBER? 10
WHAT NUMBER? 15
FOUND
WHAT NUMBER? 5
WHAT NUMBER? 16
WHAT NUMBER? 19
WHAT NUMBER? 7
WHAT NUMBER? 4
WHAT NUMBER? 17
WHAT NUMBER? 20
WHAT NUMBER? 0
ITEM= 1    VALUE= 15    LOW= 2    HIGH= 4
ITEM= 2    VALUE= 10    LOW= 3    HIGH= 0
ITEM= 3    VALUE= 5     LOW= 7    HIGH= 6
ITEM= 4    VALUE= 16    LOW= 0    HIGH= 5
ITEM= 5    VALUE= 19    LOW= 8    HIGH= 9
ITEM= 6    VALUE= 7     LOW= 0    HIGH= 0
ITEM= 7    VALUE= 4     LOW= 0    HIGH= 0
ITEM= 8    VALUE= 17    LOW= 0    HIGH= 0
ITEM= 9    VALUE= 20    LOW= 0    HIGH= 0
Ok
```

If you check back to the table we constructed earlier, you will discover that the results from this execution exactly parallel the results in that table. With only a few inserted lines we can make this routine usable for an add, change, or delete function. First, we will create a data table that is set up with the above results:

```
410 DATA 15,2,4,10,3,0,5,7,6,16,0,5,19,8,9
420 DATA 7,0,0,4,0,0,17,0,0,20,0,0
```

Now we need a loop in the program to read these into the array:

```
80 FOR I=1 TO 9
90     READ B(I,1),B(I,2),B(I,3)
100 NEXT I
110 B=9                              ' NUMBER OF NODES
```

Notice that we set B to contain the number of nodes. Originally, B was 0; but if we are starting the program with a tree already intact, we must indicate how many elements it has.

Finally, we will fix the program to give the option to add the index or not:

```
250                       INPUT "NOT FOUND, INSERT (Y OR N)";A$
260                       IF A$<>"Y" THEN 120
```

Note that we used no data editing in this example. We will let anything but Y default as no. In general that's not a good idea, but it's okay now since this is merely an exercise.

Now let's see the new program:

```
10 REM ***** PROGRAM NAME: TREESAMP
20 REM
30 REM ***** WRITTEN BY EDWARD J. COBURN
40 REM
50 REM THIS PROGRAM WILL TEST THE TREE INSERTION TECHNIQUE
60 REM
65 CLS                                    ' CLEAR THE SCREEN
70 DIM B(100,3)                           ' ARRAY FOR THE LIST
80 FOR I=1 TO 9
90     READ B(I,1),B(I,2),B(I,3)
100 NEXT I
110 B=9                                   ' NUMBER OF NODES
120 INPUT "WHAT NUMBER";X
130 IF X=0 THEN 360                       ' EXIT TO PRINT ROUTINE
140 IF B<>0 THEN 190
150     B(1,1)=X                          ' ASSIGN ROOT NODE
160     B=B+1                             ' COUNT THAT NODE
170     GOTO 120                          ' GET NEW INDEX
180                                       '
190 I=1                                   ' BEGIN SEARCH LOOP
200     IF X=B(I,1) THEN PRINT "FOUND" : GOTO 120
210     IF X>B(I,1) THEN C=3 ELSE C=2     ' SET LOW OR HIGH CODE
220                                       ' CHECK NODE
230         IF B(I,C)<>0 THEN 320
240                                       ' AREA FOR NO NEXT NODE
250             INPUT "NOT FOUND, INSERT (Y OR N)";A$
260             IF A$<>"Y" THEN 120
270             B(I,C)=B+1                ' ASSIGN NEXT NODE
280             B(B+1,1)=X                ' ASSIGN VALUE
290             B=B+1                     ' INCREASE # OF NODES
300             GOTO 120                  ' GET NEW INDEX
310             ' NEXT NODE FOUND - NEED TO CHECK AGAIN
320             I=B(I,C)                  ' SET NEW NODE CHECK
330             GOTO 200                  ' CHECK NEW NODE
340                                       '
350                                       '
360 FOR I=1 TO B
370     PRINT "ITEM=";I;"  VALUE=";B(I,1);
380     PRINT "  LOW=";B(I,2);"  HIGH=";B(I,3)
390 NEXT I
400 END
410 DATA 15,2,4,10,3,0,5,7,6,16,0,5,19,8,9
420 DATA 7,0,0,4,0,0,17,0,0,20,0,0
```

Program 13-2

Again, the only Applesoft differences are lines 65 and 210.

Let's try the program now:

```
RUN
WHAT NUMBER? 10
FOUND
WHAT NUMBER? 25
NOT FOUND, INSERT (Y OR N)? Y
WHAT NUMBER? 35
NOT FOUND, INSERT (Y OR N)? Y
WHAT NUMBER? 35
FOUND
WHAT NUMBER? 12
NOT FOUND, INSERT (Y OR N)? Y
WHAT NUMBER? 6
NOT FOUND, INSERT (Y OR N)? N
WHAT NUMBER? 0
ITEM= 1    VALUE= 15   LOW= 2    HIGH= 4
ITEM= 2    VALUE= 10   LOW= 3    HIGH= 12
ITEM= 3    VALUE= 5    LOW= 7    HIGH= 6
ITEM= 4    VALUE= 16   LOW= 0    HIGH= 5
ITEM= 5    VALUE= 19   LOW= 8    HIGH= 9
ITEM= 6    VALUE= 7    LOW= 13   HIGH= 0
ITEM= 7    VALUE= 4    LOW= 0    HIGH= 0
ITEM= 8    VALUE= 17   LOW= 0    HIGH= 0
ITEM= 9    VALUE= 20   LOW= 0    HIGH= 10
ITEM= 10   VALUE= 25   LOW= 0    HIGH= 11
ITEM= 11   VALUE= 35   LOW= 0    HIGH= 0
ITEM= 12   VALUE= 12   LOW= 0    HIGH= 0
Ok
```

Notice that the index 6 is not on the list since we indicated not to add it. Also notice that several of the zero nodes have been changed because of the new entries. For example, next high on list item 2 (value 10) is now 12. Figure 13–11 shows the initial tree and the final tree after our insertions. You should track each entry through the tree to be sure you understand what is being accomplished.

13–5
CREATING A TREE STRUCTURE PROGRAM

As in the last chapter, we will continue to use our contributions program. This time, however, few changes are necessary to the main body of the program. We will need to redo the search routine, since the routine will now do a tree search instead of an index search. But much of the rest of the program will remain unchanged. This being the case, you can reuse the program we created in the previous chapter.

Since the only part of the program that needs to be totally reworked will be the tree search, we will begin by rewriting the search module.

Tree Search Module

This module will use the same logic we used for Program 13–1, but we will need to change the array access to file access. We will also make other subtle changes from Program 13–1. The pseudocode follows; the flowchart can be seen in Figure 13–12.

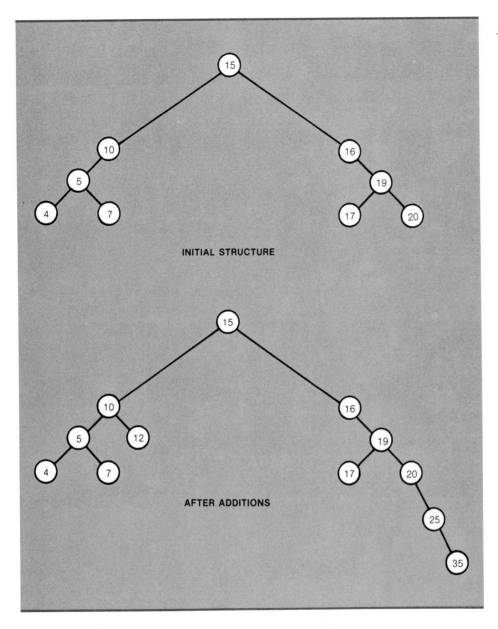

INITIAL STRUCTURE

AFTER ADDITIONS

Figure 13–11
Tree before and after
additions.

Start
IF file record count <> 1 THEN
    Set the node counter to 2 (skip over dummy record).
    Get record for checking.
    Convert the record to appropriate size (IBM and Radio Shack).
    DO-WHILE search field <> record index.
        IF record index > search field THEN
            Use left branch code.
        ELSE *(continues on page 368)*

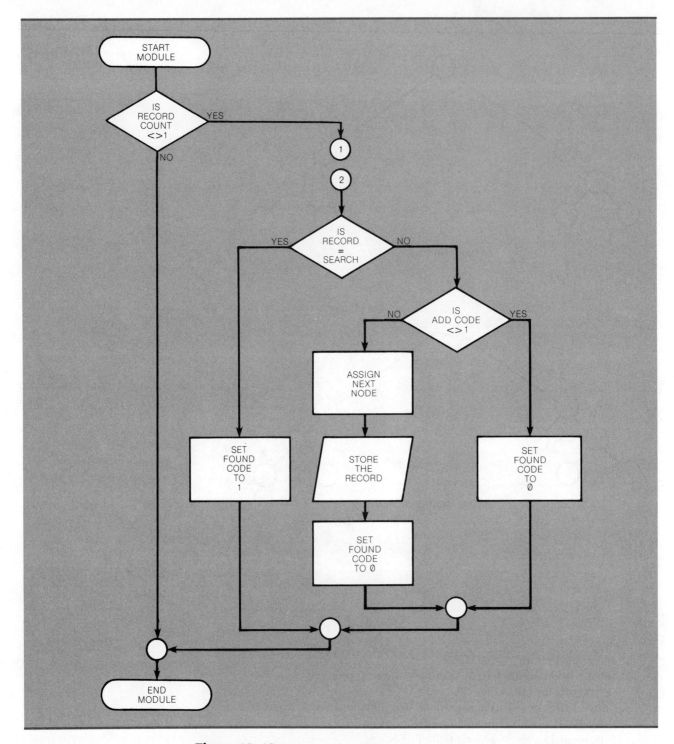

Figure 13–12
Flowchart of tree search module.

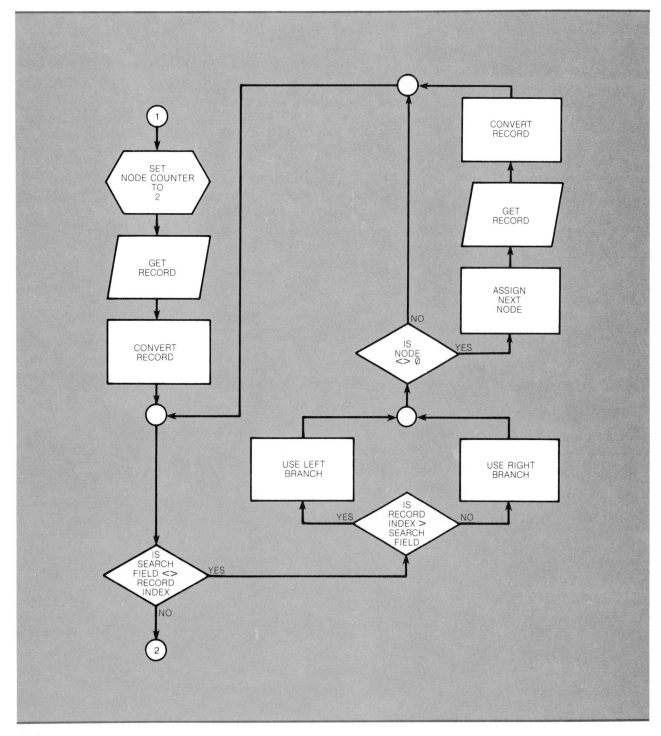

Figure 13–12
Continued

                        Use right branch code.
                    END-IF
                    IF node <> 0 THEN
                        Assign next node for record access.
                        Get record for checking.
                        Convert the record to appropriate size.
                    (ELSE)
                    END-IF
                END-DO
                IF record index = search field THEN
                    Set found code to 1 (found).
                ELSE
                    IF add code <> 1 THEN
                        Set found code to 0.
                    ELSE
                        Assign next node (low or high).
                        Store the record back.
                        Set found code to 0.
                    END-IF
                END-IF
            (ELSE)
            END-IF
            End module

The programmed module follows:

```
8970 REM
8980 REM ***** TREE SEARCH ROUTINE
8990 REM
9000 IF RECS=1 THEN RETURN              ' NO RECORD TO SEARCH
9010 TR=2                               ' BEGIN SEARCH LOOP
9020 GET #1,TR                          ' GET THE RECORD
9030 I$=MID$(F$(1),1,LEN(S$))           ' ONLY USE LENGTH OF SEARCH $
9040 IF I$=S$ THEN SC=1 : RETURN        ' FOUND THE RECORD
9050 IF I$>S$ THEN C=5 ELSE C=6         ' SET LOW OR HIGH CODE
9060 IF CVI(F$(C))<>0 THEN 9120         ' IS THERE NEXT MODE?
9070    IF IC<>1 THEN SC=0 : 9095       ' NO CHANGE IF NOT FOUND
9080        RSET F$(C)=MKI$(RECS+1)     ' ASSIGN NODE
9090        PUT #1,TR                   ' PUT RECORD BACK
9095        IC=0                        ' RESET INSERT CODE
9100        SC=0                        ' NOT FOUND CODE
9110        RETURN                      ' ALL DONE HERE
9120 TR=CVI(F$(C))                      ' ASSIGN NEXT NODE
9130 GOTO 9020                          ' GET NEXT NODE RECORD
```

Program 13–3

)))DIFFERENCES

Notice that this time the contributions amount is a string (F$(2)), as are the low and high nodes. You will see the reasoning behind this a bit later when another technique is demonstrated. The changes for Apple BASIC begin with line 9015:

```
9015 R=22 : C=1 : GOSUB 5000          : REM TO AVOID SCROLL
9020 PRINT D$;"READ TREEDATA,R";TR     : REM GET THE RECORD
9030 INPUT F$,F$(2),F$(3),F$(4),F$(5),F$(6)
```

Program continues

```
9040 IF F$=S$ THEN SC=1 : RETURN      : REM FOUND THE RECORD
9050 IF F$>S$  THEN C=5               : REM SET LOW CODE
9055 IF F$<=S$ THEN C=6               : REM SET HIGH CODE
9060 IF VAL(F$(C))<>0 THEN 9160       : REM IS THERE NEXT MODE?
9070    IF IC<>1 THEN 9130            : REM NO CHANGE IF NOT FOUND
9080       F$(C)=STR$(RECS+1)         : REM ASSIGN NODE
9090       PRINT D$;"WRITE TREEDATA,R";TR : REM PUT BACK
9094       IC=0                       : REM RESET INSERT CODE
9098       PRINT F$                   : REM PUT NAME BACK
9100       FOR J=2 TO 6
9110          PRINT F$(J)             : REM PRINT TO FILE
9120       NEXT J
9130       SC=0                       : REM NOT FOUND CODE
9140       PRINT D$                   : REM TURN OFF DISK ACCESS
9150       RETURN                     : REM ALL DONE HERE
9160 TR=VAL(F$(C))                    : REM ASSIGN NEXT NODE
9170 GOTO 9015                        : REM GET NEXT NODE RECORD
```

The Initial Module

This module will require virtually no changes from the last chapter. The heading remarks will change, as will the initial disk access (since we need only one file now). We will show the whole module only for the sake of convenience.

For the IBM and Radio Shack versions, the file length will need to be changed from 44 to 48 to allow for storage of two two-digit node numbers. For addition of the two nodes, the FIELD statement will need to be updated. Also, we will change the name of the file to TREEDATA and drop the second file OPEN on line 75. Of course, don't forget to change the REM statements to reflect the new program name and program purpose.

The programmed module follows:

```
10 REM ***** PROGRAM NAME: CONTTREE
20 REM
30 REM ***** WRITTEN BY EDWARD J. COBURN
40 REM
50 REM THE TREE STRUCTURE FILE PROCESSING PROGRAM
60 REM
70 OPEN "TREEDATA" AS #1 LEN=48
80 FIELD #1, 2 AS RF$
90 GET 1,1                         ' GET THE FIRST RECORD
100 IF CVI(RF$)=0 THEN RECS=1 ELSE RECS=CVI(RF$)
110 FIELD #1, 24 AS F$(1), 4 AS F$(2), 6 AS F$(3), 10 AS F$(4),
               2 AS F$(5), 2 AS F$(6)
120 CLS                            ' CLEAR THE SCREEN
130 PRINT TAB(10);"CONTRIBUTIONS MAINTENANCE"
140 PRINT                          ' BLANK LINE
150 PRINT "1. ADD NEW RECORDS"
155 PRINT
160 PRINT "2. CHANGE EXISTING RECORDS"
165 PRINT
170 PRINT "3. PRINT THE FILE"
175 PRINT
180 PRINT "4. EXIT THE PROGRAM"
200 P$="WHAT OPTION (1-4)"      ' PROMPT
210 L=1                         ' PROMPT LENGTH
220 GOSUB 7000                  ' PROMPT SUBROUTINE
230 IF B$>"0" AND B$<"5" THEN 270
240    M$="INPUT ERROR.  RETRY ENTRY"
```

Program 13–4

Program continues

```
250    GOSUB 6000              ' ERROR SUBROUTINE
260    GOTO 200               ' REPROMPT
270 ON VAL(B$) GOSUB 1000, 2000, 3000, 4000
280 GOTO 120
```

Program 13–4 (cont.)

)))DIFFERENCES

The Apple file length needs to be changed from 50 to 66 to allow two seven-digit node numbers to be stored. Also, we can drop line 85 since we no longer need the index file.

The Addition Module

This module also will require only a few changes. The only major changes are to delete the lines that are used to add the new index to the index file, since we are no longer using the index file. Also, we need to add 0 entries for the nodes to the end of each record. We will forgo the pseudocode and flowchart since there are few changes.

For the IBM and Radio Shack, line 1040 needs to be changed to reflect the updated FIELD specification. The lines for the index addition that need to be deleted are 1365 through 1460. We also need to insert lines 1315 and 1317 to put 0 values in F$(5) and F$(6), which are the nodes. Finally, line 1185 is added to ensure update of the nodes in the search routine.

The programmed module follows:

```
970 REM
980 REM ***** ADD MODULE
990 REM
1000 DATA CONT. NAME, 24, 3, CONT. AMOUNT, 7, 5
1010 DATA DATE OF CONT., 8, 7, PHONE NUMBER, 12, 9
1020 CLS                     ' CLEAR THE SCREEN
1030 RESTORE                 ' RESET DATA POINTER
1040 FIELD #1, 24 AS F$(1), 6 AS F$(2), 10 AS F$(3), 4 AS F$(4),
               2 AS F$(5), 2 AS F$(6)
1050 PRINT TAB(10);"CONTRIBUTIONS ENTRY"
1060 PRINT                   ' BLANK LINE
1070 FOR I=1 TO 4
1080    READ D$(I),L(I),R(I)  ' THE PROMPT, LENGTH, ROW
1090    PRINT MID$(STR$(I),2,1);". ";D$(I) ' DISPLAY PROMPT
1100    PRINT                ' BLANK LINE
1110 NEXT I
1120 FOR I8=1 TO 4
1130    L=L(I8)                        ' PROMPT LENGTH
1140    R=R(I8)                        ' ROW
1150    C=16                           ' COLUMN
1160    GOSUB 7070                     ' PROMPT SUBROUTINE
1170    IF I8<>1 THEN 1260             ' SKIP IF SEARCH OKAY
1180       S$=B$                       ' ASSIGN THE SEARCH FIELD
1185       IC=1                        ' ADD CODE FOR SEARCH
1190       GOSUB 9000                  ' SEARCH SUBROUTINE
1200       IF SC=0 THEN 1260           ' SKIP IF SEARCH OKAY
1210          M$="DUPLICATE INDEX.  REENTER"
1220          GOSUB 6000               ' ERROR SUBROUTINE
1230          R=3                      ' ROW NUMBER
1240          C=16                     ' COLUMN NUMBER
```

Program continues

Program 13–5

```
1250              GOTO 1130        ' REDO THE PROMPT
1260        G$(I8)=B$              ' STORE THE FIELD
1270 NEXT I8
1280 LSET F$(1)=G$(1)             ' ASSIGN THE FIELDS
1290 LSET F$(3)=MID$(G$(3),1,2)+MID$(G$(3),4,2)+MID$(G$(3),7,2)
1300 LSET F$(4)=MID$(G$(4),1,3)+MID$(G$(4),5,3)+MID$(G$(4),9,4)
1310 RSET F$(2)=MKS$(VAL(G$(2))
1315 RSET F$(5)=MKI$(0)
1317 RSET F$(6)=MKI$(0)
1320 PUT 1,RECS+1                 ' PUT THE RECORD
1330 FIELD #1, 2 AS RF$           ' FIELD RECORD 1
1340 RECS=RECS+1                  ' INCREASE RECORD COUNT
1350 LSET RF$=MKI$(RN)            ' SET THE FIELD
1360 PUT 1,1                      ' PUT RECORD 1
1470 P$= "DO YOU WANT TO ADD ANY MORE (Y OR N)"
1480 L=1                          ' LENGTH OF PROMPT
1490 GOSUB 7000                   ' PROMPT SUBROUTINE
1500 IF B$<>"Y" THEN RETURN
1510 GOTO 1020                    ' GET ANOTHER RECORD
```

Program 13–5 (cont.)

)))DIFFERENCES

In Applesoft, lines 1360–1480 have to be deleted. Also, line 1185 is added to ensure update of the nodes in the search module:

```
1185        IC=1                 : REM INSERT CODE
```

We need to change line 1320 to PRINT a string, not a numeric:

```
1320 PRINT F$(2)
```

And finally, we need to insert lines 1325 and 1327 to put zero values in the nodes:

```
1325 PRINT "0"                   : REM F$(5) - LOW NODE
1327 PRINT "0"                   : REM F$(6) - HIGH NODE
```

The Change Module

In this module most of the changes are cosmetic, but one is significant. Since this is a tree structure file and the only index is in the file itself, we cannot allow the user to change the index (name) without substantially altering the tree. We will discuss a bit later how to make changes, but for now, we will assume no changes to the index are possible, so we cannot allow the user to change the name. Thus, we have to change our test for the entry of the field so it will not allow entry of a one (1). The instruction in line 2310 in all versions should be changed to read:

```
2310 IF B$>"0" AND B$<>"1" AND B$<"5" THEN 2350 ' IS ENTRY OKAY
```

Of course, the prompt itself (line 2280) needs to be changed to reflect this new input:

```
2280 P$="WHAT FIELD TO CHANGE (2-4, 0 TO END)"
```

Finally, we will insert a new line for purely experimental assistance. Line 2275 will print the low and high nodes below the phone number so we can follow how the tree is being built. It will follow the same logic as our previous example; we will look at a sample display after we have discussed all the modules. For the IBM and Radio Shack, the line would read:

```
2275 PRINT "LOW =";CVI(F$(5));"   HIGH =";CVI(F$(6))
```

The Apple version would read:

```
2275 PRINT "LOW = ";F$(5);"   HIGH = ";F$(6)
```

For the IBM and Radio Shack, you will also need to delete lines 2100 and 2110, since they reassign the FIELD statement, which is no longer necessary. Then we need to change line 2060 to branch to 2120 instead of 2100. Finally, line 2045 needs to be added (all versions) to assure that the change record is not added in the search routine.

```
1970 REM
1980 REM ***** CHANGE MODULE
1990 REM
2000 P$="ENTER NAME (0 TO END)"
2010 L=24                        ' PROMPT LENGTH
2020 GOSUB 7000                  ' PROMPT SUBROUTINE
2030 IF B$ THEN RETURN           ' EXIT THE SUBROUTINE
2040 S$=B$                       ' ASSIGN SEARCH INDEX
2045 IC=0                        ' ADD CODE MUST BE ZERO
2050 GOSUB 9000                  ' SEARCH SUBROUTINE
2060 IF SC=1 THEN 2120           ' SKIP IF SEARCH FOUND
2070      M$="RECORD NOT FOUND.  RETRY"
2080         GOSUB 6000          ' ERROR SUBROUTINE
2090         GOTO 2000           ' GET INDEX AGAIN
2120 CLS                         ' CLEAR THE SCREEN
2130 PRINT TAB(10);"CONTRIBUTIONS CHANGES"
2140 PRINT                       ' BLANK LINE
2150 RESTORE                     ' RESET DATA POINTER
2160 FOR I=1 TO 4
2170      READ D$(I),L(I),R(I) ' PROMPT, LENGTH, ROW
2180      PRINT MID$(STR$(I),2,1);". ",D$(I); ' DISPLAY PROMPT
2190      R=R(I)                 ' ROW
2200      C=16                   ' COLUMN
2210      GOSUB 5000             ' CURSOR POSITIONING
2220      IF I=1 THEN PRINT F$(1)
2230      IF I=2 THEN PRINT USING "####.##";CVS(F$(2))
2240      IF I=3 THEN PRINT MID$(F$(3),1,2);"/";
                             MID$(F$(3),4,2);"/";
                             MID$(F$(3),7,2)
2250      IF I=4 THEN PRINT MID$(F$(4),1,3);"-";
                             MID$(F$(4),5,3);"-";
                             MID$(F$(4),9,4)
2260      PRINT                  ' BLANK LINE
2270 NEXT I
2275 PRINT "LOW =";CVI(F$(5));"   HIGH =";CVI(F$(6))
2280 P$="FIELD TO CHANGE (2-4, 0 TO END)"
2290 L=1                         ' PROMPT LENGTH
2300 GOSUB 7000                  ' PROMPT SUBROUTINE
2310 IF B$>"0" AND B$<>"1" AND B$<"5" THEN 2350 ' IS ENTRY OKAY?
2320      M$="INVALID ENTRY. RETRY"  ' ERROR MESSAGE
2330         GOSUB 6000          ' ERROR SUBROUTINE
2340         GOTO 2280           ' REPROMPT
2350 IF B$="0" THEN 2460         ' END CHANGES
```

Program 13–6

Program continues

```
2360 B=VAL(B$)                     ' CONVERT INPUT
2370 R=R(B)                        ' ROW
2380 C=18                          ' COLUMN
2390 L=L(B)                        ' PROMPT LENGTH
2400 GOSUB 7070                    ' PROMPT SUBROUTINE
2410 IF B=1 THEN LSET F$(1)=B$' ASSIGN FIELDS
2420 IF B=2 THEN RSET F$(2)=MKS$(VAL(B$))
2430 IF B=3 THEN LSET F$(3)=MID$(B$,1,2)+MID$(B$,4,2)+MID$(B$,7,2)
2440 IF B=4 THEN LSET F$(4)=MID$(B$,1,3)+MID$(B$,5,3)+MID$(B$,9,4)
2450 GOTO 2120
2460 PUT 1,TR                      ' DUMP OUT RECORD
2470 GOTO 2000                     ' PROMPT FOR NEW RECORD
```

Program 13–6 (cont.)

)))DIFFERENCES

Using the Apple program from the last chapter, we need to add line 2045:

```
2045 IC=0                         : REM ADD CODE MUST BE ZERO
```

Then line 2110 needs to change:

```
2110 INPUT F$(1),F$(2),F$(3),F$(4),F$(5),F$(6)
```

Then line 2242 needs to change:

```
2242    A=VAL(F$(4))             : REM FIELD TO FORMAT
```

Line 2420 needs to change to store a string:

```
2420 IF B=2 THEN F$(4)=B$
```

And line 2500 needs to change to output the string:

```
2500 PRINT F$(4)
```

Finally 2504 and 2506 need to be added:

```
2504 PRINT F$(5)
2506 PRINT F$(6)
```

The PRINT Module

This module requires only two minor changes. Line 3040 should be changed to:

```
3040 FOR I=2 TO RECS             ' TO NUMBER IN FILE
```

This ensures that the records are read from the first record after the dummy record through the end of the file. The other change is to delete line 3050 (and 3060 on the Apple) and change line 3060 (3070 on the Apple) to access record I, not the record from the index.

There is a problem with this print routine, however. Though we are able to access the file randomly, this routine will only print the file in the order that the records were added. They will not be in sequence. In order to print a sequential list of the records, we have to traverse the tree to print every record. (This would obviously be a slow process and explains why we have discussed both random access routines, indexed and tree. If you need to produce many reports that have to be in sequence, you might want to use an indexed file. If reports are not of primary concern, perhaps saving disk space by not using an index file would be more important.)

To print a sequential report, the file has to be sorted. In the next chapter we will discuss how to use the various sorting techniques currently available.

Since the changes for the print module are minor, we will not show it here.

The EXIT Module

This module is exactly the same as before. To see the pseudocode, flow-chart, and coding, refer to Chapter 11.

Testing the Program

About the only difference in the execution of this program from the last chapter is in the change routine, since we print the nodes as we display the records. Let's add a few records, chart them in a tree, and then check the nodes to make sure they are correct.

Let's add them in the following order (use whatever amounts, dates, and phone numbers you want):

```
HARROLD, SAM, RON, TOM, GEORGE, AL, FRED
```

When you display each of these entries, you should see the following low and high nodes (shown in the diagram in Figure 13–13):

NAME	LOW	HIGH
HARROLD	6	3
SAM	4	5
RON	0	0
TOM	0	0
GEORGE	7	0
AL	0	8
FRED	0	0

13–6 ADDITIONAL CONSIDERATIONS ABOUT TREES

Recall that the change routine had to be modified to not allow the name (index) to be changed. If the index can be changed, the sequence necessary for traversing the tree gets disrupted. To avoid this we simply didn't allow any changes to the name. Well, there is a relatively simple method of changing indexes in a tree that also allows deletion of records from the tree. Whenever a record needs to be removed from the tree, we simply change another field of the record to signify that the record has been deleted. In our example, perhaps we would put the code "DELETE" in the date field. Then, when the record is

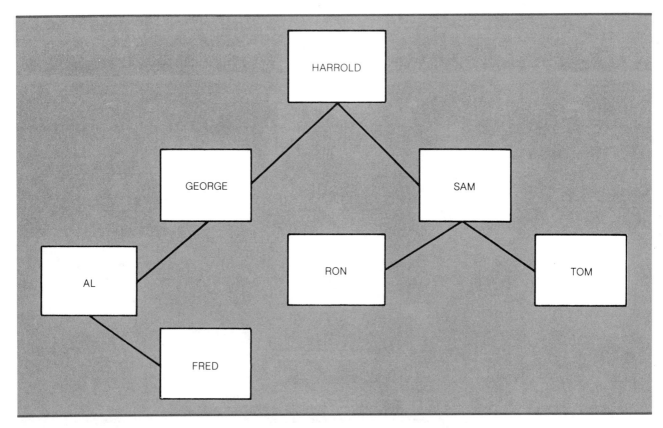

Figure 13–13
Tree structure of sample data.

read in the access routine, this field is checked to be sure it is not marked as "DELETE". We would use the same procedure to change the index. First we would find the record to change, delete it from the file, and then add back the record with the new index.

The problem with this technique is that the record, though deleted, is still in the file taking up space. This is solved by periodically using a balancing routine to balance the tree. Trees, over a period of time, have a tendency to become unbalanced; that is, there will be more entries on one side of the tree than on the other, which means it takes much more time to traverse the larger side than the smaller. It is better to have a tree that is totally balanced so that every access is as fast as possible. Routines exist to create balanced trees as records are added and deleted. But they are complicated and hardly worth the trouble unless you will be adding a large number of records to the file and the tree is very large. It is much easier to simply write a balancing program that you can use periodically to balance the tree after adding a group of records. And when you balance the tree, you can remove the records that have been marked for deletion.

We will not present a balancing program here, but the basic idea is to create a sorted list of all the indexes. You then add the records back into the tree starting at the middle and then using the middle entry of each half. Figure 13–14 shows the logic behind the balance technique.

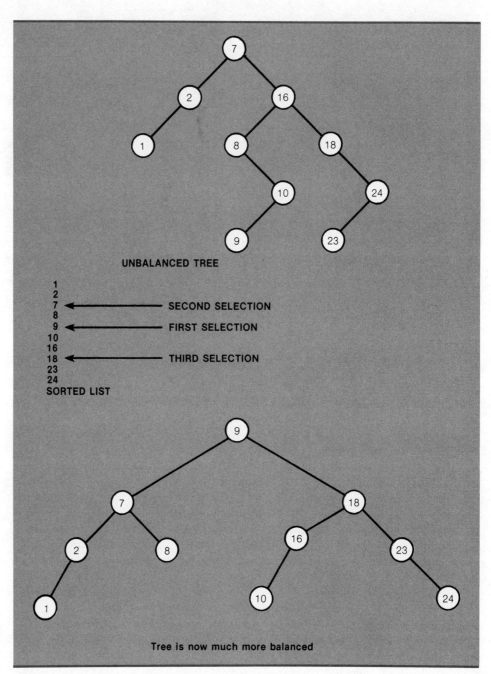

Figure 13–14
Balance technique.

Recall that earlier we used two nodes that can be virtually any length. We can store them in the IBM and Radio Shack versions in two bytes because of the FIELD statement, but in Applesoft the storage takes up considerably more space. We reserved enough room for seven-digit numbers, which allows for 9,999,999 records. Of course, a diskette would not hold anywhere near that many records, but we might very well want more records than, say, 999 and would thus need at least four bytes for the numeric storage.

There is a method that allows us to store these numbers in a much smaller storage area. By using the ASC and CHR$ commands, we can store any number up to 255 in one byte. That is, if our number is 255 or less, it will require only one byte to store; we can convert it to its ASCII character code and then get the number back with the reverse conversion. For example, suppose our record numbers for the low and high nodes are 4 and 7; we could store both of these numbers using only two bytes with the following statements:

```
10 LN$=CHR$(LN)              ' LOW NODE
20 HN$=CHR$(HN)              ' HIGH NODE
```

This will store in the string variables any number up to 256. Then, when we need the record number back, we merely use:

```
100 LN=ASC(LN$)              ' LOW NODE
110 HN=ASC(HN$)              ' HIGH NODE
```

Now suppose we have a record number higher than 255, which is quite likely since 255 is not very large. Another technique requires only two bytes of storage for each number and will allow numbers up to 65,535. To do this, we divide the number by 256 and get the integer of the quotient (answer). For example, suppose we want to store 4,925. We divide that by 256 and take the integer, which gives us 19. Then, we take that number and multiply it by 256; we subtract that from the original number to give us the amount that is left after removing all the possible multiples of 256. In our example, we multiply 19 by 256 to get 4,864; we subtract that from 4,925 to get 61. Finally, we assign the quotient (19) to one string and the amount left (61) to another string, and we have the entire number stored in two bytes. To reconstruct the original number, we first convert the strings to numerics. Then we take the first number and multiply it by 256 (19 * 256 = 4,864) and add the second number (4,864 + 61 = 4,925). This will give us our original record number back again.

Let's try another example. Suppose our record number is 2,567. First we divide the number by 256 using the following:

```
10 LN=2567
20 A=INT(LN/256)             ' LOW NODE
```

This will give us 10 for A. Then we multiply this by 256 and subtract it from the original number:

```
30 B=LN-A*256
```

This will give us 7 for B. Then we convert our two numbers (10 and 7) to strings:

```
30 A$=CHR$(A)
40 B$=CHR$(B)
```

To reconvert these strings into our record number, we would use:

```
100 A=ASC(A$)                    ' LOW NODE
110 B=ASC(B$)
```

We then multiply A by 256 and add B to get the record number:

```
120 LN=A*256+B
```

Since A is 10, A*256 gives 2560; B is 7, so LN ends up as 2567.

This technique will work for any number that needs to be stored in a minimum of space. It is, however, especially useful when we have a series of numbers that all fall within a specified range and are stored in a sequence. It can be used to store numeric arrays that have too many elements to fit within the 256 characters allowed for a record. By reducing the size necessary for each element of the array, the array becomes more manageable.

This technique can be even further expanded to allow storage of numbers up to 16,777,215 with the use of three characters, and even larger numbers can be stored with more characters. But it is usually not necessary to go beyond the two-character limit of 65,535.

SUMMARY

1. In the previous chapter we learned to use an indexed file to allow random access by some index other than the record number. In this chapter we learned to use the tree structure to do the same thing.
2. A tree structure is an index structure that is examined in sequence, but because of the construction only a few accesses are necessary to find the desired record. We used a tree with the first record in the file called the *root* and all the entries called *nodes*. The connections between the nodes are called *branches*; as we search the tree for a particular record, we are *traversing* the tree.
3. To create a tree, we first assign the root node. Then, each node is added to the tree by comparing it to the node and branching either left (for a lesser value) or right (for a larger value). This branching continues until either a match is found or the branch taken is empty. Then, if the record is found, we have an error. If it is not found, we add the record at the empty node. If we are trying to locate the record and the final branch is empty, then the record does not exist in the tree.
4. A tree has a couple of advantages over an indexed file. Since the tree requires no index file, it will generally take up less space on the disk (though the file does require two extra fields to keep track of the next lower and higher nodes). Also, the addition of records to the tree is as fast as the access. With an index file, the addition of records becomes slower as more are added. The index file, however, is better for printing a list of the records in the file. Such a list is difficult to manage with a tree.

5. The index of a record in a tree structure cannot be changed easily. It requires the deletion of the original record and the addition of a new record. The deletion of a tree structure record is best handled by storing some type of code in one of the fields (other than the index field). Then, as the records are accessed, this field is checked to see if the record is supposed to be deleted. This technique also works for actually deleting a record, rather than just changing it.

6. Deleted records can be removed when a balancing routine is run. A tree has a tendency to become lopsided over a period of time. The only way to correct this is to execute some type of balancing routine. The record deletion routine can be within the balancing routine.

7. A useful technique for storing a number in a minimum of space is to convert the number to its ASCII equivalent character and then store that character. This way, one character can store any number up to 255, and two characters can store a number up to 65,535. A third character can store any number up to 16,777,215.

GLOSSARY

Branches The connections between nodes in a tree structure.

Node An entry in a tree structure.

Root The initial entry in a tree structure.

Traversing The process of accessing the records in a tree.

Tree structure An indexing structure that does not require an index file. Access is made sequentially through a minimum of indexes in the main file.

QUESTIONS TO AID UNDERSTANDING

1. Name two differences between a tree structure file and an index file.
2. In what situation would a tree be preferable to an index file?
3. In what situation would an index file be preferable to a tree?
*4. Why can we not change an index in a tree structure without deleting and adding back the index?
5. Describe one method of deleting a record from a tree structure.
*6. Use the following list to create a tree diagram: 150, 10, 35, 165, 80, 195, 11, 0, 45, 155, 152, 88, 171, 90, 122, 149, 205, 196.
7. Use the routine created in the chapter to create a tree using the data in question 6. Use the generated tree to check your answer to 6.
*8. Write a program to randomly generate 50 numbers and insert them in a tree. Then draw a diagram depicting the entries in the tree. Check to see how balanced the tree is. Do this several times and check the balance each time.
9. Write a program to INPUT a number from 0 to 65,000 and assign it to two characters as shown in the chapter. Then reverse the process and write out the number.

10. Add a record deletion routine to the program we created in the chapter. You will need to add an entry to the initial menu and change the tree access module to look for deleted records. In the add routine, an attempt to add a deleted index should be allowed. In the change routine, no access should be allowed to a deleted record, but an error message should flash that the record has been deleted rather than just that the record was not found.

11. Change the change routine in the program in the chapter to allow a change to the index field (the name). This will require that the record be deleted and then added back. Also, the access module will have to recognize deleted records. See question 10 for more information about deleted records.

12. Return to page 350 and modify the program you wrote for question 10 to use tree processing. Use the social security number as the index.

13. Return to page 350 and rewrite the program created for question 13 to use a tree structure instead of an indexed file.

14. Change the program in this chapter to use two characters to store the low and high nodes. If you are using IBM or Radio Shack, this change will gain you no extra space in this particular instance, but you will find other uses for the technique later on in your programming.

15. Write a routine to list in sequence the records of the tree file created in the chapter. Don't sort the records, rather traverse the tree to get them in sequence.

16. Return to question 14 on page 350 and update it to use a tree structure. Change the report program to have the following format:

```
                    XYZ CORPORATION
                    EMPLOYEE LIST

NAME                ADDRESS             CITY            STATE   ZIP

ED COBURN           1400 SOUTH STREET   EL PASO         TX      76879
SARA SMITH          34567 WEST BLVD.    DENVER          CO      83789
```

QUICK QUIZ

The answers to the questions follow immediately after the quiz. Questions 1–15 are true–false, while 16–20 are multiple choice.

T F   1. The initial node of the tree is called the root node.

T F   2. As you access the various nodes of the tree, you are traversing the tree.

T F   3. The low node is the right-hand node, as we used it in the chapter.

T F   4. If the root node is 15 and the number we are accessing is 6, we would take the left branch of the tree.

T F   5. When using a tree, the records are actually stored in the file in the order that they are entered rather than in some type of sequence.

T F   6. A tree is better than an indexed file because the access is faster.

7. In our program, the numbers that represented the low and high nodes were actually one larger than their relative positions in the list since the file contains a dummy record. **T F**

8. The insertion process in an indexed file is called a bubble insert. **T F**

9. To add a record to a tree, you search for the record until you reach an empty node and then add the record at that node. **T F**

10. In the tree structure, records can be deleted by simply changing the index to the word "DELETE" and then checking for that when traversing the tree. **T F**

11. When you change a record in a tree structure, first the record is added, then the index is marked for deletion. **T F**

12. With little additional effort we could write a program to create a tree that would continually balance itself. **T F**

13. Using the CHR$ and ASC commands, we can convert a number to a character and store virtually any number in a small amount of string characters. **T F**

14. All nodes at the end of the branches will have next lower and higher node numbers as zero. **T F**

15. Index file processing can be made faster by loading the entire index into memory. **T F**

16. The first node of the tree is called the _____

    a. index   **c.** root
    b. node   **d.** none of the above

17. When it comes to actual speed of accessing records, which access method is fastest? _____

    a. random   **c.** indexed
    b. tree   **d.** all are the same

18. To change an index in a tree, which of the following steps should come first? _____

    a. Mark old record as deleted.
    b. Add new record.
    c. Access old record.
    d. Any order is okay.

19. Which of the following is *not* an advantage for using a tree file versus an index file? _____

    a. The tree usually takes less storage space.
    b. The tree is usually faster at adding indexes.
    c. The tree prints allows easier report generation.
    d. All are advantages.

20. Which of the following statements is not necessary for accessing records in the tree? _____

    a. PRINT   **c.** OPEN
    b. INPUT   **d.** all are necessary

1. T
2. T
3. F (The low node is the left side.)
4. T
5. T
6. F (Sometimes the access is faster, sometimes it is not. Adding records to a tree, however, is much faster than adding them to an index.)
7. T
8. T
9. T (A little simplified, but true.)
10. F (You can not change the index to "DELETE" or the structure will no longer be traversable.)
11. F (You would mark for deletion first since you have already located the record. It would be a waste of time to add the record and then have to relocate the old record to delete it.)
12. F (As discussed in the chapter, a self-balancing tree is difficult to pro-gram. It is easier to program an ordinary tree and then run a balancing program periodically.)
13. T
14. T (Since they are at the end of the branches, there cannot be any next nodes at all.)
15. T (Though either the index or the file itself would have to be small in order to not run out of memory.)
16. c
17. a (Strict random access is faster, since you don't need to look up the index.)
18. c (We have to start by finding the old record.)
19. c
20. a (To *access* the records, the PRINT is not needed. It is used to write records into the file. On the Apple, however, PRINT is part of the command structure.)

14 SORTING

OBJECTIVES

After completing Chapter 14, you will be able to:
- Explain what a sort is and how it is used.
- Sort a list of numbers by hand using all four sorts described in the chapter.
- Explain how each of the sorts discussed works.
- Use each of the sort procedures described in the chapter to sort a random list of numbers stored in a file.
- Use all of the techniques learned thus far to write several programs using the sorting techniques.

We have mentioned many times the desirability of having a sorted file. But just what is a sorted file or, more precisely, what is a **sort?** A sort is simply a program that arranges a set of data into a specific order.

Take our contributions file, for example. In our indexed file version, the index file is in name sequence, and we can print it that way. Suppose, however, that we want to print the list so we can tell how long it has been since a person contributed. The file would have to be listed in contributions date order. We would have to sort the file.

Many sorting techniques exist, some better than others. In this chapter we will learn how to create four different sorts: the selection sort, the bubble sort, the Shell sort, and the quicksort (the fastest).

Before we begin discussing the various techniques, we will create the input routine, output routine, and data that will be used to test all the sorts that we will use in this chapter. The input and output routines will be modules; we will present only one version of these modules since the programming necessary is virtually the same for all our versions of BASIC. The modules shown will all be written in IBM BASIC, but no changes should be necessary for the other versions, except the clear screen command, an occasional IF-THEN-ELSE statement, and the PRINT USING statement.

Note: For the time being, we will sort only numeric arrays. After we thoroughly understand the process, we will move on to processing string data, which more often requires sorting.

The Input Module

This module will READ the DATA and store it in an array. It begins by reading the first number from the DATA, which indicates how many numbers are to be put in the array and how many items there are to sort. It will then load the rest of the DATA into the array. This module is straightforward, so we will dispense with the pseudocode and flowchart.

Note: We will give each of our programs a name as we progress through the chapter. Care should be taken to always change the program name to avoid erasing an earlier sort version. The name of the following program refers to the selection sort, the first sort we will discuss.

```
10 REM ***** PROGRAM NAME: SORTSEL
20 REM
30 REM ***** WRITTEN BY EDWARD J. COBURN
40 REM
50 REM ***** PRACTICE SELECTION SORT
60 REM
70 READ NE                    ' NUMBER OF ELEMENTS
80 DIM A(NE)                  ' ARRAY TO SORT
90 FOR I=1 TO NE
100    READ A(I)              ' READ IN ARRAY
110 NEXT I
```

Program 14–1

The Output Module

This module will simply print the sorted array on the screen using a formatted output with 5 items printed on each output line. This allows a more uniform display. For the Apple version, remember to use the format module before displaying the array item.

```
870 REM
880 REM ***** OUTPUT MODULE
890 REM
895 CLS                        ' CLEAR THE SCREEN
900 J=1
910     FOR I=J TO J+4
920         PRINT USING " ### ";A(I);
930     NEXT I
940 J=J+5
950 PRINT                      ' CARRIAGE RETURN
960 IF J<NE THEN 910
970 END
```
Program 14–2

)))DIFFERENCES

On the Radio Shack Model III, line 910 will need to be:

```
910     FOR I=J TO J+9
```

And line 940 should be:

```
940 J=J+10
```

These changes are necessary to display all the lines since the Model III has only 16 lines.

On the Apple, line 895 needs to be HOME, and you will need the format routine to print line 920.

The DATA

Recall that the first number in the DATA table indicates the number of items in the table. The numbers that follow were generated randomly and then put in the DATA table. The range of numbers used was from 1 to 1000.

We could use the random number generator to generate a new list of numbers for each run of the program. We could even use an INPUT statement to determine how many numbers we want. For now, however, we want to use the same list of numbers for each run of the program. This way we can get a feel for the speeds of the various sorts, since they will be sorting the same list.

```
980 REM
985 REM ***** DATA TABLE
990 REM
1000 DATA 100
1010 DATA 403,625,556,379,775,260,14,455,694,745
1020 DATA 55,553,738,392,513,401,273,816,101,435
1030 DATA 227,537,315,446,727,605,642,22,753,2
1040 DATA 608,429,244,377,520,985,545,160,171,584
1050 DATA 500,812,258,671,516,828,693,990,795,385
1060 DATA 897,859,430,253,459,522,843,750,902,782
1070 DATA 87,484,507,369,321,541,246,581,462,389
1080 DATA 523,161,587,78,939,343,969,436,79,543
1090 DATA 677,142,310,279,460,669,266,707,495,66
1100 DATA 154,702,528,387,943,150,916,706,4,517
```
Program 14–3

Recall from Chapter 6 that one of the easiest sorts to understand is the **selection sort.** This sort scans through the array to find the smallest element. This element is then switched with the element at the beginning of the array. Take, for example, the first line of our DATA table:

```
1010 DATA 403,625,556,379,775,260,14,455,694,745
```

The selection sort used on these ten numbers would examine them to find the smallest number in the list, which is 14. Then this element is switched with the first element in the array, 403. After this, the list would be:

```
14,625,556,379,775,260,403,455,694,745
```

Then, because we know the first element is now the smallest in the array, we begin our search again at the second element, 625. This time, the low number is 260, which is switched with the starting element, 625. The list becomes:

```
14,260,556,379,775,625,403,455,694,745
```

The search then begins at the third element; 379 is now the smallest, and the list becomes:

```
14,260,379,556,775,625,403,455,694,745
```

The rest of the procedure would be as follows:

Search from position 4 finds 403, and list becomes:

```
14,260,379,403,775,625,556,455,694,745
```

Search from position 5 finds 455, and list becomes:

```
14,260,379,403,455,625,556,775,694,745
```

Search from position 6 finds 556, and list becomes:

```
14,260,379,403,455,556,625,775,694,745
```

Search from position 7 finds 625, so list doesn't change.
Search from position 8 finds 694, and list becomes:

```
14,260,379,403,455,556,625,694,775,745
```

Search from position 9 finds 745, and the list is now completely sorted:

```
14,260,379,403,455,556,625,694,745,775
```

To find the smallest item in a list, we need to set up a save variable; that is, a variable we can use to store the least value. To begin with, we will place in this variable a number larger than any number in the list. This way, when we scan through the list, any number in the list will be less than the save variable. Then, when we find a number less than the save value, it will be stored in the save variable as the smallest. This way, by the time we have scanned through the list, the save variable will contain the smallest value that was in the list.

We will also keep another variable that will have the index number of the smallest array element. This is necessary for the switching. After the item is located, the switching is done through a temporary variable, as was demonstrated for the bubble insertion technique in Chapter 12.

chapter 14 **387**

sorting

The pseudocode for this procedure follows (the flowchart is in Figure 14–1):

Start module
Set array position counter to 1.
DO-WHILE array position counter < number of elements −1.
   Initialize comparison value to 1000.
   Initialize loop counter to array position counter.
   DO-WHILE loop counter < number of elements.
     IF array item < comparison value THEN
       Comparison value = array item.
       Array marker = loop counter.
     (ELSE)
     END-IF
     Increase loop counter by 1.
   END-DO
   Switch array items.
   Increase array position counter by 1.
END-DO
End module

The program module will look like the following (remember this is only one of several modules):

```
270 REM
280 REM ***** SELECTION SORT MODULE
290 REM
300 FOR I=1 TO NE-1           ' TO ELEMENTS -1
310     CV=1000               ' COMPARISON VALUE
320     FOR K=I TO NE         ' COMPARISON LOOP
330         IF A(K)>=CV THEN 360
340         CV=A(K)           ' STORE SMALLER ITEM
350         AM=K              ' SAVE THE ARRAY SPOT
360     NEXT
370     T=A(AM)               ' STORE ITEM TO SWITCH
380     A(AM)=A(I)            ' BEGINNING ITEM DURING LOOP
390     A(I)=T                ' PUT IN SMALLEST
400 NEXT                      ' END SORT LOOP
```

Program 14–4

Notice that we removed the variables from the NEXT statements. This allows the loops to run faster; with a sort, speed is important, so any time savings helps. We will continue to do this throughout the remainder of the chapter.

Now, when you execute the program, it will seem as if it isn't doing anything. That's because there is no visual indication that anything is taking place. You may want to print something as the sort functions, perhaps the items as they are switched. The reason we have no such indicator now is that anything extraneous slows down the processing. As it is, this sort (running on the IBM) takes about fifty seconds. Pretty slow as sorts go.

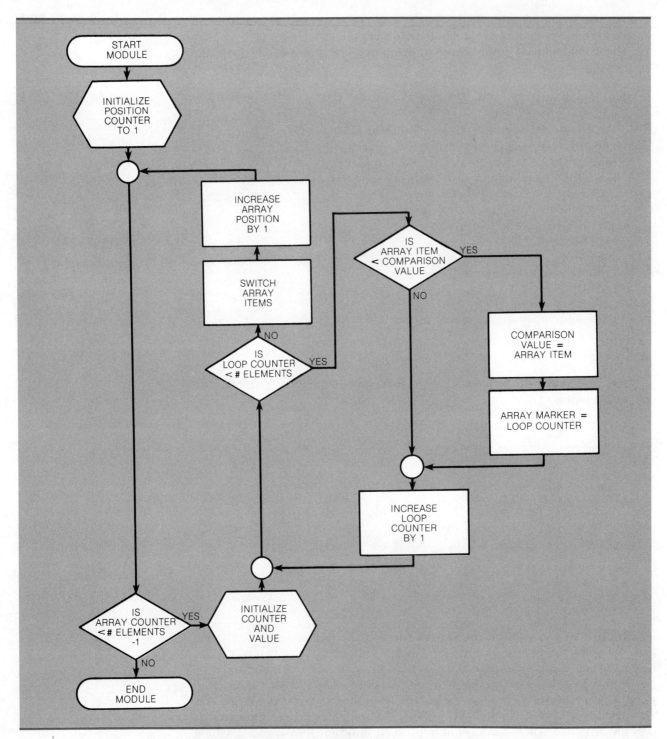

Figure 14–1
Flowchart of selection sort module.

Probably the sort most widely used by beginning programmers is the **bubble sort.** It is easy to understand and easy to write, but unfortunately it is also one of the slowest sorts.

The bubble sort starts at the bottom of the list and compares the current item with the next item. If the next item is less than the current item, the items are switched; that is, the larger item is put one step higher in the list. This way, the larger items will "bubble" their way to the top of the list. As we go through the list, we keep count of the number of switches we have done. After we are through the list, if no switches were done, the list is sorted. Otherwise, the bubbling begins again at the bottom of the list. Each time, however, we progress through one item less than the last search since the largest number will already be at the top of the list.

Let's take the first line of our DATA table again as an example. This initial list looks like:

    1010 DATA 403,625,556,379,775,260,14,455,694,745

An examination is made of the first two elements, 403 and 625. Since 625 is larger, no switch is made. Then, 625 is compared against 556. This time, the second is smaller, so the items are switched. The list becomes:

    403,556,625,379,775,260,14,455,694,745

Another look and

    403,556,379,625,775,260,14,455,694,745

Then the list stays the same since 625 is less than 775. The next comparison yields:

    403,556,379,625,260,775,14,455,694,745

And then

    403,556,379,625,260,14,775,455,694,745

Next

    403,556,379,625,260,14,455,775,694,745

Then

    403,556,379,625,260,14,455,694,775,745

And finally,

    403,556,379,625,260,14,455,694,745,775

Notice that the list is not yet sorted. All we have accomplished so far is to get the largest number, 775, to the top of the list. Now the switching begins again except we don't need to check the topmost item (775) since we already know it is the largest. The exchanges on this pass are as follows:

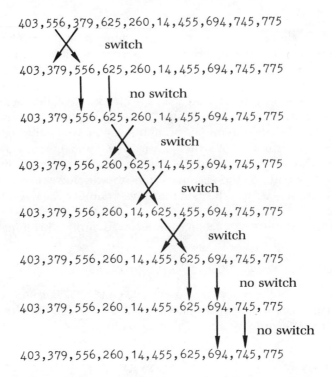

We do no comparison between 745 and 775 since we have already established that 775 is the largest item.

This process continues until either no switches are made during a pass or the pointer to the last item to switch has dropped to the bottom of the list. If no switches are made, then the list is sorted and no further examination is needed. If the pointer is at the bottom of the list, then the entire list has been switched and is sorted.

The pseudocode for the bubble sort follows (see Figure 14–2 for the flowchart):

```
Start module
Initialize array pointer to one less than the number of items.
REPEAT-UNTIL switch counter = 0 or array pointer = 0.
    Initialize switch counter to 0.
    Initialize loop counter to 1.
    DO-WHILE loop counter < array pointer.
        IF current item > next item THEN
            Switch the items.
            Increment switch counter by 1.
        (ELSE)
        END-IF
        Increment loop counter by 1.
    END-DO
    Decrement array pointer by 1.
END-REPEAT
End module
```

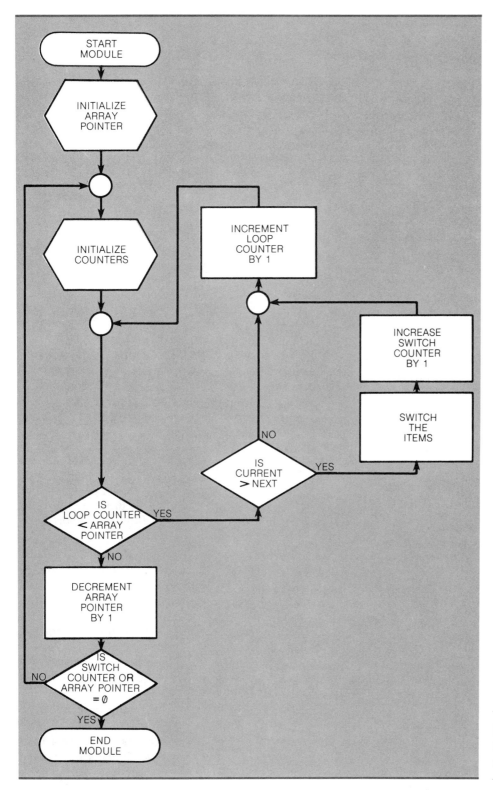

Figure 14–2
Flowchart of bubble sort module.

We will change the name of the program as follows:

```
10 REM ***** PROGRAM NAME: SORTBUBL
20 REM
30 REM ***** WRITTEN BY EDWARD J. COBURN
40 REM
50 REM ***** PRACTICE BUBBLE SORT
60 REM
```

And the sort routine will be:

```
270 REM
280 REM ***** BUBBLE SORT MODULE
290 REM
300 AP=NE-1                    ' ARRAY POINTER
310 SC=0                       ' SWITCH COUNTER
320 FOR I=1 TO AP
330     IF A(I)<=A(I+1) THEN 380
340     T=A(I)                 ' SAVE TEMPORARILY
350     A(I)=A(I+1)            ' MOVE BACK
360     A(I+1)=T               ' MOVE LARGER ITEM FORWARD
370     SC=SC+1                ' COUNT THE SWITCH
380 NEXT
390 AP=AP-1                    ' DECREMENT ARRAY POINTER
400 IF SC<>0 THEN 310          ' WERE THERE ANY SWITCHES?
```

Program 14—5

Unfortunately, when we run this sort, we find it's slower than the selection sort. The time needed to sort the list of 100 numbers has more than doubled to 113 seconds. Why, then, did we introduce this sort? For one thing, the bubble sort is easy to understand; but more importantly, it leads us into the next sort, a modified bubble sort.

14—4
THE SHELL SORT

The **Shell sort** is named after its developer, D.L. Shell. It is a modified bubble sort in that the switches in the Shell sort take place over larger distances than the "next-door" switches of the bubble sort. This turns out to be much more efficient than the method in the bubble sort. As a matter of fact, this sort technique is one of the fastest known.

The way the sort works is that a gap pointer is set up to begin at one beyond the half-way point of the array list. For example, if the array contains 100 elements, the gap pointer would be set to 51. The first item and the gap item are then compared and switched if the first item is larger. Then the second item and the gap item plus one are compared. This way, the gap always remains the same. Then the third item and the gap item plus two are compared, and so on until the gap pointer reaches the end of the array.

Next, the gap is reduced in half, and the process is repeated. For example, if there are 100 items in the array, the gap pointer would be set to 26. The first item is then compared to the gap item and switched, if necessary. Then the item pointer and gap pointer are increased, and the comparisons continue until the gap pointer is at the end of the list.

As the gap gets smaller, the number of comparisons made during a pass increases. When the gap reaches 1, the pass becomes the same as the bubble sort. The sort is complete when the gap is reduced to 0.

Let's use our first DATA statement again as a sample to sort. It begins as:

1010 DATA 403,625,556,379,775,260,14,455,694,745

Since there are ten items, the gap begins as five, and the gap pointer is set on the sixth item. Items 1 and 6 are compared and switched, if necessary. Since the first item is 403 and the gap item is 260, they would be switched and the list would become:

260,625,556,379,775,403,14,455,694,745

Then 625 is compared to 14 and switched:

260,14,556,379,775,403,625,455,694,745

Next, 556 is compared to 455 and switched:

260,14,455,379,775,403,625,556,694,745

Then 379 is compared to 694, and no switch is made. Finally, 775 is compared to 745 and switched:

260,14,455,379,745,403,625,556,694,775

Next, the gap is reduced in half (or the INT of half) to 2. Then the comparison and switching process begins again as follows:

1 and 3, no switch, and the list stays the same.
2 and 4, no switch, and the list stays the same.
3 and 5, no switch, and the list stays the same.
4 and 6, no switch, and the list stays the same.
5 and 7, switched, and the list becomes:

260,14,455,379,625,403,745,556,694,775

6 and 8, no switch, and the list stays the same.
7 and 9, switched, and the list becomes:

260,14,455,379,625,403,694,556,745,775

8 and 10, no switch, and the list stays the same.

The list now looks like:

260,14,455,379,625,403,694,556,745,775

The gap is now reduced to 1, and the switching resumes:
1 and 2, switched, and the list becomes:

14,260,455,379,625,403,694,556,745,775

2 and 3, no switch, and the list stays the same.
3 and 4, switched, and the list becomes:

14,260,379,455,625,403,694,556,745,775

4 and 5, no switch, and the list stays the same.
5 and 6, switched, and the list becomes:

14,260,379,455,403,625,694,556,745,775

6 and 7, no switch, and the list stays the same.

7 and 8, switched, and the list becomes:

14,260,379,455,403,625,556,694,745,775

The rest is sorted and requires no more switches. But we have a problem: the sort is not completed. Notice that 403 and 556 are out of order. Well, we neglected one important point about the sort. Just like the bubble sort, we have to keep track of the number of switches made during a pass; if any were made, the process is not complete. In this sort, if switches were made, the same gap is used again for another pass. Generally, with such a small selection of data, only the bubble part of the sort (when the gap is 1) needs a second pass. As you can see by examining the list, when we switch items 4 and 5 and items 6 and 7, the sort will be complete. This sort took fewer passes and, more important, fewer switches on each pass than the bubble sort.

The pseudocode for the Shell sort follows (see Figure 14–3 for the flowchart):

```
Start module
Initialize gap to the number of items.
DO-WHILE gap > 0.
   Compute new gap as integer of half of old gap.
   REPEAT-UNTIL switch counter = 0.
      Initialize switch counter to 0.
      Initialize loop counter to 1.
      DO-WHILE loop counter <= number of items − gap.
         IF current item > gap item THEN
            Switch items.
            Increment switch counter by 1.
         (ELSE)
         END-IF
         Increment loop counter by 1.
      END-DO
   END-REPEAT
END-DO
End module
```

The new program name is:

```
10 REM ***** PROGRAM NAME: SORTSHEL
20 REM
30 REM ***** WRITTEN BY EDWARD J. COBURN
40 REM
50 REM ***** PRACTICE SHELL SORT
60 REM
```

And the sort module would be:

```
270 REM
280 REM ***** SHELL SORT MODULE
290 REM
300 G=NE                          ' INITIALIZE GAP
```

Program continues on page 396

Program 14–6

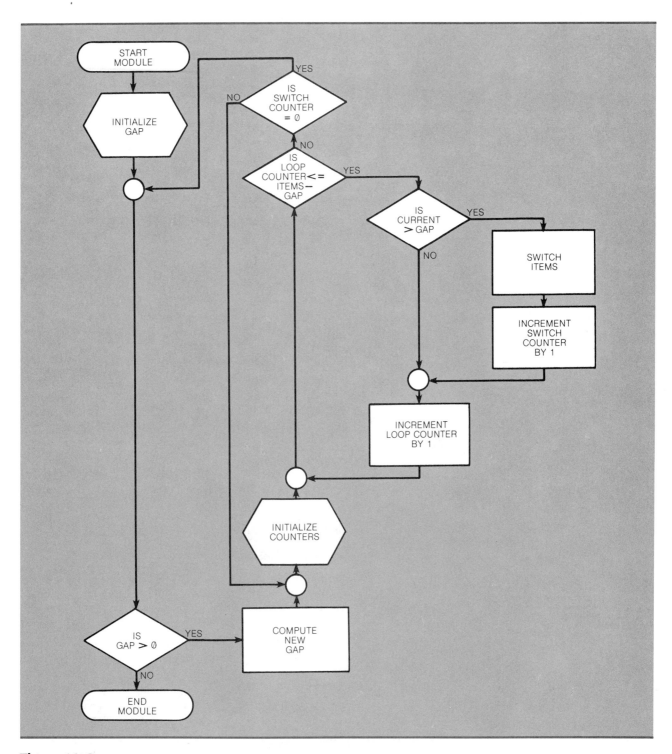

Figure 14–3
Flowchart of Shell sort module.

```
310 G=INT(G/2)                        ' COMPUTE NEW GAP
315 IF G=0 THEN 895                   ' SORT IS FINISHED
320 SC=0                              ' INITIALIZE SWITCH COUNTER
330 FOR I=1 TO NE-G
340      IF A(I)<=A(I+G) THEN 390
350      T=A(I)                       ' STORE FIRST ITEM
360      A(I)=A(I+G)                  ' MOVE GAP ITEM
370      A(I+G)=T                     ' REPOSITION FIRST ITEM
380      SC=SC+1                      ' INCREMENT SWITCH COUNTER
390 NEXT
400 IF SC<>0 THEN 320                 ' REDO LOOP IF SWITCHED
410 GOTO 310                          ' RETURN FOR NEW GAP
```

Program 14–6 (cont.)

You will notice on line 330 (the FOR statement) that the loop is from 1 to the number of items (NE) minus the gap (G) and that the comparison on line 340 is from the item number to the I + G item. For example, if the counter is 1 and the gap is 5, we compare items 1 and 6 as was demonstrated. Also notice that we included the switch counter in lines 380 and 400.

When we run this sort, the list is sorted in about 38 seconds, 12 seconds faster than the selection sort. We're improving, but we still haven't used the fastest sort available.

14–5
THE QUICKSORT

The final sort we will use is the **quicksort.** As the name implies, it is a quick sort. It was created by C.A.R. Hoare and is considered to be the best sorting method developed thus far.

The quicksort divides the list into groups called **partitions** by using an item in the middle as a **key;** all items less than the key are moved to the left, and all items larger than the key are moved to the right. This yields two partitions, which are then partitioned themselves. By continuing to partition smaller and smaller groups, eventually each partition will have only one item, and the list will be sorted.

Let's again use our first DATA statement as an example:

```
1010 DATA 403,625,556,379,775,260,14,455,694,745
```

We begin by setting up the entire list as one partition with boundaries at 1 and 10. To determine the midpoint, we add the left and right margins together and divide by 2, then take the integer. This gives us element 5 as our key, since $INT(11/2) = 5$.

Now, we begin on the left side of the partition with item 1, which is 403, and compare it to our key element, which is 775. Since 403 is less than 775, we don't want to move 403, so we move the left pointer to the next item (625) and compare again. Remember, we will move any item that is greater than the key to the other side of the partition. Since 625 is less, the pointer moves on. It will continue to move until we have found 775. The pointer will then stop since the element is no longer smaller than 775.

Now we begin with the farthest right-hand element to see if it is *less* than the key. Since 745 is less than 775, the left pointer item, 775, and the right pointer item, 745, are exchanged; the left pointer is then increased and the right pointer decreased. The left pointer now points at item 6, and the right points at item 9. We continue to check the left-hand items until we find one that is less than or equal to the key. We don't find one until we reach 775 again. At that point the right pointer is left of the left pointer, so the pass is finished since any switching would now be going in the wrong direction.

We now have two partitions: 775 is one and the other nine items are the other, as shown below:

```
403,625,556,379,745,260,14,455,694        775

          PARTITION 1              PARTITION 2
```

Since we can work with only one partition at a time, we need to save one of them. We do this by creating another array (or possibly two arrays) to use as a **stack** (discussed in more detail later) to store our partition boundaries. We always save the right partition and work with the left partition. This time, however, the right partition contains only a single element, so it is not necessary to store it (since one-element partitions are already sorted) and the stack remains empty.

We are now ready to partition the left-hand partition. We reset the pointers to the limits, this time 1 and 9. The key is again element 5, which is 745 this time. This pass will work the same way the first one did since 745 is the largest element in the partition. Therefore, we switch 745 with 694 and end up with two partitions that look like the following (remember that we already have 775 as a one-element partition):

```
403,625,556,379,694,260,14,455            745

          PARTITION 1              PARTITION 2
```

Again, there is no need to save the right partition since it contains only one element. We now partition our new left-hand partition. The left boundary becomes 1, the right boundary becomes 8; this gives us the key as element number 4, which is 379. Item 1, 403, is compared to the key and found to be larger. The right scan begins at 455, which is larger than the key so the right pointer moves back one element to 14. Since this is smaller than the key, the two items (403 and 14) are switched and we have:

```
14,625,556,379,694,260,403,455
```

Now the left pointer moves to 625, which is larger than the key, and the right pointer moves to 260 which is less than the key, so 625 and 260 are switched and we have:

```
14,260,556,379,694,625,403,455
```

Finally, the left pointer moves to 556 and the right pointer moves past 694 (since 694 is larger than the key) to 379. These items are switched, and we now have the two partitions:

```
14,260,379          556,694,625,403,455

PARTITION 1         PARTITION 2
```

Now the right partition is **pushed** onto the stack, which simply means that it is put on the top of the stack and the rest of the stack is pushed down. When a partition is used from the stack, the one on the top of the stack is used first. Our new right partition has the left margin at 4 (the first position) and the right margin at 8 (the last position).

Final partitioning of the left partition is trivial since it is already in order; so we move back to the partition stored in the stack. We begin by **popping** the partition boundaries off the stack, which means that we use the partition at the top of the stack and reset the stack counter since the stack contains one less item than it did before. (See Figure 14–4 for an illustration of how a stack works.)

Our partition boundaries are now 4 and 8, and the key is item 6, or 625. Since 556 is less than the key, the left pointer moves to 694. The right pointer finds 455, which is switched with 694; our list becomes:

        556,455,625,403,694

Then the left pointer moves to 625, and the right pointer moves to 403. The items are switched, and the pass is complete; our partitions are now:

        556,455,403   625,694

        PARTITION 1   PARTITION 2

We will do our last examination of the left partition since the right partition is already in order. The pass begins with the key as 455, the left pointer at 556, and the right pointer at 403. The items are switched, and the partition becomes:

        403,455,556

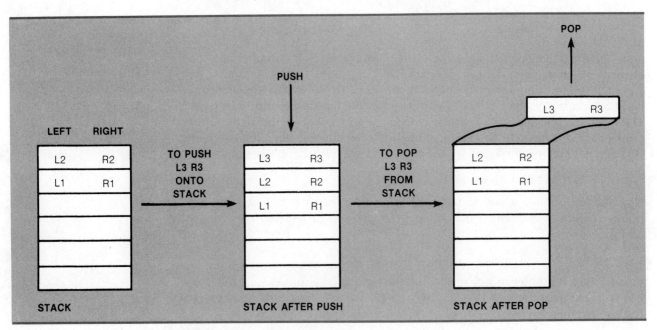

Figure 14–4
Pushing and popping a stack.

And we are finished.

This sorting technique is a bit complicated, so let's take another example before moving on to the coding. Let's use the second DATA line from our program and sort it with the quicksort technique. The list is:

```
55,553,738,392,513,401,273,816,101,435
```

This sort is summarized below:

PASS 1—boundaries are left = 1, right = 10
    key is item 6, which is 401.
Left pointer is 55, which is less than the key.
Left pointer moves to 553, which is greater than the key.
Right pointer is 435, which is greater than the key.
Right pointer moves to 101, which is less than the key.
The items 553 and 101 are switched:

```
55,101,738,392,513,401,273,816,553,435
```

Left pointer is now 738, which is greater than the key.
Right pointer is 816, which is greater than the key.
Right pointer moves to 273, which is greater than the key.
The items 738 and 273 are switched:

```
55,101,273,392,513,401,738,816,553,435
```

Left pointer is now 392, which is greater than the key.
Left pointer moves to 513, which is greater than the key.
Right pointer is 401, which is the key.
The items 513 and 401 are switched:

```
55,101,273,392,401,513,738,816,553,435
```

The pass is completed, and our partitions are:

```
55,101,273,392        401,513,738,816,435
```

The right partition is pushed onto the stack with a left margin of 5 and a right margin of 10.

PASS 2 is trivial since the partition is in sequence.

PASS 3—the partition boundaries, which are 5 and 10, are popped;
    the key is item 7, which is 738.
The left pointer is 401, which is less than the key.
The left pointer moves to 513, which is less than the key.
The left pointer moves to 738, which is the key.
The right pointer is 435, which is less than the key.
The items 738 and 435 are switched:

```
401,513,435,816,738
```

The left pointer is 816, which is greater than the key.
The right pointer is 738, which is the key.
The items 816 and 738 are switched:

401,513,435,738,816

The pass is completed, and our partitions are:

401,513,435   738,816

The right partition is in order.

PASS 4—boundaries are items 5 and 7; key is item 6, which is 513.
The left pointer is 401, which is less than the key.
The left pointer moves to 513, which is the key.
The right pointer is 435, which is less than the key.
The items 513 and 435 are switched:

401,435,513

And the partition is sorted.

All partitions are sorted, so the sort is completed. In the above examples, we skipped over the workings of the sorted partitions. Keep in mind, however, that even these sorted partitions are broken down further until all partitions are one-element partitions.

We are now ready to discuss the coding of the routine. First, let's change the name of the program to read:

```
10 REM ***** PROGRAM NAME: SORTQUIK
20 REM
30 REM ***** WRITTEN BY EDWARD J. COBURN
40 REM
50 REM ***** PRACTICE QUICKSORT
60 REM
```

The pseudocode follows (see Figure 14–5 for the flowchart):

Start module
Initialize first partition using left margin of 1
   and right margin of the number of elements.
DO-WHILE partition count > 0.
   Pop partition from the stack.
   DO-WHILE left margin < right margin.
      Determine partition middle and get key.
      Initialize left and right pointers.
      DO-WHILE left pointer <= right pointer.
         DO-WHILE left element < key.
            Move left pointer one to the right.
         END-DO
         DO-WHILE right element > key.
            Move right pointer one to the left.
         END-DO
         IF left element > right element THEN
            Swith the elements.
            Move left pointer one to right.
            Move right pointer one to left.
         (ELSE) *(continues on page 402)*

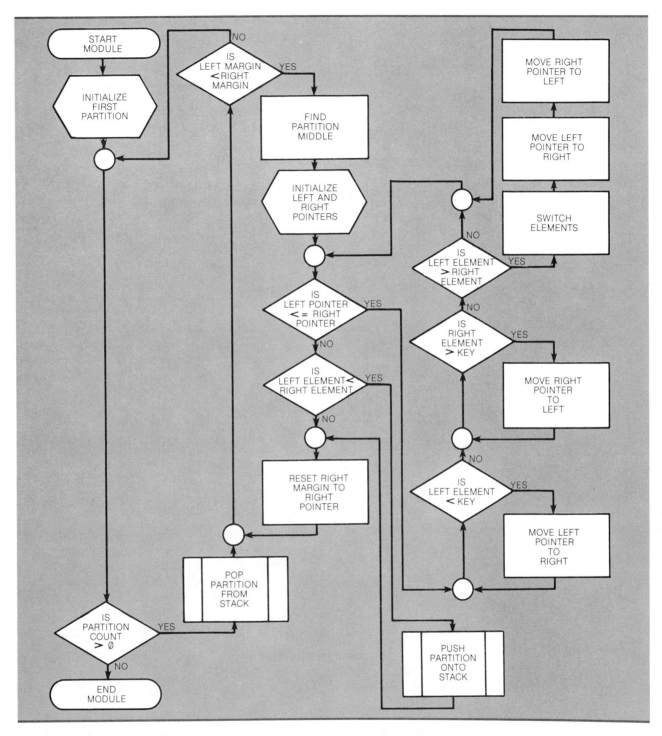

Figure 14–5
Flowchart of quicksort module.

```
            END-IF
        END-DO
        IF left element < right element THEN
            Push partition onto stack.
        (ELSE)
        END-IF
        Reset right margin to right pointer.
    END-DO
END-DO
End module
```

Notice in the flowchart that we used two predefined processes for popping from and pushing onto the stack. These processes actually consist of three statements each, which we will clarify before we continue.

Our stack actually consists of two stacks: one for the left margin of the partition and one for the right margin. In our program we will use a two-dimensional array; the first subscript will be for the element, and the second subscript will indicate whether it is the left (1) or right (2) margin. Thus, the first partition would have the left margin stored as element A(1,1) and the right margin as A(1,2) (Figure 14–6).

The procedure for pushing onto the stack consists of assigning the margins and then adding one to the stack counter. Popping from the stack requires referencing the margins to be used and reducing the stack counter.

Our quicksort module should look like Program 14–7.

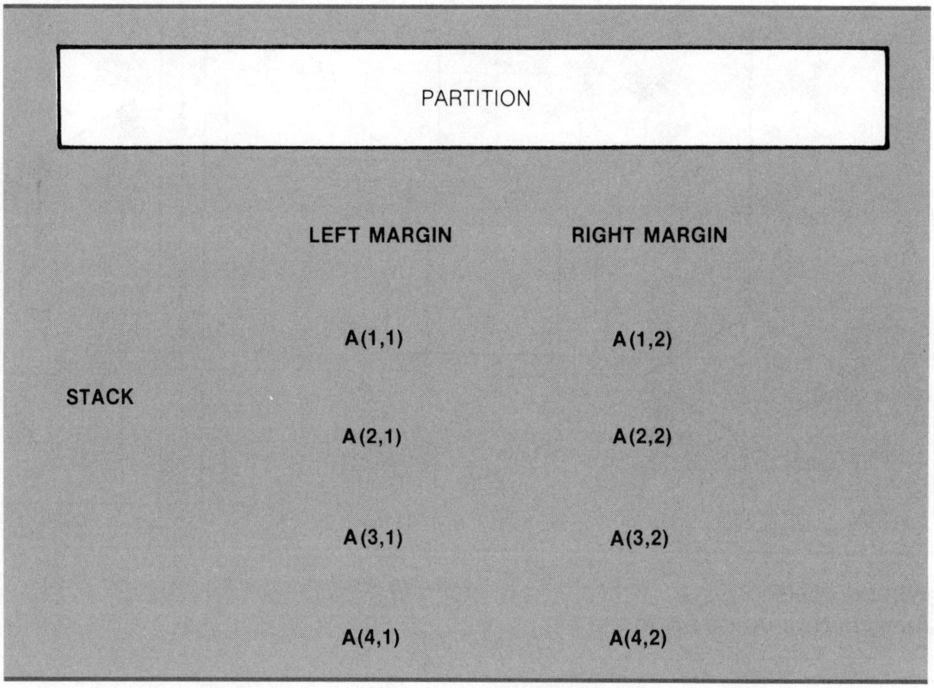

Figure 14–6
Using the array stack.

```
270 REM
280 REM ***** QUICKSORT MODULE
290 REM
300 P=1                              ' PARTITION NUMBER
310 S(P,1)=1                         ' INITIAL LEFT MARGIN
320 S(P,2)=NE                        ' INITIAL RIGHT MARGIN
325 ' ************************** POP FROM STACK
330     LM=S(P,1)                    ' USE LEFT MARGIN
340     RM=S(P,2)                    ' USE RIGHT MARGIN
350     P=P-1                        ' REDUCE THE NUMBER OF PARTITIONS
355 ' ************************** ADJUST THE PARTITION
360     PM=INT((LM+RM)/2)            ' DETERMINE PARTITION MIDDLE
370     K=A(PM)                      ' GET KEY ELEMENT
380     LP=LM                        ' INITIALIZE LEFT POINTER
390     RP=RM                        ' INITIALIZE RIGHT POINTER
400     IF A(LP)>=K THEN 430         ' IS LEFT GREATER
410         LP=LP+1                  ' MOVE LEFT POINTER
420         GOTO 400
430     IF A(RP)<=K THEN 460         ' IS RIGHT LESS
440         RP=RP-1                  ' MOVE RIGHT POINTER
450         GOTO 430
460     IF LP>RP THEN 530            ' DO ITEMS NEED SWITCHING?
470         T=A(LP)                  ' SAVE LEFT ITEM
480         A(LP)=A(RP)              ' RIGHT TO LEFT
490         A(RP)=T                  ' REPLACE RIGHT
500         LP=LP+1                  ' MOVE LEFT POINTER
510         RP=RP-1                  ' MOVE RIGHT POINTER
520     IF LP<=RP THEN 400           ' IF MARGINS OKAY DO AGAIN
530     IF LP>=RM THEN 570           ' IS POINTER OKAY?
535 ' ************************** PUSH ONTO STACK
540         P=P+1                    ' UP PARTITION COUNTER
550         S(P,1)=LP                ' LEFT MARGIN
560         S(P,2)=RM                ' RIGHT MARGIN
570     RM=RP                        ' REDO MARGIN
580     IF LM<RM THEN 360            ' IS LEFT MARGIN REACHED?
590     IF P<>0 THEN 330             ' ANY MORE IN STACK?
```

Program 14–7

This program sorts the items in about twenty seconds, an improvement of eighteen seconds over the Shell sort. This result is actually much less dramatic than with larger samples of data. With lists of 200, 300, or 500 elements the quicksort can produce startling improvements in execution time.

14–6
SORTING STRINGS

Though we used a numeric array for our practice sorts, most of the time a sort is used for string data. For example, we might want to sort our contributions file by date or a mailing list by zip code.

Only a few changes are necessary in our programs to adapt them for sorting strings. We will change the selection sort to sort strings since it is one of the easiest to understand. After we understand the modifications, we can change any of the sorts; remember, though, that the quicksort is the fastest.

Before we modify the sort module, however, we need to change the input routine to input string data instead of numbers. In the new routine we need to change line 80 to dimension a string array and line 100 to READ in the string data. The new module should look like the following (remember, we are using the selection sort):

```
10 REM ***** PROGRAM NAME: SELSTR
20 REM
```

Program 14–8

Program continues

```
30 REM ***** WRITTEN BY EDWARD J. COBURN
40 REM
50 REM ***** SELECTION SORT FOR STRING DATA
60 REM
70 READ NE                    ' NUMBER OF ELEMENTS
80 DIM A$(NE)                 ' ARRAY TO SORT
90 FOR I=1 TO NE
100    READ A$(I)             ' READ IN ARRAY
110 NEXT I
```
Program 14–8 (cont.)

The output module will also need modification to print the string array. Since we will only use ten items (we could use any number, of course), we won't need a fancy output routine. A simple FOR-NEXT loop will do:

```
870 REM
880 REM ***** OUTPUT MODULE
890 REM
895 CLS                       ' CLEAR THE SCREEN
910    FOR I=1 TO NE
920        PRINT A$(I)
930    NEXT I
970 END
```
Program 14–9

Next, we need to set up the data to be used for our array. We will use the following:

```
980 REM
985 REM ***** DATA TABLE
990 REM
1000 DATA 10
1010 DATA SAM SMITH, JOE BLOW, ED COBURN, AL SIMONS
1020 DATA FRED THOMPSON, JACK FRITZ, HARRY GARP
1030 DATA TOM JONES, PAM CONLEY, HARRISON FORD    Program 14–10
```

Finally, we need to change the sort routine to use the string array. Line 310 will have to assign the highest possible string value, which would be ZZZZZ. Then line 330, 340, 370, 380, and 390 must be changed for string data. The routine should look like the following:

```
270 REM
280 REM ***** SELECTION SORT MODULE
290 REM
300 FOR I=J TO NE-1           ' TO ELEMENTS -1
310    CV$="ZZZZZ"            ' COMPARISON VALUE
320    FOR K=I TO NE          ' COMPARISON LOOP
330        IF A$(K)>=CV$ THEN 360
340        CV$=A$(K)          ' STORE SMALLER ITEM
350        AM=K               ' SAVE THE ARRAY SPOT
360    NEXT
370    T$=A$(AM)              ' STORE ITEM TO SWITCH
380    A$(AM)=A$(I)           ' BEGINNING ITEM DURING LOOP
390    A$(I)=T$               ' PUT IN SMALLEST
400 NEXT                      ' END SORT LOOP    Program 14–11
```

Using the data in Program 14–10, when we run the program we will get a printed list:

```
AL SIMONS
ED COBURN
FRED THOMPSON
```

Program continues

```
HARRISON FORD
HARRY GARP
JACK FRITZ
JOE BLOW
PAM CONLEY
SAM SMITH
TOM JONES
Ok
```

Notice that the list is sorted. Unfortunately, it is sorted by first name rather than the standard way of sorting by last name. This is because we put the names in the DATA statement first name first. We can find the last name, as we discussed back in Chapter 7, and then sort by that. This procedure is left as an exercise at the end of the chapter.

14–7 SORTING MULTIPLE ITEMS

Generally, we need to sort records, not just single fields. When we switch items in a record sort, normally we have to switch several fields at the same time. To demonstrate this technique, we will once again change our selection sort program. We will simplify the multiple field experiment by assigning a sequence number to each of the strings we READ in. Then, when we sort the strings, we will change the sequence numbers around at the same time. To accomplish this, we will need to modify the input, output, and sort modules again. The new input module should be:

```
10 REM ***** PROGRAM NAME: SELMULT
20 REM
30 REM ***** WRITTEN BY EDWARD J. COBURN
40 REM
50 REM ***** SELECTION SORT FOR TWO FIELDS
60 REM
70 READ NE                    ' NUMBER OF ELEMENTS
80 DIM A$(NE),A(NE)           ' ARRAY TO SORT
90 FOR I=1 TO NE
100    READ A$(I)             ' READ IN ARRAY
105    A(I)=I                 ' ASSIGN SEQUENCE NUMBER
110 NEXT I
```
Program 14–12

Notice that the only changes are to the comments, line 80 to add the new array, and line 105 to assign the sequence number.

The only change to the output module will be to print the sequence number next to the string output (line 920):

```
870 REM
880 REM ***** OUTPUT MODULE
890 REM
895 CLS                       ' CLEAR THE SCREEN
910    FOR I=1 TO 10
920       PRINT A$(I),A(I)
930    NEXT I
970 END
```
Program 14–13

The DATA will not need to be changed since we are merely adding a sequence number.

The final changes we need to make are in the sort routine itself. We need to make it such that when we switch the fields, instead of switching one field, we switch both fields. This requires adding three more lines to the program to switch the numeric field. We will have the three lines follow their string counterparts. They will be lines 375, 385, and 395.

```
270 REM
280 REM ***** SELECTION SORT MODULE
290 REM
300 FOR I=J TO NE-1            ' TO ELEMENTS -1
310     CV$="ZZZZZ"            ' COMPARISON VALUE
320     FOR K=I TO NE          ' COMPARISON LOOP
330         IF A$(K)>=CV$ THEN 360
340         CV$=A$(K)          ' STORE SMALLER ITEM
350         AM=K               ' SAVE THE ARRAY SPOT
360     NEXT
370     T$=A$(AM)              ' STORE ITEM TO SWITCH
375     T=A(AM)
380     A$(AM)=A$(I)           ' BEGINNING ITEM DURING LOOP
385     A(AM)=A(I)
390     A$(I)=T$               ' PUT IN SMALLEST
395     A(I)=T
400 NEXT                       ' END SORT LOOP        Program 14-14
```

Using the data in Program 14–10 and the sequence numbers we assigned, we should get output like the following:

```
AL SIMONS        4
ED COBURN        3
FRED THOMPSON    5
HARRISON FORD    10
HARRY GARP       7
JACK FRITZ       6
JOE BLOW         2
PAM CONLEY       9
SAM SMITH        1
TOM JONES        8
Ok
```

Notice that the number printed beside the name is the relative position of each of the names in the DATA statements we used. For example, SAM SMITH is printed with a 1 because it is item 1 in the DATA statement; PAM CONLEY is item number 9 in the DATA statement, so the display shows a 9 next to her name.

This technique of sorting multiple fields can be applied to any size of record. Records with as few as two fields or as many as one hundred can be sorted using this technique. Keep in mind, however, that moving all the fields slows down the sort. It is more logical to get the sort field and associate with that the relative record number of the record in the file. Then, by sorting those two fields as we just did, we can keep the record number paired with the sort field. After the sort, it is a simple matter to read the records randomly from the file since we have the record numbers. Take our example above; if this set of data were a file and the sequence number we used were the record number, then when the sort finished we would have the record numbers with the associated fields. This is a much more time-effective method for sorting a file whose records may have many fields.

1. A sort is a program designed to arrange a list of items into alphabetical or numerical sequence. We learned how to create and use four different sorts: the selection sort, bubble sort, Shell sort, and quicksort.

2. The selection sort works by examining the list to be sorted and finding the smallest element. This item is then switched with the first item in the list. The list is then again examined for the smallest element, starting this time at the second item. When the next smaller item is found, it is switched with the second item of the list. This process continues until the last element of the array is reached. This is one of the slower processes as sorts go.

3. The bubble sort examines the list from the beginning and compares the first item with the one next to it. If the first item is larger than the next one, the items are switched. Then the second item is compared with the third and, if necessary, these items are switched. This process continues throughout the entire list. As the list is examined, a count is kept of the number of switches that were necessary. If, after one full examination of the list, no switches were made, the list is sorted. Otherwise, the sorting continues; each subsequent examination goes through the list and stops one item short of the last time. This is possible since the largest items are "bubbled" to the end. The sort ends when the only item left is the first item or when there were no switches on the pass through the list. This sort is even slower than the selection sort.

4. We looked at the bubble sort to help us understand the Shell sort. The Shell sort is much the same as the bubble sort, but the comparisons and exchanges are done over a "gap" instead of "next door" as in the bubble sort. Each time we examine the list, the gap for the comparison gets smaller; when the gap is next door, as with the bubble sort, the last examination is done and the list is sorted. We keep track of the number of switches in this sort also to determine when the sorting is finished. This is one of the fastest sorts available.

5. The fastest sort found thus far is the quicksort, which divides the list into two parts around a central key. Then all items smaller than the key are moved to the left, and all items larger are moved to the right. After this is accomplished, we have two partitions, each of which is itself partitioned. This process continues until each of the partitions is only one item long. The list is then sorted.

6. A sort is used for strings more often than for numerics. The changes required to convert our sort programs from numeric to string sorts were minor.

7. Rarely do we run a sort on a single field. Most of the time, a sort is executed on a record, so our sorts need to sort many fields at the same time. To do this, the additional fields are associated with the original list; as the original list items are exchanged, the additional field lists are also exchanged. Usually, the field to be sorted and the relative record are put together and sorted. This saves having to sort the entire file; after the sort, the records can be accessed by relative record number.

GLOSSARY

Bubble sort A sort that compares adjacent items in a list and switches them, if necessary, to move the larger item to the end of the list. After many passes through the list, the larger items are all "bubbled" to the end.

Key The central item in the quicksort around which the other items are arranged.

Partition The grouping used in the quicksort to break the list into pieces for sorting.

Pop The process of removing an item from a stack.

Push The process of putting an item into a stack.

Quicksort A sort that divides the list into two partitions around a central key and then moves all items less than the key to the left and all items greater than the key to the right. Each of these partitions is then in turn partitioned until all the par-

titions consist of only one item. The quicksort is the fastest sort technique known.

Selection sort A sort that finds the smallest item in a list and exchanges it with the first item in the list; this process continues until all the items have been moved forward to their appropriate positions.

Shell sort A variation of a bubble sort that exchanges items separated by a gap rather than adjacent items. As the sort progresses, the gap gets smaller until, on the last pass, the comparison is of adjacent items as with the bubble sort.

Sort A program designed to put a list of items into sequence.

Stack A sequential grouping for storing partitions by "pushing" them onto the stack; they are removed from the top of the stack by "popping" them off.

QUESTIONS TO AID UNDERSTANDING

1. Explain what a sort is and describe three applications in which sorts might prove useful.

*2. What is the first element in the DATA list used for?

3. 10, 35, 2, 8, 55, 22, 67, 99, 44, 56, 25, 38, 87, 3, 9. Sort this list by hand using all four sort techniques described in the chapter (the selection sort, bubble sort, Shell sort, and quicksort).

*4. What sort uses the key, and what is it used for?

*5. Change the quicksort procedure introduced in the chapter to sort the string list given in Program 14–10.

6. Change the quicksort procedure to use the string sort and the sequence number, as shown with the selection sort in the chapter.

7. Modify the quicksort program to sort the file that was set up with the tree structure program in the previous chapter. Load the entire file into four arrays and sort the arrays in conjunction.

8. Use the quicksort program to sort the tree structure file set up in the last chapter. Use only the index field and the relative record number to sort the records. Then write a print routine to access the records by relative record number and print them out.

9. Write a program to generate a list of 1000 numbers and store them in a sequential file. Then use each of the sort procedures described in the chapter to read the file into an array and sort the numbers. Record and compare the results. It will be apparent why the quicksort is the best sort to use.

10. Use the quicksort procedure to sort the indexed file we created in Chapter

12; use the contribution date as the index for the sort. Write a routine to print the list in date sequence.

11. Using the string data established in the chapter, write a routine using the quicksort that will sort the list by last name. You may have to review Chapter 7 for the technique to accomplish this.

12. Use the quicksort routine to write a program to sort the tree file we created in the previous chapter. Then write a routine to take this sorted file and create a balanced tree.

13. Use the XYZ Corporation file you created in the last chapter and write a program to enable the user to sort the file by either name, address, zip code, salary code, or employment date. If the sort selected is in name, address, or zip code order, print the report with the name, address, zip code format. If the sort selected is in salary code or employment date order, print the report with the name, birth date, pay code, employment date, and number of exemptions. (Refer back to previous chapters for the report formats.)

QUICK QUIZ

The answers to the questions follow immediately after the quiz. Questions 1–15 are true–false, while 16–20 are multiple choice.

1. A sort can be used to sort strings as well as numbers.   **T   F**

2. The Shell sort is basically a selection sort.   **T   F**

3. We always use arrays to store the lists to be sorted.   **T   F**

4. We set up the input routine to read a number from the DATA table so we   **T   F**
   would have flexibility in the number of elements in our list.

5. In the selection sort, the smallest value is found by comparing each item   **T   F**
   against the first item in the list.

6. The bubble sort works by comparing adjacent items and exchanging the   **T   F**
   items if the second item is less than the first.

7. A switch counter is used in the bubble sort to keep track of how many   **T   F**
   switches have taken place during the sort. When the counter reaches a
   certain value, we know the list is sorted.

8. Though the Shell sort is similar to the bubble sort, no switch counter is   **T   F**
   used.

9. The Shell sort begins by comparing opposite ends of the list and then mov- **T   F**
   ing the comparisons toward the middle.

10. The quicksort finds a key in the middle of the list and arranges the items **T   F**
    around that key.

11. The two partitions left after a pass in the quicksort should be virtually the **T   F**
    same size.

T F **12.** The process of storing the partition boundaries on the stack is called pushing.

T F **13.** Sorting strings is difficult because a different type of test must be set up.

T F **14.** Sorting multiple items is a simple process of switching several items instead of just one.

T F **15.** The easiest way to sort a file is to load all the fields into arrays and then sort the arrays.

_____ **16.** Which of the following sorts is the fastest?

      a. selection   **c.** quicksort

      b. bubble   **d.** Shell

_____ **17.** Which of the following sorts uses a key field?

      a. selection   **c.** quicksort

      b. bubble   **d.** Shell

_____ **18.** Which of the following sorts uses a switch counter to record the number of switches made?

      a. selection   **c.** quicksort

      b. bubble   **d.** they all do

_____ **19.** Which of the following terms is not used in reference to the quicksort?

      a. partition   **c.** switch counter

      b. key   **d.** they all are

_____ **20.** Which of the following would not be a correctly sorted list of strings?

      a. 10, 20, 30, 4, 40, 5, 52

      b. AL, ED, GEORGE, TOM, VIRGIL

      c. 10, 20, TOM, al

      d. all are correctly sorted

ANSWERS TO QUICK QUIZ

1. T
2. F (It is basically a bubble sort.)
3. T (It would be virtually impossible to sort a list without an array. The only exception to this is when we sort a file and use record numbers which act like an array.)
4. T
5. F (The smallest item is found by comparing each item against a known item that is larger than the largest possible value in the list.)
6. T
7. F (We know the list is sorted if, after one pass through the list, no switches were made, i.e., the counter is zero.)
8. F (The switch counter is used in the Shell sort for the same purpose as in the bubble sort.)
9. F (The comparisons are made over a gap, beginning at one item beyond the half-way point; the gap grows smaller with each pass, but the beginning element of each comparison is always the first element of the list.)
10. T
11. F (Though this happens sometimes, most of the time the partitions are different in size.)
12. T (It involves placing the item onto the stack and adjusting the stack counter.)

13. F (The only difference from sorting numerics is that the tests and assignments use strings instead of numerics.)
14. T (Basically, that's all there is to it.)
15. T (But it is probably the slowest way.)
16. c
17. c
18. b
19. c (The switch counter is used in the bubble and Shell sorts.)
20. d (All three lists are correct. Remember, as a string list a would put 30 before 4 since 3 is less than 4. For list c, in the ASCII sequence numbers come before capital letters and capitals come before lower-case.)

15 GRAPHICS AND COLOR

OBJECTIVES

After completing Chapter 15, you will be able to:

- Describe the three types of resolution and the uses for each.
- Explain the terminology for the graphics used on your machine.
- Demonstrate the use of graphics on your computer by writing several programs utilizing graphics techniques.

412

In previous chapters we learned how to format screens and reports to make them more pleasing to the user. Even more important, however, is that such displays allow the user to interpret the information more easily. In this chapter we will learn another approach to the display of information for ease of interpretation: use of graphics and color.

All our computers use graphics to a certain degree; the IBM and Apple also use color. We will begin with a general look at the types of computer graphics and use of color; we will then move on to the capabilities of the individual computers.

When speaking of graphics, it is customary to discuss three types of **resolution.** Resolution refers to the number of individual points on the screen that can be accessed. Each of these video screen points is called a **pixel** or **picture element.** There are three types of resolution, which allow access to a differing number of pixels: text, low, and high.

Text resolution generally allows access only to the whole array of pixels that are required to generate the textual letters shown on the screen. We used resolution of this type before when we designed a graph like the following:

```
10   !  XXXXXXXXXX
     !
5    !  XXXXX
     !
3    !  XXX
     !
6    !  XXXXX
```

We only used full characters to create this display. Each computer's display has the following number of characters, as discussed in Chapter 1:

The IBM has 24 rows by either 40 or 80 columns or 960 or 1920 positions.

The Radio Shack Model III has 16 rows by 64 columns, or 1024 positions, while the Model 4 has 24 rows by 80 columns, or 1920 positions.

The Apple has 24 rows by 40 columns, or 960 positions.

The display shown above is simple to accomplish on all our computers since they all have text resolution. All you have to do is determine the make up of the print line and the number of characters to be printed, and then print them. An example of such a program follows:

```
NEW
10 REM ***** PROGRAM NAME: TEXTGR1
20 REM
30 REM ***** TEXT RESOLUTION GRAPHICS DEMO 1
40 REM
50 REM ***** PROGRAM WRITTEN BY EDWARD J. COBURN
60 REM
70 CLS                          ' CLEAR THE SCREEN
80 FOR I = 1 TO 5
90     READ A
100    IF A<10 THEN PRINT " ";       ' EXTRA BLANK
110    PRINT A;" ";
```

Program continues   Program 15–1

```
120    PRINT "! ";
130    FOR J = 1 TO A
140        PRINT "X";
150    NEXT J
160    PRINT                        ' FOR CARRIAGE RETURN
170    IF I<5 THEN PRINT "       !" ' BETWEEN LINES
180 NEXT I
190 END
200 DATA 5,10,4,15,2
RUN
   5  ! XXXXX
      !
  10  ! XXXXXXXXXX
      !
   4  ! XXXX
      !
  15  ! XXXXXXXXXXXXXXX
      !
   2  ! XX
```
Program 15–1 (cont.)

This is simple enough, but the graph is not very instructive. It doesn't tell us anything. There should be some information displayed with the graph itself. Perhaps a scale to clarify positioning and a heading would help. Let's add these two things. We will insert lines 72 through 78:

```
72 PRINT TAB(5);"GRADE DISPLAY"
73 PRINT
74 PRINT TAB(11);"5    10    15    20"
76 PRINT TAB(5);"+-----+-----+-----+-----+"
78 PRINT TAB(5);"!"
```

To give us a heading and scale, we need to change line 170 to print the "!" after the last line of the graph:

```
170 PRINT TAB(5);"!"
```

Finally, we will insert 185:

```
185 PRINT TAB(5);"+-----+----+----+----+"
```

Now the program will look like the following:

```
10 REM ***** PROGRAM NAME: TEXTGR1
20 REM
30 REM ***** TEXT RESOLUTION GRAPHICS DEMO 1
40 REM
50 REM ***** PROGRAM WRITTEN BY EDWARD J. COBURN
60 REM
70 CLS                            ' CLEAR THE SCREEN
72 PRINT TAB(5);"GRADE DISPLAY"
73 PRINT
74 PRINT TAB(11);"5    10    15    20"
76 PRINT TAB(5);"+-----+-----+-----+-----+"
78 PRINT TAB(5);"!"
80 FOR I = 1 TO 5
90     READ A
100    IF A<10 THEN PRINT " ";      ' EXTRA BLANK
110    PRINT A;" ";
120    PRINT "! ";
130    FOR J = 1 TO A
140        PRINT "X";
```

Program continues

Program 15–2

```
150    NEXT J
160    PRINT                      ' FOR CARRIAGE RETURN
170 PRINT TAB(5);"!"
180 NEXT I
185 PRINT TAB(5);"+-----+----+----+----+"
190 END
200 DATA 5,10,4,15,2
RUN
       GRADE DISPLAY

               5    10   15   20
       +-----+----+----+----+
       !
   5   ! XXXXX
       !
  10   ! XXXXXXXXXX
       !
   4   ! XXXX
       !
  15   ! XXXXXXXXXXXXXXX
       !
   2   ! XX
       !
       +-----+----+----+----+
```

Program 15–2 (cont.)

The problem with this display is that it is not the usual method for displaying such a graph. Most bar graphs are vertical rather than horizontal. If we were to change our vertical graph to a horizontal one, it might look like the following:

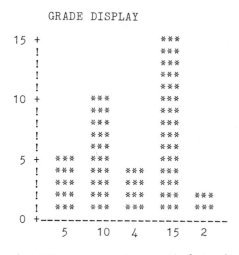

```
       GRADE DISPLAY

  15 +                   ***
     !                   ***
     !                   ***
     !                   ***
     !                   ***
  10 +         ***        ***
     !         ***        ***
     !         ***        ***
     !         ***        ***
     !         ***        ***
   5 +  ***    ***        ***
     !  ***    ***   ***  ***
     !  ***    ***   ***  ***
     !  ***    ***   ***  ***  ***
     !  ***    ***   ***  ***  ***
   0 +-----------------------------
        5     10     4    15    2
```

A program to create a vertical graph is more complicated than one for a horizontal graph. First of all, to print the data across the screen (or page) we must bring all the numbers into the machine at once. The easiest way to do this is with an array. Next, we need to begin printing the scale numbers down the side (in reverse order) to create the scale, and then compare the position of the scale with the data numbers themselves. If they match, we print the marking (***); if they don't, we print blanks (three here). The pseudocode for this program would look like the following:

Start
Read data items and store them in array.
Print heading.
Initialize counter (J) to 20.
DO-WHILE counter (J) is greater than zero.
  Print counter (J) for scale and marker.
  Initialize counter (I) to 1.
  DO-WHILE counter (I) is less than 6.
    Print "***" or blanks.
    Increase counter (I) by 1.
  END-DO
  Print blank lines.
  Decrease counter (J) by 1.
END-DO
Print graph bottom and numbers.
End

The flowchart can be seen in Figure 15–1; the program should begin by reading in the array values (we will continue to use the same values). (*Note:* You will have to reduce the height of the graph on the Radio Shack Model III since it will not fit as it is on the screen.)

```
NEW
10 REM ***** PROGRAM NAME: TEXTGR2
20 REM
30 REM ***** TEXT RESOLUTION GRAPHICS DEMO 2
40 REM
50 REM ***** PROGRAM WRITTEN BY EDWARD J. COBURN
60 REM
65 CLS                              ' CLEAR THE SCREEN
70 FOR I = 1 TO 5
80     READ A(I)
90 NEXT I
100 PRINT TAB(7);"GRADE DISPLAY"
110 PRINT                           ' BLANK LINE
120 FOR J = 15 TO 1 STEP -1         ' SCALE LOOP
130     IF J<10 THEN PRINT " ";     ' EXTRA BLANK
140     PRINT J;                    ' PRINT NUMBER
150     IF J/5=INT(J/5) THEN PRINT "+"; ELSE PRINT "!";
160     FOR I = 1 TO 5
180         IF A(I)>=J THEN PRINT "  ***"; ELSE PRINT "     ";
190     NEXT I
200     PRINT                       ' CARRIAGE RETURN
210 NEXT J
220 PRINT "  0   +--------------------------"
230 PRINT TAB(7);                   ' MOVE CURSOR TO NUMBER
240 FOR I = 1 TO 5                  ' LOOP TO PRINT NUMBERS
250     PRINT A(I);" ";
260     IF A(I)<10 THEN PRINT " "; ' EXTRA BLANK
270 NEXT I
280 PRINT                           ' CARRIAGE RETURN
290 END
300 DATA 5,10,4,15,2
```

Program 15–3

Notice on lines 130 and 260 that an extra blank is printed to keep the display in line. (A PRINT USING or edit routine could have been used instead.) The

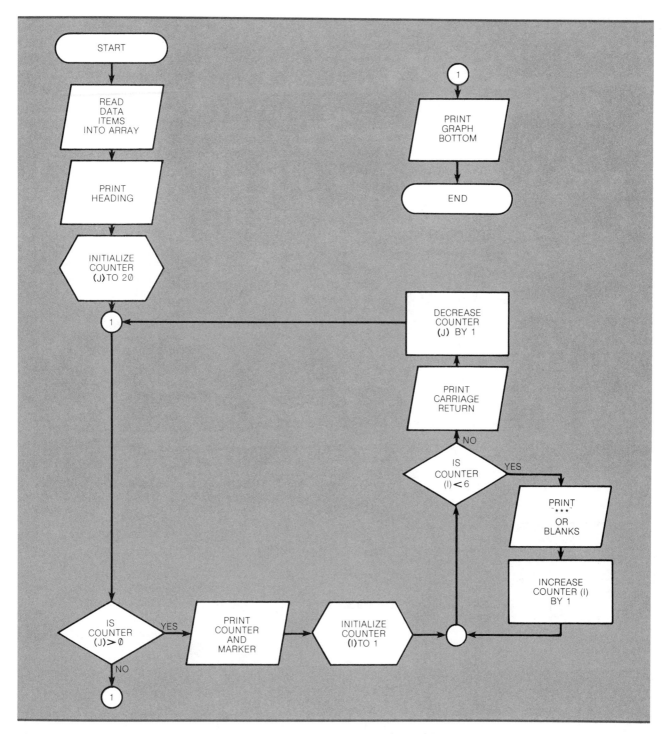

Figure 15–1
Flowchart of vertical graph.

loop from line 120 through 210 creates the display by counting down from 15 to 1; the comparison loop beginning on 160 prints the marks or blanks, depending on the value of A(I).

15–3
LOW RESOLUTION GRAPHICS

Low resolution graphics is able to access a group of pixels smaller than that used in text resolution; that is, the text character is broken up into smaller segments. Each of our machines handles low resolution graphics differently and will be discussed separately. (We will discuss low resolution graphics on the IBM in a later section.)

Low Resolution Graphics—Radio Shack

Both Radio Shack models break up their text characters into six individually accessible points that we will call **blocks.** This gives the Model III screen 128 blocks (64 * 2, numbered 0 through 127) by 48 (16 * 3, numbered 0 through 47), and the Model 4 screen 160 blocks (80 * 2) by 72 (24 * 3). Each of these individual blocks may be accessed on the Model III; predesigned graphics characters may be printed on either machine. These graphics characters are accessed by using the CHR$ function at 128–191 in the ASCII sequence. The following small program will display these characters:

```
NEW
10 REM ***** PROGRAM NAME: CHRDSPLY
20 REM
30 CLS
40 FOR I = 128 TO 191
50     PRINT CHR$(I);"   ";
60 NEXT I
70 END
```
Program 15–4

There are also other predefined characters that may be used to display special effects on the screen. Appendix G shows all characters and their corresponding ASCII code. (Predefined characters are also available on the IBM and Apple.)

The predefined blocks may be combined into graphic displays by printing the characters next to each other. For example, the following program will display a small tic-tac-toe board as shown in Figure 15–2:

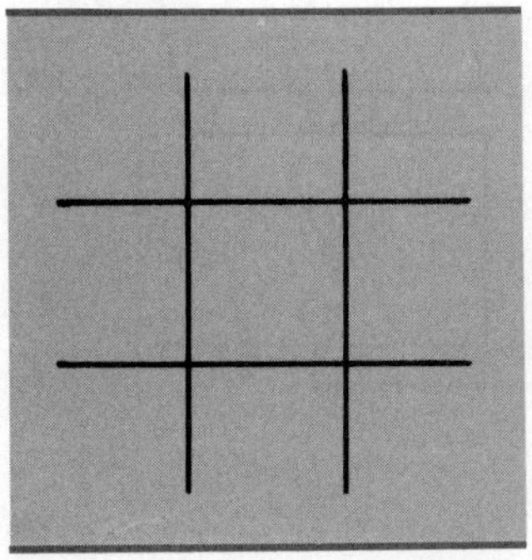

Figure 15–2
Low resolution tic-tac-toe display.

```
NEW
10 REM ***** PROGRAM NAME: TICTAC1
20 REM
30 CLS
40 PRINT "   ";CHR$(191);"   ";CHR$(191)
50 PRINT CHR$(140);CHR$(140);CHR$(140);
        CHR$(191);CHR$(140);CHR$(140);CHR$(140);CHR$(191);
        CHR$(140);CHR$(140);CHR$(140)
60 PRINT "   ";CHR$(191);"   ";CHR$(191)
70 PRINT CHR$(140);CHR$(140);CHR$(140);
        CHR$(191);CHR$(140);CHR$(140);CHR$(140);CHR$(191)
        CHR$(140);CHR$(140);CHR$(140)
80 PRINT "   ";CHR$(191);"   ";CHR$(191)
90 END
```
Program 15–5

We can do this same display on the Model III by turning on the particular pixel groups that need to be displayed. This is done by using the **SET (R,C)** command. (This command is not available on the Model 4.) The R and C refer to the row (0–127) and column (0–47). If you use a number outside these ranges, you will get an error. To display the same tic-tac-toe display would require a program like this:

```
NEW
10 REM ***** PROGRAM NAME: TICTAC2
20 REM
24 CLS
28 PRINT @(900),                 ' MOVE CURSOR OUT OF WAY
30 READ R,C
40 IF R=0 THEN 70                ' END OF DATA MARKER
50 SET (R,C)
60 GOTO 30                       ' LOOP
70 END
80 DATA 1,7,1,8,1,15,1,16
90 DATA 2,7,2,8,2,15,2,16
100 DATA 3,7,3,8,3,15,3,16
110 DATA 4,7,4,8,4,15,4,16
120 DATA 5,1,5,2,5,3,5,4,5,5,5,6,5,7,5,8,5,9,5,10,5,11,5,12
130 DATA 5,13,5,14,5,15,5,16,5,17,5,18,5,19,5,20,5,21,5,22
140 DATA 6,7,6,8,6,15,6,16
150 DATA 7,7,7,8,7,15,7,16
160 DATA 8,7,8,8,8,15,8,16
170 DATA 9,7,9,8,9,15,9,16
180 DATA 10,7,10,8,10,15,10,16
190 DATA 11,1,11,2,11,3,11,4,11,5,11,6,11,7,11,8,11,9
200 DATA 11,10,11,11,11,12,11,13,11,14,11,15,11,16
210 DATA 11,17,11,18,11,19,11,20,11,21,11,22
220 DATA 12,7,12,8,12,15,12,16
230 DATA 13,7,13,8,13,15,13,16
240 DATA 14,7,14,8,14,15,14,16
250 DATA 15,7,15,8,15,15,15,16
```

Program 15–6

Obviously, it's much easier to do it the other way. But this command gives us the flexibility to turn small blocks on and off when we need to. Speaking of "off," there's a command to do that also. If you have a graphics block that you want turned off, you simply use the **RESET(R,C)** command. There is a third command that allows the program to determine if a block is on or off. The **POINT(R,C)** command will give a value of 1 if the block is on and 0 if it is off. For example, let's change the following line in our program:

```
70 A=POINT(1,7)
```

The value of A would be 1 since (1,7) is a point we turned on with the program.

Program 15–6 can be done in a much simpler fashion since it is balanced around a central point. We merely need to determine the row and column pattern and then turn them on in one or more loops. This change is left as an exercise for the student.

This type of graphics can be used to draw circles, lines, charts, etc., simply by designating where the block should be turned on. Suppose we have a series of grades (which we have sorted into numerical sequence from 70 to 100) and we wish to plot them to observe the distribution. Figure 15–3 shows what the graph should look like; the program would look like the following:

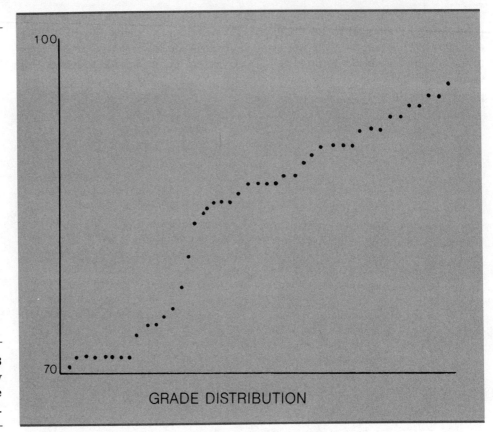

Figure 15–3
Radio Shack low
resolution grade
distribution.

```
NEW
10 REM ***** PROGRAM NAME: GRDIST
20 REM
30 REM ***** GRADE DISTRIBUTIONS
40 REM
50 REM ***** WRITTEN BY EDWARD J. COBURN
60 REM
70 CLS                         ' CLEAR THE SCREEN
80 PRINT "100";@(640),"70"     ' SCALE MARKERS
90 FOR I = 0 TO 31             ' SCALE WALL
100    SET (10,I)              ' SET THE BLOCK
110 NEXT I
120 FOR I = 11 TO 100          ' GRAPH BOTTOM
130    SET (I,31)              ' SET THE BLOCK
140 NEXT I
150 FOR I = 13 TO 99 STEP 2    ' PUT EMPTY BLOCK BETWEEN
160    READ A                  ' GET GRADE
170    B=100 - A               ' REVERSE FOR SCALE
180    SET (I,B)
190 NEXT I
200 PRINT TAB(10);"GRADE DISTRIBUTION"
210 END
220 DATA 71,72,72,72,72,72,72,72,74,75,75,76,77,79
230 DATA 82,85,86,87,88,88,88,89,90,90,90,90,91,91
240 DATA 92,93,94,94,94,94,95,95,95,96,96,97,97,98,98,99
```

Program 15–7

Notice that first we draw the outside of the graph, then read the grades from the DATA statements and plot them. Line 170 is necessary to reverse the grades, since on the machine the low numbers are at the top, not the bottom. The statement reverses the grade by subtracting it from 100 to come up with its distance from the highest possible grade. For example, if the grade is 75, the point is plotted at 25, near the bottom, while if the grade is 99, the plot is at 1, near the top.

Such a graph system could be used to plot the ups and downs of a stock purchase, the amount of products sold over a period of time, or a vast array of other numeric quantities.

Low Resolution Graphics—Apple

On the Apple, the regular screen of 40 by 24 is doubled to 40 by 48 in low resolution graphics. We will refer to each of these positions as a **block.** The bottom four lines of the screen are reserved for regular text, however, so the available area is 40 by 40. This is a nice feature that allows you to write text on the bottom of your graphics. Otherwise, you would have to design your own graphics characters to be displayed. Low resolution mode is turned on with the **GR** command.

Color is also available on those computers with a color monitor (or color TV). In low resolution, sixteen colors are available and are turned on by using the **COLOR** command. The form of the command is:

```
10 COLOR=color number
```

The color numbers are:

0 black	4 dark green	8 brown	12 green
1 magenta	5 gray 1	9 orange	13 yellow
2 dark blue	6 medium blue	10 gray 2	14 aqua
3 purple	7 light blue	11 pink	15 white

Each of the 1600 blocks is addressable individually with the **PLOT** command. The form of the command is:

```
100 PLOT C,R
```

Notice that the row and column designation (R,C) we were using before is now turned around. This is because graphing on the Apple is done on a coordinate system in which the vertical position is considered first.

Let's experiment a bit with the PLOT and COLOR commands. (Remember, color is useful only with color monitors.) We will write a short program to display the 15 colors (black is left as the background color) using the PLOT command. The program will look like the following:

```
NEW
10 REM ***** PROGRAM NAME: GRAPH1
20 REM
30 GR                       : REM TURNS ON LOW RES. GRAPHICS
40 FOR I = 1 TO 15
50    COLOR=I               : REM GIVES 1 - 15 COLOR
```

Program continues   Program 15–8

```
60      FOR J = 0 TO 39   : REM PLOTS AVAILABLE AREA
70          PLOT I*2-1,J
80          PLOT I*2,J
90      NEXT J
100 NEXT I
120 END
```

Program 15–8 (cont.)

This being an Apple program, the coding will not be indented as shown. It is only listed this way for convenience. Notice that the color is put in the loop on line 50. Then we plot two points side by side to make the color display a bit wider; very colorful, but rather slow. If all we want to do is draw lines, Applesoft has a better way to do it. **HLIN** will draw a horizontal line, and **VLIN** will draw a vertical line. The forms of the commands are:

```
100 HLIN column 1,column 2 AT row
```

and

```
110 VLIN row 1,row 2 AT column
```

The HLIN draws a line from column 1 in a row to column 2 in the same row. The VLIN draws a line from a column in row 1 to the same column in row 2. As an example of how to use these commands, let's add another small loop to our previous program:

```
120 FOR I = 1 TO 15
130     COLOR=I         : REM SETS THE COLOR
140     HLIN 1,30 AT I*2 : REM DRAWS LINE OVER DISPLAY
150 NEXT I
160 END
```

When we execute this program, we will get the same display as before (without the loop) except now new lines overlay the old lines to form a cross-hatch effect. Notice, though, how much more quickly the horizontal lines are drawn as opposed to the lines we plotted. When lines are needed, the HLIN and VLIN functions are much faster.

Now let's experiment a bit with creating graphs in the low resolution mode. Suppose we have a series of grades (listed in numerical sequence from 70–100) that we want to plot to see how they're distributed. Figure 15–4 shows how such a graph might look; the following program will create the display:

```
NEW
10 REM ***** PROGRAM NAME: GRDIST
20 REM
30 REM ***** GRADE DISTRIBUTIONS
40 REM
50 REM ***** WRITTEN BY EDWARD J. COBURN
60 REM
70 HOME                      : REM CLEAR THE SCREEN
80 GR                        : REM TURN ON GRAPHICS
85 COLOR=2                   : REM DARK BLUE
90 VLIN 1,31 AT 1            : REM SCALE WALL
100 HLIN 1,39 AT 31          : REM GRAPH BOTTOM
110 FOR I = 3 TO 39 STEP 2   : REM PUT EMPTY BLOCK BETWEEN
120     READ A               : REM GET GRADE
130     B=100 - A            : REM REVERSE FOR SCALE
140     PLOT (I,B)
```

Program continues

Program 15–9

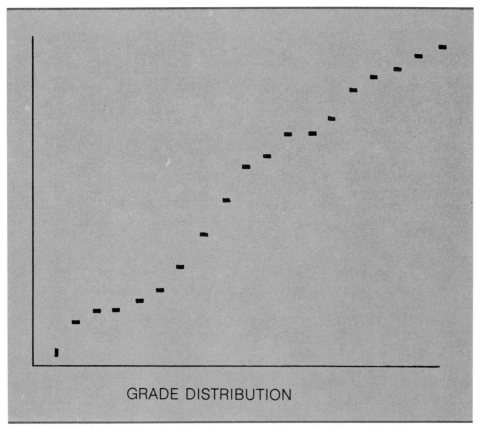

GRADE DISTRIBUTION

Figure 15–4
Apple low resolution
grade distribution.

```
150 NEXT I
160 PRINT TAB(10);"GRADE DISTRIBUTION"
170 END
180 DATA 71,74,75,75,76,77,79
190 DATA 82,85,88,89,91,91
200 DATA 92,95,96,97,98,99
```

Program 15–9 (cont.)

Notice that first we draw the outside of the graph, then read the grades from
the DATA statements and plot them. Line 170 is necessary to reverse the grades
since on the machine the low numbers are at the top, not the bottom. The
statement reverses the grade by subtracting it from 100 to come up with its
distance from the highest possible grade. For example, if the grade is 75, the
point is plotted at 25, near the bottom, while if the grade is 99, the plot is at 1,
near the top.

Such a graph system could be used to plot the ups and downs of a stock
purchase, the amount of products sold over a period of time, or a vast array of
other numeric quantities.

Before moving to low resolution graphics on the IBM, we will discuss briefly
high resolution graphics. (The reason for this will become obvious when you
read about the IBM graphics.) **High resolution** graphics is able to access each

15–4
HIGH RESOLUTION GRAPHICS

displayed pixel individually. Though generally thought of for games and other recreational activities, high resolution can be useful for creating graphics displays for many uses. We will look at a couple of these uses in the following two sections. (The Radio Shack will not be discussed since it does not have high resolution graphics without the use of a special attachment.)

Low and High Resolution Graphics—IBM

To use graphics (either low or high resolution) on the IBM, you need to use a color/graphics adapter card. The remaining discussions in this chapter apply only to computers that are so equipped.

On the IBM, the regular screen of 40 by 24 increases to 320 (numbered 0 to 319) by 200 (numbered 0 to 199) in low resolution graphics. We will refer to each of the accessible graphic positions as a **block.** To use lines 192–199, you must use the command **KEY OFF** to turn off the 25th line display. In high resolution graphics, the 80 by 24 screen is converted in the same manner to 640 by 200. That dimension is the only difference on the IBM between low and high resolution, except for the display of colors. In low resolution, four colors may be displayed on the screen simultaneously, but high resolution is strictly black and white. Text and graphics can be mixed on the IBM. This is an extremely powerful feature! The cursor is positioned using the LOCATE function, then the text characters are printed as usual.

The low resolution mode is turned on with the **SCREEN 1** command, and high resolution is turned on with **SCREEN 2.** The rest of our IBM discussion will focus on the use of low resolution graphics, since there are few differences between the two modes.

Color is available on those computers with a color monitor (or color TV). Basically eight colors are available, in two groups of four, and are turned on with a **COLOR** command. The form of the command *in text mode* is:

```
10 COLOR foreground,background,border
```

The three different color sets on the IBM in text mode are, as you can see from the COLOR statement, the foreground, background, and border. The border is displayed around the edge of the screen. The background is the rest of the screen, with the foreground being the characters (or graphics) displayed on the background (Figure 15–5). The color numbers to designate these sets are:

0	black	4	red
1	blue	5	magenta
2	green	6	gold (brown)
3	cyan	7	white (gray)

When working *in graphics mode*, the color command changes to:

```
10 COLOR background and border color,foreground palette
```

Notice that the background and border colors will be the same. Also notice that the foreground is specified second and is a **palette,** not a color. In low resolution, the colors are grouped into two different palettes numbered 0 and 1. Each palette contains three different colors and the background color. The palettes are specified as:

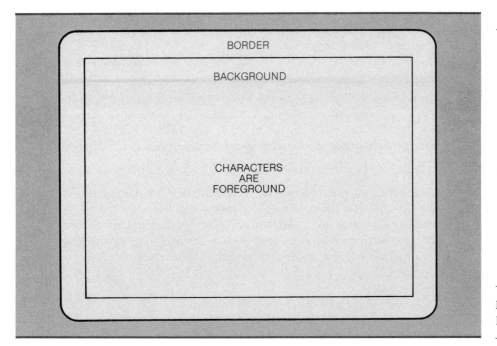

Figure 15–5
IBM screen color sets.

Palette	Color 0	Color 1	Color 2	Color 3
0	background	green	red	gold
1	background	cyan	magenta	white

For example, if we specify the color as COLOR 4,0, the background (and border) color would be red, and the foreground characters could be either red, cyan, magenta, or white. The particular foreground color is specified on the display commands.

Each of the 64,000 blocks is addressable individually with the **PSET** command. The form of the command is:

```
100 PSET (C,R),color
```

Notice that the row and column designation (R,C) we used earlier is now turned around. This is because IBM graphing is done on a coordinate system in which the vertical position is considered first. Also, the color is specified on the statement; the block that is plotted will be in the designated color.

Let's experiment a bit with the PSET and COLOR commands. (Remember, color is useful only with color monitors.) We will write a short program to display the three colors (besides the background color) using the PSET command. The program will look like the following:

```
NEW
10 REM ***** PROGRAM NAME: GRAPH1
20 REM
30 CLS                   ' CLEAR THE SCREEN
40 SCREEN 1              ' TURNS ON LOW RES. GRAPHICS
50 COLOR 0,0             ' BACKGROUND=BLACK, PALETTE 0
60 FOR I = 0 TO 200      ' PLOTS AREA
```

Program continues   **Program 15–10**

```
70     PSET (35,I),1        ' COLOR 1
80     PSET (40,I),2        ' COLOR 2
90     PSET (45,I),3        ' COLOR 3
100 NEXT I
120 END
```
Program 15–10 (cont.)

Notice that the loop merely moves the plot down the screen creating three lines, each a different color; colorful, but rather slow. If all we want to do is draw lines, the IBM has a better way to do it. The **LINE** command will draw a straight line, an empty box, or a solid color box. The form of the command is:

```
100 LINE (C,R)-(C,R),color
```

This indicates the two points between which the line will be drawn. The color at the end specifies the color of the line (using the available palette colors). If we want to draw several lines, we simply connect the end points to make an enclosed figure, such as a box or other regular (or irregular) figure. The following simple program will create an octagon (eight sides) (Figure 15–6):

```
NEW
10 REM ***** PROGRAM NAME: GRAPH2
20 REM
30 CLS                          ' CLEAR THE SCREEN
40 SCREEN 1                     ' TURNS ON LOW RES.
50 COLOR 0,0                    ' BACKGROUND BLACK-PALETTE 0
60 LINE (20,10)-(30,10),1       ' TOP LINE, GREEN
70 LINE (30,10)-(40,20),2       ' DIAGONAL, RED
80 LINE (40,20)-(40,30),1       ' RIGHT SIDE, GREEN
90 LINE (40,30)-(30,40),2       ' DIAGONAL, RED
100 LINE (30,40)-(20,40),1      ' BOTTOM LINE, GREEN
110 LINE (20,40)-(10,30),2      ' DIAGONAL, RED
120 LINE (10,30)-(10,20),1      ' LEFT SIDE, GREEN
130 LINE (10,20)-(20,10),2      ' DIAGONAL, RED
140 END
```
Program 15–11

Notice that the horizontal and vertical lines are green, and the diagonal lines are red. We could have constructed our program a bit more easily with the LINE command, using the last point specified as the beginning point on the command. Thus, line 70 could have been specified as:

```
70 LINE -(40,20),2              ' DIAGONAL, RED
```

And the rest of the program could have been done in a similar fashion.

If we wish to use the LINE command to construct a box, we merely add another specification to the LINE command. For example, the following command would draw a box on the screen in either red or magenta, depending on the palette:

```
10 LINE (10,20)-(50,70),2,B
```

Notice the B on the end. That tells the computer to make a box with one corner at (10,20) and the diagonally opposite corner at (50,70). This will be a simple outline box; if we want a solid box, all we need to do is add an F after the B:

```
10 LINE (10,20)-(50,70),2,BF
```

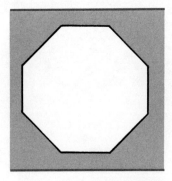

Figure 15–6
Octagon in IBM graphics.

The IBM computer graphics mode is powerful, with additional commands for drawing circles, arcs, and ellipses, and even a paint command to fill any outlined area with a specified color. We will not use any of these additional commands. If you wish to experiment with them, it is suggested that you get a book on IBM graphics; these commands can get complicated and are beyond the scope of this text.

Now let's experiment a bit with the graphics mode. Suppose we have a series of grades (we will generate them randomly from 1–99) that we want to plot to see how they're distributed. We will connect the points to make the graph more attractive. Figure 15–7 shows such a graph; the following program

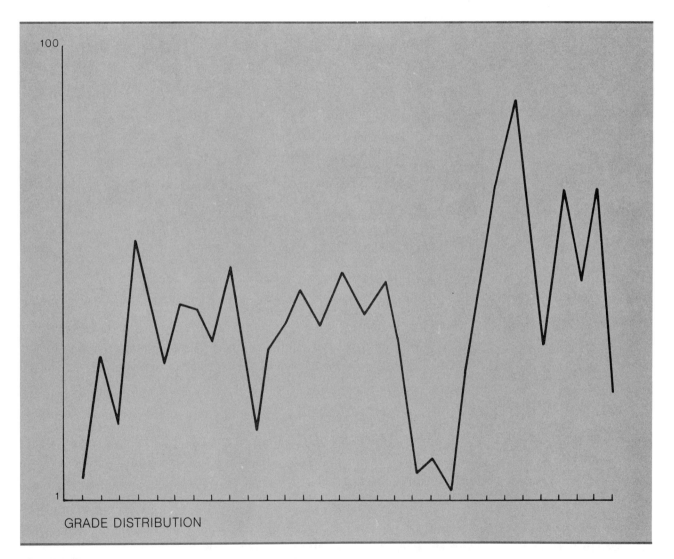

Figure 15–7
IBM high resolution graphics display.

will create the display (keep in mind that your graph will look a bit different since we are doing it randomly):

```
NEW
10 REM ***** PROGRAM NAME: GRGRPH
20 REM
30 REM ***** GRADE DISTRIBUTIONS GRAPH
40 REM
50 REM ***** WRITTEN BY EDWARD J. COBURN
60 REM
70 CLS                        ' CLEAR THE SCREEN
80 SCREEN 1                   ' TURN ON GRAPHICS
90 COLOR 0,0                  ' BACKGROUND BLACK, PALETTE 0
100 PRINT "100"               ' SCALE MARKER
110 LOCATE 14,1               ' MOVE THE CURSOR
120 PRINT "  1"               ' SCALE MARKER
130 LINE (26,1)-(26,110),2    ' GRAPH WALL
140 LINE (26,110)-(310,110),2 ' GRAPH BOTTOM
150 RANDOMIZE VAL(RIGHT$(TIME$,2))
160 B=100
170 FOR I = 36 TO 305 STEP 10 ' PUT EMPTY SPACE BETWEEN
180     A=INT(RND*99)+1        ' GET RANDOM GRADE
190     A=100 - A              ' REVERSE FOR SCALE
200     LINE (I-10),B-(I,A),3  ' PLOT LINE
210     B=A                    ' SAVE LAST POINT
220 NEXT I
230 LOCATE 16,10              ' POSITION FOR MESSAGE
240 PRINT "GRADE DISTRIBUTION"
250 END
```
Program 15–12

Notice the RANDOMIZE statement in line 150. Without this line, we would get the same display every time we ran the program. Line 180 gets the number, and line 190 is necessary to reverse the grade since on the machine the low numbers are at the top, not the bottom. The statement reverses the grade by subtracting it from 100 to come up with its distance from the highest possible grade. For example, if the grade is 10, the point is plotted at 90, near the bottom, while if the grade is 99, the plot is at 1, near the top.

Also notice how we save in the variable B (line 210) the previous plotted point so we can draw a line (line 200) from the previous point to the current point. Finally, we print the title of the graph at the bottom.

We can get an interesting effect by adding a single statement. Let's add:

```
195     PSET (I,A-1),1          ' EXTRA POINT
```

This will display a point right above where the lines intersect. It will display it in a different color so it will stand out.

Such a graph system could be used to plot the ups and downs of a stock purchase, the amount of products sold over a period of time, or a vast array of other numeric quantities.

High Resolution Graphics—Apple

In high resolution graphics on the Apple, the screen changes into a grid of 280-by-160 plotting points, with the bottom four lines left for text display as in low resolution graphics. To turn on the high resolution, we use the command **HGR** instead of the GR command. Then the COLOR and PLOT commands become **HCOLOR** and **HPLOT** to indicate high instead of low resolution. The form of the commands is otherwise the same as we used in low resolution. The colors set by the HCOLOR command vary with the particular TV or monitor used, but basically they are:

0 black 1	4 black 2
1 green (depends)	5 (depends)
2 blue (depends)	6 (depends)
3 white 1	7 white 2

Notice that only eight colors are listed now. The high resolution mode doesn't allow the use of as many colors as does the low resolution mode.

High resolution on the Apple is structured to use shapes and user-designed shape tables. We will not get into shape construction in this text. If you wish to know more about Apple high resolution graphics, it is suggested that you consult a graphics book for the Apple. We will, however, design a small graphing program to show off some of the graphing capabilities of the Apple.

Let's experiment a bit with the high resolution graphics mode. Suppose we have a series of grades (we will generate them randomly from 1–99) that we want to plot to see how they're distributed. We will connect the points to make the graph more attractive. Figure 15–8 shows such a graph; the following program will create the display (keep in mind that your graph will look a bit different since we are doing it randomly):

```
NEW
10 REM ***** PROGRAM NAME: GRGRPH
20 REM
30 REM ***** GRADE DISTRIBUTIONS GRAPH
40 REM
50 REM ***** WRITTEN BY EDWARD J. COBURN
60 REM
70 HGR                          : REM TURN ON GRAPHICS
80 HCOLOR=5                      : REM UNKNOWN COLOR
90 HPLOT 1,1 TO 1,130            : REM GRAPH WALL
100 HPLOT 1,130 TO 279,130       : REM GRAPH BOTTOM
110 B=100
120 FOR I = 14 TO 279 STEP 10    : REM PUT EMPTY SPACE BETWEEN
130     A=INT(RND(1)*99)+1        : REM GET RANDOM GRADE
140     A=100 - A                 : REM REVERSE FOR SCALE
150     HPLOT I-10,B TO I,A       : REM PLOT LINE
160     B=A                       : REM SAVE LAST POINT
170 NEXT
180 PRINT TAB(10);"GRADE DISTRIBUTION"
190 END
```
Program 15–13

Line 130 gets the number, and line 140 is necessary to reverse the grade as we discussed in the low resolution graphing section. Notice that we save the previous plotted point in the variable B (line 160) to draw a line (line 150) from the previous point to the current point. Finally, we print the title of the graph at the bottom.

We can get an interesting effect by adding a single statement. Let's add:

```
145     HCOLOR=7:HPLOT I,A-1:HCOLOR=5
```

This will display a point right above where the lines intersect. It will display it in a different color so it will stand out.

As mentioned before, such a graph system could be used to plot a wide variety of numeric quantities.

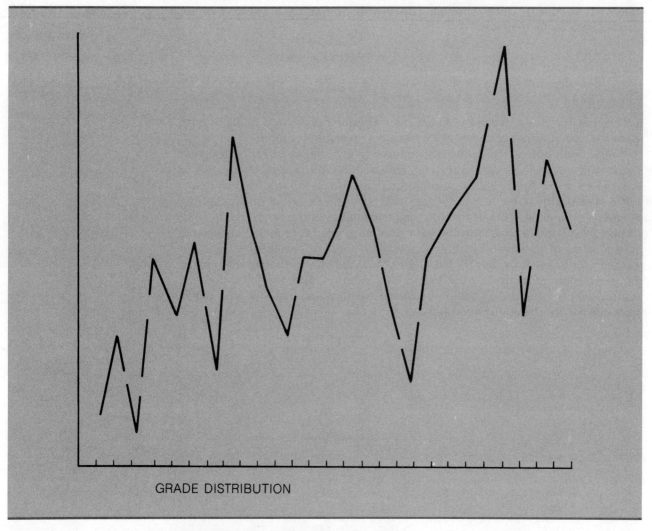

GRADE DISTRIBUTION

Figure 15–8
Apple high resolution graphics display.

SUMMARY

1. Formatting screens and reports helps the user gather information from the reports more easily. Sometimes, however, a graphic display will yield at a glance all the information that is necessary.
2. There are three different types of graphic resolution: text, low, and high. The resolution is based on the number of individual points that are accessible to the user. These points are called *pixels*.
3. Text resolution allows the programmer to access only entire characters or

character areas. This type of resolution can be used to draw bar charts and other types of displays that do not require a great deal of resolution.

4. Low resolution allows access to groups of pixels called blocks. This allows finer resolution for better graphic displays. The Radio Shack has well-defined low resolution blocks. The Apple can use sixteen colors in its low resolution mode.

5. High resolution allows the programmer to access directly each individual pixel on the screen for much more precisely constructed graphics. The IBM low resolution and high resolution modes are virtually identical, but the Apple high resolution differs a great deal from its low resolution. The Radio Shack does not have high resolution without the use of a special attachment.

GLOSSARY

Block   A group of pixels plotted in low resolution.

COLOR   The command in IBM and Apple BASIC to set the color to be displayed. Used on the Apple in the low resolution mode.

GR   The command in Apple BASIC to turn on the low resolution graphics mode.

HCOLOR   The Apple high resolution command to set the color to be displayed.

HGR   The Apple command to turn on high resolution graphics.

High resolution   The graphics mode that allows the programmer to access each pixel on the screen individually. Only the Apple and IBM have high resolution graphics without a special attachment.

HLIN   The Apple low resolution command for drawing a horizontal line.

HPLOT   The Apple high resolution command to plot a point on the screen.

KEY OFF   The IBM command to turn off the 25th line display so that it can be used for graphics display.

LINE   The IBM command to draw a line in low and high resolution graphics.

Low resolution   The graphics mode that allows groups of pixels called blocks to be accessed and plotted.

Palette   A group of colors that are used on the plotting commands in IBM low resolution graphics to designate the color of the displayed points.

Picture element   *See* **pixel.**

Pixel   A single point on the display screen.

PLOT   The Apple low resolution command to turn on a graphics block.

POINT(R,C)   The Radio Shack low resolution command to determine if a block is turned on or off.

PSET   The IBM graphics command to turn on a pixel.

RESET(R,C)   The Radio Shack command to turn off a plotted block.

Resolution   The amount of display area accessible to the programmer as a single display point.

SCREEN   The IBM command to turn on graphics. SCREEN 1 turns on low resolution graphics; SCREEN 2 turns on high resolution graphics.

SET(R,C)   The Radio Shack command to plot a block.

Text resolution   The graphics mode that allows access of only the full character areas.

VLIN   The Apple low resolution graphics command to draw a vertical line.

1. Define resolution, and explain its three different modes.
*2. Define pixel.
3. Explain how low resolution and high resolution (if your machine has it) are used on your computer.
4. Construct a horizontal bar chart (text resolution) to represent the following results of a survey on people's views of the way the country is being run. Label the chart with the abbreviation listed and use a scale to indicate range.

Totally dissatisfied	10%	TD
Dissatisfied	25%	D
Moderately satisfied	30%	MS
Satisfied	20%	S
Totally satisfied	5%	TS
No opinion	10%	NO

*5. Use the above information to create a vertical bar chart.
6. Return to Chapter 8 and use the programs in question 10 that created two files of 30 random numbers. Read the numbers in, compare them, and create a graph (only the point should be displayed on the graph) that plots the difference between the two points. (If you are using an Apple or IBM, you may wish to increase the number of points and plot them in high resolution.)
7. Return to Chapter 8 again to use the file created in question 7 to store student information and grades. Write a program to input the student records and graph their grades.
8. Use the same file discussed in question 7 and write a program to read the records in and total the number of grades in each letter grade category:

A = 90 and up
B = 80 to 89
C = 70 to 79
D = 60 to 69
F = less than 60

Finally, plot the distribution of the grades, labeling the graph appropriately.

QUICK QUIZ

The answers to the questions follow immediately after the quiz. Questions 1–15 are true–false, while 16–20 are multiple choice. (Some of these questions are machine specific.)

T F   1. Creating graphics is important because many times it is easier to glean information from an illustration than from a simple list of numbers.

2. A pixel refers to an individual picture element. **T F**

3. In text resolution, the programmer can address small groups of pixels called blocks. **T F**

4. In text resolution, the IBM has the most number of accessible positions. **T F**

5. We use vertical graphs because they are easier to construct than horizontal graphs. **T F**

6. All our machines use high resolution graphics. **T F**

7. An individual pixel is accessed in high resolution graphics. **T F**

8. The plotting functions in our versions use (column, row) instead of (row, column) as in the cursor positioning commands. **T F**

9. Color can only be used on the Radio Shack. **T F**

10. High resolution graphics cannot be done on the Radio Shack. **T F**

11. The COLOR command is used in both high and low resolution modes on the Apple. **T F**

12. The COLOR command on the IBM is the same in both the text and resolution modes. **T F**

13. Both the IBM and the Apple use different commands to access high and low resolution. **T F**

14. The Radio Shack is the only computer with predefined shapes that can be accessed in text mode. **T F**

15. The high resolution modes are more difficult to use but can be rewarding because of the much greater resolution available to the programmer. **T F**

16. The Apple uses which of the following commands to gain access to low resolution? _____
   - **a.** GR
   - **b.** HGR
   - **c.** SCREEN
   - **d.** none of the above

17. Which of the following computers does not use color? _____
   - **a.** Radio Shack
   - **b.** IBM
   - **c.** Apple
   - **d.** all three do

18. Which of the following commands is the graphics position command for the Apple? _____
   - **a.** SET
   - **b.** PSET
   - **c.** POINT
   - **d.** PLOT

19. Which command gives access to the high resolution mode on the IBM? _____
   - **a.** HGR
   - **b.** GR
   - **c.** SCREEN 1
   - **d.** none of the above

20. Which computer has access to the most pixels? _____
   - **a.** IBM
   - **b.** Apple
   - **c.** Radio Shack
   - **d.** All are the same

1. T
2. T
3. F (Block access is in low resolution.)
4. T (When the IBM is in the 80-column mode; the Radio Shack Model 4 has the same number when it is in the 80-column mode.)
5. F (We use vertical graphs because they are more commonly seen. They are actually more difficult to construct.)
6. F (Only the Apple and IBM.)
7. T
8. T (This is because they are using a coordinate system.)
9. F (Only on the Apple and IBM.)
10. T
11. F (HCOLOR is used for high resolution.)
12. F (There is a great deal of difference.)
13. T
14. F (The IBM and Apple also have predefined shapes.)
15. T
16. a
17. a
18. d
19. d (It is SCREEN 2.)
20. a

PROGRAMMING AIDS AND COMMANDS

There are several functions and commands built into the machines to make the programming task easier. This appendix explains many of these commands for each of the machines.

If you make an error when keying in a BASIC program, there are two things you can do. For one, you can rekey the line from the beginning. This will work, but it's time consuming, especially when the line is long. The other option is to use the *line editor* to modify the line that is already in the computer.

The IBM line editor's many commands are summarized below (many of the commands listed are actually keys you press to cause the particular function):

EDIT line number—the command to start the edit process.

↑ moves the cursor up one line.

↓ moves the cursor down one line.

→ moves the cursor right one character.

← moves the cursor left one character.

Ctrl/→ moves the cursor right one "word." A "word" is a character or group of characters that begins with a letter or a number and ends with a space, period, or comma.

Ctrl/← moves the cursor left one word.

Home—moves the cursor to the upper left-hand corner of the screen.

End—moves the cursor to the end of the program line.

→| moves the cursor to the next tab stop (tab stops are preset at every eight spaces).

Esc—erase the program line from the screen.

← —delete the last character that was keyed.

Ins—switch into or out of insert mode.

Ctrl/Home—clear screen and move cursor to upper left corner.

↵ —make changes to current program line permanent.

Now let's look at how to use these commands. Key in the instructions as we go along.

To begin with, key in the following line:

```
10 PRINT "GEORGE WASHINGTON IS DEAD."
```

Suppose you want to change this line. To begin the edit process you first need to enter EDIT 10. This will put the machine in edit mode, display the line number on the screen, and place the cursor on the program line where the 1 is, as follows:

<u>1</u>0 PRINT "GEORGE WASHINGTON IS DEAD."

Now suppose you want to change the name GEORGE to FRED. To do this you need to use several of the editor commands. To move the cursor over, you can simply press the right directional arrow; for example, if you press it five times, you will see:

10 PRI<u>N</u>T "GEORGE WASHINGTON IS DEAD."

Or you can press Ctrl and the right directional arrow twice to move the cursor to the end of the word PRINT (including the space after PRINT). For example, to change GEORGE you need to move to the G; press Ctrl/→ twice and then → once to get:

10 PRINT "<u>G</u>EORGE WASHINGTON IS DEAD."

Now the cursor is on the G in GEORGE. You can change the first four characters of GEORGE to FRED simply by keying them in. Now your display should look like the following:

10 PRINT "FRED<u>G</u>E WASHINGTON IS DEAD."

Of course, FREDGE has too many letters. You need to drop two letters to have FRED WASHINGTON. To do this, press the Del key twice. After this you should see:

10 PRINT "FRED WASHINGTON IS DEAD."

The final command we will discuss is the insert. The cursor should now be on the space in front of the W. Suppose you want to insert a middle initial of P. You can do this by pressing Ins to put the machine in insert mode and then keying in whatever information you need inserted. In this example, key in P. with a blank in front of the P. When you have inserted all you wish to, you need to signal to the machine that you are finished. You do this by pressing the Ins key again, and your display should be:

10 PRINT "FRED P. WASHINGTON IS DEAD."

There are several other useful options in the IBM editor. Read through the list at the beginning of this section and experiment with any we have not discussed.

The Line Editor— Radio Shack

If you make an error when keying in a BASIC program, there are two things you can do. For one, you can rekey the line from the beginning. This will work, but it's time consuming, especially when the line is long. The other option is to use the *line editor* to modify the line that is already in the computer.

The Radio Shack line editor's many commands are summarized below (many of the commands listed are actually keys you press to cause the particular function):

EDIT line number—the command to start the edit process.
A—cancels the changes and starts the edit again.
number C—changes the specified number of characters.
number D—deletes the specified number of characters.

E—ends the editing and saves all the changes.

H—hacks off the line and puts the machine in insert mode at the end of the line.

I—puts the machine in the insert mode.

number K character—kills (deletes) all the characters up to the specified number of occurrences of the specified character.

L—lists the line.

Q—quits the edit mode and cancels all changes.

number S character—searches the line for the specified occurrence of the specified character.

X—extends the line (passes the cursor to the end) and puts the machine in insert mode.

SHIFT UP-ARROW—causes escape from whatever command you are functioning under.

RETURN—records all changes and exits edit mode.

number SPACEBAR—moves the cursor the specified number of spaces to the right.

number LEFT-ARROW—moves the cursor the specified number of spaces to the left.

Now let's look at how to use these commands. Key in the instructions as we go along.

To begin with, key in the following line:

```
10 PRINT "GEORGE WASHINGTON IS DEAD."
```

Suppose you want to change this line. To begin the edit process, you need to enter EDIT 10. This will put the machine in edit mode, display the line number on the screen, and place the cursor on the program line where the P is, as follows:

```
10 ▌
```

Now suppose you want to change the name GEORGE to FRED. To do this you need to use several of the editor commands. To move the cursor over, you can simply press the space bar; for example, if you press it three times, you will see:

```
10 PRI▌
```

Or you can enter a number and then press the space bar to move the cursor that many characters over. For example, to change GEORGE you need to move over five characters more; press 5 and then the space bar, and you will have:

```
10 PRINT "▌
```

Now the cursor is on the G in GEORGE. You can change the first four characters of GEORGE to FRED by pressing C and then F to change the first character. Then you would need to press C and R to change the next character. This process is rather slow, but instead you can press 3 (we changed the G already) and then C. Now the next three characters that you press will replace the EOR in GEORGE. Press RED for FRED. Now your display should look like the following:

```
10 PRINT "FRED▮
```

Of course, GEORGE has more letters than FRED. You need to drop two letters to have FRED WASHINGTON. To do this, press the D key twice, and you will see !G!!E!. The exclamation points are simply markers to indicate which characters were deleted. You could also press 2 and then D, which would automatically delete two characters; you would then see !GE!.

After you have made a few changes, it is useful to be able to look at what you have done. An easy way to do this is to use L (for list). Press L once, and the rest of the line will list, and your display should look like:

```
10 PRINT "FRED!G!!E! WASHINGTON IS DEAD."
10 ▮
```

Now press L again to relist the line:

```
10 PRINT "FRED!G!!E! WASHINGTON IS DEAD."
10 PRINT "FRED WASHINGTON IS DEAD."
10 ▮
```

Let's use another option called the *search* and search for the W in WASHINGTON. You can do this by pressing S and then W. The cursor will then move out to the first occurrence of W, and your display will be:

```
10 PRINT "FRED ▮
```

If you press a number before the S, the cursor will search for that many characters.

The final command we will discuss is the insert. The cursor should now be on the W. Suppose you want to insert a middle initial of P. You can do this by pressing I to put the machine in insert mode and then keying in whatever information you need inserted. In this example, key in P. with a blank after the period. When you have inserted all you wish to, you need to signal to the machine that you are finished. You do this by pressing SHIFT and the up-arrow at the same time. Now press L twice, and your display should be:

```
10 PRINT "FRED P. WASHINGTON IS DEAD."
10 ▮
```

There are several other useful options in the Radio Shack line editor. The ones we have used will give you a good start. Read through list at the beginning of this section and experiment with any we have not discussed.

Before we leave the line editor discussion, it is interesting to note a couple of helpful commands that are not well documented in the Radio Shack manual. After you have edited a line, you can reedit the same line simply by pressing the period. Also, if you wish to edit the line below the current line, you can press the down-arrow to list it and then the period to edit it. The line above the current one can be listed with the up-arrow.

Error Trapping

When the computer encounters an error in your program, it will stop and tell you so. When you are writing interactive programs, this can be very disruptive. You can alleviate that problem by creating error traps to capture the errors.

Error traps are created with the ON ERROR GOTO statement. The form of the statement is:

Error traps are created with the ON ERROR GOTO statement. The form of the statement is:

```
10 ON ERROR GOTO line number
```

Whenever the program encounters an error, it will automatically branch to the line listed in the command. This statement can be placed anywhere in the program as long as it is before the error you are trying to capture. It will have no effect if the error occurs before the statement is encountered in the program.

If you set up an ON ERROR routine and in another part of the program you do not want the routine to be active, you can turn it off by issuing:

```
1000 ON ERROR GOTO 0
```

Now if an error is encountered, the program will break (stop).

To continue the program after an error routine, you use a RESUME statement after the ON ERROR is activated. Otherwise, the next time an ON ERROR is used it will not function. The RESUME statement is placed at the end of the error routine. If you want the program to retry the statement that created the error, you just use RESUME by itself:

```
1200 RESUME
```

You can direct the program to another location, however, by using a line number on the RESUME:

```
1200 RESUME 100
```

You can also use:

```
1200 RESUME NEXT
```

and the program will branch to the statement following the one where the error occurred.

Two additional commands can be useful when creating error traps. The ERL statement will let you determine the line number where the error occurred. You use PRINT ERL and the computer will display the error line, or you can use the ERL command as part of an IF-THEN-ELSE structure.

If you are constructing an error trap to catch a particular type of error, it is helpful to be able to determine what error has occurred. This is accomplished with the ERR statement on the IBM and the ERR/2 + 1 statement on the Radio Shack. This will give you the code number of the error that occurred. For the meaning of the error codes, see Appendix D.

Free Memory Display

If you wish to determine how much memory is still available for your program, you can PRINT FRE(number) and the computer will display the number of free bytes that are still available. If you use a string variable (or literal) instead of a number, the computer will reorganize string storage. This may help your string processing operate a bit faster.

AUTO Numbering

When you are keying in a program, by using the AUTO command you can have the computer automatically assign the line numbers for you. You specify the beginning line number and the amount of increment between lines. For example, suppose you want the program to begin numbering at line 100 and increment by 20, so that the next line number would be 120, then 140, and so on. You would merely enter:

```
AUTO 100,20
```

and the computer would begin with 100 as the first line number. When you are finished keying a line, simply press RETURN as always. If you wish to drop out of the AUTO mode, press the BREAK key. When you are using the AUTO command, if the computer encounters a line number already in the program, an asterisk will appear beside the number. If you do not want to change the line, press BREAK to drop out of the function.

Renumbering a Program—IBM

When you insert program lines between others, you will occasionally need to renumber the program. In IBM BASIC this can be done with the RENUM command. The form of the command is:

```
RENUM newline, startline, increment
```

The newline specifies the new line number of the first line you want to renumber. If you don't specify this, 10 is used by default. The startline specifies the line number in the original program where renumbering will start. If you omit the startline, the entire program will be renumbered. Finally, the increment specifies the increase between the lines that are renumbered. If this is not specified, 10 is used.

As an example, suppose we have a program with the line numbers 10, 20, 30, 31, 32, 34, 45, 75, 90. Let's use the command:

```
RENUM 40,32,20
```

The line numbers would now be 10, 20, 30, 31, 40, 60, 80, 100, 120. Notice that lines 10 through 31 were left alone since the startline specified 32 as the first line to renumber. Then the new line numbers start with 40 and increment by 20.

Renumbering a Program—Radio Shack

When you insert program lines between others, you will occasionally need to renumber the program. In Radio Shack BASIC this can be done with the NAME command. The form of the command is:

```
NAME newline, startline, increment
```

The newline specifies the new line number of the first line you want to renumber. If you don't specify this, 10 is used by default. The startline specifies the line number in the original program where renumbering will start. If you omit the startline, the entire program will be renumbered. Finally, the increment specifies the increase between the lines that are renumbered. If this is not specified, 10 is used.

As an example, suppose we have a program with the line numbers 10, 20, 30, 31, 32, 34, 45, 75, 90. Let's use the command:

```
NAME 40,32,20
```

The line numbers would now be 10, 20, 30, 31, 40, 60, 80, 100, 120. Notice that lines 10 through 31 were left alone since the startline specified 32 as the first line to renumber. Then the new line numbers start with 40 and increment by 20.

Program Tracing

Another interesting feature that can help debug your programs is the trace. It is turned on with the TRON command. This causes the computer to print the line number of every line it executes. For example, key in this small program:

```
NEW
5 TRON
10 PRINT "THIS IS THE FIRST LINE"
20 INPUT "PRESS RETURN TO START LOOP"
30 PRINT "THIS IS THE FIRST STATEMENT IN THE LOOP"
40 PRINT "ANOTHER STATEMENT"
50 GOTO 30
RUN
[10]THIS IS THE FIRST LINE
[20]PRESS RETURN TO START LOOP?
[30]THIS IS THE FIRST STATEMENT IN THE LOOP
[40]ANOTHER STATEMENT
[50][30]THIS IS THE FIRST STATEMENT IN THE LOOP
[40]ANOTHER STATEMENT
[50][30]THIS IS THE FIRST STATEMENT IN THE LOOP
```

This program will continue to loop as long as you let it run. If you want the trace to stop, enter TROFF either as a command or in the program.

Printing the Screen Display

You can cause the information displayed on the IBM screen to be printed on the printer by pressing the SHIFT and the Prt Sc keys at the same time. If you don't press the SHIFT key, the Prt Sc key will print an asterisk on the display. On the Radio Shack, you cause the information displayed on the screen to be printed on the printer by pressing SHIFT, down-arrow, and asterisk at the same time.

Turning on the Cursor—IBM

On the IBM, the cursor is turned off by the machine when a program is executing. (It is turned back on for an INPUT statement.) If you are using the INKEY$ command and you want the cursor to be displayed, you can use the following command:

```
10 LOCATE ,,1
```

This will leave the cursor where it is (designated by the two commas) and turn the cursor on (designated by the 1). If you are not careful and turn it off when necessary with:

```
100 LOCATE ,,0
```

you can get stray marks on the screen. You should turn it on for the INKEY$ and then off immediately upon the conclusion of the INKEY$ routine.

Turning on the Cursor—Radio Shack

On the Radio Shack, the cursor is turned off by the machine when a program is executing. (It is turned back on for an INPUT statement.) If you are using the INKEY$ command and you want the cursor to be displayed, you can use the following command:

```
10 PRINT CHR$(14);
```

This will turn the cursor on. If you are not careful and turn it off when necessary with:

```
100 PRINT CHR$(15);
```

you can get stray marks on the screen. You should turn it on for the INKEY$ and then off immediately upon the conclusion of the INKEY$ routine.

Changing the Form of the Cursor—IBM

It is occasionally useful to be able to change the form of the cursor. You can do this with the LOCATE command. The shape of the cursor can vary with the standard underline to a full block. The cursor is made up of 14 (0–13) horizontal lines on a monochrome display and 8 (0–7) lines on a color one. Using the LOCATE command you can tell the computer the beginning and ending line number for the height of the cursor. An example would be:

```
10 LOCATE ,,1,0,13
```

This would give you a full block cursor. (The 1 is to turn on the cursor.)

Changing the Form of the Cursor—Radio Shack

It is occasionally useful to be able to change the shape of the cursor. You can do this with the POKE command, which allows you to change the value of any byte in memory. Thus, it can be a very powerful command. Only use the POKE command when you are absolutely certain you know what you are doing. The command to change the cursor is:

```
POKE 16419,ASCII code of what you want
```

If you want the cursor to be a question mark, you can use the command:

```
POKE 16419,63
```

Or for an asterisk:

```
POKE 16419,42
```

If you make an error when keying in a BASIC program, there are two things you **Editing a Line** can do. For one, you can rekey the line from the beginning. This will work, but it's time consuming, especially when the line is long. The other option is to use cursor control to move the cursor to the line and modify it. The few controls for the Apple are very basic but useful.

The first step is to list the line to be modified. Then you move the cursor up to that line by first pressing the ESC key and then D. Both keys must be pressed each time to move the cursor. When you reach the line to edit, you press ESC and B to move the cursor to the left to register the first number of the line number. Only the characters that the cursor moves over will appear on the new line, so you have to make sure you get the entire line number. Then you use the right arrow to move the cursor to where you need to make your changes.

After you have positioned the cursor where it needs to be, you can then begin keying in your changes. There is no method for extending the line to make room for more characters (inserting), but you can delete a character merely by keying in a blank in place of the character.

When the computer encounters an error in your program, it will stop and **Error Trapping** tell you so. When you are writing interactive programs, this can be very disruptive. You can alleviate that problem by creating error traps to capture the errors.

Error traps are created with the ONERR GOTO statement. The form of the statement is:

```
10 ONERR GOTO line number
```

Whenever the program encounters an error, it will automatically branch to the line listed in the command. This statement can be placed anywhere in the program as long as it is before the error you are trying to capture. It has no effect if the error occurs before the statement is encountered in the program.

If you have set up an ONERR routine and in another part of the program you do not want the routine to be active, you can turn it off by issuing:

```
1000 POKE 216,0
```

Now if an error is encountered, the program will break (stop).

To continue the program after an error routine, you use a RESUME statement after the ONERR is activated. The RESUME statement is placed at the end of the error routine. If you want the program to retry the statement that created the error, the form of the statement is simply:

```
1200 RESUME
```

You can use a simple GOTO instead, but if you use a lot of error traps, this can eventually cause problems. You may recall that the PEEK (222) command will tell you what type of error occurred, or at least the code number of the error. For a list of errors and their associated code numbers, see Appendix D.

Free Memory Display   If you wish to determine how much memory is still available for your program, you can PRINT FRE(0) and the computer will display the number of free bytes that are still available.

Renumbering a Program   When you insert program lines between others, you will occasionally need to renumber the program. In Apple BASIC this can be done with the RENUMBER program found on the system disk. This renumber program is rather complicated and is well documented within the program. Therefore, we will not explain it here; it is suggested you execute and study the program instructions.

Program Tracing   Another interesting feature that can help debug your programs is the trace. In the Apple it is turned on with the TRACE command. This causes the computer to print the line number of every line it executes. For example, key in this small program:

```
NEW
5 TRACE
10 PRINT "THIS IS THE FIRST LINE"
20 INPUT "PRESS RETURN TO START LOOP"
30 PRINT "THIS IS THE FIRST STATEMENT IN THE LOOP"
40 PRINT "ANOTHER STATEMENT"
50 GOTO 30
RUN
#10   THIS IS THE FIRST LINE
#20   PRESS RETURN TO START LOOP?
#30   THIS IS THE FIRST STATEMENT IN THE LOOP
#40   ANOTHER STATEMENT
#50   #30   THIS IS THE FIRST STATEMENT IN THE LOOP
#40   ANOTHER STATEMENT
#50   #30   THIS IS THE FIRST STATEMENT IN THE LOOP
```

This program will continue to loop as long as you let it run. If you want the trace to stop, enter NOTRACE either as a command or in the program.

The trace function in the Apple has a few restrictions. If you use the trace when doing disk access, the access does not occur. That is, if you are inputting information from a disk, the machine changes the disk input to a regular input.

COMMAND SUMMARY

This appendix contains a summary of all the commands we have used in this book, along with a few commands we have not used in the book. A special feature is the inclusion of the form of the commands as used on many machines not covered in the text material. This can be helpful for program conversions from one machine to another.

This appendix is by no means exhaustive. There are many other commands that are not listed for one reason or another. For complete command coverage, check the user's manual for your particular machine.

The seven machines that are covered in the text are:

1. IBM P.C.
2. Radio Shack Model III
3. Radio Shack Model 4 (occasional differences)
4. Apple II
5. Apple II +
6. Apple IIe
7. Apple IIc

In addition, commands for the following machines are included in this Appendix:

8. Timex Sinclair 1000 and 2000
9. Atari series (400,800,600XL,800XL,1200XL)
10. NorthStar
11. CBASIC (for CP/M machines—complier BASIC)
12. MBASIC (for CP/M machines—interpretive BASIC)
13. Commodore PET, VIC 20 and 64
14. Texas Instruments 99/4A
15. Radio Shack Color Computer (occasional differences from other Radio Shacks)

All the commands are defined. If there is more than one definition for a command, the particular machine code is listed and the extra definition is listed for that machine. Reference to Radio Shack is always to both Radio Shack machines unless a specific reference is made to one of them, e.g., Radio Shack Model 4. The same is true of the three Commodore computers, the PET, VIC 20, and the 64. They will all be referred to as the PET.

AND Boolean operator for IF-THEN yielding a value of "true" only when *both* conditions are true.

APPEND *See* **MERGE.**

ASC Gives the ASCII decimal value of a string. Timex—CODE.

AUTO Will automatically number your lines as you key in a program. Used on IBM, Radio Shack, and MBASIC.

PET, Apple, Atari, NorthStar—no command.
CBASIC—word processor entry.
TI—NUMBER.

BACKUP A system command to make a backup copy of a disk. Used on Radio Shack, PET.
IBM, Apple, NorthStar—no command, requires program.
Atari—DOS command option.

CBASIC, MBASIC—CP/M command.

BASIC   A program name, rather than a command, that is entered to cause BASIC to load into memory from the disk.
IBM—BASIC or BASICA.
Radio Shack, PET—BASIC.
Apple—no command.
Atari—DOS menu command.
CBASIC—CBASIC.
MBASIC—MBASIC.

BEEP   Sounds the internal speaker on the IBM. *See also* **SOUND.**
Apple, Atari, NorthStar—PRINT CHR$(7).
PET—BELL.
Radio Shack, Timex, CBASIC, MBASIC—no command.
TI—PRINT CHR$(135).

BELL   *See* **BEEP.**

BREAK   A special command used on the TI that causes the program to stop at designated line numbers. No other version has a comparable command.

BYE   *See* **SYSTEM.**

CALL   A command to execute an assembly language subroutine. Used on IBM, Apple, NorthStar, CBASIC, MBASIC, and TI.
PET—SYS.
Timex—USR.

CAT   *See* **FILES.**

CATALOG   *See* **FILES.**

CHAIN   *See* **RUN "program name".**

CHR$ Command to convert ASCII decimal value to its character equivalent.

CHR$(4)   Control-D for Apple file handling.

CHR$(7)   *See* **BEEP.**

CHR$(135)   *See* **BEEP.**

CHR$(147)   *See* **CLS.**

CLEAR   Command to zero all numeric variables and null all string variables. Used on all but PET and CBASIC. On the Radio Shack, it also sets up string storage space.
PET—CLR.
CBASIC—no command.

CLOSE   Command to close any open files. Can designate to close a particular file. Used on all except PET. Apple requires control-D.

PET—DCLOSE.

CLR   *See* **CLEAR** for PET; *see* **ERASE** for Atari.

CLS   Command to clear the screen on IBM, Radio Shack, Timex.
Apple—HOME.
PET—PRINT CHR$(147).
NorthStar, CBASIC, MBASIC—function of terminal.
Atari—GRAPHICS.
TI—CLEAR subroutine (use CALL CLEAR).

CMD"D:drive number"—   *See* **FILES.**

CMD"S"   *See* **SYSTEM.**

CMD"X"   Cross reference of a particular string variable on the Radio Shack.
IBM, Apple, PET, Timex, Atari, NorthStar, MBASIC, TI—no command.
CBASIC—XREF.

COLOR   Set the color mode for screen output. Used on IBM, Apple, Atari, and TI. Atari also uses a SETCOLOR command. On the Apple, HCOLOR sets color for high resolution. Radio Shack III and 4, Timex, NorthStar, CBASIC, MBASIC—no command.

COMMON   Designates variables that are to retain their values as the program CHAINs another. Used on IBM, MBASIC, CBASIC.

CONCAT   *See* **MERGE.**

CONCHAR%   *See* **INKEY$.**

CONT   Will allow you to continue a program that has been stopped either by a command or by pressing the BREAK key. Used on all except CBASIC and TI.
TI—CONTINUE.
CBASIC—no command.

CVS, CVI, CVD   The commands to convert numerics stored in the FIELD buffer as strings back into their appropriate numeric equivalents. CVS is for single density, CVI is for integers, and CVD is for double density. Only the IBM and Radio Shack have these commands.

DATA   Statement to store data items to be read using the READ statement.

DATE$ Date manipulation on the IBM.
Radio Shack—TIME$.
PET—TI is only for time.
Apple, Timex, CBASIC, MBASIC, Atari—no command.

DCLOSE   *See* **CLOSE.**

DELETE Allows the deletion of blocks of program. Used on IBM, Radio Shack, and MBASIC. Also used on Apple to delete files from disk.
Apple, NorthStar—DEL.
PET, Timex, TI, Atari—no command.
CBASIC—word processor function.

DIM Allows the dimensioning of arrays. String arrays are allowed in all versions except Atari and NorthStar, which require that all strings be dimensioned before use.

DIRECTORY *See* **FILES.**

DLOAD *See* **LOAD.**

DOPEN *See* **OPEN.**

DOS *See* **SYSTEM.**

DRAWTO *See* **PLOT.**

DS The variable that contains the error number for the PET error routine (disk errors only).

DS$ The variable that contains the error number and error message for the PET error routine (disk errors only).

EDIT Will allow you to modify a program line. Used on IBM, Radio Shack, MBASIC, and NorthStar.
Apple, PET, Timex, Atari, TI—cursor controlled editing.
CBASIC—modification within word processor.

END The command that signals to the machine that your program has finished.

EOF The code used to check for the end-of-file on IBM, Radio Shack, MBASIC.
Apple—error trap (ONERR) and PEEK.
PET—STATUS (check for 64).
NorthStar—TYP.
Atari—no command.

ERASE Undimensions all arrays. Used on the IBM and MBASIC.
Atari—CLR.
Radio Shack, Apple, PET, Timex, NorthStar, CBASIC—no command.

ERL Used to print out the line number in which an error occurred. Used on IBM, Radio Shack, MBASIC.
NorthStar—ERRSET can be used for this function.
Apple, PET, Timex, Atari, CBASIC, TI—no command.

ERR Used to print out the error number when an error occurs. Used on IBM, MBASIC.
Radio Shack—ERR/2 + 1.

Apple—PEEK (222).
NorthStar—ERRSET can be used for this function.
PET, Timex, Atari, CBASIC, TI—no command.

ERROR Command used to simulate an error in order to test error routines. Used on IBM, Radio Shack, MBASIC.
Apple, PET, Timex, Atari, NorthStar, CBASIC, TI—no command.

ERRSET *See* **ON ERROR GOTO, ERL,** and **ERR.**

EXAM *See* **PEEK.**

FIELD The IBM and Radio Shack command to set up the random access record for storage into the buffer area.

FILES Will print the directory of the named drive on the IBM and MBASIC.
Radio Shack—CMD"D:drive number".
Apple—CATALOG.
PET—DIRECTOR.
NorthStar—CAT.
CBASIC—CP/M function.

FILL *See* **POKE.**

FOR-NEXT The BASIC looping function.

FRE Displays the amount of free memory available. Used on IBM, Radio Shack, Apple, PET, Atari, CBASIC, and MBASIC. On the IBM, Radio Shack, and MBASIC, FRE (string) will give amount of available string storage.
NorthStar—FREE.
Timex—no command.

FREE *See* **FRE.**

GCHAR *See* **PEEK.**

GET *See* **INKEY$.**

GET The IBM and Radio Shack command to retrieve random records from a file. The record is loaded into the FIELD buffer.

GOSUB The command to execute a subroutine.

GOTO The unconditional branch statement.

GR Apple command to set the machine in low resolution graphics mode. HGR is for high resolution.
IBM—SCREEN (1 for low, 2 for high).
Atari—GRAPHICS or GR. for several different modes.
Radio Shack III and 4, PET, Timex, NorthStar, CBASIC, MBASIC—no command.

GRAPHICS *See* **GR.**

HCHAR *See* **PLOT.**

HCOLOR *See* **COLOR.**

HGR *See* **GR.**

HLIN *See* **PLOT.**

HOME *See* **CLS.**

HPLOT *See* **PLOT.**

HTAB *See* **LOCATE.**

IF-THEN-ELSE The BASIC test function used on IBM, Radio Shack, NorthStar, CBASIC, MBASIC. The others use only the IF-THEN without the ELSE option.

INCHAR$ *See* **INKEY$.**

INKEY$ Inputs one character from the keyboard without displaying that character. Used on IBM, Radio Shack, Timex, and MBASIC.
Apple, PET—GET
NorthStar—INCHAR$
TI—KEY subroutine.
Atari—no command.
CBASIC—CONCHAR% (returns ASCII decimal code).

INPUT The statement that allows the program to receive information from the keyboard. Atari BASIC does not allow a prompt on the INPUT. (Also used by the Apple for disk input; see **INPUT#**.)

INPUT# The file input command. Used on IBM, Radio Shack, PET, MBASIC.
Apple, Atari—requires the file to be set up and then uses the INPUT statement.
CBASIC—READ#.
Timex, TI—unknown.

INSTR Function to find the first occurrence of a character in a specified string. Used on IBM, Radio Shack, and MBASIC.
TI—POS.
CBASIC—MATCH.
Apple, PET, Timex, NorthStar—no command.

INT Returns the integer of the specified variable.

KEY *See* **INKEY$.**

KEY OFF IBM command to turn off the 25th-line display.

LEFT$ String command to create a substring using a specified number of characters beginning at the left of the string. Used on all machines except the four below.
NorthStar, Atari—use different structure; A$ = B$(1,2) gives first two characters, for example.

Timex—uses modified PRINT command to display substring.
TI—SEG$.

LEN Returns the length of a string.

LET The assignment statement. The word LET is optional.

LINE *See* **PLOT.**

LIST Will allow you to display the program on the screen. All versions use this command in the same way except CBASIC, which uses a word processor.

LLIST Will allow the display of the program on the printer. Used on the IBM, Radio Shack, Timex, and MBASIC.
Apple—PR#1 and then LIST.
PET, Atari—special command structure.
NorthStar—LIST#device number.
CBASIC—word processor entry.

LOAD Brings a program from the disk into memory.
PET—DLOAD.

LOCATE The IBM direct cursor addressing command. (Also used in graphics command on Atari.)
Radio Shack—PRINT @.
Apple—HTAB and VTAB.
PET, TI—no command.
Timex—PRINT AT.
Atari—POSITION.
NorthStar, CBASIC, MBASIC—function of the terminal.

LOF The IBM and Radio Shack command to find the end of the file. It returns the record number of the last record in the file.

LPRINT The output command which causes the print to go to the printer. Used on the IBM, Radio Shack, Timex, and MBASIC.
Apple—PR#1 and then PRINT.
PET, Atari—require special commands.
CBASIC—LPRINTER.

LPRINTER *See* **LPRINT.**

LSET The command necessary to store information in the fielded variables on the IBM and Radio Shack. This command will left-justify the data in the field.

MATCH *See* **INSTR.**

MERGE Puts one file or program at the end of another. Used on the IBM and MBASIC.

Radio Shack, PET, NorthStar, TI—APPEND.

Apple—functions through RENUMBER program on SYSTEM MASTER disk.

PET—also uses CONCAT.

CBASIC—CP/M commands.

Timex, Atari—no command.

MID$ String command to create a substring using a specified number of characters beginning at a specified location of a string. Used on all machines except the four below.

NorthStar, Atari—use different structure; A$ = B$(2,2), for example, gives two characters beginning at location 2.

Timex—uses modified PRINT command to display substring.

TI—SEG$.

**MKS$, MKI$, MKD$** The commands in the IBM and Radio Shack that translate numeric variables into strings for storage in the FIELD buffer. MKS$ is for single density, MKI$ is for integers, and MKD$ is for double density.

NAME *See* **RENUM.**

NEW Clears the program out of memory. All versions use this command except the NorthStar, which uses SCR (for scratch).

NEXT *See* **FOR-NEXT.**

NOT Boolean operator for IF-THEN that yields the opposite value of the conditions.

NUMBER *See* **AUTO.**

ON . . . GOSUB Transfers control to the specified subroutine based upon the value of a specified numeric expression.

ON . . . GOTO Transfers control to the specified line number based upon the value of a specified numeric expression.

ONERR GOTO *See* **ON ERROR GOTO.**

ON ERROR GOTO The error trapping function used on IBM, Radio Shack, MBASIC.

Apple—ONERR GOTO.

Atari—TRAP.

NorthStar—ERRSET.

Timex, CBASIC, TI—no command.

OPEN Statement to open a data file.

Apple—requires use of control-D.

PET—requires special setup for disk and uses DOPEN.

OR Boolean operator for IF-THEN that yields a true value when either condition is true *or* both conditions are true.

PEEK Allows you to examine the contents of a particular byte of memory. Used on all machines except the two below.

NorthStar—EXAM.

TI—GCHAR subroutine (CALL GCHAR).

PLOT The function used on Apple, Timex, and Atari to turn on a low resolution graphics block. Can be used to draw lines on the Apple; HPLOT is used for high resolution and HLIN and VLIN for lines. Lines are drawn on the Atari with DRAWTO.

IBM—PSET and LINE for drawing lines.

Radio Shack—SET, RESET will turn off block, and POINT checks to see if a block is on or off.

TI—HCHAR and VCHAR subprograms (CALL HCHAR and CALL VCHAR).

PET, NorthStar, CBASIC, MBASIC—no command.

POINT *See* **PLOT.**

POKE Changes the value of a particular byte of memory. All machines use this command except the two below.

NorthStar—FILL.

TI—no command.

POP Command used on Apple and Atari to remove one RETURN address so that the program will RETURN back past one subroutine level.

POS *See* **INSTR.**

POS(0) The IBM command to find the cursor column position.

POSITION *See* **LOCATE.**

PR#1 or **PR#0** Turns the printer on and off on the Apple.

PRINT The output command to display information on the display screen. (Also used to print to the file on Apple and Atari; *see* **PRINT#.**)

PRINT @ *See* **LOCATE.**

PRINT# The file output command. Used on IBM, Radio Shack, PET, MBASIC.

Apple, Atari—require the file to be set up and then use the PRINT statement.

PRINT USING Data editing command. Used on IBM, Radio Shack, CBASIC, MBASIC.

NorthStar—format commands used on PRINT statement.

Apple, PET, Timex, Atari, TI—no command.

PSET *See* **PLOT.**

PUT# The output command used on the IBM and Radio Shack to write the record into the file.

READ Command to assign data to variables; the data is read from DATA statements. Also used for file setup on Apple and CBASIC.

READ# *See* **INPUT#.**

RECORD# The PET command to allow access to a particular random record number.

REM Command used to put comments in a program.

REN *See* **RENUM.**

RENUM The program renumber command used on IBM, MBASIC.
Radio Shack—NAME.
Apple, PET—no command.
TI—RESEQUENCE.
CBASIC—word processor entry.
NorthStar –REN.

RESEQUENCE *See* **RENUM.**

RESET *See* **PLOT.**

RESTORE Resets the data pointer to the beginning of the DATA line. In IBM and NorthStar BASIC, you can specify a particular line to which to restore the pointer.

RESUME Used to return to the main program from an error trap. Used on IBM, Radio Shack, and MBASIC.
NorthStar—ERRSET can be used for this function.
Apple, PET, Timex, Atari, CBASIC, TI—no command.

RETURN The statement to return to the main program from a subroutine.

RIGHT$ String command to create a substring using a specified number of characters counting backwards from the end of the string. All versions use this function except the four below.
NorthStar, Atari—use different structure; A\$ = B\$(2,2), for example, gives two characters beginning at location 2.
Timex—uses modified PRINT commmand to display substring.
TI—SEG\$.

RND Function to generate random numbers.

RSET The command necessary on the IBM and Radio Shack to store information in the field variables. This command will right-justify the data in the field.

RUN line number The program execution command that causes the program to begin executing at a particular line number.

RUN "program name" The command used in one BASIC program to cause a second program to load and execute. Used on IBM, Radio Shack, Timex, and Atari. IBM also uses CHAIN.
Apple—requires control-D.
NorthStar, CBASIC, MBASIC—CHAIN.
TI—no command.

SAVE Command to store a program on disk.
PET—DSAVE.

SCR *See* **NEW.**

SCREEN The IBM command to set the machine in graphics mode. SCREEN 1 is for low resolution; SCREEN 2 is for high resolution. *SEE also* **GR.**

SEG\$ *See* **LEFT\$, MID\$, RIGHT\$.**

SETCOLOR *See* **COLOR.**

SET *See* **PLOT.**

SOUND Generates sounds based upon certain guidelines. Used on IBM and Atari. The IBM also has PLAY command.
Apple—POKE commands.
TI—SOUND subroutine (use CALL SOUND).
Radio Shack, NorthStar, CBASIC, MBASIC—no command (*see also* **BEEP**).

STOP Command to stop the execution of a program. Prints the line number where execution stopped.

STR\$ Returns string representation of numeric expression.

STRING\$ Fills a string with any number of a specified character. Used on IBM, Radio Shack, MBASIC. Apple, PET, Timex, NorthStar, CBASIC, TI—no command.

SWAP Command to exchange the values of two variables. Used only on IBM and MBASIC.

SYS *See* **CALL.**

SYSTEM IBM and MBASIC command to drop out of BASIC down to DOS (Disk Operating System).
Radio Shack—CMD"S".
Apple—no command.

Atari—DOS or BYE.

NorthStar, TI—BYE.

CBASIC—STOP.

TAB A print alignment statement that directs the cursor to a specific column.

TI *See* **DATE$.**

TIME$. The IBM command to manipulate the time. *See also* **DATE$.**

TRAP *See* **ON ERROR GOTO.**

TROFF Turns off trace function. Used on IBM, Radio Shack, and MBASIC.

Apple—NOTRACE.

PET, Timex, Atari, NorthStar, CBASIC—no command.

TI—UNTRACE.

TRON Causes line numbers to print as the program functions. Used on IBM, Radio Shack, and MBASIC.

Apple, TI—TRACE.

PET, Timex, Atari, NorthStar, CBASIC—no command.

TYP *See* **EOF.**

UNBREAK TI command to turn off the BREAK function.

UNTRACE *See* **TROFF.**

USR *See* **CALL.**

VAL Returns the numeric value of a string.

VCHAR *See* **PLOT.**

VLIN *See* **PLOT.**

VTAB *See* **LOCATE.**

WHILE . . . WEND A command designed for the DO-WHILE structure. Used only on IBM, Radio Shack Model 4, and MBASIC.

WIDTH IBM command to change the width of the video display.

WRITE Apple command to set up a disk file to be input from.

XREF *See* **CMD"X".**

DISK ASSISTANCE

This appendix gives instructions on how to create a backup diskette for each of the computers so you will have a disk to store your programs on.

C–1
IBM

To make a copy of a disk you need to insert a disk in drive A and turn on the machine. You will then see the A> prompt. Then you simply enter DISKCOPY A: B: and the display will show:

```
Insert source diskette in drive A
Insert target diskette in drive B
Strike any key when ready
```

You need to put your target disk (the one you're copying *to*) in drive B. To eliminate the possibility of accidents, you should copy-protect your source disk (the one you are copying) by placing a small, sticky-back tab (they come in a box of diskettes) over the write-protect slot (the small slot cut in the side of the diskette). This will prevent you from accidently writing over the information on the disk should you do something wrong. This is very important.

After you have the disk write-protected, place it back in drive A and place your target disk in drive B. Now you are ready and can press any key to begin the copy process. It will take only a minute or so, and then you will have a copy of the diskette that you can use to store your programs on. You may need to delete some of the files that are already on the disk to make room for your programs.

C–2
RADIO SHACK

To make a copy of a disk, follow the procedures used to get to the TRSDOS message. Now enter BACKUP and press RETURN to begin the copying procedure. You will first be asked for the SOURCE DRIVE NUMBER. You should always use drive 0 for the source. Then you will be asked for your DESTINATION DRIVE NUMBER, which will be 1. Finally, the program will ask for the SOURCE DISK MASTER PASSWORD. The master disk you are using will have the password of PASSWORD. Before you press RETURN, you will need to put your target disk in drive 1 (the top one). To eliminate the possibility of accidents, you should copy-protect your source disk (the one you are copying) by placing a small, sticky-back tab (they come in a box of diskettes) over the write-protect slot (the small slot cut in the side of the diskette). This will prevent you from accidently writing over the information on the disk should you do something wrong. This is very important.

After you have the disk write-protected, place it in drive 0 and place your disk in drive 1. Now you are ready and can press RETURN to begin the copy process. It will take only a minute or so, and then you will have a copy of the diskette to store your programs on. You may have to delete some files from the backup diskette; many times there are system programs on the disk that take up valuable space.

Note: If the disk you put into drive 1 is not a new one, you will see:

```
DISKETTE CONTAINS DATA, USE DISK OR NOT?
```

If you are sure this is the proper disk, merely enter Y for YES and the program will do its job.

To make a copy of a disk, load the SYSTEM MASTER disk that was furnished with your Apple into drive 1 and turn on the machine. Then enter:

```
RUN COPYA
```

and press RETURN. You will then see:

```
APPLE DISKETTE DUPLICATION PROGRAM
ORIGINAL SLOT    DEFAULT = 6
```

Unless you have used a different slot for your disk drives, you merely press RETURN to see the next message (if you have a different slot, press that number, e.g., 5):

```
DRIVE   DEFAULT = 1
```

Press RETURN again to indicate that you are going to put the disk to copy from in drive 1. This is what you want. You should now see:

```
DUPLICATE SLOT   DEFAULT = 6
```

Again, unless you have used a different slot, press RETURN to see:

```
DRIVE   DEFAULT = 2
```

This indicates the drive we want to copy to, i.e., the disk that will be the duplicate. Drive 2 is what we want, so simply press RETURN. Finally you will see:

```
-- PRESS 'RETURN' KEY TO BEGIN COPY --
```

Before you press RETURN, you need to put your disk in drive 2. You should write-protect the SYSTEM MASTER using a write-protect tab (a small, sticky-back tab that comes in a box of diskettes) to cover the write-protect slot (the small slot cut in the side of the diskette). This will prevent you from accidently writing over the information on the disk should you do something wrong. This is very important.

After you have the disk write-protected, place it back in drive 1 and place your disk in drive 2.

Now you are ready and can press RETURN to begin the copy process. It will take only a minute or so, and then you will have a copy of the SYSTEM MASTER to store your programs on. You may wish to delete some of the system files from the disk to leave more room for your programs.

ERROR MESSAGES AND CODES

This appendix lists for each of our computers, the various errors that might occur and their associated error codes. When you are error trapping, you might need to look up the error number to determine the type of error trapped.

D–1
IBM

ERROR CODE	MESSAGE	ERROR CODE	MESSAGE
1	NEXT without FOR	27	Out of paper
2	Syntax error	29	WHILE without WEND
3	Return without GOSUB	30	WEND without WHILE
4	Out of data	50	Field overflow
5	Illegal function call	51	Internal error
6	Overflow	52	Bad file number
7	Out of memory	53	File not found
8	Undefined line number	54	Bad file mode
9	Subscript out of range	55	File already open
10	Duplicate definition	57	Device I/O error
11	Division by zero	58	File already exists
12	Illegal direct	61	Disk full
13	Type mismatch	62	Input past end
14	Out of string space	63	Bad record number
15	String too long	64	Bad file name
16	String formula too complex	66	Direct statement in file
17	Can't continue	67	Too many files
18	Undefined user function	68	Device unavailable
19	No RESUME	69	Communication buffer overflow
20	RESUME without error	70	Disk write-protect
22	Missing operand	71	Disk not ready
23	Line buffer overflow	72	Disk media error
24	Device timeout	73	Advanced feature
25	Device fault	--	Unprintable error
26	FOR without NEXT		

ERROR CODE	MESSAGE	ERROR CODE	MESSAGE
1	NEXT without FOR	20	Unprintable error
2	Syntax error	21	Missing operand
3	Return without GOSUB	22	Bad file data
4	Out of data	23	Disk BASIC only
5	Illegal function call	51	Field overflow
6	Overflow	52	Internal error
7	Out of memory	53	Bad file number
8	Undefined line	54	File not found
9	Subscript out of range	55	Bad file mode
10	Redimensioned array	58	Disk I/O error
11	Division by zero	62	Disk full
12	Illegal direct	63	Input past end
13	Type mismatch	64	Bad record number
14	Out of string space	65	Bad file name
15	String too long	67	Direct statement in file
16	String formula too complex	68	Too many files
17	Can't continue	69	Disk write-protect
18	NO RESUME	70	File access
19	RESUME without error		

ERROR CODE	MESSAGE	ERROR CODE	MESSAGE
0	NEXT without FOR	53	Illegal quantity
4	Disk is write-protected	69	Overflow
5	Out of data on disk data file	77	Out of memory
6	File not found	90	Undefined statement
7	Wrong column	107	Bad subscript
8	I/O error	120	Redimensioned array
9	Disk full	133	Division by zero
10	File locked	163	Type mismatch
11	Bad file name of parameter	176	String too large
12	No buffers available	191	Formula too complex
13	File type mismatch	224	Undefined function
16	Syntax error	254	Bad response to INPUT statement
22	Return without GOSUB	255	Ctrl C interrupt attempted
42	Out of data		

FINAL PROJECT IDEAS

One of the nice things about a programming class is being able to create your own programs when the class is finished. To assist in the design and creation of programs, a project at the end of each course can be invaluable. It is suggested that you come up with your own project idea. The project ideas in this appendix are only suggestions as to what types of programs (projects) you are capable of handling. If, after reading through this appendix, you come up with different ideas, by all means proceed with your own ideas.

When considering project ideas, select only those that are familiar to you. You will have to plan, write, debug, and document the program, and you cannot do that for an unfamiliar topic.

Remember, the ideas presented here are merely suggestions. If you like a topic but don't like the ideas suggested with it, use your own idea and design a project around it. The ideas presented are only meant to get your creative juices flowing. They are not intended to be the only possibilities. You may want to combine several items to come up with a unique idea. Imagination is the key here.

Finally, try to create a project that you can use in the future, perhaps something with a business application. Programming for practice is fine, but there is much greater motivation and satisfaction in creating something that will continue to be useful.

PROJECT IDEAS

1. *Inventory.* Keep track of inventory items by item number, storing them in a file. Some things to print might be an order point list (those items that need to be ordered), an inventory item list (items in inventory, how much stock, order point, etc.), and receipts list (what items are received, from whom, billing number, etc.).
2. *File maintenance.* Create a program to add, change, delete, and print items from a file of names, addresses, cities, etc. Additional programs could be created, such as a mailing labels program.
3. *Taxes.* Keep track of all IRS Schedule A deductions or simply keep a file of incomes and expenses. Write a program to generate the tax form appropriate for the filing you will do.
4. *Games.* Write a program to simulate a favorite game. A board game might be a good choice.
5. *Calendar.* Keep a file of appointments by date and time of day. Have a program that will display a particular day on the screen for viewing and possibly for editing.
6. *Telephone directory.* Keep a file of the names, phone numbers, and possibly the addresses of your friends and family. An additional program could print out a list of the file, possibly in sorted order.
7. *Design.* Create a program that will design a building or something similar on the screen or printer. If you have an IBM or Apple, you may wish to do it in low or high resolution graphics, possibly with color.

8. *Mortgage amortization.* Write a program to calculate and print out a schedule of payments for home purchase. Perhaps you can set this one up with a menu of options.

9. *Computer-aided instruction.* Write a program to teach a subject using the computer as instructor. Perhaps a program teaching math or spelling to small children would be of interest. Combining education and an enjoyable game is always challenging.

10. *Statistical applications.* The computer is a good mathematician. Take advantage of that by having the computer analyze your statistical data. Print out an appropriate report showing the results of the operations.

11. *Classroom scheduler.* Write a program that will allow you to input the number of rooms and classes and then have the program schedule the classes into the rooms for the best fit. This could also apply for dividing equipment in a plant or scheduling people in departments at a retail store.

12. *A small text editor.* Create a program that will allow you to input data to be stored, retrieved, changed, and printed.

ANSWERS TO SELECTED EXERCISES

Many of the exercises in the Questions to Aid Understanding sections have possible solutions presented here. Note, however, that only selected solutions are included. Many of the exercises are explained well in the text, and all you need to do is look up the information in the chapter. This appendix answers those questions in which there may be some doubt about the proper answer. Many programming exercises have one possible solution listed. (Remember that the solutions proposed for the programming exercises are the author's solutions. If yours do not agree, they are not necessarily wrong.) Programs listed are for the IBM PC, with only significant differences listed for the other machines.

CHAPTER 1

6. A diskette is a small plastic disk coated with a magnetic material. The disk has concentric storage circles known as tracks. Each track is broken logically into groups known as sectors. Each sector contains 256 bytes of storage.

7. A directory is a single track on the diskette reserved for the storage of names and locations of all the files and programs stored on the diskette. A directory is important because it allows the computer to keep track of where everything is stored.

CHAPTER 2

2. There are system charts and program charts. The system charts are constructed by a systems analyst and use many more symbols than do the program flowcharts. The program flowcharts are created by programmers as a visual image of the logic of the program.

6. A counter is used to determine how many times a loop has been executed in the DO-WHILE structure.

11. The flowchart can be seen in Figure F–1; the pseudocode is:

Start
Input the miles traveled.
DO-WHILE miles not negative.
   Compute the mileage rate.
   Print out the results.
   Input the miles traveled.
END-DO
End

CHAPTER 3

3. In the immediate mode the commands are executed immediately upon pressing RETURN. The commands are not stored in memory, so when the screen is cleared, all the information generated is lost. In the program mode,

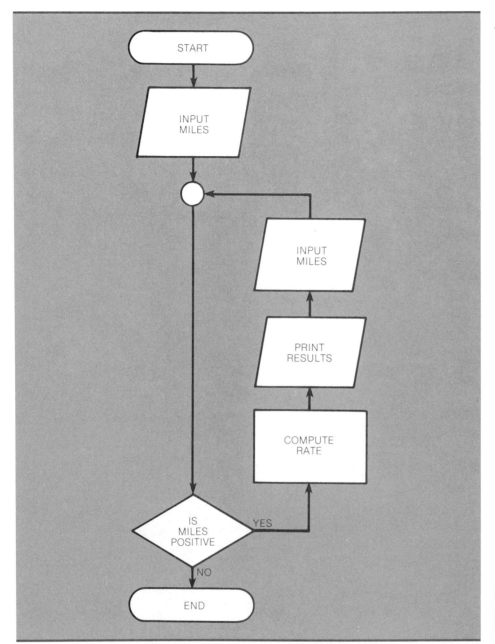

Figure F–1
Flowchart for Question 2–11.

each command has a line number on it, which causes the command to be stored in memory. Then, to execute the commands, RUN is entered.

7. a. String
   c. String
   e. Invalid (number, not variable)
   g. Numeric
   i. Invalid (Variable will not allow special characters.)

8. b. Invalid (Only the variable can be on the left-hand side of the equal sign.)
  d. Invalid (There should be an operator between the 6 and the open parenthesis.)
  f. Valid
  h. Invalid ("5", being a literal, is not compatible with a numeric.)
  j. Invalid (Incompatible since TEST is not a literal; would be valid if TEST were in quotation marks.)

11. The flowchart can be seen in Figure F–2; the pseudocode follows:

    Start
    Assign variables (5).
    Add the variables.
    Divide total by 5.
    Print the result.
    End

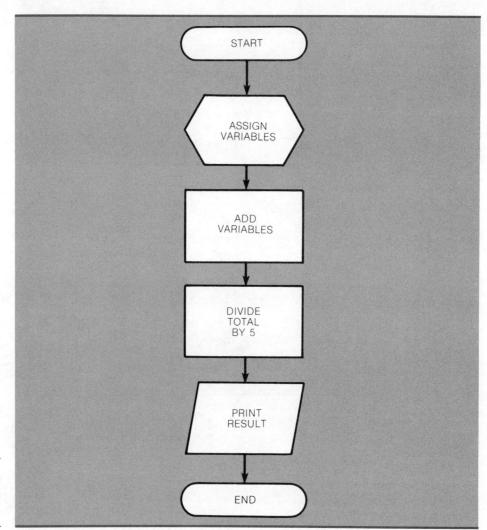

Figure F–2
Flowchart for Question 3–11.

The program should look like the following:

```
10 A=80
20 B=90
30 C=95
40 D=63
50 E=75
60 T=A+B+C+D+E
70 A=T/5
80 PRINT "THE AVERAGE IS";A
90 END
RUN
THE AVERAGE IS 80.6
Ok
```

CHAPTER 4

1. *Program* documentation consists of remarks in the program to help the programmer follow the logic of the coding. *Programmer* documentation consists of pseudocode, flowcharts, and other devices that help the programmer understand the logic of the program without looking at the actual code. *User* documentation is a manual that is prepared to help the user understand how the program functions and what is expected when the program is executed.
3. The INPUT statement can be used with a PRINT statement (a prompt) prior to the INPUT statement; this will print the prompt on the screen. Or the INPUT statement can have the prompt within the statement itself, with no prior print statement necessary.
6. (Every other line is analyzed.)
   10 Incorrect—RME is a misspelling.
   30 Correct (but two question marks would print after NAME)
   50 Correct
   70 Incorrect—the quotation mark is missing in front of MY.
   90 Correct
7. (Every other line is analyzed.)
   b. Incorrect—the semicolon should be a comma.
   d. Incorrect—the statement needs delimiters.
   f. Incorrect—there is no command since INPUT is in quotes.
10. The flowchart can be seen in Figure F–3; the pseudocode follows:

    Start
    Input the grades (3).
    Total the grades.
    Divide the total by 3.
    Print the result.
    End

    The program should look like the following:

```
10 REM ***** PROGRAM NAME: F410
20 REM
30 REM ***** GRADE PROGRAM - EXERCISE 4-10
```

Program continues

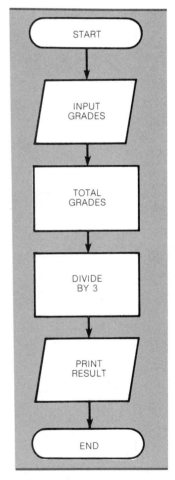

Figure F–3
Flowchart for Question 4–10.

```
40 REM
50 INPUT "KEY IN THREE GRADES";A,B,C
60 T=A+B+C
70 A=T/3
80 PRINT "THE AVERAGE IS";A
90 END
RUN
KEY IN THREE GRADES? 100, 90, 80
THE AVERAGE IS 90
Ok
```

CHAPTER 5

3. a. Branch to 110.

    Branch to 110.

    Cannot branch to 110 since branch is to 50.

    Branch to 110.

  b. Branch to 110.

    Branch to 110.

    Error—incompatible variables.

    Branch to 110.

    No branch since $A=5$ and $B=9$.

4. a. $A=10$

  c. $A=1$

6. We should use the counter variable on the NEXT statement to make it easier to match the FOR with the appropriate NEXT. This will become more important when we begin nesting the loops.

9. a. Incorrect—A and "5" are not compatible.

  c. Incorrect—THEN B is not a proper action.

  e. Incorrect—FRO should be FOR.

  g. Incorrect—incorrect symbol for relational operator.

  i. Correct

15. The flowchart can be seen in Figure F–4; the pseudocode follows:

Start

Input table size.

Print table heading.

Initialize counter to 1.

DO-WHILE counter is not greater than table size.

    Print the counter variable and the counter variable multiplied by itself.

    Increment the counter by 1.

END-DO

End

The program should look like the following:

```
10 REM ***** PROGRAM NAME: F-5-15
20 REM
30 REM ***** SQUARE TABLE - EXERCISE 5 - 15
40 REM
50 INPUT "WHAT IS THE TABLE SIZE";A
60 PRINT "NUMBER","SQUARE"
70 FOR I = 1 TO A
80    PRINT " ";I,"  ";I*I
```

Program continues on page 464

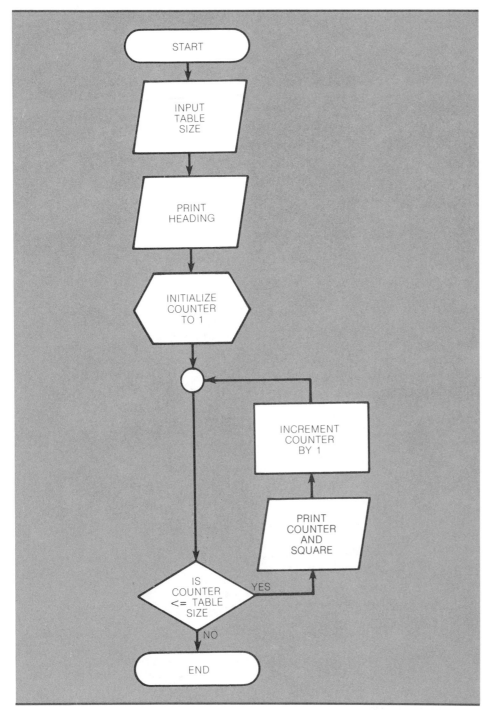

Figure F–4
Flowchart for Question 5–15.

```
90 NEXT I
100 END
RUN
WHAT IS THE TABLE SIZE? 5
NUMBER          SQUARE
     1             1
     2             4
     3             9
     4             16
     5             25
Ok
```

CHAPTER 6

3. If you always put the DATA statements at either the top or bottom of the program, they will be easy to locate when you want to change a value stored in one of the statements. Otherwise, you will have to look through the entire program to find the DATA statement that needs to be changed.

6. The RESTORE statement specifies that the DATA statement pointer should be placed to the beginning of the first DATA statement.

9. a. Incorrect—there is no line number on the RETURN statement.
   c. Incorrect—the GOSUB is misspelled.
   e. Incorrect—incomplete statement.
   g. Correct—though there are two H's in a row.
   i. Correct

10. b. Incorrect—A cannot contain HI, and B cannot contain BYE.
    d. Incorrect—there is no DATA statement.
    f. Incorrect—A cannot contain MARY.

14. The flowchart can be seen in Figure F–5; the pseudocode follows:

Start
Initialize counter to 1.
DO-WHILE counter not greater than 5.
   Read DATA into three arrays (LR, HR, D).
   Increment counter by 1.
END-DO
Initialize counter (I) to 1.
Input employee name into array.
DO-WHILE name not "END".
  Input rest of data.
  IF deductions > 3 THEN
    Set deductions to 3 (has to fit calculations).
  (ELSE)
  END-IF
  Calculate gross pay.
  Initialize tax to zero.
  Initialize counter (J) to 1.
  REPEAT-UNTIL tax is not zero.
    IF gross pay is within range THEN
      Set tax to table amount.
    (ELSE) *(continues on page 466)*

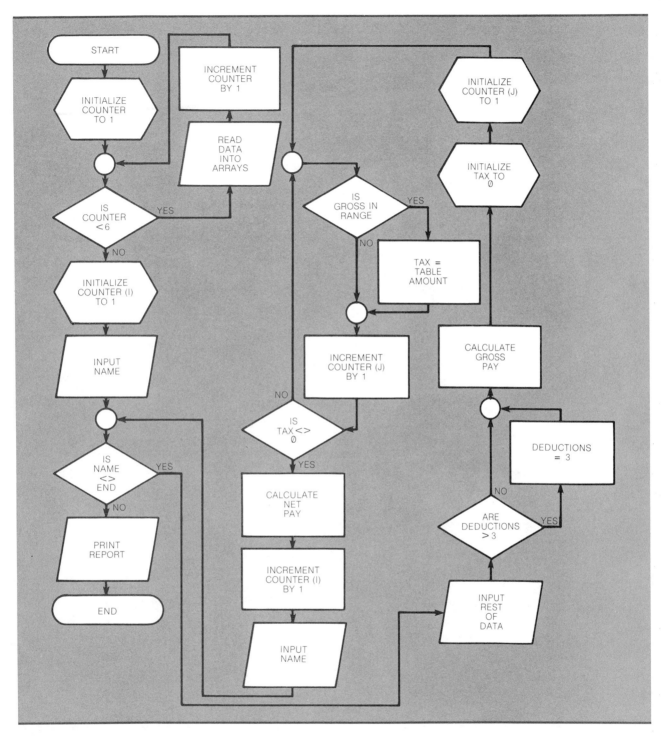

Figure F–5
Flowchart for Question 6–14.

> END-IF
> Increment counter (J) by 1.
> END-REPEAT
> Calculate net pay.
> Increment counter (I) by 1.
> Input employee name into array.
> END-DO
> Print report using arrays.
> End

The program should look like the following:

```
10 REM ***** PROGRAM NAME: F-6-14
20 REM
30 REM ***** PAYROLL PROGRAM - EXERCISE 6 - 14
40 REM
50 DIM N$(25),GP(25),TAX(25)
50 FOR I = 1 TO 5
60 ' LR IS LOW RANGE, HR IS HIGH RANGE AND D IS DEDUCTIONS
70      READ LR(I),HR(I),D(I*3-2),D(I*3-1),D(I*3)
80 NEXT I
90 I=1                                   ' LOOP COUNTER
100 INPUT "EMPLOYEE NAME";N$(I)
110       IF N$(I)="END" THEN 235  ' END-OF-DATA MARKER
120       INPUT "HOURLY RATE";R
130       INPUT "HOURS WORKED";H
140       INPUT "DEDUCTIONS";DED
150       IF DED>3 THEN DED=3           ' NECESSARY TO FIT TABLE
160       GP(I)=R*H                     ' NO WORRY ABOUT OVERTIME
170       J=1                           ' COUNTER FOR NEW LOOP
180           IF GP(I)>=LR(J) AND GP(I)<HR(J) THEN
                  TAX(I) = D((J-1) * 3 + DED)
190           J=J+1                  ' INCREMENT COUNTER
200           IF TAX(I) = 0 THEN 180    ' LOOP
210       I=I+1
220 GOTO 100
210 REM
220 REM ***** READY FOR REPORT
230 REM
235 PRINT                              ' BLANK LINE
240 PRINT "NAME         GROSS PAY       TAX     NET PAY"
250 PRINT                              ' BLANK LINE
260 FOR I = 1 TO I-1                   ' NUMBER OF ENTRIES
270     NP=GP(I)-TAX(I)
280     PRINT N$(I);TAB(13);GP(I);TAB(32);TAX(I);TAB(39);NP
290 NEXT I
300 DATA 0,100,0,0,0
310 DATA 100,200,12,9,6
320 DATA 200,400,42,30,24
330 DATA 400,800,168,120,96
340 DATA 800,99999,580,394,300
350 END
RUN

EMPLOYEE NAME? ED COBURN
HOURLY RATE? 10
HOURS WORKED? 25
DEDUCTIONS? 5
EMPLOYEE NAME? TOM SMITH
HOURLY RATE? 5.25
HOURS WORKED? 40
```

Program continues

```
DEDUCTIONS? 1
EMPLOYEE NAME? SAM GRID
HOURLY RATE? 3.56
HOURS WORKED? 35
DEDUCTIONS? 2
EMPLOYEE NAME? TAMMY JONES
HOURLY RATE? 13.62
HOURS WORKED? 40
DEDUCTIONS? 2
EMPLOYEE NAME? END

NAME            GROSS PAY      TAX      NET PAY

ED COBURN       250            24       226
TOM SMITH       210            42       168
SAM GRID        124.6          9        115.6
TAMMY JONES     544.8          120      424.8
Ok
```

CHAPTER 7

3. The LEN function will allow the programmer to determine the length of a string variable. This is useful since many times loops need to be executed through the number of characters in a string. This is only one example of the many uses for the length of a string.

6. The ASCII decimal code is the mathematical equivalent of the binary code assigned to a particular character. It is significant in that there are many character codes that are not printable keys (such as the RETURN key), and in order to use those keys in comparisons, for example, we need to be able to indicate to the machine which character we are referencing.

10. The INPUT command stops execution and waits for the user to key in some data, the INKEY$ doesn't. The INPUT command automatically prints a prompt on the screen, the INKEY$ doesn't. The length of the input on the INPUT command is virtually unlimited, the INKEY$ inputs only one character.

14. The flowchart for this can be seen in Figure F–6; the pseudocode follows:

Start
Initialize the counter to 90.
DO-WHILE counter is not less than 65.
    Print the character code.
END-DO
End

The program should look like the following:

```
10 REM ***** PROGRAM NAME: F-7-14
20 REM
30 REM ***** BACKWARDS ALPHABET - EXERCISE 7 - 14
40 REM
50 FOR I = 90 TO 65 STEP -1
60     PRINT CHR$(I);" ";
70 NEXT I
80 END
RUN
Z Y X W V U T S R Q P O N M L K J I H G F E D C B A
Ok
```

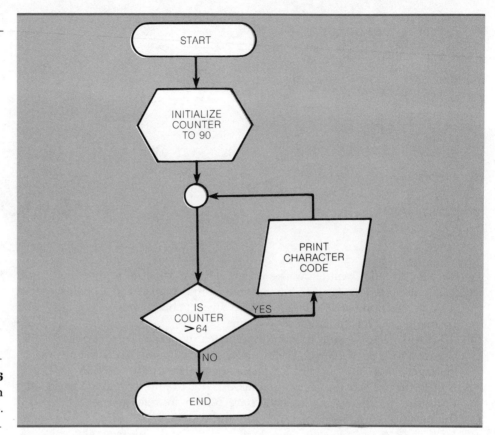

Figure F–6
Flowchart for Question
7–14.

16. The flowchart can be seen in Figure F–7; the pseudocode follows:

Start
Input word.
DO-WHILE word not "END".
  Restore data pointer.
  Initialize code to 0.
  Initialize counter to 1.
  DO-WHILE counter is less than 11.
    Read data word.
    IF input data word = read data word THEN
      Set code to 1.
      Increment counter by 1.
    (ELSE)
    END-IF
  END-DO
  IF code = 0 THEN
    Print misspelled message.
  (ELSE)
  END-IF
  Input word. *(continues on page 470)*

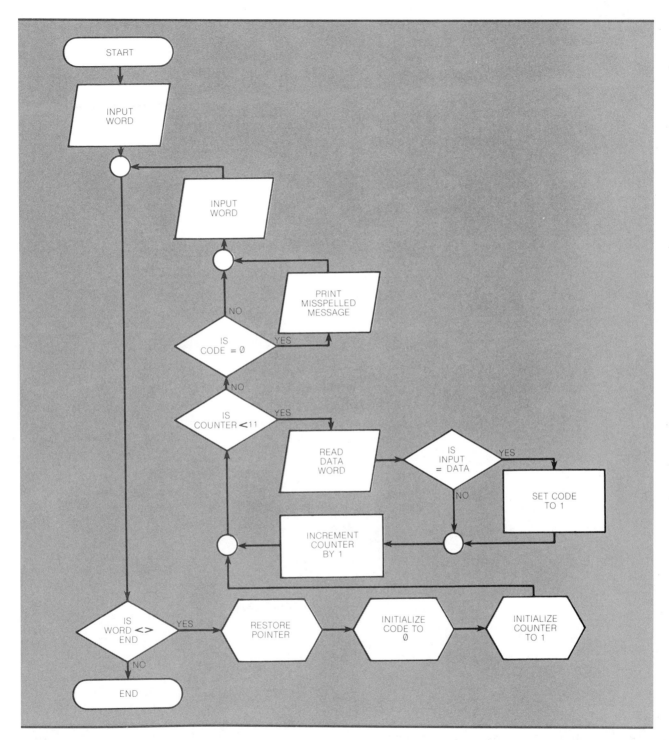

Figure F–7
Flowchart for Question 7–16.

END-DO
End

The program should look like the following:

```
10 REM ***** PROGRAM NAME: F-7-17
20 REM
30 REM ***** SPELLING CHECKER - EXERCISE 7 - 17
40 REM
50 INPUT "WHAT WORD";W$
60   IF W$="END" THEN 170       ' END-OF-DATA MARKER
70 C=0                          ' CODE
80 RESTORE
90 FOR I = 1 TO 10
100    READ D$
110    IF W$=D$ THEN C=1
120 NEXT I
130 IF C=0 THEN PRINT "WORD ";W$;" WAS MISSPELLED"
140 GOTO 50
150 REM
160 DATA HI,BYE,TOM,HELLO,PASSWORD,UP,DOWN,AROUND,IN,OUT
170 END
RUN
WHAT WORD? GEORGE
WORD GEORGE WAS MISSPELLED
WHAT WORD? HELLO
WHAT WORD? HI
WHAT WORD? HY
WORD HY WAS MISSPELLED
WHAT WORD? END
Ok
```

CHAPTER 8

1. If programs are to be written with more than a few simple data items, there must be some method of storing this data. The disk is the best solution.

4. A sequential file stores records one after another, and the records must be read back in the same order. A random file allows access to any record in the file without concern to sequence.

6A. a. Incorrect—FOR option comes second.
   c. Correct
   e. Incorrect—EXTEND should be APPEND.
   g. Correct
   i. Correct

6B. a. Incorrect—"OUTPUT" should be "O".
   c. Correct
   e. Incorrect—code should come first.
   g. Correct
   i. Correct

6C. a. Incorrect—cannot include special characters (').
   c. Correct
   e. Incorrect—must have file name, not number.
   g. Incorrect—ONERR is command, not variable name.
   i. Incorrect—must be used on PRINT statement.

10. The flowchart for the first program can be seen in Figure F–8; the pseudo-code follows:

Start
Open the file.
Initialize counter to 1.
DO-WHILE counter is less than 31.
   Generate random number between 1 and 10.
   Dump number into file.
END-DO
Close the file.
END

The program should look like the following for the IBM.

```
10 REM ***** PROGRAM NAME: F-8-10-1
20 REM
30 REM ***** RANDOM NUMBERS - EXERCISE 8 - 10
40 REM
50 REM ***** THIS IS THE DATA INPUT PROGRAM
60 REM ***** PROGRAM 1
70 REM
80 REM ***** THIS IS THE IBM VERSION
90 REM
100 OPEN "RANDOM1" FOR OUTPUT AS #1
110 FOR I = 1 TO 30
120     R=INT(RND(0)*10)+1              ' NUMBER FROM 1 TO 10
130     PRINT #1,R
140 NEXT I
150 CLOSE
160 END
```

)))DIFFERENCES

On the Radio Shack, the OPEN statement should look like:

```
100 OPEN "O",1,"RANDOM1"
```

and line 120 should be:

```
120     R=RND(10)
```

On the Apple, the OPEN statement must be three statements:

```
95 D$=CHR$(4)                   ' CONTROL-D
100 PRINT D$;"OPEN RANDOM1"
105 PRINT D$;"WRITE RANDOM1"
```

The PRINT# statement should be a PRINT:

```
130     PRINT R
```

And the CLOSE is different:

```
150 PRINT D$;"CLOSE"
```

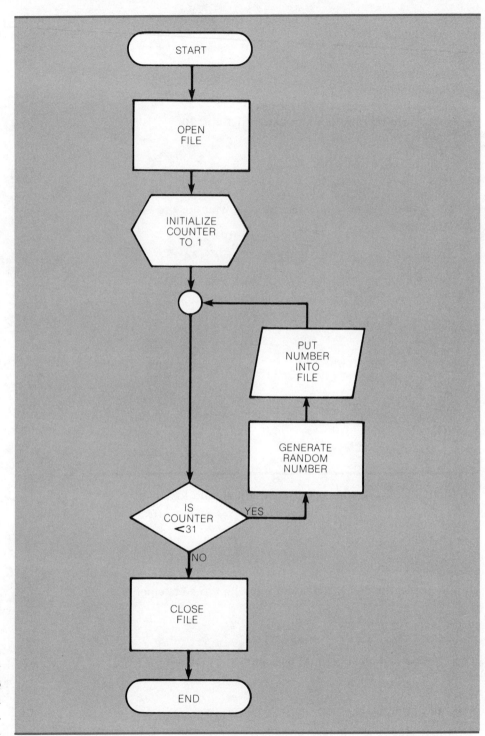

To create the second file, only the file name needs to be changed in the program, and then the program should be rerun.

The flowchart for the second program is shown in Figure F–9; the pseudocode follows:

```
Start
Open the files.
Initialize counter to 1.
DO-WHILE counter is less than 31.
   Input one number from each file.
   IF numbers match THEN
      Print number and match message.
   ELSE
      Print both numbers, difference, and mismatch message.
   END-IF
END-DO
Close the files.
End
```

The second program should look like the following:

```
10 REM ***** PROGRAM NAME: F-8-10-2
20 REM
30 REM ***** RANDOM NUMBERS - EXERCISE 8 - 10
40 REM
50 REM ***** THIS IS THE FILE INPUT PROGRAM
60 REM ***** PROGRAM 2
70 REM
80 REM ***** WRITTEN BY EDWARD J. COBURN
90 REM
100 OPEN "RANDOM1" FOR INPUT AS #1
110 OPEN "RANDOM2" FOR INPUT AS #2
120 FOR I = 1 TO 30
130     INPUT #1,N1
140     INPUT #2,N2
150     IF N1 = N2 THEN PRINT "THE NUMBER WAS";N1;
                            "AND THEY MATCHED"
        ELSE PRINT "MISMATCH, #1=";N1;" #2=";N2;
                   " DIFFERENCE=";N1-N2
160 NEXT I
170 CLOSE
180 END
```

On the Radio Shack, the OPEN statement should look like:

```
100 OPEN "I",1,"RANDOM1"
110 OPEN "I",2,"RANDOM2"
```

On the Apple, the OPEN statements need the D$ assignment and READ statements:

```
95 D$=CHR$(4)                : REM CONTROL-D
100 PRINT D$;"OPEN RANDOM1"
105 PRINT D$;"READ RANDOM1"
```

Program continues on page 475

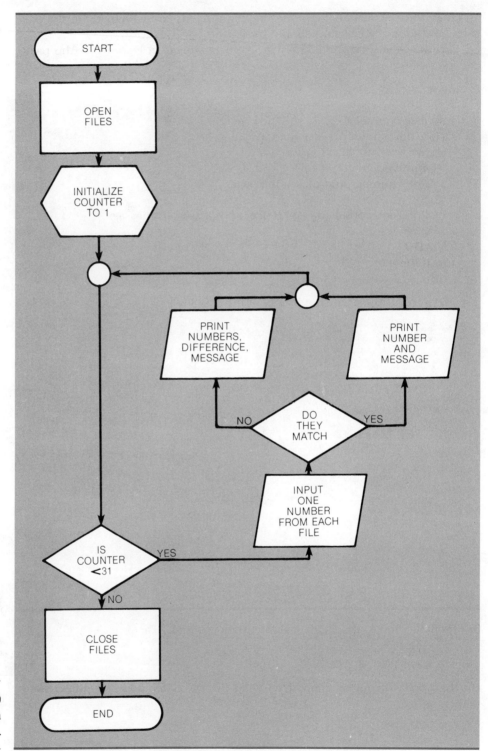

Figure F–9
Flowchart for Question
8–10 (program 2).

```
110 PRINT D$;"OPEN RANDOM2"
115 PRINT D$;"READ RANDOM2"
```

The INPUT# statements should be INPUT:

```
130      INPUT N1
140      INPUT N2
```

Line 150 needs to be two lines because of the ELSE:

```
150      IF N1 = N2 THEN PRINT "THE NUMBER WAS";N1;
                         "AND THEY MATCHED"
155      IF N1 <> N2 THEN PRINT "MISMATCH, #1= ";N1;" #2= ";N2;
                     "  DIFFERENCE= ";N1-N2
```

And the CLOSE statement needs to be:

```
170 PRINT D$;"CLOSE"
```

A sample of the output of this program would be (only a few of the 30 are listed):

```
RUN
THE NUMBER WAS 10 AND THEY MATCHED
MISMATCH, #1= 9   #2= 4   DIFFERENCE= 5
MISMATCH, #1= 1   #2= 3   DIFFERENCE= -2
MISMATCH, #1= 4   #2= 8   DIFFERENCE= -4
MISMATCH, #1= 3   #2= 7   DIFFERENCE= -4
MISMATCH, #1= 6   #2= 1   DIFFERENCE= 5
THE NUMBER WAS 4 AND THEY MATCHED
```

CHAPTER 9

4. Error messages are important because they tell the user exactly what was entered incorrectly, leaving no doubt in the user's mind about how to correct the error. Without error messages, program usage can be a very frustrating experience.

12. This program is written using DATA statements, though it could be used with the data files created previously. The purpose of this program is to practice using the screen formatting, not using data files. The flowchart is Figure F–10, the line spacing chart is Figure F–11, and the pseudocode follows:

Start
Read data items into array from DATA statements.
Read cursor positions into array from DATA statements.
Display item screen.
Input record number.
DO-WHILE record number not "END".
   Display record on screen using cursor positions.
   Input item number to change.
   DO-WHILE item number not zero.
     Input new item and print on screen using cursor position.
     Input item number to change.

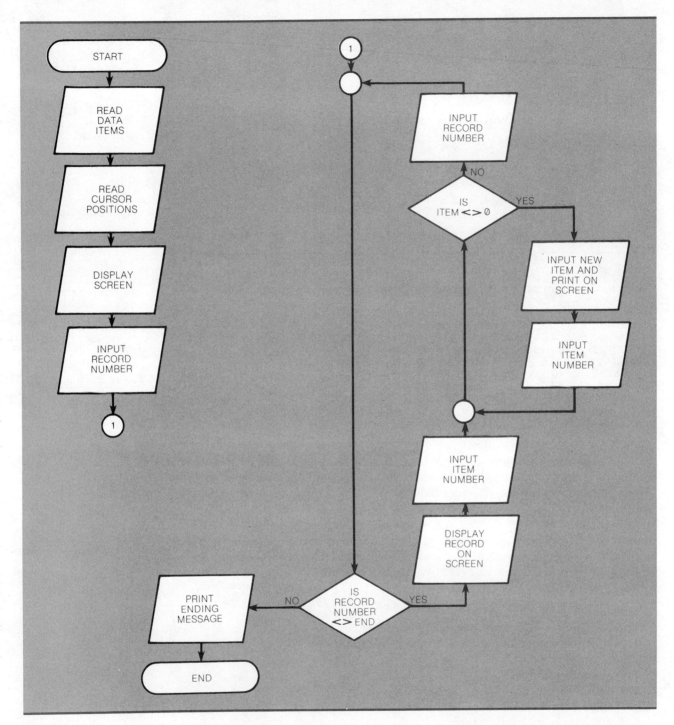

Figure F–10
Flowchart for Question 9–12.

LINE SPACING CHART
COLUMNS

```
 1                    INVENTORY MAINTENANCE
 3 YOUR OPTIONS ARE:
 5 1. INVENTORY ITEM           XXX-XX-XXXXXXX
 6 2. ITEM DESCRIPTION         XXXXXXXXXXXXX
 7 3. QUANTITY-ON-HAND             XXX,XXX
 8 4. LAST PURCHASE DATE          XX/XX/XX
 9 5. COST AT LAST PURCHASE   $XXX,XXX.XX
18 WHAT ITEM TO CHANGE (1-5, 0 TO EXIT)?
```

ROWS

Figure F–11
Design for Question 9–12.

    END-DO
    Input record number.
END-DO
Print program ending message.
End

The following is the program:

```
10 REM ***** PROGRAM NAME: F-9-12
20 REM
30 REM ***** ITEM MAINTENANCE - EXERCISE 9 - 12
40 REM
50 FOR I = 1 TO 5
60     READ I$(I),D$(I),Q(I),PD$(I),COST(I)
70 NEXT I
80 FOR I = 1 TO 5
90     READ M$(I),R(I),C(I)          ' MESSAGE,ROW,COLUMN
100 NEXT I
110 REM
120 REM ***** SCREEN DISPLAY
130 REM
140 CLS                              ' CLEAR THE SCREEN
150 PRINT TAB(10);"INVENTORY MAINTENANCE"
160 PRINT                            ' BLANK LINE
```

Program continues

```
170 PRINT "YOUR OPTIONS ARE:"
180 PRINT                                ' BLANK LINE
190 FOR I = 1 TO 5                       ' PROMPT LOOP
200     PRINT USING "#";I;               ' FIELD NUMBER
210     PRINT ".   ";M$                  ' MESSAGE
220 NEXT I
240 R=23                                 ' ROW
250 C=1                                  ' COLUMN
260 GOSUB 5000                           ' CURSOR POSITIONING
270 INPUT "WHAT INVENTORY NUMBER TO CHANGE";I$
280 REM
290 REM ***** VERIFY ITEM
300 REM
305 IF I$="END" THEN 10000               ' END-OF-DATA MARKER
310 FOR I = 1 TO 5                        ' LOCATE LOOP
320     IF I$(I)=I$ THEN 400              ' EXIT LOOP
330 NEXT I
340 M$="INVENTORY NUMBER NOT FOUND.  TRY AGAIN"
350 GOSUB 6000                           ' ERROR ROUTINE
360 GOTO 240                             ' GET INVENTORY NUMBER
370 REM
380 REM ***** DISPLAY RECORD INFORMATION
390 REM
400 R=R(1)
410 C=C(1)
420 GOSUB 5000
430 PRINT I$(I)
440 R=R(2)
450 C=C(2)
460 GOSUB 5000
470 PRINT D$(I)
480 R=R(3)
490 C=C(3)
500 GOSUB 5000
510 PRINT USING "###,###";Q(I)
520 R=R(4)
530 C=C(4)
540 GOSUB 5000
550 PRINT D$(I)
560 R=R(5)
570 C=C(5)
580 GOSUB 5000
590 PRINT USING "$###,###.##";C(I)
600 REM
610 REM ***** INPUT ITEM TO CHANGE
620 REM
630 R=23
640 C=1
650 GOSUB 5000                            ' POSITION CURSOR
660 PRINT STRING$(39," ");                ' BLANK LINE
670 GOSUB 5000
680 INPUT "WHAT ITEM TO CHANGE (1-5, 0 TO EXIT)";A
685 IF A=0 THEN 140                       ' REDISPLAY SCREEN
690 IF A>0 AND A<6 THEN 730
700 M$="INCORRECT ENTRY.  TRY AGAIN"
710 GOSUB 6000
720 GOTO 630                              ' REINPUT
730 GOSUB 5000
740 PRINT STRING$(39," ");                ' BLANK LINE
750 GOSUB 5000
```

Program continues

```
760 PRINT "ENTER NEW ";M$(A);          ' PROMPT
770 INPUT A$
780 IF A=1 THEN I$(I)=A$
790 IF A=2 THEN D$(I)=A$
800 IF A=3 THEN Q(I)=VAL(A$)
810 IF A=4 THEN D$(I)=A$
820 IF A=5 THEN COST(I)=VAL(A$)
830 GOTO 400                           ' RETURN TO DISPLAY
9000 DATA 123-BL-BG45/97,HORSE COLLAR,154,10/15/84,15.65
9010 DATA 123-BL-HT32/132,BLUE JEEP,25,10/17/83,1500.00
9020 DATA 135-BL-RD46/2,PETTICOAT,30,12/17/83,12.54
9030 DATA 400-GR-4/2,HAIR PIECE,45,01/15/82,53.45
9040 DATA 542-RE-TF14/35,POOL CUE,156,01/14/82,13.25
9050 DATA INVENTORY ITEM,5,23
9060 DATA ITEM DESCRIPTION,6,25
9070 DATA QUANTITY-ON-HAND,7,30
9080 DATA LAST PURCHASE DATE,8,29
9090 DATA COST AT LAST PURCHASE,9,27
10000 CLS                              ' CLEAR THE SCREEN
10010 PRINT "PROGRAM ENDED...."
10020 END
```

)))DIFFERENCES

First, don't forget to add the appropriate subroutines.

The only differences on the Radio Shack Model III are the row positions in lines 240 and 630.

On the Apple, line 200 doesn't need formatting at all:

```
200 PRINT I;
```

However, lines 510 and 590 do need the formatting subroutine we've used before. Also, we need to add the short routine to fill a string with blanks since lines 660 and 740 need it in addition to the Apple subroutines.

The following is a sample of the way a screen display would look after the item information had been displayed:

```
          INVENTORY MAINTENANCE

YOUR OPTIONS ARE:

1.   INVENTORY ITEM       123-RE-BG45/15
2.   ITEM DESCRIPTION        HORSE COLLAR
3.   QUANTITY-ON-HAND                 154
4.   LAST PURCHASE DATE          10/15/84
5.   COST AT LAST PURCHASE        $15.65


WHAT ITEM TO CHANGE (1-5, 0 TO EXIT)?
```

3. The asterisks allow the user to see how many characters are expected in answer to the prompt and help guide the user through the entry.

4. You might choose to use the # symbol for numeric entry, slashes for dates, and maybe $ for money entries. The only problem with such uses is that the prompt routine will be more difficult.

7. To do this routine, we will use the prompting routine we have already created (Program 10–3) and patch-correct it. (Therefore, we will not flowchart or pseudocode.) We will fix the routine so it will check a special prompt code and use the special date routine only when the prompt code is set to "D" for date. On the prompt display, instead of displaying six asterisks, we will display MM/DD/YY, and then we will input using three small loops instead of one large one. The easiest way to do that would be to make the internal loop a subroutine and call it up three times. The following routine will do the job:

```
6970 REM
6980 REM ***** PROMPT AND INPUT ROUTINE
6990 REM
7000 R=24
7010 C=1
7020 GOSUB 5000                      ' POSITION THE CURSOR
7030 PRINT STRING$(39," ");
7040 GOSUB 5000                      ' POSITION THE CURSOR
7050 PRINT P$;                       ' PRINT THE PROMPT
7060 C=LEN(P$)+2                     ' FIND THE COLUMN TO BEGIN
7070 GOSUB 5000                      ' POSITION THE CURSOR
7075 IF PC$="D" THEN PRINT "MM/DD/YY" : GOTO 7110
7080 FOR I=1 TO L
7090     PRINT "*";                  ' PRINT PROMPT MARKERS
7100 NEXT I
7110 GOSUB 5000                      ' POSITION THE CURSOR
7112 IF PC$<>"D" THEN 7120
7114 L=2 : GOSUB 7120 : MM$=B$
7115 C=POS(0)+1 : GOSUB 5000
7116 L=2 : GOSUB 7120 : DD$=B$
7117 C=POS(0)+1 : GOSUB 5000
7118 L=2 : GOSUB 7120 : YY$=B$
7119 RETURN
7120 B$=""                           ' NULL THE STRING
7130 FOR I9=1 TO L                   ' INPUT LOOP L=PROMPT LENGTH
7140     A$=INKEY$
7150     IF A$="" THEN 7140          ' CHECK FOR CHARACTER
7160     IF A$<>CHR$(8) THEN 7220        ' CHECK FOR BACKSPACE
7170         IF I9=1 THEN 7140 ' NO BACKSPACE WHEN 1ST CHAR.
7180         C=POS(0)-1          ' REDUCE THE COLUMN
7182         GOSUB 5000          ' POSITION THE CURSOR
7184         PRINT "*";          ' PRINT THE MARKER
7186         GOSUB 5000          ' POSITION THE CURSOR
7190         I9=I9-1             ' REDUCE COUNTER
7200         B$=MID$(B$,1,LEN(B$)-1)     ' DROP END CHARACTER
7210         GOTO 7140              ' GET CHARACTER AGAIN
7220     IF A$<>CHR$(13) THEN 7260       ' RETURN PRESSED?
7230         I9=L                 ' INCREASE COUNTER TO MAX
7240         PRINT STRING$(L-LEN(B$)," ");
7250         GOTO 7280            ' THIS WILL END LOOP
7260     B$=B$+A$                 ' ACCUMULATE ENTIRE STRING
7270     PRINT A$;                ' ECHO
7280 NEXT I9
7290 RETURN
```

The changes and additions to the routine (as compared to Program 10–3) are as follows:

(1) Line 7075 tests for the PC$ prompt code, and if it is D (for date), the MM/DD/YY prompt is printed instead of the asterisks, which are skipped with the GOTO.

(2) Lines 7112–7119 check for "D" again, and if the prompt code is not D, the routine will use the prompt length of 2 (L=2) and the newly created subroutine at line 7120, and then store the two-digit part of the date (either MM, DD, or YY) so that the date can be kept. The next line then causes a skip over the slash. For the Radio Shack and Apple, you will need to print the character to move the cursor to the right. On the Radio Shack, that character is 9 (CHR$(9)) and on the Apple it is 21 (CHR$(21)).

(3) Note that line 7290 was changed to a RETURN statement to make the input part of the subroutine into its own subroutine.

(4) After returning from the subroutine, the program could concatenate the three strings into one six-digit string.

CHAPTER 11

2. Random file processing, also called direct file processing, is a type of processing that allows access to each record stored in a file in any order necessary. For example, if we want to access record 15, we can do so without accessing the records in front of or behind record 15.

4. In order to find a particular record on the disk, the machine needs to know the length of the records in order to calculate the total number of bytes to bypass to get to the asked-for record. For example, if the records are each 25 bytes long and you want to access the fifth record, 100 bytes need to be skipped to get to the fifth record (4 * 25 = 100).

10. For this program we will simply modify the program from the chapter a bit. We don't need to flowchart or pseudocode it since it will be virtually the same. The program follows; we will look at the changes we made after the coding.

```
10 REM ***** PROGRAM NAME: F-11-10
20 REM
30 REM ***** PROBLEM 11-10 RANDOM FILE PROCESSING
40 REM
50 REM ***** WRITTEN BY EDWARD J. COBURN
60 REM
70 OPEN "PAYROLL" AS #1 LEN=28
80 FIELD #1, 2 AS RF$            ' DUMMY RECORD
90 GET 1,1                       ' GET THE FIRST RECORD
100 IF CVI(RF$)=0 THEN RECS=1 ELSE RECS=CVI(RF$)
110 FIELD #1, 9 AS SF$, 24 AS NF$, 1 AS CF$, 4 AS PF$
120 CLS                          ' CLEAR THE SCREEN
130 PRINT TAB(10);"PAYROLL MAINTENANCE"
140 PRINT                        ' BLANK LINE
150 PRINT "1.   ADD NEW RECORDS"
155 PRINT
160 PRINT "2.   CHANGE EXISTING RECORD"
165 PRINT
```

Program continues

```
170 PRINT "3.   PRINT THE FILE"
175 PRINT
180 PRINT "4.   EXIT THE PROGRAM"
190 PRINT
200 P$= "WHAT OPTION (1-4)"
210 L=1                              ' LENGTH OF PROMPT
220 GOSUB 7000                       ' PROMPT SUBROUTINE
230 IF B$>"0" AND B$<"5" THEN 270
240    M$="INPUT ERROR.   RETRY ENTRY"
250    GOSUB 6000                    ' ERROR SUBROUTINE
260    GOTO 200                      ' REPROMPT
270 ON VAL(B$) GOSUB 500, 2000, 3000, 4000
280 GOTO 120                         ' RETURN FOR ANOTHER INPUT
470 REM
480 REM ***** ADD MODULE
490 REM
500 CLS                              ' CLEAR THE SCREEN
510 PRINT TAB(10);"PAYROLL ENTRY"
520 PRINT                            ' BLANK LINE
530 PRINT "1. SS. NUMBER"
535 PRINT
540 PRINT "2. EMP. NAME"
542 PRINT
544 PRINT "3. SALARY CODE"
546 PRINT
548 PRINT "4. PAY RATE"
550 R=3                              ' ROW NUMBER
552 C=17                             ' COLUMN NUMBER
554 L=9                              ' SS NUMBER LENGTH
556 GOSUB 7070                       ' PROMPT SUBROUTINE
558 LSET SF$=B$                      ' ASSIGN SS NUMBER
560 R=5                              ' ROW NUMBER
570 L=24                             ' NAME LENGTH
580 GOSUB 7070                       ' PROMPT SUBROUTINE
590 LSET NF$=B$                      ' ASSIGN NAME
600 R=7                              ' ROW NUMBER
610 L=1                              ' SALARY CODE LENGTH
620 GOSUB 7070                       ' PROMPT SUBROUTINE
630 LSET SF$=B$                      ' ASSIGN SALARY CODE
632 R=9                              ' ROW NUMBER
634 L=8                              ' PAY RATE
636 LSET PF$=MKS$(VAL(B$))           ' ASSIGN AMOUNT
638 RECS=RECS+1                      ' INCREMENT RECORD NUMBER
640 PUT 1,RECS                       ' PUT THE RECORD
650 FIELD #1, 2 AS RF$               ' FIELD RECORD 1
660 LSET RF$=MKI$(RECS)              ' SET THE FIELD
670 PUT 1,1                          ' PUT RECORD 1
680 P$= "DO YOU WANT TO ADD ANY MORE (Y OR N)"
690 L=1                              ' LENGTH OF PROMPT
700 GOSUB 7000                       ' PROMPT SUBROUTINE
710 IF B$<>"Y" THEN RETURN
720 GOTO 500                         ' GET ANOTHER RECORD
1970 REM
1980 REM ***** CHANGE MODULE
1990 REM
2000 P$="RECORD NUMBER TO CHANGE (0 TO END)"
2020 L=3                             ' PROMPT LENGTH
2030 GOSUB 7000                      ' PROMPT SUBROUTINE
2040 IF VAL(B$)=0 THEN RETURN ' EXIT THE SUBROUTINE
2050 IF VAL(B$)<=RECS THEN 2080' RECORD OKAY?
2060      M$="RECORD NOT FOUND.   REENTER."
2070      GOSUB 6000                 ' ERROR SUBROUTINE
```

Program continues

```
2075       GOTO 2000              ' GET INDEX AGAIN
2080 RN=VAL(B$)+1                 ' RECORD TO ACCESS
2082 FIELD #1, 9 AS SF$, 24 AS NF$, 1 AS CF$, 4 AS PF$
2085 GET #1,RN                    ' GET THE RECORD
2090 CLS                          ' CLEAR THE SCREEN
2100 PRINT TAB(10);"PAYROLL CHANGES"
2110 PRINT                        ' BLANK LINE
2120 PRINT "1. SS. NUMBER    ";SF$
2124 PRINT
2128 PRINT "2. EMP. NAME     ";NF$
2132 PRINT
2136 PRINT "3. SALARY CODE   ";SF$
2138 PRINT
2140 PRINT "4. PAY RATE      ";CVS(PF$)
2150 P$="FIELD TO CHANGE (0 TO END)"
2160 L=1                          ' PROMPT LENGTH
2170 GOSUB 7000                   ' PROMPT SUBROUTINE
2180 IF B$>="0" AND B$<="4" THEN 2220
2190      M$="INVALID ENTRY.  TRY AGAIN"
2200      GOSUB 6000              ' ERROR SUBROUTINE
2210      GOTO 2150               ' REINPUT
2220 IF B$="0" THEN 2290          ' FIELD ENTRY
2230      IF B$="1" THEN L=9  : R=3
2240      IF B$="2" THEN L=24 : R=5
2242      IF B$="3" THEN L=1  : R=7
2244      IF B$="4" THEN L=8  : R=9
2250      C=17                    ' COLUMN
2260      GOSUB 7070              ' PROMPT SUBROUTINE
2270      IF R=3 THEN LSET SF$=B$
2272      IF R=5 THEN LSET NF$=B$
2274      IF R=7 THEN LSET SF$=B$
2276      IF R=9 THEN LSET PF$=MKI$(B$)
2280      GOTO 2090               ' REPROMPT
2290 PUT #1,RN                    ' STORE THE RECORD BACK INTO FILE
2300 GOTO 2000                    ' RETURN FOR NEW NUMBER
2970 REM
2980 REM ***** PRINT MODULE
2990 REM
3000 T=0                          ' ZERO OUT TOTAL FIELD
3005 LPRINT TAB(20);"PAYROLL LIST"
3007 LPRINT " "                   ' BLANK LINE
3020 LPRINT " SS. NUMBER  NAME";TAB(39);"PAY CODE    AMOUNT"
3030 LPRINT " "                   ' BLANK LINE
3040 FOR I=2 TO RECS              ' TO NUMBER IN FILE
3050      GET #1,I                ' GET RECORD BY NUMBER
3060      LPRINT MID$(SF$,1,3);"/";MID$(SF$,4,3);"/";MID$(SF$,7,4);
3065      LPRINT " ";NF$;TAB(43);CF$;TAB(50);
3067      LPRINT USING "#,###.##";CVS(PF$)
3070      T=T+CVS(PF$)            ' ACCUMULATE TOTAL
3080 NEXT I
3090 LPRINT TAB(51);"---------"'UNDERLINE
3100 LPRINT "TOTAL";TAB(51);USING "##,###.##";T
3110 RETURN
3970 REM
3980 REM ***** EXIT MODULE
3990 REM
4000 CLOSE #1
4010 END
```

We will not discuss the differences in the BASIC versions since this program is simply a rewrite of the program in the chapter. Instead we will discuss the differences between this program and the one in the chapter. In the beginning module, we changed the file name to PAYROLL and the file specification (the FIELD statement in the example). Finally, the heading was changed so it said PAYROLL MAINTENANCE instead of CONTRIBUTIONS MAINTENANCE. This same change was made in all the modules.

In the add module, the changes relate to adding more items for the file. Lines 520–550 were needed to list four lines on the screen instead of two. Then, lines 550–640 needed more screen access and more calls to the subroutine.

In the change module, the changes again relate to the fact that we are processing more fields. The FIELD statement (2082) is changed (not for the Apple). Then lines 2100–2140 needed upgrading to reflect the new fields. Lines 2230–2280 needed additional lines in both test groups.

Finally, in the print module, the only changes were to the column heading line and the detail line. Remember to add the subroutines where appropriate.

CHAPTER 12
1. An indexed file is easier because the records are accessed by some index other than record number. For example, a record can be retrieved not as record 4 but as the JONES record. For the programmer, it works out about the same, since indexed processing is simply an extension of random processing. But for the user, an indexed file is much easier.
3. An index file must be in sequence, or the program would have to search each index in the file. Obviously, such a search would be extremely slow.
6. If we do not search the index, a duplicate record could be added since the bubble routine does not check for duplicates.
7. The changes to Program 12–1 are fairly simple. The first thing is to change the data statements to contain strings and to change the array references in lines 80, 100, 170, 200, 230, and 270. Finally, the INPUT statement (line 140) needs to prompt for a name. We will not pseudocode or flowchart the program since the changes from Program 12–1 are minor. The changed program would look like the following:

```
10 REM ***** PROGRAM NAME: F-12-7
20 REM
30 REM ***** WRITTEN BY EDWARD J. COBURN
40 REM
50 REM THIS PROGRAM SEARCHES FOR A STRING INDEX
60 REM
70 CLS                       ' CLEAR THE SCREEN
80 DIM B$(20)                ' ARRAY FOR THE LIST
90 FOR I=1 TO 20
100      READ B$(I)          ' READ IN THE LIST
110 NEXT I
120 H=21                     ' HIGH POINT = NUMBER ITEMS + 1
130 L=0                      ' LOW POINT ALWAYS STARTS AT ZERO
140 INPUT "SEARCH FOR WHAT NAME";N$
150 C=INT(H/2)               ' C=CURRENT ITEM NUMBER
160 PRINT "* ";              ' JUST A MARKER TO INDICATE LOOPS
```

Program continues

```
170 IF N$<>B$(C) THEN 230' IS CURRENT = SEARCHED ITEM
180    PRINT "THERE IS A MATCH"
190    PRINT "SEARCHED FOR ";N$
200    PRINT "FOUND        ";B$(C)
210    GOTO 280
220 REM
230 IF N$<B$(C) THEN H=C : C=INT((L+C)/2)
                 ELSE L=C : C=C+INT((H-C)/2)
240 IF H<>C AND L<>C THEN 160      ' NOT LOW OR HIGH
250    PRINT "THERE IS NO MATCH"
260    PRINT "SEARCHED FOR    ";N$
270    PRINT "ENDED SEARCH AT ";B$(C)
280 END
290 DATA AL, BETTY, BOB, BOBBY, CALVIN
300 DATA CARL, DAN, DOUG, ED, ERVIN
310 DATA FRANK, FRED, GEORGE, HARRY, INGA
320 DATA MARY, NORMAN, PAUL, ROBERT, SAM
RUN
SEARCH FOR WHAT NAME? AL
* * * * THERE IS A MATCH
SEARCHED FOR AL
FOUND        AL
Ok
RUN
SEARCH FOR WHAT NAME? TOM
* * * * THERE IS NO MATCH
SEARCHED FOR    TOM
ENDED SEARCH AT SAM
Ok
RUN
SEARCH FOR WHAT NAME? ED
* * * * THERE IS A MATCH
SEARCHED FOR ED
FOUND        ED
Ok
```

4. Since each entry in a tree structure refers to the next item and each item is checked by value, if that value is changed, the order of the tree would no longer be valid.

6. See Figure F–12.

8. To do this program we will merely modify the program in the chapter a bit. First we will add the statement to RANDOMIZE (line 80). Then line 120 will generate a random number instead of INPUT it. Line 130 is deleted since we won't use the end-of-data marker. Finally, line 295 is added to check for the 50th number. When it is reached, the program exits the loop and prints the items from the tree. (We will not show the output, tree, flowchart, or pseudocode since they would be virtually the same as in the chapter.)

CHAPTER 13

```
10 REM ***** PROGRAM NAME: F-13-10
20 REM
30 REM ***** WRITTEN BY EDWARD J. COBURN
40 REM
50 REM THIS PROGRAM WILL RANDOMLY INSERT IN THE TREE
60 REM
65 CLS                                ' CLEAR THE SCREEN
```

Program continues

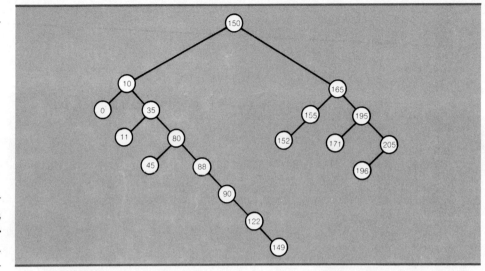

Figure F–12
Tree structure for
Question 13–6.

```
70 DIM B(100,3)                                    ' ARRAY FOR THE LIST
80 RANDOMIZE(RIGHT$(TIME$,2))
120 X=INT(RND(0)*100)+1                            ' GENERATE RANDOM NUMBER
140 IF B<>0 THEN 190
150     B(1,1)=X                                   ' ASSIGN ROOT NODE
160     B=B+1                                       ' COUNT THAT NODE
170     GOTO 120                                    ' GET NEW INDEX
180                                                 '
190 I=1                                             ' BEGIN SEARCH LOOP
200     IF X=B(I,1) THEN PRINT "FOUND" : GOTO 120
210     IF X>B(I,1) THEN C=3 ELSE C=2               ' SET LOW OR HIGH CODE
220                                                 ' CHECK NODE
230         IF B(I,C)<>0 THEN 320
240                                                 ' AREA FOR NO NEXT NODE
270             B(I,C)=B+1                          ' ASSIGN NEXT NODE
280             B(B+1,1)=X                          ' ASSIGN VALUE
290             B=B+1                               ' INCREASE # OF NODES
295             IF B=50 THEN 360                    ' EXIT LOOP
300             GOTO 120                            ' GET NEW INDEX
310             ' NEXT NODE FOUND - NEED TO CHECK AGAIN
320             I=B(I,C)                            ' SET NEW NODE CHECK
330             GOTO 200                            ' CHECK NEW NODE
340                                                 '
350                                                 '
360 FOR I=1 TO B
370     PRINT "ITEM=";I;"  VALUE=";B(I,1);
380     PRINT "  LOW=";B(I,2);"  HIGH=";B(I,3)
390 NEXT I
400 END
```

CHAPTER 14

2. As used in the chapter, it indicates to the program how many elements are in the DATA table.

4. The quicksort uses the key as a marker; all the items smaller than the key are moved to the left, and all items larger than the key are moved to the right. Then each segment is split around a new key.

5. Only a few changes to the module are needed to do the comparisons and switches on a string array instead of a numeric array. (Check the chapter for the flowchart and pseudocode.) The lines that need to be changed are 370,

400, 430, 470, 480, 490. Then we simply use the modules that have already been converted for strings to complete the program. The program follows:

```
10 REM ***** PROGRAM NAME: F-14-5
20 REM
30 REM ***** WRITTEN BY EDWARD J. COBURN
40 REM
50 REM ***** QUICKSORT FOR STRING DATA
60 REM
70 READ NE                      ' NUMBER OF ELEMENTS
80 DIM A$(NE)                   ' ARRAY TO SORT
90 FOR I=1 TO NE
100     READ A$(I)              ' READ IN ARRAY
110 NEXT I
270 REM
280 REM ***** QUICKSORT MODULE
290 REM
300 P=1                         ' PARTITION NUMBER
310 S(P,1)=1                    ' INITIAL LEFT MARGIN
320 S(P,2)=NE                   ' INITIAL RIGHT MARGIN
325 ' ************************* POP FROM STACK
330     LM=S(P,1)               ' USE LEFT MARGIN
340     RM=S(P,2)               ' USE RIGHT MARGIN
350     P=P-1                   ' REDUCE THE NUMBER OF PARTITIONS
355 ' ************************* ADJUST THE PARTITION
360     PM=INT((LM+RM)/2)       ' DETERMINE PARTITION MIDDLE
370     K$=A$(PM)               ' GET KEY ELEMENT
380     LP=LM                   ' INITIALIZE LEFT POINTER
390     RP=RM                   ' INITIALIZE RIGHT POINTER
400     IF A$(LP)>=K$ THEN 430  ' IS LEFT GREATER
410         LP=LP+1             ' MOVE LEFT POINTER
420         GOTO 400
430     IF A$(RP)<=K$ THEN 460  ' IS RIGHT LESS
440         RP=RP-1             ' MOVE RIGHT POINTER
450         GOTO 430
460     IF LP>RP THEN 530       ' DO ITEMS NEED SWITCHING?
470         T$=A$(LP)           ' SAVE LEFT ITEM
480         A$(LP)=A$(RP)       ' RIGHT TO LEFT
490         A$(RP)=T$           ' REPLACE RIGHT
500         LP=LP+1             ' MOVE LEFT POINTER
510         RP=RP-1             ' MOVE RIGHT POINTER
520     IF LP<=RP THEN 400      ' IF MARGINS OKAY DO AGAIN
530     IF LP>=RM THEN 570      ' IS POINTER OKAY?
535 ' ************************* PUSH ONTO STACK
540         P=P+1               ' UP PARTITION COUNTER
550         S(P,1)=LP           ' LEFT MARGIN
560         S(P,2)=RM           ' RIGHT MARGIN
570     RM=RP                   ' REDO MARGIN
580     IF LM<RM THEN 360       ' IS LEFT MARGIN REACHED?
590     IF P<>0 THEN 330        ' ANY MORE IN STACK?
870 REM
880 REM ***** OUTPUT MODULE
890 REM
895 CLS                         ' CLEAR THE SCREEN
910     FOR I=1 TO 10
920         PRINT A$(I)
930     NEXT I
970 END
980 REM
985 REM ***** DATA TABLE
990 REM
1000 DATA 10
1010 DATA SAM SMITH, JOE BLOW, ED COBURN, AL SIMONS
1020 DATA FRED THOMPSON, JACK FRITZ, HARRY GARP
1030 DATA TOM JONES, PAM CONLEY, HARRISON FORD
```

CHAPTER 15

2. A pixel is a single dot of resolution that can be turned on or off with a program command.

5. The flowchart for this program can be seen in Figure F–13; the screen design is shown in Figure F–14, and the pseudocode follows:

Start
Read data items and store them in array.
Print heading.
Initialize counter (J) to 50.
DO-WHILE counter (J) is not less than 1.
   Print counter (J) for scale and wall.
   Initialize counter (I) to 1.
   DO-WHILE counter (I) is not greater than 6.
     Print marker or blanks.
     Increase counter (I) by 1.
   END-DO
   Print carriage return.
   Decrease counter (J) by 5.
END-DO
Print graph bottom and labels.
End

```
10 REM ***** PROGRAM NAME: F-15-5
20 REM
30 REM ***** TEXT RESOLUTION GRAPH - EXERCISE 15 - 5
40 REM
50 FOR I = 1 TO 5
60     READ A(I)
70 NEXT I
80 PRINT TAB(6);"GOVERNMENT SATISFACTION"
90 PRINT "50% +";                    ' PRINT REFERENCE NUMBER
100 FOR J = 50 TO 1 STEP -5           ' SCALE LOOP
110    IF J<>50 THEN PRINT "    !";
120    FOR I = 1 TO 5
130       IF A(I)>=J THEN PRINT "  ***"; ELSE PRINT "     "
140    NEXT I
150    PRINT                          ' CARRIAGE RETURN
160 NEXT J
170 PRINT " 0% +--------------------------"
180 PRINT TAB(8);"TD   D   MS   S   TS   NO"
190 END
RUN
      GOVERNMENT SATISFACTION
50% +
   !
   !
   !
   !                   ***
   !          ***      ***
   !          ***      ***    ***
   !          ***      ***    ***
   !  ***     ***      ***    ***           ***
   !  ***     ***      ***    ***    ***    ***
 0% +--------------------------------
        TD    D    MS    S    TS    NO
```

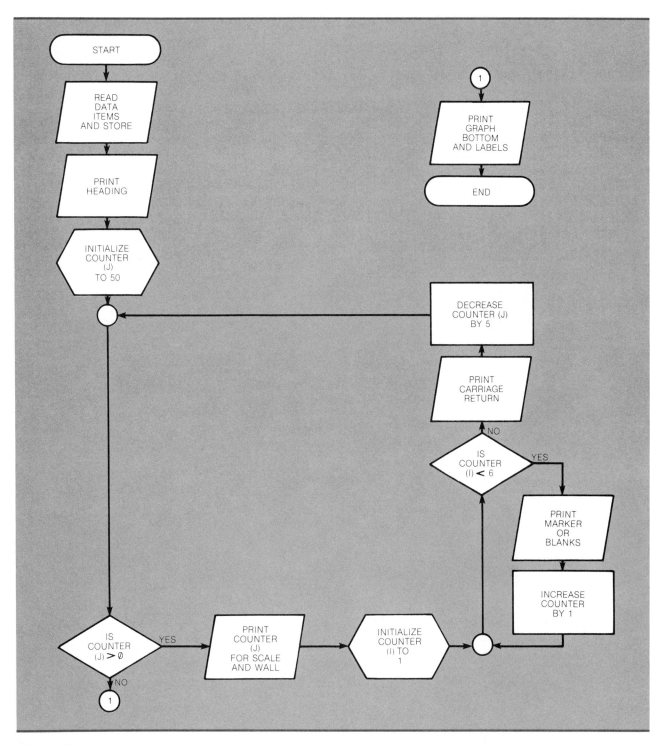

Figure F–13
Flowchart for Question 15–5.

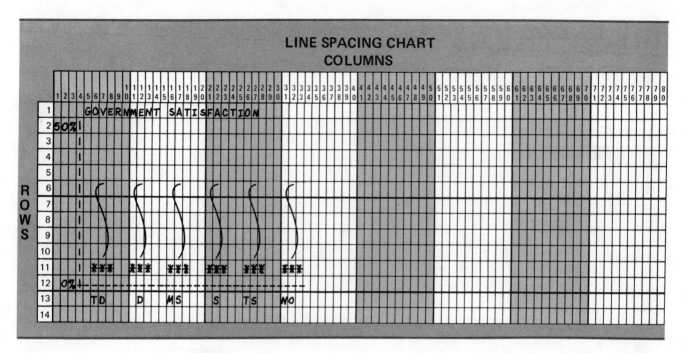

Figure F–14
Design for Question 15–5.

ASCII SEQUENCE

This appendix presents, in tabular form, the ASCII codes for each of the machines covered in this book. Most of the codes are the same for all the machines, but the nonprintable codes sometimes differ among the machines. Many graphics characters are also included.

You will often see the abbreviation N/A, meaning not-applicable. Some codes are useful only for those programming in more complex languages than BASIC (such as assembler language) and, as such, are of little use to us. The decimal code refers to the code you use to print the related character with the CHR$() command. For example, CHR$(65) will give you the character "A".

Most of the decimal codes from 32 through 127 are codes for the keyboard characters. When you press the appropriate key, the character generated has the decimal code that is listed. For example, if you press the A key, the character generated (A, of course) has the decimal code 65. Some of the other codes, such as RETURN, indicate keys that you press to generate the listed action.

The parenthetical actions listed for the IBM for the codes 7–12 and 28–31 indicate that if you press the appropriate key you will get the result listed, but if you try to use the CHR$ function, you will not get that action but a graphics character instead.

On the Radio Shack, codes 0–31 and 192–255 will generate graphics characters only if you print CHR$(21) before you try to print the characters. Note that this gives codes 0–31 a second meaning (the codes 192–255 have another meaning also). These extra graphics characters are listed at the end of the table.

DECIMAL CODE	CHARACTERS			DECIMAL CODE	CHARACTERS		
	IBM	Radio Shack	Apple		IBM	Radio Shack	Apple
0	Null	Null	Null	14	♫	Cursor on	N/A
1	☺	N/A	N/A	15	☼	Cursor off	N/A
2	☻	N/A	N/A	16	►	N/A	N/A
3	♥	N/A	N/A	17	◄	N/A	N/A
4	♦	N/A	N/A	18	↕	N/A	N/A
5	♣	N/A	N/A	19	‼	N/A	N/A
6	♠	N/A	N/A	20	¶	N/A	N/A
7	(Bell)	N/A	Bell	21	§	Use Special Characters	N/A
8	(Backspace)	Backspace	Backspace	22	▬	Use Alternate Characters	N/A
9	(Tab)	Tab	N/A				
10	(Line feed)	Line Feed	Line Feed				
11	(Cursor home)	N/A	N/A	23	↨	Double-size Characters	N/A
12	(clear screen)	N/A	N/A	24	↑	Backspace W/O Erasing	Cancel
13	RETURN	RETURN	RETURN				

DECIMAL CODE	CHARACTERS			DECIMAL CODE	CHARACTERS		
	IBM	Radio Shack	Apple		IBM	Radio Shack	Apple
25	↓	Cursor right	N/A	60	<	<	<
26	→	Cursor down	N/A	61	=	=	=
				62	>	>	>
27	←	Cursor up	N/A	63	?	?	?
28	(Cursor right)	Home cursor	N/A	64	@	@	@
				65	A	A	A
29	(Cursor left)	Erase line and start again	N/A	66	B	B	B
				67	C	C	C
				68	D	D	D
30	(Cursor up)	Erase to end of line	N/A	69	E	E	E
				70	F	F	F
31	(Cursor down)	Erase to end of display	N/A	71	G	G	G
				72	H	H	H
				73	I	I	I
32	Space	Space	Space	74	J	J	J
33	!	!	!	75	K	K	K
34	"	"	"	76	L	L	L
35	#	#	#	77	M	M	M
36	$	$	$	78	N	N	N
37	%	%	%	79	O	O	O
38	&	&	&	80	P	P	P
39	'	'	'	81	Q	Q	Q
40	(	(	(	82	R	R	R
41	)	)	)	83	S	S	S
42	*	*	*	84	T	T	T
43	+	+	+	85	U	U	U
44	'	'	'	86	V	V	V
45	-	-	-	87	W	W	W
46	.	.	.	88	X	X	X
47	/	/	/	89	Y	Y	Y
48	0	0	0	90	Z	Z	Z
49	1	1	1	91	[	[	[
50	2	2	2	92	\	\	\
51	3	3	3	93	]	]	]
52	4	4	4	94	∧	∧	∧
53	5	5	5	95	—	—	—
54	6	6	6	96	`	`	`
55	7	7	7	97	a	a	a
56	8	8	8	98	b	b	b
57	9	9	9	99	c	c	c
58	:	:	:	100	d	d	d
59	;	;	;	101	e	e	e

DECIMAL CODE	CHARACTERS		
	IBM	Radio Shack	Apple
102	f	f	f
103	g	g	g
104	h	h	h
105	i	i	i
106	j	j	j
107	k	k	k
108	l	l	l
109	m	m	m
110	n	n	n
111	o	o	o
112	p	p	p
113	q	q	q
114	r	r	r
115	s	s	s
116	t	t	t
117	u	u	u
118	v	v	v
119	w	w	w
120	x	x	x
121	y	y	y
122	z	z	z
123	{	{	{
124	|	|	|
125	}	}	}
126	~	~	~
127	⌂	±	DELETE
128	Ç	Blank	N/A
129	ü	▮	N/A
130	é	▮	N/A
131	â	▮	N/A
132	ä	▮	N/A

DECIMAL CODE	CHARACTERS		
	IBM	Radio Shack	Apple
133	à	▮	N/A
134	å	▮	N/A
135	ç	▮	N/A
136	ê	▮	N/A
137	ë	▮	N/A
138	è	▮	N/A
139	ï	▮	N/A
140	î	▮	N/A
141	ì	▮	N/A
142	Ä	▮	N/A
143	Å	▮	N/A

DECIMAL CODE	CHARACTERS			DECIMAL CODE	CHARACTERS		
	IBM	Radio Shack	Apple		IBM	Radio Shack	Apple
144	É		N/A	155	¢		N/A
145	æ		N/A	156	£		N/A
146	Æ		N/A	157	¥		N/A
147	ê		N/A	158	Pt		N/A
148	ö		N/A	159	ƒ		N/A
149	ò		N/A	160	á		N/A
150	û		N/A	161	í		N/A
151	ù		N/A	162	ó		N/A
152	ÿ		N/A	163	ú		N/A
153	Ö		N/A	164	ñ		N/A
154	Ü		N/A	165	Ñ		N/A

DECIMAL CODE	CHARACTERS			DECIMAL CODE	CHARACTERS		
	IBM	Radio Shack	Apple		IBM	Radio Shack	Apple
166	a		N/A	177			N/A
167	o		N/A	178			N/A
168	‹		N/A	179	|		N/A
169	⌐		N/A	180	⊣		N/A
170	¬		N/A	181	⊨		N/A
171	½		N/A	182	⊣|		N/A
172	¼		N/A	183	⌐		N/A
173	¡		N/A	184	¬		N/A
174	«		N/A	185	⊨|		N/A
175	»		N/A	186	||		N/A
176	░		N/A	187	⌐|		N/A

495

DECIMAL CODE	CHARACTERS			DECIMAL CODE	CHARACTERS		
	IBM	Radio Shack	Apple		IBM	Radio Shack	Apple
188	⌐		N/A	199	╟		N/A
189	╛		N/A	200	╚		N/A
190	╝		N/A	201	╔		N/A
191	┐		N/A	202	╩		N/A
192	└		N/A	203	╦		N/A
193	┴		N/A	204	╠		N/A
194	┬		N/A	205	═		N/A
195	├		N/A	206	╬		N/A
196	─		N/A	207	╧		N/A
197	┼		N/A	208	╨		N/A
198	╞		N/A	209	╤		N/A

DECIMAL CODE	CHARACTERS			DECIMAL CODE	CHARACTERS		
	IBM	Radio Shack	Apple		IBM	Radio Shack	Apple
210	⊤		N/A	221	▮		N/A
211	⊫	μ	N/A	222	▮	Ψ	N/A
212	⊨		N/A	223	▬	ω	N/A
213	⊧		N/A	224	α		N/A
214	⊓		N/A	225	β		N/A
215	╫	π	N/A	226	Γ	÷	N/A
216	╪	P	N/A	227	π	Σ	N/A
217	┘		N/A	228	Σ		N/A
218	┌	T	N/A	229	σ		N/A
219	▪	U	N/A	230	μ	∫	N/A
220	▬	Φ	N/A	231	τ		N/A

DECIMAL CODE	CHARACTERS			DECIMAL CODE	CHARACTERS		
	IBM	Radio Shack	Apple		IBM	Radio Shack	Apple
232	Φ		N/A	243	≤		N/A
233	⊖		N/A	244	⌠		N/A
234	Ω		N/A	245	⌡		N/A
235	δ		N/A	246	÷		N/A
236	∞		N/A	247	≈		N/A
237	ø		N/A	248	°		N/A
238	∈		N/A	249	•		N/A
239	∩		N/A	250	•		N/A
240	≡		N/A	251	√		N/A
241	±		N/A	252	ⁿ		N/A
242	≥		N/A	253	²		N/A

DECIMAL CODE	CHARACTERS			DECIMAL CODE	CHARACTERS		
	IBM	Radio Shack	Apple		IBM	Radio Shack	Apple
254	■		N/A	255	Blank		N/A

Radio Shack note: Codes 244–246 form a pointing hand when put together. This symbol can be used for some interesting effects. It looks like this:

As mentioned earlier, the Radio Shack will allow the display of graphics using the codes 1–31 by first printing CHR$(21). Those graphics characters are:

DECIMAL CODE	RADIO SHACK GRAPHIC	DECIMAL CODE	RADIO SHACK GRAPHIC
1		7	
2		8	
3		9	
4		10	
5		11	
6		12	

DECIMAL CODE	RADIO SHACK GRAPHIC	DECIMAL CODE	RADIO SHACK GRAPHIC
13	R	23	ẞ
14	Ä	24	ä
15	Å	25	å
16	Ñ	26	à
17	Ö	27	§
18	Ø	28	É
19	Õ	29	Æ
20	B	30	Ç
21	Ü	31	~
22	ŏ		

Ageloff, Roy, and Mojena, Richard. *Applied BASIC Programming*. Belmont, Calif.: Wadsworth, 1980.

Bent, Robert J., and Sethares, George C. *BASIC—An Introduction to Computer Programming*. Monterey, Calif: Brooks/Cole Publishing Co., 1982.

Bohl, Marilyn. *Tools for Structured Design*. Chicago: Science Research Associates, 1978.

Clark, James F., and Dunn, William O. *BASIC Programming: A Structured Approach*. Cincinnati: South-Western Publishing Co., 1983.

Coburn, Edward J. *Microcomputers: Hardware, Software, and Programming*. Indianapolis: Bobbs-Merrill, 1984.

Didday, Rich, and Page, Rex. *Using BASIC*. St. Paul, Minn.: West Publishing Co., 1981.

Haigh, Roger W., and Radford, Loren E. *BASIC for Microcomputers: Apple, TRS–80, PET*. Boston: Prindle Weber and Schmidt, 1983.

Hare, Van Court, Jr. *BASIC Programming*. New York: Harcourt Brace Jovanovich, 1982.

Kitchen, Andrew. *BASIC by Design: Structured Computer Programming in BASIC*. Englewood Cliffs, N.J.: Prentice-Hall, 1983.

Marteck, Samuel L. *BASIC*. New York: Academic Press, 1982.

Mullish, Henry. *A Basic Approach to Structured BASIC*, Second Edition. New York: John Wiley and Sons, 1983.

Norman, Robin. *Timex Sinclair 1000/ZX81 BASIC Book*. Indianapolis: Howard W. Sams, 1982.

Osborne, Adam, and Donahue, Carroll S. *PET/CBM Personal Computer Guide*, Second Edition. Berkeley, Calif.: Osborne/McGraw-Hill, 1980.

Poole, Lon. *Using Your IBM Personal Computer*. Indianapolis: Howard W. Sams, 1983.

Shelly, Gary B., and Cashman, Thomas J. *Introduction to BASIC Programming*. Fullerton, Calif.: Anaheim Publishing Co., 1982.

Spencer, Donald D. *The Illustrated Computer Dictionary*, Revised Edition. Columbus, Ohio: Charles E. Merrill, 1983.

Waite, Mitchell, and Pardee, Michael. *BASIC Programming Primer*, Second Edition. Indianapolis: Howard W. Sams, 1982.

INDEX

This index is specially constructed to be as useful as possible. There are seven different types of entries, indicating exactly where the referenced information may be found. Standard page numbers indicate that the information appears in the general text; *a* indicates that the information is found in an appendix; *f* indicates that it appears in a figure; *g* indicates that it appears in a glossary; *p* indicates that it appears in a program; *s* indicates that it appears in a summary; and *t* indicates that it appears in a table.